Examining the Cognitive and Psychological Effects of the COVID-19 Global Pandemic on High School, College, and Graduate Learners

Examining the Cognitive and Psychological Effects of the COVID-19 Global Pandemic on High School, College, and Graduate Learners

Editors

Jill D. Salisbury-Glennon
Chih-hsuan Wang
David M. Shannon
Auburn University

IAP
INFORMATION AGE PUBLISHING, INC.
Charlotte, NC • www.infoagepub.com

Library of Congress Cataloging-in-Publication Data

CIP record for this book is available from the Library of Congress
http://www.loc.gov

ISBNs: 979-8-88730-895-1 (Paperback)

979-8-88730-896-8 (Hardcover)

979-8-88730-897-5 (EPDF)

978-1-83708-564-4 EPUB

Printed and bound by CPI Group (UK) Ltd, Croydon, CR0 4YY

CONTENTS

SECTION II: UNDERGRADUATE LEARNERS

CHAPTER 1

INTRODUCTION

Examining the Cognitive and Psychological Effects of the COVID-19 Global Pandemic on High School, College, and Graduate Learners

Jill D. Salisbury-Glennon, Chih-hsuan Wang, David M. Shannon, Yan Dai, and Isabella Armstrong
Auburn University

Introductory Overview

The effects of the COVID-19 global pandemic on colleges and universities around the world have been greater than any event in recent history (Alexander et al., 2020; Rashid & Yadav, 2020). At the peak of the pandemic, 1.6 billion students at all educational levels from more than 190 countries on all continents were affected (United Nations, 2020, as cited in Daumiller et al., Chapter 20). Students missed an estimated 2 trillion hours of in-person instruction (United Nations Children's Fund et al., 2022, as cited in Daumiller et al., Chapter 20). Relatedly, over 71% of teachers felt that students were not adequately responsive to emergency remote instruction (Leech et al., 2020). During 2019–2020 alone, approximately 12 million full-time college students were impacted by the COVID-19

Examining the Cognitive and Psychological Effects of the COVID-19 Global Pandemic on High School, College, and Graduate Learners, pp. 1–9

global pandemic (IPEDS, 2020, as cited in Sherif et al., Chapter 7). At the time of this writing, we remain in the midst of this global pandemic. And thus, we are just beginning to comprehend the far-reaching effects that this pandemic will have on education into the future. This co-edited book represents one of the initial efforts to synthesize the research into the cognitive and psychological effects of the COVID-19 global pandemic on high school, college, and graduate-level learners.

Our Initial Research Into the COVID-19 Global Pandemic

This section will present a few representative research studies from our own research since the onset of the COVID-19 global pandemic. During the spring of 2020, colleges and universities around the world were abruptly closed due to the COVID-19 global pandemic. As the result of these mandated university closures, many college and university students around the world were forced to leave their campuses, and to travel to reside with family or friends, away from their college peers with whom they were used to living, on or near campus. Since many college students were now living at home with their families, Salisbury-Glennon et al. (2021) grounded their study in a social cognitive theoretical framework of self-regulated learning to investigate the effects of parental support on college students' motivation, cognitive and metacognitive strategies in the midst of this pandemic. Results from this research indicated that parental support was a statistically significant predictor of college students' motivation, which was a significant predictor of their cognitive and metacognitive strategies. Thus, parental social support was important for college students' learning during this initial phase of the pandemic, in part because many college students were now residing with their families.

In a subsequent study, Salisbury-Glennon et al. (2022) sought to further investigate the effects of these living and learning environments on college students' motivation, cognitive, and metacognitive learning strategies. The results of this study demonstrated that overall, during this unprecedented time, college students' perceived parental support while they were living at home with their parents/guardians during the spring of 2020, and their perceived peer support while they were living back on/near campus with their peers during the spring of 2021 both served to motivate these college students to use effective cognitive and metacognitive strategies. Thus, college students' prevailing social contexts served to motivate them to use effective cognitive and metacognitive learning strategies.

Grounded in social cognitive theory, Salisbury-Glennon et al. (2023) found that college students demonstrated statistically significantly higher use of motivation and cognitive learning strategies in an online learning environment. Further, the results of this study indicated that maternal social support statistically significantly predicted motivation and cognitive learning strategies. Finally, the results of this investigation demonstrated that college students' resilience significantly predicted motivation, cognitive learning strategies, and metacognitive self-regulation. Thus, the results of this study suggested that contextual variables, such as an online learning environment and maternal support, both served to significantly predict motivation, cognitive learning strategies, and metacognitive self-regulation.

To date, our team's research has demonstrated the positive effects of social support on motivation, cognitive and metacognitive strategies (e.g., Salisbury-Glennon et al., 2021; Salisbury-Glennon et al., 2022) and the effects of learning modality, social support and resilience on motivation and cognitive learning strategies (Salisbury-Glennon et al., 2023). Much of this research has been analyzed using more quantitative analyses including multivariate analyses of variance (MANOVA), structural equation modeling (SEM) and hierarchical linear regression analyses (HLM). Salisbury-Glennon et al. (2023) sought to further elucidate these complex relationships using a more qualitative research methodological approach, thematic analysis, in an effort to better understand these complex relationships. Results of thematic analyses indicated that while there were many participant comments, the results of a thematic analysis suggested three common themes: (a) *social concerns and anxiety*, as many participants mentioned feeling lonely, isolated and/or having a lack of social connection; (b) concern over the quality of their *learning, academic performance* and *preparation for a future job or career* as the result of the pandemic and online learning, and (c) a *lack of control* and/or *worry about the future*. The researchers grounded their findings in a theoretical framework of self-determination theory, as they found participant concerns regarding their *relatedness, competence and autonomy* (e.g., Deci & Ryan, 2000; Ryan & Deci, 2017). While we were conducting our own research, it became clear that there was a need for much further research into the effects of the COVID-19 global pandemic across the globe, across different developmental levels, using various research methodologies, and more diverse and underrepresented populations. Thus, the vision for this co-edited book emerged.

Overview of This Co-Edited Book

The present co-edited book serves to synthesize the research conducted by the authors with a focus on the cognitive and psychological effects of the COVID-19 global pandemic on high school, college, and graduate learners. This research has been conducted in multiple countries across multiple continents, using multiple diverse populations, using several different research methodologies, along with an emphasis on both the challenges as well as the positive outcomes that have resulted from this unprecedented event, the COVID-19 global pandemic. This co-edited book will summarize the theoretical frameworks, research methodologies, participant populations, research findings, and challenges as well as the positive outcomes of each research study. Further, this book will conclude with a more general thematic summary as well as implications for future inevitable world crises, lock-downs, and other unprecedented events. Finally, this book will be divided into three sections: Section I: High School Learners; Section II: Undergraduate Learners, and Section III: Graduate Learners.

SECTION I: HIGH SCHOOL LEARNERS

The first section of this book emphasized the cognitive and psychological effects of the COVID-19 global pandemic on high school learners. Allen et al. (Chapter 2) found that while high school students reported overwhelmingly negative impacts of the COVID-19 global pandemic, as indicated by significant ACT score declines, their research also indicated several positive effects of the COVID-19 global pandemic on high school learners such as positive and emotional skill development. Further, in Chapter 3, Fletcher et al. used a qualitative case study design based on semi-structured interviews to study the lived experiences of students who were enrolled in a High School STEM Academy. Their findings indicated that while both stakeholders and students reported significant challenges associated with the pandemic, both groups were able to make constant adjustments to create a positive learning experience. Wang et al. (Chapter 4) investigated the experiences of high school students in Taiwan in an effort to study the relations among their mental health, motivation, and self-regulated learning strategies.

SECTION II: UNDERGRADUATE LEARNERS

The second section of this co-edited book examined the cognitive and psychological effects of the COVID-19 global pandemic on undergraduate learners. Miller et al. (Chapter 5) investigated college students' perceptions of instructional practices during emergency remote learning and found that as the result of the pandemic, many of these students were more likely to choose and use online forms of instruction. In Chapter 6, Bridges and Duffy sought to examine the potential differences between first-generation college students and their continuing-generation college peers as a function of the transition to an online learning environment due to the pandemic. Sherif et al. (Chapter 7) explored the effects of the pandemic on student involvement, in particular, the campus involvement of first-generation college students. Quadlander-Goff et al. (Chapter 8) described the impact of the COVID-19 global pandemic on college students with ADHD in an effort to better understand successful interventions to help this population to succeed in the midst of challenging circumstances.

In Chapter 9, Rosen et al. sought to investigate the effects of co-rumination as a coping strategy in the midst of stressful circumstances. Tackett et al. (Chapter 10) examined the lived roles of in-service and preservice teachers with an emphasis on their constantly changing and/or increased family roles, such as childcare. Tyler et al. (Chapter 11) explored the development of resilience amongst underserved and underrepresented college students enrolled in a program based on a mentoring bridge model. In Chapter 12, Manning et al. explored the effects of emergency remote instruction on the development of nursing students' transitions to readiness for clinical work and interaction with patients. Williams and Diamond (Chapter 13) examined how multilingual students exhibited the various stages of academic acculturation in their written assignments as they emerged into online instruction. These researchers noted that this migration to online instruction was especially difficult for multilingual learners as they needed to not only adapt to a new country, but also to adapt unexpectedly to a new instructional modality.

Finally, Gutiérrez and Puga (Chapter 14) sought to identify engineering students' perspectives on both the positive and negative impacts of COVID-19 on the teaching and learning of algebra and differential equations.

SECTION III: GRADUATE LEARNERS

The third section of this co-edited book examined the cognitive and psychological effects of the COVID-19 global pandemic graduate-level learners. Yoo and Marshall (Chapter 15) explored the influence of parental status and gender on graduate students' perceived helplessness, self-efficacy, and life satisfaction. They further investigated the effects of the COVID-19 global pandemic on as a function of role strain theory (e.g., Goode, 1960) versus role accumulation theories (Sieber, 1974). Trammell et al. (Chapter 16) described the many challenges with regards to socialization, psychological well-being, and academic progress experienced by entering doctoral students at the peak of the pandemic, along with future implications and supports for students in similar situations. In Chapter 17, Cromley et al. conducted a qualitative investigation into perceived stressors experienced by doctoral students in engineering programs. Specifically, this group of researchers focused on social stressors, stressors related to international travel, and stressors related to familial challenges.

Dong et al. (Chapter 18) investigated gender differences in mental health challenges, motivation and self-regulated learning as experienced by graduate students in the midst of the pandemic. In Chapter 19, Bembenutty et al. described an intervention based on self-regulated learning strategies and academic delay of gratification that they used for teacher candidates. They found that, in the midst of these challenging circumstances, self-regulated learning and self-reflection were very helpful strategies for teacher candidates, especially after the transition to emergency remote learning. Finally, Daumiller et al. (Chapter 20), conducted a systematic meta-review of systematic reviews and meta-analyses into the cognitive and psychological effects of the COVID-19 global pandemic and present their comprehensive findings.

CONCLUSION

In closing, we would like to thank the many researchers from all over the world who came together in an effort to bring our vision to fruition and to further elucidate the cognitive and psychological effects of the COVID-19 global pandemic on high school, undergraduate and graduate learners. This collaborative effort resulted in a vast collection of research conducted across multiple continents, grounded in multiple theoretical perspectives, using multiple typical, diverse and underrepresented participant populations, and using multiple research methodologies. The present co-edited book presents also both the challenges as well as the positive outcomes found as the result of each research study as the result of the COVID-19 global pandemic. Finally, this book will conclude with a thematic summary of all the presented research as well as the implications for future crises.

REFERENCES

Alexander, B., Darby, F., Fischer, K., Jack, A. A., Le Sane, C. B., Staisloff, R., & Stout, K. A. (2020). *The post pandemic college and the future of: The academic enterprise, teaching and learning, the student experience, enrollment, business models and community colleges*. The Chronicle of Higher Education. Washington, D.C.

Allen, J., Schnieders, J. Z.-Y., Murano, D., Walton, K., Casillas, A., & Burrus, J. (2025). Effects of the COVID-19 pandemic on college and career planning, social and emotional skills, and college and career readiness: Evidence from ACT, Inc. In J. D. Salisbury-Glennon, C.-H. Wang, & D. M. Shannon (Eds.), *Examining the cognitive and psychological effects of the COVID-19 global pandemic on high school, undergraduate and graduate learners*. Information Age Publishing.

Bembenutty, H., Raffaele, C. & Pisari, D. R. (2025). A self-study on promoting self-regulated learning using technology during remote instruction. In J. D. Salisbury-Glennon, C.-H. Wang, & D. M. Shannon (Eds.), *Examining the cognitive and psychological effects of the COVID-19 global pandemic on high school, undergraduate and graduate learners.* Information Age Publishing.

Bridges, M. E. S., & Duffy, M. (2025). College during COVID-19: A mixed methods study examining undergraduate students' academic experiences and responses. In J. D. Salisbury-Glennon, C.-H. Wang, & D. M. Shannon. (Eds.), *Examining the cognitive and psychological effects of the COVID-19 global pandemic on high school, undergraduate and graduate learners.* Information Age Publishing.

Cromley, J. G., Jensen, K. J., & Mirabelli, J. F. (2025). Stresses of COVID-19 for doctoral students in engineering. In J. D. Salisbury-Glennon, C.-H. Wang, & D. M. Shannon (Eds.), *Examining the cognitive and psychological effects of the COVID-19 global pandemic on high school, undergraduate and graduate learners.* Information Age Publishing.

Daumiller, M., Rinas, R., Schoon, I., & Luftenegger, M. (2025). Cognitive and psychological effects of COVID-19: Insights from a systematic meta-review of systematic reviews and meta-analyses. In J. D. Salisbury-Glennon, C.-H. Wang, & D. M. Shannon (Eds.), *Examining the cognitive and psychological effects of the COVID-19 global pandemic on high school, undergraduate and graduate learners.* Information Age Publishing.

Deci, E. L., & Ryan, R. M. (2000). The 'what' and 'why' of goal pursuits: Human needs and the self-determination of behavior. *Psychological Inquiry, 11*, 227–268.

Dong, J., Manning, K. Q., Dai, Y., Wang, C.-H., Salisbury-Glennon, J. D., Marshall, D. T., & Trammell, D. (2025). Gender differences in graduate students' adjustment, mental health, motivation and learning strategies during the COVID-19 global pandemic. In J. D. Salisbury-Glennon, C.-H. Wang, & D. M. Shannon (Eds.), *Examining the cognitive and psychological effects of the COVID-19 global pandemic on high school, undergraduate and graduate learners.* Information Age Publishing.

Fletcher E. C., & Ford. D. Y. (2025). Examining the academic and psychological experiences of students and educational stakeholders in a high school STEM academy during the COVID-19 pandemic. In J. D. Salisbury-Glennon, C.-H. Wang, & D. M. Shannon (Eds.), *Examining the cognitive and psychological effects of the COVID-19 global pandemic on high school, undergraduate and graduate learners.* Information Age Publishing.

Goode, W. J., (1960). A theory of role strain. *American Sociological Review, 25*(4), 483–496.

Gutiérrez, V. C., & Puga D. S. E. (2025). Perspectives of engineering students on the impact of COVID-19 on the learning and teaching of algebra and differential calculus. In J. D. Salisbury-Glennon, C.-H. Wang, & D. M. Shannon (Eds.), *Examining the cognitive and psychological effects of the COVID-19 global pandemic on high school, undergraduate and graduate learners.* Information Age Publishing.

Leech, N. L., Gullett, S., Cummings, M. H., Haug, C. (2020). Challenges of remote teaching for K–12 teachers during COVID-19. *Journal of Educational Leadership in Action, 7*(1).

Manning, K. Q., Wang, C.-H., Lambert, A., Jones, M. C., Chidume, T., Dong, J., Curtis, A., & Brown. L. G. (2025). Perceptions and attitudes of nursing students' transition to remote instruction during COVID-19. In J. D. Salisbury-Glennon, C.-H. Wang, & D. M. Shannon (Eds.), *Examining the cognitive and psychological effects of the COVID-19 global pandemic on high school, undergraduate and graduate learners.* Information Age Publishing.

Miller, A. D., Vomund, J., Buehl, M. M., Brophy, N. S., & Broeckelman-Post. M. (2025). Instructional support and the student-teacher relationship in higher education: Lessons learned from students' perceptions of instruction during emergency remote learning. In J. D. Salisbury-Glennon, C.-H. Wang, & D. M. Shannon (Eds.), *Examining the cognitive and psychological effects of the COVID-19 global pandemic on high school, undergraduate and graduate learners.* Information Age Publishing.

Quadlander-Goff, E., LaPolla, M., & Marshall, D. T. (2025). The impact of the COVID-19 pandemic on college students with ADHD: Implications and interventions. In J. D. Salisbury-Glennon, C.-H. Wang, & D. M. Shannon (Eds.), *Examining the cognitive and psychological effects of the covid-19 global pandemic on high school, undergraduate and graduate learners.* Information Age Publishing.

Rashid, S., & Yadav, S. S. (2020). Impact of the COVID-19 pandemic on higher education and research. *Indian Journal of Human Development, 14*(2), 34043. https://doi.org/10.1177/0973703020946700

Rosen, L. H., Rubin, L. J., Higgins, M., & Yeatts, P. (2025). Trade-offs of seeking support for university students during the pandemic. In J. D. Salisbury-Glennon, C.-H. Wang, & D. M. Shannon (Eds.), *Examining the cognitive and psychological effects of the COVID-19 global pandemic on high school, undergraduate and graduate learners.* Information Age Publishing.

Ryan, R. M., & Deci, E. L. (2017). *Self-determination theory: Basic psychological needs in motivation, development, and wellness*. Guildford.

Salisbury-Glennon, J. D., Dai, Y., Wang, C.-H., Jang, H. S., Dong, J., Manning, K. Q., Marshall, D., & Wyckoff, C. (2023, August). *Qualitatively examining college students' anxiety, learning and motivation during COVID-19* [Poster presentation]. The 2023 Annual Convention of the American Psychological Association (APA), Washington DC.

Salisbury-Glennon, J. D., Wang, C.-H., Dai, Y. D., Jang, H.-S., Durham, K., & Shi, H. (2021). *The effects of parental relationships on motivation, learning strategies and metacognition during the COVID-19 pandemic* [Roundtable session presentation]. The annual meeting of the American Educational Research Association (AERA), Virtual Conference.

Salisbury-Glennon, J. D., Wang, C. H., Dai, Y., Jang, H. S., & Wyckoff, C. (2022). *Effects of COVID-19 on college students' social support and strategies* [Poster presentation]. The 2022 Annual Convention of the American Psychological Association (APA). Minneapolis, MN. (Virtual).

Sherif, V., Patterson, J. A., & Redger-Marquardt, C. (2025). The impact of the COVID-19 pandemic on first-generation undergraduate students' participation in campus activities. In J. D. Salisbury-Glennon, C.-H. Wang, & Shannon, D. M. (Eds.), *Examining the cognitive and psychological effects of the COVID-19 global pandemic on high school, undergraduate and graduate learners.* Information Age Publishing.

Sieber, S. D. (1974). Toward a theory of role accumulation. *American Sociological Review, 39*(4), 567–578. https://doi.org/10.2307/2094422

Tackett, S., Arrastía-Chisholm, M., & Torres, K. M. (2025). Balancing work and school during the time of COVID-19: Lessons learned from online pre- and in-service teacher training. In J. D. Salisbury-Glennon, C.-H. Wang, & D. M. Shannon (Eds.), *Examining the cognitive and psychological effects of the COVID-19 global pandemic on high school, undergraduate and graduate learners.* Information Age Publishing.

Trammell, D. L., Quadlander-Goff, E., Schoettler, N. M., Slaughter, K. F., Riel, J., & Hudson. D. L. (2025). Walking the fine line: First-Year doctoral students' experiences during COVID-19. In J. D. Salisbury-Glennon, C.-H. Wang, & D. M. Shannon (Eds.), *Examining the cognitive and psychological effects of the COVID-19 global pandemic on high school, undergraduate and graduate learners.* Information Age Publishing.

Tyler, J. M., Collins, J., Shannon, D. M., Carney, J., LaPolla, M. (2025). Underserved and underrepresented college students' resilience during COVID-19. In J. D. Salisbury-Glennon, C.-H. Wang, & D. M. Shannon (Eds.), *Examining the cognitive and psychological effects of the COVID-19 global pandemic on high school, undergraduate and graduate learners.* Information Age Publishing.

Wang, C, -H., Dai, Y., Dong, J., Manning, K. Q., Salisbury-Glennon, J. D., Tseng, C.-M., & Marshall, D. T. (2025). The effects of mental health, motivation, and learning strategies on high school students' grades during COVID-19. In J. D. Salisbury-Glennon, C.-H. Wang, & D. M. Shannon (Eds.), *Examining the cognitive and psychological effects of the COVID-19 global pandemic on high school, undergraduate and graduate learners.* Information Age Publishing.

Williams, G. M., & Diamond, M. S. (2025). Exploring the online academic acculturation of multilingual learners during COVID. In J. D. Salisbury-Glennon, C.-H. Wang, & D. M. Shannon (Eds.), *Examining the cognitive and psychological effects of the COVID-19 global pandemic on high school, undergraduate and graduate learners.* Information Age Publishing.

Yoo, H. J., & Marshall, D. T. (2025). Graduate students' mental health during COVID-19: Parenthood and gender. In J. D. Salisbury-Glennon, C.-H. Wang, & D. M. Shannon (Eds.), *Examining the cognitive and psychological effects of the COVID-19 global pandemic on high school, undergraduate and graduate learners.* Information Age Publishing.

Wentzel, K. R., Jablansky, S., & Scalise, N. R. (2021). Peer social acceptance and academic achievement: A meta-analytic study. *Journal of Educational Psychology, 113*(1), 157–180. https://doi.org/10.1037/edu0000468

CHAPTER 2

EFFECTS OF THE COVID-19 PANDEMIC ON COLLEGE AND CAREER PLANNING, SOCIAL AND EMOTIONAL SKILLS, AND COLLEGE AND CAREER READINESS

Evidence From ACT, Inc.

Jeff Allen, Joyce Zhou-Yile Schnieders, Dana Murano, Kate Walton, Alex Casillas, and Jeremy Burrus

ABSTRACT

We summarize five primary studies using data collected before the pandemic's onset and during different stages of the pandemic, concluding with ACT tests taken in spring 2022. We contribute to the understanding of the pandemic's effects by presenting research focused on high school students and examining multiple academic and interpersonal factors, including college and career readiness (at Grade 11), progress toward college and career readiness (Grades 3–10), social and emotional skill development and relationships with students' behaviors, college preparation activities, and students' perceptions

Examining the Cognitive and Psychological Effects of the COVID-19 Global Pandemic on High School, College, and Graduate Learners, pp. 11–40

of their development of academic skills, self-management skills, socialization, resilience, and college and career exploration.

Keywords: COVID-19 pandemic, college readiness, career readiness, standardized testing, social and emotional skills, academic behaviors, college preparation, college and career exploration.

INTRODUCTION

ACT, Inc. is best known for its college entrance exam but also has an active research agenda on other dimensions of college and career readiness. In addition to core academic skills, college and career navigation and social and emotional skills are key constituents of student success in school, work, and life (Camara et al., 2015). While the negative effects of the pandemic on academic performance have been well documented for elementary and middle school students (cf. Kuhfeld & Lewis, 2022; NAEP, 2022), we contribute to the understanding of the pandemic's effects by presenting research focused on high school students and examining additional academic and interpersonal factors, including college and career readiness (at Grade 11), progress toward college and career readiness (Grades 3–10), social and emotional skill development and relationships with students' behaviors, college preparation activities, and students' perceptions of their development of academic skills, self-management skills, socialization, resilience, and college and career exploration.

We summarize five primary studies using data collected before the pandemic's onset and during different stages of the pandemic, concluding with ACT tests taken in spring 2022. Table 2.1 lists the five studies, titles of the papers documenting each study (available at act.org/research), and an abbreviated title used when referring to each study. Figure 2.1 shows a timeline for the research, highlighting the dates of data collection for each study relative to pandemic milestones.

Objectives

While each of the five studies contributes uniquely to our knowledge of the pandemic's effects, the collective goal of the five studies is to understand how the pandemic affected high school students while they worked to complete high school and enter college or the workforce. A secondary goal is to understand how the pandemic's effects varied across student groups, with a special focus on groups that are underrepresented in colleges across the United States. In addition to measures of academic achievement, the

Table 2.1

Five Primary Studies

Study	Title of Research Paper(s)	Abbreviated Title
1	Examining the COVID-19 pandemic's impacts on ACT scores: Spring 2022 update	The pandemic's effects on **college and career readiness**
2	Understanding the impact of the COVID-19 pandemic on student achievement in Arkansas	The pandemic's effects on **student achievement in Arkansas**
3	Paper 1: Students have shown significant social and emotional skill development during COVID-19 Paper 2: Students' social and emotional skills and behaviors during the onset of COVID-19	**Social and emotional skills** in the time of COVID: Their development and associations with coping behaviors
4	College preparation opportunities, the pandemic, and student preparedness	**College preparation** during the pandemic
5	Disruptions and gains: Students' reflections on the effects of the pandemic	**Student reflections** on the effects of the pandemic

Figure 2.1

Research Timeline

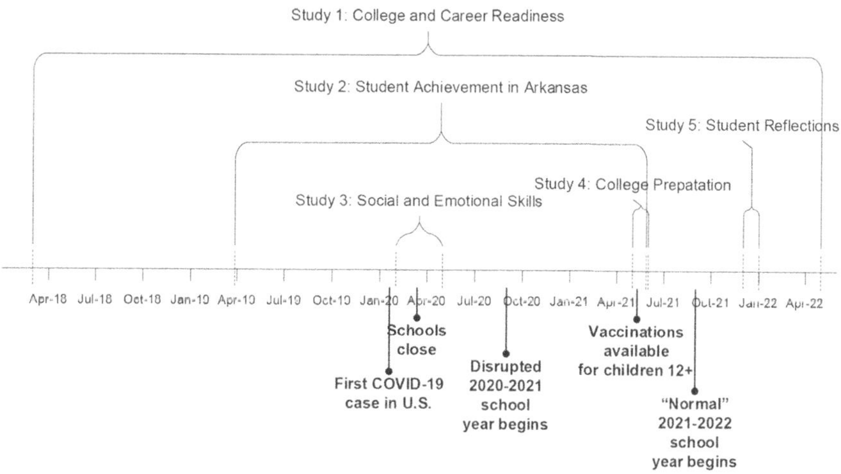

collective research examined other factors that are important for success after high school—including social and emotional skills and college preparation activities.

The objective of Study 1 was to understand the pandemic's effects on college and career readiness, as measured by the ACT test, for students who are approaching the end of their K–12 schooling experience. A secondary objective was to understand differences across sociodemographic variables in online schooling participation among high school students. Research questions addressed by Study 1 include: (1) How was students' college readiness, as measured by ACT test scores, impacted by the COVID-19 pandemic? (2) Did the level of participation in online/virtual instruction vary across demographic groups?

The objective of Study 2 was to understand the pandemic's effects on progress toward college and career readiness, as measured by standardized achievement tests for Grades 3–11. A secondary objective was to understand differences in academic growth by mode of learning (virtual, hybrid, or in-person) during the 2020–2021 academic year. Research questions addressed by Study 2 include: (1) How was students' growth towards college and career readiness impacted by the COVID-19 pandemic? (2) Did academic growth vary by mode of learning during the 2020–2021 academic year?

The objective of Study 3 was to understand students' social and emotional skill development during the onset of the pandemic. A secondary objective was to understand how students' social and emotional skill levels related to the behaviors they engaged in at the start of the pandemic. Research questions addressed by Study 3 include: (1) Did student's social and emotional skill levels change between February 2020 and April 2020, after the onset of the pandemic? (2) Did students engage in positive behaviors to cope with the onset of the pandemic, and did engagement in these behaviors vary across social and emotional skill levels?

The objective of Study 4 was to understand college-bound high school senior's participation in college preparation activities during the pandemic, the interruption of their participation due to the pandemic, and the relationship between college preparation activity participation and college application behaviors. Research questions addressed by Study 4 include: (1) Did college-bound students continue to participate in college preparation activities during the pandemic? (2) Did disparities in college preparation activities exist across student groups? (3) How was participation in college preparation activities linked to college application behaviors?

The objective of Study 5 was to understand students' perceptions of how the first year of the pandemic affected five aspects of their learning (academic learning, self-management, socializing, resilience, and college/career exploration) and key factors related to their perceptions. Research questions addressed by Study 5 include: (1) Did students perceive the pandemic as having a positive, negative or no effect on various aspects of their learning? (2) Were school-based supports and the amount of in-person learning linked to students' perceptions of disruptions and gains during the pandemic?

METHOD

All five studies are based on students who took the ACT test (and in the case of Study 2, the ACT Aspire test) but employed different target populations, sample sizes, modes of data collection, outcome measures, and data analysis techniques. In Table 2.2, we summarize the methodological features of each study.

Table 2.2

Research Methods

Study	Target Population	*N*	Mode of Data Collection	Outcome Measure	Data Analysis Technique
1	Students from high schools that administered the school-day ACT test to 11th grade students from 2018-2022	3.4 million students from 5,979 schools	ACT testing programs (mode of learning data collected by ACT registration system)	ACT test scores in English, math, reading, science, and Composite; mode of learning	Hierarchical linear regression modeling with propensity score weighting
2	Public school students from Arkansas in grades 3-11 in 2019 and 2021	246,178 students for 2021 cohort	ACT testing programs, mode of learning data collected by Arkansas Department of Education	ACT Aspire (Grades 3-10) and ACT (Grade 11) test scores in English, math, reading, science, and Composite	Hierarchical linear regression modeling with propensity score weighting
3	ACT-tested 11th and 12th grade students across the U.S. who took the February 2020 ACT test.	642 11th and 12th grade students	Online survey sent to a random sample of 30,000 students in Feb. 2020 and a follow-up survey to respondents again in Apr. 2020.	Analysis 1: Self-reported social and emotional skills at two time points Analysis 2: Behaviors at the onset of the pandemic	Analysis 1: *t*-tests, effect sizes Analysis 2: descriptive statistics, correlations

(Table continued on next page)

Table 2.2 (Continued)

Research Methods

Study	Target Population	*N*	Mode of Data Collection	Outcome Measure	Data Analysis Technique
4	ACT-tested 12th grade students who planned to enter college in 2021 and had taken the ACT test during their senior year	2,354 12th grade students	Online survey sent to a random sample of 35,000 students in May 2021	Participation in campus visits, college fairs, FAFSA workshops, and various "talk to an adult" activities, number of colleges applied to, putting down a deposit	Descriptive analysis, multiple linear regression, logistic regression
5	ACT-tested 10th—12th grade high school students who took the December 2021 ACT test.	1,893 10th-12th grade students	Online survey sent to a random sample of 31,500 students in Dec. 2021	Academic skills, grades, self-management, socializing, resilience, college/career exploration, school-based supports, mode of learning	Descriptive analysis, non-parametric tests, ordinal logistic regression, multiple linear regression

Study 1 (Allen, 2022a) relied on data from ACT school-day testing programs, so included virtually all students regardless of their college-going plans and was based on very large sample sizes. Study 1 is based on ACT state and district testing programs, in which the test is administered during the school day and all 11th grade students can test. In several states, the ACT test is used to measure academic achievement in English Language Arts (ELA), math, and science for federal accountability. Therefore, we are confident that the results are not biased due to self-selection to take the ACT test. Study 1 compared pre-pandemic test scores (spring 2018 through early March 2020) to pandemic-era scores (spring 2021 and 2022). We only included schools that tested a consistent majority of students across years, ensuring that differences across years are not due to differences in test participation across years.

Study 2 (Allen, 2022b) uses a similar research design as Study one but includes Grades 3–11 (the ACT Aspire test was administered for Grades 3–10) and is restricted to one state (Arkansas), 1 baseline year (2019), and one pandemic year (2021). Study 2 is limited to Arkansas because they are the only state that administered ACT Aspire for Grades 3–10 and because we collaborated with the Arkansas Department of Education on a special study comparing student achievement by mode of learning. While limited to one state, Study 2 provides key insights on how the pandemic's impact varied across grade levels and mode of learning (on-site, hybrid, or virtual).

Studies 3, 4, and 5 are based on surveys administered online to randomly selected groups of students who took the ACT test on a national test date (administered on Saturdays). Survey participation was voluntary, and respondents were more likely to be female and college-bound, relative to the population of all high school students. Studies 4 and 5 used weighting to make the samples more representative of their respective target populations with respect to gender, race/ethnicity, family income level, and parent education level.

Study 3 (Walton & Murano, 2020; Murano et al., 2023) examined changes in mean social and emotional skills from February 2020 to April 2020, and then examined how those skills related to specific positive coping behaviors at the onset of the pandemic. A random sample of 30,000 students who registered for the February 2020 ACT test were invited to participate in the February 2020 survey on social and emotional skills. A total of 2,010 students completed the entire survey (response rate of 7%). The 2,010 respondents were then invited to participate in an incentivized follow-up survey in April 2020, after the onset of the pandemic. The follow-up survey measured social and emotional skills as well as specific behaviors in response to the pandemic. 642 students completed the follow-up survey (response rate of 32%). The sample is disproportionately female (75%) and high achieving with a mean ACT Composite score of 25.9 (one standard deviation above the national mean).

Study 4 (Schnieders & Moore, 2022) surveyed students from the 2021 high school graduating class to examine how their college preparation activities were interrupted by the pandemic. A random sample of 35,000 students were selected from the sampling frame. A total of 2,354 college-bound students answered at least half of the required questions (response rate of 7%). In addition to descriptive statistics, we conducted regression analysis to (1) investigate factors that could help distinguish between students who participated in the activities and those who did not; (2) explore the factors related to the total number of activities that were planned but not carried out because of pandemic restrictions; (3) investigate the relationship between college preparation activities that students engaged in and their college application behaviors.

Study 5 (Schnieders, 2023) surveyed students late in 2021 to examine how the pandemic had affected them on several fronts, including academic skills, course grades, motivation to learn, and involvement in college and career exploration. A random sample of 31,500 students were selected from the sampling frame. A total of 1,893 students answered all the required questions (response rate of 6%). In addition to descriptive analyses, we also conducted a series of ordinal logistic regressions to explore the factors that could help distinguish students who perceived the pandemic as having a negative effect and those who perceived it as having no effect or a positive effect on their learning. Study 5 examined many of the same readiness domains as Studies 1–4, so is especially helpful for integrating findings across studies. Full methodological details are provided in the report for each study.

RESULTS

Study 1: The Pandemic's Effects on College and Career Readiness

We compared pre-pandemic ACT test scores (spring 2018 through early March 2020) to pandemic-era ACT test scores (spring 2021 and 2022). For each of those years, schools were included in the sample if they tested at least 75% of their 11th-grade student body. This ensures that the data are more likely to be representative of the school population. Only schools that met the 75% threshold for at least one pre-pandemic cohort (2018, 2019, or 2020) and one pandemic cohort (2021 or 2022) were included.

Table 2.3 provides the estimated ACT score declines for the 2021 and 2022 11th grade cohorts. The adjusted difference is based on a weighted hierarchical regression model and represents the estimate of the pandemic's effect on ACT test scores. Table 2.3 also includes additional measures to aid interpretation of the adjusted difference, including (1) the number of instructional months corresponding to the adjusted difference, (2) the number of college-ready students corresponding to the adjusted difference, and (3) the standardized effect size measure (*d*).

For each cohort and each subject area, ACT scores were significantly lower during the pandemic years (2021 and 2022) relative to the pre-pandemic years (2018–2020). For math, the score decline was slightly more severe for the 2022 cohort (–0.74) than it was for the 2021 cohort (–0.70). For English, reading, and science, the score declines were less severe for the 2022 cohort.

Table 2.3 shows that the ACT score declines for 2022 are comparable to receiving at least two fewer months of instruction. For math, the score declines are comparable to 3.6 fewer months of instruction for the 2021 cohort and 3.8 fewer months of instruction for the 2022 cohort. Translated to the number of students who are ready for first-year college courses, the score declines are comparable to between 1.2 (reading, 2022 cohort) and 2.9 (math, 2021 and 2022 cohorts) fewer students (per 100) who are

Table 2.3

ACT Score Changes Relative to Pre-Pandemic Cohorts, by Cohort and Score

Cohort	Score	Adjusted difference		Instructional months	College ready per 100	d
		EST	SE			
2021	Composite	–0.66	0.01	–3.0		–0.12
	English	–0.79	0.01	–2.6	–2.3	–0.12
	Math	–0.70	0.01	–3.6	–2.9	–0.14
	Reading	–0.59	0.01	–3.2	–1.6	–0.09
	Science	–0.55	0.01	–3.0	–2.1	–0.10
2022	Composite	–0.59	0.01	–2.7		–0.11
	English	–0.74	0.01	–2.4	–2.2	–0.12
	Math	–0.74	0.01	–3.8	–2.9	–0.15
	Reading	–0.42	0.01	–2.3	–1.2	–0.07
	Science	–0.44	0.01	–2.4	–1.6	–0.08

Note. EST = estimate; SE = standard error; *d* = adjusted difference in standard deviation units.

college-ready. The score declines corresponded to *d* statistics ranging from –0.07 to –0.15.

The decline in ACT Composite scores was similar for the 2022 (–0.59) and 2021 (–0.66) cohorts, suggesting that academic performance did not rebound much for the 2022 cohort. Similar to what was observed for the 2021 cohort, the 2022 score declines were least severe for students who are Asian (–0.11). The ACT Composite score declines were mostly similar across the other racial/ethnic groups (Figure 2.2). Score declines were less severe for 2022 relative to 2021 for students who are Black, two or more races, or White. Score declines were more severe for 2022 relative to 2021 for students who are Asian, Latinx, Native American, or Native Hawaiian/other Pacific Islander.

Mode of Learning Differences Across Student Groups

For students in the 2022 cohort, additional data were collected from students on their mode of learning during the school years 2020–2021 (their 10th-grade year) and 2021–2022 (their 11th-grade year). On the ACT reporting portal, students were asked two questions:

Figure 2.2

Adjusted Difference in Average ACT Composite Score Relative to Pre-Pandemic Years, by Race/Ethnicity and Year

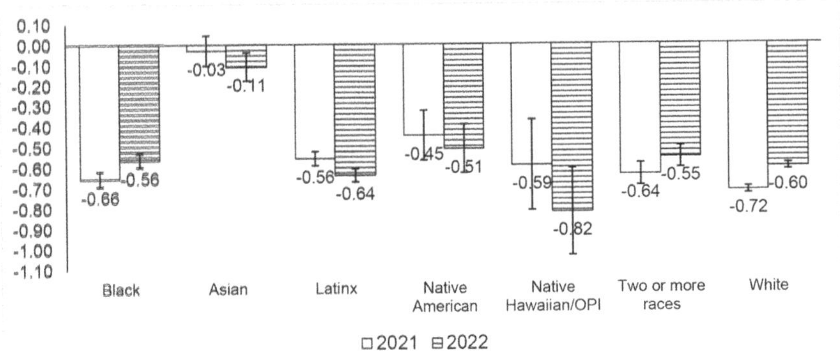

Note. The thin black lines on each bar represent 95% confidence intervals for each estimate. OPI = other Pacific Islander.

1. This school year, are you attending school online, in person (at school), or a mix of the two (hybrid)?
2. Last school year, did you attend school online, in person (at school), or a mix of the two (hybrid)?

Students were given the following response options: online only, mostly online, about the same online and in person, mostly in person, and in person only. We compared the relative frequency of the mode of learning survey responses across racial/ethnic groups. The relative frequencies of each mode of learning category are provided in Figure 2.3 for the 2020–2021 school year, which is when the students were in 10th grade and was the first full academic year that was disrupted by the pandemic.

We found that 17% of the sample learned exclusively online, 12% learned mostly online, 27% learned about the same amount online and in person, 22% learned mostly in person, and 23% learned in person only. The percentage who learned exclusively online varied dramatically across racial/ethnic groups, from 38% for students who are Asian, 33% for students who are Black, and 10% for students who are White.

During the 2020–2021 (10th grade) school year, students attended school in person 56% of the time on average. Regression analysis revealed that several demographic variables and school characteristics were collectively predictive of the level of participation in in-person schooling ($R^2 =$ 0.14). The regression coefficients (EST in Table 2.4) represent the change

Figure 2.3

Percentage in Each Mode of Learning Category During 2020–2021 School Year for 2022 Cohort, by Race/Ethnicity

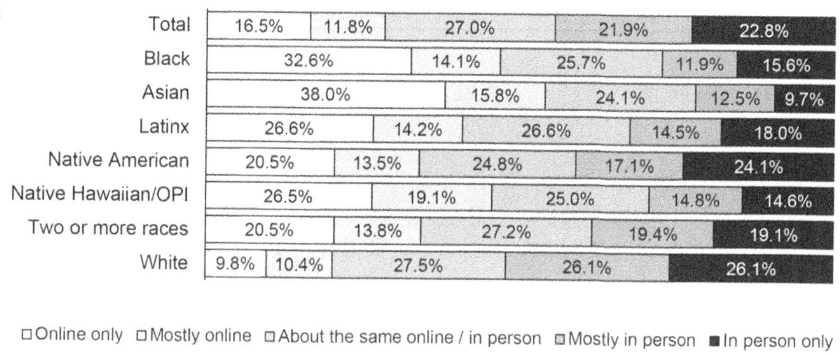

Note. OPI = other Pacific Islander.

in percentage of time spent learning in person associated with each 1-unit increase in the predictor. For example, EST = –2.38 for female gender means that the percentage of time spent learning in person was 2.38 percentage points lower for female students relative to male students. Relative to students who are White, in-person schooling percentages were lower for students from other racial/ethnic groups, especially for students who are Asian (EST = –10.56), Black (EST = –8.42), or Native Hawaiian/other Pacific Islander (EST = –6.27).

Table 2.4

Hierarchical Linear Regression Results for Predictors of In-Person Schooling During 2020–2021 School Year

Predictor	EST	SE	*t*	*p*
Intercept	51.46	0.67		
Female gender	–2.38	0.10	–24.39	< .0001
Race/ethnicity (White reference group)				
Black	–8.42	0.19	–44.83	< .0001
Asian	–10.56	0.27	–39.10	< .0001
Latinx	–4.28	0.16	–26.18	< .0001

(Table continued on next page)

Table 2.4 (Continued)

Hierarchical Linear Regression Results for Predictors of In-Person Schooling During 2020–2021 School Year

Predictor	EST	SE	*t*	*p*
Native American	–5.00	0.49	–10.19	< .0001
Native Hawaiian/OPI	–6.27	0.94	–6.65	< .0001
2 or more races	–4.56	0.22	–20.65	< .0001
School Characteristics				
School grade 11 enrollment (in hundreds)	–1.34	0.19	–7.00	< .0001
School % FRL eligible	0.03	0.01	2.52	0.012
School % URM	–0.29	0.01	–22.04	< .0001
Private school	19.99	1.19	16.85	< .0001
School locale (Urban reference group)				
Rural	15.79	0.86	18.34	< .0001
Town	13.68	0.88	15.53	< .0001
Suburban	6.47	0.82	7.91	< .0001

Note. EST = estimate; SE = standard error; t = t statistic; OPI = other Pacific Islander; FRL = free and reduced-price lunch; URM = underrepresented racial/ethnic minority.

For each one unit increase in a school's percentage of underrepresented minority students, in-person schooling percentage declined by 0.29 percentage points. The in-person schooling percentage was also lower for students at larger schools and schools serving fewer students who are eligible for free or reduced-price lunch. Relative to public schools, the in-person schooling percentage was higher for students at private schools (EST = 19.99). Relative to schools in urban locales, the in-person schooling percentage was higher for students attending school in rural (EST = 15.79), town (EST = 13.68), and suburban (EST = 6.47) locales.

Collectively, the results for the 2020–2021 school year suggest that 10th-grade students who are male, White, and attend a small private school in a rural locale that has a low percentage of underrepresented minority students were most likely to attend school in person.

Study 2: The Pandemic's Effects on Student Achievement in Arkansas

Like Study 1, this study relied on large-scale assessment data to examine effects of the pandemic on student achievement in English, math, reading, and science. Unlike Study 1, Study 2 focuses on a single state (Arkansas) and single pandemic year (2021), spans several grade levels, incorporates student growth data, and compares academic achievement by mode of learning (on-site, hybrid, or virtual).

After controlling for changes in the tested population from 2019 to 2021, we found that average ACT Aspire or ACT Composite scores declined for all grade levels, suggesting that the COVID-19 pandemic had a negative impact on student achievement in Arkansas. Figure 2.4 provides the estimated Composite score declines (in standard deviation units) by grade level. Generally, the score declines were larger for lower grade levels. For 3rd grade, Composite scores declined by 0.25 standard deviation units, which is like students' overall performance dropping from the 50th to the 40th percentile (see Figure 2.4).

Figure 2.4

Decline in Average Composite Scores for Arkansas, in Standard Deviation Units, from 2019 to 2021

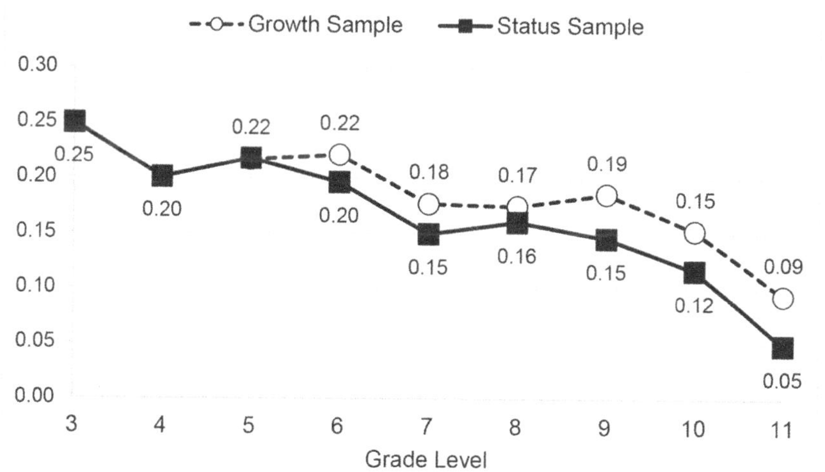

The estimated score declines based on the Growth sample (dotted line) account for prior test scores, student demographics, and school effects. The estimates based on the Status sample (solid line) account for student demographics and school effects, but not prior test scores. The Growth sample estimate is available only for 5th–11th grades, whereas the Status sample estimate is available for 3rd–11th grades. For 6th–11th grades, the declines in Composite scores are more severe for the Growth sample, suggesting that not accounting for prior test scores (Status model) may lead to understating the pandemic's impact on ACT Aspire and ACT test scores. This suggests that the estimated score declines observed for Study 1, which are based on a Status model, may understate the pandemic's impact.

Figure 2.5 provides the estimated score declines in standard deviation units, by test section and grade level. Note that the estimates are based on the Status sample for 3rd and 4th grades and the Growth sample for 5th–11th grades. Therefore, the results for 3rd and 4th grades may understate the pandemic's impact. Because they are based on different statistical models (the Growth model uses prior test scores as covariates, whereas the Status model does not), the lines between 4th and 5th grade are not connected. For 3rd–10th grades, we see that the relative score declines were much larger in math relative to the other test sections. The score declines were generally more severe for English and science than for reading. For all sections and grade levels, average scores declined from 2019 to 2021 (see Figure 2.5).

Academic Achievement Differences by Mode Of Learning

During the 2020–2021 academic year, the Arkansas Department of Education collected data on students' instructional option: on-site, hybrid,

Figure 2.5

Decline in Average Section Test Scores for Arkansas, in Standard Deviation Units, from 2019 to 2021

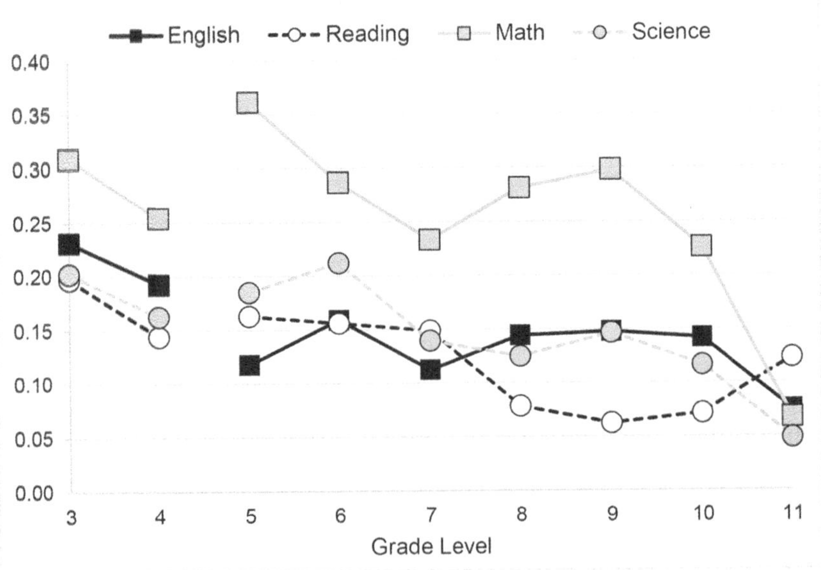

or virtual. These data were collected at 4 time points: November 15, 2020; February 15, 2021; April 15, 2021; and June 15, 2021. For analysis purposes, we considered three mode-of-learning groups:

1. All on-site: Students who were classified as on-site at all 4 time points
2. All hybrid: Students who were classified as hybrid at all 4 time points
3. All virtual: Students who were classified as virtual at all 4 time points

For all grade levels, average scores for the three mode-of-learning groups were below the scores for the 2019 pre-pandemic group (Figure 2.6). The score declines were most severe for the virtual group, followed by the hybrid group, and finally the on-site group. The differences between virtual and hybrid were generally larger than the differences between hybrid and on-site. The differences between the on-site group and the reference group are large, showing that even students in the on-site group suffered score declines relative to the pre-pandemic group. Generally, the performance gap for students who learned virtually is smaller for higher grade levels (see Figure 2.6).

Figure 2.6

Decline in Average Composite Scores for Arkansas, in Standard Deviation Units, from 2019 to 2021, by Mode of Learning Group

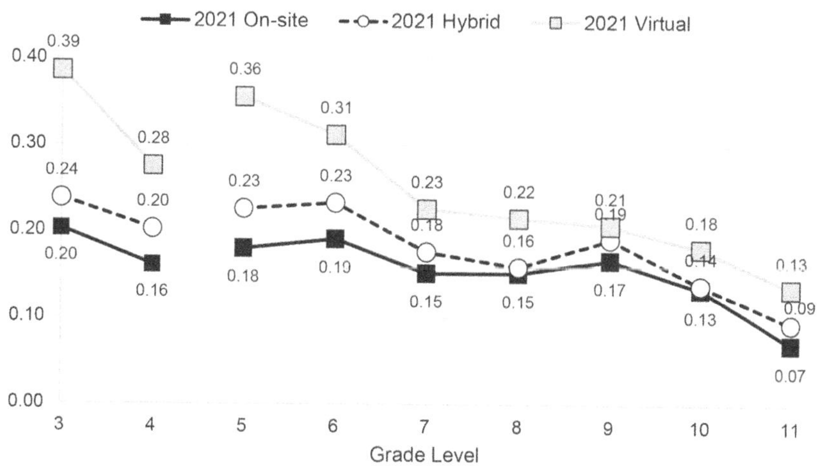

Differences across the three mode-of-learning groups were small for reading. The difference in academic growth for students who learned virtually, relative to those who learned on-site, was most severe for math.

Study 3: Social and Emotional Skills in the Time of COVID: Their Development and Associations With Coping Behaviors

Students were surveyed at two time points: Time 1 (February 8 to February 28, 2020, immediately before the COVID-19 pandemic gripped the United States) and approximately two months later at Time 2 (April 20 to May 4, 2020). At both time points, participants completed the Big Five Inventory (BFI; John & Srivastava, 1999), a 44-item measure of the Big Five personality factors with six response options ranging from *strongly agree* to *strongly disagree*. The Big Five factors—Conscientiousness, Agreeableness, Emotional Stability, Openness to Experience, and Extraversion—align directly with social and emotional (SE) skills outlined in the ACT Holistic Framework (Camara et al., 2015). Respectively, they are *Sustaining Effort, Getting Along with Others, Maintaining Composure, Keeping an Open Mind*, and *Social Connection*.

At Time 2, participants were asked on a four-point frequency scale (*never, 1–2 times per week, 3–5 times per week*, and *6–7 times per week*) to report on a variety of behaviors (e.g., initiating calls with friends and family members) to ascertain whether they had engaged in those behaviors during the onset of the pandemic. We report on 13 behaviors, all of which were considered positive, in that engaging in these behaviors indicated adapting to and positively coping with the shifting conditions caused by the onset of the pandemic.

Dependent samples *t*-tests were carried out, and standardized effect sizes were calculated to examine growth on each SE skill from Time 1 to Time 2. Students showed significant growth on four of five SE skills (see Table 2.5). Students' *Social Connection* scores were stagnant during this time, but there were significant gains for *Sustaining Effort, Getting Along with Others, Maintaining Composure*, and *Keeping an Open Mind*, with the largest gains for *Maintaining Composure* ($d = .19$).

The study did not include a pre-pandemic test-retest control group, so it is possible that the scores would have increased upon retesting in the absence of the pandemic. However, during the early stages of the pandemic, we can conclude that students improved on *Maintaining Composure* more than *Social Connection*, which could be explained by their need to face the unprecedented challenges of the pandemic while having no in-person contact with teachers and less contact with peers.

Table 2.5

Mean Social and Emotional Skill Statistics from Time 1 to Time 2

SE Skill	Time 1 *M (SD)*	Time 2 *M (SD)*	*t*	*p*	*d*
Sustaining Effort	4.35 (.74)	4.42 (.72)	3.69	<.01	.10
Getting Along with Others	4.51 (.71)	4.57 (.71)	2.80	.01	.08
Maintaining Composure	3.34 (.93)	3.51 (.86)	7.16	<.01	.19
Keeping an Open Mind	4.33 (.66)	4.37 (.69)	2.17	.03	.06
Social Connection	3.76 (.95)	3.75 (.94)	–.04	.97	–.00

Additional results suggested these five SE skills were significantly related to positive coping behaviors during the early stages of the pandemic (see Table 2.6). The largest associations were found for encouraging others to stay positive (with an average correlation across the five skills of .32). The five skills were essentially equally important for engaging in the positive behaviors, with average correlations across the 13 behaviors ranging from .18 with *Getting Along with Others* to .22 with *Sustaining Effort*.

Table 2.6

Correlations Between Social and Emotional Skills and Behavioral Frequency Items

How often do you ...	*M*	*SD*	SE	GA	MC	KO	SC
Work toward your goals?	3.08	0.85	0.40**	0.17**	0.21**	0.15**	0.25**
Set a schedule for your day?	2.70	1.06	0.30**	0.11*	0.10*	0.13**	0.22**
Complete all of your tasks and chores?	3.35	0.77	0.28**	0.15**	0.17**	0.18**	0.14**
Help family members around the house?	3.32	0.77	0.25**	0.22**	0.22**	0.24**	0.18**
Engage in activities (e.g., meditation, exercise) to help calm yourself down?	2.67	1.06	0.24**	0.15**	0.19**	0.16**	0.25**
Think about things you are grateful for?	2.91	0.94	0.31**	0.34**	0.24**	0.25**	0.26**

(Table continued on next page)

Table 2.6 (Continued)

Correlations Between Social and Emotional Skills and Behavioral Frequency Items

How often do you ...	*M*	*SD*	SE	GA	MC	KO	SC
Watch or read the news to learn more about COVID-19?	2.64	1.01	0.21**	0.15**	0.21**	0.15**	0.14**
Encourage others around you to stay positive?	2.66	0.98	0.25**	0.38**	0.25**	0.34**	0.38**
Initiate calls or video calls with friends or family members?	2.65	0.93	0.16**	0.20**	0.16**	0.21**	0.29**
How often have you...	***M***	***SD***	**SE**	**GA**	**MC**	**KO**	**SC**
Volunteered to grocery shop or run other errands for those who need help?	1.89	1.05	0.11*	0.20**	0.17**	0.17**	0.16**
Tried learning something new?	2.79	0.86	0.13**	0.13**	0.25**	0.24**	0.18**
Tried something new (e.g., a new activity, a new TV show, a new recipe)?	3.08	0.87	0.16**	0.10*	0.13**	0.20**	0.13**
Initiated a relief effort in response to COVID-19 (e.g., organized a group to make face masks)?	1.40	0.74	0.09*	0.10*	0.17**	0.12**	0.16**

Note. SE = Sustaining Effort, GA = Getting Along with Others, MC = Maintaining Composure, KO = Keeping an Open Mind, SC = Social Connection. All scales range from 1–4. *Indicates correlation is significant at the $p <. 05$ level. **Indicates correlation is significant at the $p < .01$ level.

Study 4: College Preparation During the Pandemic

We provided a list of seven activities that included common events, programs, and services that support students as they prepare for college, and these seven activities were classified into two types: "attend an event" activities and "talk with an adult" activities (Figure 2.7). Despite the pandemic restrictions, students from the class of 2021 still participated in college preparation activities, with participation rates ranging from 39% to 73% across activities. However, some plans were interrupted by the pandemic, with 46% of students reporting at least one activity or event that they had planned to participate in before the pandemic restrictions but were unable to participate in once restrictions occurred. College preparation activities most likely to be disrupted included campus visits (20%), attending a college fair (19%), talking to a college representative who visited school (15%), and participation in a FAFSA workshop (13%). The pandemic was more disruptive of "attend an event" activities compared to opportunities that involved talking with a teacher, counselor, or college representative.

Figure 2.7

Percentage of Students Participating in College Preparation Activities

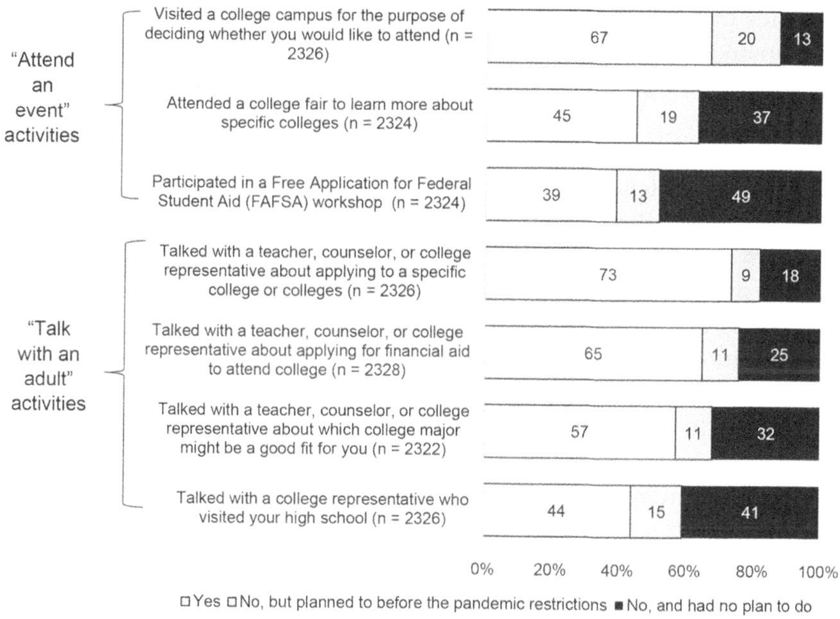

Seven logistic regression models (one for each activity) were conducted, and the results showed that with an increase in exposure to in-person learning, the likelihood of participating in all seven activities increased, after we controlled for other variables (i.e., gender, race/ethnicity, types of colleges planning to attend, ACT score, family income, parental education level, and whether students had taken college credit courses in high school). Moreover, a multiple linear regression model showed that the more in-person learning a student had, the lower the number of plans disrupted by the pandemic.

Another finding of the study was that students from certain subgroups were impacted more than others. A multiple linear regression model revealed that students from low-income families and students who were

Latinx or Asian were more likely to report higher numbers of activities that were disrupted by the pandemic, after other variables were held constant. Meanwhile, the seven logistic regression models showed that Black students were more likely to participate in six out of the seven college preparation activities than their White peers, and Black students' engagement in these activities did not appear to be disrupted by the pandemic.

Additionally, we investigated whether participating in college preparation activities was related to college application behaviors. A multiple linear regression was conducted with the number of colleges applied to as the dependent variable, with the number of "attend an event" activities participated in and number of "talk with an adult" activities participated in as independent variables, and with gender, race/ethnicity, family income, first-generation status, ACT score, types of colleges planning to attend, amount of in-person learning during the school year, taking college credit courses in high school, and academic concern due to the pandemic as covariates. Participation in "attend an event" activities and "talk with an adult" activities were both significant predictors ($p < 0.05$). After we controlled for other variables, the number of colleges applied to was expected to increase by 0.29 with each additional "attend an event" activity participated in, and to increase by 0.45 with each additional "talk with an adult" activities participated in. Moreover, a logistic regression was used to investigate whether putting down a deposit to attend a postsecondary institution was associated with participation in college preparation activities. After other variables were held constant, the number of "attend an event" activities participated in was significant at $p < 0.05$—the more "attend an event" activities a student participated in, the more likely the student had put down a deposit to attend a postsecondary institution.

Study 5: Students' Reflections on the Effects of the Pandemic

The surveyed students were provided with a list of items from various aspects of education that were relevant to their learning and development in high school, including academic learning, social and emotional learning, and college/career planning (Figure 2.8). For each item, students rated the extent to which the pandemic affected them during its first year, using a scale from –4 to 4, with a negative score indicating a decrease or loss and a positive score indicating an increase or gain.

Figure 2.8

Percentages of Students Reporting the Effects of the Pandemic

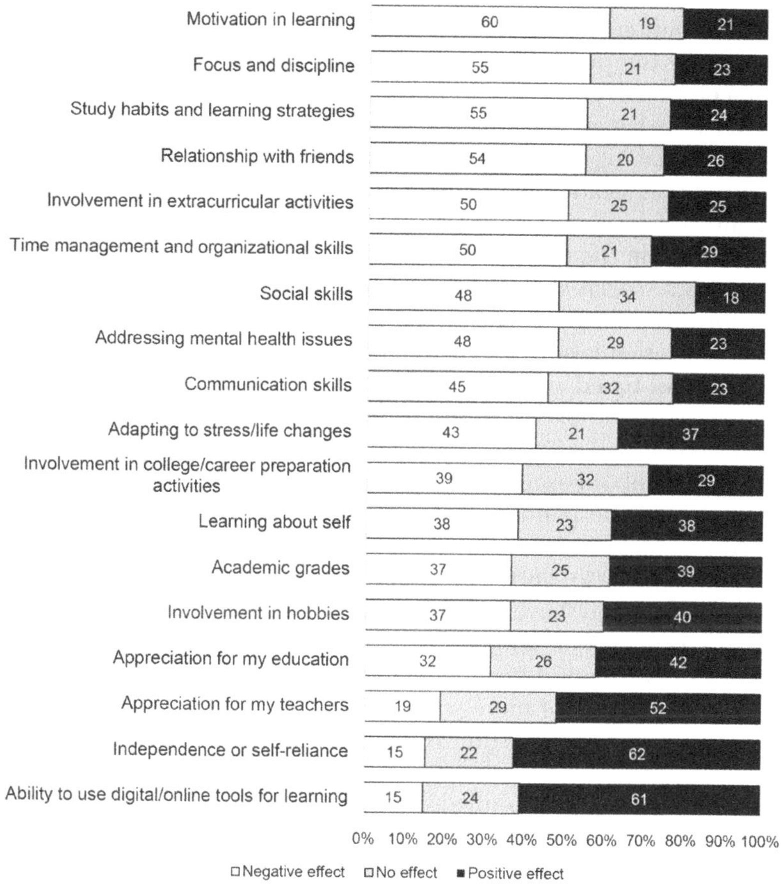

Students reported that the pandemic had a negative effect on multiple aspects of their learning (e.g., self-management, socializing, resilience, college/career exploration). Most students reported negative effects on motivation in learning (60%), focus and discipline (55%), study habits and learning strategies (55%), relationship with friends (54%), involvement in extracurricular activities (50%), and time management and organizational skills (50%).

Despite the disruptions, students also reported gains when they reflected on their learning during the first year of the pandemic. First, with the transition to online learning, 61% felt that their abilities to use digital/online tools for learning improved. Second, about 62% of students reported that they became more independent or self-reliant during the first year of the pandemic. Additionally, during the tough first year of the pandemic, 42% of students thought the pandemic had a positive effect on how much they appreciated their education. More than half (52%) reported that they had more appreciation for their teachers.

To explore the potential factors that could help distinguish students who perceived the pandemic as having a negative effect and those who perceived it as having no effect or a positive effect on their learning, a series of ordinal logistic regressions were conducted on different aspects of learning (i.e., academic learning, self-management, socializing, resilience, and college/career exploration). Each aspect of learning contained different items in the list. For example, socializing involved "relationship with friends," "social skills," and "communication skills." After we controlled for other factors (e.g., race/ethnicity, grade level, family income, parental education level), two elements stood out.

First, school-based support was a key factor. Students were provided with a list of 16 school-based supports and were asked to indicate which ones they received during the first year of the pandemic. Figure 2.9 highlights which school-based supports were more likely to be received by students during the pandemic. The supports least likely to be received included one-on-one mental health check-ins (6%), mental health outreach from educators (10%), and one-on-one academic check-ins (18%). While not all students may have needed or pursued mental health supports, the low percentages of students receiving mental health supports likely point to student mental health needs being unmet. Regression models indicated that receipt of more school-based supports was associated with a lower likelihood of reporting the pandemic having a negative effect. For every additional support a student received, their odds of reporting the pandemic having a positive or no effect on them (versus a negative effect) was increased by a factor of 1.10 for academic learning, 1.08 for self-management, 1.06 for socializing, 1.13 for resilience, and 1.09 for college/career exploration, holding constant all other variables. In other words, receiving more school-based supports was related to a lower likelihood of being negatively affected by the pandemic.

Second, the amount of in-person learning was associated with students' perceptions of the pandemic's effects, when the total number of school-based supports and other variables were held constant. For three aspects of learning, including socializing, resilience, and college/career exploration, a higher amount of in-person learning was related to a higher likelihood of students reporting the pandemic as having no effect or a positive effect on them. For every one unit increase in the amount of in-person learning, the odds of reporting the pandemic as having a positive or no effect on students (verse a negative effect) increased by a factor of 1.32 for

Figure 2.9

Percentages of Students Reporting Receiving School-Based Supports

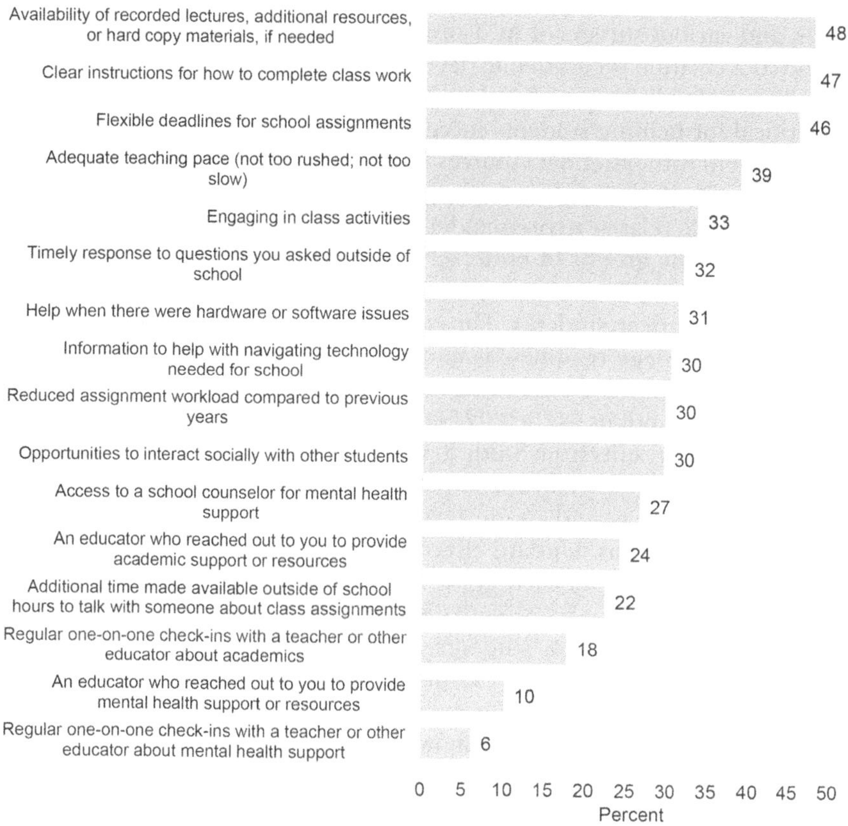

socializing, 1.11 for resilience, and 1.20 for college/career exploration. These findings indicated that more in-person learning was associated with a lower likelihood of a student perceiving the pandemic as having a negative effect on them.

CONCLUSION

The COVID-19 pandemic caused widespread disruptions to the educational system throughout the U.S. and the world, causing stress and social isolation, as well as disrupting students' academics and college and career plans. ACT, as a provider of college and career readiness solutions, was in a unique position to collect data spanning students' academic knowledge, skills, behaviors, and college preparation activities. These data came from a variety of sources: the ACT and ACT Aspire tests, data collected by a state department of education, established measures of social and emotional skills, and various surveys of ACT-tested students. These data contributed to the conversation on academic development as well as a variety of other dimensions that have not played as prominent of a role in news cycles yet are critical for helping students succeed despite the pandemic's setbacks.

Consistent with other data sources (e.g., NAEP, 2022), results from Study 1 show that ACT national test scores for 11th grade students declined in 2021 and 2022, relative to pre-pandemic years. Although scores rebounded slightly for some groups of underserved students (e.g., Black and two or more races), other student groups continued to decline, including Latinx and Native American students. Through 2022, it appears that the pandemic's effect on college readiness is most severe in math and that readiness has partially rebounded in reading and science. The 2022 cohort suffered the same interruptions as the 2021 cohort, so this result is not surprising.

Based on the results from Study 2, which focused on the student population from the state of Arkansas, both ACT Aspire and ACT scores declined for all subject areas and grade levels tested. The magnitude of score declines (expressed as standard effect sizes, *d*) suggest that the pandemic's effect was most severe for early grade levels, for math, and for students who learned virtually. In contrast, score declines were less severe for later grade levels, for reading, and for students who learned on-site. A meta-analysis by König and Frey (2022) that examined the impact of COVID-19-related school closures on student achievement and included 18 studies from the U.S. and international samples showed similar results as those obtained in Study 1 and Study 2: the pandemic had a negative impact on student achievement ($d = -0.175$), with students in primary grades more negatively affected than those in secondary grades.

In Study 3, which reported on the early effects of the pandemic (between February and April of 2020) on students' social and emotional (SE) skills, results suggest students grew in four (of five) social and emotional skills, including *Sustaining Effort*, *Getting Along with Others*, *Maintaining Composure*, and *Keeping an Open Mind*, with the largest gains on *Maintaining Composure*. In contrast, students' *Social Connection* skill scores remained flat during the same timeframe. This is consistent with what one might expect given the challenges that emerged during the onset of COVID-19. Students were adapting to a life of social distance, online learning, and—for many—watching their families struggle financially and/or emotionally. The challenging times undoubtedly required adapting, managing their emotions effectively, and maintaining composure, and we saw this pattern with the associations between the SE skills and adaptive behaviors. The study did not include a pre-pandemic test-retest control group, so it is possible that the SE skills scores would have increased upon retesting in the absence of the pandemic. Likewise, we did not test the student skills' associations with the adaptive behaviors in the absence of the pandemic. However, during the early stages of the pandemic, we can conclude that students improved on *Maintaining Composure* more than *Social Connection*, which could be explained by their need to face the unprecedented challenges of the pandemic while having no in-person contact with teachers and less contact with peers. Additionally, the *Maintaining Composure* gains were much larger than what has been reported in previous research examining SE skill development in similarly aged adolescents, despite a much shorter interval in the current study. Prior research has shown little change in the skill of *Maintaining Composure* in the absence of a major social crisis, even during spans of one to two years (Klimstra et al., 2009; Pullmann et al., 2006). Thus, in the face of COVID-19, students learned to be much more composed, and they did so quickly. A question that the data from Study 3 are not able to answer (due to their 2-month retest interval) is whether the gains in SE skills during this early stage of the pandemic may be different from gains/losses/stagnancies over the longer course of the pandemic.

Study 4 reported on missed college preparation opportunities due to the pandemic. Specifically, students reported that the college preparation activities most likely to be missed were campus visits, attending a college fair, talking to a college representative, and participating in a FAFSA workshop. Although some schools and colleges held these events virtually (EdSource, 2022), research has shown that there is a prevalent digital divide among high school students, particularly those from low-income communities and rural areas (Moore et al., 2018). Lack of access to functioning technologies and stable internet can prevent underserved groups from participating in college preparation activities and events. Although many school districts tried to mitigate these impacts by issuing school devices (e.g., Chromebooks) to all students and working with low-income families to procure internet service, it is not yet clear whether students were able to fully access these college preparation opportunities.

Finally, Study 5 asked students to reflect on their experiences during the first year of the pandemic. Most high school students agreed that several aspects of learning were disrupted, particularly their motivation to learn, focus and discipline, and study habits. Despite these negative effects on academic behaviors, only 37% of students reported negative effects (and 39% reported positive effects) on academic grades. This could be explained by accelerated grade inflation (Sanchez & Moore, 2022) and compassionate grading practices (Tamez-Robledo, 2021) implemented during the first year of the pandemic. Despite worsening academic performance, student grades were not impacted much. Additionally, students reported negative effects on socializing, resilience, and college/career exploration. These results are consistent with findings from other studies (e.g., Karaman et al., 2021; Yan et al., 2021). Despite the disruptions, students reported improved use of digital tools for learning, more independence and self-reliance, and a greater appreciation for their teachers and their education. Further, findings suggest that school-based supports (e.g., availability of recorded lectures, clear instructions for completing class work, flexible deadlines) and in-person learning were related to fewer perceived disruptions during the first year of the pandemic.

Because Study 5 assessed many of the same constructs as Studies 1–4, it helps to corroborate or shed light on other findings, including:

1. The negative effects on academic behaviors observed in Study 5 are consistent with the lower test scores observed in Studies 1 and 2.
2. Studies 2, 4, and 5 reinforce the mitigating effects of in-person instruction on academic achievement, college preparation activities, and receipt of school-based supports.
3. The demographic differences in in-person instruction observed in Study 1 imply that students who are female, from an underserved racial/ethnic group, and from an urban school were least likely to benefit from the positive effects of in-person instruction observed in Studies 2, 4, and 5.
4. Studies 3 and 5 both suggest that the pandemic's effects on *Social Connection* (e.g., "relationships with friends" from Study 5) were substantially different than its effects on *Maintaining Composure* (e.g., "adapting to stress/life changes" from Study 5).

Implications for the Future

The COVID-19 pandemic disrupted student learning in many ways (some negatively and some positively) and has prompted us to think more deeply about the structural inequities that characterize learning environments throughout the U.S. and that typically impact underserved groups disproportionally. The findings in this chapter should prompt the field and the testing industry to rethink how we can better serve *all* students, particularly those who are more vulnerable to learning disruptions (e.g., students of color, students from low-income communities, students who will be the first in their families to graduate high school and/or attend college, students in isolated rural areas). Some of these insights include:

1. Continue to incorporate digital tools for learning regardless of the setting (e.g., virtual, in-person, hybrid).

2. Help students to develop important social and emotional skills that promote maintaining composure, sustaining effort, cooperation, as well as independence and self-reliance.
3. Provide school-based supports (e.g., making lectures available as recordings, providing clear instructions for completing class work, allowing for flexible deadlines to complete assignments) to help students succeed in their academic work.
4. Provide mental health supports (e.g., one-on-one counseling, peer mentoring, online support groups) to help students cope with the variety of stressors that are known to impact their well-being and their ability to make successful academic and school-to-work transitions.
5. Move beyond one-point-in-time assessments to shorter, more frequent measures that allow stakeholders to gain a better understanding of how students' knowledge, skills, and needs are growing and/or changing, particularly during disruptions.

Further, if we are to "move the needle" on the many forms of inequity that impact student learning, it is imperative that the field and the testing industry redesign the way in which we construct assessments and learning tools by leveraging a variety of equity-based frameworks and principles to intentionally center on equity. These include:

1. Designing for equity: continuously interrogating how our development processes may have privileged some groups over others and redesigning our solutions to be more inclusive and culturally responsive
2. Asset-based: being intentional about including individuals', groups', and communities' assets and strengths to provide a more comprehensive picture and improve the efficacy of solutions
3. Expertise equity: working to disrupt the cultural bias toward academic expertise and centering on the voices of learners, practitioners, caregivers, and others with context expertise to ensure that their perspectives are valued and included in our day-to-day work and in our solutions

SUMMARY

We summarized five primary studies examining impacts of the COVID-19 pandemic on multiple domains related to college and career readiness. Some of the main findings include:

1. The pandemic-era decline in 11th grade ACT scores is comparable to three months of lost instruction and three fewer students (per 100) being ready for college algebra.
2. Test scores in Arkansas declined most in math, for younger students, and for those who learned virtually.
3. High school students showed positive social and emotional skill development at the onset of the pandemic, and these skills were associated with engagement in positive coping and prosocial behaviors.
4. Nearly half of the students in a sample of high school graduates of 2021 missed out on at least one college preparation activity due to the pandemic, including campus visits (20%) and college fairs (19%). Students who learned in-person were less likely to miss these events.
5. Students overwhelmingly reported negative impacts of the pandemic on academic behaviors, motivation, self-management, mental health, and socializing, but also noted gains in use of digital tools, self-reliance, and appreciation for education and teachers.

Additionally, we provided recommendations for how the field and the testing industry can leverage more equitable approaches to help *all* students learn and thrive despite future disruptions.

REFERENCES

Allen, J. (2022a). *Examining the COVID-19 pandemic's impacts on ACT scores: Spring 2022 update*. Technical Brief. ACT. https://www.act.org/content/dam/act/unsecured/documents/2022/R2275-COVID-19-Impacts-on-ACT-Scores-Spring-2022-Update-11-2022.pdf

Allen, J. (2022b). *Understanding the impact of the COVID-19 pandemic on student achievement in Arkansas: Comparing on-site, hybrid, and virtual modes of learning*. Technical Brief. ACT. https://www.act.org/content/dam/act/unsecured/documents/2022/R2148-Arkansas-COVID-Impact-ACT-03-2022.pdf

Camara, W., O'Connor, R., Mattern, K., & Hanson, M. A. (2015). *Beyond academics: A holistic framework for enhancing education and workplace success* (ACT Research Report No. 2015 [4]). ACT. https://www.act.org/content/dam/act/unsecured/documents/ACT_RR2015-4.pdf

EdSource. (2022). College recruiting of California students turns virtual during pandemic. https://edsource.org/2020/college-recruiting-turns-virtual-during-pandemic/641255

John, O. P., & Srivastava, S. (1999). The Big Five Trait taxonomy: History, measurement and theoretical perspectives. In L. A. Pervin & O. P. John (Eds.), *Handbook of personality: Theory and research* (2nd ed., pp. 102–138). Guilford Press.

Karaman, M. A., Eşi□, H., Tomar, İ. H., & Aliyev, R. (2021). COVID-19: Are s□hool counseling services ready? Students' psychological symptoms, school counselors' views, and solutions. *Frontiers in Psychology, 12*, 647740.

Klimstra, T. A., Hale, W. W., III, Raaijmakers, Q. A., Branje, S. J., & Meeus, W. H. (2009). Maturation of personality in adolescence. *Journal of Personality and Social Psychology, 96*(4), 898–912.

König, C & Frey, A. (2022). The impact of COVID-19-related school closures on student achievement—a meta-analysis. *Educational Measurement: Issues and Practice, 41*, 16–22.

Kuhfeld, M. & Lewis, K. (2022). *Student achievement in 2021-2022: Cause for hope and continued urgency*. NWEA Collaborative for Student Growth. https://www.nwea.org/uploads/2022/07/Student-Achievement-in-2021-22-Cause-for-hope-and-concern.researchbrief-1.pdf

Moore, R., Vitale, D., & Stawinoga, N. (2018). *The digital divide and educational equity: A look at students with very limited access to electronic devices at home*. Insights in Education and Work. ACT.

Murano, D., Walton, K. E., & Burrus, J. (2023). *Students' social and emotional skills and behaviors during the onset of COVID-19*. ACT. https://www.act.org/content/dam/act/unsecured/documents/R2293-Student-SE-Skills-and-Behaviors-During-Onset-of-COVID-19-02-2023.pdf

NAEP. (2022). *The nation's report card: Key findings of mathematics and reading grade 4 and 8*. https://www.nationsreportcard.gov/mathematics/supportive_files/2022_rm_infographic.pdf

Pullmann, H., Raudsepp, L., & Allik, J. (2006). Stability and change in adolescents' personality: A longitudinal study. *European Journal of Personality, 20*(6), 447–459.

Sanchez, E., & Moore, R. (2022). *Grade inflation continues to grow in the past decade*. ACT. https://www.act.org/content/dam/act/unsecured/documents/2022/R2134-Grade-Inflation-Continues-to-Grow-in-the-Past-Decade-Final-Accessible.pdf

Schnieders, J. Z., & Moore, R. (2022). *College preparation opportunities, the pandemic, and student preparedness: Perspectives from class of 2021 college-bound ACT test-takers*. Insights in Education and Work. ACT. https://www.act.org/content/dam/act/unsecured/documents/2022/college-preparation-opportunities-the-pandemic-and-student-preparedness.pdf

Schnieders, J. Z. (2023). *Disruptions and gains: Students' reflections on the effects of the pandemic*. ACT. https://www.act.org/content/dam/act/unsecured/documents/R2295-Disruptions-Gains-Effects-of-Pandemic-02-2023.pdf

Tamez-Robledo, N. (2021). *Pass/fail grading was an act of pandemic compassion. Is it here to stay?* https://www.edsurge.com/news/2021-05-26-pass-fail-grading-was-an-act-of-pandemic-compassion-is-it-here-to-stay

Yan, L., Whitelo□k-Wainwright, A., Guan, Q., Wen, G., Gašević, D., & Chen, G. (2021). Students' experience of online learning during the COVID-19 pandemic: A province-wide survey study. *British Journal of Educational Technology, 52*(5), 2038–2057.

Walton, K. E., & Murano, D. (2020). *Students have shown significant social and emotional skill development during COVID-19*. ACT. https://www.act.org/content/dam/act/unsecured/documents/R1843-covid-se-dev-10-2020.pdf

CHAPTER 3

EXAMINING THE ACADEMIC AND PSYCHOLOGICAL EXPERIENCES OF STUDENTS AND EDUCATIONAL STAKEHOLDERS IN A HIGH SCHOOL STEM ACADEMY DURING THE COVID-19 PANDEMIC

Edward C. Fletcher Jr.
The Ohio State University

Donna Y. Ford
The Ohio State University

ABSTRACT

To increase participation in STEM related programs and careers, education stakeholders have explored the reconfiguration of high schools into STEM

Examining the Cognitive and Psychological Effects of the COVID-19 Global Pandemic on High School, College, and Graduate Learners, pp. 41–63

theme-based career academies However, it is critical to acknowledge the academic and psychological challenges impacting high school academy students during the 2020 coronavirus pandemic, particularly for ethnically and racially diverse learners. In this study, we examined the perspectives of high school academy stakeholders as well as students in terms of the academic and psychological challenges they encountered. Further, we discuss an educational intervention to provide virtual internships for students in the STEM academies. We followed a qualitative case study design to examine the perspectives of school stakeholders and students who participated in a high school STEM academy. We conducted 25 semi-structured interviews with school stakeholders and 23 Black male academy of engineering students. Four themes emerged: *Social and Student Engagement Lacking*; *Growing Pains: School Stakeholders and Students as Adaptive Learners*; *Work-based Learning Implementation Challenges*; and *The NAF Future Ready Lab as an Intervention.* We discuss implications of our findings for educational scholars and practitioners.

Keywords: career academies, high school, pandemic, STEM, virtual learning

INTRODUCTION

To increase participation in STEM related programs and careers, education stakeholders have explored new avenues to establish a pipeline of students interested in pursuing STEM pathways at the high school level. The focus of these initiatives has been on the reconfiguration of high schools into STEM theme-based small learning communities, with objectives to enhance student motivation and engagement (Fletcher et al., 2020). To that end, one major initiative is the development of high school career academies.

Career academies are programs found within high schools featuring a college-preparatory curriculum with an embedded career theme requiring partnerships with employers and postsecondary institutions, and the integration of academic and technical content to increase rigor and relevance to students' career interests (Castellano et al., 2017). Researchers have identified the career academy as one of the most promising models for enhancing student engagement and facilitating career pursuits (Fletcher et al., 2020; Hernandez-Gantes et al., 2013). Findings from experimental studies indicate that participation in career academies results in increased student engagement, attendance, graduation rates, academic achievement, and long-term employment earnings (Kemple & Snipes, 2000).

However, it is critical to acknowledge the academic and psychological challenges impacting high school academy students during the 2020 coronavirus pandemic, particularly for ethnically and racially diverse learners from economically disadvantaged backgrounds. One of the major disruptions stemming from the 2020 coronavirus pandemic was the closure of schools across the nation. Ohio was the first state to close its schools on March 12, 2020 and every school across the United States closed by March 25, 2020, with the vast majority of schools offering online options (Chatterji & Li, 2021).

Objectives and Research Questions

In this study, we examined the perspectives of high school academy stakeholders (e.g., district and school administrators, teachers, school counselors, parents, school board members, and advisory board members) as well as students in terms of the academic (e.g., work-based learning activities, student learning) and psychological (e.g., student engagement and motivation, teachers' dispositions) challenges they encountered. Further, we discuss an educational intervention to provide virtual internships for students in the STEM academies. Through semi-structured interviews with school stakeholders and students, we examined the following research questions in this study:

1. What are the perspectives of school stakeholders regarding the academic and psychological challenges they experienced during the pandemic; and
2. What are the perspectives of students regarding the academic and psychological challenges they experienced during the pandemic?

REVIEW OF LITERATURE

Researchers have demonstrated that students in career and technical education (CTE) programs of study—including students who participate in career academies—benefit from reduced probabilities of dropping out of high school, score higher on standardized assessments, have higher graduation rates, have increased employment rates, have higher short- and medium-term earnings, and are more likely to matriculate into two-year colleges compared to non-CTE students (Brunner et al., 2021; Cellini, 2006; Dougherty, 2018; Hemelt et al., 2019; Kreisman & Stange, 2020). These benefits are likely based on a host of curricular initiatives, including students' higher engagement from studying content that is based in real-world situations and is relevant to their career interests, coursework that is connected to work-based learning opportunities, and mentorship and role models from teachers and other adults connected with their employment interests.

However, researchers have demonstrated the negative effects that online instruction can have on K–12 students, including: drops in learning

(Goldhaber et al., 2023), declines in student engagement (Herold & Kurtz, 2020), reduced standardized assessment scores (Kuhfeld et al., 2020), increased mental health and psychological issues (Liu et al., 2020), decreased graduation rates (Dougherty et al., 2022), and lower long-term educational and workforce trajectories (Kuhfeld et al., 2020). Even further, the quality of online instruction can vary based on school and neighborhood contexts, thereby, exacerbating disparities in learning opportunities and mental health issues for minoritized students (Camp & Zamarro, 2022; Hoffman, 2020).

Career academies often demand greater resources in terms of equipment and software, and require access to worksites and employer support and partnerships in the community to provide work-based learning opportunities (e.g., guest speakers, mock interviews, job shadowing, internships) to students (Fletcher et al., 2018, 2019). However, with the outbreak of the COVID-19 pandemic in the spring of 2020, many schools across the country were unable to provide their students with the acquisition of industry-recognized credentials, internships, and other work-based learning experiences (Dougherty et al., 2022; Fletcher et al., 2023). The shift from in person to online learning was challenging for career and technical education (CTE) teachers, including career academy teachers, in particular, given their reliance on more applied and hands-on pedagogical approaches that is difficult to replicate in online learning environments (Dougherty & Lombardi, 2016). This is quite concerning as it is likely to lead to diminished skill attainment and interrupt students' abilities to transition from high school to the workforce and postsecondary education (Dougherty et al., 2022). Dougherty et al. (2022) posited that, "The absence of these experiences, and the unparalleled decrease in demand for workers during the pandemic shutdowns, had the potential for massive disruptions in the skill and job experience accumulation for youth" (p. 327)

Yet, Fletcher et al. (2023) noted that the NAF (formerly known as the National Academy Foundation) created the NAF Future Ready Lab—a completely *virtual* internship experience for students. The NAF (2014) is a non-profit organization that helps build and provide technical support and professional development to a network of high school career academies across the nation. Because the NAF Future Ready Lab program specifically seeks to serve students from traditionally underserved, economically disadvantaged communities, it became clear early in the planning process that many employer partners would need to provide laptop and mobile hotspot technologies for their interns if this pivot was to be successful. Ultimately, laptops and mobile hotspots were made available to all interns participating in the NAF Future Ready Lab.

Theoretical Framework

To understand the leadership challenges for school stakeholders in a high school STEM academy during the pandemic, we relied on sense making theory as well as an ambiguity-centered approach to adaptive leadership (Heifetz, 1994; Hulme et al., 2023). Sense making is defined as a process of individuals constructing meaning within the context of a new reality. In addition, sense making refers to the process of action taken to resolve and address challenges and issues (Weick et al., 2009). Meanings are determined based on individuals' prior knowledge, values and beliefs, school norms, and culture (Spillane & Anderson, 2014). Thus, sense making enables school stakeholders and leaders to translate external demands into enacted school practices (Braun et al., 2010). During the pandemic, school stakeholders had to continually reconstruct their understanding of a quickly transforming educational and situational environment (Hulme et al., 2023).

Multiple stakeholders are involved in this dynamic and ongoing process—local and national governmental agencies, educational agencies, allied health professions, news media, and parent and community groups. During crises, school stakeholders operate under varying roles, enabling transition and adaptation to changes. These school stakeholders are essential brokers, forging bridges between organizations and varying stakeholders to implement needed changes (Kim & Kim, 2016). Using the theoretical framework of sense making as well as an ambiguity-centered approach to adaptive leadership (Heifetz, 1994), we were able to use Stanton Academy as a case study to examine the school leadership challenges and crisis management for school stakeholders in a high school STEM academy during the pandemic. Sense making occurred with both the school stakeholders and students at Stanton Academy as both groups constructed meaning within the context of a new reality, given the educational challenges that arose from the pandemic.

METHOD

Research Design

We followed a qualitative case study design to examine the experiences of both Black high school academies of engineering students and educational stakeholders as they navigated the challenges presented by the pandemic. Our research approach was interpretivist in nature and attempted to capture the meaning of participants' experiences and their sense making on educational issues (Stake, 2006; Yin, 1994). During discussions with the participants, we were able to understand and interpret the meanings of their experiences during the pandemic. The case study approach allowed for the documentation of rich descriptive information about their experiences. It is important to note that we used pseudonyms throughout our discussions to replace participant and school names as well as locations.

We studied a NAF (formerly known as the National Academy Foundation) academy of engineering (the case) operating within unique contexts (e.g., community and school district) at a distinguished level according to the NAF standards of practice. NAF continuously evaluates their high school academies to assess their level of implementation based on standards of practice. They rate academies on five levels of implementation, using the following hierarchy from highest to lowest: distinguished, model, certified, member, and under review.

NAF's educational design is based on these elements: academy development and structure, curriculum and instruction, advisory board, and work-based learning. The case study method was the most appropriate for studying students' experiences within a distinguished NAF whole school (all students participate in one of several career academy themes) magnet academy of engineering. In our case study, we relied on (interviewing participants) data-gathering methods, which were conducted virtually using zoom due to the COVID-19 pandemic.

Selection Criteria

We purposely selected Stanton Academy (pseudonym) because it was a distinguished NAF academy of engineering and its demographics were 99% Black students and 91% of them came from economically disadvantaged backgrounds. We believe Stanton Academy would help uncover how school stakeholders and students within a high fidelity (e.g., close adherence to standards in its implementation) NAF academy navigated the challenges brought on by the pandemic. Hence, the richness of the academy context and implementation of student supports helped us to answer our research objectives.

The Case: Stanton Academy

Demographics. Stanton Academy is located in the city of Stanton (population of approximately 124,000) which is 55% White, 37% African American/Black, 4% Latinx, and 3% Asian. The median income was approximately $42,000, and 19% of the community members lived below the poverty line. The Stanton Academy of Engineering is a public school with a distinguished (whole school magnet) NAF academy (one of several career themed programs) embedded within it. It is located in an urban area within the Southeastern region of the United States. Stanton Academy has approximately 969 students and 71 teachers (who were majority Black). In terms of gender, 51% of students were female and 49% were male. Concerning ethnic and racial background, 99% of students were Black and 1% were Latinx. Ninety-one percent of students qualified for free and/or reduced lunch. The graduation rate in 2020 was 97% with a student college-bound rate of 90%. Stanton Academy relied on an application system for student admission to the academy of engineering and several other career themed academies within the school. The academy of engineering also had an advisory board that was composed of 17 community members and subcommittees made up of a variety of STEM related firms that served as a primary source of employment within the local area. These local industries included environmental engineering, manufacturing industrial plants, petroleum oil refineries, chemical facilities, architectural firms, engineering consulting firms, the chamber of commerce, and STEM university faculty.

Data Collection

We conducted 4 virtual focus group interviews with 23 Black male high school academy of engineering students (n = 23) in January and February 2021. The interview protocol differed based on the stakeholder group as well as covered various domains, as this was one segment of a larger study. One of the domains of the interview protocol focused on the school stakeholder and student experiences related to the pandemic. Example interview questions for the student interviews asked the participants to: (1) Describe how the COVID-19 pandemic impacted their schooling experience; (2) How has the COVID-19 pandemic impacted their engagement and motivation in school? (3) How has the COVID-19 pandemic impacted their learning in school? And (4) what did the school do to help support you during the pandemic? Each interview lasted for 60 minutes in duration. The university's IRB approved all components of this study. We relied on the knowledge of an insider informant—the principal—to provide us with a list of participants to interview during the 3-day virtual interview.

We also conducted 11 virtual focus group interviews with 3 district administrators, 2 school administrators, 1 school board member, 1 school staff member (Registrar), 8 teachers (core academic and engineering teachers), 2 school counselors, and 8 advisory board members (comprised of postsecondary partners and business and industry representatives) (n = 25). There were five focus group interviews with: (a) one focus group for the three district administrators; (b) two focus groups with four advisory board members each; and (c) two focus groups with four teachers each. The interviews were related to school stakeholders' experiences during the pandemic. Each interview lasted for 60 minutes in duration.

Researchers' Positionalities

It is helpful to acknowledge the researchers' own inherent biases, perspectives, and frames of reference as researchers, which most likely influenced and shaped research encounters, processes, and findings. All authors are faculty (two Black men and one Black woman). The researchers have professional backgrounds in the field of career and technical/workforce education, special education (with an emphasis on gifted education), counselor education, and educational psychology. All three of the researchers have studied issues related to the impact of student participation in high school STEM-themed career academies as well as inequities in access to academically rigorous programs in schools, particularly for ethnically and racially diverse as well as students who come from economically disadvantaged backgrounds. Our perspectives and experiences led to the decision to select a NAF academy of engineering as well as Black male students as focal points in this study.

Data Analyses

All interviews were audio-recorded by the research team and transcribed verbatim (using a transcription service). We used thematic analysis to capture students' and school stakeholders' experiences. We first read the entire dataset of transcripts. After doing so, we divided the dataset into smaller meaningful segments. We then labeled each segment with a code. Afterwards, we compared each component and collapsed those with similar codes. Last, we developed themes for each code group. For example, in arriving at a theme, the entire research team first read every transcript individually. We then individually re-read each transcript to search for patterns/codes related to the experiences and motivational factors regarding participation in the academy of engineering. We met as a research team to discuss the codes that emerged. We then went back to the transcripts to select quotes that match the codes—those that accurately depicted the experiences during the pandemic for students and school stakeholders. We finally were able to discuss and agree on possible phrases/statements that represent the codes, which became our themes. Thus, the codes emerged from the data. We relied on investigator triangulation by engaging in the collective reading and analyses of transcripts. We also used interrater reliability with a threshold of 100% consensus on arriving at a theme. To that end, we reached 100% agreement on all four themes. In addition, we conducted member checks with all participants. The interviewees made no edits to the original transcripts. The applicability of the findings to other schools and students rest with the degree to which the contexts and student populations are similar to the case in this study.

RESULTS

Four themes emerged: *Social and Student Engagement Lacking*; *Growing Pains: School Stakeholders and Students as Adaptive Learners*; *Work-based Learning Implementation Challenges*; and *The NAF Future Ready Lab as an Intervention* (see Table 3.1). Students and school stakeholders reported challenges with a lack of student engagement and social interaction during the pandemic. Yet, both groups made adjustments to cope with the constantly transforming nature and disruptions precipitated by the pandemic. One of the major shifts that had to occur was in the implementation of work-based learning. To that end, the NAF was instrumental in providing an intervention (The NAF Future Ready Lab) as an intervention to enable internships to occur.

Table 3.1

Themes and Definitions that Emerge from Academy School Stakeholders and Students

Theme	Definition
Social and Student Engagement Lacking (n = 20 codes)	Students and school stakeholders reported challenges with a lack of student engagement (e.g., students not displaying their videos) and social interaction (e.g., difficulty in teachers establishing rapport with students) during the pandemic because of the shift to online teaching.
Growing Pains: School Stakeholders and Students as Adaptive Learners (n = 11 codes)	With the shift to remote learning, school stakeholders made adjustments to cope with the constantly transforming nature and disruptions precipitated by the pandemic.
Work-based Learning Implementation Challenges (n = 9 codes)	Implementing work-based learning was challenging for school stakeholders during the pandemic.
The NAF Future Ready Lab as an Intervention (n = 6 codes)	The NAF was instrumental in providing an intervention—The NAF Future Ready Lab—as an intervention to enable internships to occur.

Social and Student Engagement Lacking

Regarding the pandemic, both the school stakeholders and students discussed the challenges related to the lack of student engagement because of the needed shift to remote learning. Many of the teachers complained of the lack of engagement from students in a remote environment. One of the most substantial challenges was the issue of students who did not display their videos during class sessions. Teachers also spoke about their inability to create a positive learning environment, establish rapport with students, and develop synergistic relationships with students within an online setting. They discussed issues with students' inability to be self-directed and focus on academic work within their home environments, which oftentimes meant that students performed at lower levels and in many cases did not complete assignments. Ms. Sanders, a chemistry teacher, told us:

> It's tough to teach online sometimes because we're goin', and like you and I are face-to-face, and sometimes the kids they're—all the cameras aren't live, so you don't know what's goin' on, on the other side of the camera, until you see them actually submit work. That's a success that they try—that they are submitting some work. That's truly a success especially under these circumstances where no one's standin' over them makin' them do anything. It's a challenge to teach like that in itself ... because most online classes, you have your discussion questions, you have this, you have that, and you post to get your grades, but here, we're doin' interactive, using simulated teaching methods, so that's just a challenge to make sure that we're keeping their attention because you really don't know until you see what they're submittin' or turnin' in.

Similarly, Ms. Ferguson, a science teacher, shared:

> Keeping students engaged, both online and in person. It is a challenge, and it is a task, but we're doin' what we have to do during these times to make things work for both the teachers and the students. That's a real challenge, but it's something that we can overcome and have overcome.

Students also related to their teachers' frustrations and discussed issues learning engineering without the use of hands-on projects—at least in the early stages of the pandemic. When classes were in person, the hands-on nature of the curriculum was a source of engagement for the students. Jay, a Black male academy of engineering student articulated:

> COVID-19 affected me by taking away my hands-on learning 'cause I was able to do projects, but it wasn't hands-on projects. It was search or research a device. I really couldn't learn from that. I could learn from visual, but I need both visual and hands-on. I didn't get the hands-on, so I became lazy, and I didn't want to pay attention 'cause I wasn't having as much fun as I would, hands-on.

Mr. Leo, an advisory board member who owned his own engineering firm, explained:

> Yeah. Even beyond that—so with engineerin', you have typically the written instruction and then you have the labs and the laboratory portion of it. During the pandemic for the kids that are virtual, some of that is gonna be lost because they won't have the equipment, they won't have the on-hands direction to be able to obtain that laboratory learning.

Researchers have found that Black male career academy students choose to participate because of the hands-on nature of the curriculum (Fletcher & Cox, 2012). CJ, a Black male academy of engineering student, talked about the challenges he had with virtual learning during the pandemic.

Students also discussed the difficulties they had in reaching out for assistance and the lack of interactions they had with both teachers and their peers. CJ indicated:

> It affected my engagement because I wasn't really allowed to—since Zoom was so—or Google Meet was all new to me, it was hard to get used to it. Hard to do assignments and things like that, 'cause I like bein' hands on, doin' the work in class, bein' able to walk up to a teacher and ask for help. Yeah, it really affected me 'cause I really had to adjust to learnin' in a different way.

Jay also discussed the constant disruptions in the learning environment during the pandemic that led to a loss of learning and motivation. Students and teachers were oftentimes shifting from in person to blended to virtual instruction. Jay stated:

> Ninth grade year, half the year, I was virtual. Half of the year, I was in school. 'Cause after football season, I had just went virtual, and COVID, it messed me up in school because, when I was virtual at the house, I really wasn't paying attention. Too many distractions. Sometimes, I'd fall asleep in class, and the teacher wouldn't know, so I wasn't able to participate and able to learn. That really affected my grade and my learning experience throughout my ninth-grade year. I feel like COVID-19 really held me back a year. I feel like last year, I didn't learn as much as I could have because of the pandemic and how we had to wear masks. It took away from how we could be social, so we couldn't really be social. Half of the time, I didn't even see the faces of people I went to school with. That's how it affected me. I'd say it affected my motivation because, in the previous years, I was—I'd always be on top of my homework, doing it as soon as it's assigned. With COVID, I feel like it made me a little bit more lazy when it comes to doing schoolwork because during COVID, I had all the time in the world at the house, so I could just do my work whenever I wanted to as long as I got

> it done before the due date. In addition, students discussed the negative outcomes of participating in classes virtually.

They found the virtual environment to be isolating and missed the social interactions they were accustomed to when their classes were in person. To that end, students believed that the isolation impacted their abilities to mature as they were promoted to higher grade levels, negatively affected their work ethic, and lowered their concentration on their studies with numerous distractions from devices (e.g., smartphones). Rasheed, a Black male academy of engineering student, explained how the pandemic negatively impacted his growth, maturity, interpersonal, and social skills:

> I feel being COVID just took—when COVID hit, you just took freshmen and put 'em up where let's say 11th grade. Well, the teachers are really expecting you to 11th grade, expects you to act mature. It's hard. I feel we was rushed into maturity since we didn't have our freshman or sophomore year to really be friends, and grow as a person, and learn how life works. Since our junior year, we was like junior year. Oh, I could say it impacted me pretty regularly. Because after COVID, at the start of my 11th grade year, I was really lazy. I was on my phone a lot. I wasn't paying attention. Once my grades started to drop, I knew that I had to put my phone to the side, put all the distractions to the side, and just focus on my school work. I feel like COVID really made me lazier. I think I grew out of that right now.

While the school stakeholders and students expressed their frustrations with remote learning, they also shared with us that the pandemic inspired them to become adaptive learners and address challenges they faced. They were able to become innovative in their learning approaches and instructional strategies during the pandemic.

Growing Pains: School Stakeholders and Students as Adaptive Learners

The shift to remote learning also prompted district and school administrators to constantly adapt and problem solve. The objective of the adaptations was to ensure that all students had access to learning. Schools had to constantly shift from in person, to virtual, to blended modes of instruction. Some of the initiatives that schools developed during the pandemic included providing students with food, laptop computers, WIFI, and virtual learning platforms (e.g., Zoom). Mr. Davis, an advisory board member and executive at a large national engineering company, noted his experience with having to make continual shifts in practice from an advisory board member perspective:

> There's certainly a learning curve. I think last March when they sent the students home, there was a push to get students Chromebooks and internet hot spots if they didn't—weren't connected and didn't have it, so it's gotten better. The thing we had this morning—there's still some learning—growing pains. This morning, we were working with Miss [Gaines] at the school, and it took about—we had mock interviews, so they were scheduled from 8:30 to 11:00, but it probably took about 'til 9:15 to get everyone into their breakout rooms on Zoom and get them talking. We still do most of the same things. We switched to Zoom so the students could see us. We're blocked on the Microsoft Teams program that the school system typically uses, but it'll be interesting to see how something like the engineering symposium is done—which [Brad] is in charge of. It's been—I think from the advisory council, we're still kind of operating as if things are gonna go back to normal, but it's still an unusual year.

Dr. Jenkins, associate superintendent for the district, discussed the need for school stakeholders to be flexible given the uncertainty and constant transitions during the pandemic. He articulated:

> Well, I would say the question I asked about the challenges during the pandemic, it's just going to be continued professional development. Especially high schools are gonna have to be flexible. When you have kids that come from economically disadvantaged homes, sometimes many of 'em work. They are the caregivers of their household.... So we need to make certain, especially during this pandemic is that we be flexible, we're innovative, and we continue to provide professional development to our teachers on how to support kids who went virtual because we're probably never gonna go back to 100% brick-and-mortar. I mean, this pandemic has forced us to think outside of our boundaries. As a district, we're gonna have to make certain that we have competent teachers that are ready to provide that virtual instruction that's conducive to kids' learning styles, and that we be flexible enough.

The students who we interviewed also shared their appreciation for the efforts of district administrators in terms of the supports they provided (e.g., food, laptop computers, Wi-Fi) to ease the transition for students. Even further, the school also provided spaces (e.g., a student forum) to express their emotions and issues. Rasheed commented on his appreciation of the district and school efforts when he said:

> Yeah. I remember when the pandemic first started. I think the school offered us to come up and get free lunch for people who needed it. They gave us Chromebooks to take home, so we could still learn while during the pandemic. They gave some people access to the free internet at home if they couldn't afford it. I'd say the school has been supportive. They gave out laptops, mobile Wi-Fi's. Also, if say a student didn't have food at home,

> they was giving out breakfast from 8:00 to 11:00 in the morning, and gave out lunch. They really cared about us being at home. Then they started an emotional forum where you can tell us how you're feeling. It's called Rethink, and just keep everybody calm, and make sure nobody have any problems that they can't come to somebody about. Then they wanted to push for us to get in school as fast as possible because I know they notice how students' grades that come out ain't doing. They're virtual, and they wanted us to get back to class to help teach, and get us to learn.

Jay shared:

> I'd say the school helped—benefited us as students because during COVID, a lot of people was going through stuff, like a lot of people was being stressed out from—like some people's parents was losing jobs, not making as much money. School, they lightened the work on us to relieve some stress on the students and the teachers as well. That right there, that played a big factor when it came to school last year.

Teachers also adapted their instruction and approaches to ensure that students were able to comprehend the content. STEM courses are hands-on by nature, thus, the teachers found ways to provide hands-on learning as well as lab experiences for students in online settings. They noted that, "We had to evolve" because of the pandemic.

Rasheed also had frustrations, but he was able to adapt eventually. He discussed having issues with WIFI and how that impacted his grades:

> I feel like me dealing with COVID, COVID really hurt me growth wise because it was harder for me to learn over the computer. I was more of a in class. I had the teacher talked to me. You know what I'm saying. Them speaking to me one-on-one. Then when going to computers and having to learn through a screen, it really hurt the way I learned and all that. I feel like COVID it was really bad. I feel like I bounced back. I'm doing better now. COVID affect me mostly with my grades, 10th grade year because we were virtual. I wasn't used to being online, having to work. I had wifi problems, which I couldn't get my work turned in. Because it'll take two days for it to upload, and be able to turn in. My GPA failed that year. I had to work my hardest this year to have As and Bs to bring it back up. Now I'm trying to get back to a 3.5 GPA.

The teachers also told us that they were frustrated with the constant challenges they faced in the classroom, but tried to remain positive. They believed that remaining positive was critical in their roles as teachers and role models for their students. Thus, to ensure that students were having a positive learning experience throughout the pandemic, teachers saw it as their duty to view the pandemic as an opportunity for learning and growth.

Ms. Campbell, a business teacher, spoke about the need to have a positive mindset as well as be creative to address the perennial issues that developed throughout the pandemic:

> Our biggest challenge this year, I would have to say, has been this COVID. Tryin' to get these kids to stay motivated. Tryin' to keep the kids encouraged that we're gonna get past this. Tryin' to still give them an atmosphere that school is goin' on, and we're gonna get past this. That's the hardest challenge for some of these children. You have to realize, it's not as easy as it seems to try to do a virtual lesson when some kids don't even have a Wi-Fi hotspot. We're havin' to deal with those issues and work around those issues and make it work for us as well as for them. Challenges are gonna come and go, but as educators, that's our job to get them over that, keep them going, and teachin' to the best of our abilities.

Similarly, Ms. Ferguson, a science teacher, stated:

> It was different. Especially the initial part of it was different because I was not used to—I'm not as technologically challenged as I used to be, but I'm still not necessarily where I need to be or wanna be. I'm a work in progress. Some of those technical things were adjustments. Not seeing my students and being there and being able to be excited in that moment like I would if I was in the classroom made a difference in some of the teaching moments. I think for me, too, it's the relationships that I usually get to build with the students that I missed. There wasn't as much of that because they're online and you don't always see them. You just might see a picture of something, someone, but you don't even have that much of the interaction with them. I think that that was part of the difficulty for me.

The students also acknowledged the efforts of their teachers to ensure learning occurred. Keith, a Black male academy of engineering student, shared that he appreciated that the pandemic enabled him to be creative and innovate. He believed adaptive learning was a needed skill to have, particularly given his chosen field—engineering. Keith stated:

> It [the pandemic] impacted our school experience because we really couldn't really have any real hands-on experiences like we wanted to. I will give credit to the people, like our teachers and stuff like that because they still made a way and found a way for us to really maneuver and actually have some real experiences. I felt like it was a good thing in disguise though 'cause it was another reason to where we had to think creatively. Yeah. We had to think outside of the box to find other ways to do certain things. Personally, for me, no. It really hasn't affected my motivation because in my opinion, especially if you're going into the job field, there's gonna be a lot of wrenches that are gonna be thrown, and you have to adapt. For me, I just adapted. It really wasn't too hard.

Teachers also found positive impacts from the pandemic. Some teachers noted that the pandemic enabled students to have their own personal laptop devices. In addition, several teachers noted that parents were able to see what their children were learning in school and take part in some lessons. Mr. Gabriel, an Engineering teacher, shared with us:

> It is really cool now, since we're virtually, that the parents can see some of the things that they [their child(ren)] do because a lot of the projects we did were at school, so the parents wouldn't be able to see 'em. When we were at home, I had a lot of projects, like we'd have a note card tower. What's another one we did? These are things that you can get from the Dollar Store. We had to build a cardboard chair that you had to be able to sit in. You can get cardboard from the back of one of these stores, the Walmart, and you can only use glue and cardboard to make the chair. The parents were able to see some of the projects that we do in school 'cause they can hear us when we talk.

Mr. Gabriel further expressed:

> I wouldn't say I was glad the pandemic happened, but it was a blessing in disguise because everybody has a Chromebook now. That is huge on different things that I can cover because we used to have desktops, and it would be hard to do some of the things. Now that everybody has a Chromebook, it so much more opens up, and if they're not in school for some odd reason, they still can get the material. Those Chromebooks are clutch. [Laughter] They are really clutch. They are, so I say those Chromebooks 'cause, like I said, before the pandemic, if a kid wasn't here, they'd be behind, but now that's not the case. Every day, we have something, and you can go and review it. You can review my lectures. You can go back and rewind it. It's the Google Meet, that's huge, so like I said, I didn't want that pandemic to happen, but some of the things that came out of it were good. We had to evolve. I told the kids, "We have to evolve." It caused to evolve as teachers, and the students to evolve as well, and I think that's better for them moving forward. That was a challenge before with technology.

Work-Based Learning Challenges

One of the most important learning experiences that NAF academies provide their students is a wide array of work-based learning activities (e.g., guest speakers, mock interviews, job shadowing, internships). The NAF prioritizes internships as they understand that the internship experience is generally the most rewarding and informative experience that students gain and is a critical component of the academy experience. With the pandemic, however, implementing work-based learning was a challenge, particularly given that work-based learning generally took place in person. Mr. Alford, an advisor board member and executive of an engineering firm, spoke about this issue:

> No. We were not able to do internships this year. You can understand that because I've been working from home since last March with my job, so if they're hesitant about having full-time employees in the office right now, they're definitely not gonna bring in a high school student in too. Hopefully, with the vaccine, maybe? I don't foresee it happening in 2022, but maybe in 2023, or either we figure out some type of virtual assignment they could do, but then we would have to work with our companies to come up with suitable projects for the kids to do, where they're still learning but they can do it from a remote-type location. I think the in-person is still gonna be a challenge for a lot of our companies even if the vaccine is available widely this summer.

Yet, several of the teachers did acknowledge their efforts in implementing work-based learning activities for students virtually after the first year of the pandemic. Ms. Sanders told us about her ability to expose her students to guest speakers, who are in engineering careers, by using a virtual platform. She said:

> Most definitely. We do a lot to make sure that they get good examples, models—role models to follow. I know especially with my class, I reach out to—because it's engineering, other engineers to come in and help mentor projects. Right now we're during COVID, so everything had to be virtually, but before COVID, I would bring in engineering mentors to come in and talk to our students to guide them in their projects and just kinda be an example for 'em. More recently, one of our graduates reached out, so sometimes that happens whereas we just recently conducted a virtual interview—a questionnaire—a question session I should say, allowing a recent graduate to talk to senior engineering students who are interested in pursuing engineering and actually learn the process of setting up a little partnership so they can help some students who are actually on track applyin' to colleges for engineering to prepare them for interviews and things like that.

The NAF Future Ready Lab as an Intervention

The school stakeholders and students also acknowledged a new initiative established by NAF that facilitated the continuation of internships throughout the pandemic. The NAF Future Ready Lab model was first established in the summer of 2017 and since then has served nearly 700 high school interns throughout the county. The NAF Future Ready Lab internship model differs from a traditional internship model in that it implements a group internship experience hosted by one or more employer partners. With the outbreak of the COVID-19 pandemic in the Spring of 2020, the NAF Future Ready Lab design had to quickly pivot to address and incorporate the rapidly changing workplace health guidelines being implemented at that time. While some companies were unable to accommodate their original commitments to this program due to shifting workplace environments and staff uncertainty, 7 Future Ready Labs continued across the country and adopted a completely *virtual* experience for the 2020 interns. For example, Mrs. Martin (an advisory board member), stated:

> With the closing of businesses all over...What we've tried to do is implement virtual internships, help students really understand—takin' that virtual learning opportunity to help students understand how do you collaborate virtually? If I needed to work in a virtual team—even if it wasn't because of COVID—say my team is partly in Japan and partly here, how do I do that with efficacy? What we've tried to do is to talk with the employers and work with the employers as much as possible, those who are willing to do it, to provide virtual internships.... They're still providing internships for our students. Also looking at, in terms of the development of the academy, our students 9 through 12, looking at virtual field trips. What type of experiences can we give students right where they are? Can we collect videos from professionals? Can we get some official documents so that students can take a look at those? Really workin' with teachers to incorporate as many things as possible in the absence of being able to go somewhere.

In addition to the logistical challenges of organizing the NAF Future Ready Lab program mentioned previously, an additional, unique challenge presented by the COVID-19 pandemic was to ensure that interns had the technology to fully participate in a completely virtual experience. Since the NAF Future Ready Lab program specifically seeks to serve students from traditionally underserved, economically disadvantaged communities, it became clear early in the planning process that many employer partners would need to provide laptop and mobile hotspot technologies for their interns if this pivot was to be successful. Ultimately, laptops and mobile hotspots were made available to all interns participating in the NAF Future Ready Lab.

CONCLUSIONS

Using the theoretical framework of sense making as well as an ambiguity-centered approach to adaptive leadership (Heifetz, 1994), we were able to use Stanton Academy as a case study to examine the school leadership challenges and crisis management for school stakeholders in a high school STEM academy during the pandemic. Sense making occurred with both the school stakeholders and students at Stanton Academy as both groups constructed meaning within the context of a new reality given the educational challenges that arose from the pandemic. They were able to take action (e.g., providing food, Wi-Fi, laptop computers, and Zoom) to resolve and address challenges and issues (Weick, 2009). Throughout the pandemic school leaders and stakeholders at Stanton Academy navigated unprecedented changes and unrelenting pressures by galvanizing resources, particularly for vulnerable student populations, while operating under a high ethic of care and a shared mission of student wellbeing. For example, Stanton Academy school stakeholders had challenges engaging students in learning. This challenge was not unique to this case as schools struggled with engaging their learners across the world. To that end, researchers have demonstrated that declines in student engagement was a substantial consequence of online instruction (Herold & Kurtz, 2020).

Both the school stakeholders and students alike had to reexamine their prior knowledge, values and beliefs, school norms and culture, particularly as it relates to their conventional ways of learning via in person instruction (Spillane & Anderson, 2014). Instead, they had to learn how to navigate in a virtual educational environment which required adaptive learning and adopting new learning strategies. Thus, sense making enabled both school stakeholders and students to translate external demands (e.g., virtual learning brought on by the pandemic) into enacted school practices (e.g., learning how to learn in a virtual environment as well as accommodating students to ensure that all students had access to a conducive learning environment) (Braun et al., 2010). Thus, during the pandemic, school stakeholders and students at Stanton Academy had to continually reconstruct their understanding of a quickly transforming educational and situational environment and adjust to ensure learning occurred.

In particular, the work-based learning opportunities (e.g., guest speakers, mock interviews, job shadowing, internships) that are typically available to career academy students (Fletcher et al., 2018, 2019) had to be adjusted given the limitations on in person learning during the pandemic. This was quite challenging for both academy teachers and students given their reliance on more applied and hands-on pedagogical approaches that is difficult to replicate in online learning environments (Dougherty & Lombardi, 2016). Researchers have noted this concern as it is likely to lead to diminished skill attainment and interrupt students' abilities to transition from high school to the workforce and postsecondary education (Dougherty et al., 2022).

Yet, At Stanton Academy, multiple stakeholders were involved in this dynamic and ongoing process—from local and national governmental agencies setting policies for how learning would occur (e.g., virtual, blended, and in person) to NAF providing new ways of establishing internships through The Future Ready Lab. During the pandemic, school stakeholders (e.g., advisory board members, teachers, school counselors, school and district administrators, and students) operated under varying roles enabling transition and adaptation to changes. These school stakeholders were essential brokers, forging bridges between organizations and varying stakeholders to implement needed changes (Kim & Kim, 2016).

Implications for the Future

The pandemic had important implications for schooling and has caused both scholars and practitioners to reimagine ways to increase students' engagement and work-based learning experiences (e.g., internships), particularly with the use of emerging technologies. Thus, we are now in a particularly critical moment to reflect and prepare for the future. It is important to acknowledge the role that teachers play in the engagement of students in online settings. Thus, we recommend that school and district administrators provide teachers with professional development geared toward teaching them best pedagogical practices for teaching in online settings. Moreover, school counselors can work with administrators and teachers to ensure that students are doing well socially and psychologically by following up with them and their families to ensure students can properly engage in virtual work settings as well as providing social forums to discuss challenges and issues they may be faced with. This case study also emphasizes the importance of school stakeholders (e.g., school and district administrators, teachers, school counselors, advisory board members, parents, community members, NAF, and students) working together and collaborating to solve unprecedented challenging educational dilemmas. In the context of this case, work-based learning was a challenge for the school to offer academy students. Hence, we encourage schools to use innovative ways (e.g., virtual internships) to offer work-based learning to students and work with the community to bolster resources to support their students' continual learning.

SUMMARY

In this case study, we examined the perspectives of high school academy stakeholders (e.g., district and school administrators, teachers, school counselors, parents, school board members, and advisory board members) as well as students in terms of the academic and psychological challenges they encountered. Further, we discussed an educational intervention to provide virtual internships for students in the STEM academies. Four themes emerged: *Social and Student Engagement Lacking*; *Growing Pains: School Stakeholders and Students as Adaptive Learners*; *Work-based Learning Implementation Challenges*; and *The NAF Future Ready Lab as an Intervention.* Students and school stakeholders reported challenges with a lack of student engagement and social interaction during the pandemic. Yet, both groups made adjustments to cope with the constantly transforming nature and disruptions precipitated by the pandemic. One of the major shifts that had to occur was in the implementation of work-based learning. To that end, NAF was instrumental in providing an intervention (The NAF Future Ready Lab) as an intervention to enable internships to occur.

ACKNOWLEDGMENT

This study was funded by the National Science Foundation's EHR Core Research program, Grant/Award Number: 2000472.

REFERENCES

Braun, A., Maguire, M., & Ball, S. J. (2010). Policy enactments in the UK secondary school: Examining policy, practice and school positioning. *Journal of Education Policy, 25*(4), 547–560. https://doiorg/10.1080/02680931003698544

Brunner, E., Dougherty, S., & Ross, S. L. (2021). *The effects of career and technical education: Evidence from the Connecticut technical high school system* (Working Paper 28790). National Bureau of Economic Research.

Camp, A., & Zamarro, G. (2021). Determinants of ethnic differences in school modality choices during the COVID-19 crisis. *Educational Researcher, 51*(1), 6–16. https://doi.org/10.3102/0013189X211057562

Castellano, M., Richardson, G., Sundell, K., & Stone, J. (2017). Preparing students for college and career in the United States: The effects of career-themed programs of study on high school performance. *Vocations & Learning, 10*, 47–70. https://doi.org/10.1007/s12186 016-9162-7

Cellini, S. R. (2006). Smoothing the transition to college? The effect of tech-prep programs on educational attainment. *Economics of Education Review, 25*(4), 394–411. https://doi.org/10.1016/j.econedurev.2005.07.006

Chatterji, P., & Li, Y. (2021). Effects of COVID-19 on school enrollment. *Economics of Education Review, 83*(1), 1–5. doi:10.1016/J.ECONEDUREV.2021.102128.

Dougherty, S. M. (2018). The effect of career and technical education on human capital accumulation: *Causal evidence from Massachusetts. Education Finance and Policy, 13*(2), 119–148. https://doi.org/10.1162/edfp_a_00224

Dougherty, S., Ecton, W., Bonilla, S., & McGuinness, S. (2022). The effects of the COVID-19 pandemic and recession on career preparation during high school, *Peabody Journal of Education, 97*(3), 326–343, https://doi.org/10.1080/0161956X.2022.2079911

Dougherty, S. M., & Lombardi, A. R. (2016). From vocational education to career readiness: The ongoing work of linking education and the labor market. *Review of Research in Education, 40*(1), 326–355. https://doi.org/10.3102/0091732X16678602

Fletcher, E., & Cox, E. (2012). Exploring the meaning African American students ascribe to their participation in high school career academies and the challenges they experience. *The High School Journal, 96*(1), 4–19. https://doi.org/10.1353/hsj.2012.0017

Fletcher Jr., E. C., Dumford, A., Hernandez-Gantes, V., & Minar, N. (2020). Examining the engagement of career academy and comprehensive high school students in the United States. *The Journal of Educational Research, 113*(4), 1–15. https://doi.org/https://doi.org/10.1080/00220671.2020.1787314

Fletcher, E., Minar, N., & Rice, B. (2023). The Future Ready Lab: Maintaining students' access to internships during times of crises. *Education and Urban Society, 55*(5), 577–592. https://doi.org/10.1177/00131245211065413

Fletcher, E., Warren, N., & Hernandez-Gantes, V. (2018). Preparing high school students for a changing world: College, career, and future ready learners. *Career and Technical Education Research, 43*(1), 77–97. https://doi.org/10.5328/cter43.1.77

Fletcher, E., Warren, N., & Hernandez-Gantes, V. (2019). The high school academy as a laboratory of equity, inclusion, and safety. *Computer Science Education, 29*(4), 382–406. https://doi.org/10.1080/08993408.2019.1616457

Goldhaber, D., Kane, T., McEachin, A., Morton, E., Patterson, T., & Staiger, D. (2023). The educational consequences of remote and hybrid instruction during the pandemic. *American Economic Review: Insights, 5*(3), 377–392.

Hemelt, S. W., Lenard, M. A., & Paeplow, C. G. (2019). Building bridges to life after high school: Contemporary career academies and student outcomes. *Economics of Education Review, 68*, 161–178. https://doi.org/10.1016/j.econedurev. 2018.08.005

Herold, B., & Kurtz, H. Y. (2020, May 11). *Teachers work two hours less per day during COVID-19: 8 key EdWeek Survey findings.* Education Week. Retrieved June 24, 2020 from https://www.edweek.org/teaching-learning/teachers-work-two-hours-less-per-day-during-covid-19-8-key-edweek-survey-findings/2020/05#:~:text=Overall%2C%20the%20nation's%20teachers%20reported,were%20sharp%20disparities%20among%20districts

Heifetz, R. (1994). *Leadership without easy answers.* Harvard University Press.

Hernandez, V., & Fletcher Jr., E. C. (2013). The need for integrated workforce development systems to broaden the participation of underrepresented students in STEM-related fields. In R. Palmer & L. Wood (Eds.), *Community colleges and STEM: Examining underrepresented racial and ethnic* (pp. 37–55). Routledge.

Hoffman, J. (2020, August 13). *Young adults report rising levels of anxiety and depression in pandemic.* The New York Times. https://www.nytimes.com/2020/08/13/health/Covid-mental-health-anxiety.html

Hulme, M., Beauchamp, G., Clarke, L., Hamilton, L. (2023). Collaboration in times of crisis: Leading UK schools in the early stages of the pandemic. *Leadership and Policy in Schools, 22*(1), 161–180. https://doi.org/10.1080/15700763.2021.1917623

Kemple, J. J., & Snipes, J. C. (2000). *Career academies: Impacts on students' engagement and performance in high school.* Retrieved from Manpower Demonstration Research Corporation website: http://www.mdrc.org/publications/41/full.pdf

Kim, S., & Kim, J.-N. (2016). Bridge or buffer: Two ideas of effective corporate governance and public engagement: Bridge or buffer. *Journal of Public Affairs, 16*(2), 118–127.

Kreisman, D., & Stange, K. (2020). Vocational and career tech education in American high schools: The value of depth over breadth. *Education Finance and Policy, 15*(1), 11–44. https://doi.org/10.1162/edfp_a_0026

Kuhfeld, M., Soland, J., Tarasawa, B., Johnson, A., Ruzek, E., & Liu, J. (2020). Projecting the potential impact of COVID-19 school closures on academic achievement. *Educational Researcher, 49*(8), 549–565. https://doi.org/10.3102/0013189X20965918

Liu, J. J., Bao, Y., Huang, X., Shi, J., & Lu, L. (2020). Mental health considerations for children quarantined because of COVID-19. *The Lancet Child & Adolescent Health, 4*(5), 347–349. https://doi.org/10.1016/S2352-4642(20)30096-1

NAF. (2014). *Statistics and research: 2013–2014.* https://naf.org/wp-content/uploads/2015/04/2014NAFAnnualReport.pdf

Spillane, J. P., & Anderson, L. (2014). The architecture of anticipation and novices' emerging understandings of the principal position: Occupational sense making at the intersection of individual, organization, and institution. *Teachers College Record, 116*(7), 1–32. http://www.tcrecord.org/Content.asp?ContentId=17491

Stake, R. (2006). *Multiple case study analysis*. Guilford.

Weick, K., Sutcliffe, K., & Obstfeld, D. (2009). Organizing and the process of sensemaking. *Handbook of Decision Making, 16*(4), 83.

CHAPTER 4

THE EFFECTS OF MENTAL HEALTH, MOTIVATION, AND LEARNING STRATEGIES ON HIGH SCHOOL STUDENTS' GRADES DURING COVID-19

Chih-hsuan Wang, Yan Dai, Jianwei Dong, Kailea Q. Manning, Jill D. Salisbury-Glennon
Auburn University

Chin-Meng Tseng
Taiwan National ChiNan University

David T. Marshall
Auburn University

ABSTRACT

Learning, motivation, and strategies are critical for high school students' academic attainment and success. With the onset of the unprecedented COVID-19 global pandemic in the past three years, high school students have experienced pandemic-related anxiety, depression, and stress. All of these

Examining the Cognitive and Psychological Effects of the COVID-19 Global Pandemic on High School, College, and Graduate Learners, pp. 65–82

may adversely impact their learning motivation; and subsequently, require students to adjust their learning strategies to cope with the changes in their learning environments, such as differing course modalities and social distancing policies. The existing literature has been focusing on college students' learning in response to the pandemic. Adolescents are even more vulnerable to environmental changes and are easily prone to mental health challenges due to the physical and physiological changes that occur during this developmental stage. However, little is known regarding the impact of the COVID-19 global pandemic on high school students' mental well-being, motivation, and learning strategies. Therefore, the present study sought to disentangle the complex relationship among those factors during the COVID-19 pandemic. A total of 96 high school students who took distance learning courses during the pandemic in Taiwan fully completed the survey. The survey included demographic items, Depression, Anxiety, and Stress Scale (DASS21), selected MSLQ subscales, and their expected final grades. A structural equation model was conducted. Results indicated that high school students' mental health directly impacted their levels of motivation, which then impacted their levels of learning strategies used, and ultimately influenced their expected final grades during the pandemic. It is suggested here that mental health support is critical to help students during these challenging times and to facilitate their learning.

Beginning in March 2020, schools began to shut down in the hopes of decreasing the spread of the coronavirus. This shutdown impacted 91.3% of the world's enrolled student population (Anakpo et al., 2024). The onset of the COVID-19 global pandemic brought numerous changes for students that impacted their mental health. School campuses were closed, resulting in the loss of on-campus counseling services for many students (Zhai & Du, 2020). Further, many students had to physically leave campus, which resulted in students losing their connections with friends and losing a potentially safe space. When students were forced to stay at home, they were isolated and lost the peer socialization that they had on campus. With major changes to learning modalities (i.e., changing from in-person to virtual learning) and a loss of peer socialization, students' mental health would decline as many students experienced loneliness, uncertainty, isolation, and frustration due to these changes.

The literature examining the impact of COVID-19 on students' mental health has found evidence to support a decline in mental health, including increased stress, anxiety, and depression as a result of the COVID-19 global pandemic (Marshall, 2023; Naff et al., 2022). For example, Halliburton and colleagues (2021) conducted a mixed methods study a month after the transition to remote learning. Of the total 1,220 participants ranging from freshmen to graduate students, about two-thirds reported anxiety and depressive symptoms in the clinical cutoff scores of the mild to severe range. Approximately one third of the participants met the clinical cut-off score for mild suicidality. The three main stressors that they found related to COVID-19 included loss of routine, a lack of social contact, and work/financial stress. In their qualitative data collected, one student reported that while their mental health was already struggling, the pandemic worsened it when they were forced to move online and thus, they had a hard time handling online assignments. With the rapid shift from face-to-face to online learning formats, students may struggle to cope, which can result in confusion and ultimately in feelings of anxiety and depression. With regards to anxiety, Lischer et al. (2022) found that 85.8% of a total of 557 students reported experiencing "mild" anxiety symptoms. Specifically, the COVID-19 stressors associated with this anxiety included the financial impact of COVID-19, academic delays, the worry of becoming depressed, and worry for the health of family members.

Adolescents are even more vulnerable to environmental changes and are easily prone to mental health challenges due to physical and physiological changes in their bodies during this developmental stage. According to the data published by the World Health Organization (WHO) on November 17, 2021, around 13% of 10–19-year-olds globally experienced mental health disorders. The report highlights elevated levels of depression, anxiety, and behavioral disorders among adolescents. A survey of Taiwanese youth aged 12–17 conducted by the Child Welfare League Foundation (CWLF) in 2022 found that 17% of teenagers self-reported severe or extremely severe levels of depression. This rate surged to 23% when focusing on high school students. Additionally, these young individuals struggling with mental health issues appeared to lack the means to express their emotions or to access professional counseling resources. This highlights an urgent requirement for intervention and support. Failing to address mental health issues in this age group can have long-term consequences that extend into adulthood, impairing both physical and mental health and limiting opportunities for individuals to lead fulfilling lives.

Moreover, learning, motivation, and strategies are all critical for high school students' academic attainment. However, since the onset of the unprecedented COVID-19 global pandemic in the past three years, little is known regarding its impact on high school students' mental well-being, motivation, and learning strategies. Therefore, the present study sought to disentangle the complex relationship among these factors.

LITERATURE REVIEW

Self-Regulated Learning During COVID-19

The COVID-19 global pandemic has imposed tremendous changes in education, such as class modality changes (Castroverde & Acala, 2021), which required increased self-regulated learning for students to effectively adjust in an effort to obtain high academic achievement. Several definitions of self-regulated learning have been posited for the last 30 years. In one of the first definitions of self-regulated learning, Zimmerman (1989) defined the self-regulated learner as a learner who is a metacognitively, motivationally, and behaviorally active participant in their learning. Further, Zimmerman and Martinez-Pons (1990) suggested that self-regulated learning strategies include such methods as organizing information, using self-consequences, help-seeking, and using various learning strategies autonomously to revise the learning process.

Self-regulated learning plays a critical role in educational contexts. From the perspective of social learning theory, self-regulation is a triadic reciprocal interaction of personal, behavioral, and environmental processes (Bandura & Walters, 1977; Hadwin et al., 2017; Schunk & Di Benedetto, 2020). Self-regulated learners could use their self-generated thoughts and actions to systematically achieve their learning goals when experiencing environmental changes (Schunk & Zimmerman, 2012; Zimmerman, 2008) by self-monitoring, self-evaluating, and self-reinforcement, transforming mental abilities into academic skills through cognitive and metacognitive strategies (Zimmerman, 1998). Thus, self-regulated learning is especially important during the COVID-19 global pandemic when students face changing class modalities.

The most widely accepted self-regulated learning model assumed two important categories of self-regulated learning: (1) cognitive and metacognitive learning strategies (rehearsal, elaboration, organization, critical thinking, and metacognitive self-regulation), and (2) resource management strategies (time and study environment, effort regulation, peer learning, and help-seeking) (Pintrich et al., 1991; Pintrich, 1999). Furthermore, motivational components were found to promote and sustain self-regulated learning. Previous studies have found that self-regulated learning is positively associated with motivation and learning achievement (Brady et al., 2021; Galla et al., 2019; Hoyle & Dent, 2018; Hromalik & Koszalka, 2018). Baumeister and Vohs (2007) posited that the main beliefs of self-regulated learning included standards of desirable behavior, motivation to meet standards, and monitoring of the changed situations. In other words, self-regulated learning, together with motivational components, can play an important role in students' learning achievement when facing class modality changes. Pintrich et al. (1991) also included three general motivational components (value components, expectancy components, and affective components) related to the model of self-regulated learning and developed the Motivated Strategies for Learning Questionnaire (MSLQ).

Previous studies have found that students with class modality consistency had intensified motivation, higher levels of self-efficacy, and tended to make use of more effective learning strategies (Fogle, 2016). Astleitner (2002) found that different class modalities impacted students' critical thinking. However, there remains a paucity of research that has systematically explored students' differences in self-regulated learning and motivation as a function of class modality changes. The COVID-19 global pandemic has had a profound impact on education worldwide, forcing an unprecedented shift in class modality from traditional in-person instruction to remote and hybrid learning formats (Bozkurt & Sharma, 2020). In particular, high school students faced significant challenges as they navigated this sudden modality transition (König et al., 2020). Consequently, the development and application of self-regulated learning strategies became increasingly critical for academic success during these unprecedented times (Zimmerman & Schunk, 2014). The shift to remote and hybrid instruction required students' ability to plan, monitor, and evaluate their learning processes autonomously (Panadero, 2017), to cope with the new modality, to adapt to new learning environments, to manage their time effectively, and to stay motivated in the face of distractions and social isolation (Dai et al., 2021; Wang et al., 2020). Although some students did thrive with the new learning modalities, many students struggled to maintain their academic performance and engagement, highlighting the crucial role of self-regulated learning in the context of the COVID-19 global pandemic (König et al., 2020). Thus, educators and researchers have emphasized the need for targeted interventions and support to help high school students to strengthen their self-regulated learning skills, ultimately enhancing their resilience and adaptability in the face of ongoing and future educational challenges (Broadbent & Poon, 2021).

Mental Health Challenges and Their Impact on Motivation and Learning Strategies

High school students' mental health was negatively affected by the COVID-19 global pandemic. Studies have shown that students experienced a decline in overall well-being, with higher levels of reported stress, anxiety, and depression. These findings are supported by literature and are evident across the globe (Asanov et al., 2021; Lin, 2020; Rao & Rao, 2021; Shabna & Christuraj, 2021). Immediately after the schools' closure, Asanov et al. (2021) conducted a phone-based survey of more than 1,500 Ecuadorian high school students aged 14 to 18. The findings of their study revealed that 16% of the students experienced depression, which is 6% higher than the level of depression reported by Torres et al. (2017) in another survey study using first-year college students who were in their late adolescence. Rao and Rao (2021) conducted a study among U.S. school students to investigate changes in mental health and to identify critical stressors before and during the COVID-19 pandemic. The study found a significant decline in mental health among the population studied, with critical stressors including homework (13.2%), social isolation or lack of social interaction (8.5%), and lack of support for mental well-being (12.3%). Academic stress, identified as a key component of students' stress during COVID-19, is commonly experienced in Asian countries, due to the high expectations of parents and teachers, and the pressure associated with college entrance examinations (Jayanthi et al., 2015; Luo et al., 2020). In a school-based epidemiological survey study in China, Luo et al. (2020) examined stress among 15,055 high school students and found that academic stress was the most prevalent stressor, accounting for 58.9% of frequently reported mental health problems.

In addition to academic stress, high school students in the adolescent stage of development are vulnerable to experiencing high rates of depression and anxiety during and after enforced isolation measures. This can be explained by the fact that adolescence represents a critical phase in the development of emotional and social capacities, which are characterized by the emergence of identity formation and social relationships (Steinberg & Morris, 2001). Research suggests that adolescents are more susceptible to social isolation and loneliness (Santini et al., 2021). A 2021 survey conducted by the Centers for Disease Control and Prevention (2023) found that 42% of U.S. adolescents reported experiencing persistent feelings of sadness or loneliness, including 57% of females and 29% of males. The COVID-19 global pandemic has disrupted adolescents' daily routines, primarily through school closures and social distancing measures, causing a detrimental impact on their social experiences. Consequently, many adolescents have been forced to adapt to substantial changes, leading to elevated stress and anxiety levels (Loades et al., 2020).

Previous research has indicated that academic stress is one of the key sources of mental health issues among adolescents (Rao & Rao, 2021). However, there is limited research on how each mental health component impacts learning, motivation, and self-regulated learning strategies among high school students. According to Muris (2002), there is a negative correlation between school-related anxiety and academic self-efficacy in students with an average age of 15 years. This association is particularly evident in the negative impact of anxiety on students' perceived capability in learning, which supports the notion that self-efficacy is a domain-specific construct, as proposed by Bandura (1986). In a meta-analysis of depression and attributions in learning, Gladstone and Kaslow (1995) suggested that adolescents who identified with higher levels of depression tended to express their attributions as *learned helplessness*, ultimately relating to negative learning efforts and outcomes. *Learned helplessness*, as described by

Bodiford et al. (1988), is a state that arises when an individual repeatedly experiences an unfulfilled situation, eliciting the false belief that they are unable to control the outcome. As a result, the individual may fail to put in effort due to a sense of a perceived lack of control.

Promoting motivation and self-regulated strategies may be an effective approach to prevent the adverse impact of mental health issues on students' learning outcomes. Fostering a mastery goal structure, or intrinsic motivation, can positively facilitate using metacognitive and cognitive strategies to improve learning outcomes. Moning and Roelle (2021) randomly assigned 166 ninth grade students into two different goal structure groups. Results showed that the task outcomes were significantly higher in students who embedded mastery goals in the learning protocol writings than in the performance goal group, with control of the previous ability. Lin (2020) studied 1,060 junior high school students in Taiwan and found that excessive use of the internet became more prevalent during the lockdown period when classes were shifted online. The study revealed that young adolescents experienced difficulties with learning motivation, failed to regulate their internet use effectively, and instead resorted to maladaptive coping mechanisms to cope with their stresses.

While some studies have examined the link between motivation and self-regulated learning strategies (Li et al., 2022; Moning & Roelle, 2021), less is known regarding how mental health issues affect motivation, learning strategies, and ultimately academic outcomes. Understanding the types of mental health issues that adolescents struggle with, particularly during the COVID-19 pandemic period, can offer strategies to mitigate the negative impact of mental health challenges on learning and academic achievement.

Hypothesized Model

Much of the existing literature has focused on college students' learning in response to the COVID-19 global pandemic. Adolescents are even more vulnerable to environmental changes and are more predisposed to mental issues due to their physical and physiological changes that occur during this developmental stage (Steinberg, 2005). However, little is known regarding the impact of the COVID-19 global pandemic on high school students' mental well-being, motivation, and learning strategies. Therefore, this study sought to disentangle the complex relationship among those variables during the COVID-19 pandemic. The present study aimed to explore high school students' self-regulation and motivation during class modality changes. Specifically, for self-regulated learning, we focus on critical thinking, metacognitive self-regulation, and resource management strategies (i.e., help-seeking, time and study management, peer learning, and effort regulation). For motivational components, we focus on intrinsic and extrinsic motivation, and self-efficacy, as assessed by The Motivated Strategies for Learning Questionnaire (MSLQ; Pintrich, 1991). It is hoped that the results of the present study can help educational professionals to better understand the impact of class modality changes on high school students' self-regulated learning and motivation. Our hypothesized model is presented in Figure 4.1.

Figure 4.1

Hypothesized Model

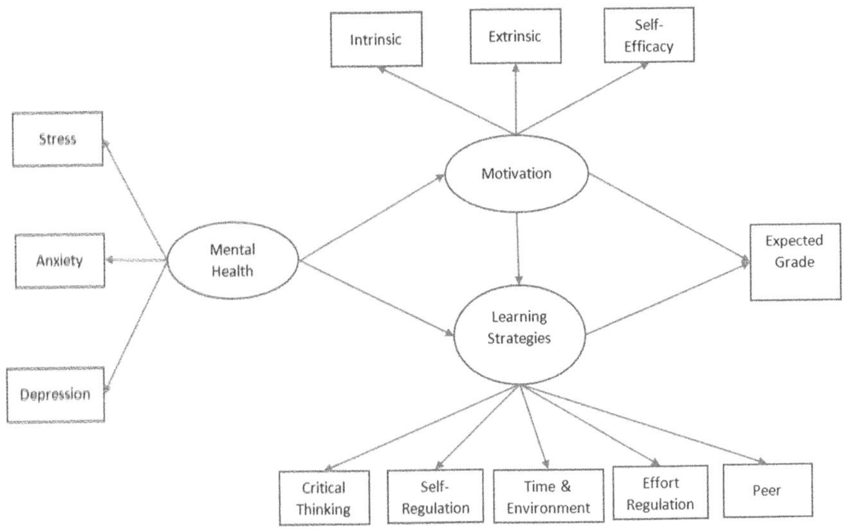

METHOD

Procedure and Participants

A convenience sampling procedure was utilized in this study. High school teachers in Taiwan facilitated the process of the study. During the school lockdown, an anonymous online survey invitation was emailed to high school teachers in May and June of 2020. These teachers could decide whether to distribute the survey invitation to their students. Participation in the survey was entirely voluntary, with students having full discretion to join. The study complied with international research guidelines, having secured approval from an Institutional Review Board (IRB) in the United

States. In this instance, the requirement for parental consent was waived. Students who decided to participate in the study reviewed the consent information online and decided whether they wanted to complete the survey. They could withdraw from participation at any time by closing the browser before submitting their responses.

One hundred and forty-one high school students in Taiwan responded to the anonymous online survey. Among those responses, 96 students completed all survey items, with a survey usable rate at 68.09%. Thirty-eight of them were male (39.6%), and 55 female students (57.3%). Three students declined to indicate their gender identity (3.1%). They were 10–12th graders (10th grade: n = 11, 11.5%; 11th grade: n = 70, 72.9%; 12th grade: n = 15, 15.6%) with a mean age of 17.53 years (SD = 0.94). Seventy students (72.9%) were enrolled in primary distance courses while 26 students (27.1%) were enrolled in hybrid classes during the COVID pandemic shutdown in Taiwan.

Measures

The anonymous survey included three sections: Depression, Anxiety and Stress Scale-21 items (DASS-21), subscales selected from Motivational Strategies and Learning Questionnaire (MSLQ), and demographic questions.

The *DASS-21* was developed by Lovibond and Lovibond (1995) to measure participants' mental health. It includes 21 items, 7 items to measure participants' level of depression, 7 items to measure the level of anxiety, and 7 items to measure the level of stress. Participants respond to those items by indicating if the item "*did not apply to me at all*" to "*applied to me very much, or most of the time.*" The higher scores indicate a higher level of depression, anxiety, and/or stress. Research indicated that the construct validity and internal consistency reliability of DASS-21 were good (Thiyagarajan et al., 2022). The internal consistency Cronbach's alpha in the current study was .83–.91.

The *MSLQ* was developed by Pintrich and his colleagues (Pintrich et al., 1993). It consists of 81 Likert type items on which the participant selects one number on a scale that ranges from 1 (*not at all true me*) to 7 (*very true of me*). Higher scores indicate a higher level of motivation and learning strategies. The current study selected the intrinsic goal orientation, extrinsic goal orientation, and self-efficacy subscales from the motivational scale as well as critical thinking, metacognitive self-regulation, time and study environment, peer learning, and effort regulation subscales from the learning strategies scale. The internal consistency reliability of the MSLQ subscales ranged .62–.93. The internal consistency Cronbach's alpha in the current study was .63–.94 (Table 4.1).

The demographic items included sex, grade level, age, learning modality, and the GPA of the participants during the pandemic lockdown in Taiwan.

Table 4.1

Reliability Results for Each Subscale

Scale	# of Items	Reliability Evidence	Cronbach's α
DASS-21			
Depression	7	.92	.90
Anxiety	7	.87	.83
Stress	7	.89	.91
Motivation			
Intrinsic	4	.74	.81
Extrinsic	4	.62	.81
Self-Efficacy	8	.93	.94
Learning Strategies			
Critical Thinking	5	.80	.80
Self-Regulation	12	.79	.85
Time & Environment	8	.76	.77
Effort Regulation	4	.69	.63
Peer Learning	3	.76	.80

RESULTS

A covariance-based structural equation model (SEM) was utilized to analyze the relationship among mental health, motivation, and learning strategies on high school students' expected grades during the pandemic lockdown in Taiwan. Chi-square statistics and fit indices, GFI, CFI, TLI, NFI, RMR, and RMSEA were used to evaluate the hypothesis model fit. If the model statistics and model fit indices of the hypothesized model indicate a poor fit, the model can be improved by trimming non-significant paths or adding correlations between variables based on the modification indices (Hox & Bechger, 1998; Kline, 2010). Each process of improvement and re-evaluation is repeated until an adequate model fit is reached (Hox & Bechger, 1998). In this research, the results for the hypothesized model indicated a poor fit, $\chi^2(52) = 184.409$, $p < .001$, $\chi^2/df = 3.546$, GFI = .763, CFI = .814, TLI = .764, NFI = .763, RMR = .097, RMSEA = .164. After respecifying the model based on the modification indices and removing non-significant paths one-by-one, the final model indicated a good fit, $\chi^2(44) = 63.363$, $p = .029$, $\chi^2/df = 1.44$, GFI = .900, CFI = .973, TLI = .959, NFI = .918, RMR = .067, RMSEA = .068 (Figure 4.2). Each path coefficient, factor loading, and R^2 were shown in Figure 4.2. R^2 represents the percentage of the variance of the dependent variable explained by the independent variables in the model. All of the paths reached statistical significance ($p < .05$), and each path coefficient demonstrated practical effectiveness (standardized $\beta > .3$). Based on the final model, mental health negatively impacted the level of motivation for high school students who took online or hybrid classes during the pandemic lockdown. The level of their motivation positively impacted the level of strategies used while taking those online or hybrid classes, and finally positively impacted their expected grades.

High school students who experienced higher levels of depression, anxiety, or stress had lower levels of motivation for working on their course work. The lower levels of motivation also led to lower levels of and poorer quality learning strategies used in taking online or hybrid courses, which eventually resulted in the belief that they would not receive good grades. On the other hand, high school students who did not experience depression, anxiety or stress during the pandemic lockdown usually had higher levels of motivation to complete their course work and utilized higher levels and efficient learning strategies, which led to them receiving higher grades.

DISCUSSION

The final model's results revealed that mental health issues indirectly affected expected grades by influencing motivation and learning strategies. Motivation played a crucial role in mitigating the negative effects of mental health problems on high school students' academic performance.

As shown in Figure 4.2, self-efficacy demonstrated the highest factor loading on the latent variable among the three subcomponents of motivation, with a loading score of .921. Intrinsic motivation followed with a loading score of .725, and extrinsic motivation had the lowest loading score of 0.589. This finding is valuable in guiding teachers to develop their instructional strategies by focusing on promoting self-efficacy and intrinsic motivation among high school students, particularly in online classes. The finding is consistent with previous research. Mesman et al. (2021) systematically reviewed 24 research articles to promote multisystem resilience among adolescents with mental health issues. Mastery motivation is a crucial factor in the resilience multisystem, a dynamic process of adaption or recovery in the context of coping with risks and self-regulation. Mastery motivation, advocated by intrinsic interests, can serve as a promotive or protective factor on self-regulation to achieve a better goal.

High school students lacking in motivation fail to elicit self-regulated strategies. She et al. (2021) used SEM to reveal the association between COVID-19 pandemic stress, academic stress, depression, and internet game disorder. Data were collected among 3,136 adolescents in 13 secondary schools in Hong Kong from September to November of 2020. There was a significant and positive path that COVID-19 stress indirectly impacted depression and excessive use of internet games through the mediation of academic stress. Participants who reported high levels of COVID-19 stress were found to be worried about schooling, dissatisfied with online learning, and playing games to avoid engaging in learning behavior and to alleviate anxiety. With the absence of motivation, depression and excessive internet game disorder correlated and suggested that playing games fails to improve mental health.

The COVID-19 pandemic has had a significant impact on the mental health and well-being of adolescents. As such, it is important for schools, mental health professionals, and policymakers to use research findings to develop effective strategies to support adolescent mental health during and after the pandemic. One such strategy could involve the implementation of mental health screening and intervention programs to identify and support students who may be struggling with mental health challenges. Additionally, school administrators and interventionists should prioritize regulating the use of digital devices, given the link between excessive internet use and mental health issues.

Research on adolescent mental health during the COVID-19 pandemic is crucial to understanding the pandemic's impact on this vulnerable population. The disruptions caused by the pandemic have the potential to have long-lasting effects on mental health and well-being. Therefore, it is essential to continue research to develop effective strategies to support adolescent mental health and mitigate the negative impacts of the pandemic on this group.

CONCLUSION

The current study explored the relationships among mental health, motivation, and learning strategies on high school students' expected grades during the COVID-19 global pandemic lockdown in Taiwan. The finding of this study plays a dual role in contributing to the field of education. First, it emphasizes the pressing issue of mental health and its indirect impact on learning outcomes. As the prevalence of mental health issues among high school students increases, their ability to self-regulate, stay motivated, and to perform well academically is significantly hindered. The present results indicated that if students experienced higher levels of mental health challenges, they had lower levels of motivation and learning strategies used, which eventually impacted their overall learning and performance. Mental health support is critical to help students during these challenging times and to facilitate their learning. In this regard, the study urges educators and stakeholders to acknowledge and address these issues that impact students' learning experiences, primarily by ensuring that necessary support systems are in place.

Moreover, another contribution of this research is advocating for the adoption of mastery learning goals. It underscores the importance of fostering self-efficacy and intrinsic motivation among high school students, especially in the context of online classes. Amid the rise of the online learning context, it becomes more crucial than ever to foster an environment that promotes the mastery of content rather than performance-oriented goals or extrinsic motivation. This approach ensures that adolescent students are intrinsically driven, equipped with adequate self-efficacy, and engaged in more self-regulated learning strategies.

SUMMARY

The COVID-19 global pandemic has profoundly impacted various aspects of adolescents' lives, but no discipline has been more impacted than education. However, it is important to note that this unprecedented pandemic presents both challenges and opportunities in studying adolescent mental health issues, motivation, and self-regulated learning strategies. The sudden shift to online learning has imposed new demands on students to self-regulate their learning, which can be challenging for many adolescents. Some students struggled to maintain motivation and attention in a home environment with potential distractions and without the physical presence of teachers, classmates and the necessary technology. Despite these challenges, the move to online learning has catalyzed an accelerated focus on teaching and learning in the digital environment and adopting evolving pedagogical approaches. Moreover, this shift to more online learning has underscored the necessity for a robust mental health support system for adolescents, for promoting research into fostering resilience and self-regulation and for developing adaptability in the face of adversities that bear long-term benefits.

Figure 4.2

Results for Final Model

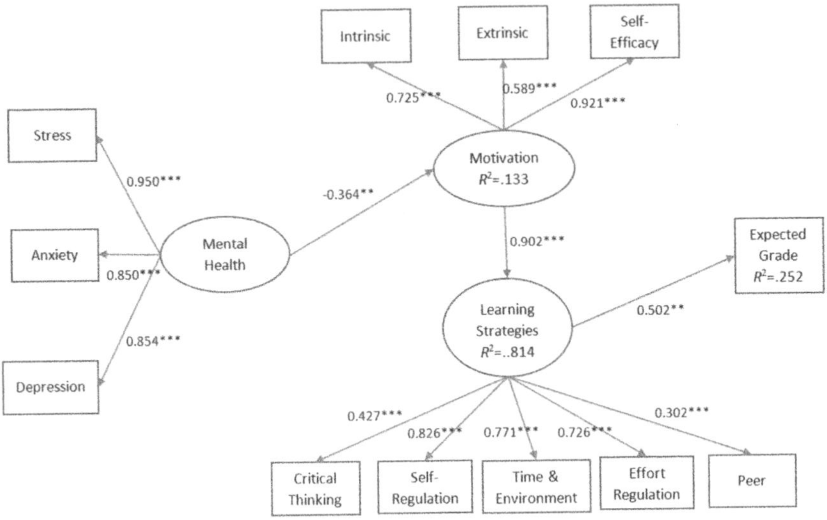

N=96, χ^2=63.363, *df*=44, p=.029, χ^2/*df*=1.44, *GFI*=.900, *CFI*=.973, *TLI*=.959, *NFI*=.918, *RMR*=.067, *RMSEA*=.068

REFERENCES

Anakpo, G., Nkungwana, S., & Mishi, S. (2024). Impact of Covid-19 on school attendance in South Africa: Analysis of sociodemographic characteristics of learners. *Heliyon, 10*(7), e29096. https://doi.org/10.1016/j.heliyon.2024.e29096

Asanov, I., Flores, F., McKenzie, D., Mensmann, M., & Schulte, M. (2021). Remote-learning, time-use, and mental health of Ecuadorian high-school students during the COVID-19 quarantine. *World Development, 138*, 105225. https://doi.org/10.1016/j.worlddev.2020.105225

Astleitner, H. (2002). Teaching critical thinking online. *Journal of Instructional Psychology, 29*(2), 53–76. http://www.u.arizona.edu/~rgolden/teachingCriticalThinking.pdf

Bandura. A. (1986). *Social foundations of thought and action: A social cognitive theory*. Prentice Hall.

Bandura, A., & Walters, R. H. (1977). *Social learning theory* (Vol. 1). Englewood Cliffs.

Baumeister, R. F., & Vohs, K. D. (2007). Self-regulation, ego depletion, and motivation. *Social and Personality Psychology Compass, 1*(1), 115–128. https://doi.org/10.1111/j.1751-9004.2007.00001.x

Bodiford, C. A., Eisenstadt, T. H., Johnson, J. H., & Bradlyn, A. S. (1988). Comparison of learned helplessness cognitions and behavior in children with high and low scores on the Children's Depression Inventory. *Journal of Clinical Child Psychology, 17*(2), 152–158. https://doi.org/10.1207/s15374424jccp1702_7

Bozkurt, A., & Sharma, R. C. (2020). Emergency remote teaching in a time of global crisis due to Corona Virus pandemic. *Asian Journal of Distance Education, 15*(1), i–iv.

Brady, A. C., Kim, Y. E., & Cutshall, J. (2021). The what, why, and how of distractions from a self-regulated learning perspective. *Journal of College Reading and Learning, 51*(2), 153–172. https://doi.org/10.1080/10790195.2020.1867671

Broadbent, J., & Poon, W. L. (2015). Self-regulated learning strategies & academic achievement in online higher education learning environments: A systematic review. *The internet and higher education, 27*, 1–13. https://doi.org/10.1016/j.iheduc.2015.04.007

Castroverde, F., & Acala, M. (2021). Modular distance learning modality: Challenges of teachers in teaching amid the Covid-19 pandemic. *International Journal of Research studies in Education, 10*(8), 7–15. https://doi.org/10.5861/ijrse.2021.602

Centers for Disease Control and Prevention. (2023). *Youth risk behavior survey: Data summary & trends report.* https://www.cdc.gov/healthyyouth/data/yrbs/pdf/YRBS_Data-Summary-Trends_Report2023_508.pdf

Dai, Y., Lin, X., Su, S., & Li, L. (2021). The online learning academic achievement of Chinese students during the COVID-19 pandemic: The role of self-regulated learning and academic entitlement. *International Journal of Psychology and Educational Studies, 8*(3), 116–127. https://doi.org/10.52380/ijpes.2021.8.3.384

Fogle, T. T. (2016). *Class modality, student characteristics, and performance in a community college introductory STEM course* [Doctoral dissertation, Capella University].

Galla, B. M., Shulman, E. P., Plummer, B. D., Gardner, M., Hutt, S. J., Goyer, J. P., & Duckworth, A. L. (2019). Why high school grades are better predictors of on-time college graduation than are admissions test scores: The roles of self-regulation and cognitive ability. *American Educational Research Journal, 56*(6), 2077–2115. https://doi.org/10.3102/0002831219843292

Gladstone, T. R., & Kaslow, N. J. (1995). Depression and attributions in children and adolescents: A meta-analytic review. *Journal of Abnormal Child Psychology, 23*, 597–606. https://doi.org/10.1007/BF01447664

Hadwin, A., Järvelä, S., & Miller, M. (2017). Self-regulation, co-regulation, and shared regulation in collaborative learning environments. In D. H. Schunk & J. A. Greene (Eds.), *Handbook of self-regulation of learning and performance* (pp. 83–106). Routledge. https://doi.org/10.4324/9781315697048-6

Halliburton, A. E., Hill, M. B., Dawson, B. L., Hightower, J. M., & Rueden, H. (2021). Increased stress, declining mental health: Emerging adults' experiences in college during COVID-19. *Emerging Adulthood, 9*(5), 433–448. https://doi.org/10.1177/21676968211025348

Hox, J. J., & Bechger, T. M. (1998). An introduction to structural equation modeling. *Family Science Review, 11*, 354–373. https://doi.org/10.1080/01688638808402800

Hoyle, R. H., & Dent, A. L. (2018). *Developmental trajectories of skills and abilities relevant for self-regulation of learning and performance*. Routledge/Taylor & Francis Group. https://doi.org/10.4324/9781315697048-4

Hromalik, C. D., & Koszalka, T. A. (2018). Self-regulation of the use of digital resources in an online language learning course improves learning outcomes. *Distance Education, 39*(4), 528–547. https://doi.org/10.1080/01587919.2018.1520044

Jayanthi, P., Thirunavukarasu, M., & Rajkumar, R. (2015). Academic stress and depression among adolescents: A cross-sectional study. *Indian Pediatrics, 52*, 217–219. https://doi.org/10.1007/s13312-015-0609-y

Kline, R. B. (2010. *Principles and practice of structural equation modeling* (3rd ed.). Guilford Press. https://doi.org/10.1080/10705511.2012.687667

König, J., Jäger-Biela, D. J., & GlutschGlutsch, N. (2020). Adapting to online teaching during COVID-19 school closure: Teacher education and teacher competence effects among early career teachers in Germany. *European Journal of Teacher Education, 43*(4), 608–622. https://doi.org/10.1080/02619768.2020.1809650

Li, S., Zheng, J., Huang, X., & Xie, C. (2022). Self-regulated learning as a complex dynamical system: Examining students' STEM learning in a simulation environment. *Learning and Individual Differences, 95*, 102–144. https://doi.org/10.1016/j.lindif.2022.102144

Lin, M. P. (2020). Prevalence of internet addiction during the COVID-19 outbreak and its risk factors among junior high school students in Taiwan. *International Journal of Environmental Research and Public Health, 17*(22), 8547. https://doi.org/10.3390/ijerph17228547

Lischer, S., Safi, N., & Dickson, C. (2022). Remote learning and students' mental health during the Covid-19 pandemic: A mixed-method enquiry. *Prospects, 51*, 589–599. https://doi.org/10.1007/s11125-020-09530-w

Loades, M. E., Chatburn, E., Higson-Sweeney, N., Reynolds, S., Shafran, R., Brigden, A., Linney, C., McManus, M. N., Borwick, C., & Crawley, E. (2020). Rapid systematic review: The impact of social isolation and loneliness on the mental health of children and adolescents in the context of COVID-19. *Journal of the American Academy of Child & Adolescent Psychiatry, 59*(11), 1218–1239. https://doi.org/10.1016/j.jaac.2020.05.009

Lovibond, S. H., & Lovibond, P. F. (1995*). Manual for the depression anxiety & stress scales* (2nd ed.) Psychology Foundation.

Luo, Y., Cui, Z., Zou, P., Wang, K., Lin, Z., He, J., & Wang, J. (2020). Mental health problems and associated factors in Chinese high school students in Henan province: A cross-sectional study. *International Journal of Environmental Research and Public Health, 17*(16), 5944. https://doi.org/10.3390/ijerph17165944

Marshall, D. T. (2023). COVID-19 and school closures: A narrative review of pediatric mental health impacts. *Journal of School Choice, 171*, 67–76. https://doi.org/10.1080/15582159.2023.2201734

Mesman, E., Vreeker, A., & Hillegers, M. (2021). Resilience and mental health in children and adolescents: An update of the recent literature and future directions. *Current Opinion in Psychiatry, 34*(6), 586. https:// 10.1097/YCO.0000000000000741

Moning, J., & Roelle, J. (2021). Self-regulated learning by writing learning protocols: Do goal structures matter?. *Learning and Instruction, 75*, 101486. https://doi.org/10.1016/j.learninstruc.2021.101486

Muris, P. (2002). Relationships between self-efficacy and symptoms of anxiety disorders and depression in a normal adolescent sample. *Personality and Individual Differences, 32*(2), 337–348. https://doi.org/10.1016/S0191-8869(01)00027-7

Naff, D., Williams, S., Furman-Darby, J., & Yeong, M. (2022). The mental health impacts of COVID-19 on PK–12 students: A systematic review of emerging literature. *AERA Open, 8*(1), 1–40. https://doi.org/10.1177/23328584221084722

Panadero, E. (2017). A review of self-regulated learning: Six models and four directions for research. *Frontiers in Psychology, 8*, 422. https://doi.org/10.3389/fpsyg.2017.00422

Pintrich, P. R. (1991). A manual for the use of the Motivated Strategies for Learning Questionnaire (MSLQ). https://doi.org/10.1037/t09161-000

Pintrich, P. R. (1999). The role of motivation in promoting and sustaining self-regulated learning. *International Journal of Educational Research, 31*(6), 459–470. https://doi.org/10.1016/s0883-0355(99)00015-4

Pintrich, P. R., Smith, D. A. F., Garcia, T., & Mckeachie, W. J. (1993). Reliability and predictive validity of the motivated strategies for learning questionnaire(MSLQ). *Educational and Psychological Measurement, 53*(3), 801–813. https://doi.org/10.1177/0013164493053003024

Rao, M. E., & Rao, D. M. (2021, July). The mental health of high school students during the COVID-19 pandemic. *Frontiers in Education, 6*. https://doi.org/10.3389/feduc.2021.719539

Santini, S. I., Pisinger, V. S. C., Nielsen, L., Madsen, K. R., Roffey, S., Thygessen, L. C., & Meilstrup, C. (2021). Social disconnectedness, loneliness, and mental health among adolescents in Danish high schools: A nationwide cross-sectional study. *Frontiers in behavioral neuroscience, 15*, 632906. https://doi.org/10.3389/fnbeh.2021.632906

Schunk, D. H., & DiBenedetto, M. K. (2020). Motivation and social cognitive theory. *Contemporary Educational Psychology, 60*, 101832. https://doi.org/10.1016/j.cedpsych.2019.101832

Schunk, D. H., & Zimmerman, B. J. (Eds.). (2012). *Motivation and self-regulated learning: Theory, research, and applications*. Routledge. https://doi.org/10.4324/9780203831076

Shabna, S., & Christuraj, P. (2021). Psychosocial problems among adolescents during COVID 19 lockdown. *Turkish Online Journal of Qualitative Inquiry, 12*(9).

She, R., Wong, K., Lin, J., Leung, K., Zhang, Y., & Yang, X. (2021). How COVID-19 stress related to schooling and online learning affects adolescent depression and Internet gaming disorder: Testing conservation of resources theory with sex difference. *Journal of Behavioral Addictions, 10*(4), 953–966. https://doi.org/10.1556/2006.2021.00069

Steinberg, L. (2005). Cognitive and affective development in adolescence. *Trends in Cognitive Sciences, 9*(2), 69–74. https://doi.org/10.1016/j.tics.2004.12.005

Steinberg, L., & Morris, A. S. (2001). Adolescent development. *Annual Review of Psychology, 52*(1), 83–110. https://doi.org/10.1146/annurev.psych.52.1.83

Thiyagarajan, A., James, T. G., & Marzo, R. R. (2022). Psychometric properties of the 21-item Depression, Anxiety, and Stress Scale (DASS-21) among Malaysians during COVID-19: A methodological study. *Humanities & Social Sciences Communications, 9*, 1–8. https://doi.org/10.1057/s41599-022-01229-x

Torres, C., Otero, P., Bustamante, B., Blanco, V., Díaz, O., & Vázquez, F. L. (2017). Mental health problems and related factors in Ecuadorian college students. *International Journal of Environmental Research and Public Health, 14*(5), 530. https://doi:org/10.3390/ijerph14050530

Wang, C. H., Salisbury-Glennon, J. D., Dai, Y., Lee, S., & Dong, J. (2022). Empowering college students to decrease digital distraction through the use of self-regulated learning strategies. *Contemporary Educational Technology, 14*(4), ep388. https://doi.org/10.30935/cedtech/12456

Wang, X., Hegde, S., Son, C., Keller, B., Smith, A., & Sasangohar, F. (2020). Investigating mental health of U.S. college students during the COVID-19 pandemic: Cross-sectional survey study. *Journal of Medical Internet Research, 22*(9), e22817. https://doi.org/10.2196/22817

World Health Organization. (2021). *Mental Health of Adolescents*. https://www.who.int/news-room/fact-sheets/detail/adolescent-mental-health

Zhai, Y., & Du, Xue (2020). Addressing collegiate mental health amid COVID-19 pandemic. *Psychiatry Research, 288*, 113003. https://doi.org/10.1016/j.psychres.2020.113003

Zimmerman, B. J. (1989). A social cognitive view of self-regulated academic learning. *Journal of Educational Psychology, 81*(3), 329. https://doi.org/10.1037/0022-0663.81.3.329

Zimmerman, B. J. (1998). Academic studying and the development of personal skill: A self-regulatory perspective. *Educational psychologist, 33*(2–3), 73–86. https://doi.org/10.1207/s15326985ep3302&3_3

Zimmerman, B. J. (2008). Investigating self-regulation and motivation: Historical background, methodological developments, and future prospects. *American Educational Research Journal, 4-5*(1), 166–183. https://doi.org/10.3102/0002831207312909

Zimmerman, B. J., & Martinez-Pons, M. (1990). Student differences in self-regulated learning: Relating grade, sex, and giftedness to self-efficacy and strategy use. *Journal of Educational Psychology, 82*(1), 51–59. https://doi.org/10.1037/0022-0663.82.1.51

Zimmerman, B. J., & Schunk, D. H. (2014). *Educational psychology: A century of contributions: A Project of Division 15 (Educational Psychology) of the American Psychological Society*. Routledge. https://doi.org/10.4324/9781315734255

SECTION II

UNDERGRADUATE LEARNERS

CHAPTER 5

INSTRUCTIONAL SUPPORT AND THE STUDENT-TEACHER RELATIONSHIP IN HIGHER EDUCATION

Lessons Learned From Students' Perceptions of Instruction During Emergency Remote Learning

Angela D. Miller, Jeffrey Vomund, Michelle M. Buehl, Nate S. Brophy, and Melissa Broeckelman-Post
George Mason University

ABSTRACT

Instructional support for students and high-quality student-teacher relationships in higher education settings are necessary for student achievement and well-being in any classroom setting. These aspects may be even more important in an online setting. Student perceptions of the learning environment are a valuable lens to understand effective teaching in a classroom or online. Consideration of students' perceptions of their instructors and the structure of their online classes during the transition to emergency remote learning

Examining the Cognitive and Psychological Effects of the COVID-19 Global Pandemic on High School, College, and Graduate Learners, pp. 85–107

(ERL) during the COVID-19 pandemic is key for stakeholders in undergraduate education as the demand for and enrollment in online courses climbs post-pandemic. The lessons we can learn from student reports of online course support, instructor competence and commitment, and their learning satisfaction and dissatisfaction can inform and improve instruction. Additionally, lessons from the crisis highlight the importance of the emotional aspects of teaching and learning, which are also inherent in psychological and social theories of motivation. Findings from both quantitative and qualitative analyses from data provided by students (N = 935) in an introductory undergraduate Communication course center on the pivotal role of the instructor and how students perceive interactions with their instructor. Student perceptions of the learning environment are directly related to their basic psychological need satisfaction. Differences between classrooms with easy versus difficult transitions are investigated.

Keywords: motivation, higher education

Students' perceptions of the learning environment are a critical factor in developing the behaviors and attitudes that support their wellness and achievement. These perceptions may even be more central to student success than the actual instructional strategies that teachers intend (Bandura, 1986; Urdan, 2004). Student perspectives on learning are dependent on the instructional context (Tai et al., 2019) and can differ based on the course modality (e.g., face-to-face, online). Since the COVID-19 pandemic, there has been a rise in the number of online courses being offered and a shift in the students who elect to enroll in online modalities (National Center for Education Statistics, n.d.). Many theories of motivation and conceptualizations of the student-teacher relationship have not been tested within this teaching modality and within this new student population.

Much can be learned from the initial semester of transition to emergency remote learning (ERL) with respect to what students need and want from their instructors to be motivated in this online environment. The purpose of this chapter is to examine students' perceptions of the transition semester vis-à-vis the courses that undergraduate students found to have the easiest and the most difficult transitions from face-to-face to online. Examining students' perceptions within the theoretical framework of needs satisfaction and dissatisfaction of self-determination theory (SDT; Deci & Ryan, 1991), we can begin to understand what aspects of the student-teacher relationship and which strategies of instructional support are most salient for online learning. Although the online transition was an emergency, key traits of previous work on student-teacher interactions and instructional support stand out and deserve more focus in our research moving forward from the pandemic.

LITERATURE REVIEW

Basic human need satisfaction and need dissatisfaction or need frustration are key to learning and teaching in both face-to-face and online settings (e.g., Demir et al., 2019; Filak & Nicolini, 2018; Ryan & Deci, 2020). Research on student perceptions suggests a number of essential ideas that involve both emotional and instructional aspects of teaching. According to SDT, there are three basic psychological needs to support or thwart thriving (Ryan & Deci, 2017): (a) need for autonomy in one's own experiences and actions, (b) need for a sense of competence to complete and execute tasks, and (c) need for relatedness or feelings of connectedness to others. In face-to-face educational contexts, needs satisfaction has been positively related to student motivation and learning outcomes (Grolnick & Ryan, 1989; Kusurkar et al., 2013). Wang et al. (2019) found that, compared to face-to-face courses, students in online courses reported lower levels of need satisfaction and higher levels of need dissatisfaction (frustration). Although the positive correlation between need satisfaction and need dissatisfaction (frustration) that the authors found in the online course may be partly explained to measurement bias due to usage of bipolar scales; they did note that the finding may also be partly due to perceived lower quality of teaching in online courses or perceived lack of social presence and interactions. Students' perceptions of lack of interaction and presence have been confirmed in other studies of online learning (Bowers & Kumar, 2015).

Basic Psychological Needs

The three basic needs are facilitated in a learning environment by the instructor. Instructors' abilities to transition their face-to-face courses to ERL impacted both students' learning experiences and instructor's ability to not only deliver content but also to connect with their students. Instructors who have been able to fulfill students' basic psychological needs in a face-to-face setting may struggle with the shift to online. Instructional practices to build student competence, support autonomy, and facilitate students' experience of relatedness with peers and the instructor may have been lost in the transition or may not work in the same manner as in a face-to-face setting. Previous research has found that students in online courses typically feel less supported than those in face-to-face settings (Kelly et al., 2007). Even though online learning could provide more flexibility and autonomy to students (Broadbent & Poon, 2015), it may be more difficult for students who lack the self-regulation skills necessary to manage their own learning (Bradley et al., 2017).

Instructor Competence and Commitment

Students' perceptions of their instructor's competence and commitment have been shown to impact educational outcomes. Undergraduate students' perceptions of lower pedagogical competence on the part of their instructor have been associated with students' increased acceptance of cheating (Murdock et al., 2007). Further, perceptions of instructor competence have predicted affective engagement (Kordrostami & Seitz, 2022) and academic achievement in college undergraduates taking online classes (Frisby et al., 2013). To our knowledge, no study has examined the relationship of instructor competence and commitment to students' basic psychological needs satisfaction and frustration. Because perceived instructor competence influences student outcomes in both in-person and online settings, we expect that it will relate positively to students' needs satisfaction and negatively to the frustration of their basic psychological needs.

Online Supportive Course Design

Student satisfaction and motivation have been shown to be moderated by their perceptions of teacher academic support (Naseer & Rafique, 2021), and elements of course design have been positive predictors of students course satisfaction in an ERL context (Patwardhan et al., 2020). Also, course design can contribute to the academic support students receive (Clinkenbeard, 2022). Reeve and Cheon (2021) demonstrated that elements of course design can provide students with autonomy supportive classroom structures. Thus, we expect student perceptions of an online supportive course design will positively predict satisfaction of students' basic psychological needs and negatively predict needs frustration, and that higher student ratings of online supportive course design will be associated with easier transitions to ERL.

Online Readiness

Students' perceptions of their readiness for online learning have been shown to affect student satisfaction with courses in higher education (Kumar, 2021). Further, the online readiness subscales of "self-directed learning" and "learner control" (Huang et al., 2010) are related to student success in virtual learning environments (Kirmizi, 2015). Student perceptions of instructors meeting their basic psychological needs have also been shown to improve achievement in courses (Kusurkar et al., 2013), and their satisfaction with academic major (Schenkenfelder et al., 2020). To the best of our knowledge, to date, no one has studied the relationship between online readiness and students' satisfaction or frustration of their basic psychological needs. Therefore, we expect that students with greater online readiness will also have an easier transition to ERL and will perceive higher needs satisfaction and lower needs frustration from their instructors.

Student Perceptions of Instruction During ERL

Empirical research into student perceptions of ERL has only recently begun to emerge in the literature. The results thus far suggest that students missed the classroom community, motivation, and focus that came from in-person learning (Iluzada & Talbert, 2022). However, O'Connor and Lee (2023) found that students who were given small group work during ERL— meant to address these precise concerns—did not always use these structures to their full potential. Instead, many students witnessed or participated in social loafing, that is, allowing others to contribute to group tasks and keeping cameras off to make non-engagement easier. Of even more concern is Stewart et al.'s (2022) finding that students perceived limited improvements in remote learning environments, classroom structure, processes, and student support from spring 2020 to fall 2020.

With the COVID-19 pandemic and ERL, students' perceptions of instructors' competence and commitment may have been shaken in an already fragile environment. Examining what contributes to the satisfaction and frustration of students' psychological needs in this transitional environment may be particularly informative to better understanding the role of the student-teacher relationship and instructional support in online as well as in face-to-face learning.

Research Questions

1. Are there differences in students' needs satisfaction and needs frustration between courses perceived as difficult transitions to online learning as compared to those courses perceived as easy transitions?
2. Do perceptions of the online instructional context predict students' need satisfaction and need frustration? Are these relationships moderated by students' online learning skills?
3. How do students describe the learning experiences in best verus worst case transitions? What instructional strategies are referenced by students in their discussion of the transition?

METHODS

Procedures

All students enrolled in sections of an introductory communication course at a large public university completed a pre-course online survey during the first two weeks of the semester, where demographic data was collected. Halfway through the semester, the COVID crisis reached the United States; the remainder of the semester was taught exclusively online. A post-course online survey was developed after the online transition and administered during the final two weeks of the semester. All students enrolled in the targeted courses completed the post-course survey.

Participants

Participants were undergraduate students (N = 935; 45.1% female) at a large mid-Atlantic university with an average age of 19.75 (SD = 3.25). The majority of students were freshman (56.8%), followed by sophomores (25.9%), juniors (10.3%), and seniors (6.7%). Students were asked to report their race/ethnicity and could indicate more than one response. The sample was 42.6% White, 32.3% Asian, 15.3% Black, 13.4% Hispanic, 6% Middle Eastern or North African, and 1.1% Pacific Islander. Additionally, 61.2% indicated English was their first language and 34.7% were first generation college students.

Measures

Responses to Likert-type item surveys as well as open-ended items were collected. At the end of the semester, students were asked to identify the course that had "the easiest or most successful online transition" and the course that had the "hardest or more difficult online transition," and then to respond to a series of Likert items on a scale for 1 = Strongly Disagree to 5 = Strongly Agree for each of the two courses.

Psychological Needs Satisfaction and Frustration

The Basic Psychological Needs Scale (BPNS; Chen et al., 2015), adapted for online learning, was used to assess the SDT components of competence, relatedness, and autonomy with valances for satisfaction and frustration. Latent variable models indicated strong convergent validity with loadings ranging from .35 to .93 in the easiest transition courses and from .44 to .94 in the most difficult transitions. Discriminant validity was indicated with correlations from .32 to .66 in both models. Reliability indicated by omega in the latent models ranged from .88 to .91.

Perceived Teacher Competence

Perceived teacher competence was assessed using a nine-item scale (Murdock et al., 2001). Sample items include, "The instructor's presentation of the material is well organized," and, "My instructor is well prepared for class." Reliability for the easiest transition courses was $\alpha = .92$ and in the hardest course transition $\alpha = .94$.

Online Supportive Course Design

Fifteen items were originally created to identify structural elements that students perceived as being supportive of learning during the transition to emergency remote teaching. Items were based on previous research about online learning and researcher teaching experience in online and face to face contexts. Sample items included, "I was given clear instructions for what I needed to do," and, "My instructor was available to me if I had questions." Factor analyses for both the easiest and most difficult transition were completed using principal axis factoring with promax rotation. In both samples, 7 items were retained loading on one factor with a reliability of .74 in the easiest transition courses and .85 in the most difficult transition. Correlation with teacher competence and commitment was moderate in the easiest transition ($r = .60$) and strong ($r = .80$) in the difficult transition, suggesting separate constructs in best case scenarios and overlap with teacher characteristics in contexts that are more difficult to navigate as a learner.

Online Readiness

Self-directed learning and online learner control scales from the Online Readiness Scale (Huang et al., 2010) were used to assess students' preparedness for online learning. Sample items include, "I feel confident in using online tools (email, discussion) to effectively communicate with others," and "I can direct my own learning progress." There were eleven items total with good reliability ($\alpha = .82$).

Qualitative Data Collection

Students responded to three open-ended items asking them to describe their experience during remote learning and to focus on helpful and not helpful instructor behaviors. The questions were as follows:

1. Tell us about your experience transitioning from on-campus classes to online classes partway through the semester. What was your experience like in all of your classes?
2. What challenges or obstacles made it hard to complete your coursework? (e.g., personal circumstances, internet reliability, access to materials, health issues, other constraints)
3. What did some faculty members do that was especially helpful or not helpful?

RESULTS

Descriptive Statistics

Students reported on basic psychological needs satisfaction and frustration for the course, which was labeled as most difficult transition and also for the course that was the easiest transition (Table 5.1). Students reported a moderate amount of online skills overall (Table 5.2). Perceptions of teacher competency and online course design were higher in the easiest transition course than the most difficult transition course (Table 5.2). Correlations (Table 5.3) between dimensions of self-determination satisfaction and frustration were low to moderate, with slightly strong correlations among dimensions in the hardest transition courses. The strongest correlation was between perceived teacher competency and online course support, indicating that students' perceptions of teacher competency were related to an instructor's ability to transition their course online in an organized and well-structured format.

Differences Between Easiest and Most Difficult Transitions (RQ1)

Dependent *t*-tests were used to examine differences in each of the three subscales (autonomy support, relatedness, and competence). All mean differences were statistically significant (Table 5.1). As anticipated, frustration was highest in the most difficult transition courses and satisfaction was significantly higher in the easiest transition courses. Overall, relatedness was

Table 5.1

Mean and Standard Deviations of BPN for Hardest and Easiest Transition

	Easiest Transition	Hardest Transition	Effect Size
Item	*M (SD)*	*M (SD)*	*d*
Frustration			
Autonomy	2.75 (.85)	3.45 (.90)	.66
Relatedness	2.26 (.78)	2.51 (.87)	.33
Competence	2.24 (.91)	3.14 (1.06)	.82
Satisfaction			
Autonomy	3.72 (.79)	2.74 (.85)	.92
Relatedness	3.23 (.94)	2.74 (.95)	.44
Competence	4.17 (.69)	3.12 (1.00)	.97

Table 5.2

Descriptive Statistics

	Easiest Transition		Hardest Transition	
Variables	α	*M (SD)*	α	*M (SD)*
Online Skills	.84		3.56 (.71)	
Teacher Competency	.92	4.37 (0.60)	.94	3.55 (0.98)
Online Course Design	.74	4.36 (0.54)	.85	3.42 (0.94)

Table 5.3

Correlations

Variables	1	2	3	4	5	6	7	8	9
Online Skills	—	.21*	.27*	–.28*	–.25*	-.37*	.32*	.26*	.41*
2. Teacher Competency	.21*	—	.77*	–.38*	–.32*	-.31*	.52*	.33*	.56*
3. Online Course Support	.24*	.60*	—	–.34*	–.30*	-.35*	.50*	.37*	.58*
Frustration									
4. Autonomy	–.15*	–.36*	–.26*	—	.34*	.48*	–.52*	-.21*	–.48*
5. Relatedness	–.15*	–.31*	–.28*	.39*	—	.34*	–.25*	-.43*	–.34*
6. Competence	–.20*	–.29*	–.27*	.58*	39*	—	–.37*	-.28*	–.66*

(Table continued on next page)

Table 5.3 (Continued)

Correlations

Variables	1	2	3	4	5	6	7	8	9
Satisfaction									
7. Autonomy	.24*	.45*	.43*	–.47*	–.24*	-.35*	—	.50*	.66*
8. Relatedness	.16*	.26*	.27*	–.19*	–.34*	-.11*	.45*	—	.46*
9. Competence	.31*	.49*	.45*	–.46*	–.31*	-.59*	.63*	.32*	—

*$p < .001$. Correlations in the lower diagonal are the easiest transition and in the upper diagonal are the hardest transition.

lower than feelings of competence in both the easy and difficult transitions, lower than autonomy in the easiest transition and equivalent to autonomy in the hardest transition courses.

Perceptions of Instructional Context Predict Basic Psychological Needs (RQ2)

Confirmatory factor analysis verified the latent factors of Basic Psychological Needs Satisfaction and Basic Psychological Needs Frustration. The relationship between perceived classroom variables (e.g., teacher competence and commitment and online supportive course design) and the basic psychological needs constructs of satisfaction and frustration was examined using structural models with latent dependent variables and observed predictor variables. Student self-report online learning skills was also included. Hypothesized relationships were examined for both the easiest and hardest transition courses. Following Kline (2016), we used multiple fit indices to establish model fit. Criteria for excellent fit include RMSEA < .08 with a 90% confidence interval below .10 and CFI > .95.

Easiest Transition. For courses reported as the easiest transition course, the data fit the hypothesized model well, X^2 (19), = 99.16, $p < .05$, RMSEA = .07 [.05, .08], CFI =.99. Perceived teacher competence and commitment was a significant predictor of basic psychological needs, it was positively related to satisfaction (β = .39, $p < .05$) and negatively related (β = –.35, $p < .05$) to frustration. Online supportive course design was also related positively (β = .27, $p < .05$) to satisfaction and negatively (β = -13, $p < .05$) to frustration. Student self-reported online learning skills also followed this pattern (Figure 5.1).

Figure 5.1

Easiest Transition

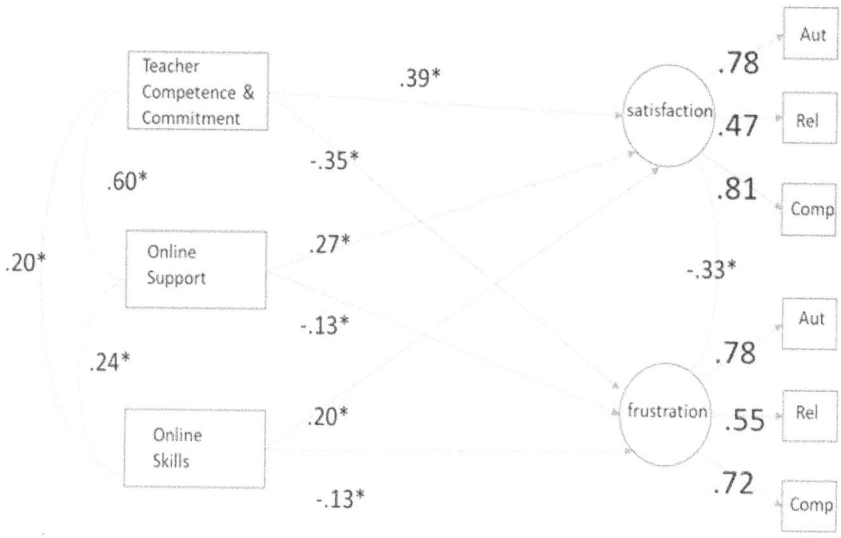

Note. *$p < .05$.

Hardest Transition. For courses reported as the hardest transition course, the data also fit the hypothesized model well, X^2 (19), = 97.19, $p < .05$, RMSEA = .07 [.06, .08], CFI =.98. Perceived teacher competence and commitment was also a significant predictor of basic psychological needs. It was again positively related to satisfaction (β = .38, $p < .05$) and negatively related (β = -.31, $p < .05$) to frustration. Additionally, online supportive course design and student online learning skills also significantly related to needs satisfaction or frustration (Figure 5.2). There was also a significant interaction effect between online supportive course design and the students' online learning skills for both satisfaction (β = .07, $p < .05$) and frustration (β = –.11, $p < .05$). Exploration of these significant interaction effects indicated that when students reported high levels of online learning skills, the relationship between online supportive course design and needs satisfaction and frustration was stronger. Directionally, the relationship with satisfaction was positive and with frustration was negative, similar to the easiest transition model. In other words, students' perceptions of the level of supportive class design was a better predictor of both needs satisfaction and needs frustration when the students' own level of online skills was higher; thus students with weaker online skills may have considered their own difficulties with functioning online as reasoning for needs frustration or satisfaction rather than or in conjunction with the instructor's course support. Indeed, the path coefficient from student's online skills to needs frustration is stronger (β = –.35) in the hardest transition as compared to the easiest transition course (β = –.13).

Figure 5.2

Hardest Transition

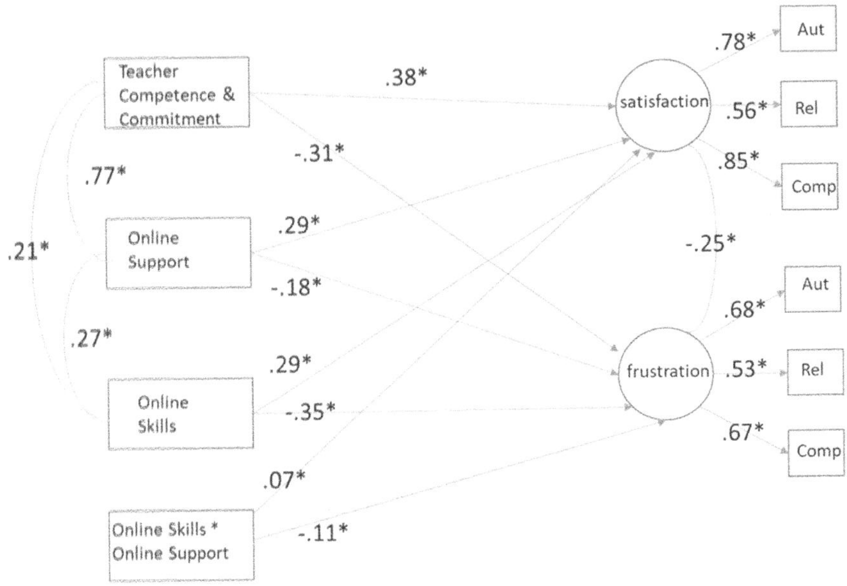

Note. *$p < .05$.

Students Perceptions of Best and Worst Transitions (RQ3)

Qualitative data adds further explanation for these relationships seen in the quantitative models. Students were asked three open-ended questions at the end of the quantitative survey given at the end of the 2020 Spring Semester during which the entire university shifted to ERL due to the COVID-19 pandemic. In total, 879 students responded to these questions. Responses to each question ranged from a single word to multiple paragraphs, with students typically responding with a sentence or two to each question.

Following Merriam and Tisdell (2016), coding occurred in three stages (i.e., open coding, axial coding, and categorization) using Dedoose 9.0.86. The second author was primarily responsible for qualitative coding, and they consulted with the first author on questions of interpretation and accuracy. To support the trustworthiness of interpretation, all authors were given access to qualitative data and invited to comment upon and ask questions regarding the coding process.

Using open coding, student perceptions were identified which noted a connection between a given instructional strategy and the ease or difficulty of the transition to ERL; however, it quickly became clear that a variety of personal circumstances also affected student perceptions of this transition. Initial codes for instructional strategies included "use of videos," "use of discussion boards," "flexibility for due dates," "regular emails," "timely feedback," "scaffolding assignments," "interactive class sessions," and "emotionally supportive." Codes for personal circumstances that students identified as impactful in their transition to ERL included "trouble with technology," "maintaining a work/life balance," "too much time at home," "difficulties with family members," and "a lack of self-regulation." Codes had analogues for both easy and difficult transitions. For instance, easier transitions were characterized by student comments which referenced regular emails, flexible due dates, and interactive virtual classrooms, whereas difficult transitions were characterized by comments referencing a lack of communication from instructors, rigid approaches to the syllabus, and only lecturing to students while online. Similarly, students' personal circumstances had positive and negative transition analogues. Positive transitions to ERL included a home with a quiet place to work, reliable technology, and an ability to manage wide swaths of unstructured time, while negative transitions referenced attempting to study in chaotic atmospheres, struggles with technology, and a lack of capacity to productively manage a sudden lack of external structure.

During axial coding, analogous codes were joined into themes. For instance, open codes such as "posted videos" and "refused to alter assignments" were both placed under the theme of "scaffolding assignments." The following themes emerged regarding instructional strategies: scaffolding assignments, multiple teaching modalities, consistent communication, timely feedback, willingness to work with individual students, proactive communication, and being flexible with due dates. Themes that arose from students' personal circumstances included: technology, work/life balance, ability to manage time effectively, family circumstances, and mental health challenges.

During the categorization phase of analysis, four overall groupings of student perceptions—two that involved teachers' instructional strategies and two that referenced students' personal circumstances—emerged as central to the ease or difficulty with which students transitioned to ERL. The instructional strategy most frequently noted as impacting students' transition was instructor flexibility: over 45% of students made some reference to the flexibility of their instructor as impacting their transition. This included flexibility in using multiple learning modalities, a willingness to adjust class timelines and procedures based on individual student needs, and an openness to different ways students could demonstrate competency in their classroom. One student comment from the flexibility category stated, *"The biggest thing that helped me was (the instructor) allowing for a flexible schedule (not requiring online meetings), by allowing us some freedom to learn the material when it was beneficial to us alleviated some stress."* However, this desire for flexibility was also thwarted at times. One student complained, *"There are also some professors who, while they say they 'understand our situation,' don't do anything to accommodate our circumstances.... [S]ome professors have refused to be flexible."*

A second pivotal instructional strategy vis-à-vis the success of students' transition to ERL involved how instructors chose to communicate with their students: 42% of all respondents noted the importance of an instructor's communication patterns as influential in the success or failure of their move to ERL. Successful transitions employed strategies such as regular emails with updates for course requirements, timely and actionable feedback on assignments that allowed for students to improve them and resubmit, and a commitment to responding to student emails. These strategies garnered such comments as, *"The quick response time on email was very helpful. Fast communication seems like the most important aspect of online classes."* We also included students' experience of interactivity under this umbrella, as students indicated that communication structures that supported meaningful dialogue with and learning from peers also improved their experience of online learning. One student wrote of the transition, *"My class experiences were actually pretty good, maybe it was because it was online, but the classes online were more interactive and my classmates and I tended to ask more questions."* When students did not feel the communication of the instructor was appropriate or timely, it tended to generate significant frustration. One student wrote, *"The biggest difficulty when completing online learning was communication with professors.... I had professors putting up assignments and then giving no further explanation on what they expect or how to complete them."* Students seemed to feel that in-person instruction lends itself to more impromptu questions of instructors and more convenient interaction with peers. Without this affordance, some online learners struggled to keep up with the course requirements.

Two categories of personal factors also greatly impacted students' experience of the transition to ERL: self-regulation and technological affordances. Just over 33% of students commented directly on their lack of self-regulation or on how much more difficult it was to get their work done without the built-in structures provided by going to an on-campus learning environment. Many comments followed along these lines: *"It was a very tough transition. I was unable to keep myself organized the way I would when I was back on campus."* Students missed the spaces and times set aside for study and struggled to put the necessary boundaries on their lives when they were always in the same physical space (i.e., their home). This daily struggle could become demotivating, resulting in even less ability to self-regulate: *"Being at home isn't the best learning environment for me as it's hard to focus and stay motivated. At home all my brain wants to do is be in break mode and schoolwork seems less crucial. While I'm trying to pay attention in class, there are a lot more distractions going on such as people walking around, knocking on my door, and so forth."*

Many students struggled with the executive functioning demands of fully online learning (Harel-Gadassi, 2022). The lack of gathering in the same physical space strained not only young adults' self-regulation but also their technology—both their capacity to operate their technology correctly and the limits of the technology itself. Fully 30% of students noted that trouble with technology had a negative impact on their experience of ERL. Some students referenced their inability to use the technology effectively, such as these comments about the biggest challenge in the transition to ERL: *"Just being able to figure out different types of technology"*; and, *"I was a bit confused to do all work with technology and sometimes the technology was not working well."* However, many students also struggled with the technology itself noting that *"spotty internet"* or *"unreliable connectivity"* made just accessing online videos a struggle.

These two struggles—lack of self-regulation and issues with technology—often conspired together to make ERL that much more difficult. One student stated, *"I felt so unmotivated. My mom and dog are very distracting and at home I have no proper area to do my work. I also get very distracted by my family and just technology. Also, internet access too, I don't have the best Wi-Fi in my house."* For some students, the physical campus provides not only necessary environmental affordances to support their work, it also provides the technological affordances—the up-to-date, physical hardware—to make regular access to online resources possible.

DISCUSSION

Students' perceptions of the learning environment including their perceptions of the instructors' competence and commitment as well as their perceptions of the teacher's behaviors used in the online support course design are indicative of the students' basic psychological needs satisfaction and frustration during the height of the COVID pandemic. However, much of what was learned in this hectic semester regarding student-teacher relationships and instructional support can be carried forward in the post COVID era. A survey of 1,413 U.S. higher education students found 73% "somewhat" or "strongly" (46%) agreed that they would take fully online courses in the future (MacKenzie, 2021). Previous research on student perceptions of instruction references many of the things noted by students in both qualitative and quantitative analyses including scaffolding of assignments for student success, supportive classroom environments that allow students to have sufficient control of their learning, and providing feedback (e.g., Girard & Lemoyne, 2018; Pekrun, 2016; Schenke at al., 2015). In courses where the students viewed the transition as easiest, positive perceptions associated positively with satisfaction and negatively with frustration. But, in courses where the transition to online was more difficult, the students' own online skills moderated the relationship between the online course design and the students' satisfaction or frustration. When the students' own online learning skills were lower, there was a weaker connection between the perceived supportive efforts of the teacher and satisfaction or frustration; however, when the students' own online skills were stronger, so was the relationship between the perceived instructor supports and satisfaction and frustration. In other words, the students' own lack of online skills exacerbated any problems the instructor may have had in making the transition to online emergency teaching.

The personal circumstances that students discussed as impacting their transition to ERL may also be relevant to a broader educational context. When the pandemic hit and in-person learning simply ended, many students and universities found themselves with technology (old computers) and technological knowledge (How to use Zoom?) desperately in need of an upgrade. Although online students are less likely to be caught off guard in the current milieu, it is worth noting that students enrolled in fully online degree programs trend slightly lower income, older, more likely to have a family, and more likely to be students of color than traditional, in-person learners (Venable, 2022); thus, they may have less access to the most current technology than traditional, in-person learners. It is one thing to alert would-be students of the technological requirements of an online class, but it is another if students are penalized because their technology may not be adequate to the demands of remote learning. Moreover, as online learners are more likely to have families and jobs than their in-person counterparts, self-regulation—already identified as an issue in the transition to online learning—may become even more critical. Instructors who are attuned to helping their students succeed may reflect on the self-regulatory supports they can embed into their assignments, which may serve as proactive supports to student success (Dabbagh & Kitsantas, 2012; Song & Kim, 2021).

Surprisingly, in this emergency transition, students did report fairly high levels of perceived teaching competence even in the most difficult transition course (M = 3.55); however, it is worth noting that the standard deviation in both of the perceived teaching variables, competency and online supports, were almost double the amount of variability found in the easiest transitions. This suggests that although, on average, instructors were perceived as doing a reasonable job, there was a lot of variability in students' perceptions. It is highly likely that many students were empathetic to the difficult situation of the COVID crisis and were less critical than in a typical online setting.

Implications for the Future

The COVID-19 pandemic accelerated the already growing phenomenon of online learning in higher education (Bamforth, 2021). As a result, students have increasing options to take courses in online or hybrid contexts. Thus, although the move to ERL forced many students who would not have chosen online learning to become virtual learners, increasing numbers of students in higher education are choosing to learn in an online context. Similarly, ERL forced many instructors to adapt to an online context, and now more instructors have the option (and the responsibility) to adapt their teaching to the virtual environment. For these reasons, the perspective of students from ERL may offer important insights to instructors in an increasingly online milieu. Online materials need to allow for collaboration, communication, interaction, and feedback.

In no uncertain terms, our students told us that they value—and expect—instructor flexibility in an online environment. Research suggests that flexibility is one of the important reasons students choose online learning (Venable, 2022). Often, this flexibility is interpreted as the flexibility to "attend" lectures when they are available, for instance, after work or when their children are asleep. However, the comments from our students suggest that the expectation of flexibility goes beyond class attendance. Instead, student perceptions of instructor flexibility that positively impacted their learning experience included flexibility regarding due dates, teaching modalities, and even how students demonstrated knowledge of class content. Previous literature suggests that this pedagogical flexibility satisfies students' needs for autonomy supportive environments which provide necessary structure but also significant relevant choice so that students can co-create their learning experience to make it more meaningful (Cheon et al., 2020). Thus, flexibility is not only about making learning more convenient, or possible, for students whose lives have many other demands, but also about helping students build more meaning into their educational experience.

Added structure and increased communication and feedback were also frequently noted in the qualitative data. Students discuss their perceptions of caring and commitment in greater detail, indicating that they felt a stronger sense of belonging and support from those instructors. Many students also discussed helpful strategies used by instructors, including videos that helped them scaffold their learning and multiple options for student interaction through chat apps, online discussions, and group assignments.

The demand for increased pedagogical flexibility also suggests why students so often commented upon the value of instructors' proactive communication as improving their experience of learning. If students value flexibility as circumstances change, this implies that the syllabus distributed at the semester's beginning has become a less reified and more developing document. Flexibility requires more frequent communication, and our students perceived that as primarily the purview of the instructor. Although instructors may object to the demands of more emails and reminders for students when due dates are already listed in the syllabus, our student responses suggest they feel more competent and connected when instructors are frequent and proactive communicators. Again, the literature affirms this insight: when students feel uninformed their competence and relatedness needs are likely to be frustrated (Hartnett, 2015). This suggests that frequent and proactive communication with students is a critical task for instructors who want to support students' motivation and effort.

Limitations of the current study include measures that were adapted to meet the needs of this transition study. Attempting to measure student perceptions during the transition semester did not allow time for rigorous item development and validation procedures. Furthermore, some student perceptions captured here in both quantitative and qualitative data may not be equivalent to student perceptions in the post pandemic era. Undoubtably, how students experienced the transition to online learning does likely influence their likelihood to enroll in future online coursework as well as impact their expectations of online instruction and learning.

Conclusion: Challenges and Opportunities

As we move beyond the pandemic, the results from this study highlight some specific challenges and opportunities with respect to student-teacher relationships and the way that instructor intentions and expectations are communicated to support better student outcomes in online courses. Given that student perceptions provide the necessary lens to be able to influence student achievement and well-being in online learning, careful and meaningful consideration of student perceptions is key to any intervention, instructional factor, or emotional aspect of the classroom.

Student expectations overall are one area of challenge for continued online learning opportunities. Specifically, as we move beyond the pandemic and ERL, students may have greater expectations for quality online instruction (i.e., they may have been more forgiving of online instruction in an ERL context). COVID-19 and ERL provided an opportunity for instructors to experience online instruction. Moving forward, instructors will need to continue to develop and hone their skills for online instruction.

Providing students the desired flexibility while being fair to all, maintaining structure, and supporting students' overall learning and experience also represents another challenge to navigate. For instance, extending deadlines automatically may not be wise if assignments build on each other or if core skills are needed to be successful on assignments due later in the semester. There is still a need for students to develop self-regulatory skills for future success outside of the classroom. Students taking an agentic approach and advocating for the flexibility they need offers an opportunity for instructors to discuss their expectations with students and to provide rationales for when flexibility is or is not provided. Moreover, it may be easier for instructors to be flexible and communicative in a non-emergency state. Instructors themselves were managing a big shift with the pandemic and ERL, including personal health, family, and work issues, many instructors teaching online for the first time and not by choice. In a non-emergency state, instructors can be prepared to be flexible in intentional and planned ways, perhaps taking better advantage of various tools that can aid with communication (e.g., use of announcement, videos, and other interactive tools in LMS systems). The results of this investigation highlight the importance of making changes with an eye to how such changes might relate to students' needs for competence, autonomy, and relatedness.

Student access to technology and or reliable internet is also a continued challenge as is the development of online learning skills. These challenges present opportunity for explicit discussion around the skills needed to be successful in online courses. Additional consideration can also be given to the supports that institutions of higher education can provide (e.g., quiet place to take online classes with reliable internet) and what skills should be explicitly taught as part of the curriculum (e.g., self-regulation skills; skills for online learning).

As we move beyond the pandemic, attention to student teacher relationship and the way that instructor intentions and expectations are communicated online are key to better student outcomes. Student perceptions provide the necessary lens to be able to influence student achievement and well-being in online learning settings. Careful and meaningful consideration of student perceptions is key to many instructional as well as emotional aspects of the learning environment. This examination of students' perceptions of learning from this emergency remote learning period provide critical information as higher education faces increased demand and enrollment in online courses in the post pandemic world.

REFERENCES

Bamforth, E. (2021, April 29). *Online college enrollment growth outpaces real-world institutions*. EdScoop. https://edscoop.com/online-institutions-enrollment-outpaces-real-world-college-thanks-part-time-students/

Bandura, A. (1986). *Social foundations of thought and action: A social cognitive theory*. Prentice-Hall.

Bowers, J., & Kumar, P. (2015). Students' perceptions of teaching and social presence: A comparative analysis of face-to-face and online learning environments. *International Journal of Web-Based Learning and Teaching Technologies, 10*(1), 27–44. https://doi.org/10.4018/ijwltt.2015010103

Bradley, R. L., Browne, B. L., & Kelley, H. M. (2017). Examining the influence of self-efficacy and self-regulation in online learning. *College Student Journal, 51*, 518–530.

Broadbent, J., & Poon, W. L. (2015). Self-regulated learning strategies and academic achievement in online higher education learning environments: A systematic review. *The Internet and Higher Education, 27*, 1–13. http://dx.doi.org/10.1016/j.iheduc.2015.04.007

Chen, B., Vansteenkiste, M., Beyers, W., Boone, L., Deci, E. L., Van der Kaap-Deeder, J., Duriez, B. Lens, W., Matos, L., Mouratidis, A., Ryan, R. M., Sheldon, K. M., Soenens, B., Van Petegem, S., & Verstuyf, J. (2015). Basic psychological need satisfaction, need frustration, and need strength across four cultures. *Motivation and Emotion, 39*, 216–236. https://doi.org/10.1007/s11031-014-9450-1

Cheon, S. H., Reeve, J., & Vansteenkiste, M. (2020). When teachers learn how to provide classroom structure in an autonomy-supportive way: Benefits to teachers and their students. *Teaching and Teacher Education, 90*, 103004. https://doi.org/10.1016/j.tate.2019.103004

Clinkenbeard, J. E., & Bonsangue, M. V. (2022). Academic outcomes and experiences of freshman students in mathematics courses during the COVID-19 pandemic. *The Learning Assistance Review, 27*(1). 15–54.

Dabbagh, N., & Kitsantas, A. (2012). Personal learning environments, social media, and self-regulated learning: A natural formula for connecting formal and informal learning. *The Internet and Higher Education, 15*(1), 3–8.

Deci, E. L., & Ryan, R. M. (1991). A motivational approach to self: Integration in personality. In R. A. Dienstbier (Ed.), *Current theory and research in motivation, Vol. 38. Nebraska Symposium on Motivation, 1990: Perspectives on motivation* (pp. 237–288). University of Nebraska Press.

Demir, M., Burton, S., & Dunbar, N. (2019) Professor-student rapport and perceived autonomy support as predictors of course and student outcomes. *Teaching of Psychology, 46*(1), 22–23. https://doi.org/10.1177/0098628318816132

Filak, V. F., & Nicolini, K. M. (2018). Differentiations in motivation and need satisfaction based on course modality: A self-determination theory perspective. *Educational Psychology, 38*(6), 772–784.

Frisby, B. N., Limperos, A. M., Record, R. A., Downs, E., & Kercsmar, S. E. (2013). Students' perceptions of social presence: Rhetorical and relational goals across three mediated instructional designs. *Journal of Online Learning and Teaching, 9*(4), 468–480.

Girard, S., & Lemoyne, J. (2018). Analyzing the contribution of student-perceived motivational climate to predict student goal adoption in physical education: Testing invariance relative to teacher-induced climate. *Physical Educator, 75*(4), 701–724. https://doi.org/10.18666/tpe-2018-v75-i4-8197

Grolnick, W. S., & Ryan, R. M. (1989). Parent styles associated with childrens' self-regulation and competence in school. *Journal of Educational Psychology, 81*(2), 143–154. https://doi.org/10.1037/0022-0663.81.2.143

Harel-Gadassi, A. (2022). For whom is distance learning suitable? The relationship between distance learning, executive functions, and academic achievements. *Universal Journal of Educational Research, 10*(2), 129–136. https://doi.org/10.13189/ujer.2022.100202

Hartnett, M. (2015). Influences that undermine learners' perceptions of autonomy, competence and relatedness in an online context. *Australian Journal of Educational Technology, 31*(1), 86–99. https://doi.org/10.14742/ajet.1526

Huang M. L., Chou C., Chen, C. H., & Own, Z. Y. (2010) Learner readiness for online learning: scale development and student perceptions. *Computers & Education* 55, 1080–1090. https://doi.org/10.1016/j.compedu.2010.05.004

Iluzada, C., & Talbert, T. L. (2022). Learning, course satisfaction, and community in the time of COVID-19: Student perceptions of the switch to emergency remote teaching. *InSight: A Journal of Scholarly Teaching, 17*, 65–82. https://eric.ed.gov/?id=EJ1353684

Kelly, H. F., Ponton, M. K., & Rovai, A. P. (2007). A comparison of student evaluations of teaching between online and face-to-face courses. *The Internet and Higher Education, 10*(2), 89–101. https://doi.org/10.1016/j.iheduc.2007.02.001

Kirmizi, O. (2015). The influence of learner readiness on student satisfaction and academic achievement in an online program at higher education. *The Turkish Online Journal of Educational Technology, 14*(1), 133–142.

Kline, R. B. (2016). *Principles and practice of structural equation modeling* (4th ed.). Guilford.

Kusurkar, R. A., Cate, T. J. T., Vos, C. M. P., Westers, P., & Croiset, G. (2013). How motivation affects academic performance: A structural equation modelling analysis. *Advances in Health Sciences Education, 18*(1), 57–69. https://doi.org/10.1007/s10459-012-9354-3

Kordrostami, M., & Seitz, V. (2022). Faculty online competence and student affective engagement in online learning. *Marketing Education Review, 32*(3), 240–254. https://doi.org/10.1080/105280008.2021.1965891

Kumar, S. P. (2021). Impact of online learning readiness on students' satisfaction in higher educational institutions. *Journal of Engineering Education Transformations, 34*(0), 64–70. https://doi.org/10.16920/jeet/2021/v34i0/157107

MacKenzie, L. (2021, April 26). *Students want online learning options post-pandemic*. Inside Higher Ed. https://www.insidehighered.com/news/2021/04/27/survey-reveals-positive-outlook-online-instruction-post-pandemic

Merriam, S. B., & Tisdell, E. J. (2016). *Qualitative research: A guide to design and implementation* (6th ed.). John Wiley & Sons.

Murdock, T. B., Hale, N. M., & Weber, M. J. (2001). Predictors of cheating among early adolescents: Academic and social motivations. *Contemporary Educational Psychology, 26*(10), 96–115. https://doi.org/10.1006/ceps.2000.1046

Murdock, T. B., Miller, A. D., & Goetzinger, A. (2007). Effects of classroom context on university students' judgments about cheating: Mediating and moderating processes. *Social Psychology of Education: An International Journal, 10*(2), 141–169. https://doi.org/10.1007/s11218-007-9015-1

Naseer, S., & Rafique, S. (2021). Moderating role of teachers' academic support between students' satisfaction with online learning and academic motivation in undergraduate students during COVID-19. *Education Research International*, Article 7345579. https://doi.org/10.1155/2021/7345579.

National Center for Education Statistics, (n.d.). *Fast facts: Distance learning*. https://nces.ed.gov/fastfacts/display.asp?id=80

O'Connor, P. A., & Lee, R. (2023). 'We can't see your slides!' Undergraduate psychology students' perceptions of emergency remote teaching. *Psychology Teaching Review, 29*(1), 25–36. https://doi.org/10.53841/bpsptr.2023.29.1.25

Patwardhan, V., Rao, S., Thirugnanasambantham, C., & Prabhu, N. (2020). Community of Inquiry (CoI) framework and course design as predictors of satisfaction in emergency remote teaching: Perspectives of hospitality management students. *Journal of E-Learning & Knowledge Society, 16(4)*, 94–103. https://doi.org/10.20368/1971-8829/1135315

Pekrun, R. (2016). Academic emotions. In Kathryn R. Wentzel & David B. Miele (Eds.), *Handbook of motivation at school* (2nd ed., pp. 120–144). Routledge. https://doi.org/10.4324/9781315773384-8

Reeve, J., & Cheon, S. H. (2021). Autonomy-supportive teaching: Its malleability, benefits, and potential to improve educational practice. *Educational Psychologist, 56*(1), 54–77. https://doi.org/10.1080/00461520.2020.1862657

Ryan, R. M., & Deci, E. L. (2017). *Self-determination theory: Basic psychological needs in motivation, development and wellness*. Guildford.

Ryan, R. M., & Deci, E. L. (2020). Intrinsic and extrinsic motivation from a self-determination theory perspective: Definitions, theory, practices and future directions. *Contemporary Educational Psychology, 61*, Article 10860. https://doi.org/10.1016/j.cedpsych.2020.101860

Schenke, K., Lam, A. C., Conley, A. M., & Karabenick, S. A. (2015). Adolescents' help seeking in mathematics classrooms: Relations between achievement and perceived classroom environmental influences over one school year. *Contemporary Educational Psychology, 41*, 133–146. https://doi.org/10.1016/j.cedpsych.2015.01.003

Schenkenfelder, M., Frickey, E. A., & Larson, L. M. (2020). College environment and basic psychological needs: Predicting academic major satisfaction. *Journal of Counseling Psychology, 67*(2), 265–273. https://doi.org/10.1037/cou0000380

Song, D., & Kim, D. (2021). Effects of self-regulation scaffolding on online participation and learning outcomes. *Journal of Research on Technology in Education, 53*(3), 249–263. https://doi.org/10.1080/15391523.2020.1767525

Stewart, W. H., Baek, Y., & Lowenthal, P. R. (2022). From emergency remote teaching (ERT) to sustained remote teaching (SRT): A comparative semester analysis of exchange students' experiences and perceptions of learning online during COVID-19. *Online Learning, 26*(2), 170–197. https://doi.org/10.24059/olj.v26i2.2661

Tai, J. H. M., Bellingham, R., Lang, J., & Dawson, P. (2019). Student perspectives of engagement in learning in contemporary and digital contexts. *Higher Education Research & Development, 38*(5), 1075–1089. https://doi.org/10.1080/07294360.2019.1598338

Urdan, T. (2004). Predictors of academic self-handicapping and achievement: Examining achievement goals, classroom goal structures, and culture. *Journal of Educational Psychology, 96*(2), 251–264. https://doi.org/10.1037/0022-0663.96.2.251

Venable, M. A. (2022). *2022 Online education trends report.* Best Colleges. https://res.cloudinary.com/highereducation/images/v1647967676/BestColleges.com/2022_Online-Education_Trends-Report/2022_Online-Education_Trends-Report.pdf

Wang, C., Hsu, H. K., Bonem, E. M., Moss, J. D., Yu, S., Nelson, D. B., Levesque-Bristol, C. (2019). Need satisfaction and need dissatisfaction: A comparative study of online and face-to-face learning contexts. *Computers in Human Behavior*, 95, 114–125. https://doi.org/10.1016/j.chb.2019.01.034

CHAPTER 6

COLLEGE DURING COVID-19

A Mixed Methods Study Examining Undergraduate Students' Academic Experiences and Responses

Mary Elizabeth Sewell Bridges
East Carolina University

Melissa C. Duffy
University of South Carolina

ABSTRACT

COVID-19 ushered in a new set of challenges for many university students. First-generation students in particular already face barriers to academic success, and COVID-19 likely exacerbated these challenges. This mixed-methods study aimed to: (1) provide a better understanding of the impact of COVID-19 on undergraduate students' experiences overall; (2) examine impact over fall 2020 and spring 2021; and (3) explore potential differences between first-generation students and their continuing-generation peers. Participants completed an online survey (N = 345) and follow-up interview (n = 15). Quantitative analysis indicated a greater overall impact of COVID-19 in fall 2020 compared to spring 2021, and revealed the impact on students' experiences of stress, interactions with friends and family, and daily routines

Examining the Cognitive and Psychological Effects of the COVID-19 Global Pandemic on High School, College, and Graduate Learners, pp. 109–137

decreased from fall 2020 to spring 2021. Results also suggested first-generation students reported lower impact than their continuing generation peers regarding experiences of stress, interactions with friends and family, and daily routines. Qualitative data illustrated the impact on social, emotional, motivational, and academic facets of school and highlighted coping strategies used in response to challenges faced. Given these insights, institutions should examine ways to further support students in areas most impacted in order to promote academic success.

Keywords: COVID-19, college students, first-generation college students, coping

INTRODUCTION

The COVID-19 pandemic has had a profound impact on education delivery worldwide, including higher education. In March 2020, institutions were forced to abandon normal operations and to send millions of college students home, relying on online instruction (Aucejo et al., 2020; Brown, 2020). This sudden change impacted students in a variety of ways, including financial hardship, impairment of psychological well-being, and increased academic challenge (Bono et al., 2020; Clabaugh et al., 2021; Kecojevic et al., 2020; Lederer et al., 2020; Patterson et al., 2021; Son et al., 2020). Initial research also suggests first-generation (FG) college students may have been particularly impacted as the pandemic served to exacerbate existing inequalities. Compared to their continuing generation (CG) peers, FG students experienced greater financial hardships, increased living and technology expenses, more difficulty with online learning, heightened experience of mental health disorders, and additional concerns about their ability to continue enrollment in response to the pandemic (Barber et al., 2021; Davis et al., 2021; Soria et al., 2020). As COVID-19 variants (Delta, Omicron) extended the impact for college students and higher education institutions, students faced continued stressors including, prolonged remote instruction, social distancing, and loss of loved ones due to COVID-19 (Fruehwirth et al., 2021; Sirrine et al., 2021; Son et al., 2020).

While research continues to emerge on the impact of COVID-19, the majority of the early work focused on K–12 settings. Limited studies were conducted within higher education settings and those that did take place in higher education settings typically focused on psychological consequences, rather than students' academic experiences. Initial explorations of the academic impact revealed that worry about academics was one of the largest contributors to increased stress/anxiety and many students reported related difficulties with concentration, motivation, and online learning (Klein et al., 2021; Son et al., 2020; Unger & Meiran, 2020; Wang et al., 2020).

Given the enduring and evolving nature of the pandemic, it is important to fully understand the impact of COVID-19 on students' college experience, paying particular attention to populations that have historically faced barriers to academic success and persistence, specifically first-generation students. First-generation students typically demonstrate lower graduation and retention rates compared to their continuing-generation peers (National Center for Education Statistics [NCES], 2018). Additional insights can help to guide institutional program development and policy decisions in response to students' challenges and needs.

OBJECTIVES

Although initial research has provided some insights into the impact of COVID-19, there is a need to further examine college students' experiences during this unique event. As such, the purpose of this mixed methods study was to examine the impact of COVID-19 on college students' academic experiences during the first full academic year of the pandemic (fall 2020 to spring 2021). This represents a unique time frame in which it was clear that the pandemic was no longer temporary and at the same time presented a relatively new learning experience (primarily online) for most students. A second goal was to examine potential differences in the impact of COVID-19 among FG and CG students as emerging research indicated that this may be a particularly at-risk group. In the following sections, we describe existing research examining COVID-19's impact, experiences unique to first-generation students, and draw on theories of stress and coping, as well as self-determination to frame the current study, which aims to better understand college students' academic challenges experienced during the first full academic year of the pandemic.

REVIEW OF LITERATURE

COVID-19 Impact

Much of the preliminary research on COVID-19 in higher education has focused on the impact to students' mental health and well-being. Studies across U.S. institutions indicated that students experienced increased stress, depression, and anxiety (e.g., Browning et al., 2021; Halliburton et al., 2021; Lee et al., 2021; Reyes-Portillo et al., 2022; Son et al., 2020). Qualitative research also indicated that students were experiencing increased worry and anxiety, feelings of loneliness and isolation, and added academic, personal, and financial stress (Farris et al., 2021; Hoyt et al.,

202; Kaur et al., 2022). Prior to the pandemic, studies demonstrated high levels of stress can result in poor grades on exams, lower academic performance generally, diminished motivation, burnout, dropout, and decreased mental health (Frazier et al., 2018; Hubbard et al., 2018; Lee & Jang, 2015; Pascoe et al., 2019). Early research on the impact of COVID-19 suggests the pandemic may have exacerbated many of the traditional challenges college students face, highlighting the need for a greater understanding of the impact on students' experiences.

While online learning was pervasive, it appears to also be a contributor to students' negative academic experience and learning loss. During the mandatory lockdown, learning loss varied based on access to remote learning, the quality of online instruction, support at home, and level of engagement (Farris et al., 2021; Son et al., 2020). Many students reported that the added stress of online learning was linked to difficulty adjusting online, increased workload, limited interaction with or understanding from faculty, and lack of social connection with peers (Aguilera-Hermida, 2020; Barber et al., 2021; Clabaugh et al., 2021; Farris et al., 2021; Halliburton et al., 2021; Lemay et al., 2021). By fall 2020, approximately 31% of higher educational institutions in the U.S. were utilizing fully online or primarily online instruction, 22% employed a hybrid model, and 31% were operating fully or primarily in-person. By spring 2021, 41% had moved to primarily or fully online, 20% were utilizing a hybrid or hyflex model, and 36% were primarily or fully-in-person (C2i, 2021). Although the COVID-19 vaccine was widely available to college students by spring 2021 (Moody, 2021), many institutions continued to rely on hybrid models and online learning. Some research suggests students have decreased interest in remote instruction based on their experiences during COVID-19, which impacts enrollment and persistence (Barber et al., 2021). According to the National Student Clearinghouse Research Center (2022), enrollment loses due to the pandemic represent a 5.1% decline over the last two years.

As the pandemic has continued, so have the financial burdens for many students. Students reported losses in internships opporunitities, job offers, and delayed graduation (Hagedorn et al., 2020; Lederer et al., 2020; Son et al., 2020). Many students also reported reductions in work hours or employment loss (Akin-Odanye et al., 2020; Reyes-Portillo et al., 2022). COVID-19 has impacted college students in a variety of ways, but research suggests that some students have experienced greater impact than others. Emerging research suggests that the negative effects of the pandemic have been exacerbated among first generation, low-income, and students of color (Aucejo et al., 2020; Barber et al., 2021; Lederer et al., 2020; Soria et al., 2020).

COVID-19 and First-Generation Students

Approximately 33% of college students are first-generation (NCES, 2018). FG students are typically defined as individuals whose parent/guardians either did not enroll in postsecondary education or did not earn a four-year degree (Cataldi et al., 2018). They are more likely to come from low-socioeconomic backgrounds and often include historically underrepresented ethnic or racial groups (Center for First-Generation Student Success, 2017; Gibbons et al., 2019; House et al., 2020; Toutkoushian et al., 2021). Higher education serves as an avenue of social mobility for FG students, opening up career and financial opportunities that they may not otherwise have access to. However, research suggests FG students face additional challenges in college (e.g., lack of family support, increased financial demands, being less academically prepared) compared to their CG peers that can threaten their academic achievement, persistence, and overall well-being (e.g., Cataldi et al., 2018; House et al., 2020; Pratt et al., 2017; Radunzel, 2018; Toutkoushian et al., 2021). FG students often complete college at lower rates than their CG peers with only 27% earning a bachelor's degree within four years after enrolling compared to 42% of CG students (RTI, 2019). The difficulties these students face can also compound when students' FG status intersects with other marginalized identities (e.g., race, gender, age, socioeconomic status) leading to lower self-efficacy and increased stress (House et al., 2020; Ives & Castillo-Montoya, 2020).

Prior to COVID-19, FG students were already working to balance academic demands while working more hours than their CG peers. FG students also indicated feeling disconnected from campus and their peers and unaware of or unwilling to use resources available (e.g., Atherton, 2014; RTI International, 2019; Soria & Stebleton, 2012; Yee, 2016). In terms of COVID-19 impact, initial studies suggest FG students share many of the difficulties faced by their CG peers (e.g., adjusting to online learning, decrease in motivation, increased mental health concerns), but have had to manage additional barriers (e.g., housing insecurity, increased work demands, added financial burdens) unique to their FG status (e.g., Barber et al., 2021; Davis et al., 2021; Rodríguez-Planas, 2022; Soria et al., 2020). Many FG students reported that the move to online learning increased academic demands and found it difficult to balance school and additional responsibilities at home, such as helping care for siblings, caring for their own children, working more to support family (Barber et al., 2021; Soria et al., 2020). Some FG students reported having limited access to the internet or increased technology costs (Barber et al., 2021; Davis et al., 2021; Soria et al., 2020). Taken together, these added stressors can place greater challenges that make it difficult to cope with or manage the changes in instructional delivery and learning environment. In the following section, we discuss theoretical frameworks to help us to better understand how students are likely to respond to stressful events, such as learning and instructional changes due to COVID-19.

Theoretical Frameworks

Lazarus and Folkman's (1984) transactional model of stress and coping suggests an individual's experience with stress is a dynamic process that involves a transaction between multiple systems within the individual (i.e., affective, psychological, neurological, physiological, and cognitive) and their environment (Lazarus & Folkman, 1984; Folkman, 2010). A key aspect of this theory is that the stress response is considered a subjective experience, influenced by appraisals—both the initial perception of external stressors (primary appraisal), which may be perceived as a threat, as well as the resources to deal with stress, such as coping strategies (secondary appraisal). After an initial appraisal, an individual assesses how they might change or accept the situation. Stress or distress is experienced when the individual perceives that the demands exceed or tax resources (Folkman, 2010). It is worth noting that not all stress is detrimental. In fact, exposure to moderate amounts of stress may be necessary for developing effective coping skills (Leebens & Williamson, 2017). Coping strategies, such as self-regulation and help-seeking are also important in situations of uncontrollable adversity (Masten, 2014). While COVID-19 likely activated students' stress response, there may be variations in how students appraised and responded to the related stressors.

In examining the impact of COVID-19, it is important to consider not just how students are feeling (stress and coping) but also how they are engaging or disengaging. Self-determination theory (SDT) provides a helpful framework for examining the impact of COVID-19 on student motivation and engagement (Deci & Ryan, 2000; Ryan & Deci, 2020). According to SDT, motivation differs according to the extent to which three needs are met: autonomy, competence, and relatedness. The need for autonomy refers to the independent choice to become involved in a behavior; the need for competence is achieved when individuals experience success or satisfaction while learning a new skill, and this success promotes engagement; and relatedness is the need for belonging or connection (Ryan & Deci, 2020). It is likely all three of these needs have been challenged for students as a result of COVID-19. The way in which individuals perceive obstacles and view opportunities influences subsequent motivational processes and behaviors similar to appraisals of stress. Taken together, these theories can help to understand student responses to the pandemic. Drawing from theory and the need to more closely examine first-generation student experiences, the following research questions were proposed: (RQ1) How did COVID-19 impact students' experiences? (RQ2) Were there changes in COVID-19 impact over time? (RQ3) Were there differences in COVID-19 impact between FG and CG students? Findings can help to improve student supports especially for more at-risk learner groups, adapt to educational changes moving forward, and prepare for similar events that may occur in the future.

METHODOLOGY

Research Design

This study used an *explanatory sequential mixed methods design*, which involves a quantitative phase, followed by a qualitative phase (Creswell & Creswell, 2018; Fetters, 2019; Plano Clark & Ivankova, 2016). This design allowed for an analysis of the overall impact of COVID-19 (quantitative), followed by a more in-depth investigation into the *nature* of its impact on the academic experience (qualitative). Semi-structured individual interviews were conducted to further explore *how* COVID-19 impacted academics and the use of coping strategies to adapt to the changes by asking participants to expand on their responses from the initial survey. Given the uniqueness and immediacy of the pandemic, the goal was to understand students' perspectives by adopting a more emergent or inductive approach.

Participants

Undergraduate students (N = 345) from two southeastern U.S. universities participated in the study. Institutional Review Board approval was obtained from both institutions and students were recruited through undergraduate psychology and education courses. Extra credit was offered by undergraduate course instructors when applicable. Otherwise, participants were entered into a draw for a chance to win $50 gift certificate. A small compensation was offered at one institution to participants for completing interviews. The sample was predominately white (n = 239, 68.1%), female (n = 290, 82.6%), freshmen (n = 140, 39.9%), with a mean age of 20.1 years (SD = 3.55). The number of FG students (n = 71, 20.2%) was representative of the FG student populations at both institutions. Participant demographics are reported in Table 6.1. The larger sample from the survey (n = 229) served as the selection pool to recruit participants for follow-up interviews (n = 15), using convenience sampling. The sample for interviews was predominately white (n = 14, 93%), female (n = 13,

Table 6.1

Demographic Characteristics of Survey Participants

Variable	Total $N = 345$ (%)	Fall 2020 $n = 229$ (%)	Spring 2021 $n = 116$ (%)
Gender			
Woman	290 (82.6)	190 (83.0)	100 (86.2)
Man	51 (14.5)	36 (15.7)	15 (12.9)
Prefer to self-describe	1 (0.3)	1 (0.4)	– –
Prefer not to say	3 (0.9)	2 (0.9)	1 (0.9)
Ethnicity			
Black/African American	65 (18.5)	35 (15.3)	30 (25.9)
White	239 (68.1)	164 (71.6)	75 (64.7)
Asian	11 (3.1)	8 (3.5)	3 (2.6)
American Indian/Alaskan Native	1 (0.3)	1 (0.4)	– –
Hispanic/Latinx	7 (2.0)	5 (2.2)	2 (1.7)
Multiethnic	21 (6.0)	15 (6.6)	6 (5.2)
Other	1 (0.3)	1 (0.4)	– –
Classification			
Freshmen	140 (39.9)	113 (49.3)	27 (23.3)
Sophomore	74 (21.1)	44 (19.2)	30 (25.9)
Junior	74 (21.1)	36 (15.7)	38 (32.8)
Senior	56 (16.0)	36. (15.7)	20 (17.2)
Other (second degree)	1 (1.7)	– –	1 (0.9)
Age			
Mean	20.10 –	19.33 –	21.62 –
SD	3.55 –	1.56 –	5.42 –
Parental Education			
Less than High School Diploma	11 (3.1)	8 (3.5)	3 (2.6)
High School Diploma	61 (17.4)	39 (17.0)	22 (19.0)
Some College	95 (27.1)	58 (25.3)	37 (31.9)
Bachelor's Degree	108 (30.8)	73 (31.9)	35 (30.2)
Master's Degree	53 (15.1)	38 (16.6)	15 (12.9)
Doctoral or Professional Degree	17 (4.8)	13 (5.7)	4 (3.4)

87%), junior (n = 8, 53%), and had a mean age of 20.3 years (SD = 1.09), which was relatively representative of the larger sample. Demographic characteristics for interview participants are presented in Table 6.2.

Table 6.2

Demographic Characteristics of Interview Participants

Variable	Total N = 15 (%)
Gender	
Woman	13 (86.7)
Man	2 (13.3)
Ethnicity	
Black/African American	1 (6.7)
White	14 (93.3)
Classification	
Freshmen	3 (20.0)
Sophomore	1 (6.7)
Junior	8 (53.3)
Senior	3 (20.0)
Age	20.2 –
Mean	1.09 –
SD	

Measures

Demographics. A demographic questionnaire was administered to collect information on gender identity, ethnicity, age, year of study, major, SAT/ACT scores, GPA, and parents'/guardians' highest level of education (used to determine student FG or CG status).

Coronavirus Impact Scale (CIS). An adapted version of the CIS (Stoddard & Kaufman, 2020) was used to assesses the impact of COVID-19 on daily routines, family income/employment, stress, access to food, mental health care, and social support, family discord, immediate/extended family members and close friends and academic performance (added for this study).[1] Likert scale items ranged from 1 ("no change") to 4 ("severe"). We also included an open-ended question with the following prompt: "In what ways has the COVID-19 pandemic impacted your academics or access to social supports? (if any)." The overall COVID-19 psychosocial impact score represented summed responses to Likert scale items (using the adapted version, scores could range from 9 to 36, with higher scores indicating greater impact). Given that CIS was a new scale developed in response to the pandemic, there is limited information about reliability and validity; however, several COVID-19 studies have used this tool (Dewa et al., 2021; Félix et al., 2021; Machado et al., 2020) and it is registered with the NIH OBSSR suite of common instruments (NIH, 2021). Analysis of internal scale consistency demonstrated an acceptable level of reliability ($\alpha = .82$).

Procedure

Questionnaires were administered via SurveyMonkey, a secure online survey tool. The survey link was distributed in fall 2020 (Data Round 1) and spring 2021 (Data Round 2) to different groups of students. At the time of the fall data collection, both campuses had moved the majority of courses online or to a hybrid model (i.e., some online, some face-to-face), were implementing mask mandates, and required students to distance themselves socially both in and out of the classroom. At the time of spring data collection, there was a return to more face-to-face learning, though many courses remained online and in a hybrid model, and there was an ease of additional COVID restrictions (i.e., masking, social distancing). In the broader context of the pandemic, COVID vaccines were available by the spring. Semi-structured interviews were conducted following the first round of data collection. Interview participants were asked a series of follow-up questions to explore how COVID-19 impacted academic experiences and responses to changes. Interviews were conducted by two members of the research team (one for each site) via password-protected Zoom meetings. Each interview lasted approximately 25–35 minutes and was recorded via Zoom and transcribed.[2]

Coding and Analysis

Open-ended survey and interview responses were coded using thematic analysis involving several rounds of review to develop codes and identify emergent themes (Saldaña, 2013). The process included: familiarity with the data, generating initial codes, searching for themes, reviewing themes, defining and naming themes, and producing the report (Braun & Clarke, 2006). Two members of the research team began by using the interview question headings (i.e., COVID-19 impact on academics, COVID-19 impact on social supports) to review the qualitative data and develop a coding key, which included areas of impact and whether the impact was positive or negative. To establish credibility of interview codes, the two coders randomly selected a sample of seven transcripts, representing 47% of the interview data. Percent agreement was calculated and demonstrated 100% agreement. To establish credibility of open-ended survey codes, two coders randomly selected a sample of 50 responses representing 53% of the survey data and demonstrated 96% agreement. Discrepancies were resolved through discussion. Quantitative analyses were conducted using the Statistical Package for Social Sciences (SPSS), Version 27.

RESULTS

(RQ1) How Did COVID-19 Impact Students' Experiences?

In terms of overall CIS score, the mean for the sample was 20.31 (SD = 5.38) out of 36. The largest area of impact reported by students was stress (72.2% reported moderate to severe), followed by interactions with family and friends (62% reported moderate to severe), daily routines (57.6% reported moderate to severe), and academics (56.2% reported moderate to severe). These four items representing the greatest areas of impact (over 50% of the sample reported moderate-to-severe impact for each item) were selected for subsequent analysis. Areas with less pervasive impact included stress and discord in the family (46.3% reported moderate to severe) and family income (38.8% reported moderate to severe), followed by access to mental health services (16.7% reported moderate to severe) and access to healthcare (17.1% reported moderate to severe). Access to food was least impacted (9.6% reported moderate to severe). See Figure 6.1 for CIS results.

Responses from open-ended survey questions from each data round (Data Round 1, n = 200; Data Round 2, n = 94) and individual interviews (N = 15) illustrated 4 key areas of impact: (1) academic, (2) emotional, (3) motivational, and (4) social, which we used to describe results below. *Academic* impact referred to students' understanding of course material, course performance, and general academic experience; *emotional* impact referred to students' feelings, especially related to academics, *motivational* impact referred to students' desire to complete work or perform well in a course; and *social* impact referred to sources of support and changes to how students interacted with these supports.

Open-ended survey responses. Analysis of open-ended survey responses (n = 294) to the COVID-19 question revealed that 41% of participants indicated a negative academic impact due to COVID-19. As one student wrote, "Adapting to the new way of learning and being a student has been

Figure 6.1

COVID Impact Areas

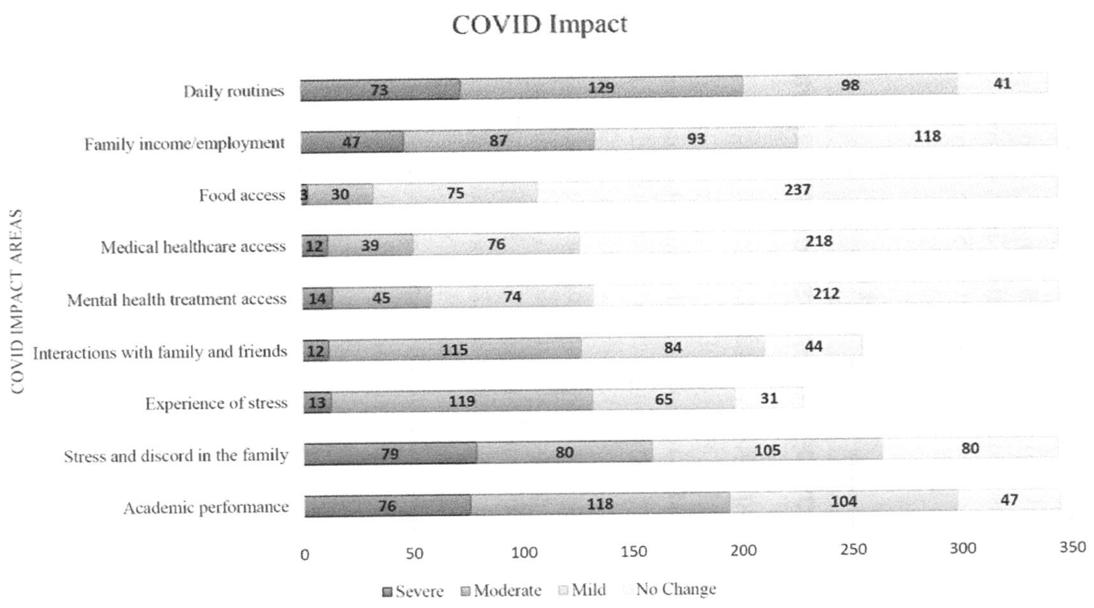

Note. The numbers in the figure represent the number of participants who selected each response option (no change, mild, moderate, or severe) for each category, illustrating the level of impact across the areas measured.

very difficult while trying to keep up with the normal course load." The majority of respondents (52%) cited online learning as a contributor to the negative impact COVID-19 had on their academics. One student wrote, "COVID-19 has impacted my academics severely. Due to COVID-19 almost everything is online, and I have issues learning that way ... when we had to switch to online my grades drastically dropped." Another noted, "COVID-19 has affected my academics in that the majority of my classes are online. I don't get the opportunity to establish a relationship with my professors or even ask them questions in a lot of cases. I feel like I'm on my own a lot of time with my studies and the course content." Other areas impacted included: social (35% reported negative impact), emotional (16% reported negative impact), and motivational (15% reported negative impact). The social impact included reduced contact with peers both in and outside of the classroom and difficulty making new friends as illustrated in the following quote: "Socially I have been impacted because I transferred schools and have barely been able to meet new people, due to the lack of un person classes." The emotional impact largely centered around heightened personal and academic stress, while the motivational impact translated to increased levels of procrastination, inability to maintain attention and focus. Students commented, "I have lost my ability to maintain routine and feel lost with time. Due to this, I am often overwhelmed and anxious" and "I feel burnt out and worn down and I know if COVID never hit I would be so much more motivated and excited to be at college." A few participants (4%) indicated a positive impact of COVID-19 on social supports, online learning, motivation, and emotion. For example, as one student wrote, "It has given everyone a reason to support each other and work together." Another noted: "Online classes meant staying at home this semester, which I prefer, instead of going back to school." Some students (9%) indicated COVID-19 had no impact on their academics or access to social support.

Interviews. Analysis of interviews ($n = 15$) also illustrated a largely negative impact across all identified themes. Similar to survey responses, in terms of academics, the majority of students described a negative impact (93%) with many noting issues with online learning. One student stated, "I have to actually have a physical person there to help teach it to me. So, it was a stressful time with that class [online], because I realized that I was going to fail." Interaction with faculty was both positively and negatively impacted by COVID-19. Some noted challenges: "I feel like, it's definitely been a little more difficult to build relationships with my professors because of like, zoom and everything," whereas others observed benefits: "Academic support, I'm not gonna lie, I would say it's definitely increased it, ironically, because it's so much easier now to hop on a FaceTime with someone, your professor, another student, anyone, and get that help ... literally anyone because everyone's at their computer now." Social supports were another area where both positive and negative impacts were observed. Many students (73%) commented on difficulties connecting with others: "I'm like, wow, I wish I could just see you. Like, I don't want to be having to do this when I'm like, a mile away from you. And it's very disheartening when you want to be there be and be with people." Those who indicated a positive impact of COVID-19 (27%) cited changes in their interpersonal relationships. One student noted, "when we shifted to all online, I went back home for multiple months. So I got more of the physical connection with my family." In terms of emotional impact, the majority of interview participants (93%) described a negative experience. A student stated: "just sitting back and kind of doing nothing has just been kind of draining emotionally, mentally and physically." Another student noted, "this semester has been, I don't know, just like very, even though I haven't done much, it's been very taxing on me. I feel drained." Finally, many interview participants (47%) cited motivation was also negatively impacted as illustrated in the following quotes: "I guess you would say then, in terms of motivation, it's 0 out of 100; I have no motivation anymore." and another mentioned, "I want to quit, I don't want to do anymore.... I don't want to be a failure." Table 6.3 illustrates additional exemplars from interviews by theme.

Table 6.3

COVID-19 Impact Themes and Exemplars From Semi-Structured Interview

Theme	Defined	Impact	Exemplars
Academic	Impact on student understanding of course material, impact on grades, impact on general academic experience	Positive (n = 6)	"I feel like being online, they (faculty) talked to us more, they communicated and wanted to check up on us more, which I don't think we would have had if we were in person. So it was nice, maybe connecting, and having more like nice, maybe connecting, and having more like deeper relationships with your teachers."
			"Academically, ironically, it hasn't been the worst thing, because there is nothing to do but study."
		Negative (n = 14)	"Academically, I've had to shift my way of learning in a way, I'm very much a face to face, let's talk through it process out loud type of person. I don't do well with just kind of reading an article and having to process through it independently, and not being able to get feedback. And because of COVID, a lot of classes have been online. So that's kind of what we've been given. So that's been very difficult,"

(Table continued on next page)

Table 6.3 (Continued)

COVID-19 Impact Themes and Exemplars From Semi-Structured Interview

Theme	Defined	Impact	Exemplars
			"I honestly feel like I didn't probably get as much out of the classes as I usually did. Because I'm so used to being fully immersed in classes and having small group discussions and things like that, which we could do on zoom. But it just wasn't the same. And it wasn't as engaging honestly."
Emotional	Impact on student feelings about the course or academics. Includes experiences of stress and anxiety.	Negative (n = 14)	"this semester has been, I don't know, just like very, even though I haven't done much, it's been very taxing on me. I feel drained."
			"My daily routine has been thrown out of whack so much that my sleep schedule is non-existent. I try to wake up for class and end up getting a major migraine or pass out during class on Zoom."
Motivational	Impact on student desire to complete work or do well in a course. Includes attention and persistence.	Positive (n =4)	"...when we shifted to all online, I went back home for multiple months. So I got more of the physical connection with my family, I spent a lot of time like every I mean, I was with my family every day."
		Negative (n = 11)	"I think it's definitely impacted, like the people I interact with, like, I think, a lot of times it can, I like to get out of my bubble, like, I'm pretty extroverted and I like to talk to people who, like, aren't in my major, you know, to see people in my sorority, and it's definitely like, cut down on who I've seen this semester, because there's that added pressure of like, God forbid, that I'm the person who brings like, COVID into a hospital."

When asked about their response to academic challenges or setbacks, several participants described ways in which they coped with difficulties. Participants noted strategies that involved regulation of their behavior, motivation, emotion, and attention. For example, one student described help-seeking: "I feel like maybe I could reach out to my teachers more to develop that more one-on-one relationship, especially now, because this semester, my classes are online, more than they were last semester." Other strategies included finding a balance between academics and activities that

Table 6.4

Coping Responses Illustrated in Semi-Structured Interviews

Coping Responses	Details
Adaptive	
Found creative ways to connect with others	Reconnected with friends through online video game playing, social media platforms (i.e., Snapchat, TikTok), and socially distanced gatherings when it was safe to do so.
Sought out academic services	Used tutoring and academic center resources as well as actively reaching out to faculty and teaching assistants.
Created reward systems to increase motivation and reduce stress	Applied various schedules of reinforcement to combat lower motivation and procrastination. Created a balance between academic demands and stress relieving activities.
Used teletherapy during quarantine	Participants engaged with mental health resources either continuing therapy or utilizing resources for the first time.
Accepted current circumstances and engaged more with social supports	Accepted changes that occurred as a result of COVID. Intentionally engaged more with supports including online study groups and regular virtual meetings with family and friends.
Maladaptive	
Increased substance use	Used alcohol as a way to deal with academic stress related to online learning.
Negative attributions regarding self and others	Engaged in negative self-talk and experienced lower self-efficacy in response to academic challenges due to COVID. Negative perceptions of faculty instructional methods and responses.

reduce stress. A student noted, "I feel like I've responded good and bad. And I just kind of gotten to the point where I'm letting myself like, okay, it's fine to take a step back from school and just chill with friends for a week, or for a night or two and just not worry about freaking out about everything." Another mentioned, "That's like the main thing that really kept me going was doing stuff that I enjoy to keep myself happy and take my mind off of things." Table 6.4 provides a summary of adaptive and maladaptive coping strategies described during the interviews.

(R2) How Has the Overall Impact of COVID-19 Changed Over Time?

An independent samples *t*-test revealed a statistically significant difference in CIS Score between fall 2020 and spring 2021, $t(192) = 1.98$, $p = .05$; $d = 0.24$) with fall showing greater COVID-19 impact ($M = 20.74$, $SD = 4.91$) than spring ($M = 19.45$, 6.12).[3] With respect to the four areas most impacted by COVID-19 between fall and spring, a one-way MANOVA revealed a significant effect of time overall, Wilks' $\lambda = .96$, F (4, 336) = 3.795, $p < .05$, partial $n^2 = .04$). Specifically, univariate analysis revealed significant decreases in experiences of stress $F(1, 339) = 14.03$, $p < 0.001$, interactions with family and friends, $F(1, 339) = 7.71$, $p = .006$, and daily routines, $F(1, 339) = 4.10$, $p = .044$ between fall and spring. There were no significant changes in impact on academic performance, $F(1, 339) = 2.81$, $p = .095$.

An exploratory analysis of qualitative data from open-ended survey responses ($n = 294$) also illustrated a larger negative impact in the fall. Interactions with family and friends were explicitly mentioned by more participants in the fall ($n = 23$) compared to spring ($n = 10$). One student in fall 2020 wrote, "It has caused me to be isolated from friends and family. Stressed about getting sick or getting some(one) I love sick. And also stressed about when life will go back to normal." Experiences of stress were mentioned more by fall respondents ($n = 57$) as one wrote, "Feelings of stress and anxiety have exacerbated being overwhelmed by school. I can't be with my friends to destress/socialize the same way." Similar responses were noted in the spring ($n = 28$), but some students seemed to have adjusted. One student wrote: "the stress has been unreal and I have had to learn how to deal with things very differently ... but I'm making it."

In fall 2020, one student wrote, "COVID-19 has affected my academics in that the majority of my classes are online. I don't get the opportunity to establish a relationship with my professors or even ask them questions in a lot of cases. I feel like I'm on my own a lot of time with my studies and the course content." Similarly, in spring 2021, a student wrote, "the burnout is severe because a lot of professors expect us to just watch videos they post and learn it ourselves it seems like." It is worth noting more students reported no impact in spring 2021 (14%) compared to fall 2020 (6%) supporting the lessened impact over time.

(R3) How Has COVID-19 Impacted FG Students' Compared to Their CG Peers?

An independent samples *t*-test revealed there was not a statistically significant difference in the overall CIS score of FG students compared to CG,

Table 6.5

COVID Impact Scale Means by Student Status

COVID Scale Item	*Total* *M (Std. Dev.)*	*FG* *M (Std. Dev.)*	*CG* *M (Std. Dev.)*
Daily Routines	2.69 (.94)	2.41 (.97)	2.76 (.92)
Family Income	2.18 (1.05)	2.23 (1.11)	2.17 (1.04)
Food Access	1.42 (.69)	1.52 (.73)	1.39 (.67)
Medical/ Healthcare Access	1.55 (.83)	1.68 (.91)	1.52 (.80)
Mental Health Access	1.60 (.86)	1.62 (.88)	1.59 (.86)
Interaction w/ Family & Friends	2.80 (1.01)	2.51 (1.04)	2.87 (.98)
Experiences of Stress	3.01 (.96)	2.72 (.97)	3.08 (.95)
Stress/Discord in Family	2.46 (1.09)	2.39 (1.04)	2.48 (1.10)
Academic Performance	2.65 (.97)	2.55 (.97)	2.67 (.97)
COVID Impact	20.31 (5.38)	19.62 (5.91)	20.49 (5.22)

Note. FG represents first-generation student status. CG represents continuing generation student status. COVID Impact Scale item scores could range from 1 to 4 with higher scores indicating greater impact. COVID Impact overall scores could range from 9 to 36 with higher scores indicating greater impact.

$t(343) = 1.210, p > .05$. However, results of a one-way MANOVA examining the four areas most impacted revealed a statistically significant effect of student status (Wilks' $\lambda = .97$, $F\ (4, 336) = 3.084, p < .05$, partial $n^2 = .04$). Specifically, FG students reported significantly lower impact compared to CG students in experiences of stress, $F\ (1, 339) = 7.81, p = .005$, daily routines $F\ (1, 339) = 7.96, p = .005$, and interactions with family and friends $F\ (1, 339) = 7.03, p = .008$. The impact on academic performance did not significantly differ between the two groups, $F(1, 339) = .930, p = .335$. Table 6.5 includes CIS means for FG and CG status.

An exploratory analysis of qualitative data from open-ended survey responses ($N = 294$) comparing responses of FG students ($n = 55$) to their CG peers (n = 239) did not reveal major differences between groups and suggested similar impact as noted in the quantitative analysis. For example, 47% of open-ended responses from FG students noted a negative impact related to distance learning similar to 50% of open-ended responses from CG students who also commented on this across fall and spring. Consistency among the two groups was found across the key areas of impact (academic, social, motivational, emotional). Although the impact on academic performance was not found to be significantly different in this sample, some of the survey responses are reflective of the impact of COVID-19 on FG students seen in the literature. One FG student wrote, "It has impacted my academics because we can't even go to class. It is very hard not to get distracted when you are constantly surrounded by your family." Another noted, "I don't have access to internet at home so when COVID-19 got severe they closed down all local library, which really impacted me; often times I had to sacrifice some of my schoolwork because I had no internet to do it." These student responses may represent the impact that COVID-19 had on magnifying the unique challenges that FG students face in accessing resources that support academic achievement.

CONCLUSION

The purpose of this study was to explore the impact of COVID-19 on college students' academic experiences during the first full academic year of the pandemic. Additionally, this study also explored the impact on a vulnerable student population, first-generation students. Results from quantitative data suggest the overall impact of COVID-19 appeared most salient in fall 2020 and became less severe as the pandemic continued. COVID-19 had a considerable negative impact on students' lives particularly related to daily routines, experiences of stress, and interactions with friends and family, and academics. As the pandemic persisted, the academic impact remained constant for students, while daily routines, experiences of stress, and interactions with friends and family appeared to lessen. In the spring, vaccines were made available and quarantine restrictions eased, which may have contributed to the decreased impact of COVID-19 on daily and social aspects of life. While many campuses continued to shift to more in-person learning opportunities, others remained online or used a hybrid model for students. Considering the overwhelmingly negative response to online learning found in this study, this may explain the consistency seen in the academic impact on students.

Review of qualitative data illuminated four key areas of impact: academic, emotional, motivational, and social. Over half of the participants indicated a negative academic impact due to COVID-19, and both quantitative and qualitative data suggest the impact was sustained over time. Students largely connected the academic impact to difficulties in adjusting to online learning, disconnection from learning with peers, increased workload, decreased confidence, and lack of communication with or direct access to faculty. Students also emphasized the need to engage with faculty and peers in the learning environment and suggested online learning was an isolating experience at times. While students did not indicate significant changes in their academic performance overall, several felt that the online format made courses more difficult, that they spent more time learning independently, and perceived an increased workload compared to face-to-face courses. Students also reported reduced motivation, difficulty concentrating, and increased procrastination, all largely connected to online learning.

The negative emotional impact indicated by both survey and interview participants referenced high levels of stress and anxiety, as well as frustration over missing out on the "college experience." For first-year students, this meant a non-traditional start to college. They cited missed opportunities to make new friends or attend social and athletic events. Upper-level students shared similar concerns over missing out on their traditional senior year experiences. Students described feeling overwhelmed, frustrated, defeated, and lonely. Relatedly, the social impact of COVID-19 concentrated on limited access to and interaction with friends and family. Our findings are consistent with research conducted early in the pandemic and subsequent studies that have followed. COVID-19 research in higher education suggests one of the largest contributors to increased stress/anxiety was worry about academics and many students reported related difficulties with concentration, motivation, and online learning (e.g., Farris et al., 2021; Halliburton et al., 2021; Kaur et al., 2022; Son et al., 2020; Unger & Meiran, 2020).

Results of our analysis of the impact on FG students compared to their CG peers is not as consistent with findings from other COVID-19 FG research studies (e.g., Barber et al., 2021; Davis et al., 2021; Soria et al., 2020). Specifically, results did not reveal a significant difference in academic impact between FG and CG peers, and while there were significant differences in the impact on daily routines, stress, and interactions with family and friends, FG students actually reported lower impact in these areas than CG peers. There are two reasons that might help to explain this somewhat unexpected finding. First, some studies have shown FG students indicate higher levels of resilience as they enter college (Alvarado et al., 2017). It is possible the higher levels of resilience FG students have developed as a result of adversity faced prepared them in some way to navigate these new challenges. Second, since many FG students traditionally live at home, it is also possible that the move off campus early in the pandemic did not impact their daily routines or interactions with friends and family to the same degree as their CG peers (Soria et al., 2020). Future research could utilize qualitative data to further examine differences found in the impact of COVID-19 on FG students compared to their CG peers.

The findings of this study largely support Lazarus and Folkman's (1984) transactional model of stress—while key themes did emerge in terms of stressors, not all students conveyed the same reaction to change in learning and instructional methods. In fact, despite the overwhelming negative impact reported, some participants cited positive impacts of the pandemic and employed adaptive coping responses to COVID-19. Some students noted difficult courses were restructured in a helpful way and appreciated the flexibility of having all of their courses online allowed for more study time. Others cited how professors checked in on them more and were generally more understanding of academic difficulties they were experiencing as a result of the pandemic. The mandatory lockdown resulted in more time at home with family for some students, allowing for the deepening of relationships and increased access to support. The shared experience of the pandemic also increased support for one another among their peers and promoted a sense of community during a challenging time. Some students also indicated their ability to persist through the pandemic difficulties enhanced their self-efficacy. It is worth noting that some students responded with less adaptive coping strategies, such as increased substance use, negative beliefs about abilities, or attributing academic difficulties solely to faculty.

The findings of the study also largely align with Deci and Ryan's (2000) self-determination theory (SDT). Students reported disengagement or negative impacts on academic performance that were tied to feeling less confident in their ability to learn effectively under the new conditions (competence), having limited options to access supports (relatedness) and not being able to learn in the manner they preferred (autonomy). Despite these challenges, some students responded with adaptive and innovative ways to meet their basic psychological needs. Students reported taking advantage of academic resources more during COVID-19 (i.e., tutoring, virtual meetings with professors, online study sessions). During quarantine, students also indicated that they reached out to others and found innovative ways of connecting, such as social media, online technology, and socially-distanced meet ups.

IMPLICATIONS FOR THE FUTURE

COVID-19 was an unexpected and unprecedented event that impacted students in a variety of ways. This study adds to the literature by offering a better understanding of how COVID-19 impacted college students' academic experiences during a year of the pandemic. The use of both quantitative and qualitative data in this study provides deeper insight into factors contributing to students' experiences. The academic impact of COVID-19 was largely centered around the shift to online learning, which presented many challenges for students. This finding is supported by COVID-19 literature examining the academic impact (Aguilera-Hermida, 2020; Barber et al., 2021; Clabaugh et al., 2021; Farris et al., 2021; Halliburton et al., 2021; Lemay et al., 2021). Students in this study indicated that the online learning environment made them feel isolated and disconntected from the faculty and their peers. As institutions continue to use online platforms as a delivery method, consideration should be given to providing opportunities for students to develop meaningful relationships with faculty and to engage with their peers. This could be facilitated through intentional interactions between faculty and students using a variety of mediums (e.g., personalized emails, videos, blogs, synchronous online discussion sessions), as well as actively promoting opportunities for students to collaborate (e.g., student peer groups, class chat-groups, small-group activities). Additionally, developing online assignments and activities that promote student autonomy (e.g., choice on assignment format, option to adjust weight of assignments) and competence (e.g., metacognitive reflection, detailed feedback, low-stakes assignments early in course) could serve to combat some of the loss of confidence students reported experiencing as a result of online learning and may also serve to positively impact student motivation and combat procrastination (Ryan & Deci, 2020). In order to implement some of these changes, institutions should also consider a collaborative approach to redesigning online curriculum and instruction that includes faculty, instructional designers, and teaching and learning center staff (Nworie, 2021). It is important to recognize these changes will require institutional support, especially for faculty who also faced their own set of challenges during the pandemic (e.g., Cutri et al., 2020; Johnson et al., 2020).

The results of this study also suggest that institutions should evaluate resources available to students, such as online forms of non-academic support (e.g., counseling services, job placement, mentoring, technology support; Nworie, 2021) and adequate staff to manage increased mental health needs of diverse student populations (Priestley et al., 2021). College students reported heightened stress and anxiety levels as a result of COVID-19; therefore, there is a need to ensure campus resources that support both students' academic pursuits as well as overall emotional well-being. Responses from participants who successfully navigated these adverse experiences can provide important insight into necessary interventions and support made available to students. Students in this study employed a variety of adaptive coping strategies, including use of teletherapy and academic services offered. It is encouraging that the results of this study suggest the impact of COVID-19 is lessening over time. Nevertheless, institutions have an opportunity to use what has been learned about the impact of COVID-19 to support students in reconnecting to the campus and to prepare for similar events moving forward.

There are limitations to the study that are important to note and can help to identify areas for future research. First, we relied on self-report measures, which may be susceptible to cognitive biases. Collecting behavioral measures of student engagement and instructor feedback would help to triangulate data and provide insights into learning processes. Second, we collected data during the first full academic year of the pandemic; however, additional data collection could examine longer-term impacts. Additionally, our two data rounds contained different groups of students; a repeated-measures/longitudinal design would allow a more robust and reliable comparison of change over time. Finally, we opted to use a more emergent approach to the study given the evolving and unpredictable nature of the pandemic; however, future work could directly test students' stress appraisals, as well as coping and resilience strategies. Similarly, our exploration of the impact on first-generation students emerged as the project progressed. In future work, it would be beneficial to include questions more tailored to FG students to examine how they adjusted. Given that research suggests low-income students and students of color were largely impacted by COVID-19 (e.g., Molock & Parchem, 2021; Rodríguez-Planas, 2022), future research should also seek to obtain a more diverse sample to better understand the unique experiences of these students. Despite the limitations, we believe that this study paves the way for future research examining college students' response to stress and the impact on their academic experience.

SUMMARY

The findings from this research highlight the importance of attending to the psychosocial impact of COVID-19 on college students' experience, including academic, emotional-motivational, and social facets. Given that the shift to online learning was a challenge for many, institutions should consider which educational tools best help instructors and students to maintain connection and optimize learning in these environments. Students are also likely to benefit from mental health and academic resources that help to build learning and emotion regulation strategies. Despite these areas for development, student feedback indicated potential opportunities for growth and resilience, such as building new ways to connect with peers, instructors, and family. Our hope is that resources in higher education continue to be improved upon to equip college educators and students with the tools needed to successfully navigate these types of unexpected events in the future.

REFERENCES

Aguilera-Hermida, A. P. (2020). College students' use and acceptance of emergency online learning due to covid-19. *International Journal of Educational Research Open*, *1*, 100011. https://doi.org/10.1016/j.ijedro.2020.100011

Akin-Odanye, E. O., Kaninjing, E., Ndip, R. N., Warren, C. L., Asuzu, C. C., Lopez, I., Muiruri, C., & Vilme, H. (2021). Psychological impact of covid-19 on students at institutions of higher learning. *European Journal of Education Studies*, *8*(6), 112–128. https://doi.org/10.46827/ejes.v8i6.3770

Alvarado, A., Spatariu, A., & Woodbury, C. (2017). Resilience & emotional intelligence between first generation college students and non-first generation college students. *FOCUS on Colleges, Universities & Schools*, *11*(1), 1–10. https://doi.or/10.1155/2012/490647

Atherton, M. C. (2014). Academic preparedness of first-generation college students: Different perspectives. *Journal of College Student Development*, *55*(8), 824–829. https://doi.org/10/1353/csd.2014.0081

Aucejo, E. M., French, J. F., Araya, M. C., & Zafar, B. (2020). The impact of COVID-19 on student experiences and expectations: Evidence from a survey. *Journal of Public Economics*, *191*, 1–15. https://doi.org/10.1016/j.jpubeco.2020.104271

Barber, P. H., Shapiro, C., Jacobs, M. S., Avilez, L., Brenner, K. I., Cabral, C., Cebreros, M., Cosentino, E., Cross, C., Gonzalez, M. L., Lumada, K. T., Menjivar, A. T., Narvaez, J., Olmeda, B., Phelan, R., Purdy, D., Salam, S., Serrano, L., Velasco, M. J., … Levis-Fitzgerald, M. (2021). Disparities in remote learning faced by first-generation and underrepresented minority students during COVID-19: Insights and opportunities from a remote research experience. *Journal of Microbiology & Biology Education*, *22*(1), 1–25. https://doi.org/10.1128/jmbe.v22i1.2457

Bono, G., Reil, K., & Hescox, J. (2020). Stress and wellbeing in college students during the COVID-19 pandemic: Can grit and gratitude help? *International Journal of Wellbeing*, *10*(3), 39–57. https://doi.org/10.5502/ijw.v10i3.1331

Brown, C. (2020, April 9). *Readying for the future: Covid-19, higher ed, and fairness*. Lumina Foundation.

Browning, M. H. E. M., Larson, L. R., Sharaievska, I., Rigolon, A., McAnirlin, O., Mullenbach, L., Cloutier, S., Vu, T. M., Thomsen, J., Reigner, N., Metcalf, E. C., D'Antonio, A., Helbich, M., Bratman, G. N., & Alvarez, H. O. (2021). Psychological impacts from COVID-19 among university students: Risk factors across seven states in the United States. *PLOS ONE*, *16*(1), e0245327, 1–27. https://doi.org/10.1371/journal.pone.0245327

Cataldi, E., Bennett, C., & Xianglei, C. (2018). *First-generation students: College access, persistence, and postbachelor's outcomes*. National Center for Educational Statistics. https://nces.ed.gov/pubs2018/2018421.pdf

Center for First-Generation Student Success. (2017, December 1). *First-generation students: Approaching enrollment, intersectional identities, & asset-based success.* https://firstgen.naspa.org/blog/first-generation-students-approaching-enrollment-intersectional-identities-and-asset-based-success

Clabaugh, A., Duque, J. F., & Fields, L. J. (2021). Academic stress and emotional well-being in United States college students following onset of the COVID-19 pandemic. *Frontiers in Psychology, 12*, 1–8. https://doi.org/10.3389/fpsyg.2021.628787

College Crisis Initiative (C2i). (2021). *Davidson College.* https://collegecrisis.shinyapps.io/dashboard/

Creswell, J. W., & Creswell, J. D. (2018). *Research design: qualitative, quantitative, and mixed methods approaches* (5th ed.). Sage.

Davis, C. R., Hartman, H., Turner, M., Norton, T., Sexton, J., Méndez, D., & Méndez, J. (2021). Listen to the feedback of students: First-generation college students voice inequalities in schooling brought on by the covid-19 pandemic. *Journal of College Student Retention: Research, Theory & Practice,* 152102512110663. https://doi.org/10.1177/15210251211066302

Deci, E. L., & Ryan, R. M. (2000). The "what" and "why" of goal pursuits: Human needs and the self-determination of behavior. *Psychological Inquiry, 11*(4), 227–268. https://doi.org/10.1207/s15327965pli1104_01

Dewa, L. H., Crandell, C., Choong, E., Jaques, J., Bottle, A., Kilkenny, C., Lawrence-Jones, A., Di Simplicio, M., Nicholls, D., & Aylin, P. (2021). CCopeY: A Mixed-methods coproduced study on the mental health status and coping strategies of young people during COVID-19 UK lockdown. *Journal of Adolescent Health, 68*(4), 666–675. https://doi.org/10.1016/j.jadohealth.2021.01.009

Farris, S. G., Kibbey, M. M., Fedorenko, E. J., & DiBello, A. M. (2021). A qualitative study of COVID-19 distress in university students. *Emerging Adulthood, 9*(5), 462–478. https://doi.org/10.1177/21676968211025128

Félix, S., de Lourdes, M., Ribeiro, I., Cunha, B., Ramalho, S., Vaz, A. R., Machado, P. P. P., & Conceição, E. (2021). A preliminary study on the psychosocial impact of COVID-19 lockdown in post-bariatric surgery women: the importance of eating behavior, health care access, and social support. *Current Psychology, 40*(12), 6275–6281. https://doi.org/10.1007/s12144-021-01529-6

Fetters, M. D. (2020). *The mixed methods research workbook: Activities for designing, implementing, and publishing projects.* Sage.

Folkman, S. (2010). *Stress, health, and coping: Synthesis, commentary, and future directions.* Oxford Handbooks Online. https://doi.org/10.1093/oxfordhb/9780195375343.013.0022

Frazier, P., Gabriel, A., Merians, A., & Lust, K. (2018). Understanding stress as an impediment to academic performance. *Journal of American College Health, 67*(6), 562–570. https://doi.org/10.1080/07448481.2018.1499649

Fruehwirth, J. C., Biswas, S., & Perreira, K. M. (2021). The covid-19 pandemic and mental health of first-year college students: Examining the effect of COVID-19 stressors using longitudinal data. *PLOS ONE, 16*(3), e0247999. https://doi.org/10.1371/journal.pone.0247999

Gibbons, M. M., Rhinehart, A., & Hardin, E. (2019). How first-generation college students adjust to College. *Journal of College Student Retention: Research, Theory & Practice*, *20*(4), 488–510. https://doi.org/10.1177/1521025116682035

Hagedorn, R. L., Wattick, R. A., & Olfert, M. D. (2021). "My entire world stopped": College students' psychosocial and academic frustrations during the COVID-19 pandemic. *Applied research in quality of life*, 1–22. https://doi.org/10.1007/s11482-021-09948-0

Halliburton, A. E., Hill, M. B., Dawson, B. L., Hightower, J. M., & Rueden, H. (2021). Increased stress, declining mental health: Emerging adults' experiences in college during COVID-19. *Emerging Adulthood*, *9*(5), 433–448. https://doi.org/10.1177/21676968211025348

House, L. A., Neal, C., & Kolb, J. (2019). Supporting the mental health needs of first generation college students. *Journal of College Student Psychotherapy*, *34*(2), 157–167. https://doi.org/10.1080/87568225.2019.1578940

Hoyt, L. T., Cohen, A. K., Dull, B., Maker Castro, E., & Yazdani, N. (2021). "Constant stress has become the new normal": Stress and Anxiety Inequalities Among U.S. College Students in the Time of COVID-19. *Journal of Adolescent Health*, *68*(2), 270–276. https://doi.org/10.1016/j.jadohealth.2020.10.030

Hubbard, K., Reohr, P., Tolcher, L., & Downs, A. (2018). Stress, mental health symptoms, and help-seeking in college students. *Psi Chi Journal of Psychological Research*, *23*(4), 293–305. https://doi-org.pallas2.tcl.sc.edu/10.24839/2325-7342.JN23.4.293

Johnson, N., Veletsianos, G., & Seaman, J. (2020). U.S. faculty and administrators' experiences and approaches in the early weeks of the COVID-19 pandemic. *Online Learning*, *24*(2), 6–21. https://doi.org/10.24059/olj.v24i2.2285

Stoddard, J., & Kaufman, J. (2020). *Coronavirus Impact Scale*. https://www.nlm.nih.gov/dr2/Coronavirus_Impact_Scale.pdf

Kaur, J., Chow, E., Ravenhurst, J., Snyder, T., Pennell, S., Lover, A. A., & Goff, S. L. (2022). Considerations for meeting students' mental health needs at a U.S. university during the covid-19 pandemic: A qualitative study. *Frontiers in Public Health*, *10*. https://doi.org/10.3389/fpubh.2022.815031

Kecojevic, A., Basch, C. H., Sullivan, M., & Davi, N. K. (2020). The impact of the COVID-19 epidemic on mental health of undergraduate students in New Jersey, cross-sectional study. *PLOS ONE*, *15*(9), e0239696, 1–16. https://doi.org/10.1371/journal.pone.0239696

Klein, P., Ivanjek, L., Dahlkemper, M., Jeličić, K., Geyer, M. A., Kü□hemann, S., & Susac, A. (2021). Studying physics during the COVID-19 pandemic: Student assessments of learning achievement, perceived effectiveness of online recitations, and online laboratories. *Physical Review Physics Education Research*, *17*(1), 010117-1-010117–11. https://doi.org/10.1103/physrevphyseducres.17.010117

Lazarus, R. S., & Folkman, S. (1984). *Stress, appraisal, and coping*. Springer.

Lederer, A. M., Hoban, M. T., Lipson, S. K., Zhou, S., & Eisenberg, D. (2020). More than inconvenienced: The unique needs of U.S. college students during the Covid-19 pandemic. *Health Education & Behavior, 48*(1), 14–19. https://doi.org/10.1177/1090198120969372

Lee, J., & Jang, S. (2015). An exploration of stress and satisfaction in college students. *Services Marketing Quarterly, 36*(3), 245–260. https://doi.org/10.1080/15332969.2015.1046774

Lee, J., Solomon, M., Stead, T., Kwon, B., & Ganti, L. (2021). Impact of COVID-19 on the mental health of U.S. college students. *BMC Psychology, 9*(1). https://doi.org/10.1186/s40359-021-00598-3

Leebens, P. K., & Williamson, E. D. (2017). Developmental psychopathology: Risk and resilience in the transition to young adulthood. *Child and Adolescent Psychiatric Clinics of North America, 26*(2), 143–156. https://doi.org/10.1016/j.chc.2016.12.001

Lemay, D. J., Bazelais, P., & Doleck, T. (2021). Transition to online learning during the COVID-19 pandemic. *Computers in Human Behavior Reports, 4*, 100130. https://doi.org/10.1016/j.chbr.2021.100130

Machado, P. P. P., Pinto-Bastos, A., Ramos, R., Rodrigues, T. F., Louro, E., Gonçalves, S., Brandão, I., & Vaz, A. (2020). Impact of COVID-19 lockdown measures on a cohort of eating disorders patients. *Journal of Eating Disorders, 8*(1). https://doi.org/10.1186/s40337-020-00340-1

Masten, A. S. (2014). *Ordinary magic: Resilience in development.* Guilford Press.

Molock, S. D., & Parchem, B. (2021). The impact of COVID-19 on college students from communities of color. *Journal of American College Health*, 1–7. https://doi.org/10.1080/07448481.2020.1865380

Moody, J. (2021, August 12). *Colleges requiring a coronavirus vaccine for fall.* U.S. News and World Report. https://www.usnews.com/education/best-colleges/articles/colleges-requiring-a-coronavirus-vaccine-for-fall-what-to-know

National Center for Education Statistics (NCES). (2018, February). *First-generation students college access, persistence, and post bachelor's outcomes.* https://nces.ed.gov/pubs2018/2018421.pdf

National Institutes of Health (NIH). (2021). *National Public Health Emergency and Disaster Research Response.* https://dr2.nlm.nih.gov/

National Student Clearinghouse Research Center. (2022, January 13). *Current term enrollment estimates.* https://nscresearchcenter.org/current-term-enrollment-estimates/

Nworie, J. (2021, May 19). Beyond COVID-19: What's next for online teaching and learning in higher education? *EDUCAUSE.* https://er.educause.edu/articles/2021/5/beyond-covid-19-whats-next-for-online-teaching-and-learning-in-higher-education

Pascoe, M. C., Hetrick, S. E., & Parker, A. G. (2019). The impact of stress on students in secondary school and higher education. *International Journal of Adolescence and Youth, 25*(1), 104–112. https://doi.org/10.1080/02673843.2019.1596823

Patterson, Z. R., Gabrys, R. L., Prowse, R. K., Abizaid, A. B., Hellemans, K. G. C., & McQuaid, R. J. (2021). The influence of COVID-19 on stress, substance use, and mental health among postsecondary students. *Emerging Adulthood, 9*(5), 516–530. https://doi.org/10.1177/21676968211014080

Plano Clark, V., & Ivankova, N. (2016).*Mixed methods research: A guide to the field.* Sage. https://doi: 10.4135/9781483398341

Pratt, I. S., Harwood, H. B., Cavazos, J. T., & Ditzfeld, C. P. (2017). Should I stay or should I go? Retention in first-generation college students. *Journal of College Student Retention: Research, Theory & Practice, 21*(1), 105–118. https://doi.org/10.1177/1521025117690868

Priestley, M., Broglia, E., Hughes, G., & Spanner, L. (2021). Student perspectives on improving mental health support services at university. *Counselling and Psychoptherapy Research, 22*(1), 197–206. https://doi.org/10.1002/capr.12391

Radunzel, J. (2018). Examining retention and transfer in relation to incoming student data for first-generation and continuing-generation students: What differences exist? *Journal of College Student Retention: Research, Theory & Practice, 23*(2), 214–242. https://doi.org/10.1177/1521025118813516

Reyes-Portillo, J. A., Masia Warner, C., Kline, E. A., Bixter, M. T., Chu, B. C., Miranda, R., Nadeem, E., Nickerson, A., Ortin Peralta, A., Reigada, L., Rizvi, S. L., Roy, A. K., Shatkin, J., Kalver, E., Rette, D., Denton, E. G., & Jeglic, E. L. (2022). The psychological, academic, and economic impact of COVID-19 on college students in the epicenter of the pandemic. *Emerging Adulthood, 10*(2), 473–490. https://doi.org/10.1177/21676968211066657

Rodríguez-Planas, N. (2022). Hitting where it hurts most: COVID-19 and low-income urban college students. *Economics of Education Review, 87*, 1–8. https://doi.org/10.1016/j.econedurev.2022.102233

RTI International. (2019). *First year experience, persistence, and attainment of first-generation college students.* NASPA. https://firstgen.naspa.org/files/dmfile/FactSheet-02.pdf

Ryan, R. M., & Deci, E. L. (2020). Intrinsic and extrinsic motivation from a self-determination theory perspective. Definitions, theory, practices, and future directions. *Contemporary Educational Psychology*, 61. https://doi.org/10.1016/j.cedpsych.2020.101860

Saldaña, J. (2013). *The coding manual for qualitative researchers* (3rd ed.). Sage.

Sirrine, E. H., Kliner, O., & Gollery, T. J. (2021). College student experiences of grief and loss amid the COVID-19 global pandemic. *OMEGA – Journal of Death and Dying*, 003022282110274, 745–764. https://doi.org/10.1177/00302228211027461

Son, C., Hegde, S., Smith, A., Wang, X., & Sasangohar, F. (2020). Effects of COVID-19 on college students' mental health in the United States: Interview survey study. *Journal of Medical Internet Research, 22*(9), e21279. https://doi.org/10.2196/21279

Soria, K. M., Horgos, B., Chirikov, I., & Jones-White, D. (2020). *First-generation students' experiences during the COVID-19 pandemic*. SERU Consortium, University of California—Berkeley and University of Minnesota. https://escholarship.org/content/qt19d5c0ht/supp/First-Generation_Students.pdf

Soria, K. M., & Stebleton, M. J. (2012). First-generation students' academic engagement and retention. *Teaching in Higher Education, 17*(6), 673–685. https://doi.org/10.1080/13562517.2012.666735

Stebleton, M. J., Soria, K. M., & Huesman, R.L.(2014), First-generation students' sense of belonging, mental health, and use of counseling services at public research universities. *Journal of College Counseling, 17*, 6–20. https://doi.org/10.1002/j.2161-1882.2014.00044.x

Stoddard, J., & Kaufman, J. (2020). *Coronavirus Impact Scale*. https://www.nlm.nih.gov/dr2/Coronavirus_Impact_Scale.pdf

The College Crisis Initiative (C2i). (2021). *Davidson College*. https://collegecrisis.shinyapps.io/dashboard/

Toutkoushian, R. K., May-Trifiletti, J. A., & Clayton, A. B. (2019). From "first in family" to "first to finish": Does college graduation vary by how first-generation college status is defined? *Educational Policy, 35*(3), 481–521. https://doi.org/10.1177/0895904818823753

Unger, S., & Meiran, W. (2020). Student attitudes towards online education during the covid-19 viral outbreak of 2020: Distance learning in a time of social distance. *International Journal of Technology in Education and Science, 4*(4), 256–266. https://doi.org/10.46328/ijtes.v4i4.107

Wang, C., Pan, R., Wan, X., Tan, Y., Xu, L., McIntyre, R. S., Choo, F. N., Tran, B., Ho, R., Sharma, V. K., & Ho, C. (2020). A longitudinal study on the mental health of general population during the COVID-19 epidemic in China. *Brain Behavior and Immunity, 87*, 40–48. https://doi.org/10.1016/j.bbi.2020.04.02

Yee, A. (2016). The unwritten rules of engagement: Social class differences in undergraduates' academic strategies. *The Journal of Higher Education, 87*(6), 831–858. https://doi.org/10.1353/jhe.2016.0031

ENDNOTES

1. Collection of information regarding personal diagnosis of COVID-19 was removed to protect health privacy.
2. Data was collected as part of a larger research project on academic emotions; here we focus on responses related to the impact of COVID.
3. Survey was administered to different group of participants in fall and sprin

CHAPTER 7

THE IMPACT OF THE COVID-19 PANDEMIC ON FIRST-GENERATION UNDERGRADUATE STUDENTS' PARTICIPATION IN CAMPUS ACTIVITIES

Victoria Sherif, Jean A. Patterson, and Chelsea Redger-Marquardt
Wichita State University

ABSTRACT

This chapter, which is part of a larger study focused on the role of campus involvement in first-generation undergraduate students' leadership and academic achievement, presents findings on the impact of the COVID-19 pandemic on first generation students' current and future participation in campus activities. The average student reported being only occasionally involved in campus activities. Overall, students expressed having fewer campus participation opportunities during the pandemic. Traditional age first-generation students (18–23) felt the pandemic affected their involvement

Examining the Cognitive and Psychological Effects of the COVID-19 Global Pandemic on High School, College, and Graduate Learners, pp. 139–169

more so than adult learners (24+), who were less likely to be involved even before the pandemic. Campus involvement is important for student success; thus, university administrators need to be cognizant of ways to encourage first-generation students to become involved in campus life.

Keywords: first-generation undergraduate students, student leadership,

student engagement, campus activities

The COVID-19 pandemic has radically shifted the nature of educational systems worldwide, especially institutions of higher education. During the 2019–2020 academic year, approximately 12 million full-time college students were impacted by the novel virus (IPEDS, 2020). In response to the global pandemic to ensure public health and safety, traditional classroom education was moved into the distance learning environment (UNESCO, 2020; U.S. Department of Education, 2020).

The shift from a traditional to distance approach to education has affected various aspects of student experiences, including academic performance, social interactions and relationships, finances and financial security, and mental health (Hamlin & Barney, 2022; Huckins et al., 2020; Luo et al., 2017; Marinoni, 2020; Neuwirth et al., 2021; Reyes-Portillo, 2022; Salta et al., 2021). Indeed, multiple recent studies have reported that the COVID-19 pandemic has had adverse effects on students' academic success and academic expectations, especially among students from disadvantaged backgrounds (Aucejo et al., 2020; Limniou et al., 2021; Lederer et al., 2021; Tejedor et al., 2020; Rodríguez-Planas, 2020). Research conducted by Aucejo et al. (2020), Lee et al. (2021), and Rodríguez-Planas (2022) found that due to the pandemic, academic performance significantly decreased among top-performing low-income and first-generation student groups. The semester GPA of these student groups was expected to be lower by 30%. Also, nearly 50% of low-income and first-generation students were predicted to take a gap year leading to the delay in their graduation (Rodríguez-Planas, 2022). Likewise, students of color along with students who had someone close to them test positive for COVID-19 had increased probability of reporting a decrease in their achievement score (Kimaru et al., 2023).

The achievement gap between traditional and underrepresented students also partly attributed to limited socialization and networking opportunities worsened by the pandemic (Mishra, 2020). Many college students reported feeling isolated and strained (Vaterlaus et al., 2021). Consequently, the lack of physical, social interaction and presence in classrooms and on campus influenced students' engagement and led to a sense of isolation and disconnect, thus resulting in a high dropout rate for online learners (Bawa, 2016; Jaggars, 2011). Although friendships among undergraduate college students and their social interactions with instructors deteriorated, there was a reported improvement in romantic relationships among students and intergenerational relationships between students and their families (Goodwin et al., 2020; Herbenick et al., 2020; Lindberg et al., 2020). According to Gallegos et al. (2020), the latter was found to decrease students' stress levels, substance misuse, and overall negative impact of COVID-19 changes.

In addition to strained interpersonal relationships with peers and educators due to the pandemic, undergraduate students experienced job loss or reduced working hours (Aucejo et al., 2020; Birmingham et al., 2021; Gewalt et al., 2022). Prior to COVID-19, 54% of full-time undergraduate students were employed on campus (National Center for Education Statistics, 2022). During the pandemic, universities and colleges across the United States, Germany, and China implemented cost-cutting strategies including student job cuts (Gewalt et al., 2022; Kocsis, 2020; Raaper & Brown, 2020; Zheng et al., 2022). Substantial campus-based job loss for students and their families elevated students' financial hardship (Lederer et al., 2021). Sudden loss of household income increased worries about losing housing (Jones et al., 2021) and increased anxiety, stress, and concern for graduation and future career success (Hamlin & Barney, 2022; Gonzalez-Ramirez et al., 2021).

These disruptions in students' academic, social, and financial aspects of their lives adversely impacted mental health, resulting in an exacerbation of preexisting mental health risks. Prior to the pandemic, research recorded an elevation in depression, anxiety, stress, and suicidality among undergraduate students (Chen et al., 2019; Cornish et al., 2017; Eisenberg et al., 2013; Lipson et al., 2019; Liu et al., 2019). Current literature indicates tremendously worsened trends in students' mental well-being, associating COVID-19 with elevated stress, depression, restless sleep, difficulties coping, frustration, worry, and hopelessness (Birmingham et al., 2021; Reyes-Portillo et al., 2022; Son et al., 2020). A study conducted by Browning et al. (2022) predicted that being a woman between 18 and 24 years of age, having poor general health, having a screen time for more than 8 hours per day, and knowing someone impacted by COVID-19 caused elevated mental health challenges. This worsening in anxiety and depression coupled with decreased connection in peer support systems and sense of belonging to campus resulted in lowered academic achievement (Hu et al., 2022; Son et al., 2020) and heightened risk for mood disorders and suicidal behaviors (Conrad et al., 2021; Reyes-Portillo et al., 2022).

While research reports the negative impact of the pandemic on student mental health, socialization, and academic achievement and engagement in learning (Lee et al., 2021; Mucci-Ferris et al., 2021; Potts, 2021; Vaterlaus et al., 2021; Salta et al., 2022; Wester et al., 2021; Wu & Teets, 2021), it fails to inform the role of COVID-19 on student on-campus engagement. Furthermore, the literature focuses predominantly on traditional, underrepresented racial minority, or low-income undergraduate students, paying little attention to students from non-traditional backgrounds (i.e., first-generation) (Davis et al., 2021; Soria et al., 2020). First-generation college students (FGCS) are those whose parent(s)/guardian(s) have not attained a bachelor's degree from a college or university (Gibbons & Woodside, 2014; Stuber, 2011). Between 30% and 50% of all undergraduate students nationwide are considered first generation college students (Cataldi et al., 2018; Redford & Mulvaney Hoyer, 2017). Data collected in the 2015–16 academic year noted Whites (46%) comprised the highest percentage of FGCS, followed by Hispanic/Latinx (25%), Black (18%), Asian (6%), and students of other races (5%) (Center for First-Generation Student Success, 2018).

Despite these isolated characteristics, the term FGCS is inclusive and represents an overlap of multiple identities (Bettencourt et al., 2020; Garriott et al., 2021; Goldstein & Lopez, 2021; Ngyen & Ngyen, 2018; Tevis & Griffen, 2014). According to Collins (2015), intersecting identities capture race, gender, class, sexuality, ethnicity, nation, ability, and age as co-constructing phenomena. Often, FGCS are found to be from underrepresented populations, lower socioeconomic background, and of older age (Engle & Tinto, 2008; Ives & Castillo-Montoya, 2020; Jackson et al., 2022; Ngyen & Ngyen, 2018; Santa-Ramirez et al., 2022).

Higher education is responding to the increased presence of FGCS on their campuses by providing academic and social supports to improve their retention and persistence to degree completion (Whitley et al., 2018). Much of the literature on FGCS, however, tends to be deficit-oriented; it highlights the challenges and obstacles these students confront, such as lack of college readiness, financial instability, limited family support, and issues with social integration on the college campus (Engle, 2007; Falcon, 2015; Mehta et al., 2011; Stebleton & Soria, 2013). Despite university efforts to support FGCS, they retain a marginalized status on campus (Stuber, 2011). FGCS also tend not to be involved in campus activities (Patterson et al., 2021).

As campus involvement plays a positive role in student leadership and academic achievement of traditional students (Astin, 1993; Day, 2017; Dugan & Komives, 2010; Kulp et al., 2021; Riutta & Teodorescu, 2014; Roddenberry, 2017; Rosch & Stephens, 2017; Thomas et al., 2021; Vetter et al., 2019), there is a critical need to better understand how FGCS' campus involvement were supported and sustained in general and the context of the COVID-19 pandemic. If colleges and universities are committed to providing support for FGCS to successfully complete their bachelor's degrees, it is important to clarify if these students engage in campus life and, if so, how. This chapter emerged as a result of a larger survey-based study aimed to explore the impact of student engagement on leadership and academic achievement of undergraduate FGCS. In the context of this chapter, we explored the following research question: What are the perspectives of undergraduate FGCS on the impact of COVID-19 in their participation in campus activities? As follows, we are to present findings pertaining to FGCS' involvement in campus activities during and post-pandemic. The findings revealed occasional involvement in campus activities prior to the pandemic, with even fewer opportunities for extra-curricular learning and networking during the pandemic. Participation in campus activities among traditional age FGCS was impacted the most.

STUDENT INVOLVEMENT

Student involvement through campus activities plays a critical role in creating campus community, connecting co-curricular programming, and fostering student development and learning. College campuses have continuously sought increased student involvement in campus activities and leadership opportunities. In addition, campus activities offer extensive learning experiences available through clubs, student government, involvement activities, and organizations. Increased involvement on campus is valued, as scholarly literature has consistently demonstrated the critical role of involvement in overall student development and success.

The impact of student involvement in campus activities on overall student development is observed in such areas as student leadership, improved learning, persistence in completing a college degree, and psychosocial well-being. According to Astin (1999), the student engagement in social and academic aspects of higher education fosters positive student experience and learning. The greater student involvement in college, the greater will be personal development, academic achievement, and professional readiness (Astin, 1993; Zhou, 2017).

Involvement in campus activities significantly increases the development of professional skills (Bowden et., 2021; Nash et al., 1973). Student involvement enhances self-esteem, self-confidence, interpersonal, and leadership skills (Pascarella & Terenzini, 1991; Rosch & Collins, 2017). As highlighted by Rosch and Collins (2017), highly engaged students often experience the improvement in their leadership self-efficacy, motivation to lead, and leadership capacity. Furthermore, students who are active in campus activities acquire extensive experience in collective decision-making, communication with peers, conflict resolution, innovation, and organizational management (Griffith & Dunham, 2015).

Equally important, academic achievement and retention are the ultimate products of involvement as they indicate that the student was active and engaged in curricular and extracurricular opportunities to the extent of degree completion and graduation (Tinto, 2017). Specifically, involvement of undergraduate students on college has been linked to improved learning outcomes (Garland, 2010; Hyer, 2019; Mitchell et al., 2015; Moore et al., 1998; Ullah & Wilson, 2007) and persistence and retention (Finn, 2006; Kuh et al., 2008; Moreira et al., 2013; Zhou, 2017). Student involvement is also associated with increased student academic achievement (Carini et al., 2006; Finn & Rock, 1997; Kuh, 2009). Participation in campus activities translates into improved social skills and leads to increased engagement in classroom and support systems (Kimbark et al., 2017). In addition, time management and decision making learned while participating in campus activities are linked to improved study skills (Fowler & Boylan, 2010). It has a positive relationship with goal orientation (Bakker et al., 2015), self-regulation (Cho & Kim, 2013), and motivation (Oga-Baldwin & Nakata, 2017). The extent to which each of one of these skills is developed through campus participation predisposes the student for success in learning, positive interaction with faculty, and reliable peer support system.

As participation in campus activities is marked by tremendous personal and professional growth, it is also linked to psychosocial well-being (Knifsend, 2020; Martin, 2000). Academic and extracurricular programs are impactful for students in interpersonal skill development, self-confidence, and self-awareness (Clark et al., 2015) and, as a result, benefit student psychosocial and mental health (Kilgo et al., 2016). According to Busseri et al. (2006) and Buckley and Lee (2021), the amount of time spent on activities across campus is related with the positive psychosocial outcomes including sense of belonging, lowered anxiety, and increased quality of friendships.

Although there are numerous definitions of student involvement, scholars agree that student involvement is a complex, multidimensional, and broad construct comprising emotional and behavioral aspects (Appleton et al., 2008; Ben-Eliyahu et al., 2018; Eccles, 2016; Fredricks & McColskey, 2012; Kahu, 2013). Specifically, emotional involvement pertains to emotional reactions and relationships with and within an educational organization, including enjoyment of being involved, interest in involvement, and positive attitude towards involvement. Behavioral involvement, on the contrary, refers to active participation in college activities, positive conduct and behavior in learning and interactions with peers and instructors, along with intentional effort and observable action employed to participate on campus (Bond et al., 2020).

For the current study and chapter, as it is hardly possible to comprehensively examine every aspect of the student involvement construct

(Kahu, 2013), it was important to begin with a clear definition of student involvement (Boekaerts, 2016; Solomonides, 2013). The understanding adheres to a common definition of student involvement by Astin (1993, 1999) and Kuh (2001, 2008, 2009): the amount of time and effort students devote to on-campus activities that contribute to students' positive college experiences, desired academic and social outcomes, and the intentional institutional programming available for student involvement. In this light, both students and colleges play an active role in designing educationally purposeful campus activities. In addition, according to Komives (2019), higher education institutions are responsible for ensuring that student involvement is mutually beneficial to the student and the college community.

FIRST-GENERATION COLLEGE STUDENTS

Students who are first in their family to pursue an undergraduate degree comprise one third of the U.S. college-attending student body (Whitley et al., 2018). These first-generation students begin their academic journey with a number of skills that help them succeed in college (Gillen-O'Neel, 2021; Jehangir, 2010). For instance, FGCS have high levels of academic intrinsic motivation (Brookover et al., 2021). According to Orbe (2004), being a FGCS is motivating in itself. Similarly, research conducted by Wang (2014) indicated that many FGCS are motivated internally and by their family members to pursue their academic goals and serve as role models for their siblings. Further study (Vega, 2016) revealed that motivation to excel in college was instilled at a young age.

Strongly correlated with student motivation (Brooks et al., 2012), FGCS show resilience. In a study by Brookover et al. (2021), FGCS navigated the stressors of college enrollment and academics in part due to their self-direction, sense of ownership, and self-determination. FGCS resilience was also observed through setting and meeting academic goals, seeking out needed academic support and resources, and taking a responsibility for their academic success.

In addition to high motivation and resilience, positive attitudes and dispositions of FGCS foster their success in college. Demetriou et al. (2017) found that these students were flexible and willing to adapt to a new academic and social environment of higher education, felt independent, and perceived challenges as opportunities for growth. Along with these dispositions, positive risk-taking fostered students' coping with challenges, setting of academic and career goals, development of autonomy, and solidifying their occupational identities.

Current systems of higher education, however, are not always set up to foster FGCS success. Despite having personal assets, FGCS also face unique challenges in college, including lower graduation, financial constraints, limited available cultural and social capital, and extracurricular engagement (Stebleton & Soria, 2013). As institutions of higher education face pressure to expand enrollments and retain students from diverse and underserved backgrounds, they find it particularly difficult to graduate FGCS (Lowery-Hart & Pacheco, 2011; Phipps, 2020). Statistics show that there is a significant gap in postsecondary attendance for FGCS comparing to their traditional peers (Redford & Mulvaney Hoyer, 2017). For examples, only six percent of FGCS first attended 4-year postsecondary institutions comparing to 28% of continuing-generation peers. Furthermore, only 27% of undergraduate FGCS will attain their college degree within four years (Whitley et al., 2018) in comparison to 62.3% of continuing-generation students, whose parent(s) attended college (National Student Clearinghouse Research Center, 2022).

Along with the lower enrollment and graduation rates, several other differences are found between FGCS and their continuing-generation peers. These differences are interconnected and often hinder FGCS' academic success and degree attainment. For instance, FGCS are more likely to have more work responsibilities, and a lower socioeconomic status (Garcia, 2010; Saenz et al., 2007), educational aspirations, and social capital (Evans et al., 2020; Ward et al., 2012).

In addition, these students are to experience more academic challenges when comparing to other student groups, including limited academic preparation (Balemian & Feng, 2013; Borrero, 2011; Falcon, 2015; Majer, 2009; Martinez at al., 2009; Strand, 2013). Increased academic workload frequently causes stress due to the need for time management (Conley & Hamlin, 2009; Magallanes, 2020). That, coupled with limited financial resources, negatively impacts FGCS academic effectiveness and degree completion. As research has shown, these students tend to work more and study less than their non-first-generation peers due to financial resources and knowledge, family dependence on their income, and feasibility of college cost (Chen, 2005; Pascarella et al., 2004; Rehr et al., 2022).

The scarce pre-pandemic literature on FGCS on-campus engagement also suggests that these students tend to be less engaged overall and less likely to participate in diverse campus activities (Frederick et al., 2018; Pike et al., 2009). FGCS have been found to have consistently lower social involvement and academic engagement (Lundberg et al., 2007; Pike et al., 2003) and lower sense of belonging (Stebleton et al., 2014) compared to their continuing-generation peers. According to the Center for First-Generation Student Success (2018), only 46% of FGCS participated in extra-curricular clubs compared to 65% of continuing-generation students.

Gaps in on-campus involvement persist with FGCS progression throughout college. In research conducted by Pike et al. (2011) and Terenzini et al. (1996) first-year FGCS had lower levels of engagement with collaborative learning, faculty, and extracurricular activities. Pascarella et al. (2004) also reported limited engagement of second- and third-year students as it pertained to activities outside of classroom. Research by Pike et al. (2011) further highlighted limited interactions between senior FGCS and their peers, faculty, and staff related to enriching educational and social experiences. It was revealed that FGCS are less likely to participate in learning communities, research projects with faculty, capstone experience, and internship opportunities (National Survey of Student Engagement, 2017).

As FGCS tend to perceive the college environment as less supportive due to their employment and financial obligations, progressing through college and making meaningful connections with their peers outside of classroom continue to be restricted (D'Amico & Dika, 2013; Moschetti & Hudley, 2015; Pascarella et al., 2004). This limited involvement on campus (Fischer, 2007; Gibson & Slate, 2010) negatively impacts FGCS motivation to engage and participate in service-learning or leadership programs (Pulliam & Sasso, 2016). As colleges and universities continue to enroll new FGCS students and strive to support current FGCS on their pathway to success, there is a need for better understanding and addressing of FGCS involvement considering its impact on persistence, resilience, motivation, professional preparation, academic outcomes, and social relationships among continuing-generation students as discussed above. With institutions of higher education navigating the post-pandemic educational terrain, examining FGCS on-campus participation and the impact of the COVID-19 pandemic could inform the extent of FGCS involvement overall and identify the areas in need of improvement in supporting and fostering these students' engagement.

METHODS AND PARTICIPANTS

This study employed a survey-based approach. The survey was designed to include three sections: student involvement, student leadership, and student demographics. The student demographics section consisted of multiple-choice questions pertaining to student year in college, area of study, age, race, student status (i.e., online, transfer, traditional, etc.), living arrangement, and gender with nonbinary options. The leadership section of the survey aimed to explore respondents' level of agreement with statements pertaining to student knowledge of leadership, motivation to learn about and practice leadership, attitudes towards leadership development and practice, and experiences as leaders (Sherif, 2018, 2019).

The student involvement section of the survey was comprised of Likert scale and multiple choice-type items examining student current and prior involvement in campus activities, types of activities involved, nature of involvement/role (i.e., participant of activity on campus, member of planning team, and leader of planning team), and the extent to which the pandemic impacted student involvement (Komives, 2019; NACA, 2021). The scale was piloted with undergraduate continuing-generation students. Individual interviews were conducted with survey respondents to determine questions' relevance, clarity, appropriateness of wording, scale length, applicability of response choices, and potential response errors. In addition, we evaluated the questionnaire flow, adequacy of instruction, trustworthiness, and timeliness of survey completion (Hatry et al., 1998; Nardi, 2006; Saris & Gallhofer, 2007). Upon administering the survey to the sample group, the calculated value for Cronbach's Alpha was $\alpha = .94$ ($N = 28$).

The study was conducted at a 4-year public Midwestern teaching university. The reported enrollment of FGCS for fall 2020 was 4,206 students, who accounted for 45% of its undergraduate population. This conducted study was funded by National Association for Campus Activities and approved by the Institutional Review Board. The contact information (i.e., email addresses) of prospective respondents was obtained through the university registrar. The survey was distributed in spring 2021 to the overall university's FGCS population via Qualtrics. The respondent pool was adjusted to 4,173 to reflect inapplicability, opted out population, bounced and failed email addresses, etc. The survey was completed by 862 students with the overall response rate of 20.7%. Participation in the study was incentivized by offering $25 gift card through random drawing.

Descriptive and inferential statistics were employed to analyze the data in SPSS (v.28). The majority of respondents identified themselves as female (71.3%, $n = 556$), 26.5% identified as male ($n = 207$), and 1.0% ($n = 8$) selected "Other" gender category. Nine respondents "preferred not to say." They were predominantly White/Caucasian (56.0%, $n = 437$), followed by Asian (9.7%, $n = 76$) and Black or African American (6.9%, n=54); the "Other race" category was selected by 12.9% ($n = 101$). Over half of the respondents were between 18 and 23 years of age (traditional) (60.9%, $n = 473$), with 38.9% ($n = 302$) being 24 years old and older (adult learners).

The sample was represented by 16.6% ($n = 127$) first-year (freshman), 18.8% ($n = 144$) second-year (sophomore), 27.3% ($n = 209$) third-year (junior), and 34.2% ($n = 292$) fourth-year (senior) students. The sample was representative of students pursuing an undergraduate degree in education and social studies (23.8%, $n = 186$), liberal arts (22.3%, $n = 174$), health professions (20.4%, $n = 159$), engineering and STEM (16.0%, $n = 125$), and business and communication (15.6%, $n = 122$). The average GPA score was 3.2 (n = 691, SD = 0.61). The background of the respondents was representative of the university's overall FGCS population. These data and background characteristics also reflected the national demographic trends (Cataldi et al., 2018; Center for First-Generation Student Success, 2018).

FINDINGS

Participation on Campus

FGCS participants were asked to indicate the extent of their involvement in campus activities on a 4-point Likert scale ranging from (1) "I am not involved in any campus activities" to (4) "I have been involved in campus activities in the past but not at this moment." The results indicated that respondents were occasionally involved in campus activities (M = 1.73, SD = .93). Interestingly, slightly over 50% of respondents regardless of race, gender, and age reported not participating in any campus activities (52.7%, n = 452). Active current involvement in campus activities was reported predominantly by students who identified as African American (17.5%, n = 10), female (11.9%, n = 102), and traditional (17.8%; n = 84). Students representing liberal arts (32.5; n = 33) and engineering/STEM professions (26.5%; n = 27) reported being most actively involved. Responses pertaining to the current on-campus involvement were equally distributed among first-, second-, third-, and fourth-year students.

Respondents were also asked to identify student engagement activities they were part of on campus. Educational events (i.e., workshops, invited guest lectures, etc.) were reported by 18.6% (n = 160) followed by social and hobby-based clubs (i.e., book clubs, theater, etc.) (18.1%, n = 156) and multicultural activities (i.e., multicultural fairs, multicultural discussion groups, diversity parades, etc.) (11.8%, n = 102). Being a member of fraternity/sorority organizations was reported by 8.9% of students (n = 77). Interestingly, students who identified as African American (28.1%, n = 16) or Asian (25.0%, n = 19) predominately participated in multicultural activities, while respondents who identified as White were mainly engaged in educational events (18.3%, n = 80). The responses also varied by gender, with male participants being mostly involved with social and hobby-based clubs (23.2%, n = 48) and female participants being mostly involved in educational events (19.8%, n = 110). Traditional students were mostly involved with social and hobby clubs (23.7%, n = 111) compared to 15.2% (n = 46) of adult learners who reported their active participation was in educational events. A shift in interest in campus activities was noted among first-, second-, third-, and fourth-year students (see Table 7.1), where freshmen were mainly interested in participating in hobby/

social clubs and residence hall activities, and sophomore, junior, and senior students were more actively involved in educational events and social clubs. Participation in professional events was reported the highest among fourth-year students.

Table 7.1

Involvement in Campus Activities by Year in College (Top 4 Activities)

Activity	Year in College			
	Freshman	Sophomore	Junior	Senior
	n	*n*	*n*	*n*
Hobby/ Social Club	29	23	42	49
Residence Hall Activities	17	9	15	18
Educational Events	18	29	48	54
Multicultural Events	10	23	26	33
Professional Events	7	9	20	32

The capacity in which respondents participated in past and current on-campus activities described above varied. Slightly over half of students (53.6%, $n = 462$) reported being a participant, followed by 34.7% ($n = 299$) of students who served as a member of an event/activity planning team and 25.5% ($n = 220$) who were leading named activities. No variation in reported capacities was found based on race, gender, and age. However, respondents' involvement was moderately positively related with their on-campus involvement as a leader of student-centered activities ($r(220) = .31, p = < .001$) (see Table 7.2). The respondents who were actively involved on campus often indicated taking a leadership role in enrichment activities.

Respondents' current involvement on campus also had a moderate positive relationship with their involvement in planning of campus activities as a leader in the future ($r(855) = .38, p = < .001$). This finding suggests that those who led student-focused activities had a stronger interest in continuing in their leadership role in activity planning. Furthermore, a moderate positive relationship was found between being a participant in events/activities and their planning ($r(296) = .5, p = < .001$) and between being a participant and leading events/activities ($r(220) = .5, p = < .001$). Planning events/activities also had a positive strong relationship with serving as a leader of named activities ($r(211) = .8, p = < .001$).

Table 7.2

Association* Between Agreement Ratings Pertaining to Involvement Capacity

Survey Item	*"I have been actively involved in campus activities"*	*"I would be interested in participating in planning of campus activities as a leader"*
"I have been actively involved on campus as a leader of planning team"	0.31	0.8
"I would be interested in participating in planning of campus activities as a leader"	0.38	1
"I have been actively involved on campus as a participant of planning team"	1	0.5

Note. $*p < 0.01$. Only significant correlations were displayed.

COVID-19 Pandemic and Student Involvement

Survey respondents were asked if the COVID-19 pandemic impacted student participation in campus activities on a Likert scale from (1) "Strongly Disagree" to (5) "Strongly Agree." The results indicated that the respondents were neutral about the COVID-19 impact on their on-campus involvement ($M = 3.4$, $SD = 1.3$). However, nearly half of the respondents agreed and strongly agreed that COVID-19 impacted their participation in campus activities (50.4%, $n = 457$), whereas 22.1% ($n = 189$) indicated no impact of COVID-19 on their campus involvement. The highest level of agreement on the COVID-19 impact on student involvement was found among traditional (60.3%, $n = 285$), Asian (56.5%, $n = 43$), first-year (47.5%; $n = 48$) and fourth-year (35.6%; $n = 79$) students compared to participating adult learners (34.4%, $n = 104$) who had the lowest rating of "Agree" and "Strongly Agree." No statistically significant relationship was found between students' year in school, field of study, and the agreement rating of the impact of COVID-19 on student involvement.

Those respondents who were impacted by the COVID-19 pandemic reported being impacted mainly as a participant (67.0%, $n = 447$) and a leader (21.1%, $n = 141$). They also indicated having fewer extracurricular learning opportunities due to the pandemic (43.9%, $n = 293$). In addition, 19.6% ($n = 169$) reported being most involved on campus before the global pandemic.

Interestingly, as shown in Table 7.3, there was a positive moderate relationship between student pre-pandemic participation in campus activities and the ratings of impact of the pandemic on student current participation ($r(666) = .24, p = < .001$). The participants who were actively engaged in campus activities before global "shutdown" had a stronger sense of agreement about the negative impact of COVID-19 on their current on-campus involvement. Furthermore, student age negatively moderately correlated with the level of agreement on the COVID-19 impact on student involvement on campus ($r(776) = -.28, p = < .001$). Specifically, older students were less likely to report the negative impact of COVID-19 on their participation on campus, which is also reflected in the findings discussed above.

Table 7.3

Association* Between Agreement Ratings Pertaining to Participation in Campus Activities

Survey Item	*"The COVID-19 pandemic impacted my involvement on campus"*	*"Please indicate your interest in being involved in campus activities"*
"I have been actively involved in campus activities"	0.24	0.38
Age	–0.28	–0.36
"The COVID-19 pandemic impacted my involvement on campus"	1	0.28

Note. *$p < 0.01$. Only significant correlations were displayed.

When respondents were asked about future participation in campus activities, 38.0% (n = 327) indicated their interest in learning more about campus activities, (20.7% (n = 178) were unsure about their interest, (and 17.9% (n = 155) were interested in participating on campus in the future. Among those who had interest in being part of campus activities, 14.9% (n = 128) were considering participating in event planning as a member and 7.9% (n = 68) were considering participating as a leader. The least interest in being involved on campus in the future was recorded among adult learners. This is evident in a negative moderate correlation between student age and their interest in participating in campus activities ($r(776) = -.36, p = < .001$) (see Table 7.3).

There was a positive moderate relationship between student interest in participating in campus activities after the pandemic and the ratings of the COVID-19 impact on student involvement on campus ($r(855) = .28$,

$p = < .001$). This could indicate that students who had fewer opportunities to participate in campus activities due to COVID-19 were more interested in becoming involved on campus after the pandemic. Furthermore, future student on-campus involvement had a positive moderate relationship with the extent of their current involvement in campus activities ($r(855) = .38, p = < .001$). It was also positively moderately correlated with participants' involvement before the pandemic ($r(665) = .17, p = < .001$). Those respondents who were the most involved on campus before COVID-19 and who have been currently participating in campus activities had a higher interest in getting involved in the future.

CONCLUSIONS AND IMPLICATIONS

The findings indicate that study participants occasionally engaged in campus activities that were offered in the form of social and hobby-based clubs and educational events, and less frequently, yet still consistently, in multicultural events. Overall, the FGCS respondents' involvement in campus activities was somewhat impacted by the COVID-19 pandemic, although this was different for the adult learners represented in the sample. They reported little impact of the pandemic on their on-campus participation compared to traditional respondents. This finding may be related with their reported limited involvement prior to the pandemic.

Due to the COVID-19 pandemic, FGCS, as demonstrated in this chapter, were only occasionally involved in campus activities. Compounded with the global COVID-19 pandemic, students experienced even fewer opportunities to engage on campus. They had limited access to learning opportunities and extracurricular activities as participants, members of planning team, and leaders. This especially negatively influenced traditional, Asian, and younger students and those who participated in and led the planning of campus activities prior to the pandemic.

Most studies on the impact of the COVID-19 pandemic have focused on the disruption to teaching and learning that took place at the beginning of the pandemic in March 2020 (Kiebler & Steward, 2022; Potts, 2021), whereas this chapter provides a snapshot of how the pandemic affected FGCS' participation in campus activities. As the number of FGCS continues to grow on college campuses, student involvement in campus activities becomes a wider-used venue for increasing FGCS success and retention. Specifically, on-campus engagement can not only foster FGCS connection to academic support resources, but can also support student sense of belonging, career choice, and professional networking that could lead to alleviation of financial barriers.

On the positive side, there was a large group of FGCS representing all years of college who have been engaged in campus activities as either participant or leader or both. Although this finding contradicts the existing research suggesting low on-campus participation among FGCS, it is encouraging. This finding may be related to the increasing need to belong and motivation to succeed in college, especially among third- and fourth-year students. Furthermore, those who reported being negatively impacted by the pandemic had a high interest in participating in campus activities post-pandemic.

Although the extent of participation in campus activities varied among FGCS, it is important to understand that COVID-19 impacted these students differently based on their reported age, race, field of study, and year in college. Nevertheless, many of the respondents planned to engage on campus more. This, in turn, can foster their feeling of connection with peers and campus culture (Pratt et al., 2019; Ryan & Deci, 2016).

Campus Involvement Strategies and Considerations

As student affairs and advising practitioners, it is important to note that FGCS generally indicated a desire for engagement. With this desire, colleges and universities have the opportunity to more fully engage these students in campus life. Based on our study findings and conclusions, we propose the following strategies for consideration: (1) student awareness, (2) tailored campus engagement, and (3) reigniting student engagement.

Student Awareness

FGCS, particularly the traditional-aged students, desire to be involved in campus activities. Thus, college and university personnel need to ensure students are aware of such opportunities available to them. Multiple and targeted modalities of communication, such as social media, newsletters, emails, and so on, need to be employed to ensure FGCS receive the message about possible participation. As the study indicated, students of color, males and females, traditional and non-traditional FGCS all have different interests and needs within the broad array of campus program offerings. Thus, it will be important for college and university personnel to tailor the message for different FGCS identity groups who have different interests to increase their involvement.

Tailored Campus Engagement

Given that FGCS have various and intersecting identities and in turn different interests, it would behoove college and university personnel to tailor their campus engagement offerings to their varying needs and interests. An important starting point is opening dialogue with the FGCS to understand what kinds of engagement they find meaningful and of value (Caruth, 2018). In order to effectively support and foster student engagement, FGCS voices elevating their unique needs and challenges must be heard (Risisky et al., 2022). Having these voices heard may help with (re-)engagement of those whose participation in campus activities was impacted the most.

The study's findings demonstrated that students of color preferred culturally relevant programming, that female and non-traditional FGCS preferred educationally focused programming, and that male students preferred social programming. It is also interesting to note that juniors and seniors were more involved in social/hobby clubs, educational events, and professional events than freshman and sophomore students. These findings indicate that a one-size-fits-all approach will not yield the highest level of campus engagement.

Reigniting Student Engagement

FGCS campus engagement was minimal prior to the pandemic interfering with and disrupting their education. For non-traditional students, campus engagement was virtually nonexistent due to work and family obligations outside of school. Now that campuses returned to normal, there is an opportunity for practitioners to rethink how they engage students. Furthermore, as part of the reigniting process it will be important to attend to the fact that student plans, paths, or goals were interrupted. For example, students might not have had the opportunity for a signature experience or program that has traditionally been offered at a specific time in their academic plan. Some educational experiences and programs are unique to a university whereas others are typical across university settings (e.g., sophomore year leadership academy, on-site internship placements or shadowing opportunities, student teaching, rituals or ceremonies in fraternity or sorority life, study abroad). Regardless of the program, these engagements represent milestones and touchpoints for the college student experience.

In some instances, it might work to reignite that engagement by expanding the target population (e.g., expanding the sophomore leadership academy to also include juniors and seniors impacted by the pandemic). In other instances, a student's academic plan might require a student to "miss out" on this experience and for universities to provide a different on-ramp for renewed or first-time engagement (e.g., forgoing a shadowing experience and moving a student directly into an internship). Lessons learned from remote instruction and the virtual environment could be applied to campus engagement as another way to reignite FGCS campus engagement. This will require intentional design and re-design of campus involvement and services with the goal of reigniting engagement for this population of students.

Limitations

One of the limitations of the presented findings was the purposeful sampling technique, which likely skewed the interpretation and findings toward experiences of students bounded by one 4-year public teaching institution. The selection of a sample of only first-generation students at a particular university presents a limitation in terms of drawing conclusions about whether the findings are specific to the status only or are driven by other, intersecting, identities. Furthermore, the study did not account for student income.

Another important limitation is associated with the self-reporting nature of the data collection instrument. This includes the risk of respondents to report on socially desirable self-descriptions (Paulhus, 2002). Furthermore, the student involvement section of the survey focused on examining the extent and type of student participation in campus activities and did not account for further exploration of student motivation of involvement and/or sense of belonging.

Future Research Considerations

Colleges and universities embraced a new post-pandemic reality. First, research opportunities abound for understanding retrospectively how the pandemic affected campus engagement for first-generation graduate students, out-of-state/out-of-region students, and transfer students and based on institutional type (i.e., community college, private college, 4-year public teaching/research institutions). Second, it would be beneficial to expand the current study with qualitative inquiries allowing for a deeper analysis and further understanding of FGCS' academic and social integration. Third, other important factors, such as motivation for (non-) participation, career aspirations or goals, and classroom involvement, were missing from this study. Research incorporating these additional factors could more accurately reveal the extent of FGCS participation on campus with the focus on their status and intersecting identities. Fourth, the findings shared in this chapter captured FGCS involvement towards the end of the COVID-19 pandemic. Future research could expand knowledge on longitudinal effects by comparing these results to the more recent ones. Last, considering the large number of third- and fourth-year FGCS survey respondents, it might be beneficial to further examine the role of their engagement on career choices, career placement, and professional success post-graduation.

REFERENCES

Astin, A. W. (1993). *What matters in college? Four critical years revisited*. Jossey-Bass.

Astin, A. W. (1999). Student development: A developmental theory for higher education. *Journal of College Student Personnel, 40*(5), 518–529.

Appleton, J. J., Christenson, S. L., & Furlong, M. J. (2008). Student engagement with school: Critical conceptual and methodological issues of the construct. *Psychology in the Schools, 45*(5), 369–386. https://doi.org/10.1002/pits.20303

Aucejo, E. M., French, J. F., Ugalde Araya, M. P., & Zafar, B. (2020). *The impact of COVID-19 on student experiences and expectations: Evidence from a survey. (Working paper No. 27392)*. National Bureau of Economic Research. https://www.nber.org/papers/w27392

Bakker, A. B., Vergel, A. I. S., & Kuntze, J. (2015). Student engagement and performance: a weekly diary study on the role of openness. *Motivation and Emotion, 39*(1), 49–62. https://doi.org/10.1007/s11031-014-9422-5

Balemian, K., & Feng, J. (2013, July). *First generation students: College aspirations, preparedness and challenges* [Paper presentation]. The CollegeBoard Advanced Placement Annual Conference, Las Vegas, NV. https://files.eric.ed.gov/fulltext/ED563393.pdf

Bawa, P. (2016). Retention in online courses: Exploring issues and solutions—a literature review. *Sage Open, 6*(1), 1–11. https://doi.org/10.1177/2158244015621777

Ben-Eliyahu, A., Moore, D., Dorph, R., & Schunn, C. D. (2018). Investigating the multidimensionality of engagement: Affective, behavioral, and cognitive engagement across science activities and contexts. *Contemporary Educational Psychology, 53*, 87–105. https://doi.org/10.1016/j.cedpsych.2018.01.002

Bettencourt, G. M., Mansour, K. E., Hedayet, M., Feraud-King, P. T., Stephens, K. J., Tejada, M. M., & Kimball, E. (2022). Is first-gen an identity? How first-generation college students make meaning of institutional and familial constructions of self. *Journal of College Student Retention: Research, Theory & Practice, 24*(2), 271–289. https://doi.org/10.1177/1521025120913302

Birmingham, W. C., Wadsworth, L. L., Lassetter, J. H., Graff, T. C., Lauren, E., & Hung, M. (2021). COVID-19 lockdown: Impact on college students' lives. *Journal of American College Health, 71* (3), 879–893. https://doi.org/10.1080/07448481.2021.1909041

Boekaerts, M. (2016). Engagement as an inherent aspect of the learning process. *Learning and Instruction, 43*, 76–83. https://doi.org/10.1016/j.learninstruc.2016.02.001

Bond, M., Buntins, K., Bedenlier, S., Zawacki-Richter, O., & Kerres, M. (2020). Mapping research in student engagement and educational technology in higher education: a systematic evidence map. *International Journal of Educational Technology in Higher Education, 17*(2), 2–30. https://doi.org/10.1186/s41239-019-0176-8

Borrero, N. (2011). Shared success: Voices of first-generation college-bound Latino/as. *Multicultural Education, 18*(4), 2430.

Bowden, L. L.-H., Tickle, L., & Naumann, K. (2021). The four pillars of tertiary student engagement and success: a holistic measurement approach. *Studies in Higher Education, 46*(6), 1207–1224. https://doi.org/10.1080/03075079.2019.1672647

Brookover, D. L., Hanley, E. M., Boulden, R., & Johnson, K. F. (2021). "I want to be a first": Student, family, and school factors influencing first-generation student college readiness. *School Community Journal, 31*(1), 41–64.

Brooks R., Brooks S., & Goldstein S. (2012). The power of mindsets: Nurturing engagement, motivation, and resilience in students. In S. Christenson, A. Reschly, & C. Wylie (Eds.), *Handbook of research on student engagement* (pp. 541–562). Springer.

Browning, Larson, L., Sharaievska, I., Rigolon, A., McAnirlin, O., Mullenbach, L., Cloutier, S., Vu, T., Thomsen, J., Reigner, N., Metcalf, E., D'Antonio, A., Helbich, M., Bratman, G., & Olvera Alvarez, H. (2021). Psychological impacts from COVID-19 among university students: Risk factors across seven states in the United States. *PloS One, 16*(1), 1–27. https://doi.org/10.1371/journal.pone.0245327

Buckley, P., & Lee, P. (2021). The impact of extra-curricular activity on the student experience. *Active Learning in Higher Education, 22*(1), 37–48. https://doi.org/10.1177/1469787418808988

Busseri, M. A., Rose-Krasnor, L., Willoughby, T., & Chalmers, H. (2006). A longitudinal examination of breadth and intensity of youth activity involvement and successful development. *Developmental Psychology, 42*(6), 1313–1326. https://doi.org/10.1037/0012-1649.42.6.1313

Carini, R. M., Kuh, G. D., & Klein, S. P. (2006). Student engagement and student learning: Testing the linkages*. *Research in Higher Education, 47*(1), 1–32. https://doi.org/10.1007/s11162-005-8150-9

Caruth, G. D. (2018). Student engagement, retention, and motivation: Assessing academic success in today's college students. *Participatory Educational Research, 5*(1), 17–30. https://doi.org/10.17275/per.18.4.5.1

Cataldi, E. F., Bennett, C. T., & Chen, X. (2018). *First-generation students: College access, persistence, and postbachelor's outcomes*. National Center for Education Statistics.

Center for First-Generation Student Success (2018). *First-Generation college students: Demographic characteristics and postsecondary enrollment fact sheet*. https://firstgen.naspa.org/files/dmfile/FactSheet-01.pdf

Chen, X. (2005). *First generation students in postsecondary education: A look at their college transcripts* (NCES 2005–171). U.S. Department of Education, National Center for Education Statistics.

Chen J. A., Stevens C., Wong S. H. M., & Liu C. H. (2019). Psychiatric symptoms and diagnoses among US college students: A comparison by race and ethnicity. *Psychiatric Services, 70*(6), 442–449. https://doi.org/10.1176/appi.ps.201800388

Cho, M.-H., & Kim, B. J. (2013). Students' self-regulation for interaction with others in online learning environments. *The Internet and Higher Education, 17*, 69–75. https://doi.org/10.1016/j.iheduc.2012.11.001

Clark, G., Marsden, R,. Whyatt, J. D., Thompson, L., & Walker, M. (2015). "It's everything else you do ...": Alumni views on extracurricular activities and employability. *Active Learning in Higher Education, 16*(2), 133–147. https://doi.org/10.1177/1469787415574050

Collins, P. H. (2015). Intersectionality's definitional dilemmas. *Annual Review of Sociology, 41*(1), 1–20.

Conley, P. A., & Hamlin, M. L. (2009). Justice-learning: Exploring the efficacy with low-income, first-generation college students. *Michigan Journal of Community Service Learning, 16*, 309–342. https://doi.org/10.37333/001c.29628.

Conrad, R. C., Hahm, H. C., Koire, A., Pinder-Amaker, S., & Liu, C. H. (2021). College student mental health risks during the COVID-19 pandemic: Implications of campus relocation. *Journal of Psychiatric Research, 136*, 117–126. https://doi.org/10.1016/j.jpsychires.2021.01.054

Cornish P. A., Berry G., Benton S., Barros-Gomes P., Johnson D., Ginsburg R., Whelan B., Fawcett E., & Romano V. (2017). Meeting the mental health needs of today's college student: Reinventing services through Stepped Care 2.0. *Psychological Services, 14*(4), 428–442. https://doi.org/10.1037/ser0000158

Davis, C. R., Hartman, H., Turner, M., Norton, T., Sexton, J., Mendez, D., & Mendez, J. (2021). "Listen to the feedback of students": First-generation college students voice inequalities in schooling brought by the COVID-19 pandemic. *Journal of College Student Retention: Research, Theory, and Practice, 0*(0), 1–25. https://doi.org/10.1177/15210251211066302

Day, D. (2017). *Student engagement and on campus involvement* [Honors thesis, Salisbury University]. Salisbury, MD. https://mdsoar.org/bitstream/handle/11603/10931/DayDana_Fall2017.pdf?sequence=1&isAllowed=y

D'Amico, M. M., & Dika, S. L. (2013). Using data known at the time of admission to predict first-generation college student success. *Journal of College Student Retention: Research, Theory & Practice, 15*(2), 173–192. https://doi.org/10.2190/cs.15.2.c

Demetriou, C., Meece, J., Eaker-Rich, D., & Powell, C. (2017). The activities, roles, and relationships of successful first-generation college students. *Journal of College Student Development 58*(1), 19–36. https://doi.org/10.1353/csd.2017.0001.

Dugan, J. P., & Komives, S. R. (2010). Influences on college students' capacities for socially responsible leadership. *Journal of College Student Development, 51*, 525–549. https://doi.org/10.1353/csd.2010.0009

Eccles, J. (2016). Engagement: Where to next? *Learning and Instruction, 43,* 71–75. https://doi.org/10.1016/j.learninstruc.2016.02.003

Eisenberg D., Hunt J., & Speer N. (2013). Mental health in American colleges and universities: Variation across student subgroups and across campuses. *The Journal of Nervous and Mental Disease, 201*(1), 60–67. https://doi.org/10.1097/nmd.0b013e31827ab077

Engle, J. (2007). Postsecondary access and success for first-generation college students. *American Academic, 3*(1), 25–48.

Engle J., & Tinto V. (2008). *Moving beyond access: College success for low-income, first-generation students.* Pell Institute for the Study of Opportunity in Higher Education.

Evans, R., Stansberry, D., Bullington, K. E., & Burnett, D. (2020). First in college: A qualitative exploration of experiences of first-generation students. *Inquiry: The Journal of the Virginia Community Colleges, 23*(1), 1–32.

Falcon, L. (2015). Breaking down barriers: First-generation college students and college success. *Innovation Showcase, 10*(6), 1–5.

Finn, J. (2006). *The adult lives of at-risk students: The roles of attainment and engagement in high school* (NCES 2006-328). U.S. Department of Education, National Center for Education Statistics. https://nces.ed.gov/pubs2006/2006328.pdf

Finn, J. D., & Rock, D. A. (1997). Academic success among students at risk for school failure. *Journal of Applied Psychology, 82*(2), 221–234. https://doi.org/10.1037/0021-9010.82.2.221

Fischer, M. J. (2007). Settling into campus life: Differences by race/ethnicity in college involvement and outcomes. *The Journal of Higher Education, 78*(2), 125–161. https://doi.org/10.1080/00221546.2007.11780871

Fredricks, J. A., & McColskey, W. (2012). The measurement of student engagement: A comparative analysis of various methods and student self-report instruments. In S. L. Christenson, A. L. Reschly, C. Wylie, S. L. Christenson, A. L. Reschly, & C. Wylie (Eds.), *Handbook of research on student engagement* (pp. 763–782). Springer.

Frederick, M., Sasso, P. A., & Maldonado, J. (2018). *The dynamic student development meta-theory: A new model for student success.* Peter Lang.

Fowler, P., & Boylan, H. (2010). Increasing student success and retention: A multidimensional approach. *Journal of Developmental Education, 34*(2), 2–10.

Gallegos, M., Zalaquett, C. ., Luna Sánchez, S. E. ., Mazo-Zea, R., Ortiz-Torres, B., Penagos-Corzo, J. C., Portillo, N., Torres Fernández, I., Urzúa, A., Morgan Consoli, M., Polanco, F. A., Florez, A. M., & Lopes Miranda, R. (2020). Coping with the coronavirus (Covid-19) pandemic in the Americas: Recommendations and guidelines for mental health. *Revista Interamericana De Psicología/Interamerican Journal of Psychology, 54*(1), e1304. https://doi.org/10.30849/ripijp.v54i1.1304

Garcia, V. (2010). First-generation college students: How co-curricular involvement can assist with success. *The Vermont Connection, 31*(1). https://scholarworks.uvm.edu/tvc/vol31/iss1/6

Garriott, P. O., Ko, S.-J. "Stella," Grant, S. B., Jessen, M., & Allan, B. A. (2021). When race and class collide: Classism and social-emotional experiences of first-generation college students. *Journal of College Student Retention: Research, Theory & Practice*, *0*(0). https://doi.org/10.1177/1521025121995483

Garland, A. M. (2010). *Assessing the relationship between student involvement and academic performance in higher education* [Master's thesis, Western Kentucky University]. Bowling Green, KY.

Gewalt, S. C., Berger, S., Krisam, R., Krisam, J., & Breuer, M. (2022). University students' economic situation during the COVID-19 pandemic: A cross-sectional study in Germany. *PloS one*, *17*(10), e0275055. https://doi.org/10.1371/journal.pone.0275055

Gibbons, M. M., & Woodside, M. (2014). Addressing the needs of first-generation college students: Lessons learned from adults from low-education families. *Journal of College Counseling*, *17*(1), 21–36. https://doi.org/10.1002/j.2161-1882.2014.00045.x

Gibson, A. M., & Slate, J. R. (2010). Student engagement at two-year institutions: Age and generational status differences. *Community College Journal of Research and Practice*, *34*(5), 371–385. https://doi.org/10.1080/10668920802466384

Gillen-O'Neel, C. (2021). Sense of belonging and student engagement: A daily study of first- and continuing-generation college students. *Research in Higher Education*, *62*, 45–71. https://doi.org/10.1007/s11162-019-09570-y

Goldstein, S. B., & Lopez. H. N. (2021). An intersectional investigation of study abroad intent among Latino/a and White first-generation students. *Frontiers: The Interdisciplinary Journal of Study Abroad*, *33*(2), 1–16. https://doi.org/10.36366/frontiers.v33i2.534

Gonzalez-Ramirez, J., Mulgueen, K., Zealand, R., Silverstein, S., Mulqueen, C., & BuShell, S. (2021). Emergency online learning: College students' perceptions during the COVID-19 pandemic. *College Student Journal*, *55*(1), 29–46.

Goodwin, R., Hou, W. K., Sun, S., & Ben-Ezra, M. (2020). Quarantine, distress and interpersonal relationships during COVID-19. *General Psychiatry*, *33*(6), 1–5. https://dx.doi.org/10.1136%2Fgpsych-2020-100385

Griffith, B. A., & Dunham, E. B. (2015). *Working in teams: Moving from high potential to high performance*. Sage. https://doi.org/10.4135/9781506300153

Hamlin, A. R., & Barney, S. T. (2022). The impact of COVID-19 on U.S. college students, and how educators should respond. *Research in Higher Education*, *42*, 1–16. https://files.eric.ed.gov/fulltext/EJ1347721.pdf

Hatry, H. P., Marcotte, J. E., van Houten, T., & Weiss, C. H. (1998). *Customer surveys for agency managers: What managers need to know*. The Urban Institute Press.

Herbenick, D., Hensel, D.J., Eastman-Mueller, H., Beckmeyer, J., Fu, T.-C., Guerra-Reyes, L., & Rosenberg, M. (2022). Sex and relationships pre- and early- COVID-19 pandemic: Findings from a probability sample of U.S. undergraduate students. *Archives of Sexual Behavior*, *51*, 183–195. https://doi.org/10.1007/s10508-021-02265-5

Hu, K., Godfrey, K., Ren, Q., Wang, S., Yang, X., & Li, Q. (2022). The impact of the COVID-19 pandemic on college students in USA: Two years later. *Psychiatry Research*, *315*. https://doi.org/10.1016/j.psychres.2022.114685

Huckins, J. F., DaSilva, A. W., Wang, W., Hedlund, E., Rogers, C., Nepal, S. K., Wu, J., Obuchi, M., Murphy, E. I., Meyer M. L., Wagner, D. D., Holtzheimer, P. E., Campbell, A. T. (2020). Mental health and behavior of college students during the early phases of the COVID-19 pandemic: Longitudinal smartphone and ecological momentary assessment study. *Journal of Medical Internet Research, 22*(6), e20185. https://doi.org/10.2196/20185

Hyer, C. (2019). *Student involvement and the impact on academic success* [Doctoral dissertation, Boise State University]. Boise, ID.

IPEDS. (2020). *Integrated postsecondary education data system.* Google Scholar. https://nces.ed.gov/ipeds/use-the-data

Ives J., & Castillo-Montoya M. (2020). First-generation college students as academic learners: A systematic review. *Review of Educational Research, 90*(2), 139–178. https://doi.org/10.3102/0034654319899707

Jackson, A., Colson-Fearon, B., & Versey, H. S. (2022). Managing intersectional invisibility and hypervisibility during the transition to college among first-generation women of color. *Psychology of Women Quarterly, 46*(3), 354–371 https://doi.org/10.1177/03616843221106087

Jaggars, S. S. (2011). Online learning: Does it help low-income and underprepared students? *CCRC Working Paper No. 26.* https://ccrc.tc.columbia.edu/media/k2/attachments/online-learning-help-students.pdf

Jehangir, R. (2010). Stories as knowledge: Bringing the lived experience of first-generation college students into the academy. *Urban Education, 45*(4), 533–553. https://doi.org/10.1177/00420 8591037235 2

Jones, H. E., Manze, M., Ngo, V., Lamberson, P., & Freudenber, N. (2021). The impact of the COVID-19 pandemic on college students' health and financial stability in New York City: Findings from a population-based sample of City University of New York (CUNY) students. *Journal of Urban Health, 98*, 187–196. https://doi.org/10.1007/s11524-020-00506-x

Kahu, E. R. (2013). Framing student engagement in higher education. *Studies in Higher Education, 38*(5), 758–773. https://doi.org/10.1080/03075079.2011.598505

Kiebler, J. M., & Stewart, A. J. (2022). Student experiences of the COVID-19 pandemic: Perspectives from first-generation/lower-income students and others. *Analyses of Social Issues and Public Policy, 22*(1), 198–224. https://doi.org/10.1111/asap.12288

Kilgo, C. A., Mollet, A. L., & Pascarella, E. T. (2016). The estimated effects of college student involvement on psychological well-being. *Journal of College Student Development, 57*(8), 1043–1049. https://doi.org/10.1353/csd.2016.0098

Kimaru, L. J., Habila, M. A., Mantina, N. M., Lopez, D. N., & Melton, F. (2023). The impact of COVID-19 on academic performance among college-level students. *Journal of American College Health*, 1–7. https://doi.org/10.1080/07448481.2022.2155052

Kimbark, Peters, M. L., & Richardson, T. (2017). Effectiveness of the student success course on persistence, retention, academic achievement, and student engagement. *Community College Journal of Research and Practice, 41*(2), 124–138. https://doi.org/10.1080/10668926.2016.1166352

Knifsend, C. A. (2020). Intensity of activity involvement and psychosocial well-being among students. *Active Learning in Higher Education, 21*(2), 116-127. https://doi.org/10.1177/1469787418760324

Kocsis, Zs. (2020). A hallgatoi munkavallalas mint a lemorzsolodas egyik lehetseges tenyezoje [Student unemployment as one of the possible factors of dropout]. *Educatio, 29*(2), 295–304.

Komives, S. R. (2019). Engagement with campus activities matters: Toward a new era of educationally purposeful activities. *The Journal of Campus Activities Practice and Scholars*hip, *1*(1), 14–25. https://doi.org/10.52499/2019003

Kuh, G. D. (2001). Assessing what really matters to student learning: Inside the national survey of student engagement. *Change: The Magazine of Higher Learning, 33*(3), 10–17. https://doi.org/10.1080/00091380109601795

Kuh, G. D. (2009). What student affairs professionals need to know about student engagement. *Journal of College Student Development, 50*(6), 683–706. https://doi.org/10.1353/csd.0.0099

Kuh, G. D., Cruce, T. M., Shoup, R., Kinzie, J., & Gonyea, R. M. (2008). Unmasking the effects of student engagement on first-year college grades and persistence. *The Journal of Higher Education, 79*(5), 540–563. https://doi.org/10.1080/00221546.2008.11772116

Kulp, A. M., Pascale, A. B., & Grandstaff, M. (2021). Types of extracurricular campus activities and first-year students' academic success. *Journal of College Student Retention: Research, Theory & Practice, 23*(3), 747–767. https://doi.org/10.1177/1521025119876249

Lederer, A. M., Hoban, M. T., Lipson, S. K., Zhou, S., & Eisenberg, D. (2021). More than inconvenienced: The unique needs of U.S. college students during the COVID-19 pandemic. *Health Education & Behavior, 48*(1), 14–19. https://doi.org/10.1177/1090198120969372

Lee, J., Solomon, M., Stead, T., Kwon, B., & Ganti, L. (2021). Impact of COVID-19 on the mental health of US college students. *BMC Psychology, 9*(95), 2–10. https://doi.org/10.1186/s40359-021-00598-3

Limniou, M., Varga-Atkins, T., Hands, C., & Elshamaa, M. (2021). Learning, student digital capabilities and academic performance over the COVID-19 pandemic. *Education Sciences, 11*(361), 1–15. https://doi.org/10.3390/educsci11070361

Lindberg, L. D., Bell, D. L., & Kantor, L. M. (2020). The sexual and reproductive health of adolescents and young adults during the COVID-19 pandemic. *Perspectives on Sexual and Reproductive Health, 52*(2), 75–79. https://doi.org/10.1363/psrh.12151

Lipson, S. K., Lattie, E.G., & Eisenberg, D. (2019). Increased rates of mental health service utilization by U.S. college students: 10-year population-level trends (2007-2017*). Psychiatric Services, 70*(1), 60–63. https://doi.org//epdf/10.1176/appi.ps.201800332

Liu C. H., Stevens C., Wong S. H. M., Yasui M., & Chen J. A. (2019). The prevalence and predictors of mental health diagnoses and suicide among US college students: Implications for addressing disparities in service use. *Depression and Anxiety, 36*(1), 8–17. https://doi.org/10.1002/da.22830

Lowery-Hart, R., & Pacheco, G. Jr, (2011). Understanding the first-generation student experience in higher education through a relational dialectic perspective. *New Directions for Teaching and Learning, 2011*(127), 55–68. https://doi.org/10.1002/tl.457

Lundberg, C. A., Schreiner, L. A., Hovaguimian, K. D., & Miller, S. S. (2007). First-generation status and student race/ethnicity as distinct predictors of student involvement and learning. *Journal of Student Affairs Research and Practice, 44*, 57–83. https://doi.org/10.2202/1949-6605.1755

Luo, N., Zhang, M., & Qi, D. (2017). Effects of different interactions on students' sense of community in e-learning environment. *Computers & Education, 115*, 153–160. https://doi.org/10.1016/j.compedu.2017.08.006

Majer, J. M. (2009). Self-efficacy and academic success among ethnically diverse first- generation community college students. *Journal of Diversity in Higher Education, 2*(4), 243–250. https://doi.org/10.1037/a0017852

Magallanes, M. (2020). *The academic challenges of first-generation college students within a four-year institution* [Master's thesis, Taylor University]. Upland, IN.

Marinoni, G., Land, H. V., & Jensen, T. (2020). *The impact of COVID-19 on higher education around the world: AU Global survey report.* International Association of Universities, France.

Martin L. M. (2000). The relationship of college experiences to psychosocial outcomes in students. *Journal of College Student Development, 41*(3), 292–301.

Martinez, J. A., Sher, K. J., Krull, J. L., & Wood, P. K. (2009). Blue-collar scholars? Mediators and moderators of university attrition in first-generation college students. *Journal of College Student Development, 50*, 87–103.

Mehta, S. S., Newbold, J. J., & Rourke, M. A. (2011). Why do first-generation students fail? *College Student Journal, 45*, 20–35.

Mishra, S. (2020). Social networks, social capital, social support and academic success in higher education: A systematic review with a special focus on 'underrepresented' students. *Educational Research Review, 29*. https://www.sciencedirect.com/science/article/abs/pii/S1747938X1830304X?via%3Dihub

Mitchell, D.; Soria, K. M.; Daniele, E. A.; & Gipson, J. A. (2015). *Student involvement & academic outcomes: Implications for diverse college student populations*. Peter Lang. https://doi.org/10.3726/978-1-4539-1467-0

Moore, J., Lovell, C. D., McGann, T., & Wyrick, J. (1998). Why involvement matters: A review of research on student involvement in the collegiate setting. *College Student Affairs Journal, 17*(2), 4–17.

Moschetti, R. V., & Hudley, C. (2015). Social capital and academic motivation among first-generation community college students. *Community College Journal of Research and Practice, 39*(3), 235–251. https://doi.org/10.1080/10668926.2013.819304

Moreira, P. A., Dias, P., Vaz, F. M., & Vaz, J. M. (2013), Predictors of academic performance and school engagement—integrating persistence, motivation and study skills perspectives using person-centered and variable-centered approaches. *Learning and Individual Differences, 24*, 117–125. https://doi.org/10.1016/j.lindif.2012.10.016

Mucci-Ferris, M., Grabsch, D., & Bobo, A. (2021). Positives, negatives, and opportunities arising in the undergraduate experience during the COVID-19 pandemic. *Journal of College Student Development, 62*(2), 203–218. https://doi.org/10.1353/csd.2021.0017

Nardi, P.M. (2006). *Doing survey research* (2nd ed). Pearson.

Nash, R. J., & Agne, R. M. (1973). Career Education: Earning a living or living a life? *The Phi Delta Kappan, 54*(6), 373–378. http://www.jstor.org/stable/20189371

National Association for Campus Activities (NACA). (2021). *Research agenda.* https://www.naca.org/ProDev/Documents/ResearchAgenda.pdf

National Center for Education Statistics. (2022). College student employment. *Condition of Education*. U.S. Department of Education, Institute of Education Sciences. https://nces.ed.gov/programs/coe/indicator/ssa.

National Student Clearinghouse Research Center (2022, November*). Completing college: National and state reports*. Report No. 11. https://nscresearchcenter.org/wp-content/uploads/Completions_Report_2022.pdf

National Survey of Student Engagement. (2017). Engagement insights: Survey findings on the quality of undergraduate education—Annual results 2017. *Indiana University Center for Postsecondary Research*. http://nsse.indiana.edu/NSSE_2017_Results/pdf /NSSE_2017_Annual_Results.pdf

Neuwirth, L. S., Jovic, S., & Mukherji, B. R. (2021). Reimagining higher education during and post-COVID-19: Challenges and opportunities. *Journal of Adult and Continuing Education, 27(*2), 141–156. https://doi.org/10.1177/1477971420947738

Ngyen, T.-H., & Ngyen, B. M. D. (2018). Is the "First-Generation Student" term useful for understanding inequality? The role of intersectionality in illuminating the implications of an accepted—yet challenged—term. *Review of Research in Education, 42*(1), 146–176. https://doi.org/10.3102/0091732x18759280

Oga-Baldwin, W. Q., & Nakata, Y. (2017). Engagement, gender, and motivation: a predictive model for Japanese young language learners, *System, 65*, 151–176. https://doi.org/10.1016/j.system.2017.01.011

Orbe, M. P. (2004). Negotiating multiple identities within multiple frames: An analysis of first-generation college students. *Communication Education, 53*(2), 131–149. https://doi.org/10.1080/0363452041000168240l

Pascarella, E., & Terenzini, P. (1991). *How college affects students: Findings and insights from twenty years of research*. Jossey-Bass.

Pascarella, E. T., Pierson, C. T., Wolniak, G. C., & Terenzini, P. T. (2004). First-generation college students: Additional evidence on college experiences and outcomes. *The Journal of Higher Education, 75*(3), 249–176. https://doi.org/10.1353/jhe.2004.0016

Patterson, J. A., Akella, N., Rangel, M., Stegman, M., & Stubblefield, D. (2021). *Telling their stories: First-generation college students' academic and social integration at a midwestern university* [Paper presentation]. American Educational Research Association, Virtual.

Paulhus, D. L. (2002). Socially desirable responding: The evolution of a construct. In H. I. Braun, D. N. Jackson, & D. E. Wiley (Eds.), *The role of constructs in psychological and educational measurement* (pp. 49–69). Lawrence Erlbaum Associates.

Phipps, S. S. (2020). *The relationships between college interventions and first-generation students' academic success at a large Tier I institution* [Doctoral dissertation, University of Houston]. Houston, TX.

Pike, G. R., Kuh, G. D., & Gonyea, R. M. (2003). The relationship between institutional mission and students' involvement and educational outcomes. *Research in Higher Education, 44*, 241–261.

Pike, G. R., Kuh, G. D., & Massa-McKinley, R. C. (2009). First-year students' employment, engagement, and academic achievement: Untangling the relationship between work and grades. *NASPA Journal, 45*(4), 1012–1034. https://doi.org10.2202/1949-6605.2011

Pike, G. R., Kuh, G. D., & McCormick, A. C. (2011). An investigation of the contingent relationships between learning community participation and student engagement. *Research in Higher Education, 52*, 300–322. https://doi.org/10.1007/s11162-010-9192-1

Potts, C. (2021). Seen and unseen: First-year college students' sense of belonging during the Covid-19 pandemic. *College Student Affairs Journal, 39*(2), 214–224. https://files.eric.ed.gov/fulltext/EJ1317816.pdf

Pratt, I. S., Hardwood, H. B., Cavazos, J. T., & Ditzfeld, C. P. (2019). Should I stay or should I go? Retention in first-generation college students. *Journal of College Student Retention: Research, Theory, & Practice, 21*(1), 105–118. https://doi.org/10.1177/1521025117690868

Pulliam, N., & Sasso, P. A. (2016). Building institutional capacity for college access and success: Implications for enrollment management. *Higher Education Politics & Economics, 2*(1), 1–36. https://doi.org/10.32674/hepe.v2i1.19

Raaper, R., & Brown, C. (2020). The COVID-19 pandemic and the dissolution of the university campus: Implications for student support practice. *Journal of Professional Capital and Community, 5*(3/4), 343–349.

Redford, J., & Mulvaney Hoyer, K. M. (2017). *First-generation and continuing-generation college students: A comparison of high school and postsecondary experiences* (NCES 2018-009). National Center for Education Statistics.

Rehr, T. I., Regan, E. P., Abukar, Z., & Meshelemiah, J. C. A. (2022). Financial wellness of first-generation students. *College Student Affairs Journal, 40*(1), 90–105. https://doi.org/10.1353/csj.2022.0007

Reyes-Portillo, J. A., Warner, C. M., Kline, E. A., Bixter, M. T., Chu, B. C., Miranda, R., Nadeem, E., Nickerson, A., Peralta, A. O., Reigada, L., Rizvi, S. L., Roy, A. K., Shatkin, J., Kalver, E., Rette, D., Denton, E., Shatkin, J., Kalver, E., Rette, D., Denton, E-G., & Jeglic, E. L. (2022). The psychological, academic, and economic impact of COVID-19 on college students in the epicenter of the pandemic. *Emerging Adulthood, 10*(2), 473–490. https://doi.org/10.1177/21676968211066657

Risisky, D., Duff, E., & Espinet, J. (2022). College students' perceptions on safety measures and campus engagement during the COVID-19 pandemic. *Journal of American College Health*, 1–9. https://doi.org/10.1080/07448481.2022.2138717

Riutta, S., & Teodoresku, D. (2014). Leadership development on a diverse campus. *Journal of College Student Development, 55*(8), 830–836. https://doi.org/10.1353/csd.2014.0082

Roddenberry, C. (2017). The value and challenges of using web conferencing technology to integrate online students into campus activities. *Journal of Educational Multimedia and Hypermedia, 26*(4).

Rodríguez-Planas N. (2022). COVID-19, college academic performance, and the flexible grading policy: A longitudinal analysis. *Journal of Public Economics, 207*, 104606. https://doi.org/10.1016/j.jpubeco.2022.104606

Rosch, D. M., & Collins, J. D. (2017). The significance of student organizations to leadership development. *New Directions for Student Leadership, 2017*(155), 9–19.

Rosch, D. M., & Stephens, C. M. (2017). Campus involvement as a predictor for durable leadership development in conjunction with leadership program participation. *Journal of College Student Development, 58*(7), 1107–1112. https://doi.org/10.1353/csd.2017.0087

Ryan, R. M., & Deci, E. L. (2016). Facilitating and hindering motivation, learning, and well-being in schools: Research and observations from self-determination theory. In K. R. Wentzel & D. B. Miele (Eds.), *Handbook on motivation at schools* (pp. 96–119). Routledge.

Saenz, V. B., Hurtado, S., Barrera, D., Wolf, D., & Yeung, F. (2007). *First in my family: A profile of first-generation college students at four-year institutions since 1971*. Higher Education Research Institute, University of California.

Salta, K., Paschalidou, K., Tsetseri, M., & Koulougliotis, D. (2022). Shift from a traditional to a distance learning environment during the COVID-19 pandemic: University students' engagement and interactions. *Science & Education, 31*(1), 93–122. https://doi.org/10.1007/s11191-021-00234-x

Santa-Ramirez, S., Wells, T., Sandoval, J., & Koro, M. (2022) Working through the experiences of first-generation students of color, university mission, intersectionality, and post-subjectivity, *International Journal of Qualitative Studies in Education, 35*(2), 109–124. https://doi.org/10.1080/09518398.2020.1783012

Saris, W. E., & Gallhofer, I. N. (2007). *Design, evaluation, and analysis of questionnaires for survey research*. John Wiley.

Sherif, V. (2018). Voices that matter: Rural high school youth on leadership. *Research in Educational Administration and Leadership: International Perspectives on Team Leadership Special Issue, 3*(2). https://eric.ed.gov/?id=EJ1207465

Sherif, V. (2019). Modeling youth leadership: An integration of personality development theories and ethics. *Journal of Leadership Education*. https://journalofleadershiped.org/jole_articles/modeling-youth-leadership-an-integration-of-personality-development-theories-and-ethics/

Solomonides, I. (2013). A relational and multidimensional model of student engagement. In E. Dunne, & D. Owen (Eds.), *The student engagement handbook: Practice in higher education* (pp. 43–58). Emerald.

Son, C., Hegde, S., Smith, A., Wang, X., & Sasangohar, F. (2020). Effects of COVID-19 on college students' mental health in the United States: Interview survey study. *Journal of Medical Internet Research, 22*(9), 1–14. https://doi.org/10.2196/21279

Soria, K.M., Horgos, B., Chirikov, I., & Jones-White, D. (2020). *First-generation students' experiences during the COVID-19 pandemic*. Student Experiences in the Research University (SERU) Consortium. https://conservancy.umn.edu/handle/11299/214934

Stebleton, M., & Soria, K. (2013). Breaking down barriers: Academic obstacles of first-generation students at research universities. *The Learning Assistance Review, 17*(2), 7–19.

Stebleton, M. J., Soria, K. M., & Huesman, R. L. (2014). First-generation students' sense of belonging, mental health, and use of counseling services at public research universities. *Journal of College Counseling, 17*, 6–20. https://doi.org/10.1002/j.2161-1882.2014.00044.x

Strand, K. (2013). *Making sure they make it! Best practices for ensuring the academic success of first-generation college students*. CIC/Walmart College Success Awards Report. https://files.eric.ed.gov/fulltext/ED561082.pdf

Stuber, J. M. (2011). Integrated, marginal, and resilient: Race, class, and the diverse experiences of white first-generation college students. *International Journal of Qualitative Studies in Education, 24*(1), 117–136. https://doi.org/10.1080/09518391003641916

Thomas, N. S., Barr, P. B., Hottell, D. L., Adkins, A. E., & Dick, D. M. (2021). Longitudinal influence of behavioral health, emotional health, and student involvement on college student retention. *Journal of College Student Development, 62*(1), 2–18. https://dx.doi.org/10.1353/csd.2021.0001

Tejedor, S., Cervi, L.; Pérez-Escoda, A., Jumbo, F. T. (2020). Digital literacy and higher education during COVID-19 lockdown: Spain, Italy, and Ecuador. *Publications, 8*(48), 1–17. https://doi.org/10.3390/publications8040048

Terenzini, P. T., Springer, L., Yaeger, P. M., Pascarella, E. T., & Nora, A. (1996). First-generation college students: Characteristics, experiences, and cognitive development. *Research in Higher Education, 37*, 1–22. https://doi.org/10.1007/bf01680039

Tevis, T., & Griffen, J. (2014). Absent voices: Intersectionality and college students with physical disabilities. *Journal of Progressive Policy & Practice, 2*(3), 239–254.

Tinto, V. (2017). Reflections on student persistence. *Student Success, 8*(2), 1–8. https://doi.org/10.5204/ssj.v8i2.376

Ullah, H., & Wilson, M. A. (2007). Students' academic success and its association to student involvement with learning and relationships with faculty and peers. *College Student Journal, 41*(4), 1192--1202.

UNESCO. (2022, April). *Education: From disruption to recovery*. https://en.unesco.org/covid19/educationresponse.

U.S. Department of Education, Office of Civil Rights. (2020, May). *Questions and answers for postsecondary institutions regarding the COVID-19 national emergency*. [OCR-00118]. https://www2.ed.gov/about/offices/list/ocr/docs/20200512-qa-psi-covid-19.pdf

Vaterlaus, J. M., Shaffer, T., & Pulsipher, L. (2021). College student interpersonal and institutional relationships during the COVID-19 pandemic: A qualitative exploratory study. *The Social Science Journal*. https://doi.org/10.1080/03623319.2021.1949553

Vega, D. (2016, September). "Why not me?" College enrollment and persistence of high-achieving first-generation Latino college students. *School Psychology Forum, 10*(3). https://thrive.arizona.edu/sites/default/files/Why%20Not%20Me%20-%20College%20Enrollment%20and%20Persistence%20of%20High-Achieving%20First-Generation%20Latino%20College%20Students.pdf

Vetter, M. K., Schreiner, L. A., McIntosh, E. J., & Dugan, J. P. (2019). Leveraging the quantity and quality of co-curricular involvement experiences to promote student thriving. *Journal of Campus Activities Practice and Scholarship, 1*(1), 39–51. https://doi.org/10.52499/2019006

Wang, T. R. (2014). "I'm the only person from where I'm from to go to college": Understanding the memorable messages first-generation college students receive from parents. *Journal of Family Communication, 14*, 270–290. https://doi.org/10.1080/15267431.2014.908195

Ward, L., Siegel, M. J., & Davenport, Z. (2012). *First-generation college students: Understanding and improving the experience from recruitment to commencement*. Wiley.

Wester, E. R., Walsh, L. L., Arango-Caro, S., & Callis-Duehl, K. L. (2021). Student engagement declines in STEM undergraduates during COVID-19-driven remote learning. *Journal of Microbiology and Biology Education, 22*. https://doi.org/10.1128/jmbe.v22i1.2385

Whitley, S. E., Benson, G., & Wesaw, A. (2018). *First-generation student success: A landscape analysis of programs and services at four-year institutions*. Center for First-Generation Students' Success. https://firstgen.naspa.org/2018-landscape-analysis

Wu, F., & Teets, T. S. (2021). Effects of the COVID-19 pandemic on student engagement in a general chemistry course. *Journal of Chemical Education, 98*(12), 3633–3642. https://doi.org/10.1021/acs.jchemed.1c00665

Zheng, S., Wu, G., Zhao, J., & Chen, W. (2022). Impact of the COVID-19 epidemic anxiety on college students' employment confidence and employment situation perception in China. *Frontiers in Psychology, 13*, 980634.

Zhou, J. (2017). *Impact of engagement on the academic performance and persistence of first-year college students at a four-year public institution* [Doctoral dissertation, Florida State University]. Tallahassee, FL.

CHAPTER 8

THE IMPACT OF THE COVID-19 PANDEMIC ON COLLEGE STUDENTS WITH ADHD

Implications and Interventions

Emma Quadlander-Goff
Troy University

Madeline LaPolla and David T. Marshall
Auburn University

ABSTRACT

Students diagnosed with attention-deficit/hyperactivity disorder (ADHD) struggle with a multitude of problems in postsecondary education, such as submitting assignments in a timely manner, organizing coursework, and staying focused during lectures. The COVID-19 pandemic greatly impacted those who already struggled with postsecondary education, resulting in the exacerbation of symptoms that impacted academic performance and decreased rates of graduation. We conducted a systematic review of the literature focused on the impact of COVID-19 on postsecondary students diagnosed with ADHD, as well as successful interventions that alleviate

Examining the Cognitive and Psychological Effects of the COVID-19 Global Pandemic on High School, College, and Graduate Learners, pp. 171–194

ADHD symptoms. Interventions that target academic-related impairment can provide a basis for increasing success rates amongst college students diagnosed with ADHD. The chapter concludes with a descriptive case study to demonstrate how instructors and counselors can gain further insight into the challenges experienced by this population and the interventions that can offer them assistance.

Keywords: attention-deficit/hyperactivity disorder, COVID-19, college students, instructors, counselors

INTRODUCTION

The COVID-19 pandemic forced postsecondary campuses to close for in-person instruction in March 2020 and pivot to remote instruction for the remainder of the 2020 Spring Semester. On many campuses, online instruction continued well into the 2020–2021 academic year, forcing many students to learn almost exclusively online for the span of a year (Birmingham et al., 2023). The effects of the pandemic resulted in college students diagnosed with attention-deficit/hyperactivity disorder (ADHD) to face a range of challenges (Meaux et al., 2009). Specifically, individuals diagnosed with ADHD report executive functioning deficits along with sluggish cognitive tempo, which can influence performance at work or in school (Kamradt et al., 2022; Rosello et al., 2020). College students diagnosed with ADHD struggle with procrastination and avoidance, along with emotional dysregulation and issues related to self-esteem (Bodalski et al., 2022). Such struggles were uniquely impacted by the effects of the pandemic.

The global pandemic presented new academic and mental health stressors for college students with ADHD. For those who had been previously struggling with a neurodevelopmental disorder, like ADHD, the pandemic negatively impacted their well-being and worsened their symptoms (Ando et al., 2021; Foster et al., 2023). Some of these symptoms, like inattention, may have even increased one's risk of contracting the virus as they made it more difficult to consistently follow safety protocols (Merzon et al., 2022; Rosenthal et al., 2022). Additionally, the safety procedures implemented by colleges increased anxiety (Seddio et al., 2022), loneliness (Laslo-Roth et al., 2020), and depressive symptoms (Kertzscher et al., 2022) for students with ADHD. Further, support systems often available to students, like campus resources, faculty, and peers, became less accessible as a result of enforced social distancing protocols. Such systems are particularly important to students with neurodevelopmental disorders (i.e., ADHD) and contribute to their success in postsecondary education (Hoyle et al., 2022).

While students with a documented diagnosis often receive accommodations in coursework, researchers have determined that such accommodations do not always assist in improving the student's academic performance (Jansen et al., 2017; Lefler et al., 2023). Thus, identifying interventions that can be utilized by instructors and mental health professionals can improve the coursework experiences of college students with ADHD. The purpose of this chapter is to share findings from a systematic review of the literature that explores how students diagnosed with ADHD fared academically during the pandemic, as well as to propose interventions including cognitive behavioral therapy (CBT) techniques and applicable accommodations that have been successful in helping this population. The chapter concludes with a descriptive case study that can serve as a guide for assisting students with ADHD.

CRITERIA FOR ADHD

ADHD is a neurodevelopmental disorder characterized by inattention (trouble concentrating, easily distracted, forgetfulness), hyperactivity (increased energy, trouble remaining still, increased talkativeness, restlessness), and impulsivity (trouble with self-control and acting without thinking) that impairs personal functioning and development in two or more domains of life (American Psychiatric Association [APA], 2013). To qualify for an official diagnosis of ADHD, an individual must have six or more symptoms related to inattention and/or hyperactivity/impulsivity that must also be present for at least six months. These symptoms also need to have been present prior to the individual being 12-years-old. Additionally, there are three subtypes of ADHD: predominantly hyperactive-impulsive presentation, predominantly inattentive presentation, or combined presentation.

As a neurodevelopmental disorder, ADHD symptoms must be present during early stages of development and is therefore predominantly first diagnosed in children (APA, 2013). Within the United States, it is estimated that about 6 million (9.8%) of children between the ages 3–17 have been diagnosed with ADHD with the largest age group being those 12–17 years old (13%) (Centers for Disease Control and Prevention [CDC], 2019; Danielson et al., 2022). Both Black and White non-Hispanic children are more likely to be diagnosed with ADHD than Hispanic or Asian children, and ADHD is more likely to be diagnosed in boys (13%) than girls (6%) (CDC, 2019). Additionally, children diagnosed with ADHD frequently receive comorbid diagnoses of mental, emotional, or behavioral disorders (64%) with behavioral or conduct problems being the most prevalent (52%).

Prevalence rates of adults with ADHD vary. According to the *Diagnostic and Statistical Manual* (5th ed.; DSM-5), the prevalence rate of ADHD is about 2.5% in adults (APA, 2013). Chung et al. (2019) found that the prevalence rates of ADHD in U.S. adults increased from 0.43% in 2006 to 0.96% in 2016; this represented an increase of 123.3% in the diagnosis of ADHD in adults, compared to an increase of 26.4% in children during the same time span. Globally, it is estimated that almost 140 million adults have persistent, or childhood-onset adult ADHD (2.58%) and 366.3 million adults have symptomatic ADHD (6.76%) as of 2020 (Song et al., 2021). Overall, these rates demonstrate the relative commonality of ADHD within the adult population, which constitutes the necessity for further investigation into the impact of the disorder in areas such as education and the COVID-19 pandemic.

ADHD AND COLLEGE STUDENTS

ADHD is an early on-set disorder, referring to a diagnosis in childhood that can follow into adulthood (Barkley et al., 2015; Wood et al., 2021). However, there is conflicting evidence on the diagnosis of ADHD including incidence of misdiagnosis, over-diagnosis, and under-diagnosis. Many ADHD diagnoses made in college rely on self-reported symptoms (Wood et al., 2021). DuPaul et al. (2009) stated that approximately 2 to 8% of college students in the United States are diagnosed with ADHD. However, a more recent study that examined 24 colleges across nine countries suggested that approximately 16% of students were diagnosed with ADHD (Mak et al., 2021).

ADHD can have substantial effects on a young adult's academic career. According to Nugent and Smart (2014), postsecondary students diagnosed with ADHD exhibit lower grade point averages (GPAs) and an increased likelihood of dropping out of their educational program. Nugent and Smart (2014) state that "college is often the time when individuals transition from adolescence to adulthood, and postsecondary education is characterized by greater organizational demands and the absence of close parent or teacher support" (p. 1787), which influences a student's ability to complete coursework. The major life transition that occurs from secondary to postsecondary education can influence a student's ability to cope with symptoms of ADHD. A recent study suggests that inattentive symptoms are the primary factor related to academic problems for university students diagnosed with ADHD (Hartung et al., 2022).

A review of the literature suggests that the ADHD-related symptoms that influence a student's experiences in academia include emotional dysregulation (Barkley et al., 2015; Bodalski et al., 2022), sluggish cognitive tempo (Kamradt et al., 2022), rates of lower self-efficacy (Waite et al., 2022), and higher rates of impairment and procrastination (Wood et al., 2021). Specifically, emotional dysregulation, which is a deficit of executive functioning, can partially account for the relationship between ADHD symptoms in college students and procrastination (Bodalski et al., 2022). Sluggish cognitive tempo, including slowed thinking and daydreaming, are frequently experienced by those diagnosed with childhood and adult ADHD, and are linked to struggles with time-management and organization (Kamradt et al., 2022). Furthermore, self-efficacy, defined as an individual's belief that they can implement a specific behavior, is substantially lower among young adults diagnosed with ADHD that are attending college (Waite et al., 2022).

Accommodations

College students (i.e., under the age of 25; U.S. Department of Education, 2022) diagnosed with ADHD enrolled in postsecondary education are challenged with a multitude of issues, including disappointment with their grades, dropping courses, and decreased scores on college entrance exams (Barkley, 2015). A similar study revealed that university students who struggle with negative thought processes and worry often experience challenges in lifestyle due to issues with time management and have continuous dissatisfaction with relationships and academic performance (Kwon et al., 2018). Moreover, students with ADHD experience other challenges related to the college setting, such as higher levels of binge drinking (Garcia et al., 2020; Mochrie et al., 2020) and problematic gaming (Lefler et al., 2022). Mochrie et al. (2020) found that college students with ADHD that are transitioning into the postsecondary academic environment reported increased depressive symptoms and more frequent engagement in substance abuse.

Each of the presented findings suggests an increased need for mental health professionals and instructors to develop and implement interventions and provide accommodations that support the academic growth of college students with ADHD. Additionally, Waite et al. (2022) note that young adults with ADHD could benefit from additional resources focused on academic success, including specified accommodations and mental health support. According to Terras (2020), disability accommodations serve two purposes: "to access the content and comprehend it" (p. 185). Prior literature that documents ADHD accommodations suggests that typical accommodations provided to students include additional examination time, modification of classroom seating, and peer note taking (Lovett & Lewandowski, 2015). Another study found that accommodations provided in postsecondary education for ADHD often rely on minimal data related to symptomatology, with more accommodations offered than originally requested (Harrison & Armstrong, 2022). To reduce these accommodation issues, Weis et al. (2021) recommends that students diagnosed with ADHD seek an evaluation completed by a psychologist as opposed to a primary care physician, and that these psychologists should rely on data from an evidence-based assessment to identify specific accommodations that target ADHD symptoms. It is important that instructors create an inclusive classroom environment that incorporates accommodations for students with ADHD (Bustamante et al., 2021). Symptom specific accommodations suggested by psychologists can provide further support and clarification to instructors focused on meeting student's needs in the learning environment.

METHODS

The purpose of this chapter is twofold: (1) to explore the impact that the COVID-19 pandemic had on college students diagnosed with ADHD and (2) to better understand successful interventions for this population. A comprehensive search of relevant literature published between 2020 and 2022 was conducted to locate peer-reviewed published studies that explored ADHD, college students, and COVID-19. Databases utilized in the search were selected based on the inclusion of mental health and educational peer-reviewed journals. The following databases were searched for this study: PsychINFO, EBSCO, PubMED, Google Scholar, ERIC, and PsycArticles. The following search terms were used in combination for this study: *Attention-deficit/hyperactivity disorder*, *ADHD*, *adult ADHD*, *college students*, *young adults*, *COVID-19*, *coronavirus*, *accommodations*, *asynchronous learning*, *interventions*, *postsecondary education*, and *impairment*. A total of 41 peer-reviewed journal articles were reviewed for this chapter. We present the results of a comprehensive review of the symptoms of ADHD among college students and the impact of COVID-19 on college students diagnosed with ADHD. Selection criteria for articles included articles published between 2020 and 2022, and those whose study had a predominant focus on ADHD with a population focus of young adults; studies that analyzed ADHD in childhood were excluded. The review of the literature aimed to address the following questions:

1. What has been the impact of the COVID-19 pandemic on university and college students diagnosed with ADHD?
2. What interventions have been successful for treating and accommodating university and college students diagnosed with ADHD?

COLLEGE STUDENTS WITH ADHD AND THE IMPACT OF COVID-19

Mandatory quarantines and enforced social-distancing practices aimed at combating the spread of the virus led to sudden changes in educational practices. Most collegiate institutions switched from in-person learning to an online format, which allowed students to continue the semester while remaining physically safe from the virus (Crawford et al., 2020). However, while these measures may have kept individuals from contracting COVID-19, they made students more "unsafe" from mental health issues. These academic changes, combined with the uncertainties caused by the pandemic, contributed to increased negative mental health, including heightened stress, anxiety, and depression (Torales et al., 2020). Further, students already struggling with preexisting mental illnesses, such as ADHD, were uniquely vulnerable to the impacts of the pandemic, and had to navigate managing both the symptoms of their condition with the nuances of the global disaster (Foster et al., 2023).

Many adults with ADHD experienced increased emotional distress during the pandemic (Adamou et al., 2020). Due to the nature of the symptoms of ADHD (inattention, hyperactivity, and impulsivity), individuals with ADHD were found to struggle more with various safety protocols, including washing hands, quarantining, and wearing a face mask as such symptoms made it hard to engage in these behaviors and increased risk for exposure (Merzon et al., 2022). For instance, inattentiveness may result in difficulty remembering to adhere to such protocols as wearing a mask or washing one's hands, resulting in a failure to engage in these practices, and increasing the risk of contracting the virus. College students with ADHD were found to experience greater difficulties with online learning than those without ADHD due to increased loneliness, and decreased college and peer support (Laslo-Roth et al., 2022). Sarid and Lipka (2023) found that college students with ADHD had decreased academic self-efficacy during the pandemic. Further, college students with ADHD experienced heightened anxiety as a result of the ADHD symptoms (Seddio et al., 2022).

The pandemic had a predominantly negative impact on individuals with ADHD (Ando et al., 2021; Behrmann et al., 2022). Behermann and colleagues (2022) conducted a systematic review of the literature which focused on the mental health impact of the pandemic on individuals (children, adolescents, and adults) with ADHD and found reports of negative behavioral (i.e., inattention, hyperactivity, impulsivity), psychological (i.e., depression, anxiety, stress, trauma), emotional (i.e., boredom, sadness, irritability), social (i.e., isolation) and other outcomes (i.e., poor sleep). However, not everyone was negatively impacted. Behermann et al. uncovered some positive outcomes within their review, such as lowered anxiety and increased feelings of hope. A qualitative study conducted in Japan found both positive and negative impacts of the pandemic amongst adults with ADHD that related specifically to the quarantine measures enacted during the pandemic (Ando et al., 2021). Some of the positive aspects included better time management, increased self-discipline, and lowered fatigue while remaining in place. Negative impacts included worsening ADHD symptoms (i.e., inattention), increased negative emotions (i.e., frustration and stress), and increased internal struggles (i.e., worries, concerns, and boredom). Some of this could be attributed to issues related to screen time as the pandemic forced individuals to mediate more of their communication and information consumption, smartphone addiction (Toma et al., 2022) and problematic internet use (Zhao et al., 2021) among college students and adolescents with ADHD.

Research regarding the impact of the COVID-19 pandemic in college students with ADHD is limited, yet revealing of two consistent themes: the impact of COVID-19 on female students with ADHD and reduced access to resources. Moreover, some studies specifically explore the impact of the pandemic on women of various ages, including those with ADHD, which is interesting when one considers that men are more likely to be diagnosed with ADHD than women (CDC, 2019). Yet, females were identified within the literature as being a population uniquely vulnerable to the harmful effects of the pandemic. Thus, one theme that emerged was the unique impact that the COVID-19 pandemic had on women with ADHD, including those who were college-aged. Second, research suggests that college and college-aged students with ADHD had reduced access to important on-campus sources of support that would otherwise have served as protective factors in navigating the struggles of college, which was a result of enforced online learning. As such, college-aged students with ADHD, particularly women, may benefit uniquely from various interventions and increased sources of support to better promote academic success during periods of great difficulty.

There is a limited amount of literature exploring the impact of learning modality (online/hybrid/face-to-face) on postsecondary students with ADHD that were enrolled in postsecondary programs during the COVID-19 pandemic. One study's findings suggest that postsecondary students with ADHD experienced lower academic self-efficacy during COVID-19 (Sarid & Lipka, 2023). Terras (2020) suggests that postsecondary students with ADHD completing online coursework struggled with developing student-instructor relationships, completing large projects, and meeting deadlines. Thus, we can speculate that the transition from the face-to-face learning environment to strictly online coursework as a result of the COVID-19 pandemic may have exacerbated symptoms of ADHD and created additional barriers to successfully completing coursework.

Female Students With ADHD

Foster and colleagues (2023) explored various mental health concerns, including ADHD, in young adults from 2018–2021, and found that only women had significant increases in prevalence rates of ADHD during the pandemic. One study in particular found that women with ADHD (compared to women without ADHD) had decreased psychological quality of life, with decreased emotional well-being, increased stress and anxiety, and lowered physical quality of life with increased sleep problems as a result of the pandemic (Engel-Yeger, 2022). Though the study did not specifically focus on college-aged women, their sample of women with ADHD did include 46 Israeli women between the ages of 19–60 (M = 27.64). Participants (women, college students, 70% with ADHD) reported that the stress of the pandemic negatively impacted their ability to form relationships with others at school, relationships that could be especially beneficial to students with developmental disabilities (i.e., ADHD) in forming connections for possible resources (Hoyle et al., 2022). Thus, college-aged women with ADHD appeared to be impacted uniquely by the effects of the pandemic and may have been unable to access resources otherwise available to them to aid in managing such concerns.

Close relationships were identified as highly important and valuable resources to college-aged women with developmental disabilities (70% with ADHD) when beginning college (Hoyle et al., 2022). Such relationships provided support, guidance, and encouragement during the transitional period into college, especially during hard times. However, the social distancing protocols enacted during the pandemic limited one's ability to form such relationships with peers and faculty members that could act as supports. Additionally, struggles with ADHD symptoms, such as inattention, further decreased one's ability to maintain important relationships with others, as it was hard to focus one's attention on the formation and sustainability of the relationship when there was infrequent interaction with the other—out of sight, out of mind.

These difficulties and other effects of the coronavirus pandemic on adults with ADHD, including college students, have led researchers to recognize the need for improved interventions and resources aimed at supporting this population during particularly difficult periods (Engel-Yeger, 2022; Laslo-Roth et al., 2022). It is important for those who may act as sources of support, including instructors and counselors, to be well-equipped to help students with ADHD during stressful periods.

Access to Resources

Reduced access to care and support systems from the pandemic further negatively impacted both men and women with ADHD. Individuals struggling with neurodevelopmental disorders, including ADHD, experienced significant increases in depressive symptoms as a result of limited access to medical care during the pandemic (Kertzscher et al., 2022). When compared to college students without ADHD, Israeli college students with

ADHD reported higher rates of loneliness and learning difficulties (Laslo-Roth et al., 2022). Such difficulties were connected to perceived decreased support from one's institution, though increased feelings of hope helped to mediate these effects.

Summary

The unforeseen circumstances of the pandemic led to an exacerbation of ADHD symptoms in college students. These students had arduous college experiences in which they were expected to adjust learning preferences. Students with ADHD also reported increases in symptoms related to other mental disorders. Moreover, students struggled with not only adjusting to online delivery methods of coursework but also establishing and maintaining relationships with others in addition to accessing institutional resources. Instructors and counselors should consider interventions that will support college students with ADHD in the academic setting.

INTERVENTIONS FOR INSTRUCTORS

A review of the literature on college students diagnosed with ADHD indicates that interventions targeting ADHD symptoms can be effective in increasing student success in postsecondary education. Although the most common interventions utilized to treat ADHD are psychostimulant medications (Molina et al., 2020), behavioral interventions (Solanto & Scheres, 2021), or a combination of both (Wilens & Dodson, 2004), an exploration of specific interventions that instructors and counselors may use are provided and described in Table 8.1.

Opening the Dialogue

The first step in assisting students in postsecondary education that have ADHD is to begin the conversation. Bustamante et al. (2021) states that instructors should ask students about their learning preferences and skills, by providing context in syllabi and carving out class time dedicated to these areas for discussion. Conversing with students regarding their learning preferences that can be accommodated in the educational environment should be prioritized to support their learning endeavors and will demonstrate that the instructor is approachable. To create an environment of inclusivity, instructors may also incorporate open invitations into class discussion regarding the student's needs (Bustamante et al., 2021; Hogan

Table 8.1

Interventions for Working With College Students With ADHD

Applicable Profession	Intervention	Description
Instructor	Opening the Dialogue	Ask students about learning preferences and their skills to focus on building accommodations
Instructor	Scaffolding	Provide guidance on instruction by creating a schedule structure that reviews content and sets expectations
Instructor	Body Doubling	Students partner with another individual on work either in the classroom or via an online platform
Instructor	Time Management & Technology	Utilization of online platforms to assist students in maintaining focus for a duration of time
Counselor	Cognitive Behavioral Therapy	Increase executive functioning through developing skills in time management, planning, and organization
Counselor	Token Economies	Using rewards to motivate the student to complete coursework

& Sathy, 2022). This discussion with students can occur as a group and or one-on-one with the student diagnosed with ADHD, depending on student comfortability.

Scaffolding

A second approach that instructors can utilize is scaffolding content of coursework to assist the student in staying on track. Scaffolding is an approach that can be seamlessly integrated into an instructor's coursework planning and can provide students with ADHD increased guidance related to instruction. Instructors can incorporate schedule structure by stating these components in the syllabi and reviewing them at the beginning of lectures. For example, instead of having students write a paper that is due at the end of the semester, have students submit assignments related to the paper throughout the semester. Not only will the increased amount of feedback benefit all students academically (Love & Marshall, 2022), the scaffolded assessments will especially help students with ADHD stay on track throughout the semester.

According to Bustamante et al. (2021), instructors should consider scaffolding by providing expectations for students, discuss examination preparation, and build connections between topics for students with ADHD. The concept of scaffolding in pedagogy has origins from Vygotsky's (1978) zone of proximal development theory, which describes what the student can learn independently versus with the help of others. Scaffolding refers to the initial support provided by another to a student, fading over time, to which the student can take full responsibility for their learning (Van de Pol et al., 2013). Instructors teaching students with ADHD may implement scaffolding by incorporating interactions into the learning environment through small group work (Van de Pol et al., 2013) and whole class teaching (Smit et al., 2013). Furthermore, Bustamante et al. (2021) states that "scaffolding can tell students what to expect in class, how to prepare for class and exams, and can allow students to see how each lesson relates to a main topic and the connections between main topics" (p. 574). With regard to scaffolding, students with ADHD benefit most from contingent support by the instructor, wherein the instructor monitors student learning consistently as opposed to fading support (Van de Pol et al., 2019).

Body Doubling

Another method that instructors may incorporate into the classroom to assist college students with ADHD is a technique called body doubling. Body doubling is a strategy aimed at increasing productivity by incorporating the presence of another individual in order to reduce distraction and maintain focus (Attention Deficit Disorder Association, 2022). Body doubling can be integrated into work in the classroom or on virtual platforms such as Zoom (Rogers, 2023). With the transition of learning from synchronous to asynchronous or remote, body doubling has increased momentum. Body doubling has been represented across social media platforms or apps for people with ADHD that are working. Apps such as Flown, FocusMate, and Flow Club can be utilized by students with ADHD to facilitate this. These apps offer methods of "virtual coworking" in which individuals can schedule sessions with one another, start a video call, outline goals or objectives for the session, and work together (FocusMate Inc., 2023). There is limited literature regarding the effectiveness of body doubling. However, as clinicians that treat college students diagnosed with ADHD, we have found that body doubling has demonstrated positive outcomes with regard to success in academia. Instructors may incorporate body doubling into pedagogical practices by pairing students to work together in class or assisting students with scheduling study sessions outside of class. Additional research is needed to empirically explore the efficacy of this practice.

Time Management and Technology

As students transitioned from receiving lectures in-person to remotely, instructors modified teaching methods to serve virtual learning. The use of technology in the classroom has continued to increase, and this was exacerbated by the COVID-19 pandemic. A study conducted by Fichten et al. (2022) that assessed technological preferences for students with ADHD suggested that online quiz platforms were preferred, as they assisted students in maintaining attention. Furthermore, other technological applications available for those struggling with time management, including *Pomodoro Timer, Interval Timer, and Stay on Task*, can be utilized (Fichten et al., 2022). Lastly, instructors and mental health professionals can suggest that students use online calendars or agendas to assist in time management, task completion, and attendance to classes or appointments (Fichten et al., 2022).

INTERVENTIONS FOR COUNSELORS

There are also interventions that counselors can employ to help students with ADHD. Two such interventions include cognitive behavioral treatment techniques and token economies.

Cognitive Behavioral Therapy

Cognitive behavioral therapy (CBT) techniques that focus on increasing executive functioning, such as assisting students in developing time management skills, planning, and organizing lecture materials, have proven to be helpful for college students diagnosed with ADHD (Hartung et al., 2022; Solanto & Scheres, 2021). Moreover, psychoeducation on the disorder increases feelings of normalization and validation (Solanto & Scheres, 2021). It is widely known that accommodations are a priority choice when students enter postsecondary education with ADHD (Harrison & Armstong, 2022), with federal regulations that denote that ADHD is a disabling condition (U.S. Department of Justice, 2016). However, Weis et al. (2019) note that misdiagnosis or lack thereof is a limitation since accommodations can contribute to further academic issues. Thus, it is suggested that counselors requesting accommodations for college students with ADHD provide additional information such as a specific description of the student's functional limitations, the appropriateness and duration of the accommodation, and data in support of the accommodations (Weis et al., 2019). There is minimal information regarding treatment interventions for college students with ADHD navigating academic environments during COVID-19.

Token Economies

An intervention that counselors may incorporate into the learning environment is the use of a token economy by utilizing rewards. According to Kallweit et al. (2019), the integration of rewards into tasks can increase motivation and activation. Token economies utilize a "consequence strategy awards of points or tokens for desirable behavior (positive contingency reinforcement) and may condition significant impairments to display inappropriate behaviors such as withdrawal of a previously gained token (response cost)" (Coelho et al., 2015, p. 2). CBT can be integrated with token economies by "using either positive contingency reinforcement rewarding appropriate behavior or negative reinforcement in the form of response costs by withdrawing a token" (Coelho et al., 2015, p. 6). For example, counselors can provide psychoeducation on token economies by teaching college students with ADHD to identify rewards that can serve as motivators and a method of accountability for completing coursework. Moreover, counselors teach students to remove the reward if tasks are not met. Although token economies are often implemented with children and adolescents in education, counselors can teach college students with ADHD how to utilize rewards independently.

CASE STUDY—JENNA

Jenna[1] is a 19-year-old Caucasian female obtaining her bachelor's degree at a four-year public university. Jenna is a sophomore, entering the fall semester of her second year in the business college for her major in accounting. Jenna was a freshman during the 2019–2020 academic year and during the spring semester, the COVID-19 pandemic required her university to transition from in-person coursework to remote learning. During the fall semester of the 2020–2021 academic year, Jenna reports that she has greatly struggled adjusting to remote coursework and that her classes consist of synchronous and asynchronous instruction.

Jenna states that she has experienced the following symptoms: careless mistakes, disorganization, avoidance, being easily distracted, forgetfulness, talking excessively, and impatience. Specifically, Jenna has reported that she frequently makes careless mistakes on graphs, struggles with managing and organizing her time in a manner that she can complete coursework, avoiding weekly discussions and semester projects, not being able to focus on one task at a time, and forgetting to attend remote classes held on Zoom. She has had instructors "call her out" for talking too much during class and has generally been impatient when collaborating with peers on group projects. Jenna notes that she experienced most of these symptoms prior to the pandemic; however, with the transition to remote coursework, Jenna states that her symptoms are debilitating. Jenna stated that she was diagnosed with ADHD during her senior year of high school. Jenna reached out to a psychiatrist her senior year of high school as she learned from friends that her academic struggles were abnormal. Jenna is not currently taking medication to treat her ADHD and has just started counseling. Jenna has requested help from her university instructors to help with her management of ADHD symptoms, as she fears that she "will fail most of her classes if she doesn't get this under control."

Applications for Instructors

Instructors that are working with Jenna on managing and completing coursework can implement the following strategies. First, the instructor could host a discussion either in-person or online to talk about the student's preferred methods of learning. The instructor may also meet with Jenna one-on-one to have a conversation about her concerns regarding her ADHD. The instructor can infuse scaffolding and structure into the in-person or online classroom by creating a structured syllabus, carving out time for breakout rooms and group conversations, and facilitating discussion boards. Next, the instructor can develop a course requirement for the students to engage in body-doubling, by providing students with a schedule in which they can work with another student for a specified time on coursework; this will also integrate the use of a timer. Through these interventions, Jenna will be able to engage more frequently, set expectations for herself and attendance, and save her energy for timed interactions. Once Jenna and the university receive specified accommodations from a mental health professional, the instructor can meet with Jenna to ensure the accommodations are enacted and support Jenna's learning experience(s).

Applications for Counselors

A counselor providing therapy can work with Jenna on developing time management skills and organizing coursework by using an agenda or planner. More specifically, a counselor may ask Jenna to bring in her planner and sit down together to plan out each day of the following week. Next, it is suggested that the counselor provide Jenna with psychoeducation on ADHD, including symptoms, prevalence, biological basis, and methods of treatment. Third, the counselor should consider referring Jenna to a psychologist for evaluation to identify appropriate accommodations. The counselor may correspond with the psychologist to determine areas that need to be focused on in treatment and targeted by accommodations. Lastly, the counselor can teach Jenna about the use of a token economy in which Jenna will identify a rewards system and integrate rewards as positive reinforcement in relation to completing assignments.

Applications for Both Instructors and Counselors

Jenna may also benefit from improved relationships with others within her community, as these may serve as sources of support during her collegiate career. Instructors can assist students like Jenna in this by providing them with campus resources for academic assistance (e.g., tutors and strategists), and others that encourage involvement in student organizations and in forming connections with fellow classmates. Additionally, Jenna's counselor can assist her with developing community connections by providing community-based resources and brainstorming social activities that Jenna can become involved in within her community (e.g., religious groups, book clubs, recreational activities, volunteering opportunities). Lastly, counselors should also explore any social anxiety or stress that Jenna may have in forming new connections.

Instructors and counselors can utilize interventions that target and alleviate ADHD symptoms to support college students in coursework. Specifically, instructors can focus on creating inclusive environments by incorporating open dialogue in the classroom, scaffold course content to increase guidance and structure, and integrate technology to facilitate interactions. Moreover, body doubling can be added to course content to assist students with ADHD in focusing on assignments. On the other hand, counselors can incorporate CBT techniques, collaborate with other professionals on identifying student-specific accommodations, and integrate token economies to assist students with ADHD in postsecondary education. CBT techniques can help students with ADHD increase executive functioning, a major factor that causes challenges for this population. The provided case study demonstrates how these interventions can be adapted to a student's specific situation.

IMPLICATIONS FOR FUTURE RESEARCH

As of this writing,[2] there is a scarcity of research exploring the experiences of college students with ADHD during the COVID-19 pandemic.

Past research has already demonstrated the unique academic struggles individuals in college may face as a result of their ADHD symptoms (e.g., Lefler et al., 2017). Research has also shown that stressful events, such as a global pandemic, can exacerbate such symptoms (Foster et al., 2023). In general, college students faced intense and sudden changes over the course of the pandemic, especially in the beginning when campuses closed down, teaching modalities transitioned from in person to online, and students were forced to return home (Crawford et al., 2020). Despite these facts, the experience of college students with ADHD during the pandemic is not well understood. Thus, more research is necessary to explore these experiences and better understand ways to support students during such times and during the current post-pandemic era.

Additionally, prevalence rates show that ADHD is diagnosed statistically more in boys than girls (APA, 2013; CDC, 2019). Yet, the research that does exist on the topic of college students with ADHD during the pandemic assesses women more than men (Engel-Yeger, 2022; Foster et al., 2023; Hoyle et al., 2022; Kertzscher et al., 2022; Laslo-Roth et al., 2020). This may be due to the additional struggles women may face during such events and the intersectionality of these identities (gender and ADHD), which may require more specialized prevention and intervention strategies to foster growth and well-being during such difficult times. However, there still remains a need to better understand how male college students with ADHD fared during the shifts and changes of the pandemic to inform ways to support this group as well. Further, the intersection of different identities (e.g., socioeconomic status) and ADHD should also be explored.

Regardless of gender, all college students had to leave their campuses and the traditional in-person collegiate experience due to the restrictions put in place to mitigate the spread of COVID-19. This change shifted more than just teaching methods as socialization and the formation of relationships between students and peers, and students and faculty diminished. Such relationships have been identified by students with developmental disabilities (such as ADHD) as a source of support during the transition to college (Hoyle et al., 2022). Being completely online and fully socially distanced from others meant the development of such connections was limited, leaving students with ADHD without the resources and strengths that come from such. More research may be valuable to better assess ways to increase social connectivity. Apart from the pandemic, this may also be informative for students with ADHD attending online college programs who already are distanced from peers, faculty, and other college resources. Such resources include both instructors and counselors, which further informs the need to consider these future research suggestions both within the context of the classroom and counseling.

The impact of the pandemic extends further than postsecondary education does. High school students diagnosed with ADHD have also been impacted by the pandemic (Breaux et al., 2022; ; Marshall, 2024; Marshall & Pressley, 2024; Naff et al., 2022; Sibley et al., 2021). This population also experienced reduced motivation, difficulties with online learning, and social isolation, all significantly worse than before the pandemic. This is important given that these students will matriculate into college soon. Recognizing the challenges of transitioning from high school to college is imperative for instructors and counselors providing support to students with ADHD, instructors and counselors may consider integrating the provided interventions into secondary education to smooth the transition process.

CONCLUDING THOUGHTS

College students with ADHD face unique challenges during their postsecondary education. Such challenges were greatly impacted and intensified by the effects of the COVID-19 pandemic. This review of the literature explored the impact of the pandemic on college students with ADHD. Much of the current literature focuses on outcomes for female students with ADHD and the impact of diminished access to necessary resources. Finally, the review considered these findings within the context of a fictional case study, providing resources for instructors and counselors to better assist college students with ADHD. Although research is presently limited on this topic, it is necessary to explore the needs of this population and to establish research aimed at providing them with greater support. This review contributes to this growing body of research and offers research-based interventions that may be utilized for this purpose.

REFERENCES

Adamou, M., Fullen, T., Galab, N., Mackintosh, I., Abbott, K., Lowe, D., & Smith, C. (2020). Psychological effects of the COVID-19 imposed lockdown on adults with attention deficit/hyperactivity disorder: Cross-sectional survey study. *JMIR Formative Research, 4*(12). https://doi.org/10.2196/24430

American Psychiatric Association [APA] (2013). Attention-deficit/hyperactivity disorder. In *Diagnostic and statistical manual of mental disorders* (5th ed.). https://doi.org/10.1176/appi.books.9780890425596.

Ando, M., Takeda, T., & Kumagai, K. (2021). A qualitative study of impacts of the COVID-19 pandemic on lives in adults with attention deficit hyperactive disorder in Japan. *International Journal of Environmental Research and Public Health, 18*, 1–10. https://doi.org/10.3390/ijerph18042090

Attention Deficit Disorder Association. (2022, October 24). *The body double: A unique tool forgetting things done.* https://add.org/the-body-double/

Barkley, R. A. (2015). *Attention-deficit hyperactivity disorder: A handbook for diagnosis & treatment.* Guilford Press.

Behrmann, J. T., Blaabjerg, J., Jordansen, J., Jensen de López, K. M. (2022). Systematic review: Investigating the impact of COVID-19 on mental health outcomes of individuals with ADHD. *Journal of Attention Disorders, 26*(7), 959–975. https://doi.org/10.1177/10870547211050945

Birmingham, W. C., Wadsworth, L. L., Lassetter, J. H., Graff, T. C., Lauren, E., & Hung, M. (2023). COVID-19 lockdown: Impact on college students' lives. *Journal of American College Health, 71*(3), 879–893. https://doi.org/10.1080/07448481.2021.1909041

Bodalski, E. A., Flory, K., Canu, W. H., Willcutt, E. G., & Hartung, C. M. (2022). ADHD symptoms and procrastination in college students: The roles of emotion dysregulation and self-esteem. *Journal of Psychopathology and Behavioral Assessment* https://doi.org/10.1007/s10862-022-09996-2

Bodalski, E. A., Neger, E. N., Bridges, R. M., Gleason, L. D. L., Anzalone, C., & Flory, K. (2022). A new organizational and study skills intervention for college students with ADHD. *Cognitive and Behavioral Practice, 29*(2), 411–424. https://doi.org/10.1016/j.cbpra.2020.09.005

Breaux, R., Dunn, N. C., Langberg, J. M., Cusick, C. N., Dvorsky, M. R., & Becker, S. P. (2022). COVID-19 resulted in lower grades for male high school students and students with ADHD. *Journal of Attention Disorders, 26*(7), 1011–1017. https://doi.org/10.1177/10870547211044211

Bustamante, C., Chini, J. J., & Scanlon, E. (2021). Supporting students with ADHD in introductory physics courses: Four steps for instructors. *The Physics Teacher, 59*(573). https://doi.org/10.1119/10.0006465

Centers for Disease Control and Prevention [CDC] (2019). *Data and statistics about ADHD.* https://www.cdc.gov/ncbddd/adhd/data.html

Chung, W., Jiang, S. F., Paksarian, D., Nikolaidis, A., Castellanos, F. X., Merikangas, K. R., & Milham, M. P. (2019). Trends in the prevalence and incidence of attention-deficit/hyperactivity disorder among adults and children of different racial and ethnic groups. *JAMA Network Open, 2*(11), e1914344. https://doi.org/10.1001/jamanetworkopen.2019.14344

Coelho, L. F., Barbosa, D. L. F., Rizzutti, S., Muszkat, M., Bueno, O. F. A., & Miranda, M. F. (2015). Use of cognitive behavioral therapy and token economy to alleviate dysfunctional behavior in children with attention-deficit hyperactivity disorder. *Frontiers in Psychiatry, 6*(167), 1–9. https://doi.org/10.3389/fpsyt.2015.00167

Crawford, J., Butler-Henderson, K., Rudolph, J., Malkawi, B., Glowatz, M., Burton, R., Magni, P. A., & Lam, S. (2020). COVID-19" 20 countries' higher education intra-period digital pedagogy responses. *Journal of Applied Learning & Teaching, 3*(1), 9–28. https://doi.org/10.37074/jalt.2020.3.1.7

Danielson, M. L., Holbrook, J. R., Bitsko, R. H., Newsome, K., Charania, S. N., McCord, R. F., Kogan, M. D., & Blumberg, S. J. (2022). State-level estimates of the prevalence of parent-reported ADHD diagnosis and treatment among U.S. children and adolescents, 2016 to 2019. *Journal of Attention Disorders, 26*(13), 1685–1697. https://doi.org/10.1177/10870547221099961

DuPaul, G. J., Weyandt, L. L., O'Dell, S. M., & Varejao, M. (2009). College students with ADHD: Current status and future directions. *Journal of Attention Disorders, 13*(3), 234–250. https://doi.org/10.1177/1087054709340650

Engel-Yeger, B. (2022). Emotional status and quality of life in women with ADHD during COVID-19. *OTJR: Occupation, Participation and Health, 42*(3), 219–227. https://doi.org/10.1177/15394492221076516

Fichten, C. S., Havel, A., Jorgensen, M., Wileman, S., Harvison, M., Arcuri, R., & Ruffolo, O. (2022). What apps to postsecondary students with attention deficit hyperactivity disorder actually find helpful for doing schoolwork? An empirical study. *Journal of Education and Learning, 11*(5), 44–54. https://doi.org/10.5539/jel.v11n5p44

FocusMate, Inc. (2023). *How it works.* https://www.focusmate.com/how-it-works

Foster, S., Estévez-Lamorte, N., Walitza, S., & Mohler-Kuo, M. (2023). The impact of the COVID-19 pandemic on young adults' mental health in Switzerland: A longitudinal cohort study from 2018–2021. *International Journal of Environmental Research and Public Health, 20,* 1–113. https://doi.org/10.3390/ijerph20032598

Garcia, M., Rouchy, E., Galéra, C., Tzourio, C., & Michel, G. (2020). The relation between ADHD symptoms, perceived stress and binge drinking in college students. *Psychiatry Research, 284,* 112689. https://doi.org/10.1016/j.psychres.2019.112689

Harrison, A. G., & Armstrong, I. (2022). Accommodation decision-making for post-secondary students with ADHD: Treating the able as disabled. *Psychological Injury and Law, 15*(4), 367–384. https://doi.org/10.1007/s12207-022-09461-1

Hartung, C. M., Canu, W. H., Serrano, J. W., Vasko, J. M., Stevens, A. E., Abu-Ramadan, T. M., Henning, C., Summerfeldt, L. J., & Parker, D. A. J. (2022). ADHD and academic success in university students: The important role of impaired attention. *Journal of Attention Disorders, 26*(6), 893–901.

Hogan, K. A., & Sathy, V. (2022). *Inclusive teaching: Strategies for promoting equity in the college classroom.* West Virginia University Press.

Hoyle, J. N., Laditka, J. N., & Laditka, S. B. (2022). "Eventually I'm gonna need people": Social capital among college students with developmental disability. *Research in Developmental Disabilities, 127,* 1–11. https://doi.org/10.1016/j.ridd.2022.104270

Jansen, D., Petry, K., Ceulemans, E., van der Oord, S., Noens, I., & Baeyens, D. (2017). Functioning and participation problems of students with ADHD in higher education: Which reasonable accommodations are effective? *European Journal of Special Needs Education, 32*(1). https://doi.org/10.1080/08856257.2016.1254965

Kallweit, C., Pauecke, M., Straub, M., & Exner, C. (2019). Adult ADHD: Influence of physical activation, stimulation, and reward on cognitive performance and symptoms. *Journal of Attention Disorders, 25*(6), 809–819. https://doi.org/10.1177/1087054719845050

Kamradt, J. M., Eadeh, H.-M., & Nikolas, M. A. (2022). Sluggish cognitive tempo as a transdiagnostic link between adult ADHD and internalizing symptoms. *Journal of Psychopathology and Behavioral Assessment, 44*, 699–712. https://doi.org/10.17077/etd.005966

Kertzscher, L., Kohls, E., Baldofski, S., Moeller, R., Schomerus, G., & Rummel-Kluge, C. (2022). Managing the COVID-19 pandemic in people with mental disorders: An exploratory telephone interview study in a psychiatric outpatient department. *Comprehensive Psychiatry, 116*, 1–9. https://doi.org/10.1016/j.comppsych.2022.152313

Kwon, S. J., Kim, Y., & Kwak, Y. (2018). Difficulties faced by university students with self-reported symptoms of attention-deficit hyperactivity: A qualitative study. *Child and Adolescent Psychiatry and Mental Health, 12*(1), 12–20. https://doi.org/10.1186/s13034-018-0218-3

Laslo-Roth, R., Bareket-Bojmel, L., & Margalit, M. (2022). Loneliness experience during distance learning among college students with ADHD: The mediating role of perceived support and hope. *European Journal of Special Needs Education, 37*(3), 220–234. https://doi.org/10.1080/08856257.2020.1862339

Lefler, E. K., Sacchetti, G. M., & Del Carlo, D. I. (2017). ADHD in college: A qualitative analysis. *ADHD Attention Deficit and Hyperactivity Disorders, 8*, 79–93. https://doi.org/10.1007/s12402-016-0190-9

Lefler, E. K., Alacha, H. F., Vasko, J. M., Serrano, J. W., Looby, A., Flory, K., & Hartung, C. M. (2022). Sex differences in ADHD symptoms, problematic gaming, and impairment in college students. *Current Psychology*. https://doi.org/10.1007/s12144-022-03469-1

Lefler, E. K., Alacha, H. F., Weed, B. M., Reeble, C. J., & Garner, A. M. (2023). Professor and peer perceptions of requests for academic accommodations in college: An examination of ADHD and specific learning disorder. *Psychological Reports*. https://doi.org/10.1177/00332941231156821

Love, S. M., & Marshall, D. T. (2022). Video feedback and instructor social presence in an asynchronous online course. *Journal of Effective Teaching in Higher Education, 5*(2), 43–58. https://doi.org/10.36021/jethe.v5i2.324

Lovett, B. J., & Lewandowski, L. J. (2015). *Testing accommodations for students with disabilties: Research-based practice*. American Psychological Association.

Mak, A. D. P., Lee, S., Sampson, N. A., Albor, Y., Alonso, J., Auerbach, R. P., Baumeister, H., Benjet, C., Bruffaerts, R., Cuijpers, P., Ebert, D. D., Gutierrez-Garcia, R. A., Hasking, P., Lapsley, C., Lochner, C., & Kessler, R. C. (2021). ADHD comorbidity structure and impairment: Results of the WHO world mental health surveys international college student project (WMH-ICS). *Journal of Attention Disorders, 26*(8), 1078–1096. https://doi.org/10.1177/10870547211057275

Marshall, D. T. (2024). COVID-19 and school closures: A narrative review of pediatric mental health impacts. *Journal of School Choice, 18*(1), 67–76. https://doi.org/10/1080/15582159.2023.2201734

Marshall, D. T., & Pressley, T. (2024). *Lessons of the pandemic: Disruption, innovation, and what schools need to move forward.* The Guilford Press.

Meaux, J. B., Green, A., & Broussard, L. (2009). ADHD in the college student: A block in the road. *Journal of Pediatric and Mental Health Nursing, 16*(3), 248–256. https://doi.org/10.1111/j.1365-2850.2008.01349.x

Merzon, E., Weiss, M. D., Cortese, S., Rotem, A., Schneider, T., Craig, S. G., Vinker, S., Cohen, A. G., Green, I., Ashkenazi, S., Weizman, A., & Manor, I. (2022). The association between ADHD and the severity of COVID-19 infection. *Journal of Attention Disorders, 26*(4), 491–501. https://doi.org/10.1177/10870547211003659

Mochrie, K. D., Whited, M. C., Cellucci, T., Freeman, T., & Corson, A. T. (2020). ADHD, depression, and substance abuse risk among beginning college students. *Journal of American College Health, 68*(1), 6–10. https://doi.org/10.1080/07448481.2018.1515754

Molina, B. S. G., Kipp, H. D., Joseph, H. M., Engster, S. A., Harty, S. C., Dawkins, M., Lindstrom, R. A., Bauer, D. J., & Bangalore, S. S. (2020). Stimulant diversion risk among college students treated for ADHD: Primary care provider prevention training. *Academic Pediatrics, 20*(1), 119–127. https://doi.org/10.1016/j.acap.2019.06.002

Naff, D., Williams, S., Furman-Darby, J., & Yeung, M. (2022). The mental health impacts of COVID-19 on PK–12 students: A systematic review of emerging literature. *AERA Open, 8*(1), 1–40. https://doi.org/10.1177/23328584221084722

Nugent, K. & Smart, W. (2014). Attention-deficit/hyperactivity disorder and postsecondary students. *Neuropsychiatric Disease and Treatment, 10,* 1781–1791. http://doi.org/10.2147/NDT.S64136

Rogers, K. (2023, February 13). *The benefits of 'body doubling' when you have ADHD, according to the experts.* CNN Health. https://www.cnn.com/2023/02/13/health/adhd-body-doubling-productivity-benefits-wellness/index.html

Rosello, B., Berenguer, C., Baixauli, I., Mira, A., Martinez-Raga, J., & Miranda, A. (2020). Empirical examination of executive functioning, ADHD associated behaviors, and functional impairments in adults with persistent ADHD, remittent ADHD, and without ADHD. *BMC Psychiatry, 20*(134), 1–12. https://doi.org/10.1186.s12888-020-02542-y

Rosenthal, E., Franklin-Gillette, S., Jung, H. J., Nelson, A., Evans, S. W., Power, T. J., Yerys, B. E., Dever, B. V., Reckner, E., & DuPaul, G. J. (2022). Impact of COVID-19 on youth with ADHD: Predictors and moderators of response to pandemic restrictions on daily life. *Journal of Attention Disorders, 26*(9), 1223–1234. https://doi.org/10.1177/10870547211063641

Sarid, M., & Lipka, O. (2023). The relationship between academic self-efficacy and class engagement of self-reported LD and ADHD in Israeli undergraduate students during COVID-19. *European Journal of Psychology,* 1–22. https://doi.org/10.1007/s10212-023-00677-6

Sibley, M. H., Ortiz, M., Gaias, L. M., Reyes, R., Joshi, M., Alexander, D., & Graziano, P. (2021). Top problems of adolescents and young adults with ADHD during the COVID-19 pandemic. *Journal of Psychiatric Research, 136*, 190–197. https://doi.org/10.1016/j.jpsychires.2021.02.009

Seddio, K., Pollack, D., Crawford, H., & Lewis, J. (2022). Attention-deficit/hyperactivity disorder (ADHD) and anxiety during the COVID-19 pandemic: Implications for internalizing behaviors in college students. *Journal of American College Health*. https://doi.org/10.1080/07448481.2022.2069469

Solanto, M. V., & Scheres, A. (2021). Feasibility, acceptability, and effectiveness of a new cognitive-behavioral intervention for college students with ADHD. *Journal of Attention Disorders, 25*(14), 2068–2082. https://doi.org/10.1177/1087054720951865

Song, P., Zha, M., Yang, Q., Zhang, Y., Li, Z., & Rudan, I. (2021). The prevalence of adult attention-deficit hyperactivity disorder: A global systematic review and meta-analysis. *Journal of Global Health, 11*(04009). https://doi.org/10.7189/jogh.11.04009

Smit, J., van Eerde, H. A. A., Bakker, A. (2013). A conceptualisation of whole-class scaffolding. *British Educational Research Journal, 39* (5), 817–834. https://doi.org/10.1002/berj.3007

Terras, K. (2020). Comparing disability accommodations in online courses: A cross-classification. *Journal of Educators Online, 17*(2), 175–187.

Toma, R. A., Anderson, C. A., Matichescu, M., Frant, A., Almajan-Guta, B., Candea, A., & Bailey, K. (2022). Effects of media use, smart phone addiction, and adult ADHD symptoms on wellbeing of college students during the COVID-19 lockdown: Dispositional hope as a protective factor. *Frontiers in Psychology, 13*, 1019976. https://doi.org/10.3389/fpsyg.2022.1019976

Torales, J., O'Higgins, M., Castaldelli-Maia, J. M., & Ventriglio, A. (2020). The outbreak of COVID-19 coronavirus and its impact on global mental health. *International Journal of Social Psychiatry, 66*(4), 317–20. https://doi.org/10.1177/0020764020915212

U.S. Department of Education. (2022). *Characteristics of postsecondary students* (No. 3). https://nces.ed.gov/programs/coe/pdf/2022/csb_508.pdf

U.S. Department of Justice. (2016). Amendment of Americans with Disabilities Act Title II and Title III regulations to implement ADHD Amendments Act of 2008; Final Rule. Federal Register, 81, 53204-53243.

Van de Pol, J., Volman, M., & Beishuizen, J. (2013). Scaffolding in teacher-student interaction: A decade of research. *Educational Psychology Review, 22*(3), 271–297. https://doi.org/10.1007/s10648-010-9127-6

Van de Pol, J., Mercer, N., & Volman, M. (2019). Scaffolding student understanding in small-group work: Students' uptake of teacher support in subsequent small-group interaction. *Journal of the Learning Sciences, 28*(2), 206–239. https://doi.org/10.1080/10508406.2018.1522258

Vygotsky, L. S. (1978). *Mind society—The development of higher psychological processes*. Harvard University Press. https://doi.org/10.1080/10508406.2018.1522258

Waite, R., Buchanan, T., & Leahy, M. (2022). Assessing ADHD symptoms among young adults in the university with the ASRS v1.1: Examining associations with social anxiety and self-efficacy. *International Journal of Disability, Development and Education, 69*(5), 1631–1644. https://doi.org/10.1080/1034912x.2020.1825643

Weis, R., Hombosky, M. L., Schafer, K. K., Shulman, D. & Tull, J. K. (2021). Accommodation decision-making for postsecondary students with ADHD: Implications for neuropsychologists. *Journal of Clinical and Experimental Neuropsychology, 43*(4), 370–383. https://doi.org/10.1080/13803395.2021.1918645

Wilens, T. E., & Dodson, W. (2004). A clinical perspective of attention-deficit/hyperactivity disorder into adulthood. *The Journal of Clinical Psychiatry, 65*, 1303–1313. http://doi.org/10.4088/JCP.v65n1003

Wood, W. L., Lewandowski, L. J., & Lovett, B. J. (2021). Profiles of diagnosed and undiagnosed college students meeting ADHD symptom criteria. *Journal of Attention Disorders, 25*(5), 646–656. https://doi.org/10.1177/1087054718824991

Zhao, Y., Jiang, Z., Guo, S., Wu, P., Lu, Q., Xu, Y., Liu, L., Su, S., Shi, L., Que, J., Sun, Y., Sun, Y., Deng, J., Meng, S., Yan, W., Yuan, K., Sun, S., Yang, L., Ran, M., Kosten, T. R., … Shi, J. (2021). Association of symptoms of Attention Deficit and Hyperactivity with problematic internet use among university students in Wuhan, China during the COVID-19 pandemic. *Journal of Affective Disorders, 286*, 220–227. https://doi.org/10.1016/j.jad.2021.02.078

ENDNOTES

1. The case of Jenna is fictitious and was created to demonstrate the application of ADHD interventions.
2. July 2023.

CHAPTER 9

TRADE-OFFS OF SEEKING SUPPORT FOR UNIVERSITY STUDENTS DURING THE PANDEMIC

Lisa H. Rosen, Linda J. Rubin,
Meredith Higgins, and Paul Yeatts
Texas Woman's University

ABSTRACT

This study examined the relationship between co-rumination, perceived friendship closeness, perceived coronavirus threat, depression, and psychological distress in emerging-adult women during the COVID-19 pandemic. We hypothesized that co-rumination would indirectly influence depression and psychological distress through perceived friendship closeness and perceived coronavirus threat. Participants completed assessments between July and October 2020. Perceived coronavirus threat was positively associated with both depression and psychological distress. Friendship closeness was negatively associated with depression, but was not significantly related to psychological distress. Tests of indirect effects indicated that there were significant indirect effects from co-rumination to depression through both coronavirus threat and perceived friendship closeness. There was also a sig-

Examining the Cognitive and Psychological Effects of the COVID-19 Global Pandemic on High School, College, and Graduate Learners, pp. 195–215

nificant indirect effect from co-rumination to psychological distress through perceived coronavirus threat, but not through perceived friendship closeness. Implications and future research directions are discussed.

INTRODUCTION

Emerging adults may be substantially impacted by the many stressors associated with the pandemic. The spread of COVID-19 and the declaration of a pandemic in March 2020 dramatically altered the lives of almost everyone. The instability and stress associated with the pandemic may have been especially pronounced for college students in emerging adulthood, a developmental period already characterized by uncertainty, and made especially difficult with the added confusion and behavioral limitations resulting from the pandemic (Germani et al., 2020). Emerging adulthood spans from 18 years to 29 years of age, and is a time of identity exploration, self-focus, and feeling in-between adolescence and adulthood (Arnett et al., 2014). When stressed, college students tend to rely on their friends, and may be most likely to turn to them as a source of support (Barry et al., 2016). Social support from friends often serves as a protective factor; however, negative adjustment outcomes may result when supportive interactions between friends involve co-rumination or excessive discussion of problems (Boren, 2013; Landphair & Preddy, 2012; Rose, 2002; Rose et al., 2022; Spendelow et al., 2017). Given that female friendships are more intimate in nature than male friendships (Maccoby, 1998; Roy et al., 2010) and co-rumination has been found to be more prevalent among girls and women (Rose, 2002; Spendelow et al., 2017), the current study examined co-rumination in women as has been done in past research (e.g., Byrd-Craven et al., 2008; Byrd-Craven et al., 2010; Rankin et al., 2018; Starr & Davila, 2007). Specifically, the current study seeks to examine the adaptive as well as maladaptive outcomes of support-seeking (i.e., co-rumination) among college students during the pandemic.

GOALS, OBJECTIVES, STATEMENT OF PROBLEM

The current study examined college students' co-rumination with friends during the COVID-19 pandemic. During this stressful period, co-rumination was likely to occur given that college students turn to friends when faced with difficulties (Barry et al., 2016), and the pandemic created a wide range of problems (e.g., issues with work, academics, and family; Cao et al., 2020). Based on past research documenting the adjustment trade-offs associated with co-rumination (Haggard et al., 2010; Rose et al., 2007;

Spendelow et al., 2017), we sought to test the hypothesis that co-rumination surrounding the pandemic would be associated with benefits as well as costs, which has important implications for the mental health of college students. In terms of positive outcomes, we hypothesized that co-rumination with a close friend regarding pandemic-related problems would be associated with greater perceived friendship closeness. Conversely, we hypothesized that negative effects of co-rumination, including greater perceived coronavirus threat, would emerge. Both coronavirus threat and friendship closeness were examined as mediators of the relation between co-rumination and psychological maladjustment (i.e., depression and psychological distress). We hypothesized that perceived friendship closeness would be negatively associated with psychological maladjustment, and that perceived coronavirus threat would be positively associated with psychological maladjustment.

LITERATURE REVIEW

Co-Rumination and Adjustment

Although originally examined in children's friendships, the study of co-rumination has been extended to other developmental periods, including college students (DiGiovanni et al., 2023; Rose et al., 2007; Spendelow et al., 2017; Starr, 2015). The term co-rumination was coined by Rose in 2002, who defined co-rumination as "excessively discussing personal problems within a dyadic relationship ... characterized by frequently discussing problems, discussing the same problem repeatedly, mutual encouragement of discussing problems, speculating about problems, and focusing on negative feelings" (p. 1830). Rose has further described co-rumination as "lying at the intersection of self-disclosure and rumination" (Rose et al., 2007, p. 1020). Rather than ruminating about a problem alone, co-rumination occurs within a dyadic relationship, such as a close friendship, as partners disclose their thoughts and feelings centering on problems (Rose, 2002; Rose et al., 2007). Importantly, co-rumination is more extreme and repetitive in nature than are normative forms of self-disclosure. Co-rumination is also characterized by intense focus on negative affect and lack of attention to problem-solving (Haggard et al., 2011; Starr, 2015).

Co-rumination has been examined in observational studies with adolescents as well as college students (Byrd-Craven et al., 2010; Rose et al., 2014). In these investigations, friends elicited and encouraged problem talk through a number of mechanisms, including asking a question, showing support, requesting additional information, or offering a similar experience. As such, discussions in which partners engaged in co-rumination often involved perseverating on the problems, focusing on the accompanying negative affect, and hypothesizing about potential causes and consequences (Byrd-Craven et al., 2010; Rose, 2002, Rose et al., 2014).

Seeking social support is routinely viewed as adaptive (Barry et al., 2016); however, certain forms of social support seeking, such as co-rumination, are associated with negative outcomes (Rose et al., 2007; Spendelow et al., 2017, Starr, 2015; Whitton & Kuryluk, 2013). Across childhood through adulthood, studies have documented adjustment trade-offs associated with co-rumination (Rose et al., 2007; Spendelow et al., 2017). In terms of beneficial outcomes, co-rumination is associated with perceived closeness and positive friendship quality (Rose, 2002; Rose et al., 2007). There are also costs associated with co-rumination; consistently, co-rumination has been associated with depression and anxiety (Landphair & Preddy, 2012; Rose, 2002; Rose et al., 2007). A recent meta-analysis documented the relationship between co-rumination and internalizing problems and found that neither age nor gender moderated this relationship, though co-rumination was higher among females than males (Spendelow et al., 2017).

Similar adjustment trade-offs are found in examinations of co-rumination in different contexts, such as work and healthcare settings. Co-workers may discuss problems at work in the attempt to decrease stress (Boren, 2013; Haggard et al., 2011). Although such interactions may be associated with greater relationship quality, co-rumination in the workplace predicts perceived global stress and burnout. The university setting may present similar challenges to the workplace (e.g., deadlines, group projects).

Co-rumination can occur through multiple communication modalities (Keshishian et al., 2016; Murdock et al., 2019). For a sample of college students, there was a strong association between face-to-face co-rumination and co-rumination via phone calls (r = .75) and text messaging (r = .73), and all these forms of co-rumination were linked to positive friendship quality (Keshishian et al., 2016). In another sample of American college students, co-rumination over mobile phones was linked to anxiety and depression; however, this finding did not hold for Italian college students (Murdock et al., 2019). These findings suggest that co-rumination occurs via phone calls and text messaging in American samples holds important implications for college students, which is a group for whom mobile phone ownership is ubiquitous (Pew Research Center, 2019). Further, these findings of co-rumination occurring via different communication modalities also have important implications for examining discussions of problems during the COVID-19 pandemic, when social distancing guidelines were in place, possibly rendering in-person co-rumination less likely.

COVID-19 and Adjustment

The World Health Organization declared the COVID-19 outbreak to be a pandemic in March 2020, and noted that widespread fear and anxiety surrounding the novel coronavirus was to be expected (World Health Organization, 2020). In spring 2020, the majority of Americans reported fear of contracting this new and potentially life-threatening disease (Saad, 2020). Furthermore, about 20% of Americans reported having experienced a physical reaction when thinking about the pandemic (Keeter, 2020). As a great deal about COVID-19 remained unknown, feelings of uncertainty and worry about the future were common (Killgore et al., 2020; Torales et al., 2020). In line with this fear, the pandemic profoundly affected daily life and social behavior (Arslan et al., 2020), as discussed below, with a focus on college students.

Perhaps, most notably, the pandemic limited face-to-face social interactions. Individuals became isolated during lockdown, and even as restrictions eased, social distancing guidelines affected the ability to connect in person (Arslan et al., 2020; Galea et al., 2020). Many found new ways to socialize virtually, and nearly half of emerging adults reported attending online social gatherings (Schaeffer & Raine, 2020). Although immunology experts urged the public to engage in social distancing as one of the key behaviors needed to stop the spread of COVID-19, there was variability in the extent to which individuals actually socially distanced. Emerging adults were less likely to comply with social distancing guidelines, perhaps due to self-focus as well as greater use of heuristic processing (Moore et al., 2020; Wang & Li, 2020).

For many, the pandemic was associated with financial strain (Arslan et al., 2020). Those in emerging adulthood may have been most likely to experience financial loss because many worked in the service-sector, which was greatly affected by the pandemic (Fry et al., 2020; Schaeffer & Raine, 2020). In a survey of American adults, those in emerging adulthood were most likely to indicate that they or someone in their home had lost their job or experienced a pay cut; more than half of those 18 to 29 years of age indicated that they or someone in their household has experienced job and/or wage loss (Schaeffer & Raine, 2020). As shortages of household items occurred during the pandemic, some changed their shopping behavior and became prone to panic buying, which may have resulted in further financial stress (Escolà-Gascón et al., 2020).

Due to job loss and/or closing college campuses, many college students moved home to live with their parents (Cao et al., 2020; Fry et al., 2020; McMillan, 2020). Interestingly, more than half of emerging adults resided at home with parents during summer 2020, which was a higher rate than during the Great Depression (Fry et al., 2020). Given that emerging adults spend more time with peers than parents and are working toward financial independence (Barry et al., 2016; Lanz & Serido, 2020), moving back home may have been especially stressful. Nagata (2020) suggested that "college students have returned home unexpectedly, after a period of living independently in dorms, and thus feel that they have regressed" (p. 297). College students may have provided sources of support for their parents in the pandemic, but there may have also been greater family conflict (Wu et al., 2020).

In terms of college students moving home, the transition from face-to-face courses to remote schooling was often an additional stressor (Cao et al., 2020; Gillis & Krull, 2020; Liu et al., 2020). Many students faced technological issues, such as limited internet access. Students cited a number of factors affecting their academic work during the pandemic, including distractions at home, lack of private workspace, and COVID-related anxieties. Correspondingly, students frequently reported difficulty concentrating on their work and remaining motivated (Gillis & Krull, 2020). Some students expressed concerns that the pandemic would delay their academic progress (Cao et al., 2020).

Given the stress associated with the pandemic, concern and fear surrounding COVID-19 were common, and mental health challenges increased (Czeisler et al., 2020; Liu et al., 2020; Skalski et al., 2020; Szkody et al., 2020; Ye et al., 2020). Emerging adults reported greater distress than any other age group in March 2020, with one-third of emerging adults classified as being in the high distress group (Schaeffer & Raine, 2020). Those 18 to 24 years of age reported the highest of levels anxiety, depression, substances used to cope with the pandemic, and suicidal ideation in June 2020, with nearly three-fourths of those surveyed in this age group reporting at least one mental health concern (Czeisler et al., 2020). Many American emerging adults reported feelings of loneliness during the pandemic (Lisitsa et al., 2021; Merolla et al., 2021), with 43% reporting elevated levels of depression and 45% reporting elevated levels of anxiety (Liu et al., 2020). Germani and colleagues (2020) suggested that "COVID-19 has crucially affected emerging adults' work, study, social lives, and caring responsibilities in a time of personal and interpersonal change" (p. 6). Emerging adults may have also been especially affected, given that this developmental period is ordinarily characterized by uncertainty and striving for independence, and the pandemic brought further instability and insecurity about the future as well as reduced autonomy due to pandemic-related restrictions (Germani, Buratta, Delvecchio, & Mazzeschi, 2020; Germani, Buratta, Delvecchio, Gizzi, & Mazzeschi, 2020).

In times of great stress, such as that associated with the pandemic, social support can often be protective (Inauen & Zhou, 2020); however, certain forms of social support, including those that are co-ruminative in nature can be maladaptive (Boren, 2013; Haggard et al., 2010; Rose et al., 2007). Some research has suggested that social support seeking may be associated with lower levels of maladjustment during the pandemic (Grey et al., 2020; Yu et al., 2020). As is the case in past research, the effects of social support may be complex, and other findings have indicated that peer support did not protect against the negative effects of COVID-19 on mental health (Liu et al., 2020; Szkody et al., 2020).

Current Study

Examining co-rumination as a risk factor for college students is critically important because the manner in which pandemic-related challenges are handled has the potential to affect their developmental trajectory (Morgan, 2019). College students faced incredible challenges during the pandemic, including financial loss and academic hardship (Fry et al., 2020). Many may have felt powerless, and as if they socially and emotionally regressed because of reduced autonomy due to restrictions and having to move back home (Nagata, 2020). Under these conditions, communication with friends was limited to electronic mediums (Juvonen et al., 2021). Consequently, it is not surprising that emerging adults have reported the highest levels of distress during the pandemic (Czeisler et al., 2020; Liu et al., 2020; Schaeffer & Raine, 2020). By examining whether co-rumination is an adaptive or maladaptive strategy for dealing with pandemic-related stress, the current study has the potential to guide interventions to assist college students in navigating the challenges faced during the transition to adulthood.

METHOD

Participants

Participants included 593 (559 female) undergraduate students at a public university, primarily for women. The age of the sample ranged from 18 to 29 years (M = 19.20, SD = 2.01). Participants reported their race/ethnicity as follows: 38.4% Hispanic; 24.8% White, non-Hispanic; 20.9% Black or African American, non-Hispanic; 12.9% Asian, non-Hispanic; and 3% other, which is representative of the university community. Given that the sample was 94% female, analyses were limited to data from female undergraduates, which is consistent with previous research on co-rumination (e.g., Byrd-Craven et al., 2008; Byrd-Craven et al., 2010; Rankin et al., 2018; Starr & Davila, 2007). The demographics of the sample were representative of students enrolled in undergraduate psychology courses and the student body of the university from which it was drawn.

Procedure

Participants were recruited from undergraduate psychology courses and received research participation credits for their participation. Students chose from a list of available studies and other research-related opportunities, such as writing literature reviews. Students from introduction to general psychology classes were part of the participant pool, and given that this is a core course, demographics of the participant pool mirror the demographics of the university. Participants provided informed consent and completed a series of questionnaires online via a secure webpage. Questionnaires included measures of co-rumination, friendship closeness, perceived coronavirus threat, depression, and psychological distress. All data were collected between July and October 2020.

Measures

Co-Rumination

Co-rumination was assessed using the 27 item Co-Rumination Questionnaire (CRQ, Davidson et al., 2014; Rose, 2002). Participants responded to items (e.g., "we spend most of our time together talking about problems that my friend or I have") on a 5-point scale ranging from 1 (*not at all true*) to 5 (*really true*). Participants were instructed to answer the questions in relation to discussions of problems tied to COVID-19 with their closest friend. The CRQ was reliable with the current sample, Cronbach's $\alpha = .96$.

Friendship Closeness

Friendship closeness was assessed with the Network of Relationships Inventory (NRI, Buhrmester & Furman, 2008). Participants rated their relationship with their best friend on five positive relationship features (i.e., companionship, disclosure, emotional support, approval, satisfaction) and five negative relationship features (i.e., conflict, criticism, pressure, exclusion, dominance) using a 1 (*never or hardly at all*) to 5 (*always or extremely much*). Each relationship feature was assessed with three items;

sample items include "How happy are you with your relationship with this person" for satisfaction and "How often do you and this person disagree and quarrel with each other?" for conflict. Higher scores indicate higher friendship closeness. The NRI was reliable for the current sample, Cronbach's α = .87, and has been used to assess relationship quality during the pandemic (Donker et al., 2020).

Perceived Coronavirus Threat

The newly developed Perceived Coronavirus Threat Questionnaire was used to measure fear of COVID (Conway et al., 2020). Participants responded to six items (e.g., "I am afraid of the coronavirus (COVID-19); "Thinking about the coronavirus (COVID-19) makes me feel threatened") on a 1 (*not true of me at all*) to 7 (*very true of me*) scale. The Perceived Coronavirus Threat Questionnaire was reliable with the current sample, Cronbach's α = .85.

Depression

The Center for Epidemiologic Studies Depression Scale (CESD, Radloff, 1977) was used to assess symptoms of depression. This scale consists of 20 questions measuring feelings and behaviors associated with depression from the past week (e.g., "I felt sad"; "I felt everything I did was an effort") to which participants respond on a 4-point Likert scale from 0 (*rarely or none of the time, less than 1 day*) to 3 (*most or all of the time, 5-7 days*). The CESD was reliable for the current sample, Cronbach's α = .89, and this measure has been used to assess depression during the COVID-19 pandemic (Kim et al., 2020).

Psychological Distress

A measure of psychological distress was adapted from The Coronavirus Health and Impact Survey (CRISIS, Nikolaidis et al., 2020). Participants indicated how they felt over the past two weeks on a five-point scale ranging from 1 (*not at all*) to 5 (*extremely*) for the following five items: "How worried were you generally"; "How fidgety or restless were you"; "How fatigued or tired were you"; "How irritable or easily angered were you"; and "How lonely were you." The measure was reliable with the current sample, Cronbach's α = .83.

RESULTS

Descriptive statistics and correlations are presented in Table 9.1. Initially, all variables were checked for standard assumptions of normality. Mahalanobis distance was calculated to test for multivariate normality (Henson, 1999). No serious departures from univariate or multivariate normality were found in the current sample. Analysis of missing value patterns using Little's Missing Completely at Random test (MCAR; Little, 1988) was non-significant, indicating that missing values were missing completely at random. Finally, the measurement model was tested to confirm that latent variables were accurately defined. All items were significantly related to prescribed latent factors ($p < .001$), and measurement model fit was adequate, χ^2 (2,992) = 9,721.70 ($p < .001$), RMSEA = .06, 90% CI [.06 – .06]), CFI = .74, SRMR = .07.

Table 9.1

Correlations and Descriptive Statistics

	Mean (SD)	1	2	3	4	5
1. Co-rumination	3.06 (.89)	–	.11*	.19**	.13**	.04
2. Friendship Closeness	2.14 (1.02)		–	–.02	–.11*	–.16**
3. Perceived coronavirus threat	4.45 (1.45)			–	.35**	.15**
4. Psychological distress	4.06 (.51)				–	.59**
5. Depression	21.22 (10.61)					–

Note. *$p < .05$, **$p < .01$

Structural equation modeling using Mplus v8 was conducted to test the hypothesized model, and to specifically examine potential indirect effects. Figure 9.1 illustrates the model that was tested, showing that co-rumination affected psychological distress and depression indirectly through perceived coronavirus threat and perceived friendship closeness. All standardized path coefficients and corresponding p values are included in Table 9.2. Goodness-of-fit statistics indicated adequate fit overall (Kenny, 2020), χ^2

(2,995) = 9,728.80 (p < .001), RMSEA = .06, 90% CI [.06 - .06]), CFI = .74, SRMR = .07. Taken together, fit indices indicated that model fit was acceptable (Hooper et al., 2008). Results indicated that co-rumination had a significant, positive relationship with both mediators (i.e., perceived coronavirus threat and friendship closeness), $p < .001$. Perceived coronavirus threat was positively, significantly related to both depression and psychological distress, $p < .001$. However, friendship closeness was negatively, significantly related to depression ($p = .02$), but was not significantly related to psychological distress ($p = .17$). Tests of indirect effects indicated that there were significant indirect effects from co-rumination to depression through both coronavirus threat ($p = .002$) and perceived friendship closeness ($p = .04$). There was also a significant indirect effect from co-rumination to psychological distress through perceived coronavirus threat ($p < .001$), but not through perceived friendship closeness ($p = .32$).

Figure 9.1

Mediated Model

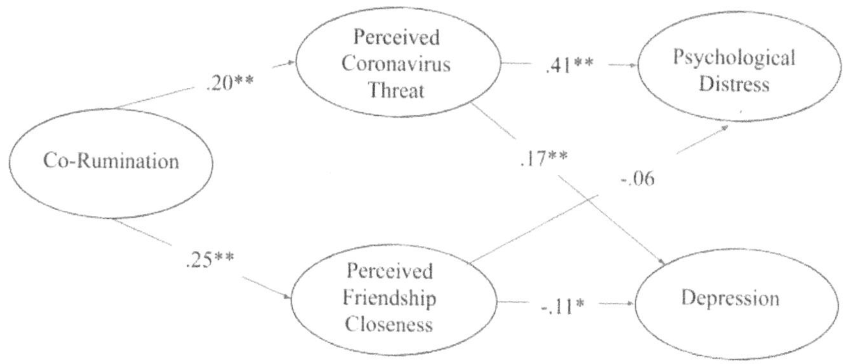

Note. *p < .05. **p < .01

Table 9.2

Structural Equation Model Results

	R^2	β	*SE*	*P*
Depression on	.04*			
Perceived coronavirus threat		.17**	.05	< .001
Friendship closeness		–.11*	.05	.02
Psychological Distress on	.17**			

(Table continued on next page)

Table 9.2 (Continued)

Structural Equation Model Results

	R^2	β	*SE*	*P*
Perceived coronavirus threat		.41**	.04	< .001
Friendship closeness		–.06	.05	.17
Perceived coronavirus threat on	.04*			
Co-rumination		.20**	.05	< .001
Friendship closeness on	.07**			
Co-rumination		.25**	.04	< .001

Note. Standardized estimates (β) are displayed. R^2 represents the total amount of variance explained in each endogenous latent variable.

$^*p < .05$. $^{**}p < .01$.

CONCLUSIONS

Based on the current study's findings, co-rumination appeared to contribute to friendship closeness for college students, while simultaneously increasing depression and psychological distress. Results provided support for the hypothesized adjustment trade-offs associated with co-rumination, and they extended previous research findings to include women college students during the pandemic. Although sharing pandemic-related concerns with a close friend may have been intended to relieve stress, the current findings suggested that such discussions may have actually increased fears surrounding coronavirus. Pandemic-related fear has dramatically affected college students' daily lives (Arslan et al., 2020; Escolà-Gascón et al., 2020) and has been linked with mental health concerns (Liu et al., 2020; Skalski et al., 2020; Szkody et al., 2020). Discussing pandemic-related concerns may have increased fear of the coronavirus, which in turn, negatively affected adjustment. In the current study, co-rumination reported by college students predicted depression and psychological distress indirectly through perceived coronavirus threat. Consistent with past research (Landphair & Preddy, 2012; Rose et al., 2007; Spendelow et al., 2017), co-rumination appeared to have negative mental health consequences. College students have reported high levels of distress during the pandemic, including symptoms of anxiety and depression (Czeisler et al., 2020; Schaeffer & Raine, 2020). Current findings suggested that co-rumination may be contributing to mental health concerns during the pandemic, at least among women in college.

Despite the negative outcomes associated with co-rumination, consistent with past research (e.g., Rose et al., 2007; Spendelow et al., 2017), there were also benefits linked to this process for women college students during the pandemic. Co-rumination was positively associated with perceived friendship closeness. Although originally examined in childhood friendships (Rose, 2002), co-rumination among close friends during emerging adulthood may positively predict relationship quality. In the current study, perceived friendship closeness was negatively associated with depression, but counter to the hypotheses, was not significantly associated with psychological distress. There was a significant indirect effect from co-rumination to depression through perceived friendship closeness, which is in line with findings that social support may play a protective role during the COVID-19 pandemic (Grey et al., 2020; Inauen & Zhou, 2020; Yu et al., 2020).

The findings for social support and co-rumination appear to be mixed. Given the repetitive nature of co-rumination, the consequences may outweigh the benefits (Spendelow et al., 2017). Co-rumination predicted psychological distress through perceived coronavirus threat, but no significant indirect effect was found via perceived friendship closeness. Although both perceived coronavirus threat and perceived friendship closeness mediated the relationship between co-rumination and depression, the negative indirect effect via perceived coronavirus threat was stronger than the positive indirect effect via perceived friendship closeness. That is, the positive outcome of co-rumination was somewhat outweighed by the negative outcomes for women college students. These findings further underscore how the effects of social support may be complex, with some research suggesting that peer support does not buffer against the negative effects of the pandemic on adjustment (Liu et al., 2020; Szkody et al., 2020). Supportive relationships characterized by high levels of co-rumination may not be protective in nature due to the intense and perseverating focus on problems and negative affect, though college women may be comforted by feelings of closeness in their friendships.

All results must be interpreted with consideration of the study's methodological limitations. First, co-rumination focused on a self-identified close friendship dyad and was reported by only one member of the dyad. Although investigations of co-rumination commonly focus on only one member of a close friendship dyad (e.g., Boren, 2014; Keshishian et al., 2016; Starr et al., 2015), examining both friendship partners as well as different types of relationships (e.g., multiple friendship partners, siblings) may have provided a more comprehensive view of this process.

An additional limitation was that the current study focused only on women's friendships, as is consistent with past research (e.g., Byrd-Craven et al., 2008; Byrd-Craven et al., 2010; Rankin et al., 2018; Starr &

Davila, 2007). Even though meta-analytic work suggested that gender does not moderate the relationship between co-rumination and internalizing problems (Spendelow et al., 2017), this is the first known investigation of co-rumination surrounding pandemic-related problems, and gender differences remain to be examined during this unprecedented time. Women may co-ruminate to a greater extent than men regarding pandemic-related problems, which would mirror findings related to general problem talk (Rose, 2002; Spendelow et al., 2017); however, this remains to be empirically examined.

There are also limitations associated with the study measures. We used the Co-Rumination Questionnaire (Davidson et al., 2014; Rose, 2002), which is most commonly employed in investigations of co-rumination. However, as the pandemic limited face-to-face interaction (Arslan et al., 2020; Galea et al., 2020; Grey et al., 2020), it would have been interesting to assess the manner in which co-rumination was unfolding (e.g., phone calls, text messaging; Keshishian et al., 2016; Murdoch et al., 2019). We did not use a well- validated measure of psychological distress, but rather adapted our measure from The Coronavirus Health and Impact Survey (Nikolaidis et al., 2020). Still, we selected this measure as it was part of the PhenX COVID-19 library of recommended measures to examine the effects of COVID-19, and as such will enable comparison with other studies conducted during the pandemic (PhenX Toolkit, 2020).

Despite these limitations, this study has important strengths. This is the first known investigation of co-rumination among college students during the COVID-19 pandemic. Life dramatically changed when COVID-19 began to spread, and resulted in a wide range of challenges for college students, including concerns with work, academics, and family (Arslan et al., 2020; Cao et al., 2020; Galea et al., 2020; Grey et al., 2020). When faced with challenges such as these, emerging adults tend to turn to their friends as a source of support (Barry et al., 2016). The current study showed that discussing pandemic-related issues with a close friend may be positively associated with relationship quality. Although these interactions likely stem from the desire to reduce pandemic-related stress, the current study suggests the opposite outcome; co-ruminative exchanges may have led to greater perceived coronavirus threat, which may in turn, predict psychological maladjustment.

IMPLICATIONS FOR FUTURE

Future research is needed to better understand the nature and consequences of co-rumination during the pandemic. In particular, observational studies would provide researchers with the opportunity to examine what college students perceive to be the most pressing concerns, as the pandemic has had lasting implications for students' college experiences. Longitudinal research is needed to understand the long-term consequences of the pandemic, which have been predicted based on the negative effects of past epidemics on mental health (Galea et al., 2020). Co-rumination during the pandemic may exacerbate these long-term consequences on mental health, and longitudinal investigations are needed to examine these associations.

The current findings hold important implications for the well-being of women college students during times of stress, such as the COVID-19 pandemic. The manner in which emerging adults handle these challenges may influence their developmental trajectory as they navigate the transition to adulthood (Morgan, 2019) and potentially have long-lasting, generational effects, as the pandemic and its fallout will have impacted every woman in college who is alive today. Support from friends has the potential to serve a protective function (Barry et al., 2016). However, social support can also be maladaptive at times. The current study suggested that although co-rumination during the pandemic was associated with perceived friendship closeness, it also predicted perceived coronavirus threat, which in turn, may result in depression and psychological distress. This finding is in line with Landphair and Preddy's (2012) assertion that "because of its focus on the negative, co-rumination may cause more harm than good" (p. 19). These findings may inform work with college students and emerging adults. Discouraging co-rumination might be associated with negative outcomes, as there can be benefits from sharing concerns with a supportive peer or partner (Landphair & Preddy, 2012; Muller et al., 2019). Rather, college students should be encouraged to develop problem-solving skills, as this has the potential to resolve concerns before co-rumination commences (Rose et al., 2022). Additionally, college students should be encouraged to engage in supportive discussions focused on generating solutions to pandemic-related problems, rather than focusing on negative affect (Landphair & Preddy, 2012). Constructive discussions have the potential to foster coping strategy development, which would benefit college students during times of stress (Leipold et al., 2019; Muller et al., 2019).

SUMMARY

College students are going through a period of transition and may have been more affected than others by the many stressors associated with COVID-19. The current study examined the effects of social support-seeking for college students during the pandemic. College students tend to rely on their friends when stressed, and social support from friends can serve as a protective factor. However, negative adjustment outcomes may result when supportive interactions between friends involve co-rumination, or excessive discussion of problems without an approach that includes problem-solving. Results provided support for the hypothesized adjustment trade-offs associated with co-rumination and extended previous research findings to include college students during the pandemic. As college students have been particularly affected by the COVID-19 pandemic, adaptive coping strategies and constructive forms of social support may be key to fostering resilience during the transition to adulthood amid this time of great stress. The challenge remains for university faculty and staff to help foster resilience in their students by helping them create authentic connections with others.

REFERENCES

Arnett, J. J., Žukauskienė, R., & Sugimura, K. (2014). The new life stage of emerging adulthood at ages 18-29 years: implications for mental health. *The Lancet. Psychiatry*, *1*(7), 569–576. https://doi.org/10.1016/S2215-0366(14)00080-7

Arslan, G., Yıldırım, M., Tanhan, A., Buluş, M., & Allen, K. (2020). Coronavirus stress, optimism-pessimism, psychological inflexibility, and psychological health: Psychometric properties of the Coronavirus Stress Measure. *International Journal of Mental Health and Addiction*, 1–17. https://doi.org/10.1007/s11469-020-00337-6

Barry, C. M., Madsen, S. D., & DeGrace, A. (2016). *Growing up with a little help from their friends in emerging adulthood.* In J. J. Arnett (Ed.), *Oxford library of psychology. The Oxford handbook of emerging adulthood* (pp. 215–229). Oxford University Press.

Boren, J. P. (2013). The relationships between co-rumination, social support, stress, and burnout among working adults. *Management Communication Quarterly*, *28*(1), 3–25. https://doi.org/10.1177/0893318913509283

Buhrmester, D. & Furman, W. (2008). The Network of Relationships Inventory: Relationship Qualities Version. Unpublished measure, University of Texas at Dallas.

Byrd-Craven, J., Geary, D. C, Rose, A. J., & Ponzi, D. (2008). Co-ruminating increases stress hormone levels in women. *Hormones and Behavior*, *53*(3), 489–492. https://doi.org/10.1016/j.yhbeh.2007.12.002

Byrd-Craven, J., Granger, D. A., & Auer, B. J. (2011). Stress reactivity to co-rumination in young women's friendships: Cortisol, alpha-amylase, and negative affect focus. *Journal of Social and Personal Relationships*, *28*(4), 469–487. https://doi.org/10.1177/0265407510382319

Cao, W., Fang, Z., Hou, G., Han, M., Xu, X., Dong, J., & Zheng, J. (2020). The psychological impact of the COVID-19 epidemic on college students in China. *Psychiatry Research*, *287*, 112934–112934. https://doi.org/10.1016/j.psychres.2020.112934

Conway, L. G., III, Woodard, S. R., & Zubrod, A. (2020, April 7). *Social psychological measurements of COVID-19: Coronavirus Perceived threat, government response, impacts, and experiences questionnaires*. https://doi.org/10.31234/osf.io/z2x9a

Czeisler, M. É., Lane, R. I., Petrosky, E., Wiley, J. F., Christensen, A., Njai, R., Weaver, M. D., Robbins, R., Facer-Childs, E. R., Barger, L. K., Czeisler, C. A., Howard, M. E., & Rajaratnam, S. (2020). Mental health, substance use, and suicidal ideation during the COVID-19 Pandemic–United States, June 24-30, 2020. *MMWR. Morbidity and Mortality Weekly Report*, *69*(32), 1049–1057. https://doi.org/10.15585/mmwr.mm6932a1

Davidson, C. L., Grant, D. M., Byrd-Craven, J., Mills, A. C., Judah, M. R., & Lechner, W. V. (2014). Psychometric properties of the Co-Rumination Questionnaire. *Personality and Individual Differences*, *70*, 171–175. https://doi.org/10.1016/j.paid.2014.07.002

DiGiovanni, A. M., Cornelius, T., & Bolger, N. (2023). Decomposing variance in co-rumination using dyadic daily diary data. *Social Psychological and Personality Science*, *14*(5), 636–646. https://doi.org/10.1177/19485506221116989

Donker, M. H., Mastrotheodoros, S., & Branje, S. (2020, October 13). *Development of parent-adolescent relationships during the COVID-19 pandemic: The role of stress and coping*. https://doi.org/10.31234/osf.io/urmt9

Escolà-Gascón, Á., Marín, F.-X., Rusiñol, J., & Gallifa, J. (2020). Measuring psychosocial reactions to COVID-19: The COVID Reaction Scales (COVID-RS) as a new assessment tool. *Frontiers in Psychology*, *11*, 1–12. https://doi.org/10.3389/fpsyg.2020.607064

Fry, R., Passel, J. S., & Cohn, D. (2020, September 4). *A majority of young adults in the U.S. live with their parents for the first time since the Great Depression*. Pew Research Center. https://www.pewresearch.org/fact-tank/2020/09/04/a-majority-of-young-adults-in-the-u-s-live-with-their-parents-for-the-first-time-since-the-great-depression/

Galea, S., Merchant, R. M., & Lurie, N. (2020). The mental health consequences of COVID-19 and physical distancing: The need for prevention and early intervention. *JAMA Intern Med*, *180*(6), 817–818. https://doi.org/10.1001/jamainternmed.2020.1562

Germani, A., Buratta, L., Delvecchio, E., & Mazzeschi, C. (2020). Emerging adults and COVID-19: The role of individualism-collectivism on perceived risks and psychological maladjustment. *International Journal of Environmental Research and Public Health*, *17*(10), 3497. https://doi.org/10.3390/ijerph17103497

Germani, A., Buratta, L., Delvecchio, E., Gizzi, G., & Mazzeschi, C. (2020). Anxiety severity, perceived risk of COVID-19 and individual functioning in emerging adults facing the pandemic. *Frontiers in Psychology*, *11*, 567505–567505. https://doi.org/10.3389/fpsyg.2020.567505

Gillis, A., & Krull, L. M. (2020). COVID-19 remote learning transition in spring 2020: Class structures, student perceptions, and inequality in college courses. *Teaching Sociology*, *48*(4), 283–299. https://doi.org/10.1177/0092055X20954263

Grey, I., Arora, T., Thomas, J., Saneh, A., Tohme, P., & Abi-Habib, R. (2020). The role of perceived social support on depression and sleep during the COVID-19 pandemic. *Psychiatry Research*, *293*, 113452–113452. https://doi.org/10.1016/j.psychres.2020.113452

Haggard, D. L., Robert, C., & Rose, A. J. (2010). Co-rumination in the workplace: Adjustment trade-offs for men and women who engage in excessive discussions of workplace problems. *Journal of Business and Psychology, 26*(1), 27–40. https://doi.org/10.1007/s10869-010-9169-2

Henson, R. K. (1999). Multivariate normality: What is it and how is it assessed? *Advances in Social Science Methodology, 5*, 193–211. https://doi.org/10.1017/CBO9781107415324.004

Hooper, D., Coughlan, J., & Mullen, M. (2008, September). Evaluating model fit: A synthesis of the structural equation modelling literature. In *7th European Conference on research methodology for business and management studies* (Vol. 2008, pp. 195–200).

Inauen, J., & Zhou, G. (2020). Health and well-being in the early stages of the Covid-19 pandemic: Insights from applied psychology. *Applied Psychology : Health and Well-Being, 12*, 937–940. https://doi.org/10.1111/aphw.12245

Juvonen, J., Schacter, H. L., & Lessard, L. M. (2021). Connecting electronically with friends to cope with isolation during COVID-19 pandemic. *Journal of Social and Personal Relationships, 38*(6), 1782–1799. https://doi.org/10.1177/0265407521998459

Keeter, S. (2020, March 30). *People financially affected by COVID-19 outbreak are experiencing more psychological distress than others.* Pew Research Center. https://www.pewresearch.org/fact-tank/2020/03/30/people-financially-affected-by-covid-19-outbreak-are-experiencing-more-psychological-distress-than-others/

Keshishian, A. C., Watkins, M. A., & Otto, M. W. (2016). Clicking away at co-rumination: co-rumination correlates across different modalities of communication. *Cognitive Behaviour Therapy, 45*(6), 473–478. https://doi.org/10.1080/16506073.2016.1201848

Killgore, W.D.S, Taylor, E. C., Cloonan, S. A., & Dailey, N. S. (2020). Psychological resilience during the COVID-19 lockdown. *Psychiatry Research, 291*, 113216–113216. https://doi.org/10.1016/j.psychres.2020.113216

Kim, A. W., Nyengerai, T., & Mendenhall, E. (2020). *Evaluating the mental health impacts of the COVID-19 pandemic in Urban South Africa: Perceived risk of COVID-19 infection and childhood trauma predict adult depressive* Symptoms. https://doi.org/10.1101/2020.06.13.20130120

Landphair, J., & Preddy, T. (2012). More than talk: Co-rumination among college students. *About Campus, 17*(3), 18–22. https://doi.org/10.1002/abc.21082

Lanz, M., & Serido, J. (2020). Financial and life instability: Obstacles to and opportunities for emerging adult development and future well-being. *Emerging Adulthood, 8*(6), 439–442. https://doi.org/10.1177/2167696820951042

Leipold, B., Munz, M., & Michéle-Malkowsky, A. (2019). Coping and resilience in the transition to adulthood. *Emerging Adulthood*, 7(1), 12–20. https://doi.org/10.1177/2167696817752950

Lisitsa, E., Benjamin, K. S., Chun, S. K., Skalisky, J., Hammond, L. E., & Mezulis, A. H. (2020). Loneliness among young adults during the COVID-19 pandemic: The mediational roles of social media use and social support seeking. *Journal of Social and Clinical Psychology, 39*(8), 708. https://doi.org/10.1521/jscp.2020.39.8.708

Little, R. J. (1988). A test of missing completely at random for multivariate data with missing values. *Journal of the American Statistical Association, 83*(404), 1198–1202. https://doi.org/10.2307/2290157

Liu, C. H., Zhang, E., Wong, G., Hyun, S., & Hahm, H. C. (2020). Factors associated with depression, anxiety, and PTSD symptomatology during the COVID-19 pandemic: Clinical implications for U.S. young adult mental health. *Psychiatry Research, 290*, 113172. https://doi.org/10.1016/j.psychres.2020.113172

Kenny, D. (2020, June 5). *Measuring model fit*. http://www.davidakenny.net/cm/fit.htm

Maccoby, E. E. (1998). *The two sexes: Growing up apart, coming together*. Harvard University Press.

McMillan, S. J. (2020). COVID-19 and strategic communication with parents and guardians of college students. *Cogent Social Sciences, 6*(1), 1–19. https://doi.org/10.1080/23311886.2020.1843836

Merolla, A. J., Otmar, C., & Hernandez, C. R. (2021). Day-to-day relational life during the COVID-19 pandemic: Linking mental health, daily relational experiences, and end-of-day outlook. *Journal of Social and Personal Relationships, 38*(8), 2350–2375. https://doi.org/10.1177/02654075211020137

Moore, R. C., Lee, A., Hancock, J. T., Halley, M., & Linos, E. (2020). Experience with social distancing early in the COVID-19 pandemic in the United States: Implications for public health messaging. *medRxiv: The Preprint Server for Health Sciences*. https://doi.org/10.1101/2020.04.08.20057067

Morgan, E. M. (2019). Does your research really matter? Revitalizing public engagement in the study of emerging adulthood. *Emerging Adulthood, 7*(6), 383–390. https://doi.org/10.1177/2167696818782308

Muller, F., Hagedoorn, M., Soriano, E. C., Stephenson, E., Smink, A., Hoff, C., DeLongis, A., Laurenceau, J., & Tuinman, M. (2019). Couples' catastrophizing and co-rumination: Dyadic diary study of patient fatigue after cancer. *Health Psychology, 38*(12), 1096–1106. http://doi.org/10.1037/hea0000803

Murdock, K. K., Gorman, S., & Robbins, M. (2014). Co-rumination via cellphone moderates the association of perceived interpersonal stress and psychosocial well-being in emerging adults. *Journal of Adolescence, 38*, 27–37. https://doi.org/10.1016/j.adolescence.2014.10.01

Nagata, J. M. (2020). Supporting young adults to rise to the challenge of COVID-19. *Journal of Adolescent Health, 67*(2), 297–298. https://doi.org/10.1016/j.jadohealth.2020.04.020

Nikolaidis, A., Paksarian, D., Alexander, L., DeRosa, J., Dunn, J., Nielson, D. M., Droney, I., Kang, M., Douka, I., Bromet, E., Milham, M. P., Stringaris, A., & Merikangas, K. R. (2020). The Coronavirus Health and Impact Survey (CRISIS) reveals reproducible correlates of pandemic-related mood states across the Atlantic. *medRxiv: The Preprint Server for Health Sciences*. https://di.org/10.1101/2020.08.24.20181123

Pew Research Center. (2019, June 12). *Mobile fact sheet*. https://www.pewresearch.org/internet/fact-sheet/mobile/

PhenX Toolkit. (2020). *COVID-19 research collections*. https://www.phenxtoolkit.org/collections/view/8

Radloff, L. S. (1977). The CES-D scale: A self-report depression scale for research in the general population. *Applied Psychological Measurement, 13*, 385–401. https://doi.org/10.1177%2F014662167700100306

Rankin, A., Swearingen-Stanborough, C., Granger, D. A., & Byrd-Craven, J. (2018). The role of co-rumination and adrenocortical attunement in young women's close friendships. *Psychoneuroendocrinology, 98*, 61–66. https://doi.org/10.1016/j.psyneuen.2018.07.027

Rose, A. J. (2002). Co–rumination in the friendships of girls and boys. *Child Development, 73*(6), 1830–1843. https://doi.org/10.1111/1467-8624.00509

Rose, A. J., Carlson, W., & Waller, E. M. (2007). Prospective associations of co-rumination with friendship and emotional adjustment. *Developmental Psychology, 43*(4), 1019–1031. https://doi.org/10.1037/0012-1649.43.4.1019

Rose, A. J., Schwartz-Mette, R.A., Glick, G. C., Smith, R. L., & Luebbe, A. M. (2014). An Observational Study of Co-Rumination in Adolescent Friendships. *Developmental Psychology, 50*(9), 2199–2209. http://dx.doi.org/10.1037/a0037465

Rose, A. J., Smith, R. L., Schwartz-Mette, R. A., & Glick, G. C. (2022). Friends' discussions of interpersonal and noninterpersonal problems during early and middle adolescence: Associations with co-rumination. *Developmental Psychology, 58*(12), 2350–2357. https://doi.org/10.1037/dev0001445

Roy, R., Benenson, J. F., & Lilly, F. (2000). Beyond intimacy: Conceptualizing sex differences in same-sex friendships. *The Journal of Psychology, 134*, 93–101. https://doi.org/10.1080/00223980009600852

Saad, L. (2020, April 16*). In U.S., more fear COVID-19 illness than financial harm.* Gallup. https://news.gallup.com/poll/308504/fear-covid-illness-financial-harm.aspx

Schaeffer, K., & Raine, L. (2020, June 16). *Experiences with the COVID-19 outbreak can vary for Americans of different ages.* Pew Research Center. https://www.pewresearch.org/fact-tank/2020/06/16/experiences-with-the-covid-19-outbreak-can-vary-for-americans-of-different-ages/

Skalski, S., Uram, P., Dobrakowski, P., & Kwiatkowska, A. (2020). The link between ego-resiliency, social support, SARS-CoV-2 anxiety and trauma effects. Polish adaptation of the Coronavirus Anxiety Scale. *Personality and Individual Differences, 17*, 110540. https://doi.org/10.1016/j.paid.2020.110540

Starr, L. R. (2015). When support seeking backfires: Co-rumination, excessive reassurance seeking, and depressed mood in the daily lives of young adults. *Journal of Social and Clinical Psychology, 34*(5), 436–457. https://doi.org/10.1521/jscp.2015.34.5.436

Starr, L. R., & Davila, J. (2007). Clarifying co-rumination: Associations with internalizing symptoms and romantic involvement among adolescent girls. *Journal of Adolescence, 32*(1), 19–37. https://doi.org/10.1016/j.adolescence.2007.12.005

Spendelow, J. S., Simonds, L. M., & Avery, R. E. (2017). The relationship between co-rumination and internalizing problems: A systematic review and meta-analysis. *Clinical Psychology and Psychotherapy, 24*(2), 512–527. https://doi.org/10.1002/cpp.2023

Szkody, E., Stearns, M., Stanhope, L., & McKinney, C. (2020). Stress-buffering role of social support during COVID-19. *Family Process, 60*, 1002–1015. https://doi.org/10.1111/famp.12618

Torales, J., O'Higgins, M., Castaldelli-Maia, J. M., & Ventriglio, A. (2020). The outbreak of COVID-19 coronavirus and its impact on global mental health. *International Journal of Social Psychiatry, 66*(4), 317–320. https://doi.org/10.1177/0020764020915212

Wang, K., & Li, S. (2020). Who is willing to engage in social gatherings during the Coronavirus Disease 2019 lockdown? A curvilinear relationship between age and heuristic processing. *Frontiers in Psychology, 11*. https://doi.org/10.3389/fpsyg.2020.586408

Whitton, S. W., & Kuryluk, A. D. (2013). Intrapersonal moderators of the association between relationship satisfaction and depressive symptoms: Findings from emerging adults. *Journal of Social and Personal Relationships, 30*(6), 750–770. https://doi.org/10.1177/0265407512467749

World Health Organization (2020, July 31). *Rolling updates on the coronavirus disease (COVID-19)*. https://www.who.int/emergencies/diseases/novel-coronavirus-2019/events-as-they-happen

Wu, M., Xu, W., Yao, Y., Zhang, L., Guo, L., Fan, J., & Chen, J. (2020). Mental health status of students' parents during COVID-19 pandemic and its influence factors. *General Psychiatry, 33*(4), e100250. https://doi.org/10.1136/gpsych-2020-100250

Ye, Z., Yang, X., Zeng, C., Wang, Y., Shen, Z., Li, X., & Lin, D. (2020). Resilience, social support, and coping as mediators between COVID-19-related stressful experiences and Acute Stress Disorder among college students in China. *Applied Psychology : Health and Well-Being*. https://doi.org/10.1111/aphw.12211

Yu, H., Li, M., Li, Z., Xinag, W., Yuan, Y. L., Liu, Y., Li, Z., & Xiong, Z. (2020). Coping style, social support and psychological distress in the general Chinese population in the early stages of the COVID-19 epidemic. *BMC Psychiatry, 20*(1), 426–426. https://doi.org/10.1186/s12888-020-02826-3

CHAPTER 10

BALANCING WORK AND SCHOOL DURING THE TIME OF COVID-19

Lessons Learned From Online Pre- and In-Service Teacher Training

Samantha Tackett
Florida State University

Meagan Arrastía-Chisholm
Valdosta State University

Kelly M. Torres
The Chicago School

ABSTRACT

The ongoing COVID-19 pandemic objectively affected the teaching of educational psychology during the 2019–2020 academic year. Subjectively, however, the pandemic affected learning to varying degrees. Uncertainties of the continual and long-term impact of COVID-19 require that educator preparation programs examine their current online instructional approaches

Examining the Cognitive and Psychological Effects of the COVID-19 Global Pandemic on High School, College, and Graduate Learners, pp. 217–239

to understand how to effectively structure virtual learning that reflects the academic needs of pre- and in-service teachers. In this study, responses from pre- and in-service teachers ($n = 211$) enrolled in educational psychology courses across five semesters were collected and analyzed to explore the lived experiences of the pre- and in-service teachers engaged in teacher education courses during the COVID-19 pandemic. In general, the students were satisfied with the course organization, assignments, increased knowledge, and instructor. Negative effects included interruptions to their field practicums, stressful situations within the home while caring for family members, difficulty with balancing multiple roles within the confinement of their homes, increased coursework activity, and lower self-efficacy with learning online. Implications for supportive mental health and resiliency policies and practices in higher education are discussed.

Keywords: COVID-19, teachers, teacher training, online learning,

Bronfenbrenner's ecological systems theory, self-efficacy, resilience

INTRODUCTION

In 2020, the global impact of COVID-19 resulted in academic institutions abruptly needing to close their campuses. In fact, Blankenberger and Williams (2020) described the spread of COVID-19 as a catastrophe that had extensive impacts on higher education. Educational institutions were not adequately prepared for the global lockdown, which negatively affected their faculty and students. In particular, university and college faculty needed to swiftly transform their on-ground courses to online modalities in order to allow college students to complete their program requirements. Allen et al. (2020) predicted that the long-term impact of the ongoing pandemic will have significant ramifications. Indeed, the pandemic exposed university shortcomings and the necessity of promoting professional development training opportunities focused on digital technologies (Rashid & Yadav, 2020).

College students who enroll in university teacher preparation courses are often referred to as preservice or in-service teachers. Preservice teachers are those students completing initial teacher education training for certification; whereas in-service teachers often return to college to pursue advanced degrees and/or endorsement opportunities. Through preservice teacher preparation coursework, students gain valuable experiences of connecting course content to classroom settings (e.g., classroom management, working with culturally and linguistically diverse learners; Rutt et al., 2020). These experiences are typically offered in person but were disrupted during the COVID-19 pandemic impacting preservice teachers access to in classroom preparation. Further, pursuing additional coursework allows in-service teachers the opportunity to expand their knowledge and expertise in specific subject areas or teaching methodologies. Ultimately, by gaining specialized skills, in-service teachers can better serve their students and meet the diverse needs of learners in their classrooms (Schneider & Costner, 2021).

This chapter discusses the use of Bronfenbrenner's ecological systems theory (1979, 2005) to interpret the lived experiences of the pre- and in-service teachers engaged in teacher education courses during the COVID-19 pandemic. The importance of the study discussed in this chapter is its evidentiary contribution of the lived experience of preservice and in-service teachers in a predominantly rural region of the United States during the height of the COVID-19 pandemic.

REVIEW OF THE LITERATURE

General College Student Reactions to Online Learning

College students traditionally enroll in course modalities that they feel most comfortable completing or that best accommodate their daily schedules and responsibilities. The evolution of diverse learning formats has resulted in researchers investigating college student learning outcomes in different educational modalities (e.g., face-to-face, online). Distance learning formats with college students have been found to be as effective as face-to-face learning contexts (Nguyen, 2015) and, with some college student populations, even the preferred learning context (Aguilera-Hermida, 2020). Furthermore, due to the advent of innovative learning technologies, the widespread adoption of the internet, and the need for a digitally trained workforce, online education is expected to continue to increase in popularity (Palvia et al., 2018). However, students may feel anxious and uncertain about how to effectively perform in online learning settings. As online education may rapidly become more commonplace and widespread throughout the foreseeable future for a variety of reasons including future pandemics, Bao (2020) recommended that faculty determine how to mitigate students' levels of anxiety when needing to transition quickly to online deliveries of education.

A number of human, economic, and technological factors can influence an individual's confidence and experience with online and remote learning contexts. For example, individuals' levels of motivation, access to reliable internet and technology, and allocation of time available for online and remote learning can impact their ability to perform in these academic settings (Adnan & Anwar, 2020; Almahasees et al., 2021; Chiu et al., 2021; Thanasi-Boce, 2021). In the next section, we discuss a study of K–12 students that experienced learning losses associated with human (e.g., developmental needs, family/relationship support), economic, and technological influences (e.g., technology divide). Studies with online college students (Aguilera-Hermida, 2020; Saadé & Bahli, 2005) have found similar challenges experienced by students in self-efficacy with technology, self-regulation, and home conditions, resources, relationships.

Impact of Remote and Hybrid Instruction

During this time, the use of remote and hybrid instruction affected students across educational systems: college students, as well as the K–12 students who the preservice teachers were training to serve. A group of researchers from the National Bureau of Economic Research used testing data from 2.1 million students in 10,000 schools across 49 states to explore the role of remote and hybrid instruction in "widening gaps in achievement by race and school poverty" (Goldhaber et al., 2022, p. 3). By comparing pre-pandemic (fall 2017–2019) students' achievement gains to the gains accomplished during the pandemic (fall 2019–fall 2021), they identified remote instruction as a primary factor of widening achievement gaps: "we find that the shift in instructional mode was a primary driver of widening achievement gaps by race/ethnicity and by school poverty status.... [H]igh-poverty schools experienced 50 percent more achievement loss than low-poverty schools" (Goldhaber et al., 2022, p. 2). Similar to other educational research studies (Camp & Zamarro, 2021; Oster et al., 2021), they observed that students within high-poverty schools tended to be Black and Hispanic. Compared to low- or mid-poverty schools, the students enrolled in high-poverty schools experienced a higher frequency of remote instruction and 5.5 more weeks of remote instruction (Goldhaber et al., 2022).

Across all the school categories, the effect of shifting to hybrid or remote instruction was negative, "implying that even at low-poverty (high income) schools, students fell behind growth expectations when their schools went remote or hybrid" (Goldhaber et al., 2022, p. 11). The achievement losses were found to be substantially larger for students enrolled in mid- and high-poverty schools than for students enrolled in low-poverty schools. Their analysis identified implications for the recovery of students in high-poverty schools/districts with greater incidents of remote instruction in 2020–21, as they "will need to spend nearly all of their federal aid on academic recovery to help students recover from pandemic-related achievement losses" (Goldhaber et al., 2022, p.13).

The COVID-19 pandemic brought about unprecedented challenges for teacher education students, particularly with the sudden shift to online learning. Many teacher education programs had to transition to virtual platforms, causing significant adjustments and struggles for students pursuing their degrees. One of the main challenges faced by teacher education students during online learning was the lack of face-to-face interaction and hands-on experiences (Piccolo et al., 2021). Teaching is a profession that heavily relies on personal connections and classroom dynamics, making it difficult to replicate these aspects in a virtual environment. Students missed the opportunity to observe experienced teachers, engage in in-person discussions, and practice teaching in real classrooms, which are crucial for their development as educators (Thomas et al., 2021).

The phenomenological approach of this study is to understand and describe the participants' lived experience. The study discussed within this chapter addresses a gap in the literature for the ecological systems perspective of the lived experience of pre- and in-service teachers during the COVID-19 pandemic.

THEORETICAL FRAMEWORK

The ecological theory of Bronfenbrenner (1979, 2005) is especially useful for conceptualizing teacher learning and teacher education during the COVID-19 pandemic. This ecological systems theory focuses on how individuals' inherent qualities and environments interact to influence their development. Given that the pandemic has affected both pre- and in-service teachers' environments across roles (e.g., student, teacher, parent, child, citizen, consumer, employee), this theory provides both the worm's- and bird's-eye view of student learning experiences. Its primary focus is to understand "mutual accommodation throughout the life course," the changing properties in one's immediate setting, and how the relations between settings and large contexts are embedded (Bronfenbrenner, 2005, p. 107).

The ecological perspective offers the researcher a look into the college experience as it extends beyond the college campus (Kitchen et al., 2019). This framework encompasses five nested systems (i.e., microsystem, mesosystem, exosystem, macrosystem, and chronosystem) that reflect relationships considered being hierarchal and reflective of the individual (McLinden, 2017). The nested systems range in proximity to the student. The closest context is the microsystem and the most distal is the macrosystem, with the mesosystem encompassing the interactions of two or more microsystems. Individuals operate within microsystems which are the most intimate, such as one's family and place of work. The macrosystems in which individuals operate include greater systems, like their school system or the larger community culture. Daily life is also affected by exosystems which are more intimate than the greater macrosystems but include influences shared by many individuals. Exosystems exist outside the individual but exert control over them, nonetheless. Some examples may include social media and the employers of parents or spouses. Lastly, the chronosystem comprises aspects of our shared experience during this time in history, such as access to technology and the COVID-19 pandemic. This ecological theory has been used to understand how technology affects development (Navarro & Tudge, 2022), how COVID-related grief has impacted children (Chachar et al., 2021), and how to manage COVID-related stress for younger learners (Zhou, 2020). Using this ecological lens, we examine the lived experiences of the pre- and in-service teachers engaged in teacher education courses during the COVID-19 pandemic.

METHODS

The methodology for this study involved exploring data sources for themes with a phenomenological approach. Inductive analysis was used to identify phenomena among students' self-reported experiences in combination with descriptive course results. This allowed the researchers to understand more about the experiences of the pre- and in-service teachers taking coursework during the COVID-19 pandemic. Written responses from 211 pre- and in-service teachers enrolled in educational psychology courses were analyzed in this study. Data were collected across five semesters during the COVID-19 pandemic from learners taking undergraduate and graduate level educational psychology as part of their educator preparation program. Participants came from a variety of majors, including elementary education, middle grades education, and special education.

Participants

This study was conducted at a public university located in a rural area in the southeast United States. The preservice teachers within this study were undergraduate students enrolled in teacher education programs of study and teaching practicums. The in-service teachers within this study were graduate students enrolled in teacher education programs of study and teaching practicums. In-person instruction at this university was disrupted in parallel with the public K–12 education in the predominantly rural region. These courses were deemed hybrid due to the change in modality. By the next academic school year, in-person instruction mostly resumed for undergraduate students, including preservice teachers. However, graduate coursework had been online before the pandemic began. Despite this consistency, the graduate students were all in-service teachers facing the realities of the pandemic in their daily teaching practice in predominantly rural and moderate to high poverty school locations. Because of the uncertain nature of the pandemic, the authors did not implement practices outlined by Kim (2020) and others for either group of students.

Procedures

All data were collected using an online learning management system using the same procedures as other assignments in the course. Students were prompted for written responses over seven timepoints during their courses with open-ended questions. This allowed the instructor to check in with students and gauge whether the course was meeting their needs. Examples of questions include the following: "How do you feel about the precautions to prevent COVID-19 infections?" and "How are the special conditions related to COVID-19 (e.g., physical distancing, plexiglass, masks, canceling of large gatherings) affecting you personally and/or your academic performance?" These check-in data enabled insight into students' experiences across timepoints throughout the semester. The three coauthors then analyzed the data in the following months after the course had ended.

Data Analysis

Pursuant to LeCompte et al. (1993), this qualitative approach involves scanning data for categories of a particular phenomenon and then searching for relationships that may exist among categories. To identify common categories, all COVID-19 student self-reported data were compared, aggregated, and ordered. Once all categories were identified, relationships were determined within the data structure of the ecological model. Frequency of each category were calculated to identify most prevalent themes. Next, all core categories were compiled and summarized. To enhance the reliability of this study, triangulation methods were employed (e.g., participant completed course, completed course surveys). Particularly, multiple researchers reviewed and discussed the initial categorization processes to ensure agreement across all codes and categories. For this study, the themes were categorized according to the level of Bronfenbrenner's theory.

RESULTS

In this section, we outline the 12 themes identified in students' writings and align them with each level of Bronfenbrenner's theory. Table 10.1 lists each of the 12 themes and a representative quote from students' data. In Figure 10.1, we have summarized the frequency of themes identified within students' written responses across all timepoints ($N = 247$). After coding statements and constructing overall themes, we tallied the frequencies to identify the primary points discussed by students. Over the pandemic time period, we observed that 11 different components of students' experiences with COVID represent 78% of the coded data, whereas one theme, *No Impact*, represents 22% of the responses. Overall, 36% of the data related to one's personal well-being (e.g., emotional/psychological impact, fatigue, social distancing) and concern or care for those immediately within their environment (e.g., taking care of family members, protecting those with weakened immune systems). Students' concerns and challenges with their academic performance and online learning context represented about 16% of the data. Lastly, comments regarding wearing a mask, adapting/adjusting to the situation, and pursuing/receiving a vaccine represented 26% of the data. The next discussion of data incorporates the themes into the five levels of Bronfenbrenner's ecological systems theory.

Table 10.1

Example Statements From Student Data

Theme	Example statements from data
Emotional/ Psychological Impact	"I'm so overwhelmed that it is difficult to function."
Fatigue	"I am so exhausted by the time that I get home each day."
Feelings of Disconnect/Social Isolation	"I very much so looking forward to football games as well as other large social gatherings my freshman year that I sadly will not be able to participate in due to the current situation. As well as being in large lecture halls with my peers and having to take classes online once a week has affected me academically."
Concerned with COVID Exposure	"It is difficult because I avoid seeing family and doing public activities, but I go to work every day and I am exposed at school. It is very stressful."
Family/Friends Contracting COVID	"Thus far, all my in-laws including my husband have had COVID. During that time, I never had any symptoms and was negative when I got tested... I have had two family members die from COVID. One was a cousin, and one was an uncle (ages 47 and 69)."
Social Distancing	"It creates a barrier for myself and my students in the classroom. Young students thrive on social interaction, and they are unable to interact and socialize with their friends from other classes while at recess due to COVID-19 regulations. Also, students are not allowed to eat lunch in the lunchroom this year, they are eating lunch and breakfast in the classroom. Students are strictly confined to our classroom and the students within our class. This creates a lot of unnecessary "drama" amongst students."

(Table continued on next page)

Table 10.1 (Continued)

Example Statements From Student Data

Theme	Example statements from data
Academic Performance	"It is affecting me academically, I'm more of a physical learner, so me taking online classes may be a little more difficult."
Teaching/Learning Modality	"The conditions have made it harder for me, I do not function well with online classes, or hybrid. I honestly have struggled to keep up, as I think that I have gotten a lot of work done, then there is more. I just feel like I cannot keep up at times."
Wearing a Mask	"The biggest thing that affects me is that the masks affect how I sign. I am a Deaf education major and needing to use ASL every day. But a big component of the language is facial movements and expressions, with a mask covering half my face I lose a lot of the language. On top of that one can confuse signs due to not being able to tell placement."
Adjustment/ Adapt/ Overcome	"I have designated a specific spot for school in my home, so that I do not associate my room with school."
Vaccine	"We are slowly returning to normal operations at my school. The majority of my family has been vaccinated and we are returning to more normal activities."
No Impact	"None of these things are particularly affecting me personally or academically."

Figure 10.1

Percentage of COVID-19 Themes Across All Timepoints

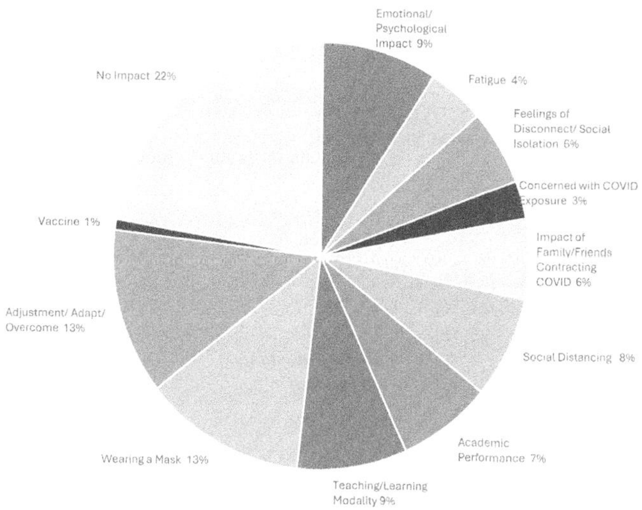

In Figure 10.2, the theory is applied to the two groups of educators with brief examples of the relevant components for the educators at each level, this should be evident in their writings and concerns while taking coursework. A comparison of the two groups shows that preservice and in-service teachers expressed very different perspectives and experiences within the micro- and mesosystems, as illustrated in the data. Commonalities between the groups were also found, including a general decline in concerns surrounding COVID-19 over time. A number of themes were identified across data points that characterized the experiences of pre- and in-service teachers during the COVID-19 pandemic, including changes to their microsystems, mesosystems, and shared challenges across macrosystems.

Figure 10.2

Bronfenbrenner's Ecological Theory Applied to Pre- and In-Service Teachers During COVID-19

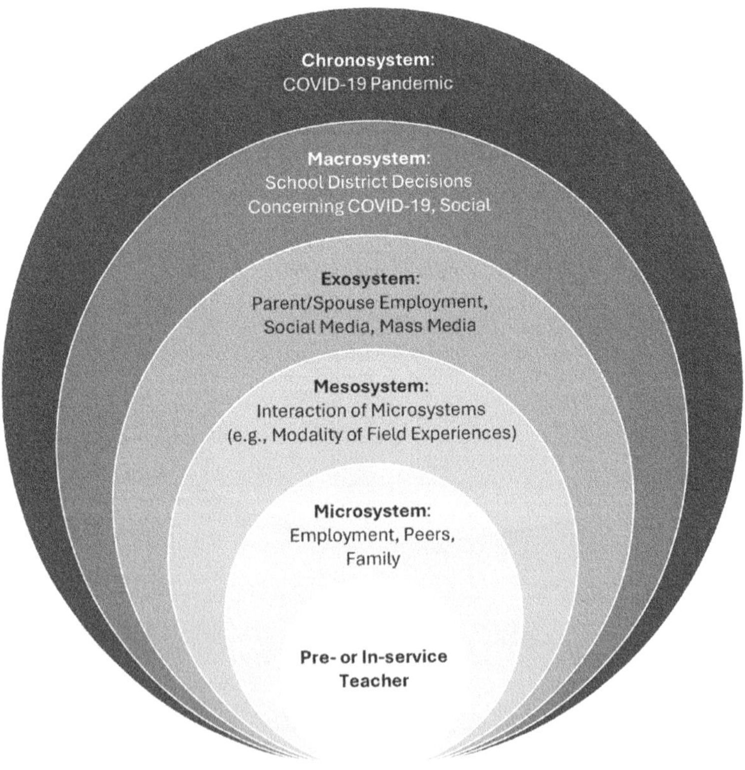

Participants reported similar negative experiences, including interruptions to their field practicums, stressful situations while balancing coursework with taking care of family members, and low self-efficacy with learning through online modalities. In other words, participants had many shared characteristics across their own microsystems. However, these negative experiences decreased over the semesters, and none of the participants expressed any distress by the most recent data collection. In particular, participants reported negative experiences occurring most frequently in the 2020 Fall Semester, with fewer occurrences in their 2021 Spring Semester coursework.

Microsystems: Psychosocial Issues, Family Roles, and Grief

Bronfenbrenner (1979) described a microsystem as a "pattern of activities, roles, and interpersonal relations" that occur in a particular setting (p. 22). Given that this community of pre- and in-service teachers were spread out geographically, they all experienced their own individual setting while logging in from home during the pandemic.

Both pre- and in-service teachers reported the impact that the pandemic had on their overall health and stress. One participant commented, "I have experienced fatigue. I have attributed this to my increased workload with school and work." In-service teachers were more likely to report negative experiences due to increased or constantly changing family roles in the way of childcare, taking care of sick family members, and increased workload at their teaching jobs. Preservice teachers were more likely to report missing the interaction with peers during class because of the shift to online instruction. Grief from loss was also expressed by both preservice and in-service teachers, as well as anxiety and other psychosocial stressors. As shown in Figure 10.3, these concerns within the microsystems of the students varied in frequency over time with feelings of disconnection increasing over the academic school year, yet emotional and psychological impact decreasing over time.

Mesosystems: Teaching/Learning Across Modalities and Field Experiences

Given one's microsystem, a learner then participates in a mesosystem, "the interrelations among two or more settings," bringing their roles from home and work with them as they function as a student (Bronfenbrenner, 1979, p. 25). For pre- and in-service teachers, the mesosystem of the

Figure 10.3

Microsystem Themes for COVID Experience Over Time

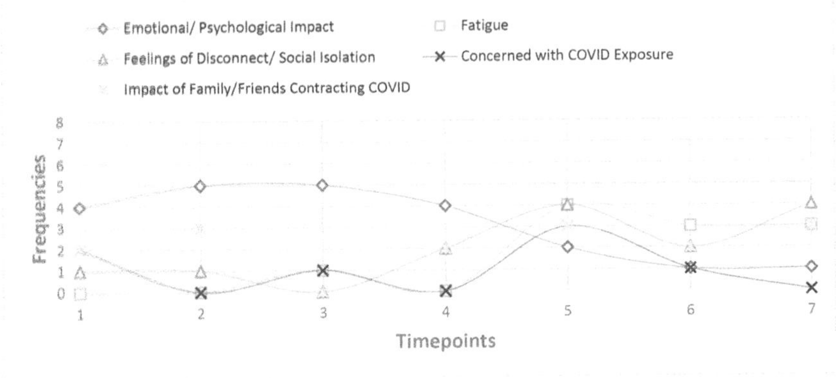

university course is especially complex, with their attitudes about teaching and learning constantly informing and being informed by their roles across microsystems. In particular, many students' roles as students, parents, and teachers overlapped and conflicted during this time. This mesosystem of the course was specifically and strictly restricted to the online or virtual learning realm, as compared to most semesters during which courses were hybrid. Given the expectation of face-to-face interactions, it is not surprising that the preservice teachers were extremely disappointed with not having face-to-face field experiences. This was especially true in the first semester, in which the onset of the pandemic quickly disrupted the field experience, leaving a portion of students without any face-to-face experience to draw from.

For the 2020 Fall Semester, some participants expressed concerns regarding their need to continue being enrolled in online coursework. This concern was illustrated by participants reporting that the additional stress of the pandemic had affected their grades. Participants felt that some aspects of the online course structures did not contribute to their academic success. This was especially true for the preservice teachers, who were less accustomed to taking online coursework, as most in-service teachers take coursework exclusively online. Participant comments highlighted the challenges online learning had on collaborative learning experiences. Particularly, some participants perceived online group work as being less effective. For example, one preservice teacher reported, "I have had to move study groups online which is ok but not an ideal substitute for the real thing."

In-service teachers completing endorsement coursework also experienced concerns with teaching during the pandemic. One in-service teacher shared that "Because of it I was not able to teach face to face, I have had to teach online. This created more work for myself at school and I fell behind in many of my assignments for my courses, including this one." In essence, the modality of the course and work changing over time proved to be challenging for this teacher while in school. However, concerns both about academic performance and teaching/learning modalities decreased in frequency across the school year, as shown in Figure 10.4.

Figure 10.4

Mesosystems Themes for COVID Experience Over Time

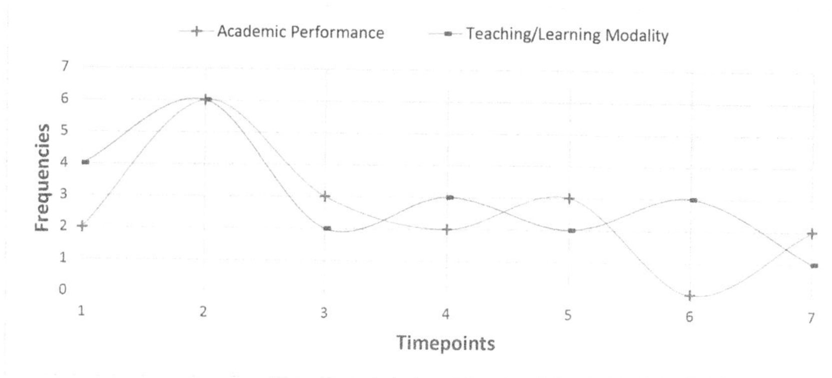

Macrosystems: Vaccination, Masks, and Social Distancing

During this study, the participants operated within unique macrosystems, meaning that events affected and were affected by what happened across settings (Bronfenbrenner, 1979). For example, as people in surrounding areas got infected with COVID, policies changed in public and private schools. As policies changed, individuals' behaviors and attitudes shifted. These policies varied across states, cities, counties, and districts. Some cultural influences from the macrosystem may have been at play, as seen by the differences in responses to COVID in schools across developed nations (Khanal et al., 2021). For example, some K–12 schools remained closed, while others remained open after the spring of 2020. This had a direct impact on the modality of field experience, as well as pre- and in-service teachers' ability to focus on coursework with the demands of childcare and work.

Additionally, in-service teachers expressed barriers when interacting with their students. During classroom interactions, an in-service teacher indicated that "Masks have been a great barrier in teaching my students guided reading" and that "students rely heavily on watching your mouth movements and that is also how you can assist them with their words and sounds." When returning to in-person teaching, another in-service teacher commented that she experienced high levels of stress when teaching students who were not required to wear masks. In-service teachers also discussed the impact that being confined to their classrooms had on student behavior. For instance, one participant indicated that the need to remain in the classroom for breakfast and lunch created "unnecessary drama amongst the students." Again, these policies within the macrosystem varied across participants but shaped their experiences both at home as students and parents and at work/school as teachers and student teachers. Both social distancing and mask usage concerns peaked during the middle of each semester, as shown in Figure 10.5. As vaccines and boosters became more available to this population, a few students expressed feeling more at ease towards the end of the spring semester.

Figure 10.5

Macrosystems Themes for COVID Experience Over Time

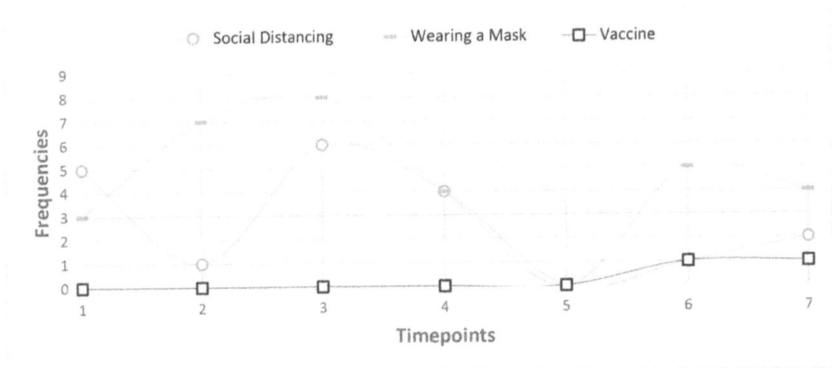

No Impact

Interestingly, the data collection at timepoints 2, 3, and 4 resulted in three, zero, and zero student statements, respectively, reporting "no impact" by COVID. However, the "no impact" statements dramatically increased during the data collection at timepoints 5, 6, and 7, which were 13, 14, and 18, respectively. Despite this upward trend, students consistently indicated that they had to overcome challenges, adapt, and adjust their learning in response to COVID-19 (see Figure 10.6). Although the majority of the statements (78%) within the data identified specific issues, challenges, stressors, or concerns as a result of the COVID pandemic, a minority of the coded statements (22%) across all seven timepoints identified that COVID had no impact on them and how they operated. It is important to note that the absence of impact occurred across system levels from the participants' perspectives.

Figure 10.6

No Impact Theme for COVID Experience Over Time

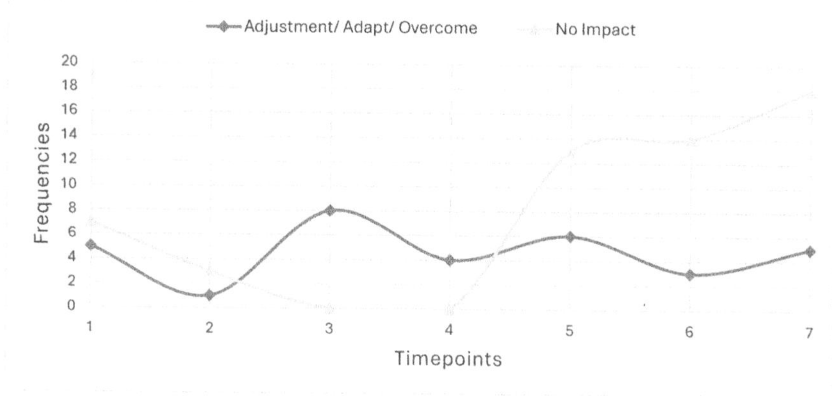

CONCLUSIONS

Friga (2020) reported that a survey conducted by the Chronicle of Higher Education found 84% of university presidents predicted a decline in enrollment in new and continuing students. Data collected recently by the National Student Clearinghouse Research Center (2023) revealed continual downward trends in higher education enrollment. These trends, however, are showing to be more reflective of on-ground undergraduate pre-pandemic numbers. However, the ultimate educational impact of COVID is still unknown, and institutions of higher education are bracing for the long-term ramifications from the global shutdowns and personal and communal trauma.

Gramlich (2023) recently summarized the findings of four national surveys conducted by the Pew Research Center between March 2020 and September 2022. The culmination of data revealed that young adults (18–29), women, people in lower-income households, and adults with a disability (or chronic health condition) were much more likely to have experienced high psychological distress since March 2020. University enrollment predominantly consists of young adults in undergraduate and graduate programs of studies and consistently trends upward with higher undergraduate enrollment rates of people who identify as women or females than men or males (Conger, 2015). The preservice and in-service teachers in our study were young adults, identified as women, and people in lower-income households who have experienced high psychological distress and enrolled as current members of a college cohort.

The next college student cohorts arriving are the teenagers who matriculated through high school during the pandemic. For this student group, the Pew Research Center found they reported their mental health *as not good most of the time or always* throughout the pandemic (March 2020–September 2022). Certainly, business as usual will not be successful with these pandemic and post-pandemic college student cohorts (future pre- and in-service teachers), who have experienced abnormal mental-health strain. In fact, the top request received from student participants in the Active Minds Young Adult Mental Health Survey (2020) was for higher education leadership "to prioritize student mental health and help students heal, process, and recover" (p. 1). Alongside academic achievement, post-secondary educators and administrators are engaging students with opportunities to develop wellness practices, self-care habits, and stress-management skills (Brown & Kafka, 2020). With the realities of post-traumatic stress, there is an opportunity for post-traumatic growth to be shepherded by courses (e.g., Changing Minds, Changing Lives at University of Massachusetts at Amherst), resilience programs (e.g., Student Resilience Project at Florida State University), and student affairs programming (e.g., Road to Wellbeing at Boston University).

Although many universities are in the process of transitioning back to normal educational practices, there is still much uncertainty associated with the future and the long-term impact of the COVID-19 pandemic on institutional practices and policies (Crawford et al., 2020). In particular, institutions of higher education need to consider how their student and faculty populations are able to adapt to online learning and ensure that they have the expertise to navigate new learning platforms that encompass rigorous learning experiences. University leaders and faculty should also consider the substantial longer-term impacts of the pandemic and how they are able to better structure curricula and program degree requirements to support student learning experiences. Particularly, the impacts of COVID-19 on university students were significant and varied and included disruption of academic schedules, mental health challenges, financial difficulties, and challenges with diverse learning modalities (Adedoyin & Soykan, 2020; Feng & Zhang, 2021; Fletcher et al., 2023; Gómez-Garcí et al., 2022), resulting in unforeseen outcomes that prompted higher education faculty and administrators to further examine how they can ensure continual future support for a changing educational landscape.

Bronfenbrenner's ecological systems theory provides a foundation for understanding the importance of various systems and contexts and how individuals develop and function through different life events, including college experiences (Kitchen et al., 2019). Throughout the pandemic, schools and colleges closed, parents lost jobs, and students from pre-kindergarten to college lost learning opportunities, access to technology, stabilizing routines, and social and emotional supports. Bronfenbrenner's ecological systems theory illuminates the various systems and contexts that encompass one's life experiences. This is supported by the National Academies of Sciences, Engineering, and Medicine (NASEM, 2023) report that highlights multiple research findings with detrimental outcomes across numerous domains of well-being (e.g., economic resources, education, food, housing, physical and mental health, social and emotional support) for children, students, and families, especially for minoritized populations and those with fewer economic resources (Feng & Zhang, 2021; Fletcher et al., 2023; Goldhaber et al., 2022; Gramlich, 2023; Oster et al., 2021). It has now been well documented that "students at all levels missed learning, though the greatest losses were among students without access to in-person schooling, children from minoritized populations, and those from low-income households" (Coker et al., 2023, para. 6).

Through the multiple layers of nested systems in the Bronfenbrenner theory, ranging from the individual's immediate environment to broader societal factors, the magnitude of the pandemic's impact becomes more evident. Within this study, participants described how the pandemic had disrupted their routines and relationships within their immediate environments. They further shared how the impact of social distancing and remote learning had altered the way they interacted with others, often leading to feelings of disconnection and frustration from a lack of access to educational experiences such as field experiences and group work activities. Remote learning and school closures created unexpected difficulties that negatively affected participants' grades, overall health (e.g., elevated levels of stress and fatigue), and access to impactful learning experiences (e.g., face-to-face field experiences). Within the context of this current study, the inclusion of Bronfenbrenner's ecological systems theory provided a useful framework for understanding the complex and interconnected impacts of the COVID-19 pandemic on students and their environments. Ultimately, by recognizing the multiple systems and contexts that shape individuals' experiences, we can better understand the challenges that they face and develop more effective strategies for supporting their educational pursuits and well-being. Ross and Locke (2023) proposed that Bronfenbrenner's ecological systems theory provides higher education leaders with a unique approach to student support through the implementation of strategies that mitigate stress and reduce recovery time.

Implications for the Future

Prior to the pandemic, many universities were experiencing a declining enrollment trend for face-to-face or traditional courses and substantial uptakes in online courses. The sudden and necessary transition to online learning may result in a continual increase in higher education enrollment in online coursework and programs. As a result, the impact of the pandemic has provided universities with a prime opportunity to restructure their online teaching approaches to accommodate the growing online student enrollment that has already been predicted to occur in the next decade and that has now been accelerated by the COVID-19 pandemic. Furthermore, we know that the learning environment (i.e., microsystem, mesosystem, exosystem, macrosystem, and chronosystem) influences how and what students learn, as well as their personal development across the life course (Bronfenbrenner, 2005).

In addition to the impacts on university students, COVID-19 has also had a significant impact on field experience requirements. Specifically, aspiring teachers had to adapt to a rapidly changing educational landscape, with many facing unique challenges as they navigated remote learning, limited student engagement, and reduced opportunities for in-person classroom experience (Garcia-Morales et al., 2021; Oliveria et al., 2021). However, the pandemic also had positive impacts on field experiences in the increased use of technology in education. As institutions of higher education shifted to online learning, faculty and students were able to gain valuable experience in virtual instruction, online assessment, and digital communication technology, which is likely to continue to play an important role in all educational sectors. Furthermore, innovative technologies have advanced how teacher education curricula are structured, allowing for more immersive virtual experiences (Torres & Tackett, 2017). For example, teacher education curricula have expanded to include virtual reality and 360 videos to further prepare preservice and in-service teachers on topics including classroom management (Theelen et al., 2020), presence and empathy (Han et al., 2022), and working with diverse learners (Yakubova et al., 2021).

Summary

The COVID-19 pandemic had a significant impact on college students in a variety of ways. With the move to online learning, many students faced challenges in staying focused and motivated, as well as dealing with technical difficulties and internet access issues. In addition, students struggled with the lack of in-person interaction with peers and faculty, leading to feelings of isolation and disconnection (Handel et al., 2020). Notably, preservice teachers were presented with unique challenges associated with field placements. Many teacher training programs require preservice teachers to complete a certain number of hours of in-person teaching experience in real classrooms. Indeed, Keefe (2020) highlighted that the pandemic made it difficult to find placements or to gain the necessary experience due to social distancing restrictions and school closures. Limited interaction with students also posed unique challenges in the development of more complex teaching skills (e.g., classroom management, student engagement). However, the COVID-19 pandemic illustrated the importance of understanding the interconnectedness between different systems and the need for a coordinated response at all levels. For example, universities had to proactively determine how to best support students' learning and emotional well-being during emergency remote instruction (Fletcher et al., 2023).

The pandemic also underscored the importance of resilience, or the ability to adapt and cope with stress and adversity. Resilience is a key concept in Bronfenbrenner's ecological systems theory (Wosnitza et al., 2021), as it emphasizes the importance of the various systems and contexts in which individuals develop and how they can support individuals' ability to adapt and thrive. For example, participants in this study demonstrated resilience in their ability to acclimate to online learning and in their descriptions of adjusting to a new normal. In the context of the pandemic, resilience can take many forms, such as the ability to adapt to remote learning, find new ways to connect with others, and seek out resources and support when needed. Although resilience was not a focus of this current study, future research of pre- and in-service teachers' perceived resilience and the perceived impact of a university's practices on their resilience is of value.

While Bronfenbrenner's ecological systems theory is not necessarily a recent theory, it is well-suited as a theoretical context for the present study. Bronfenbrenner's theory provides a valuable lens through which to understand the impact of the COVID-19 pandemic on individuals and their environments (Brigandi et al., 2022). For example, understanding the impact to learners creates an opportunity for higher education to provide adequate support in stressful and uncertain situations. By recognizing the interconnectedness of different systems and the importance of resilience, we can better support individuals and communities during future challenging times.

REFERENCES

Active Minds. (2020). *Recommendations for prioritizing student mental health and campus-wide healing and recovery during COVID-19*. https://www.activeminds.org/wp-content/uploads/2020/06/COVID-19-Position-Statement.pdf

Adedoyin, O. B., & Soykan, E. (2020). Covid-19 pandemic and online learning: The challenges and opportunities. *Interactive Learning Environment, 31*(2), 863–875. https://doi.org/10.1080/10494820.2020.1813180

Aguilera-Hermida, A. P. (2020). College students' use and acceptance of emergency online learning due to COVID-19. *International Journal of Educational Research Open, 1*, 100011. https://doi.org/10.1016/j.ijedro.2020.100011

Allen, J., Rowan, L., & Singh, P. (2020). Teaching and teacher education in the time of COVID-19. *Asia-Pacific Journal of Teacher Education, 48*(3), 233–236. https://doi.org/10.1080/1359866X.2020.1752051

Almahasees, Z., Mohsen, K., & Amin, M. O. (2021). Faculty's and student's perceptions of online learning during COVID-19. *Frontiers in Digital Education, 12*(6). https://doi.org/10.34190/ejel.19.5.2475

Adnan, M., & Anwar, K. (2020). Online learning amid the COVID-19 pandemic: Students' perspectives. *Journal of Pedagogical Sociology and Psychology, 2*(1), 45–51.

Bao, W. (2020). COVID-19 and online teaching in higher education: A case study of Peking University. *Human Behavior and Emerging Technologies*. https://onlinelibrary.wiley.com/doi/epdf/10.1002/hbe2.191

Blankenberger, B., & Williams, A. M. (2020). COVID and the impact on higher education: The essential role of integrity and accountability. *Administrative Theory & Praxis, 42*(3), 404–423.

Brigandi, C. B., Spillance, N. K., Rambo-Hernandez, K. E., & Stone, J. (2022). Teaching in the time of COVID-19: A biological systems theory approach. *Frontiers in Education, 25*(7). https://doi.org/10.3389/feduc.2022.964492

Bronfenbrenner, U. (1979). *The ecology of human development: Experiments by nature and design*. Harvard University Press.

Bronfenbrenner, U. (2005). *Making human beings human: Bioecological perspectives on human development*. Sage.

Brown, S., & Kafka, A. C. (2020). Covid-19 has worsened the student mental-health crisis. Can resilience training fix it?. *The Chronicle of Higher Education, 11*. https://www.chronicle.com/article/covid-19-has-worsened-the-student-mental-health-crisis-can-resilience-training-fix-it/

Camp, A., & Zamarro, G. (2021). Determinants of ethnic differences in school modality choices during the COVID-19 crisis. *Educational Researcher, 51*(1), 6–16.

Chachar, A. S., Younus, S., & Ali, W. (2021). Developmental understanding of death and grief among children during COVID-19 pandemic: Application of Bronfenbrenner's bioecological model. *Frontiers in Psychiatry, 12*. https://doi.org/10.3389/fpsyt.2021.654584

Chiu, T. K. F., Lin, T. J., & Lonka, K. (2021). Motivating online learning: The challenges of COVID-19 and beyond. *The Asia-Pacific Education Research, 30*, 189–190. https://doi.org/10.1007/s40299-021-00566-w

Coker, T. R., Cheng T. L., Ybarra, M. (2023). Addressing the long-term effects of the COVID-19 pandemic on children and families: A report from the national academies of sciences, engineering, and medicine. *Journal of the American Medical Association, 329*(13), 1055–1056. https://doi.org/10.1001/jama.2023.4371

Conger, D. (2015). High school grades, admissions policies, and the gender gap in college enrollment. *Economics of Education Review, 46*, 144–147. https://doi.org/10.1016/j.econedurev.2015.03.003

Crawford, J., Butler-Henderson, K., Rudolph, J., & Glowatz, M. (2020). COVID-19: 20 countries' higher education intra-period digital pedagogy responses. *Journal of Applied Teaching and Learning, 3*(1), 1–20. https://doi.org/10.37074/jalt.2020.3.1.7

Feng, Y., & Zhang, Y. (2021). Evaluation and analysis of mental health level of college students with financial difficulties under the background of COVID-19. *Frontiers in Psychology, 12*. https://doi.org/10.3389/fpsyg.2021.649195

Fletcher, T. L., Jefferson, J. P., Boyd, B., Park, S. E., & Crumpton-Young, L. (2023). Impact of COVID-19 on sense of belonging: Experiences of engineering students, faculty, and staff at Historically Black Colleges and Universities (HBCUs). *Journal of Engineering Education*. https://doi.org/10.1002/jee.20512

Friga, P. N. (2020). Under Covid-19, university budgets like we've never seen before. *The Chronicle of Higher Education, 20*. https://www.chronicle.com/article/under-covid-19-university-budgets-like-weve-never-seen-before/

Goldhaber, D., Kane, T. J., McEachin, A., Morton, E., Patterson, T., & Staiger, D. O. (2022). *The consequences of remote and hybrid instruction during the pandemic*. National Bureau of Economic Research. https://doi.org/10.3386/w30010

Garcia- Morales, V. J., Garrido-Moreno, A., & Martin-Rojas, R. (2021). The transformation of higher education after the COVID disruption: Emerging challenges in an online learning scenario. *Frontiers in Psychology, 12*, 616059. https://doi.org/10.3389/fpsyg.2021.616059

Gómez-Garcí, G., Ramos-Navas-Parejo, M., de la Cruz-Campos, J. C., & Rodriguez-Jiménez, C. (2022). Impact of COVID-19 on university students: An analysis of its influence on psychological and academic factors. *International Journal of Environmental Research Public Health, 19*(16), 10433. https://www.ncbi.nlm.nih.gov/pmc/articles/PMC9407859/

Gramlich, J. (2023). *Mental health and the pandemic: What U.S. surveys have found*. Pew Research Center's Social & Demographic Trends Project. https://policy-commons.net/artifacts/3456460/mental-health-and-the-pandemic/4256833/

Han, I., Shin, H. S., Ko, Y., & Shin, W. S. (2022). Immersive virtual reality for increasing presence and empathy. *Journal of Computer Assisted Learning, 38*(4), 1115–1126. https://doi.org/10.1111/jcal.12669

Handel, M., Stephan, M., Glaswer-Zikuda, M., Kopp, B., Bedenlier, S., & Ziegler, A. (2020). Digital readiness and its effects on higher education students' socio-emotional perceptions in the context of the COVID-19 pandemic. *Journal of Research on Technology in Education, 54*(2), 267–280. https://doi.org/10.1080/15391523.2020.1846147

Keefe, E. S. (2020). Learning to practice digitally: Advancing pre-service teachers' preparation via virtual teaching and coaching. *Journal of Technology and Teacher Education, 28*(2), 223–232.

Khanal, P., Bento, F., & Tagliabue, M. (2021). A scoping review of organizational responses to the COVID-19 pandemic in schools: A complex systems perspective. *Education Sciences, 11*(3), 115.

Kim, J. (2020). Learning and teaching online during Covid-19: Experiences of student teachers in an early childhood education practicum. *International Journal of Early Childhood, 52*(2), 145–158.

Kitchen, J. A., Hallet, R. E., Perez, R. J., & Rivera, G. J. (2019). Advancing the use of ecological systems theory in college student research: The ecological systems interview tool. *Journal of College Student Development, 60*(4), 381–400.

LeCompte, M. D., Preissle, J., & Tesch, R. (1993). *Ethnography and qualitative design in educational research*. Academic Press.

McLinden, M. (2017). Examining proximal and distal influences on the part-time student experience through an ecological systems theory. *Teaching in Higher Education, 22*(3), 373–388.

National Academies of Sciences, Engineering, & Medicine. (2023). *Addressing the long-term effects of the COVID-19 pandemic on children and families.* https://doi.org/10.17226/26809

National Student Clearinghouse Research Center. (2023). *National student clearinghouse research center's regular updates on higher education enrollment.* https://nscresearchcenter.org/stay-informed/

Navarro, J. L., & Tudge, J. R. (2022). Technologizing Bronfenbrenner: Neo-ecological theory. *Current Psychology*, 1–17. https://doi.org/10.1007/s12144-022-02738-3

Nguyen, T. (2015). The effectiveness of online learning: Beyond no significant difference and future horizons. *Journal of Online Learning and Teaching, 11*(2), 309–319.

Oliveria, G., Teixeira, J. G., Torres, A., & Morais, C. (2021). An exploratory study on the emergency remote education experience of higher education students and teachers during the COVID-19 pandemic. *British Journal of Educational Technology, 52*(4), 1357–1376. https://doi.org/10.1111/bjet.13112

Oster, E., Jack, R., Halloran, C., Schoof, J., McLeod, D., Yang, H., Roche, J., & Roche, D. (2021). Disparities in learning mode access among K–12 students during the COVID-19 pandemic, by race/ethnicity, geography, and grade level—United States, September 2020–April 2021. *Morbidity and Mortality Weekly Report, 70*(26), 953–958. https://doi.org/10.15585/mmwr.mm7026e2

Palvia, S., Aeron, P., Gupta, P., Mahapatra, D., Parida, R., Rosner, R., & Sindhi, S. (2018). Online education: Worldwide status, challenges, trends, and implications. *Journal of Global Information Technology Management, 21*(4), 233–241.

Piccolo, D. L., Livers, S. D., & Tipton, S. L. (2021). Adapting student teaching during the COVID-19 pandemic: A comparison of perspectives and experiences. *The Teacher Educator, 56*(3), 229–249. https://doi.org/10.1080/08878730.2021.1925382

Rashid, S., & Yadav, S. S. 2020. Impact of COVID-19 pandemic on higher education and research. *Indian Journal of Human Development, 14*(2), 340–343. https://doi.org/10.1177%2F0973703020946700

Ross, P. M., Scanes, E., & Locke, W. (2023). Stress adaptation and resilience of academics in higher education. *Asia Pacific Education Review,* 1–21. https://doi.org/10.1007/s12564-023-09829-1

Rutt, A., Mumba, F., & Kibler, A. (2020). Preparing preservice teachers to teach science to English learners: A review. *Journal of Research in Science Teaching, 5*(5), 625–660. https://doi.org/10.1002/tea.21673

Saadé, R., & Bahli, B. (2005). The impact of cognitive absorption on perceived usefulness and perceived ease of use in on-line learning: an extension of the technology acceptance model. *Information & Management, 42*(2), 317–327. https://doi.org/10.1016/j.im.2003.12.013

Schneider, E., & Costner, K. M. (2021). The impact of virtual ESOL endorsement courses for in-service educators during the COVID-19 pandemic. *Southeastern Regional Association of Teacher Educators Journal, 30*(2), 2. https://files.eric.ed.gov/fulltext/EJ1339971.pdf

Thanasi-Boce, M. (2021). The role of the instructor, motivation, and interaction in building online learning satisfaction during the COVID-19 pandemic. Electronic *Journal of e-Learning, 19*(5), 401–415. https://doi.org/10.34190/ejel.19.5.2475

Theelen, H., van den Beemt, A., & den Brok, P. (2020). Enhancing authentic learning experiences in teacher education through 360-degree videos and theoretical lectures: Reducing pre-service teachers' anxiety. *European Journal of Teacher Education, 45*(2), 230–249. https://doi.org/10.1080/02619768.2020.1827392

Thomas, M. A., Norgaard, M., Stambaugh, L. A., Atkins, R., Kumar, A. B., & Farley, A. L. P. (2001). Online involvement for Georgia student teachers during Covid-19. *Frontiers in Psychology, 12.* https://doi.org/10.3389/fpsyg.2021.648028

Torres, K. M., & Tackett, S. (2017). Preparing pre-service teachers to meet the unique academic needs of 21st century learners. In O. Dreon & D. Polly (Eds.), *Teacher education for ethical professional practice in the 21st century,* 334–358. IGI Global. https://doi.org/10.4018/978-1-5225-1668-2.ch015

Wosnitza, F. P., Beltman, S., & Mansfield, C. F. (2021). Resilience in education: Concepts, contexts, and connections. *Educational Review, 73*(6), 798–798.

Yakubova, G., Kellems, R. O., Chen, B. B., & Cusworth, Z. (2021). Practitioner's attitudes and perspectives toward the use of augmented and virtual reality technologies in the education of students with disabilities. *Journal of Special Education Technology, 37*(2). https://doi.org/10.1177/01626434211004445

Zhou, X. (2020). Managing psychological distress in children and adolescents following the COVID-19 epidemic: A cooperative approach. *Psychological Trauma: Theory, Research, Practice, and Policy, 12*(S1), S76. https://doi.org/10.1037/tra000075

CHAPTER 11

UNDERSERVED AND UNDERREPRESENTED COLLEGE STUDENTS' RESILIENCE DURING COVID-19

Jessica Meléndez Tyler
Vanderbilt University

Joanna Collins
Virginia Tech University

David Shannon
Auburn University

Jamie Carney
Auburn University

Madeline LaPolla
Auburn University

ABSTRACT

This chapter investigates the resilience and academic focus of undergraduate STEM students from disadvantaged backgrounds in the Alabama Black Belt

Examining the Cognitive and Psychological Effects of the COVID-19 Global Pandemic on High School, College, and Graduate Learners, pp. 241–269

region during the COVID-19 pandemic. The transition to online learning impacted instruction quality, leading to academic challenges for students. However, implementing a mentoring Bridge Model supported and positively influenced students' ability to balance responsibilities, academic performance, and confidence in remote work. Social issues, peer relations, and time management emerged as significant predictors of resilience. These findings can improve instructional methods, especially for students from disadvantaged backgrounds.

Keywords: undergraduate students, resilience, academic focus, COVID-19, mentoring Bridge Model

INTRODUCTION

Higher education is crucial in providing opportunities for upward mobility and access to resources, particularly for disadvantaged students (Ro et al., 2021). However, these students often face numerous challenges, including limited resources, financial constraints, and systemic barriers, which can hinder their academic progress and success. The COVID-19 pandemic has had a profound impact on all aspects of academic life, especially for disadvantaged students in higher education (Conrad et al., 2021; Lederer et al., 2021; Parker et al., 2021; Valladolid, 2021; Wilson et al., 2021). The sudden shift to online learning, campus closures, and the pandemic's broader social, economic, and psychological effects have presented significant student obstacles (Back et al., 2021; Usher et al., 2021; Valladolid, 2021).

The transition to online instruction occurred abruptly, with limited preparation and support for both students and faculty (Bird et al., 2022; Parker et al., 2021). Moreover, disadvantaged students, particularly those in science programs with laboratory requirements, faced additional challenges due to lacking access to essential tools and resources (Back et al., 2021; Parker et al., 2021; Wang et al., 2021b). Additionally, economic limitations have affected students' ability to acquire necessary resources and to participate effectively in online learning (Parker et al., 2021; Usher et al., 2021). The closure of campuses disrupted the social connectedness that students experienced, leading to feelings of isolation and reliance on virtual interactions (Ro et al., 2021; Wolcutt, 2022). Moreover, the loss of campus support systems has exacerbated mental health issues and academic burnout (Back et al., 2021; Ro et al., 2021). Disadvantaged college students, including underrepresented groups, have faced increased vulnerabilities and adverse health outcomes during the pandemic (Johns & Hawkes, 2020; Lancaster & Arango, 2021; Lederer et al., 2021). The uncertainty surrounding the pandemic and the transition to remote learning have contributed to anxiety, stress, and concerns about academic and career outcomes (Ang et al., 2022; Saulnier et al., 2022). The closure of campuses also eliminated crucial support systems that students relied on for their well-being (Ro et al., 2021; Strayhorn, 2012).

In response to these challenges, the Mentoring Bridge Model has been implemented to support underrepresented minority and lower-income students in STEM disciplines, offering academic and social support through peer mentoring (Dunn et al., 2021; Qazi et al., 2016). This model aims to enhance students' resilience, time management, and persistence, enabling them to navigate the academic and social challenges exacerbated by the pandemic. This chapter examined the impact of COVID-19 on the resilience of disadvantaged students who participated in the Bridge Model during the initial two years of the pandemic (2020–2022). It investigated the influence of academic focus, confronting social issues, time management, Bridge Model perceptions, and persistence on students' resilience. The study aimed to gain insights into students' experiences and to inform the development of targeted support systems by analyzing data from four different semesters within this period. Understanding the factors contributing to student resilience and academic focus is crucial for addressing disadvantaged students' challenges and promoting equitable outcomes in higher education. By identifying effective strategies and support mechanisms, universities can bridge the educational opportunity gap and better assist students from disadvantaged backgrounds navigate adversity.

Goals, Objectives, and Statement of the Problem

As we continue to address the mental and academic challenges that college students faced during the COVID-19 pandemic, it is crucial to examine its overall impact, particularly among lower-income students and those from underrepresented and underserved minority backgrounds. This chapter discusses factors that have influenced students' resilience, self-regulation, and learning outcomes during the transitional period of the pandemic. Additionally, we sought to explore the types of support that colleges provided and how these interventions influenced students' coping strategies and academic achievements. This study examined variables such as academic focus, the ability to address social issues, effective time management, perceptions of the bridge model, and persistence in relation to resilience. By comparing these variables across different semesters, we aimed to comprehensively understand students' experiences during the COVID-19 pandemic and inform future strategies and interventions for improved outcomes.

REVIEW OF THE LITERATURE

Preliminary research has been conducted to examine the effects of the COVID-19 pandemic on higher education, focusing on understanding the role of resilience in these outcomes (Parker et al., 2021). Resilience encompasses students' ability to adapt to online academic learning and the factors influencing their successful transition during these challenging times. Research has also shed light on the academic and psychological issues experienced by students during the COVID-19 pandemic, including burnout and engagement (Schaufeli et al., 2002; Wang et al., 2021a), motivation and learning (Usher et al., 2021), and distress and prevention behaviors (Kuhn et al., 2022). These studies underscored the significance of resilience as a personal and psychological resource that students utilized to navigate the impact of COVID-19 and the changes it brought to their academic pursuits and personal lives (Kuhn et al., 2022; Wang et al., 2021a).

Online Learning

Students experienced a sudden and unexpected transition to online learning during the COVID-19 pandemic. According to Muilenburg and Berge (2005), effective online learning includes eight areas: facilitator issues, social interaction, study skills, technological skills, learner motivation, time and support for studies, cost and internet access, and technical issues. In a study examining these factors and the COVID-19 pandemic, the most prominent learning barriers for students were social interaction and learning motivation barriers (Le & Van Kieu, 2022). Additionally, with the sudden shift to online learning during the pandemic, online teaching often meant more independent work and homework and less instructor-student engagement, which promoted a lack of academic focus and commitment (Oliveira et al., 2021; Wang et al., 2021b).

While some research shows that there are no significant differences in students' learning outcomes in online learning versus traditional learning settings (Back et al., 2021; Wladis et al., 2015), attrition rates for online classes suggest that individual differences in student experience, background, and motivation may contribute to student matriculation and success when participating in online classes (Bird et al., 2022; Muilenburg & Berg, 2005; Wladis et al., 2015). For example, Bird et al. (2022) employed two difference-in-differences frameworks to examine the impact of transitioning to virtual instruction on course completion among Virginia community college students. The findings revealed a significant decrease of 6.7 percentage points in course completion rates following the shift to virtual instruction. Interestingly, the online teaching experience of faculty members did not act as a mitigating factor in this study for the adverse effects associated with the transition to virtual teaching.

In contrast, Usher et al. (2021) highlighted that high instructor quality, support, and understanding in navigating the adjustment to online learning was crucial to coping with the challenges of the pandemic. For students accustomed to face-to-face learning within the classroom, the transition to online learning during COVID-19 was a difficult adjustment, with students feeling exhausted, depressed, unmotivated, isolated, anxious, and unfocused (Back et al., 2021; Oliveira et al., 2021; Parker et al., 2021; Ro et al., 2021; Son et al., 2020; Wang et al., 2021b). In another study by Krendl (2023), the mental health outcomes of 111 undergraduates at a large Midwestern university were examined before and after the onset of the pandemic. The results indicated a significant association between heightened levels of stress and loneliness and worsening symptoms related to anxiety and depression. This finding underscores the impact of increased stress and social isolation on college students' mental well-being during the pandemic. These considerations highlight the challenges students had to navigate during COVID-19, compounded for students from under-represented and marginalized groups.

Students From Disadvantaged Backgrounds in COVID-19

The COVID-19 pandemic created a myriad of unfortunate circumstances for college students. Amid these circumstances, students from disadvantaged backgrounds struggled with higher risks of contracting COVID-19 (Blanco et al., 2022), maintaining school commitments, and remaining in school as dropout rates were high among vulnerable student populations (Back et al., 2021; Lackner, 2023). In addition, with remote learning, access to the internet and technology became equivalent to access to education, negatively affecting students from disadvantaged backgrounds (Luong & Arnold, 2020). Science, technology, engineering, and mathematics (STEM) students from disadvantaged backgrounds encountered increased challenges in their educational environments, which included insufficient accommodations and faculty/peer support, preparation, professional skills, and discrimination issues (Dunn et al., 2021).

A study of college student persistence during the COVID-19 outbreak in 2020 found that new students, men, minoritized students, and part-time students had the highest withdrawal rates, with part-time Black male students being the most vulnerable to midsemester withdrawal (Lacker, 2023). In addition, Liu et al. (2022) highlighted studies that demonstrated female and sexual minority students reporting higher levels of anxiety and depression during the pandemic (see Chirikov et al., 2020; and Wang et al., 2020). Lederer and colleagues (2021) also noted the additional challenges students of color faced during COVID-19, with discrimination and xenophobia increasing during a turbulent time of social unrest. This chapter highlights how disadvantaged students utilize resilience despite being affected by these factors.

Resilience and Academic Persistence

Resilience has been linked to coping and outcomes of adversity (Masten, 2018; Smith et al., 2008; Wang et al., 2021a). Resilience research has often focused on strengths-based models, specifically on factors individuals may possess that encourage more desirable outcomes when facing adversity (American Psychological Association [APA], 2012; Masten, 2018; Valladolid, 2021). Resilience corresponds to coping with difficulties and setbacks, which can include the social, psychological, and academic effects of COVID-19 (Cassidy, 2016; Martin & Marsh, 2006; Wang et al., 2021a). Student coping behaviors during COVID-19 suggest resilience may be critical to academic outcomes and personal coping.

Resilience, self-regulation, and academic focus have previously been shown to contribute to academic resilience (Caporale-Berkowitz et al., 2022; Hartley, 2011; Usher et al., 2021). *Academic resilience* is the ability to address or overcome acute and chronic adversity related to one's educational and academic development (Cassidy, 2016; Martin, 2013). This concept is relevant to the changes students experienced during COVID-19. Specifically, following Tinto's (1975, 1987, 1993, 2017) interactionalist theory of student persistence, academic and social integration levels can directly impact persistence and retention until graduation.

Tinto's interactionalist theory of student persistence (Tinto, 2017) provides valuable insights into how the COVID-19 pandemic has impacted undergraduate students. The sudden transition to remote learning and campus closures due to COVID-19 had profound implications for students' integration and engagement. Losing in-person interactions with faculty and peers deprived students of the supportive networks and sense of belonging crucial for their academic success. The isolation from the shift to online education created challenges in maintaining social connections and accessing necessary resources, contributing to feelings of disconnection and reduced engagement. The prolonged disruption and the constant changes in instructional modalities introduced a high level of uncertainty into students' educational experiences. This increased uncertainty, isolation, and limited access to support systems significantly impacted students' resilience and ability to persist in their studies.

Considering Tinto's (2017) theory, the COVID-19 pandemic disrupted the critical integration processes for student persistence. The loss of face-to-face interactions, reduced access to campus resources and heightened uncertainties undermined students' sense of belonging and hindered their academic progress. Since resilience is not considered a trait, but one's ability to utilize previously acquired coping skills to manage a current stressor, knowing how this relates to students' coping during COVID-19 is essential (Anasuri & Anthony, 2018; Son et al., 2020; Usher et al., 2021). In addition, studies early into COVID-19 demonstrated that students struggled to manage all the stressors associated with the pandemic and the transitions in their academic lives (Zhai & Du, 2020).

This struggle included increased mental health issues (Bladek, 2021; Usher et al., 2021). Mental health issues can also correspond with lowered resilience and coping skills (Moore et al., 2021; Tope-Banjoko et al., 2020). Furthermore, resilience may be a component of persistence and academic focus that correlates with students' overall academic success (Warren & Hale, 2020). Understanding how resilience may have influenced students during COVID-19 may provide a process for considering how to facilitate and support students moving forward in both online and in-person learning formats. For instance, this may include the use of supportive mentorship programs.

Mentoring

Research has consistently shown that mentoring relationships can positively impact various aspects of students' academic experiences and outcomes (Lee & Cramond, 1999). Mentoring programs have been recognized as valuable interventions in higher education; these programs aim to enhance students' academic engagement, motivation, self-efficacy, and sense of belonging, ultimately contributing to improved academic achievement, retention rates, and degree completion (Campbell & Campbell, 1997). Mentoring programs particularly benefit disadvantaged students, offering them personalized support and guidance to overcome barriers and achieve academic success. Research conducted by Crisp and Cruz (2009) demonstrated that mentoring interventions positively impact the academic outcomes of underrepresented minority students, including increased retention rates and improved grades. Similarly, a study by Campbell and Campbell (1997) found that mentoring relationships fostered a sense of belonging and connectedness among disadvantaged students, leading to higher engagement and motivation to persist in their academic pursuits.

Moreover, mentoring has been found to contribute to developing critical skills and knowledge essential for academic success. In their work, Allen and Eby (2007) highlighted that mentoring programs can provide disadvantaged students access to information, resources, and opportunities they may not have otherwise been exposed to. This exposure helps students navigate the academic landscape, make informed decisions, and develop the necessary skills for effective learning and self-advocacy. These findings underscore the significance of mentoring as a valuable tool for enhancing disadvantaged students' educational experiences and success in higher education.

Overall, these components may provide an essential consideration as students address and understand the impact of COVID-19 on all aspects of their academic and personal lives. It also can provide a critical context for exploring how colleges and universities must provide academic, social, and learning supports to facilitate students' academic outcomes through online learning (Daumiller et al., 2021; Tinto, 2017; Welbeck & Torres, 2019). The Bridge Model (Dunn et al., 2021) was an innovative approach to support STEM students and their resilience during the COVID-19 pandemic. This flexible, comprehensive program provides a multilayered support system and experiences contributing to academic resilience, including mentoring and social integration. The authors present a study on disadvantaged students during COVID-19 and how a mentoring model enhanced their resilience during the transition to online learning.

METHODS

Participants

Three hundred and thirty-one undergraduate students from 10 higher education institutions, including 3 community colleges and 7 four-year universities, including three Historically Black Colleges and Universities (HBCUs), participated in this study. All undergraduate students participating in a National Science Foundation (NSF) funded project focused on broadening participation in STEM disciplines were invited to provide feedback on their experiences at the end of each semester. The specific programs included in this study were Louis Stokes Alliance for Minority Participation (LSAMP) and the Students in Science, Technology, Engineering, and Mathematics-Making to Achieve Excellence and Recognition (SSTEM-MAKERS) Project. All students participated in the Mentoring Bridge Model for SSTEM described earlier. A summary of participant characteristics for each of the 4 semesters is found in Table 11.1. Participants were most likely to be enrolled at a 4-year institution, identify as female and be a junior or senior. The sample was diverse in race, with over 75% identifying as African American each semester.

Table 11.1

Sociodemographic Characteristics of Participants

Participant Characteristics	Spring 2020 (*N* = 105) *N* (%)	Fall 2020 (*N* = 86) *N* (%)	Spring 2021 (*N* = 64) *N* (%)	Spring 2022 (*N* = 76) *N* (%)
Type of Institution				
2-year college	12 (11.4%)	10 (11.6%)	4 (6.3%)	6 (7.9%)
4-year HBCU	32 (30.5%)	29 (33.7%)	18 (28.1%)	24 (31.6%)
4-year non-HBCU	54 (51.4%)	46 (53.5%)	36 (56.3%)	35 (46.1%)
Not reported	7 (6.7%)	1 (1.2%)	6 (9.4%)	9 11.8%)
Academic Status				
Freshman	11 (10.5%)	12 (13.9%)	7 (10.9%)	6 (7.9%)
Sophomore	30 (28.6%)	14 (16.3%)	14 (21.9%)	12 (15.8%)
Junior	31 (29.5%)	30 (34.9%)	17 (26.6%)	19 (25%)
Senior	28 (26.7%)	30 (34.9%)	23 (35.9%)	32 (42.1%)
Not reported	5 (4.8%)	7 (8.2%)	3 (4.7%)	6 (7.9%)
Gender				
Female	57 (54.3%)	51 (59.3%)	34 (53.1%)	36 (47.4%)
Male	39 (37.1%)	33 (38.4%)	27 (42.2%)	32 (42.1%)
Prefer not to answer/not reported.	9 (8.6%)	9 (10.5%)	3 (4.7%)	8 (10.5%)
Race				
American Indian or Alaskan Native	4 (3.8%)	4 (4.7%)	1 (1.6%)	2 (2.6%)
Asian	7 (6.7%)	7 (8.1%)	6 (9.4%)	3 (3.9%)
Black or African American	81 (77.1%)	74 (86.0%)	54 (84.4%)	61 (80.3%)
Native Hawaiian or Pacific Islander	1 (0.9%)	1 (1.2%)	0	0
White	13 (12.4%)	12 (13.9%)	6 (9.4%)	9 (11.8%)
Other (bi/multi-racial, Caribbean)	1 (0.9%)	0	0	1 (1.3%)
Prefer not to answer/not reported.	6 (5.7%)	7 (8.1%)	3 (4.7%)	6 (7.9%)
Ethnicity				
Hispanic	6 (5.7%)	6 (6.9%)	2 (3.1%)	5 (6.6%)
Non-Hispanic	88 (83.4%)	77 (89.5%)	53 (82.8%)	65 (85.5%)
Prefer not to answer/not reported.	11 (10.5%)	10 (11.6%)	9 (14.1%)	6 (6.6%)

Data Collection

Following IRB approval, feedback was gathered from participating students through anonymous online surveys. Measured constructs in the study included resilience, academic focus, college persistence, issues and challenges, time management, and overall Bridge Model perceptions. Resilience was measured using the Brief Resilience Scale (Smith et al., 2008), and persistence was measured using the College Persistence Questionnaire (Davidson et al., 2009). Other constructs were measured using scales tailored to the projects' goals and were developed by project leaders. Reliability estimates were determined for each scale over the four semesters and were very supportive. More specifically, the median reliabilities (r) were .752 for resilience, .749 for academic focus, .733 for social issues, .759 for time management, .876 for persistence, and .965 for Bridge Model Outcomes.

RESULTS

The study results show that the abrupt transition to remote learning during the COVID-19 pandemic had varying impacts on college students' academic experiences. In a follow-up assessment, students perceived that their abilities had either remained the same or slightly improved since the transition to remote learning. The fall of 2021 was marked by positive changes in students' ability to balance responsibilities, overall academic performance, and confidence in working remotely. Similarly, in the spring of 2021, students reported improvements in working remotely, confidence in learning remotely, their ability to learn online, and the quality of the learning process. In terms of resilience, students initially demonstrated moderate levels in the spring of 2020. Still, as the pandemic persisted, they reported facing more significant challenges in coping with stress, bouncing back from setbacks, and recovering from difficulties.

The multiple regression analyses explored the variables related to resilience during the pandemic. Academic focus consistently emerged as a positive predictor of resilience across all four semesters. Confidence in facing social issues and relating to peers was a significant predictor in the spring of 2020 and 2021, while time management was a positive predictor in the fall of 2020 and spring of 2022. Overall perceptions of the Bridge Model, which refers to the support and resources provided by their colleges, positively contributed to resilience in the spring of 2022. The findings suggest that while the transition to remote learning had challenges, students could adapt and perceive improvements in various aspects of their academic experience. Factors such as academic focus, confidence in social interactions, time management, and support from the Bridge

Model played essential roles in promoting resilience during the pandemic. Additional findings will shed light on the factors influencing the resilience of disadvantaged students during the initial two years of the pandemic.

Transition During COVID and Resilience

In March 2020, students transitioned to remote learning. This abrupt transition impacted the quality of instruction, with 60.4% of students describing a decline in quality. Over half (54%) also described a decline in the quality of their academic and other work responsibilities. On the other hand, the quality of project-related experiences was not as impacted, with just 26.7% reporting a decline in the quality of their project activity and 25% in the quality of mentoring. In addition, students reported remaining in contact with their advisor, other students in their cluster, and other students in their classes.

During a follow-up in the 2020–21 academic year, students were asked to report how they changed academically since the abrupt transition to remote learning in the spring of 2020. This change was examined using a 5-point response scale (1 = much worse now, 2 = worse now, 3 = about the same, 4 = better now, 5 = much better now). Overall, students generally believed their abilities stayed the same or slightly improved. In the fall of 2021, students reported the most positive changes in their ability to balance different responsibilities ($M = 3.35$), overall academic performance ($M = 3.30$), and confidence in working remotely ($M = 3.24$). In the spring of 2021, all reported improvement, with the greatest being related to working remotely ($M = 3.7$), confidence in learning remotely ($M = 3.59$), ability to learn online ($M = 3.57$), and the quality of the learning process ($M = 3.43$). In response to items from the Brief Resilience Scale (Smith et al., 2008), students indicated moderate levels of resilience with an overall average of 3.54 in the spring of 2020. As COVID persisted through the spring of 2022, students reported having a more challenging time making it through stressful events, a more difficult time snapping back, and a long time overcoming setbacks in their life (see Table 11.2).

Thus, the fall of 2021 was marked by positive changes in students' ability to balance responsibilities, overall academic performance, and confidence in working remotely. Similarly, in the spring of 2021, students reported improvements in working remotely, confidence in learning remotely, ability to learn online, and the quality of the learning process. In terms of resilience, students initially demonstrated moderate levels in the spring of 2020. Still, as the pandemic persisted, they reported facing more significant challenges in coping with stress, bouncing back from setbacks, and recovering from difficulties.

Table 11.2

Brief Resilience Scale (Spring 2020–Spring 2022)

	Spring 2020 (n = 105)		Fall 2020 (n = 86)		Spring 2021 (n = 64)		Spring 2022 n = 76)	
	M	*SD*	*M*	*SD*	*M*	*SD*	*M*	*SD*
I tend to bounce back quickly after hard times.	3.88	1.09	3.83	1.01	4.03	.983	4.10	.919
I have a hard time making it through stressful events. (r)	3.18	1.27	2.94	1.17	2.82	1.28	2.87	1.28
It does not take me long to recover from a stressful event.	3.58	1.13	3.47	1.06	3.47	1.19	3.69	1.07
It is hard for me to snap back when something bad happens. (r)	3.67	1.08	3.15	1.22	3.08	1.28	3.01	1.32
I usually come through difficult times with little trouble.	3.29	1.08	3.48	1.05	3.34	1.14	3.67	1.11
I tend to take a long time to get over setbacks in my life. (r)	3.69	1.07	3.16	1.18	3.05	1.20	2.84	1.28
Overall Scale	**3.54**	**.821**	**3.34**	**.671**	**3.33**	**.697**	**3.32**	**.714**

Note: 5-point agreement scale (SD, D, N, A, SA)

Variables Related to Resilience

Multiple regression analysis was used to examine variables in relation to resilience for four different semesters during the COVID-19 pandemic. More specifically, the variables of academic focus, ability to face social issues, time management, Bridge Model perceptions, and persistence were examined in relation to resilience and compared among the four different terms using a backward elimination multiple regression. Each regression began by fitting the full model and eliminated variables with a greater than 10% probability of an association by chance alone ($p > .10$) to arrive at a final restricted model. The alpha level was set *a priori* to $\alpha = 0.05$.

Overall, the four full regression models were statistically significant, with moderate to large effect sizes (R2) ranging from 23.9% in the spring of 2020 to 40.3% in the spring of 2022. Each model was reduced to models restricted to variables meeting the criteria for inclusion described above. These final models were statistically significant, with effect sizes ranging from 22.1% in the spring of 2020 to 38.1% in the spring of

2021. Standardized coefficients (Betas) were estimated for each predictor variable. The resulting statistically significant Betas in the final model ranged from .228 to .494. The predictor of academic focus was retained in the four regression models, indicating that students more focused on their educational process expressed greater resilience. During the spring of 2020 and 2021, students indicating more confidence to face social issues and relate to peers was a statistically significant predictor of resilience, while time management was retained as a positive predictor in the fall of 2020 and the spring of 2022. Overall. Bridge Model perceptions were also a positive predictor in the spring of 2022. These results, including full and final model R^2 values, standard errors of estimate, and standardized regression coefficients (Betas), are summarized in Table 11.3.

Table 11.3

Summary of Regression Analysis by Academic Term

Full Model	Spring 2020	Fall 2020	Spring 2021	Spring 2022
R^2	.239	.359	.391	.403
Standard Error of Estimate	.736	.554	.547	.576
F	6.208***	9.738***	7.443***	9.463***
Predictor Variables	B^a	B^a	B^a	B^a
Academic Focus	.256*	.210	.472***	.252
Social Issues	.238*	.121	.221	–.117
Time Management	.064	.374**	.108	.194
Bridge Model Perceptions	–.084	–.121	–.028	.246*
Persistence	.099	.055	-.022	.243
Final Model				
R^2	.221	.342	.381	.378
Standard Error of Estimate	.734	.552	.538	.579
F	14.460***	23.36***	18.783***	14.615***

(Table continued on next page)

Table 11.3 (Continued)

Summary of Regression Analysis by Academic Term

Full Model	Spring 2020	Fall 2020	Spring 2021	Spring 2022
Predictor Variables	*B*[a]	*B*[a]	*B*[a]	*B*[a]
Academic Focus	.298**	.210*	.494***	.316**
Social Issues	.275**		.228*	
Time Management		.451***		.265**
Bridge Model Perceptions				.251*
$R2$ Difference	.018	.017	.010	.025
F	.7805	.7691	.3175	1.4656

a-effect sizes (small = .10, medium = .30, large = .50)

$*p < .05, ** p < .01, *** p < .001$

Subsequent regressions were examined further to explore the relationship between academic focus and resilience (see Table 11.4). Using a backward elimination approach, each full regression model was reduced to a subset of predictors with statistically significant models and effect sizes ranging from 16.5% in the spring of 2020 to 43.9% in the spring of 2021. Consistent with the four regressions, those students who considered withdrawing from at least one class indicated less resilience. During the first two semesters, students who expressed having trouble concentrating on their academic work also indicated less resilience.

However, other items were found to be positively associated with resilience. For example, dedicating more time to academic responsibilities (spring 2020) and staying connected to peers (fall 2020) was positively associated with resilience. In the spring of 2021, students reported being focused, motivated to learn in their classes, and committed to completing their degree on time, indicating higher resilience levels. One year later, in the spring of 2022, focusing on academics, being motivated to learn, and staying in contact with peers were associated with higher levels of resilience.

Academic focus consistently emerged as a positive predictor of resilience across all four semesters. Confidence in facing social issues and relating to peers was a significant predictor in the spring of 2020 and 2021, while time management was a positive predictor in the fall of 2020 and spring of 2022. Overall perceptions of the Bridge Model, which refers to the support and resources provided by their colleges, positively contributed to resilience in the spring of 2022. The findings suggest that, while the transition to remote learning had challenges, students could adapt and perceive improvements in various aspects of their academic experience. Factors such as academic focus, confidence in social interactions, time management, and support from the Bridge Model played essential roles in promoting resilience during the pandemic.

Table 11.4

Academic Focus and Resilience

	Spring 2020	Fall 2020	Spring 2021	Spring 2022
Full Model				
R^2	.201	.296	.479	.441
Standard Error of Estimate	.766	.598	.567	.583
F	2.646**	3.482***	4.694***	5.049***
Final Model				
R^2	.165	.263	.439	.427
Standard Error of Estimate	.757	.591	.556	.569
F	4.24***	7.950***	11.170***	10.276***
Academic Focus Items (Final Model)	*B*[a]	*B*[a]	*B*[a]	*B*[a]
I have been focused on my academics			.302*	.369*
I have been motivated to learn in my classes			.485**	.444**
I am having trouble concentrating on my academic work	–.203*	–.252**		

(Table continued on next page)

Table 11.4 (Continued)

Academic Focus and Resilience

	Spring 2020	Fall 2020	Spring 2021	Spring 2022
I have considered withdrawing from at least one class	–.234**	–.187*	–.474***	–.380**
I have not spent as much time on my coursework				–.236 (p = .084)
I am committed to completing my degree on time		.180a	.243*	
I have dedicated more time to my academic responsibilities	.178*			
I have stayed connected with my peers		.246*		.336**
I am confident that I am learning what I need to know in my classes				
I plan to enroll in courses next semester/term.				

a-effect sizes (small =.10, medium = .30, large =.50)

$^*p < .05$, $^{**}p < .01$, $^{***}p < .001$

DISCUSSION

The study provides valuable insights into how the transition to remote learning during the COVID-19 pandemic impacted disadvantaged college students' academic experiences, resilience, and persistence. Tinto's (2017) model of student motivation and resilience highlights self-efficacy, sense of belonging, and perceptions of the curriculum as critical factors influencing student persistence. The findings of this study align with Tinto's model, indicating that factors such as academic focus, confidence in social interactions, effective time management, and institutional support were crucial in promoting resilience during the pandemic. Understanding these factors can help educational institutions develop strategies to support students' resilience and enhance their academic experiences in times of crisis.

The study's findings suggest that the sudden shift to remote learning had varying effects on students' academic quality and sense of belonging. While most students reported a decline in the quality of instruction and their academic responsibilities, project-related experiences and mentoring were less affected. Variables that contributed to student persistence included access to support from the institution, such as advising, structured strategies (including faculty and peer mentoring), meaningful course assignments, and feelings of engagement and connection. The results highlight the importance of social connections during this challenging period, as students maintained contact with advisors, peers, and classmates. These findings are consistent with previous research emphasizing the impact of quality instruction, communication with instructors, self-efficacy in coursework, and social connectedness (Schindler & Boney, 2022).

Academic focus consistently emerged as a positive predictor of resilience across all four semesters, indicating that students who prioritized their educational process and trusted the curriculum displayed higher levels of resilience. Notably, students demonstrated moderate levels of resilience in the spring of 2020, likely influenced by the perceived short-term nature of online learning and the uncertainty surrounding the pandemic's trajectory. However, as the pandemic persisted, students reported facing increased challenges in coping with stress and rebounding from setbacks, indicating a cumulative impact on resilience.

Confidence in facing social issues and relating to peers was a significant predictor in both the spring of 2020 and 2021, underscoring the importance of social support and interpersonal connections in fostering resilience. The participants' overall perceptions of the Bridge Model, representing the support and resources provided by their colleges, also positively contributed to resilience, particularly in the spring of 2022. This highlights the significance of institutional support in promoting student resilience. The study suggests that feeling connected, cared for, and guided by mentors profoundly impacted the undergraduate experience for these individuals, enabling them to adapt and thrive during the pandemic. Effective time management skills were also found to positively contribute to resilience during the fall of 2020 and spring of 2022, emphasizing the role of self-efficacy and time management in building resilience (Schwarzer & Warner, 2013). These skills helped participants maintain a sense of control over their responsibilities and foster optimism about their education despite the challenges posed by the pandemic.

CONCLUSIONS

This chapter presents preliminary research on the impact of unexpected transitioning to online learning on students from diverse backgrounds with consideration of the other dynamics students faced during COVID-19. Specifically, the study examined the impact of the Bridge Model (Dunn et al., 2021), an educational mentorship initiative focused on increasing support to disadvantaged undergraduate STEM students during a global pandemic when remote learning became a standard instructional mode. Additionally, the study considered how academic resilience was fostered through this program within the context of the unique factors that arose from the pandemic. Finally, the implications from the preliminary results provide valuable educational insights aimed at increasing the support of disadvantaged students and increasing factors that promote academic resilience.

The study examined several educational factors. The impact of quality of instruction was explored, with results from this study demonstrating that the quality of instruction initially declined. Still, with contact and support from peers and mentors, more long-term adverse outcomes appeared to be nominal. This is supported by the literature, which shows that contact and interaction with peers, educators, and mentors effectively decreases feelings of isolation and enhances the clarity of goals (Inman, 2020; Morse et al., 2022). Moreover, students reported increased management of their time and responsibilities throughout the pandemic, which supports that students can possess academic resilience and focus once healthy habits are established (Schindler & Boney, 2022). However, as the semesters, pandemic, and remote learning persisted, students in this study reported difficulty maintaining their sense of resilience, meaning-making, and ability to bounce back from adversity, which parallels research on the effects of ongoing turmoil and stress (Browning et al., 2021; Piltch-Loeb et al., 2021). Lastly, students in the study who were more focused on their academic duties and professional relationships could block out external and environmental stressors expressed greater resilience. This poses an additional challenge for disadvantaged students, as they may lack the privileges necessary to prioritize their academic obligations over personal responsibilities and needs.

Faculty also reported difficulty transitioning to remote learning unexpectedly, which can directly impact students' experiences and success (Oliveira et al., 2021; Parker et al., 2021). Administrators and institutions can provide horizontal mentoring, support, and resources for faculty and students in structured and recurring meetings, addressing possible emotional and procedural challenges (Dunn et al., 2021; Parker et al., 2021; Yang et al., 2022). This can include stress and time management, student support advice, faculty preparation, and awareness of continuing issues (Dunn et al., 2021; Patterson & Patterson, 2009). While educators have learned to work remotely, they may be experiencing misalignment between professional and personal identity demands, directly impacting mentorship and the academic environment (Yang et al., 2022).

These findings have important implications for college counseling centers and professionals serving the college population. These individuals must understand disadvantaged students' challenges, including financial constraints, limited access to resources, familial responsibilities, and systemic barriers. Recognizing the significant impact of these factors on students' academic experiences and resilience is essential. Additionally, it is crucial to consider the intersectionality of students' identities, such as race, ethnicity, gender, socioeconomic status, ability status, and first-generation status, as these factors shape their unique challenges and strengths.

College counseling centers should address various aspects of student well-being to support disadvantaged students, including mental health, stress management, time management, study skills, and self-care. Helping students develop essential skills in academic success and resilience, such as effective time management, goal setting, problem-solving, self-advocacy, and self-regulation, is vital. Workshops and individual sessions focused on building these skills can be beneficial. Collaboration with other campus departments, such as academic advisors, financial aid offices, tutoring services, and career development centers, is crucial to ensure a coordinated and holistic approach to student support. Active engagement with disadvantaged student populations through targeted outreach, workshops, presentations, and awareness campaigns can promote mental health and resilience within these communities. Building relationships with student organizations, faculty, and staff can enhance support and reach a broader audience. Implementing these strategies will enable college counseling centers to support disadvantaged students in enhancing their academic resilience and overall well-being. As we continue to address the psychological and academic outcomes college students face during this challenging time, it remains essential to provide them with the necessary support to navigate these challenges (Morse et al., 2022).

Limitations and Lessons Learned

Nevertheless, there were limitations to this quantitative study and lessons learned that warrant consideration. First, the participant pool only included STEM students in the Alabama Black Belt, defined as a region in the South historically driven by cotton production and the presence of African Americans (Prior & Wong, 2022). Thus, results on academic resilience from samples of other underrepresented groups may vary based on remote learning experiences and geographic and social locations. Additionally, as only STEM programs were considered, students in other areas of education (i.e., liberal arts, business, psychology) may have varying academic experiences due to the pandemic, and, therefore, may report different academic resilience-related factors. Other limitations were found due to the sample size; three hundred and thirty-one students from 10 institutions participated in the study. However, over the four semesters of this study, the average number of participants from each semester was 82.75. This may have been due to the limited number of students initially involved in these STEM programs and the ability to maintain encouraging participation across the four semesters. The hardships of the pandemic outside of academics could have negatively impacted their ability to continue being involved in the study, which also relates to the ability of the researchers to remain in contact with the participants.

IMPLICATIONS FOR THE FUTURE

A robust understanding of the college student experience is critical to enhancing student support, focus, and resilience and improving collegiate-level pedagogy. It is also important to understand these issues within the context of the COVID-19 pandemic and to consider ways to foster resilience during and outside turmoil. Resilience is a product of a larger context, often requiring systemic changes and accountability, including within educational institutions (Tinto, 2017; Wolcott, 2022). The study for this chapter emphasized the importance of social support, institutional resources, and effective time management skills in promoting resilience among disadvantaged college students. These findings highlight the need for interventions and support systems that foster positive relationships, provide guidance and resources, and empower students to develop self-efficacy and time management skills.

Understanding these factors can help educational institutions to develop strategies to support disadvantaged students' resilience and to enhance their academic experiences during times of crisis. Despite the transition to remote learning challenges, disadvantaged students could adapt and perceive improvements in their academic experiences by focusing on critical factors that contribute to resilience. To help disadvantaged students thrive, institutions must implement crisis plans, establish horizontal and vertical mentorship programs to engage skill building (e.g., time management and organizational skills) (Dunn et al., 2021), employ flexible teaching methods with high-value curricula, prioritize student self-efficacy, and foster a supportive campus culture. Specifically, research suggests that pedagogical and mentoring interventions are impactful, particularly for students who may be at risk due to environmental, cultural, or historical factors (Inman, 2020). Also, students who felt psychological capital and campus belonging reported a lower likelihood of experiencing adverse mental health effects due to COVID-19 and their learning process (Ro et al., 2021; Wang et al., 2021a). Disadvantaged college students (e.g., first-generation, students with disabilities, or undocumented students) would benefit from their institutions' increased attention to cultivating campus community and connection, increased focus on educating faculty about early warning systems of academic and psychological struggle (Tinto, 2017), and increased knowledge of academic and professional etiquette to foster a flourishing academic environment.

It is recommended that higher education administrators provide outreach services to students of specific high-vulnerable groups (Browning et al., 2021; Liu et al., 2022). Through a multicultural feminist lens, mentorship interventions can focus on the lack of power and expertise disadvantaged students experience within their educational process and advocate for and promote student growth through robust relational engagement and exploration (Inman, 2018, 2020). As reflected in this study and chapter, college educators intentionally joining students in peer mentorship and cooperative learning methods may be crucial in student academic resilience and perception of belonging through unexpected adversity (like the COVID-19 pandemic). Mentorship as a partnership between college educators and students may help strengthen student connections to a rich and creative learning environment, empower them to capitalize on their skills, and provide support and meaningful interaction to overcome challenges (Inman, 2020; Wang et al., 2021b).

Further, with the small numbers of minority faculty in higher education, cross-cultural mentorship relationships are prevalent (Harris & Lee, 2019). Harris and Lee (2019) advise cross-cultural mentorship relationships utilizing an advocate-mentor model that focuses on broaching issues underrepresented students face in higher education. A mentor is a role model and advocate, helping disadvantaged students bridge the gap in their academic and professional pursuits by fostering healthier habits and resilience. The Bridge Model (Dunn et al., 2021), a novel approach, offers mentorship and support strategies to disadvantaged students, addresses funding and personal barriers, and promotes mandatory attendance to academic resources, such as tutoring and networking events. This approach enables disadvantaged and underrepresented students to connect interpersonally and professionally weekly (for, on average, 2–3 hours weekly with a faculty member or graduate student), enhance academic focus, and develop important skills like time management and social integration.

Educators have now learned to complete their jobs remotely out of necessity through the pandemic, but identity issues arise through a misalignment between professional and personal identity demands (Yang et al., 2022). The authors recommend support from institutional administrators, promoting small group environments to enhance engagement (Wang et al., 2021b) and leadership related to stress management and professional effectiveness in times of crisis (Patterson & Patterson, 2009). Institutions must also overtly and continuously communicate normalizing messaging within the curriculum that academic struggles are common and that students can learn to be successful through campus resources even after the pandemic (Tinto, 2017). This can demonstrate to faculty their long-term value to the institution and an often-underutilized resource for student support while they experience the traumatic effects of a global pandemic (Lederer et al., 2021). College educators and administrators can also cultivate academic resilience through a growth mindset and finding ways to feel "heard, valued, and supported" (Wolcott, 2022, p. 477).

These results can also illuminate focus areas for college counseling centers, faculty, and professional helpers who serve the college population. With emerging adulthood full of many personal and professional changes (Bladek, 2021; Morse et al., 2022), faculty, college counselors, and professional helpers can aid in this adjustment period by addressing the identity challenges and habits of daily living of college students. Providing college students with a hope and resilience framework can improve college retention, learning outcomes, and coping with mental health issues associated with college learning (Kuhn et al., 2022; Valladolid, 2021). Seeking professional help and therapy has become more normalized for younger generations. Still, students may perceive their difficulties as not severe enough to pursue services (Son et al., 2020) or inaccurately view help-seeking behavior as a failure to fit into college, so institutions must proactively support these students (Tinto, 2017).

Faculty, college counselors, and professional helpers can directly aid college students and their academic success and resilience through psychoeducation and behavioral rehearsal on strategies for resilience, value sorting, task-oriented coping strategies (Valladolid, 2021), habit stacking, perspective-taking or cognitive reappraisal (Browning et al., 2021), stress management, time management, and relationship-building skills. The authors also recommend challenging beliefs about impression management, belonging, worth, perfectionism, rigidness, and overcontrol to help promote resilience and performance in college students. Encouragement of students to find sources of comfort like spiritual practices, mindfulness, and self-soothing techniques can also be practical, along with active forms of coping, decreasing avoidant or problem-solving coping.

Future research on academic resilience in undergraduate students should consider exploring such within undergraduates from different programs than STEM. These results show that students in STEM programs from underrepresented backgrounds could be resilient in overcoming some of the struggles connected to an abrupt change in their educational experience. To increase the generalizability of these results, the study should be replicated, considering this same population in other non-STEM educational disciplines. Students in those fields may have unique needs separate from those in STEM programs. For instance, educational programs require student-teaching experiences to graduate, which continued to be a requirement even during the pandemic, though it was done online instead of in person (Back et al., 2021). Students in these education programs experienced negative emotions such as disappointment and uncertainty during their online student teaching experiences. Such experiences and those of students in other programs may have unique implications for academic resilience, persistence, and focus.

SUMMARY

The enrollment of first-generation students in higher education is increasing (Ramos, 2019), with underrepresented and disadvantaged students facing significant barriers, particularly in STEM fields (Gehringer et al., 2022; Rainey et al., 2018). The attrition rates for first-generation students of color are high, highlighting the need for strategies to support them (Ramos, 2019). This chapter contributes to understanding the challenges and resilience of disadvantaged students in online learning. Despite difficulties, students showed resilience in their academic programs. Future research should explore the impact of online learning on academic resilience. This chapter emphasizes the role of faculty and administrators in supporting students through innovative approaches like the Bridge Model (Dunn et al., 2021). Further research should examine the factors contributing to academic resilience in these programs and explore their application in other university support systems.

REFERENCES

Allen, T. D., & Eby, L. T. (2007). *The Blackwell handbook of mentoring: A multiple perspectives approach*. Blackwell.

Anasuri, S., & Anthony, K. (2018). Resilience levels among college students: A comparative study from two southern states in the USA. *IOSR Journal of Humanities and Social Science, 23*(1), 52–73. https://doi.org/10.1016/10.9790/0837-2301035273

Ang, W. H. D., Chew, H. S. J., Dong, J., Yi, H., Mahendren, R., & Lau, Y. (2022). Digital training for building resilience: Systematic review, meta-analysis, and meta-egression. *Stress and Health, 38*(5), 848–869. https://doi.org/10.1002/smi.3154

American Psychological Association (APA). (2012). *Building your resilience*. https://www.apa.org/topics/resilience

Back, M., Golembeski, K., Gutiérrez, A., Macko, T., Miller, S., & Pelletier, D. L. (2021). "We were told the content we delivered was not as important": Disconnect and disparities in world language student teaching during COVID-19. *System, 103*, 1–11. https://doi.org/10.1016/j.system.2021.102679

Bird, K. A., Castleman, B. L., & Lohner, G. (2022). Negative impacts from the shift to online learning during the COVID-19 crisis: Evidence from a statewide community college system. *EdWorkingPaper*, 20–299. Retrieved from Annenberg Institute at Brown University. https://doi.org/10.26300/gx68-rq13

Bladek, M. (2021). Student well-being matters: Academic library support for the whole student. *The Journal of Academic Librarianship, 47*(3), 2–10. https://doi.org/10.1016/j.acalib.2021.102349

Blanco, T., Floyd, B., Mitchell, B., & Hughes, R. (2022). Varied institutional response to COVID-19: An investigation of U.S. colleges' and universities' reopening plans for fall 2020. *AERO Open, 8*(1), 1–18. https://doi.org/10.3886/E164401V1

Browning, M., Larson L.R., Sharaievska, I., Rigolon, A., McAnirlin, O., Mullenbach L., Cloutier, S., Vu, T. M., Thomsen, J., Reigner, N., Metcalf, E. C., D'Antonio, A., Helbich, M., Bratman, G. N., & Alvarez, H. O. (2021). Psychological impacts from COVID-19 among university students: Risk factors across seven states in the United States. *PLoS ONE, 16*(1), e0245327. https://doi.org/10.1371/journal.pone.0245327

Caporale-Berkowitz, N. A., Boyer, B. P., Muenks, K., & Brownson, C. B. (2022). Resilience, not grit, predicts college student retention following academic probation. *Journal of Educational Psychology, 114*(7), 1654–1669. https://doi.org/10.1037/edu0000721

Cassidy, S. (2016). The Academic Resilience Scale (ARS-30): A new multidimensional construct measure. *Frontiers in psychology, 7*, 1787. https://doi.org/10.3389/fpsyg.2016.01787

Campbell, T. A., & Campbell, D. E. (1997). Faculty/student mentor program: Effects on academic performance and retention. *Research in Higher Education, 38*, 727–742.

Chirikov, I., Soria, K. M, Horgos, B., & Jones-White, D. (2020). *Undergraduate and graduate students' mental health during the COVID-19 pandemic*. UC Berkeley, Center for Studies in Higher Education. https://escholarship.org/uc/item/80k5d5hw

Conrad, R. C., Hahm, H., Koire, A., Pinder-Amaker, S., & Liu, C. H. (2021). College student mental health risks during the COVID-19 pandemic: Implications of campus relocation. *Journal of Psychiatric Research, 136*, 117–126. http://dx.doi.org/10.1016/j.jpsychires.2021.01.054

Crisp, G., & Cruz, I. (2009). Mentoring college students: A critical review of the literature between 1990 and 2007. *Research in Higher Education, 50*, 525–545. https://doi.org/10.1007/s11162-009-9130-2

Daumiller, M., Rinas, R., Hein, J., Janke, S., Dickhäuser, O., & Dresel, M. (2021). Shifting from face-to-face to online teaching during COVID-19: The role of university faculty achievement goals for attitudes towards this sudden change, and their relevance for burnout/engagement and student evaluations of teaching quality. *Computers in Human Behavior, 118*, 106677. https://doi.org/10.1016/j.chb.2020.106677

Davidson, W., Beck, H., & Milligan, M. (2009). The College Persistence Questionnaire: Development and validation of an instrument that predicts student attrition. *Journal of College Student Development, 50* (4), 373–390. https://doi.org/10.1353/csd.0.0079

Dunn, C., Shannon, D., McCullough, B., Jenda, O., Qazi, M., & Pettis, C. (2021). A mentoring bridge model for students with disabilities in science, technology, engineering, and mathematics. *Journal of Postsecondary Education and Disability, 34*(2), 163–177.

Gehringer, T. A., Folberg, A. M., & Ryan, C. S. (2022). The relationships of belonging and task socialization to GPA and intentions to re-enroll as a function of race/ethnicity and first-generation college student status. *Journal of Diversity in Higher Education, 15*(6), 744–754. https://doi.org/10.1037/dhe0000306

Harris, T. M., & Lee, C. N. (2019). Advocate-mentoring: A communicative response to diversity in higher education. *Communication Education, 68*(1), 103–113. https://doi-org/10.1080/03634523.2018.1536272

Hartley, M. T. (2011). Examining the relationships between resilience, mental health, and academic persistence in undergraduate college students. *Journal of American College Health, 59*(7), 596–604. http://doi.org//10.1080/07448481.2010.515632

Inman, A. G. (2018). Social justice mentoring and scholarship: Building a community of leaders and advocates. *The Counseling Psychologist, 46*(8), 1040–1054. https://doi.org/10.1177/0011000018817908

Inman, A. G. (2020). Culture and positionality: Academy and mentorship. *Women & Therapy, 43*(1–2), 112–124. https://doi.org/10.1080/02703149.2019.1684678

Johns, S., & Hawkes, S. (2020). A look at empathy, university belonging, and intersectionality: How to support a diverse student body amid the COVID-19 crisis. *Journal of Interdisciplinary Studies in Education, 9*(2), 10–13. https://doi.org/10.32674/jise.v9i2.2407

Krendl, A. C. (2023). Changes in stress predict worse mental health outcomes for college students than does loneliness; Evidence from the COVID-19 pandemic. *Journal of American College Health, 71*(1), 40–43. https://doi.org/10.1080/07448481.2021.1887198

Kuhn, T., Vander Horst, A., Gibson, G., Cleveland, K., Wawrosch, C. Hunt, C. Woolverton, C., & Hughes, J. (2022). Distress and prevention behaviors during the COVID-19 pandemic among college students: The moderating role of resilience. *International Journal of Behavioral Medicine. 29*, 524–529. http://doi.org/10.1007/s12529-021-10034-w

Lackner, E. (2023). Community college student persistence during the COVID-19 crisis of spring 2020. *Community College Review, 51*(2), 193–215. https://doi.org/10.1177/00915521221145304

Lancaster, M., & Arango, E. (2021). Health and emotional well-being of urban university students in the era of COVID-19. *Traumatology, 27*(1), 107–117. https://doi.org/10.1037/trm0000308

Le, T. T. K., & Van Kieu, N. (2022). An investigation into barriers in online learning during the pandemic: View from students at a vocational college. In *2022 10th International Conference on Information and Education Technology (ICIET)* (pp. 199–203). IEEE.

Lederer, A. M., Hoban, M. T., Lipson, S. K., Zhou, S., & Eisenberg, D. (2021). More than inconvenienced: The unique needs of U.S. college students during the COVID-19 pandemic. *Health Education & Behavior, 48*(1), 14–19. https://doi.org/10.1177/1090198120969372

Lee, J., & Cramond, B. (1999). The positive effects of mentoring economically disadvantaged students. *Professional School Counseling, 2*(3), 172–178.

Liu, Y., Frazier, P. A., Porta, C. M., & Lust, K. (2022). Mental health of US undergraduate and graduate students before and during the COVID-19 pandemic: Differences across sociodemographic groups. *Psychiatry Research, 309*, 114428. https://doi.org/10.1016/j.psychres.2022.114428

Luong, J., & Arnold, R. (2020). Creating a digital learning community: Four key considerations for remote learning during a pandemic. An *International Conference on Engineering, Technology, and Education*, 786–791. https://doi.org/10.1109/TALE48869.2020.9368385

Martin, A. J. (2013). Academic buoyancy and academic resilience: Exploring 'everyday' and 'classic' resilience in the face of academic adversity. *School Psychology International, 34*(5), 488–500. https://doi.org/10.1177/0143034312472759

Martin, A. J., & Marsh, H. W. (2006). Academic resilience and its psychological and educational correlates: A construct validity approach. *Psychology in the Schools, 43*(3), 267–281. https://doi.org/10.1002/pits.20149

Masten, A. S. (2018). Resilience theory and research on children and families: Past, present, and promise. *Journal of Family Theory & Review, 10*(1), 12–31. https://doi.org/10.1111/jftr.12255

Moore, S. E., Wierenga, K. L., Prince, D. M., Gillani, B., & Mintz, L. J. (2021). Disproportionate impact of the COVID-19 pandemic on perceived social support, mental health and somatic symptoms in sexual and gender minority populations. *Journal of Homosexuality, 68*(4), 577–591. https://doi.org/10.1080/00918369.2020.1868184

Morse, J. L., Lee, H., Haddock, S. A., & Henry, K. L. (2022). Meaning in life trajectories among college students: Differential effects of a mentoring program. *Journal of Happiness Studies, 23*(1), 285–302. https://doi-org/10.1007/s10902-021-00399-w

Muilenburg, L. Y., & Berge, Z. L. (2005). Student barriers to online learning: A factor analytic study. *Distance Education, 26*(1), 29–48. https://doi.org/10.1080/01587910500081269

Oliveira, G., Grenha Teixeira, J., Torres, A., & Morais, C. (2021). An exploratory study on the emergency remote education experience of higher education students and teachers during the COVID-19 pandemic. *British Journal of Educational Technology, 52*(4), 1357–1376. https://doi.org/10.1111/bjet.13112

Parker, S., Hansen, M., & Bernadowski, C. (2021). COVID-19 campus closures in the United States: American student perceptions of forced transition to remote learning. *Social Sciences, 10*(62), 1–18. http://dx.doi.org/10.3390/socsci10020062

Patterson, J. L., & Patterson, J. H. (2009). Staying positive in negative times. *Educational Leadership, (67)*2, 1.

Piltch-Loeb, R., Merdjanoff, A., & Meltzer, G. (2021). Anticipated mental health consequences of COVID-19 in a nationally representative sample: Context, coverage, and economic consequences. *Preventative Medicine, 145*, 1–9. http://dx.doi.org/10.1016/j.ypmed.2021.106441

Prior, J. W., II, & Wong, D. W. S. (2022). Exploring different dimensions in defining the Alabama Black Belt. *GeoJournal, 87*(3), 1525. https://doi.org/10.1007/s10708-020-10325-x

Qazi, M. Shannon, D., Jenda, O., McCullough, B., Griffin, G., & Lunn, A. (2016). A mentoring bridge model to prepare students with disabilities in the STEM fields at Tuskegee University. *Journal of Women and Minorities in Science and Engineering, 22*(3), 183–197. https://doi.org/10.1615/JWomenMinorScienEng.2016015452

Rainey, K., Dancy, M., Mickelson, R., Stearns, E., & Moller, S. (2018). Race and gender differences in how sense of belonging influences decisions to major in STEM. *International Journal of STEM Education, 5*, 10. https://doi.org/10.1186/s40594-018-0115-6

Ramos, B. N. (2019). Moving from access to success: How first-generation students of color can build resilience in higher education through mentorship. *Vermont Connection, 40*(1), 55–61. https://scholarworks.uvm.edu/tvc/vol40/iss1/9

Ro, A., Rodriguez, V. E., & Enriquez, L. E. (2021). Physical and mental health impacts of the COVID-19 pandemic among college students who are undocumented or have undocumented parents. *BMC Public Health, 21*(1), 1580.

Saulnier, K.G., Koscinski, B., Volarov, M., Accorso, C., Austin, M.J., Suhr, J.A., & Allan, N. (2022). Anxiety sensitivity and intolerance of uncertainty are unique and interactive risk factors for COVID-19 safety behaviors and worries. *Cognitive Behaviour Therapy, 51*, 217–228. http://dx.doi.org/10.1080/16506073.2021.1976819

Schaufeli, W. B., Martinez, I. M., Pinto, A. M., Salanova, M., Bakker, A. B. (2002). Burnout and engagement in university students: A cross-national study. *Journal of Cross-Cultural Psychology. 33*(5), 464–481. https://doi.org/10.1177/0022022102033005003.

Schindler, V. P., & Boney, J. D. (2022). Characteristics contributing to graduation for university students with DSM-5 diagnoses after completion of a mentoring program. *Mentoring & Tutoring: Partnership in Learning, 30*(1), 124–141. https://doi.org/10.1080/13611267.2022.2031085

Schwarzer, R., & Warner, L. M. (2012). Perceived self-efficacy and its relationship to resilience. In *Resilience in children, adolescents, and adults: Translating research into practice* (pp. 139–150). Springer.

Smith, B., Dalen, J., Wiggins, K., Tooley, E., Christopher, P., & Bernard, J. (2008). The Brief Resilience Scale: Assessing the ability to bounce back. *International Journal of Behavioral Medicine, 15*, 194–200. https://doi.org/10.1080/10705500802222972

Son, C., Hegde, S., Smith, A., Wang, X., & Sasangohar, F. (2020). Effects of COVID-19 on college students' mental health in the United States: Interview survey study. *Journal of Medical Internet Research, 22*(9). http://dx.doi.org/10.2196/21279

Strayhorn, T. L. (2012). *College students' sense of belonging: A key to educational success for all students*. Routledge. https://doi.org/10.4324/9780203118924

Tope-Banjoko, T., Davis, V., Morrison, K., Fife, J., Hill, O., & Talley, C. (2020). Academic resilience in college students: Relationship between coping and GPA. *Anatolian Journal of Education, 5*(2), 109–120. https://doi.org/10.29333/aje.2020.529a

Tinto, V. (1975). Dropout from higher education: A theoretical synthesis of recent research. *Review of Educational Research, 45*, 89–125. https://www.jstor.org/stable/1170024

Tinto, V. (1987). *Leaving college: Rethinking the causes and cures of student attrition*. University of Chicago Press.

Tinto, V. (1993). *Leaving college: Rethinking the causes and cures of student attrition*. (2nd ed.). University of Chicago Press. https://doi.org/10.7208/chicago/9780226922461.001.0001

Tinto, V. (2017). Reflections on student persistence. *Student Success, 8*(2), 1–8. https://doi.org/10.5204/ssj.v8i2.376

Usher, E. L., Golding, J. M., Han, J., Griffiths, C. S., McGavran, M. B., Brown, C. S., & Sheehan, E. A. (2021). Psychology students' motivation and learning in response to the shift to remote instruction during COVID-19. *Scholarship of Teaching and Learning in Psychology*. Advance online publication. http://dx.doi.org/10.1037/stl0000256

Valladolid, V. (2021) The role of coping strategies in the resilience and well-being of college students during COVID-19 pandemic. *Philippine Social Science Journal, 4*(2), 30–42. https://doi.org/10.52006/main.v4i2.342

Warren, J. M., & Hale, R. W. (2020). Predicting grit and resilience: Exploring college students' academic rational beliefs. *Journal of College Counseling, 23*(2), 154–167. https://doi.org/10.1002/jocc.12156

Wang, J., Bu, L., Li, Y., Song, J., & Li, N. (2021a). The mediating effect of academic engagement between psychological capital and academic burnout among nursing students during COVID-19 pandemic: A cross-sectional study. *Nurse Education Today. 101*, 1–6. https://doi.org/10.1016/j.nedt.2021.104938

Wang, Y., Stein, D., & Shen, S. (2021b). Students' and teachers' perceived teaching presence in online courses. *Distance Education, 42*(3), 373–390. https://doi.org/10.1080/01587919.2021.1956304

Wang, X., Hegde, S., Son, C., Keller, B., Smith, A., & Sasangohar, F. (2020). Investigating mental health of US college students during the COVID-19 pandemic: Cross-sectional survey study. *Journal of Medical Internet Research. 22*(9). https://doi.org/10.2196/22817.

Welbeck, R., & Torres, R. (2019). The male student success initiative: Investing in the success of men of color. *MDRC*. https://eric.ed.gov/?id=ED599692

Wilson, O. W., Holland, K. E., Elliott, L. D., Duffey, M., & Bopp, M. (2021). The impact of the COVID-19 pandemic on US college students' physical activity and mental health. *Journal of Physical Activity and Health, 18*(3), 272–278. https://doi.org/10.1123/jpah.2020-0325

Wladis, C., Conway, K. M., & Hachey, A. C. (2015). The online STEM classroom—Who succeeds? An exploration of the impact of ethnicity, gender, and non-traditional student characteristics in the community college context. *Community College Review, 43*(2), 142–164.

Wolcutt, M. (2022). Damaged, discouraged and defeated? How mindset may offer hope for healing. *Medical Education, 56*(5), 477–479. https://doi.org/10.1111/medu.14740

Yang, S., Shu, D., & Yin, H. (2022). "Teaching, my passion; publishing, my pain": Unpacking academics' professional identity tensions through the lens of emotional resilience. *Higher Education, 84*(2), 235–254. https://doi.org/10.1007/s10734-021-00765-w

Zhai, Y., & Du, X. (2020). Mental health care for international Chinese students affected by the COVID-19 outbreak. *The Lancet Psychiatry*, 7(4), e22. https://doi.org/10.1016/S2215-0366(20)30089-4

CHAPTER 12

PERCEPTIONS AND ATTITUDES OF NURSING STUDENTS' TRANSITION TO REMOTE INSTRUCTION DURING COVID-19

Kailea Q. Manning, Chih-hsuan Wang, Ann Lambert, Meghan C. Jones, Tiffani Chidume, Jianwei Dong, Amy Curtis, and Lynn Greenleaf Brown
Auburn University

ABSTRACT

Higher education institutions suddenly transitioned from face-to-face to remote learning environments during the outbreak of the COVID-19 Pandemic. Nursing is a discipline that thrives on skills and direct personal communication. Undergraduate nursing students were not prepared for professional training via an online modality. Although they were considered a digital generation, taking nursing courses online was different from generic electronic device use. Shifting to a remote learning environment also meant the loss of face-to-face clinical training and opportunities to practice skills in a "hands-on" manner. Nursing students were left with concerns regarding their ability to perform skills adequately and to find a job after graduating. This chapter includes two studies that were designed to help us to better understand nursing students' experience with technology and their perceptions of readiness during remote learning. The first study uses the extended technology acceptance model (ETAM) to explore undergraduate nursing

Examining the Cognitive and Psychological Effects of the COVID-19 Global Pandemic on High School, College, and Graduate Learners, pp. 271–295

students' perceptions of the levels of technology competency, self-management, self-efficacy, usefulness of remote learning management system (LMS), ease of use of LMS, attitude toward LMS, intention and actual use of LMS, and their expected grades. Results indicated that as faculty adjusted their teaching methods to using remote technologies, undergraduate nursing students were challenged to increase their self-management behaviors. However, they may have also gained confidence in their technical competence by taking greater ownership and responsibility for their learning. The second study explores how students perceived their readiness in clinical training and if this changed after their first semester, before an instructional nursing skills camp, and after the camp ended. The results revealed that students' overall perceptions of readiness in performing the skills required for their first clinical service were significantly higher after completing the bootcamp. Taken together, educators and researchers can use the obtained information from each study to help ensure that nursing students are successful in their programs, whether they are in-person or remote.

Keywords: nursing education, remote learning, self-directed learning, technology acceptance model

The coronavirus disease (COVID-19) has caused havoc worldwide, hospitalizing tens of thousands of individuals (Centers for Disease Control [CDC], 2020) since December 2019. As COVID-19 continued to spread in spring 2020, many U.S. states implemented measures to slow the spread of the virus, from city-wide curfews and shut-downs to "Stay-At-Home" mandates. Higher education institutions were no different, as they were deeply impacted by the effects of COVID-19, resulting in widespread campus closures. Meanwhile, higher education institutions initiated contingency plans for a transition from face-to-face to remote instruction. Plans included how to communicate and provide lessons to students, conduct meetings, and proctor exams, all either remotely, or in a hybrid modality. With nursing students transitioning to a remote learning environment due to the pandemic, there was a major disruption to the health profession's education and clinical training (Murphy, 2020), as the health profession's education is predominantly a hands-on, interactive field. Nursing students are accustomed to attending classes on-campus, practicing in the skills and simulation labs, as well as learning together in the lecture halls. Faculty were used to utilizing experiential learning modules to promote student engagement in the classroom setting. Hence, understanding students' perception and impact on nursing education during this transition is important.

Self-Directed Learning in Remote Settings

For many professional schools, such as nursing, the unexpected changes due to the pandemic took a devastating toll. Nursing is a profession that thrives on skills and direct, personal communication. During the severe acute respiratory response syndrome (SARS) outbreak of 2003, nursing schools in Canada ceased classroom instruction and initiated virtual instruction. Reflecting back on this time, faculty remember the uncertainty and fear that arose as students were pulled from clinical placements, then from the classroom setting (University of Toronto, 2013). Faculty also stated that communication was essential in all aspects of the course: staying abreast of current information related to the virus, disseminating the information, and addressing student concerns regarding their education and transition to remote learning (University of Toronto, 2013).

Similar to Canadian students experiencing the SARS outbreak, U.S. nursing students were concerned about clinical experiences and faculty struggled to convert in-person classroom time to a remote instruction format, such as Zoom sessions during the coronavirus pandemic. There were added barriers for students and faculty members who considered themselves technologically challenged. In 2010, Gordon et al. determined key competencies needed to transition from face-to-face to remote learning, including the establishment of a Virtual Private Network, assessment and possible upgrade of bandwidth, configuration and use of audiovisual equipment, and familiarity of the learning management tools and functionality. Johns Hopkins University developed a useful guide regarding adjusting in-person courses for remote learning in response to the COVID-19 pandemic. The guidelines include setting realistic expectations, establishing frequent communication, maintaining focus on the learning objectives, and preparing content with the chosen method of technology in mind (Cruickshank, 2020).

Remote learning is not a new concept and is a great option for some curricula, but the nature of nursing school itself infers some level of socialization and hands-on learning. In Smith et al.'s (2009) study, instructors explained that the field of nursing is a "human care-giving activity" which requires nurses to have human relations skills. The nursing instructors suggested that teaching students how to be culturally sensitive is a critical component which is not easily achieved through remote learning. Additionally, remote learning is not set up to thoroughly support nursing education in teaching skills application and critical thinking because there is a lack of ability to provide feedback through "real-time" interactions between students and faculty (Smith et al., 2009). Further, nursing education offers students a clinical environment to develop and practice their nursing skills. Clinical education is a fundamental component for nursing which is not easily translated through remote learning. Nursing students have voiced that remote simulation and virtual environments do not provide the same level of learning and practice that face-to-face patient interaction does (Michel et al., 2021). Despite these challenges, according to Karaman's

(2011) survey of 1041 Registered Nurses in a distance bachelor's degree program, participants viewed remote learning opportunities as suitable for their work requirements and personal needs. This result indicated that regardless of the clinical concerns specific to the nursing education context, participants had positive attitudes towards remote courses and considered them as appropriate opportunities for continuous training.

Self-directed learning (SDL) refers to the student's ownership and taking responsibility for their own learning. Knowles (1975) defined SDL theory as a process where individuals take initiative to learn, with or without the help of others, such as faculty and other students. He proposed that, as learners mature, they become increasingly self-directed. SDL includes self-management, self-monitoring, and motivation (Yuan et al., 2012). More specifically, the process includes the student setting goals for learning, selecting individualized strategies, identifying appropriate learning resources, and evaluating learning outcomes. Readiness for SDL is individualized and varies along a continuum (Guglielmino, 1977) and is described by Wiley (1983) as the degree to which the student maintains the attitudes, abilities and personality characteristics that are required for SDL. Self-directed learning is not preferred for all students and may cause some anxiety and frustration with coursework. Due to the COVID-19 pandemic, nurse educators and students were acutely thrust into remote teaching and learning, which required some measure of self-directed learning.

SDL plays an important role in successful online education (Zhu, 2021). Online learning requires that students manage their time, learning, and study strategies on their own, resulting in a necessity for increased levels of SDL compared to traditional environments (Khalid et al., 2020). Studies indicated that self-management is especially important during remote learning (Um & Jang, 2021; Wang et al., 2013). Self-management was positively correlated with college students' engagement, course satisfaction and learning outcomes during the pandemic (Awabdeh & Albashtawi, 2023; Um & Jang, 2021). The elements of self-management have also been found to be positively related to student's participation in online learning (Kop & Fournier, 2011). Within undergraduate nursing students during the pandemic, self-directed learning was found to be positively related to satisfaction with online learning and academic achievement (Kim et al., 2020). When considering online learning, the relationship between SDL and technology also becomes relevant. Multiple studies indicate a positive relationship between SDL and the acceptance of technology. For example, Lai et al. (2020) found that students who worked in an environment where teachers encouraged and integrated the use of technology were more likely to engage in SDL. Similarly, a study conducted in a medical school revealed that medical students in a learning environment where SDL was encouraged were also more likely to utilize different forms of technology to engage in SDL (Zheng, 2022). Pan (2020) illustrates that students who were more likely to accept technology and perceive themselves as technology efficacious, or technically competent, displayed a more positive attitude towards SDL. Technical competencies, which refer to an individual's confidence in using computer technology in learning, should be considered as crucial aspects of student readiness for remote learning (Hung et al., 2010; Yu, 2018; Yu & Richardson, 2015). Students with higher technological competence are more likely to navigate online platforms, utilize various digital tools, and easily access resources, ultimately leading to engaging with course materials effectively and efficiently (Koyuncuoglu, 2022).

However, possessing these competencies alone does not guarantee academic success. Wei and Chou (2020) conducted a structural equation modeling study in Taiwan with a sample of 354 college students enrolled in asynchronous remote learning courses. The researchers found a direct relationship between computer/internet self-efficacy and course satisfaction, and a partial effect on academic performance (Hung et al., 2010). Specifically, the results showed that while computer/internet self-efficacy positively predicted remote discussion scores, it did not have any significant impact on exam group project scores. Although factors such as computer proficiency, internet connectivity, and the ability to navigate learning management systems (LMS) play a role in the remote learning experience, having technological skills alone will not ensure better learning outcomes.

Despite the inconclusive impact on learning outcomes, technologically competent students demonstrate higher confidence, ability, and satisfaction with using digital communication tools for more effective collaboration with their peers and instructors (Wei & Chou, 2020). Yu and Richardson (2015) also describe technology competencies as self-efficacy in remote learning environments. Furthermore, students with higher technological competence are likely to overcome technology challenges and adapt to various learning platforms. These attitudes, usage tendencies, and usage confidence are components of the technology acceptance model, which is discussed in the following section.

Extended Technology Acceptance Model (TAM)

The technology acceptance model (TAM) was developed by Davis et al. (1989). It adopted two theoretical frameworks, the theory of reasoned action (TRA) by Ajzen and Fishbein (1980) and the theory of planned behavior (TPB) by Ajzen (1991), to examine an individual's attitudes, subjective norms, and perceived behavioral control. According to Ajzen, attitude is an individual's positive or negative evaluation of performing a specific behavior. Attitudes significantly affect one's behaviors, as they are more likely to act on behaviors that align with positive attitudes and less likely to engage in behaviors that align with negative attitudes. Subject norm refers to the social pressure or expectations an individual perceives from their surrounding social environment regarding a specific behavior or action. Perceived behavioral control is the last component involved in the theory's development, which considers that individuals who feel little to no control over their behaviors, on some occasions, would not intend and actually put their behaviors into action. These factors are often used to predict an individual's behavioral intention and their actual behavior toward technology use (Ajzen, 1991; Davis et al., 1989; Fathema, 2013; Ajzen & Fishbein, 1980; Barki & Hartwick, 1994).

TAM has been widely used in various fields, especially in the healthcare field (Kalayou et al., 2020; Karaman, 2011; Kuo et al., 2013; Rho et al., 2015) to assess technology acceptance and has been shown to be effective in predicting behavior intentions and technology adoption. The acceptance of using technology among nursing school students can be contextualized in terms of their perceptions of its usefulness and ease of use, affecting their attitudes towards, intentions to use, and actual use of technology. The TAM model may provide insight into the students' transition to remote learning (Karaman, 2011; Tung & Chang, 2008; Williamson & Muckle, 2018). Nursing schools are under pressure to adopt technology and integrate it into their teaching environments to facilitate active and meaningful learning experiences. Williamson and Muckle (2018) argue that it is fundamental to recognize that technology integration does not guarantee successful learning outcomes; readiness is the key factor. Higher acceptance of technology indicates higher readiness and is more likely to result in positive learning outcomes. Tung and Chang (2008) proposed that understanding users' perspectives and barriers is crucial in promoting e-learning tools among nursing students. They used structural equation modeling and examined the factors that influence nursing students' intention to select remote courses in Taiwan. The study found that computer self-efficacy, system compatibility, perceived usefulness, and perceived information quality were significant positive predictors of behavioral intention. On the other hand, computer anxiety and perceived financial cost had a negative impact. The findings highlight that nursing schools need to provide appropriate training and support to enhance students' computer self-efficacy and system compatibility while also addressing anxiety and financial cost concerns to facilitate the adoption of e-learning among nursing students.

The success of remote learning in nursing schools is highly dependent on the acceptance of technology by nursing students. TAM provides a framework for understanding the factors that influence the adoption and use of technology in distance learning. By examining the changes in perceptions, attitudes, and intentions towards distance learning over time,

TAM can inform strategies to promote technology acceptance and improve the effectiveness of remote learning.

The TAM framework can be used to help determine the students' intent to use and actual use of technology during remote learning. The TAM model considers the following factors: student's perception of ease of use, perceived usefulness, and the student's attitude toward using the technology (Fathema, 2013). In other words, a person's intent to use and actual use can be predicted by the person's perception of use and ease of use. The TAM model may provide insight to the students' transition to remote learning.

Nursing Students' Perceived Readiness

Nursing education relies heavily on face-to-face interactions to teach students critical skills related to nursing and for clinical placements which provide necessary clinical experience. With the abrupt transition to remote education, students lost these traditional learning experiences. Therefore, it is imperative that educators understand how this change influenced students' perceptions of readiness in clinical training. Clinical training is a foundational component for nursing curricula because it allows students to implement their theoretical knowledge and gain practical application skills (Dunn & Hansford, 1997). Clinical training and placements are vital for helping nursing students become confident and comfortable performing skills they will use every day in the nursing profession. Further, clinical training allows nursing students to practice in a safe environment that is more similar to "real world" situations than what they learn in the classroom setting.

Clinical training is a necessary and important part of nursing education; however, it is also identified as one of the most stressful times by nursing students (Moscaritolo, 2009). Even before the pandemic, nursing students have been found to experience more stress and anxiety than students within other disciplines (Fitzgerald & Konrad, 2021; De Los Santos, et al., 2021). The basic stress and anxiety provoked by clinical training in nursing education compounded with the effect of the pandemic halting face-to-face meetings has resulted in a higher intention of quitting nursing school because students fear they will not be prepared for their future field and careers (Fitzgerald & Konrad, 2021). Michel et al. (2021) conducted a qualitative study of undergraduate nursing students' perceptions of nursing education during the pandemic. Their results found that students felt moving to virtual education and losing in-person clinical training put them at a deficit for finding a job in the future and one student stated that, "learning ... in a completely virtual setting has made me feel incredibly underprepared when it comes to many basic nursing skills" (p. 907). Student's comfort and confidence levels in their ability to perform the skills pertinent to their work illustrates the importance of understanding how the pandemic influenced their perception of readiness.

Ultimately, nursing education is rarely conducted in a fully remote learning environment, as it is traditionally intended to be a hands-on method of training. In this remote learning modality, nursing students are not able to receive the hands-on clinical instruction that they expect, which may impact their perceived readiness. This chapter will examine two studies to better understand nursing students' perceptions of remote learning due to the pandemic and how this environment impacted their perceptions of clinical readiness. The first study was conducted to examine the relationship between students' perceptions and attitudes in taking remote courses and their expected grades, whereas the second study was to examine students' perceived readiness of clinical training during the COVID-19 pandemic.

STUDY 1 METHOD

This study focused on the perceptions and attitudes of students enrolled in hands-on nursing courses at the end of the semester while the course transitioned from face-to-face to remote only instruction due to the COVID-19 Pandemic. The Institutional Review Board approved the study. Participants were students enrolled in three nursing courses during spring 2020 in a southeastern university. Students attended course sessions in the traditional face-to-face format until the courses were transitioned to remote delivery immediately after spring break, as the pandemic dictated these process changes. Data were collected as an anonymous survey hosted by Qualtrics.

Participants

A total of 137 students from three nursing courses participated in this study. Two responses were removed due to large missing data points. A total of 135 valid surveys were retained for data analysis with a usable response rate of 98.54%. The participants' ages ranged from 20 to 33 years old, with a mean age of 21.50 years (SD = 1.35). One hundred and twenty-four students (1.2%) were female, and 131 (96.3%) were White. The majority of participants were seniors (n = 91, 66.9%) while the rest were juniors. Thirty-seven students (27.2%) were taking "*Acute Care across the Lifespan*," 66 of them (48.5%) were taking "*Professional Nursing Leadership in Microsystems*," and 32 of them (23.5%) were taking "*Chronic Conditions across the Lifespan*." Eighty students (58.5%) indicated that their expected grade would be an A, 37 of them (27.2%) estimated a B, while others (n = 18, 13.2%) expected a C (M = 3.46, SD = 0.72). Their average reported GPA was 3.55 (SD = 0.25).

Instruments

Participants in this study answered questions from four components: Self-Management Scale, Technology Competencies Scale, extended TAM measures, and basic demographic questions.

Self-Management Scale. Fisher et al. (2001) developed the Self-Directed Learning Readiness Scale to investigate students' readiness to take remote nursing courses. The current study adopted this Self-Management subscale with a total of 13 items. Items were rated on a 5-point Likert-type scale ranging from "*Strongly Disagree*" (1) to "*Strongly Agree*" (5). Students who received higher scores on this scale had a higher level of self-management in their learning. The internal consistency Cronbach's Alpha in the original study was .86, while in the current study were .89 and .90, indicating the scores were reliable.

Technology Competencies Scale. The scale was adopted from the Technical Competencies subscale in Student Online Learning Readiness Instrument (SOLR) by Yu and Richardson (2015) and Yu (2018). Items were measured on a 5-point Likert-type scale ranging from "*Strongly Disagree*" (1) to "*Strongly Agree*" (5) with a total of 6 items. Students receiving higher scores on this scale had a higher level of confidence using computer technologies in their learning. The internal consistency reliability Cronbach's Alpha in the original study was .88, and it was .87 and .88 in the current study, indicating the scores were reliable.

Extended TAM Measures. Items in the extended TAM scale were adapted from Fathema (2013). She conducted a study to investigate college students' perceptions and attitudes toward taking remote courses using a learning management system. The scale includes seven variables, System Quality, Facilitating Conditions, Perceived Self-Efficacy, Perceived Ease of Use, Perceived Usefulness, Attitudes toward Use, and Behavioral Intention to Use, with a total of 25 items. Items were rated on a five-point Likert-type scale ranging from "*Strongly Disagree*" (1) to "*Strongly Agree*" (5). Students receiving higher scores on this scale had more positive perceptions and attitudes towards using a learning management system to take a traditional hands-on nursing course remote. The internal consistency reliability of Cronbach's Alpha in Fathema's (2013) study ranged from .87 ~.96. In the current study, the Cronbach's Alpha ranged from .80 ~.94.

Demographic Questions. Seven demographic questions were included in the survey, including age, educational classification, gender, ethnicity, the hands-on nursing course they were taking, expected grade, overall GPA, and two questions asking how often they used Canvas to take the course at the beginning and at the end of the remote course.

Procedure

The nursing course instructors sent out the email survey invitation with an anonymous online survey link provided by researchers to their students. Students received the invitation email from their instructor the week before the end of the semester and completed the survey by clicking the anonymous survey link. Two reminders were sent to the students a week and two weeks after the initial survey invitation. Students responded regarding their perceptions and attitudes when they initially, and unexpectedly, transitioned to remote instruction and at the end of the semester.

Data Analysis

A path analysis using the structural equation modeling (SEM) technique with covariance-based and maximum likelihood estimation was utilized in examining and evaluating the relationship between students' perceptions and attitudes in taking the courses and their expected grades during the COVID-19 pandemic. The responses were evaluated using a hypothesized model developed from the literature review (Figure 12.1). The fit of the model was assessed using model fit indices, including Goodness-of-Fit Test (Chi-square statistic), Goodness-of-Fit Index (GFI), Comparative Fit Index (CFI), Tucker Lewis Index (TLI), Normed Fit Index (NFI), and Root Mean Square of Error Estimation (RMSEA). The general cut-off value for the indices were larger than .95 for CFI and TLI, and less than .08 for RMSEA (Hair et al., 2006). When the evaluation of the hypothesized model indicates a poor fit, two strategies: (1) removing non-significant paths using the trimming process; and/or (2) adding relationships between variables based on the modification indices can be used to improve the model (Hox & Bechger, 1998; Kline, 2010; Ullman & Bentler, 2013). After adding or removing one path at a time, the model needs to be re-evaluated until it reaches an adequate fit (Hox & Bechger, 1998).

RESULTS FOR STUDY 1

Data was downloaded from Qualtrics and missing values were replaced by the regression method. After data screening, it was analyzed using the SPSS and AMOS. Table 12.1 presents the descriptive statistics and correlation results. The full theoretical model, including all potential paths among variables, was first evaluated. After eliminating non-significant paths and adding relationships between variables according to modification indices, a final model was obtained.

Table 12.1

Descriptive Statistics and Correlations for Study Variables (n = 135)

	M	*SD*	1	2	3	4	5	6	7	8	9	10	11
1. Self-Management	3.48	0.51	---										
2. Tech Competency	3.67	0.78	.35***	---									
3. System Quality	3.73	0.76	.41**	.50***	---								
4. Facilitating	3.46	0.85	.31***	.35***	.49***	---							
5. Self-Efficacy	3.86	0.98	.52***	.44***	.61***	.29***	---						
6. Ease to Use	3.98	0.76	.39***	.43***	.73***	.42***	.66***	---					
7. Usefulness	3.53	0.99	.28***	.38***	.61***	.49***	.62***	.51***	---				
8. Attitude	3.62	1.01	.43***	.41***	.70***	.30***	.74***	.63***	.77***	---			
9. Intend to Use	3.91	0.82	.38***	.52***	.70***	.49***	.57***	.65***	.57***	.65***	---		
10. Actual Use	7.63	0.95	.36***	.10*	.25***	.11**	.20***	.27***	.10**	.27***	.24***	---	
11. Expected Grade	3.46	0.72	.11**	-.12**	.08*	-.05	.25***	.13**	.17***	.21***	.05	.08*	---

$* p < .05$; $** p < .01$; $*** p < .001$

Overall, model fit was excellent, indicating a strong fit of the model. The Chi-square test was statistically significant, $c^2(17) = 53.09, p < .001, c^2/df = 3.12$, while other fit indices indicated a good fit, GFI =.99, CFI =.99, TFI = .97, NFI = .99, RMSEA = .056, and all of the path coefficients were statistically significant ($p < .05$). Several of the paths demonstrated practical significance ($\beta > 0.3$) (Table 12.2).

Table 12.2

Regression Weight Estimates

			Std. est.	Unstd. Est.	*S.E.*	*p*
Self-Efficacy	←	Tech Competent	.142	.179	.036	<.001
Self-Efficacy	←	System Quality	.538	.690	.043	<.001
Ease of Use	←	Facilitating	.329	.293	.027	<.001
Ease of Use	←	Self-Efficacy	.342	.265	.023	<.001
Usefulness	←	System Quality	.320	.412	.051	<.001
Usefulness	←	Facilitating	.219	.253	.030	<.001
Usefulness	←	Ease of Use	–.108	–.140	.047	.003
Usefulness	←	Self-Efficacy	.440	.442	.036	<.001
Attitude to Use	←	System Quality	.620	.822	.039	<.001
Attitude to Use	←	Self-Manage	.183	.363	.058	<.001
Intention Use	←	System Quality	.430	.462	.040	<.001
Intention Use	ß	Facilitating	.166	.159	.028	<.001
Intention Use	←	Attitude to Use	.276	.224	.028	<.001
Actual Use	←	System Quality	.110	.246	.100	.014
Actual Use	←	Intention Use	.117	.146	.049	.003
Actual Use	←	Self-Manage	.317	.596	.073	<.001
Expected Grade	←	System Quality	.320	.178	.045	<.001
Expected Grade	←	Facilitating	–.105	–.089	.035	.012
Expected Grade	←	Self-Manage	.151	.215	.059	<.001
Expected Grade	←	Tech Competent	–.244	–.227	.039	<.001

According to the final model, the results are as follows (Figure 12.1).

1. *Factors related to Expected Final Grade*. The actual use had no influence on students' expected grade. Only students' confidence in time management, setting learning goals, and organizing and prioritizing their learning and work (Self-Management) and their satisfaction toward taking nursing hands-on courses through Canvas (System Quality) had positive impacts on their expected final grade. Their confidence in using computer technology to take the remote course (Technology Competencies) and their perceptions of support they received in using Canvas to take the course (Facilitating Condition), negatively influenced their expected final grade.
2. *Factors related to Actual Use, Intention to Use, and Attitude toward Use*. Students' satisfaction toward taking hands-on nursing courses through Canvas (System Quality), their confidence in time management, setting learning goals, and organizing and prioritizing their learning and work (Self-Management), and their intention to use Canvas to take the course (Intention Use) had a positive impact on their actual use of Canvas. In addition, students' satisfaction toward taking courses through Canvas (System Quality), perceived support for using Canvas to take courses (Facilitating Condition), and their attitude toward taking courses through Canvas (Attitude) had a positive impact on their intention to take courses in Canvas. Further, students' satisfaction toward taking courses through Canvas (System Quality) and their confidence in time management, setting learning goals, and organizing and prioritizing their learning and work (Self-Management) had positive impacts on their attitude toward using Canvas.
3. *Factors related to Perceived Usefulness and Ease of Use*. Students' satisfaction toward taking courses through Canvas (System Quality), perceived support for using Canvas to take courses (Facilitating Condition), perception of how easy it is to use Canvas to take remote courses (Ease of Use), and their self-efficacy in using Canvas to take a hands-on nursing course (Self-Efficacy) impacted their perceptions of the usefulness of Canvas to take a remote, hands-on nursing course, whereas their perceived support for using Canvas to take courses (Facilitating Condition) and confidence in taking remote nursing courses (Self-Efficacy) also had impacts on their perception of ease of use.
4. *Factors related to Self-Efficacy*. Students' satisfaction toward taking courses through Canvas (System Quality) and their technology competency (Tech Competent) influenced their perceived self-efficacy in taking remote hands-on nursing courses in the final models.

The results from the final model indicated that nursing students' confidence and ability in time management, setting learning goals, and organizing and prioritizing their learning and work (Self-Management) and confidence in using computer technology to take a remote course (Technology Competencies) played important roles in their expected final grade. Those two factors directly and indirectly via some factors in the extended TAM model influenced nursing students' expected final grade. In addition, their Self-Management beliefs and intention to use Canvas to take the course impacted their actual behavior in logging into Canvas to take the course.

Figure 12.1

Final Model

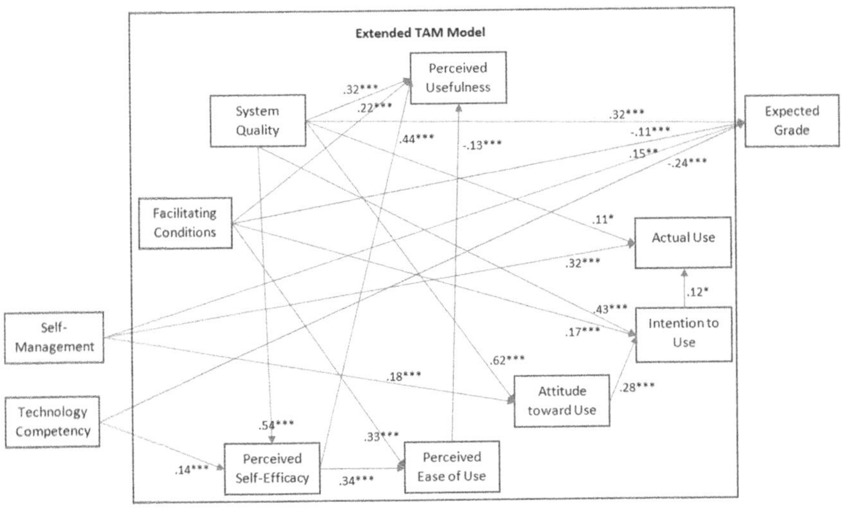

$\chi2(16) = 53.09$, $p = .005$, $\chi2/df = 2.16$; GFI = .99, CFI = .99, TLI = .98, NFI = .99, RMSEA = .041

* $p \leq .05$; ** $p < .01$; *** $p < .001$

STUDY #2 METHOD

This study aims to understand how students perceived their readiness in clinical training and if this changed after their first semester, before an instructional nursing skills camp, and after the camp ended. The Institutional Review Board at the institution approved the study. This study takes place at a southeastern university in 2020 during the COVID-19 pandemic, with all first-year undergraduate nursing students. Data were collected utilizing the online survey platform, Qualtrics.

Participants

A total of 16 undergraduate nursing students completed the study. The selection criteria for this study consisted of participants who were 18 years of age or older and those who were undergraduate nursing students. The anonymous survey link was sent out to the students participating in a face-to-face boot camp after the university locked down and before they went to the clinics for practicum.

The sample consisted solely of females who largely identified as White (n = 15, 93.75%), with one participant (6.25%) identifying as Asian. The sample had an average age of 20.38 years (SD = 1.46). All 16 participants reported starting their nursing program in the summer of 2020. Overall, the sample had relatively high levels of experience with shadowing where 14 participants (87.50%) indicated they had shadowed before entering their program. Of the 14 students, five had volunteered and nine had observed in a hospital or clinic setting. Only two participants (12.50%) in the sample reported they had no experience with shadowing prior to beginning their nursing program. When asked about their in-patient experience, six participants (37.50%) reported they did have experience, while nine (56.25%) reported they did not, and one could not remember. Finally, only six (37.50%) participants in the sample reported having a family member who is a medical professional.

Intervention: Skills Bootcamp

Students admitted during the summer and fall semesters of 2020 that they did not have any direct hands-on skills in the lab or direct patient care in the hospital or long-term care facilities. These students received didactic and laboratory content online via Zoom and Panopto recordings. Faculty understood how important hands on, kinesthetic, skills are in nursing curricula, thus a skills bootcamp was developed.

Faculty felt that it was important for students to receive in person lab sessions to review skills and practice safety procedures prior to being assigned an inpatient clinical rotation. Eight hours of lab were assigned, per student, spanning over two instructional days. They were assigned times to report to the skills lab. Prior to reporting to the skills lab, students were assigned clinical skills videos (Panopto recordings of faculty demonstrating specific skills) to view. Once in the lab, students were divided into small groups (groups of 6–8) with one instructor facilitating clinical skills. These skills included: medication administration (oral, intramuscular, subcutaneous, and intradermal), vital signs, and head to toe physical examination. Students practiced medication administration on low fidelity manikins and task trainers. They practiced site identification, vital signs, and head to toe assessment skills on each other during the assigned lab time. Small group instructors provided feedback and allowed for students to correct mistakes and validate skills in real-time.

Instruments

Clinical Learning Environment Comparison Survey 2.0 (CLECS 2.0). To capture the undergraduate nursing students' perception of readiness in clinical training the CLECS 2.0 (Leighton, 2015) survey was adopted. The CLECS 2.0 measure was developed to assess how well students believe their learning needs are being met in three different areas: the traditional clinical environment, in a face-to-face simulation environment, and in a computer-based simulation environment. Studies have provided evidence that the CLECS is reliable and valid (Leighton, 2015; Leighton et al., 2021). Due to the context of the present study, the measure was modified to assess the student's perceptions of readiness for each learning need before the beginning of summer (i.e., before they began the nursing program), before a skills camp was held, and after attending the skills camp.

The prompt for the survey was adapted to read, "Please rate each statement based on the levels of your perceptions of readiness in performing each activity." The original measure includes a 4-point response scale ranging from "*Not Met*" (1) to "*Well Met*" (4). However, for the purpose of this study, the response scale was revised to range from "*Not Ready at All*" (1) to "*Very Ready*" (4). Finally, three items were modified in order to fit the students' activities and seven items were removed because they could not be applied to the activities the students performed during the practicum, for example, changing, "Identifying short- and long-term goals for the patient," to read "Identifying short- and long-term nursing goals." The final scale consisted of 22 items.

Demographic Questions. Eight demographic questions were included in the survey such as age, sex, and ethnicity. Additionally, students were asked if they had shadowed before entering their nursing program, if they had any in-patient experience, and if they had family members who are medical professionals. A final question inquired if medical TV shows or movies influenced their readiness to provide care.

Procedure

The Skills Bootcamp was implemented in the fall of 2020 and spring of 2021 during students' second semester in the nursing curriculum. Students were provided the anonymous survey link at the end of the face-to-face bootcamp they attended. They were asked to rate their perceptions of readiness at the beginning of the summer, before the 2-day intensive face-to-face skills bootcamp, and at the end of the bootcamp.

RESULTS FOR STUDY 2

The current study explored nursing students' perception of readiness in their clinical ability to perform the skills pertinent to their work. Data were analyzed using related-samples Friedman's analysis of variance by ranks with the Statistical Package for the Social Sciences (SPSS) version 29. Results indicated that students' overall perceptions of readiness in performing the skills required for their first clinical service were significantly higher after completing the bootcamp, $p < .001$. Table 12.3 presents the results for all items.

Table 12.3

Related-Samples Friedman's Analysis of Variance by Ranks Results for Each Item (n = 16)

	Pre	Mid	Post	χ^2	Pairwise
	M (SD)	*M (SD)*	*M (SD)*	*df* = 2	Comparison
Preparing to care for patients.	1.31 (0.60)	2.06 (0.44)	2.69 (0.48)	24.53***	Pre<Mid<Post
Interacting with patients.	1.94 (0.77)	2.31 (0.70)	2.88 (0.62)	18.87***	Pre=Mid<Post
Providing information and support to patient's family.	1.38 (0.62)	2.00 (0.52)	2.31 (0.48)	19.63***	Pre<Mid=Post
Understanding patient's pathophysiology.	1.50 (0.52)	3.06 (0.68)	3.19 (0.54)	27.71***	Pre<Mid=Post
Identifying patient's problems.	1.25 (0.45)	2.44 (0.63)	2.75 (0.58)	26.92***	Pre<Mid=Post
Developing plans of care for patients.	1.13 (0.34)	2.44 (0.73)	2.69 (0.70)	26.26***	Pre<Mid=Post
Performing appropriate patient assessment.	1.13 (0.35)	2.73 (0.46)	3.33 (0.49)	28.00***	Pre<Mid=Post
Identifying short- and long-term nursing goals.	1.25 (0.58)	2.50 (0.63)	2.81 (0.54)	28.00***	Pre<Mid=Post
Discussing patient's developmental needs.	1.44 (0.63)	2.75 (0.58)	2.88 (0.50)	26.91***	Pre<Mid=Post
Discussing patient's psychosocial needs.	1.31 (0.60)	2.38 (0.62)	2.69 (0.60)	24.18***	Pre<Mid=Post

(Table continued on next page)

Table 12.3 (Continued)

Related-Samples Friedman's Analysis of Variance by Ranks Results for Each Item (n = 16)

	Pre	Mid	Post	χ^2	Pairwise
	M (SD)	*M (SD)*	*M (SD)*	*df* = 2	Comparison
Discussing patient's spiritual needs.	1.69 (0.79)	2.94 (0.68)	3.06 (0.68)	26.91***	Pre<Mid=Post
Discussing patient's cultural needs.	1.69 (0.60)	2.81 (0.54)	2.81 (0.54)	28.00***	Pre<Mid=Post
Able to perform verbal or written documentation of patient care provided.	1.56 (1.03)	2.44 (0.96)	2.81 (0.91)	23.23***	Pre<Mid=Post
Reacting calmly to changes in my patient's condition.	1.75 (0.78)	2.44 (0.73)	2.50 (0.73)	17.43***	Pre<Mid=Post
Knowing what to do if I make an error in my care.	1.31 (0.60)	2.69 (0.87)	2.94 (0.77)	23.46***	Pre<Mid=Post
Being confident in my decisions.	1.38 (0.62)	2.25 (0.68)	2.69 (0.60)	19.84***	Pre<Mid=Post
Having an instructor available to me.	1.69 (0.79)	2.75 (0.86)	3.00 (0.82)	21.39***	Pre<Mid=Post
Feeling challenged and stimulated.	2.50 (1.16)	3.13 (0.72)	3.31 (0.70)	12.09**	Pre<Post Pre=Mid Mid=Post
Receiving immediate feedback on performance.	2.50 (1.03)	3.00 (0.63)	3.25 (0.58)	14.00***	Pre<Post Pre=Mid Mid=Post
Feeling confident in my abilities.	1.31 (0.70)	2.38 (0.62)	3.00 (0.73)	26.46***	Pre<Mid=Post
Feeling supported by instructor and peers when making care related decisions.	2.00 (1.07)	2.80 (0.94)	3.13 (0.92)	13.35**	Pre<Post Pre=Mid Mid=Post
Improving my critical thinking skills with experience.	2.07 (1.16)	2.93 (0.80)	3.33 (0.72)	19.63***	Pre<Mid=Post

DISCUSSION

Taken together, both studies offered important information regarding students' attitudes and perceptions towards remote nursing education and clinical readiness due to this learning modality.

With regards to the first study, there are multiple possibilities that may have contributed to the relationship between students' perceptions and attitudes toward remote nursing courses. First, students' confidence in time management, setting learning goals, and organizing and prioritizing their learning and work while taking remote nursing courses may be representative of a false perception of their own abilities. Students may not recognize the inherent barriers to transitioning to remote learning, such as setting aside time for their remote coursework without distractions. As mentioned previously, SDL is imperative for online learning, especially compared to that of traditional face-to-face classes (Um & Jang, 2021; Wang et al., 2013). Based on an SDL framework, these results may suggest that the nursing students had higher perceived levels of SDL prior to the pandemic from their brief encounters with taking a few online courses or planning their study schedules. However, after transitioning to a fully remote setting in which the students must control the majority of their own environment, their abilities related to SDL (e.g., self-management, self-monitoring and motivation) may have been lower than they expected. For example, if they are working from a home that is shared with roommates or family, they must account for potential distractions and create a plan to protect their time for learning.

Additionally, it is critical to remember that this transition to remote learning occurred during a global pandemic. There are family and societal factors at play that may further complicate students' dedicated time for learning. Individual students reported personal challenges to faculty, such as the loss of a loved one, due to COVID-19, where traveling to the funeral complicated their ability to login to the remote course as required. As nursing students were not attending any activities on campus, they were not required to report a diagnosis of COVID-19. It is possible that students themselves, or family members, were personally affected by COVID-19. Dealing with the illness themselves or supporting a sick family member may have further impeded their ability to manage their time and prioritize their learning needs.

At the beginning of the course, students considered using the learning management system provided by the university to be worthwhile. Students had positive attitudes in using it, and were satisfied with the functions, content, and interaction within the remote learning environment. Each of these factors were rated lower by the end of the course. The decline in positive attitudes could be related to many of the challenges described earlier in the discussion. At the beginning of the course, students did not know what to expect and may have had a more optimistic outlook towards remote learning, whereas after completing the course over several weeks, their optimism could have been overcome by a more realistic view of the challenges posed by remote learning. When considering the TAM model, components such as perceived usefulness and positive attitudes towards technology would likely result in more positive outcomes. However, it may be more important to consider the readiness of the students as a key factor when interpreting these results (Williamson & Muckle, 2018). Students may have been open to technology and initially perceived their LMS as useful because of their experiences up to the start of the pandemic, however; after transitioning to complete online education, their level of readiness may not have been high enough for feelings of success. Actual use is the only factor that was significantly higher at the end of the semester. This finding is not surprising and can be explained by the increase in activity required to submit final work, such as final papers, projects, and reflective logs. This final flurry of activity and influx of assignments may be reflective of poor self-management skills, which students rated lower at the end of the semester.

When examining students' perceptions of readiness for clinical skills in the second study, results revealed they were higher after completing the intensive bootcamp. This trend may illustrate the difficulties which nursing students faced with the switch to remote clinical training. Multiple studies conducted during the COVID-19 pandemic found that nursing students often reported struggling with remote learning formats, found remote learning to be more demanding and stressful, and felt remote learning was inadequate at teaching student's clinical skills (Michel et al., 2021; Oducado & Estoque, 2021). With the importance placed on hands-on clinical training, the thought of learning these skills via online education may have been stress inducing and anxiety provoking for nursing students. Based on the TAM model, these students likely did not perceive the remote technology to be useful or easy to use in clinical training situations. Further, these students may have faced low computer self-efficacy and higher computer anxiety. With all of these factors at play, the problem of a perceived lack of ability and therefore, a lack of readiness can occur. It should be noted that at a foundational level, regardless of perceptions or acceptance of technology, nursing education is typically a hands-on curriculum which the pandemic heavily disrupted. In a previous study, one nursing student explained that a lack of in-person patient experiences have made it difficult to practice valuable nursing skills because they have had to practice on pillows or stuffed animals and another student stated that remote clinical training gave students the training hours required, but that they were "no real substitute" for in-person learning experiences (Michel et al., 2021, p. 907).

Conclusion

Nursing students' education abruptly transitioned from face-to-face to remote instruction as the COVID-19 pandemic directly affected their academic lives. The alternate model of remote delivery for instruction was essential to protect the health and safety of students while ensuring uninterrupted academic progress. As faculty adjusted their teaching methods utilizing remote technologies, students were challenged to increase their self-management behaviors and may have increased their confidence in technical competence with more ownership and responsibility for their own learning. Furthermore, the transition to remote learning suspended face-to-face clinical experiences for these nursing students, which have been evidenced as a critical component for nursing education. Students reported a decrease in perceived readiness for clinical work until they received in-person training during the intensive bootcamp. These studies illustrate the difficulties nursing students faced with the transition to remote learning and the lack of clinical experience which negatively influenced their readiness to perform important skills in their field.

Implications

Educators and researchers can use the obtained information from each study to help ensure that nursing students are successful in their programs, whether they are in-person or remote. Data collected based on the TAM measures regarding students' behaviors and actual use of their learning management system can assist in future curriculum development to improve the students' experience. Further, integrating information learned about students' perceptions of readiness for clinical training may also be beneficial to develop an effective program and curriculum. It may also be important for educators to consider implementing some kind of camp or exercise utilizing a face-to-face skills lab whenever nursing education is held remotely. Additionally, educators must address the students' technology concerns in order to prepare for a similar pivot to online education, if necessary, in the future.

SUMMARY

The COVID-19 pandemic forced a rapid shift to remote learning in nursing education, presenting numerous challenges and opportunities for students and educators. Understanding the perceptions and attitudes of nursing students during this transition could help educators to address the difficulties and leverage the opportunities to enhance learning experiences. The absence of in-person clinical training and skills labs may hinder students' development of essential practical skills required in the nursing profession. However, remote learning can offer nursing students greater flexibility in accessing learning materials and potentially reaching nursing students who have full-time jobs. The transition encourages educators to explore new teaching approaches, interactive remote modules, and collaborative tools to expose nursing students to a broader range of resources, enriching their knowledge and understanding.

REFERENCES

Ajzen, I. (1991). The theory of planned behavior. *Organizational behavior and human decision processes, 50*(2), 179–211. https://doi.org/10.1016/0749-5978(91)90020-T

Ajzen, I., & Fishbein, M., (1980). *Understanding attitudes and predicting social behavior*. Prentice-Hall.

Awabdeh, A. A., & Albashtawi, A. H. (2023). Predictable factors that help students engagement in online EFL classroom and their relationship to self-management. *International Journal of Emerging Technologies in Learning, 18*(1), 4–18. https://doi.org/10.3991/ijet.v18i01.35257

Barki, H., & Hartwick, J. (1994). Measuring user participation, user involvement, and user attitude. *MIS quarterly, 18*(1), 59–82. https://doi.org/10.2307/249610

Centers for Disease Control. (2020). Coronavirus Disease 2019. Cases in the U.S. https://www.cdc.gov/coronavirus/2019-ncov/cases-updates/cases-in-us.html

Cruickshank, S. (2020). *How to adapt courses for online learning: A practical guide for faculty*. Johns Hopkins University HUB. https://hub.jhu.edu/2020/03/12/how-to-teach-online-courses-coronavirus-response/

Davis, F. D., Bagozzi, R. P., & Warshaw, P. R. (1989). User acceptance of computer technology: A comparison of two theoretical models. *Management science, 35*(8), 982–1003. https://doi.org/10.1287/mnsc.35.8.982

De Los Santos, J. A. A., Labrague, L. J., & Falguera, C. C. (2021). Fear of COVID-19, poor quality of sleep, irritability, and intention to quit school among nursing students: A cross-sectional study. *Perspectives in Psychiatric Care, 58*(1), 71–78. https://doi.org/10.1111/ppc.12781

Dunn, S. V., & Hansford, B. (1997). Undergraduate nursing students' perceptions of their clinical learning environment. *Journal of advanced nursing, 25*(6), 1299–1306. https://doi.org/10.1046/j.1365-2648.1997.19970251299.x

Fathema, N. (2013). *Structural equation modeling (SEM) of an extended technology acceptance model (TAM) to report web technology adoption behavior in higher education institutions* [Doctoral dissertation, Auburn University]. AUETD. https://etd.auburn.edu/bitstream/handle/10415/3889/Doctoral%20Dissertation_Nafsaniath%20Fathema_11_08_2013.pdf?sequence=2&isAllowed=y

Fitzgerald, A., & Konrad, S. (2021, April). Transition in learning during COVID-19: Student nurse anxiety, stress, and resource support. *Nursing Forum, 56*(2), 298–304. https://doi.org/10.1111/nuf.12547

Fisher, M., King, J., & Tague, G. (2001). Development of a self-directed learning readiness scale for nursing education. *Nurse Education Today, 21,* 516–525. https://doi.org/10.1054/nedt.2001.0589

Gordon, J., Weiner, E., McNew, R., & Trangenstein, P. (2010). Teaching during a Pandemic event: Are universities prepared? *MEDINFO 2010, 160,* 620–624. https://doi.org/10.3233/978-1-60750-588-4-620

Guglielmino, L. M. (1977). *Development of the self-directed learning readiness scale*. University of Georgia.

Hox, J. J., & Bechger, T. M. (1998). An introduction to structural equation modeling. *Family Science Review, 11*, 354–373.

Hung, M. L., Chou, C., Chen, C. H., & Own, Z. Y. (2010). Learner readiness for online learning: Scale development and student perceptions. *Computers & Education, 55*(3), 1080–1090. https://doi.org/10.1016/j.compedu.2010.05.004

Kalayou, M. H., Endehabtu, B. F., & Tilahun, B. (2020). The applicability of the modified technology acceptance model (TAM) on the sustainable adoption of eHealth systems in resource-limited settings. *Journal of Multidisciplinary Healthcare, 13*, 1827–1837. https://doi.org/10.2147/JMDH.S284973

Karaman, S. (2011). Nurses' perceptions of online continuing education. *BMC Medical Education, 11*, 1–6. https://doi.org/10.1186/1472-6920-11-86

Khalid, M., Bashir, S., & Amin, H. (2020). Relationship between self-directed learning (sdl) and academic achievement of university students: A case of online distance learning and traditional universities. *Bulletin of Education and Research*, *42*(2), 131–148.

Kim, S., Jeong, S. H., Kim, H. S., & Jeong, Y. J. (2022). Academic success of online learning in undergraduate nursing education programs in the COVID-19 pandemic era. *Journal of Professional Nursing*, *38*, 6–16. https://doi.org/10.1016/j.profnurs.2021.10.005

Kline, R. B. (2010). Promise and pitfalls of structural equation modeling in gifted research. In B. Thompson & R. F. Subotnik (Eds.), *Methodologies for conducting research on giftedness* (pp. 147–169). American Psychological Association. https://doi.org/10.1037/12079-007

Knowles, M. S. (1975). *Self-directed learning: A guide for learners and teachers.* Association Press

Kop, R., & Fournier, H. (2011). New dimensions to self-directed learning in an open networked learning environment. *International Journal of Self-Directed Learning*, *7*(2), 1–18.

Koyuncuoglu, D. (2022). Analysis of digital and technological competencies of university students. *International Journal of Education in Mathematics, Science, and Technology (IJEMST), 10*(4), 971–988. https://doi.org/10.46328/ijemst.2583

Kuo, K. M., Liu, C. F., & Ma, C. C. (2013). An investigation of the effect of nurses' technology readiness on the acceptance of mobile electronic medical record systems. *BMC medical informatics and decision making, 13*, 1–14. https://doi.org/10.2147/JMDH.S284973

Lai, Y., Saab, N., & Admiraal, W. (2022). Learning strategies in self-directed language learning using mobile technology in higher education: A systematic scoping review. *Education and Information Technologies, 27*(6), 7749–7780. https://doi.org/10.1007/s10639-022-10945-5

Leighton, K. (2015). Development of the clinical learning environment comparison survey. *Clinical Simulation in Nursing, 11*(1), 44–51. https://doi.org/10.1016/j.ecns.2014.11.002

Leighton, K., Kardong-Edgren, S., Schneidereith, T., Foisy-Doll, C., & Wuestney, K. A. (2021). Meeting undergraduate nursing students' clinical needs: a comparison of traditional clinical, face-to-face simulation, and screen-based simulation learning environments. *Nurse Educator, 46*(6), 349. https://doi/org/10.1097/NNE.0000000000001064

Moscaritolo, L. M. (2009). Interventional strategies to decrease nursing student anxiety in the clinical learning environment. *Journal of Nursing Education, 48*(1), 17–23. https://doi.org/10.3928/01484834-20090101-08

Michel, A., Ryan, N., Mattheus, D., Knopf, A., Abuelezam, N. N., Stamp, K., Branson, S., Hekel, B., & Fontenot, H. B. (2021). Undergraduate nursing students' perceptions on nursing education during the 2020 COVID-19 pandemic: A national sample. *Nursing Outlook, 69*(5), 903–912. https://doi.org/10.1016/j.outlook.2021.05.004

Murphy, B. (2020). COVID-19: How the virus is impacting medical schools. *Am Med Assoc.*

Oducado, R. M., & Estoque, H. (2021). Online learning in nursing education during the COVID-19 pandemic: Stress, satisfaction, and academic performance. *Journal of Nursing Practice, 4*(2), 143–153. https://doi.org/10.30994/jnp.v4i2.128

Pan, X. (2020). Technology acceptance, technological self-efficacy, and attitude toward technology-based self-directed learning: Learning motivation as a mediator. *Frontiers in Psychology, 11*, 564294. https://doi.org/10.3389/fpsyg.2020.564294

Rho, M. J., Kim, H. S., Chung, K., & Choi, I. Y. (2015). Factors influencing the acceptance of telemedicine for diabetes management. *Cluster Computing, 18*, 321–331. https://doi.org/10.1007/s10586-014-0356-1

Smith, G. G., Passmore, D., & Faught, T. (2009). The challenges of online nursing education. *The Internet and Higher Education, 12*(2), 98–103. https://doi.org/10.1016/j.iheduc.2009.06.007

Tung, F. C., & Chang, S. C. (2008). Nursing students' behavioral intention to use online courses: A questionnaire survey. *International Journal of Nursing Studies, 45*(9), 1299–1309. https://doi.org/10.1016/j.ijnurstu.2007.09.011

Ullman, J. B., & Bentler, P. M. (2013). Structural equation modeling. In J. A. Schinka, W. F. Velicer, & I. B. Weiner (Eds.), *Handbook of psychology: Research methods in psychology* (pp. 661–690). John Wiley & Sons.

University of Toronto. (2013). *Teaching in a time of crisis: SARS and the impact on U of T's faculty of nursing*. https://bloomberg.nursing.utoronto.ca/news/teaching-in-a-time-of-crisis-sars-and-the-impact-on-u-of-ts-faculty-of-nursing/

Wei, H-C., & Chou C. (2020) Online learning performance and satisfaction: Do perceptions and readiness matter?. *Distance Education, 41*(1), 48–69. https://doi.org/10.1080/01587919.2020.1724768

Williamson, K. M., & Muckle, J. (2018). Students' perception of technology use in nursing education. *CIN: Computers, Informatics, Nursing, 36*(2), 70–76. https://doi.org/10.1097/CIN.0000000000000396

Yu, T. (2018). Examining construct validity of the Student Online Learning Readiness (SOLR) instrument using confirmatory factor analysis. *Online Learning, 22*(4), 277–288. http://dx.doi.org/10.24059/olj.v22i4.1297

Yu, T., & Richardson, J. C. (2015). An exploratory factor analysis and reliability analysis of the Student Online Learning Readiness (SOLR) instrument. *Online Learning, 19*(5), 120–141. http://dx.doi.org/10.24059/olj.v19i5.593

Yuan, H. B., Williams, B. A., Fang, J. B., & Pang, D. (2012). Chinese baccalaureate nursing students' readiness for self-directed learning. *Nurse Education Today, 32*(4), 427–431. https://doi.org/10.1016/j.nedt.2011.03.005

Um, N. H., & Jang, A. (2021). Antecedents and consequences of college students' satisfaction with online learning. *Social Behavior and Personality: An International Journal, 49*(8), 1–11. https://doi.org/10.2224/sbp.10397

Wang, C.-H., Shannon, D. M., & Ross, M. B. (2013). Students' characteristics, self-regulated learning, technology self-efficacy, and course outcomes in web-based courses. *Distance Education, 34*, 302–323. https://doi.org/10.1080/01587919.2013.835779

Wiley, K. (1983). Effects of a self-directed learning project and preference for structure on self-directed learning readiness. *Nursing Research, 32*(3), 181–185.

Zheng, B. (2022). Medical students' technology use for self-directed learning: Contributing and constraining factors. *Medical Science Educator, 32*(1), 149–156 https://doi.org/10.1007/s40670-021-01497-3

Zhu, M. (2021). Enhancing MOOC learners' skills for self-directed learning. *Distance Education, 42*(3), 441–460. https://doi.org/10.1080/01587919.2021.1956302

CHAPTER 13

EXPLORING THE ONLINE ACADEMIC ACCULTURATION OF MULTILINGUAL LEARNERS DURING COVID

Gwendolyn M. Williams and Mary S. Diamond
Auburn University

ABSTRACT

This study examined how multilingual students exhibited the various stages of academic acculturation, as evidenced through their written assignments both at the beginning and the end of the semesters after they had become accustomed to online instruction. The research questions for this study were as follows: What were the essences of the challenges that the students encountered when they migrated to online English learning? What strategies did the students find to be most helpful in adjusting to learning English through an online platform? This research used thematic analysis to study the subjects' sensemaking of their experience of transitioning to an online learning model. The chapter will describe findings of various student experiences from their frustration with language issues, technology issues, interaction challenges, and instructional distractions before offering practical suggestions to address the concerns revealed in the study's data.

Keywords: online learning, multilingual students, English instruction

Examining the Cognitive and Psychological Effects of the COVID-19 Global Pandemic on High School, College, and Graduate Learners, pp. 297–317

INTRODUCTION

While online instruction in the field of language education has been a well-established and researched field for several decades (Lim & Aryadoust, 2022), the unexpected transition to online instruction showed that many international students struggled to adapt to the new learning context. Previous research has explored the linguistic and cultural challenges that multilingual learners (MLs) have encountered in online instruction (Bailey & Lee, 2020; Sailsman, 2020), the lack of student preparedness for online learning (Kaya, 2021), the requisite tech skills and online learning practices needed to be a successful online language learner (Bich & Lian, 2021; Harrison et al., 2018), and the learning effectiveness of online instruction for MLs (Emelyanova & Voronina, 2017). However, these research studies have not examined student perceptions during the unique context of the COVID migration to online learning when there was no time to have a structured transition for students to ease into online learning. Therefore, this study seeks to understand how students adapted to their new learning environment. Such data will provide insight into experiences of MLs during the pandemic to inform teacher development about online pedagogy.

Statement of the Problem

While most of the pandemic research literature has focused on the teacher perspectives of shepherding ML students through the transition to online instruction while learning the technology skills themselves (Abdel Latif, 2022; Sprague et al., 2022), such research has not addressed the experience of ML students during the same era. Although transferring from in-person instruction to online schooling has been explored in a previous study as part of a planned or gradual migration (Kebritchi et al., 2017), the context of the pandemic changed the dynamics of the transition as students learned to study in a new virtual environment during a sudden migration to online instruction (Bailey & Lee, 2020; Li, 2022). International students faced a double challenge in that they were living in a foreign country while also studying in an unfamiliar environment of online instruction with little preparation or guidance (Han et al., 2022; Koo et al., 2021). Students had to master the norms of schooling in the new culture as well as learn the processes and expectations for studying in the new online context (Bailey & Lee, 2020; Sailsman, 2020). Therefore, the problem is a lack of knowledge about the perceptions of international students in an emergency remote teaching context. This gap hinders instructors from creating and facilitating learning while acknowledging the unique circumstances in which the international students were studying.

Academic acculturation refers to the process of personal change that results from contact between two cultures as an individual becomes part of a new group while simultaneously influencing the group members' norms of academic practice through sharing one's own lived experiences and scholarly acumen (Jiang et al., 2010). Specifically, academic acculturation focuses on the changes in the individual's mannerisms and dispositions (Neumann et al., 2023). While academic acculturation is a complicated endeavor of making sense of competing emotional, social, and academic factors all the while feeling confused and unsure about decision making (Elliot et al., 2016), the acculturation process is heightened when the dual influences of geographical cultures and technological cultures interact to shape how an individual develops appropriate behaviors for their current environment (Brunton & Jeffrey, 2014; Cao et al., 2021). The construct of academic acculturation includes several different elements, such as language issues (Bai & Wang, 2022), autonomous learning (Emelyanova & Voronina, 2017), and social challenges (Bich & Lian, 2021), each of which contribute to the overall adjustment to a new educational environment. Failure to adjust in any of these areas could result in confusion, feelings of incompetence, or loneliness for the international student (Antoniadou & Quinlan, 2020; Bastien et al., 2018; Brunton & Jefferey, 2014).

In the context of the current study, international students had arrived at the university expecting to engage in in-person classes and community social opportunities (Li & Middlemiss, 2022). Instead, these students became isolated in their off-campus housing with their only connection to socialization and learning occurring through online platforms. Other international students in the same classes chose not to remain in the United States during the lockdown and instead returned to their native countries to engage in learning from the comforts of home. However, despite the social support that the international students gained from their families (Azaola, 2020), studying from different countries meant that international students had to attend synchronous classes in their time zones, often resulting in extremely early morning classes.

This diversity in student demographics underscores how environmental factors influence MLs' learning (Han et al., 2022). Understanding the variety of experiences encountered during the transition online will enable educators to design and deliver instruction that responds to the MLs' perspectives. The research questions were as follows: What challenges did the students encounter when they migrated to online English learning? What strategies did the students find to be most helpful to learning English through an online platform? To answer these questions, the researchers analyzed reflective writing about the experience of the transition written by MLs from the beginning of their experience in emergency remote teaching and the end of the term after they had acclimated to their new learning context. This study used written reflections as data samples because they portray life experiences, expertise, conclusions, and perspectives which are experimental (Ramlal & Augustin, 2020). Given the novel context of the rapid transition to online learning, reflections provided insights into the students' interpretations of their new learning venues and procedures. Through the process of thematic analysis (Braun & Clarke, 2021; Nowell et al., 2017), the researchers identified the patterns occurring across both data sets to explore the findings of this research.

The authors of this study were two European American women who were interested in studying the academic acculturation of international students as they adjusted to studying in online courses in English. The one researcher was an associate professor whose research focused teaching English learners as they learned to adjust to studying academic content areas in a foreign culture. The second researcher was an instructor at an intensive English program who taught English learners in academic English classes needed to matriculate at an undergraduate university program. Since the researchers had completed a study that examined how instructors of English learners had responded to the transition to online instruction during the pandemic, they also wanted to explore international students' experiences with the goal of helping future ML students acclimate to online learning.

Review of the Literature

The following section will describe previous research on the various components of academic acculturation to provide an understanding of the issues that influence MLs in their transition from in-person to online instruction. An awareness of the unique issues for MLs in online instruction is important for designing culturally and linguistically relevant instruction (Hollie, 2017) that also incorporates technology training to socialize the MLs into the norms of online learning (Kung, 2017). Therefore, this review addresses the linguistic challenges, autonomous learning issues, and social issues in online instruction for MLs explored in previous studies.

Linguistic Challenges

First, language plays a prominent role in academic acculturation online in that the level of language proficiency can prevent the ML from communicating in the host language in both the receptive and productive modes of language (Bai & Wang, 2022; Bastien et al., 2018). The ability to comprehend academic lectures and discussions can be challenging because of the rate of speech or the unfamiliar accents of their peers or instructors (Cao et al., 2021). Previous research has indicated that international students may only understand 20–30% of the lectures during the first year of a study abroad (Bai & Wang, 2022; Brunton & Jeffrey, 2014; Koo & Jiang, 2022). Additionally, MLs may encounter increased difficulty verbally contributing their thoughts to class discussions, since they may not have access to their peers' verbal or nonverbal cues to support their linguistic interaction in an online setting (Bai & Wang, 2022; Cao et al., 2021; Kebritchi et al., 2017). Similarly, the amount of reading and writing required for online academic classes can prove onerous for ML students because of the complexity of the text structure and vocabulary contained therein (Bastien et al., 2018; Sailsman, 2020). MLs with lower English proficiency have a greater cognitive task to accomplish because they first must comprehend the language before they can master the instructional content (Brunton & Jeffrey, 2014). Added to the cognitive load of academic study in a second language, MLs who are inexperienced in critical thinking may also struggle with reading (Jabeen et al., 2019). Overall, the language difficulties in an online environment can inhibit the MLs' acculturation into a successful learning experience (Emelyanova & Voronina, 2017).

Autonomous Learning Challenges

In addition to language issues, academic acculturation can present autonomous learning challenges to ML students. Autonomous learning refers to the degree to which language learners are directing their own learning (Chong & Reinders, 2022). While international students display a high degree of independence in that they are living and studying far away from their home culture (Marginson, 2014), the level of initiative may not manifest itself in academic behavior. Previous research determined that autonomous learning is the most challenging part of online instruction for MLs (Bailey & Lee, 2020). To begin with, readiness for distance learning affects MLs' interaction and success in online courses (Kaya, 2021). Online courses often expect MLs to be independent learners to succeed with minimal instructional coaching (Kung, 2017; Sailsman, 2020). However, Harrison et al. (2018) claimed that many MLs may not be tech savvy enough to independently participate in a learning management system (LMS) and may need more technological training. When students feel that their learning is increasing their proficiencies or skill set, MLs are more likely to become more independent learners (Bich & Lian, 2021). Despite the potential for self-directed learning in an online context, instruction may lack access to either teacher presence or online teacher resources (Bich & Lian, 2021). The reduced immediacy of contact places the onus for solving problems on learners as they respond to the challenges that they encounter and engage in independent practice to master course content (Emelyanova & Voronina, 2017). The amount of time that students are engaged in individualized exercises can compensate for the reduction in contact hours for ML students (Emelyanova & Voronina, 2017). Overall, research indicates that ML students who are more autonomous learners are more successful in online instruction (Bich & Lian, 2021; Kaya, 2021; Sailsman, 2020).

Due to the significance of time management in the development of ML autonomy (Jabeen et al., 2019), the cultural concept of time affects online study in different ways. First, the notion of firm deadlines may not be prevalent in various cultures, so ML students may not be familiar with punitive consequences for late assignments (Bai & Wang, 2022). Additionally, if students log on to their learning management system from different time zones, synchronous interaction becomes difficult to schedule and usually results in asynchronous communication (Harrison et al., 2018). In prior studies, some ML students acknowledged the delayed response creates time to construct responses (Bailey & Lee, 2020), others missed the immediacy of instant feedback to motivate the students to complete the assignments on time (Harrison et al., 2018; Li, 2022). Overall, time factors into online instruction through learning communication procedures and meeting assignment deadlines.

Social Challenges

Social challenges can inhibit academic acculturation for online MLs learners because stronger interpersonal connections lead to greater academic acculturation (Neumann et al., 2023). While some ML students may be accustomed to more passive roles as students (Cao et al., 2021; Koo & Jiang, 2022), research underscores the importance of interaction in online language learning (Bich & Lian, 2021; Kebritchi et al., 2017; Li, 2022). However, many MLs feel that online instruction does not provide the students with enough communication with their peers (Harrison et al., 2018; Li, 2022). Students must be deliberately engaged and committed to communicating with their instructor and peers for successful online learning (Bastien et al., 2018; Sailsman, 2020). In a prior study, many MLs had expected more oral interaction online, but instead had encountered content that heavily relied on written materials (Harrison et al., 2018). To cultivate the norms for online interaction, technology can simulate face-to-face communication in an online setting and can provide a greater sense of community for ML students (Bich & Lian, 2021; Sailsman, 2020). Technological tools that support such interaction for MLs have been interactive blogs and chat functions (Aslan & Citfci, 2019), video conferences and project-based learning (Bich & Lian, 2021). While the tools to achieve communication vary across settings, online learning offered students a welcoming environment in the harsh isolation that was prevalent during the pandemic (Li, 2022).

Social support, an essential component of academic success (Bastien et al., 2018), can occur through multiple channels at institutional, instructional, and peer levels of interaction (Elliot et al., 2016; Jabeen et al., 2019; Xing et al., 2020). Brunton and Jeffrey's (2014) research concluded that forming social relationships can alleviate feelings of isolation, give the students a boost in their confidence, and improve their academic performance. Research has argued that institutions have the obligation to support ML students who are sojourning in the host country (Bai & Wang, 2022; Xing & Bolden, 2019). Strategies to facilitate the acculturation of ML students to campus life can include offering opportunities for student engagement (Elliot et al., 2016), providing facilities for student recreation (Slaten et al., 2016) and hosting academic orientation programs (Cao et al., 2021; Wang & Hannes, 2014). Despite the beneficent goals of such practices, MLs have commented that institutional practices often do not last long enough to provide appropriate levels of support (Brunton & Jeffrey, 2014). To extend this assistance, research suggests that instructors can record their lectures so that MLs can relisten to the lecture (Bai & Wang, 2022), provide project-based learning in which MLs would interact with local students (Bich & Lian, 2021), or offer alternative assignments to allow student choices (Xing & Bolden, 2019). Lastly, Aslan and Ciftci (2019) stated that creating joint writing projects, such as wikis, can enhance collaboration between MLs and their peers to foster the acculturation process. The degree of social support is significant to academic acculturation because MLs' degree of well-being is often correlated to scholarly achievement (Neumann et al., 2023).

Technological Challenges

Research indicates that MLs' level of technological expertise influences their performance in online instruction (Emelyanova & Voronina, 2017; Koo & Jiang, 2022). The degree of competency often depends on the availability of tech resources, access to network connectivity, or the personal affordability of technology in their home country (Harrison et al., 2018; Jin et al., 2022; Li, 2022). While previous experience with technology influences the degree of technology usage in the future (Jin et al., 2022), mastering online learning often requires time and guided practice to become a fully proficient participant (Li, 2022). Bich and Lian (2021) concluded that the investment of time required to learn technological skills yields dividends in terms of ease of focus, learner initiative, class participation, and peer collaboration. Furthermore, awareness of various technology applications can provide more diverse opportunities to cater to specific learning preferences for MLs (Harrison et al., 2018). Given online instruction's dependence on technology, digital factors impacted all the forementioned challenges to MLs' academic acculturation.

METHODS

In this study, we examined student reflective writing to analyze the acculturation issues that ML students encountered when they transitioned from in-person to online instruction. After receiving approval from the institutional review board, we examined reflective writing assignments collected from 30 subjects over a three-semester time span. Given the nature of found data (Ang et al., 2013), the exact demographics of the group cannot be known. However, the writing prompts asked students to reflect on their online experience (see Appendix A). One assignment directly asked students to describe their experiences with the online migration after the first week. Other assignments prompted students to compose reflective essays about their experiences in the course, with responses about online learning included in the data set. Although previous research has explored teacher preparation for online instruction (Codreanu, 2020; Pawan et al., 2016), far fewer studies have explored the challenges that MLs have in adjusting to online instruction (Bailey & Lee, 2020; Bich & Lian, 2021). Such qualitative data could be useful to inform more student-centered online instruction for MLs.

Participants

The subjects for this study were international students enrolled in various English language classes at a large university in the southeastern United States. The students' English proficiency levels ranged from an intermediate intensive English program with 20 instructional hours a week to an advanced pathway program in which students studied English for 6 to 10 hours a week, depending on English skill level, in addition to academic content courses leading to an undergraduate degree. The courses selected for inclusion in this study were an advanced writing course for advanced pathway students, a high intermediate integrated skills class for other pathway students, and an intermediate reading/writing course for intensive English program students. The researchers, one of whom was the instructor of the aforementioned courses, coded the various reflections to denote the assignment submission period, thereby providing a chronological context for the findings in relation to the start of the pandemic.

Data Analysis

The researchers used thematic analysis to determine the common themes in the data (Braun & Clarke, 2021; Nowell et al., 2017). Each of the researchers read the data sets individually to become aware of the scope of our data corpus before reaching a consensus of the dominant themes of the data (Pigden & Jegede, 2020), which were language, socialization, technology, and learning. After analyzing whether the trends suggested a coherent pattern upon which to structure our research framework (Nowell et al., 2017), we determined that the themes mapped to many of the components of academic acculturation (Bai & Wang, 2022, Jiang et al., 2010). We then reviewed the themes to ensure that they represented the data while still being flexible to allow change if warranted (Neuendorf, 2018). The themes in the data focused on the following parts of the model of academic acculturation as applied to an online context: linguistic challenges, autonomous learning challenges, and interactional struggles. Originally, technology was a distinct category; upon further examination, researchers dispersed that data among the other categories since that theme ran throughout all themes. While originally designated as learning challenges, we renamed the category autonomous learning to capture the scope of the data more accurately. Next, we engaged in thorough descriptions of the data that supported each theme to ensure the data thoroughly fit into the specific category (Nowell et al., 2017). Triangulation of the findings occurred through analysis of the multiple data sets. The final remaining themes of the data were linguistic challenges, autonomous learning challenges, and social challenges.

FINDINGS

Linguistic Challenges

This study revealed that students determined that language activities that they completed in the face-to-face classroom became more difficult in an online context. One such student remarked, "When we took classes online, we lacked better communication with classmates and teachers. Although online classes can also enable us to communicate, I think it is definitely less effective than communicating in the classroom." Given reduced contextual clues in an online setting (Kebritchi et al., 2017), students struggled to establish the meaning of the words that they were using. Such a comment correlates with a previous finding that MLs who feel that technology strengthens their language growth are more motivated to participate in online instruction (Emelyanova & Voronina, 2017). Another student stated, “When recording a video to a computer instead of speaking to an audience, this is not a public speech,” thereby noting that the move to online instruction affected the authenticity of the context of language production. The subject continued by explaining that “although I can understand this helpless move, but my public speaking ability has not been exercised and improved.” The lack of progress frustrated the subjects who wanted to become more fluent in their oral language development. Such sentiments echoed the findings of Bich and Lian (2021) whose study indicated that students did not feel that their oral proficiency improved during online instruction. Other students in this study stated that online instruction enabled them to develop their language skills, as noted in the following comment:

> I do have hard time to organize an essay, I’m not good at turning my opinion into an essay. This class helps me develop this skill and gives me lots of chances to practice. I think writing skill is necessary and it will help me directly for my future life in the college. Honestly, I’m not good at remote learning, but I’m ok with [this] course.

As this quote demonstrates, students were able to look past the linguistic challenges of online learning to identify how technology could facilitate their understanding of the English language.

Autonomous Learning Challenges

Many of the subjects had not experienced online learning before and described the transition to virtual instruction as a loss of the familiar structured classroom learning environment. One of the comments from the data stated “the bad influence is that we are losing a study atmosphere. It was my first time to use Zoom so I am not familiar with it and cannot follow the professor’s order instantly.” Another subject also noted this unease with the new format of instruction by explaining “many activities and speeches cannot be conducted in the class. And another problem is that I often forget to do discussion.” Such a comment highlights the significance of student autonomy in the shift from teacher centered instruction to online student-centered instruction (Li, 2022). While student independence was a prevalent outcome of online learning in this study, subjects stated that technology issues prevented the students from actively engaging in the learning management system (Bich & Lian, 2021). One subject noted the following:

> After we started the remote learning, I can hardly do as active as before because of the network issue. Not only the teacher has that, the technology issue also happened on me which caused I can hardly hear and understand what the teacher was saying and teaching.

Therefore, although technology facilitated instruction, it also presented the learner with new challenges and distractions that were not present during in-person instruction (Li, 2022). One student described the situation as follows:

> Another disadvantage is because I am in my bedroom and there are too many stuff that attracts me more than the online class. So, I think for the people like me that are easy to be attracts by other stuffs, that's a disadvantage and also a challenge.

MLs had to develop the willpower to avoid distractions and focus on content mastery during their online instruction.

Despite the new norms of online pedagogy, some students felt that the online learning experience was not that different from the learning that they encountered in in-person instruction as expressed by one who noted, "Learning remotely is pretty much same as learning in school, as long as you keep all the information in your mind and use your time more wisely." Many subjects affirmed that caveat of time management and described various distractions from studying the content (Bailey & Lee, 2020). Another student concurred that they felt that online instruction dramatically influenced their learning in that "online classes reduce our learning efficiency because we always need to take some time to debug our camera and microphone." The challenge of mastering the technology to facilitate their instruction was a struggle for students until they achieved a working knowledge of the programs and apps needed to participate. To counter such loss of focused learning, Bich and Lian (2021) suggest that online learners need increased teacher guidance to employ technology applications to improve their language proficiency.

Students' academic and social success are related to each other in complex ways (Bastien et al., 2018). For example, the subjects in this study had just begun to adjust to the interactional norms of their classroom instructors when their online migration impacted both their academic and overall acculturative stress. As one student explained, "if we have class inside classroom with our professor, we are able to rise [*sic*] our hands and ask, but online class, it is hard to ask question." Students needed to learn another set of interactional norms to continue building the necessary social instructional support for both large group classes and supplemental study sessions. As another student noted on social networking and classroom interaction, "[this city] is a new place for me. I have never been here before. I can chat with teachers, classmates, and friends on the Internet, but it seems that face-to-face conversation can make the relationship between two people better." Accordingly, the MLs acknowledged simultaneously adjusting to both of their new environments (Koo et al., 2021). Other students were more enthusiastic with their discovery of state-of-the-art technology to support traditional social and academic connections for learning as one of the subjects described as follows:

> The pandemic has brought new study [method] where teachers and students can hear and see each other, and study groups can be arranged online, making lessons easier … we can have group discussions, … I have study groups for all my film assignments, and my team members and I meet at Zoom to discuss our film assignments. It's a new experience.

While this innovative instruction was exciting for some subjects, many valued the teacher presence of their instructors during their daunting transition to online learning (Pawan et al., 2016). One student reflected that "I recognize the interest of many teachers when they constantly sending emails to reassure as well as for instructions on how to join the online class or the assignments to be completed." Students perceived these interactional supports as being both part of the new learning environment—breakout rooms, for example—and being due to supportive teacher presence. Though the methods of academic and social interaction shifted, students developed new skills and strategies to build the necessary online connections with each other and with their instructors.

DISCUSSION

Findings from this study revealed that students experienced difficulties communicating with both instructors and their peers due to language issues. While some of those difficulties stem from overall lower language proficiency, many of the students found that online learning stifled their language growth due to the differences in instructional practices. At least initially, the students felt that the online exercises did not result in the same language growth gained from in-person instruction. However, students' focus on the technology may have diverted the attention from the dual foci of language and content. Additionally, since familiar in-person language exercises may not translate into online learning, the unease of learning through the new pedagogy may have affected the students' perception of their language proficiency growth.

This study demonstrated that student mastery of technological tools in online instruction required continuous faculty support. For many students in this study, the tools were new mechanisms for them, so formal instruction about the procedures for using the technology was key to participating in the online classroom. While students needed an initial primer on participating online (Harrison et al., 2018), such training did not always address the challenges that the students encountered in their online learning. Therefore, students would often seek assistance from their instructors or peers to overcome technical barriers to learning. Such a phenomenon highlights the instructors' need for technological training to avoid waiting for outsourced technology assistance to address the students' technical issues (Bailey & Lee, 2020). Additionally, obstacles in technology access required workarounds to continue instruction for students who were in other countries.

The autonomous learning concerns that emerged from this study showed that students developed personal strategies to overcome distractions within the online learning environment. Disruptions came from a variety of sources, including objects in their learning environment and digital resources such as social media or external sites (Li, 2022). Additionally, students experienced physical discomfort from enduring long class periods with little physical movement or from participating in non-traditional working hours in a different time zone (Bich & Lian, 2021; Li, 2022). The individualized responses to perceived problems empowered the ML students to take more initiative to downplay the elements that threatened to divert the students' attention from their online learning. Although previous research has noted the propensity for digital distractions in online learning (Bailey & Lee, 2020; Li, 2022), the current study went beyond this to analyze how students exhibited their own initiative to devise personalized strategies to help them remain focused despite the temptation to wander from their studies. This deliberate individualized approach was more successful than adopting a prescribed practice from an outsider simply because the strategy was specific to fend off the distraction.

Findings from this study revealed the students had to cultivate new norms of interacting in an online community. Specifically, while previous research has documented that in-person pedagogy does not translate directly into online instruction (Aslan & Ciftci, 2019), this research concluded that student behavior for online learning did not correspond to the expectations of learning online. To address this mismatch, students must be socialized in the norms of participating in online instruction. This study also affirmed early studies that found that a lower English proficiency hindered the MLs' interaction in an online setting. However, this research also demonstrated that some students still desired the social support that they had become accustomed to from their face-to-face instruction.

The data in the current study presented several different limitations. First, the limited sample size may not be generalizable to larger populations. The unique circumstances of the sudden migration to online learning also may be non-replicable because lessons learned from the pandemic would inform a future emergency remote learning experience. In contrast to the context of intensive English classes in this study, data from university content area classes might yield significantly different data from more proficient ML students. Finally, found data does not allow for researchers to direct the data for research purposes (Ang et al., 2013), so the elicitation of data from this study did not specifically respond to the research questions.

Conclusions

In conclusion, this study revealed specific challenges that ML students experienced as they adjusted to online instruction. Initially, the unfamiliarity with recent technology hindered MLs from learning since they diverted their attention to operating the technology and could not focus solely on content competency. In addition, the technology issues compounded the linguistic challenges inherent in the online environment. At the same time, supplemental LMS resources, like recordings of class sessions, served to bolster the progress of other students. Furthermore, after the initial acculturation period, students employed the technology with relative ease and were able to refocus their attention on course content.

More importantly, the data showed that the students who developed their own personal strategies to become independent learners were more autonomous, adjusting to their new norms in an online learning environment. MLs who took the initiative to devise their own strategies for deflecting external distractions were better able to remain focused on instruction. For instance, some students had to adjust to living in one time zone while studying for up to 20 hours a week in a different time zone. Such proactive behavior provides a positive model of strategies to mentor multilingual students into online learning. This study also showed that students had to learn different norms to maintain connections with their instructors and peers as they struggled with the isolation of remote instruction. The migration to online learning interrupted students' academic acculturation to U.S. classrooms, so they had to use new strategies to build social support to sustain their academic progress within and outside of their class meetings. This study offers insight for both instructors and multilingual students who are seeking successful learning experiences in the online English language classroom.

Explicit acknowledgement of the challenges of academic and technological acculturation processes, as articulated in the literature, can allow students to situate themselves in the variety of responses to the challenges and develop strategies to overcome them. By identifying the issues that the ML students encountered, current educators can better prepare ML students for online learning through assignments that help the students to engage in productive struggles while simultaneously developing content and technological expertise. For example, as seen in the current study, ML students could produce reflective texts that focus on the challenges they are facing with their online learning while still meeting the course outcome of writing narrative genres. This study provides insight into students' perspectives about online instruction so that teachers can proactively address the obstacles identified in the current study.

Implications

Given the challenges experienced by the students in this study, there are several suggestions for mitigating these obstacles. For example, early and ongoing incorporation of digital interactions, supplemental resources and online tools within a face-to-face course can prepare students for a sudden migration. Though the online-only circumstances of the 2020 COVID-19 landscape have evolved, many institutions are now using e-learning days and online class meetings to address situational disruptions like weather-related closures now that e-learning is a viable educational venue. Therefore, we conclude this chapter through offering the following suggestions for instructors of online ML students.

Practical Suggestions

- **Include clear, detailed assignment descriptions with rubrics and instructions for using the LMS.**

While clear instructions are always important, in online learning environments, well-defined assignment descriptions with specific rubrics can provide guidance to complete course requirements. Similarly, providing detailed directions for how to find assignments, submit assignments, and view teacher feedback can benefit all students while providing necessary support to those new to the course, context, or LMS.

- **Provide redundant resources so students can have multiple sources of input to facilitate content mastery.**

Instructors who provide course content through multiple modalities can mitigate linguistic challenges for MLs by reinforcing content in the students' stronger skill area such as listening, speaking, reading, or writing. For example, a student who finds reading difficult can watch and listen to course video files to understand course content. In addition to the variety of content stimuli, asynchronous access can allow students to engage with the course on their own time or access the material multiple times to reinforce content learning to overcome learning challenges like technology issues, unfamiliarity with online platforms, and time zone differences.

- **Plan for meaningful interaction and community building during synchronous online instruction.**

Instructors must incorporate interactive activities into online learning courses to build community. Combining online discussions in breakout rooms with discussion board posts reinforces the benefits of each mode of interaction. Students who prefer to discuss with classmates can use technology features to simulate face-to-face interaction while others who favor written communication will also feel supported. The asynchronous nature of the online discussion boards is inclusive of students who may face network or time zone issues as well.

- **Maintain consistent teacher presence throughout the course.**

For international students studying online, a strong teacher presence supports their success. In situations where students transition online quickly, a consistent, clear teacher presence in the course can recreate some in-person learning environment safeguards within their online courses. For example, if an instructor maintains contact with students whose network issues prevent them from attending the synchronous sessions, the students can still experience the kind of guidance an instructor can provide in traditional classroom settings. Further, by preserving a tangible presence through assignment and assessment feedback, instructors can support students who may be reluctant or unable to participate in class sessions. Finally, by sharing video recordings of the class sessions, students can see their classmates and instructors interact online, providing both resources for students and the kinds of academic behavioral modeling of an instructor's presence.

- **Incorporate other devices, so they are tools, not temptations.**

In the data, students specifically mentioned how phones and other devices were tempting distractions. To minimize such distractions, instructors can incorporate devices into face-to-face instruction to prepare students for online learning technologies and in-class strategies. For example, many academic activities, such writing workshops, group research investigations, and other activities, can incorporate tech applications. Additionally, students could review concepts and compete in class activities like Kahoot, Quizlet, or Nearpod on their phones. Such strategies can reduce the allure of devices in both in-person and online instruction.

REFERENCES

Abdel Latif, M. M. (2022). Coping with COVID-19-related online English teaching challenges: Teacher educators' suggestions. *ELT Journal, 76*(1), 20–33. https://doi.org/10.1093/elt/ccab074

Ang, C. S., Bobrowicz, A., Schiano, D. J., & Nardi, B. (2013). Data in the wild: Some reflections. *Interactions, 20*(2), 39–43. https://doi.org/10.1145/2427076.2427085

Antoniadou, M., & Quinlan, K. M. (2020). Thriving on challenges: how immigrant academics regulate emotional experiences during acculturation. *Studies in Higher Education, 45*(1), 71–85. https://doi.org/10.1080/03075079.2018.1512567

Aslan, E., & Ciftci, H. (2019). Synthesizing research on learner perceptions of CMC use in EFL/ESL writing. *CALICO Journal, 36*(2), 100–118. https://doi.org/10.1558/cj.34818

Azaola, M. C. (2020). Support from extended family in higher education: A narrative literature review. *Journal of Further and Higher Education, 44*(8), 1065–1079. https://doi.org/10.1080/0309877X.2019.1648775

Bai, L., & Wang, Y. X. (2022). Combating language and academic culture shocks—International students' agency in mobilizing their cultural capital. *Journal of Diversity in Higher Education, 15*(2). http://dx.doi.org/10.1037/dhe0000409

Bailey, D. R., & Lee, A. R. (2020). Learning from experience in the midst of Covid-19: Benefits, challenges, and strategies in online teaching. *Computer-Assisted Language Learning Electronic Journal, 21*(2), 178–198.

Bastien, G., Seifen-Adkins, T., & Johnson, L. R. (2018). Striving for success: Academic adjustment of international students in the US. *Journal of International Students, 8*(2), 1198–1219. https://doi.org/10.32674/jis.v8i2.143

Bich, T. N. C., & Lian, A. (2021, December). Exploring challenges of major English students towards learning English speaking skills online during COVID-19 pandemic and some suggested solutions. In *18th International Conference of the Asia Association of Computer-Assisted Language Learning (AsiaCALL–2-2021)* (pp. 135–144). Atlantis Press.

Braun, V., & Clarke, V. (2021). *Thematic analysis: A practical guide*. Sage.

Brunton, M., & Jeffrey, L. (2014). Identifying factors that influence the learner empowerment of international students. *International Journal of Intercultural Relations, 43*, 321–334. https://doi.org/10.1016/j.ijintrel.2014.10.003

Cao, C., Zhu, C., & Meng, Q. (2021). Chinese international students' coping strategies, social support resources in response to academic stressors: Does heritage culture or host context matter? *Current Psychology, 40*(1), 242–252. https://doi.org/10.1007/s12144-018-9929-0

Chong, S. W., & Reinders, H. (2022). Autonomy of English language learners: A scoping review of research and practice. *Language Teaching Research*. https://doi.org/10.1177/13621688221075812

Codreanu, F. (2020). Teaching English online: From course to practice. *Acta Technica Napocensis-Languages for Specific Purposes, 20*(3), 29–37.

Elliot, D. L., Baumfield, V., Reid, K., & Makara, K. A. (2016). Hidden treasure: Successful international doctoral students who found and harnessed the hidden curriculum. *Oxford Review of Education, 42*(6), 733–748. https://doi.org/10.1080/03054985.2016.1229664

Emelyanova, N., & Voronina, E. (2017). Introducing blended learning in the English language classroom: Students' attitudes and perceptions before and after the course. *Knowledge Management & E-Learning: An International Journal, 9*(1), 33–49. https://doi.org/10.34105/j.kmel.2017.09.003

Han, Y., Chang, Y., & Kearney, E. (2022). "It's doable": International graduate students' perceptions of online learning in the US during the pandemic. *Journal of Studies in International Education, 26*(2), 165–182. https://doi.org/10.1177/102831532110614

Harrison, R. A., Harrison, A., Robinson, C., & Rawlings, B. (2018). The experience of international postgraduate students on a distance-learning programme. *Distance Education, 39*(4), 480–494. https://doi.org/10.1080/01587919.2018.1520038

Hollie, S. (2017). *Culturally and linguistically responsive teaching and learning: Classroom practices for student success*. Shell Education.

Jabeen, R., Wang, P., & Cheng, L. (2019). Academic engagement, social integration, and academic socialization: English as an additional language in higher education. *BC TEAL Journal, 4*(1), 95–107. https://ojs-o.library.ubc.ca/index.php/BCTJ/article/view/337

Jiang, X., Di Napoli, R., Borg, M., Maunder, R., Fry, H., & Walsh, E. (2010). Becoming and being an academic: The perspectives of Chinese staff in two research-intensive UK universities. *Studies in Higher Education, 35*(2), 155–170. https://doi.org/10.1080/03075070902995213

Jin, L., Deifell, E., & Angus, K. (2022). Emergency remote language teaching and learning in disruptive times. *CALICO Journal, 39*(1), i–x. https://doi.org/10.1558/cj.20858

Kaya, S. (2021). The factors predicting students' participation in online English courses. *Eurasian Journal of Educational Research, 91*, 301–320. https://doi.org/10.14689/ejer.2021.91.14

Kebritchi, M., Lipschuetz, A., & Santiague, L. (2017). Issues and challenges for teaching successful online courses in higher education: A literature review. *Journal of Educational Technology Systems, 46*(1), 4–29. https://doi.org/10.1177/00472395166617

Koo, K., Baker, I., & Yoon, J. (2021). The first year of acculturation: A longitudinal study on acculturative stress and adjustment among first-year international college students. *Journal of International Students, 11*(2), 278–298.
Koo, K. & Jiang, M. (2022). What does it mean to take online classes as an international student during COVID-19? *Online Learning, 26*(4), 209–230. https://doi.org/10.24059/olj.v26i4.3495
Kung, M. (2017). Methods and strategies for working with international students learning online in the US. *TechTrends, 61*(5), 479–485. https://doi.org/10.1007/s11528-017-0209-x
Li, D. (2022). The shift to online classes during the COVID-19 pandemic: Benefits, challenges, and required improvements from the students' perspective. *Electronic Journal of e-Learning, 20*(1), 1–18. https://doi.org/10.34190/ejel.20.1.2106
Li, G., & Middlemiss, W. (2022). Effects of cultural intelligence and social support on adjustment of international students in higher education. *International Journal of Teaching and Learning in Higher Education, 33*(2), 143–152.
Lim, M. H., & Aryadoust, V. (2022). A scientometric review of research trends in computer-assisted language learning (1977–2020). *Computer Assisted Language Learning, 35*(9), 2675–2700. https://doi.org/10.1080/09588221.2021.1892768
Marginson, S. (2014). Student self-formation in international education. *Journal of Studies in International Education, 18*(1), 6–22. https://doi.org/10.1177/1028315313513036
Neuendorf, K. A. (2018). Content analysis and thematic analysis. In *Advanced research methods for applied psychology* (pp. 211–223). Routledge.
Neumann, H., Kozak, S., & Gil, L. (2023). The impact of academic acculturation and language proficiency on international students' university experience and academic success: A longitudinal study. *The Canadian Modern Language Review, 79*(2), 121–140. https://doi.org/10.3138/cmlr-2021-0055
Nowell, L. S., Norris, J. M., White, D. E., & Moules, N. J. (2017). Thematic analysis: Striving to meet the trustworthiness criteria. *International Journal of Qualitative Methods, 16*(1), 1–13. https://doi.org/10.1177/1609406917733
Pawan, F., Weichart, K.A. Warren, A. N. & Park, J. (2016). *Pedagogy & practice for on-line English language teacher education*. TESOL Press.
Pigden, L., & Jegede, F. (2020). Thematic analysis of the learning experience of joint honours students: Their perception of teaching quality, value for money and employability. *Studies in Higher Education, 45*(8), 1650–1663. https://doi.org/10.1080/03075079.2019.1661985
Ramlal, A., & Augustin, D. S. (2020). Engaging students in reflective writing: An action research project. *Educational Action Research, 28*(3), 518–533. https://doi.org/10.1080/09650792.2019.1595079
Sailsman, S. (2020). ESL students learning online A review of literature. *Quarterly Review of Distance Education, 21*(1), 45–52. https://www.infoagepub.com/products/Quarterly-Review-of-Distance-Education-21-1
Slaten, C. D., Elison, Z. M., Lee, J. Y., Yough, M., & Scalise, D. (2016). Belonging on campus: A qualitative inquiry of Asian international students. *The Counseling Psychologist, 44*(3), 383–410. https://doi.org/10.1177/0011000016633506

Sprague, D. R., Williamson, J., & Foulger, T. S. (2022). Design guidelines for post-COVID era preparation programs: Action steps toward technology infusion. *Journal of Technology and Teacher Education, 30*(2), 177–187.

Wang, Q., & Hannes, K. (2014). Academic and socio-cultural adjustment among Asian international students in the Flemish community of Belgium: A photo-voice project. *International Journal of Intercultural Relations, 39*, 66–81. http://dx.doi.org/10.1016/j.ijintrel.2013.09.013

Xing, D. C., & Bolden, B. (2019). Treading on a foreign land: A multiple case study of Chinese international students' academic acculturation experiences. *Student Success, 10*(3), 25. https://doi.org/10.5204/ssj.v10i3.1406

Xing, D., Bolden, B., & Hogenkamp, S. (2020). The sound of silence: A musically enhanced narrative inquiry into the academic acculturation stories of Chinese international students with low spoken English proficiency. *Journal of Curriculum and Pedagogy, 17*(1), 25–47. https://doi.org/10.1080/15505170.2019.1627616

APPENDIX A

Writing Prompts

Start of Remote Learning Class Activity—Spring 2020

For this assignment, you will enter your notes from today's breakout room discussion.

- PROMPT: Discuss your experience with online learning so far this week. Has it been overall positive or negative? Why? What are the advantages and disadvantages? What are some challenges you anticipate?

Final Writing Exam—Spring 2020

For your final in-class writing, write a reflection about your performance this semester in GLOB-1100 and other classes.

Some suggestions of content ideas are:

- What did you do well?—explain
- What did you struggle with, or what do you think you could have done better?—explain
- What lessons or skills did you develop that you think will be helpful in your future academic career?—explain

- How did the change to Remote Learning affect your performance in GLOB 1100 and your other classes?

Start of Term of Remote Learning Class Activity—Summer 2020

For this assignment, you will enter your notes from today's breakout room discussion.

- PROMPT: Discuss your experience with online learning so far. Has it been overall positive or negative? Why? What are the advantages and disadvantages? What are some challenges you anticipate?

Midterm Timed Essay Exam—Fall 2020

Essay Exam Prompt:

Write a short essay on the impact of "Topic X" on "Topic Y."

In other words, you may replace the two topics with any logical cause/effect relationship, such as (but not limited to):

1. The impact of smartphones on study habits
2. The impact of video gaming on health
3. The impact of the COVID-19 pandemic on the economy (or my life, or my family, etc.)
4. The impact of remote/online learning on academic success

CHAPTER 14

PERSPECTIVES OF ENGINEERING STUDENTS ON THE IMPACT OF COVID-19 ON THE LEARNING AND TEACHING ALGEBRA AND DIFFERENTIAL CALCULUS

Valeria Cornejo Gutiérrez and Danelly Susana Esparza Puga
Universidad Autónoma de Ciudad Juárez

ABSTRACT

We present a study whose main objective is to identify engineering students' perspectives on the impact of COVID-19 on the teaching and learning of algebra and differential calculus, as well as to explore the proposals that they suggest for similar situations. The concern arises from the high failure rates among first-semester students during the February–June 2022 period at the Autonomous University of Ciudad Juarez, which could be related to the learning experience during the COVID-19 lockdown. To gather relevant information, interviews were conducted with ten engineering students, who described their classes, expressed their emotions, evaluated, and analyzed their experiences during the lockdown, and provided conclusions

Examining the Cognitive and Psychological Effects of the COVID-19 Global Pandemic on High School, College, and Graduate Learners, pp. 319–339

and proposals for future actions. The analysis of the responses revealed a wide range of emotions experienced by the students, including frustration, anxiety, depression, joy, and hope. The students preferred face-to-face interactions with their peers and teachers to remote digital instruction. The findings highlight the need to improve teaching methods and provide training in digital tools to educators to better prepare for similar situations in the future. Additionally, the students emphasized the importance of taking personal responsibility and committing to their education. While this study has provided significant insights from some engineering students, it would be advisable to conduct broader research to verify the generalization of the findings among other students in this discipline.

Keywords: COVID-19, algebra, differential calculus, Gibbs reflective cycle

INTRODUCTION

The COVID-19 pandemic has significantly changed the world's nations' social, political, and economic landscape. The pandemic has also seriously impacted schools, teachers, and students. Mexican schools were closed due to the COVID-19 pandemic on March 30, 2020. Before this declaration, the Secretaría de Educación Pública (SEP) published an agreement in which classes were officially suspended from March 23, 2020, to April 20, 2020. Still, it was not until the second semester of 2021 that some educational institutions gradually returned to daily activities (Agreement number 02/03/20 of 2020 Secretaría de Educación Pública).

The COVID-19 pandemic has and continues to impact educational institutions, mainly affecting students and teachers. Students faced various challenges in learning mathematics in virtual environments during the closures of educational institutions (Bringula et al., 2021). On the other hand, teachers were worried about effectively serving all students and evaluating the progress of students and their commitment to schoolwork (Cusi et al., 2022; Kalogeropoulos et al., 2021). Despite finding literature on the events during the abrupt transition from in-person to virtual environments caused by the pandemic (Al-Mawee et al., 2021; Hill & Fitzgerald, 2020; Hyland & O'Shea, 2021) it is necessary to explore what is happening in the present with the return to face-to-face academic activities after practically two years of closures of educational institutions.

The research reported in this chapter will describe and analyze students' perspectives on the impact of COVID-19 on teaching and learning algebra and differential calculus. In the same way, it is desired to know possible proposals by students in case a similar situation arises. To do this, the Gibbs cycle (1988) reflective was used as a basis, focusing on learning from previous experiences and applying that knowledge in the future. This research is expected to contribute to our understanding of the impact of

COVID-19 on the teaching and learning of the aforementioned participants. Further, this research should provide helpful information that can serve to improve education in virtual environments in case of future public health crises.

The structure of this chapter is as follows. First, the statement of the problem is presented. Then, an overview of research into the impact of the COVID-19 lockdown on mathematics teaching and learning is elucidated. Subsequently, the implemented method for conducting the research is explained. Finally, the study findings and a discussion of their possible interpretations and potential implications for the future are presented.

STATEMENT OF THE PROBLEM

During the February–June 2022 semester, first-semester engineering students at the Institute of Engineering and Technology (IIT) of the Autonomous University of Ciudad Juarez (UACJ) presented high failing grades during the first, second, and third partial evaluations in the subjects of algebra and differential calculus. Comparing the failure rates of the February–June 2022 semester with those of the semesters from February–June 2019 to August-December 2021, they increased significantly.

The learning experiences afforded during the COVID-19 lockdown could potentially contribute to this situation. Figure 14.1 presents the statistics of failure rates in algebra before, during, and after the COVID-19 lockdown, while Figure 14.2 displays the failure rates in differential calculus during the same periods.

Figure 14.1

Statistics of Failure Rates in Algebra Before, During, and After The COVID-19 Lockdown

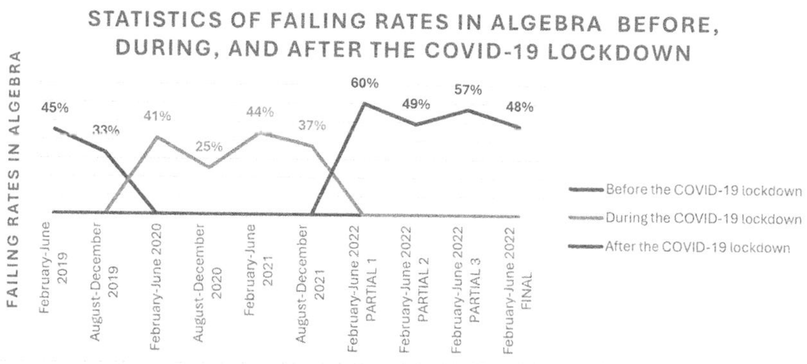

Figure 14.2

Statistics of Failure Rates in Differential Calculus Before, During, and After the COVID-19 Lockdown

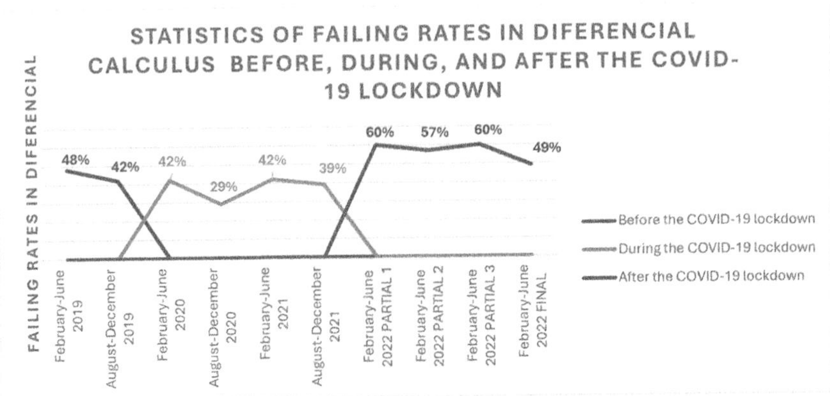

From February–June 2019 to February–June 2022, the lowest failure rate was observed during the COVID-19 lockdown in the semesters of February–June 2020 and August–December 2020, unlike the periods before the pandemic, namely February–June semesters 2019 and August–December 2019, where failure rates ranged from 33% to 49%. Additionally, a noticeable difference can be observed when students reintegrate into in-person classes, as the failure rates increased considerably compared to those during and before the COVID-19 lockdown. Therefore, the identified problem and objective of the research were to investigate what was happening and why the failure rates of first-semester students taking algebra and differential calculus classes increased upon returning to in-person courses.

Some possible causes for the decrease in failure rates during the closure of educational institutions are that students likely used various applications or math solvers during classes and exams, had access to video recordings of classes, experienced less pressure in virtual exams compared to in-person exams, and the teacher's evaluations were more accessible. However, some possible reasons will be provided later to explain the significant increase in failure rates upon returning to in-person classes after the COVID-19 lockdown.

REVIEW OF THE LITERATURE

In recent years, the COVID-19 pandemic has drastically changed how education is delivered worldwide, and mathematics education is no exception. As a result, many researchers have conducted studies to examine the impact of the pandemic on the teaching and learning of mathematics. In this context, several studies have explored the experiences of teachers and students with digital platforms and tools, the challenges and opportunities associated with remote instruction, and the potential of technology for supporting mathematics education in a post-pandemic world. This topic has generated considerable interest among researchers and practitioners in mathematics education as they seek to understand and respond to the ongoing challenges posed by the pandemic (Borba, 2021; Chan et al., 2021; Engelbrecht et al., 2023).

The confinement during the pandemic has significantly impacted millions of students and teachers. Transitioning to education in virtual environments required teachers to implement new teaching techniques (Brunetto et al., 2021). However, this transition has not been equal, as not all students have had access to virtual education, revealing the existing social inequalities in the world. Furthermore, some teachers have expressed concerns about the digital divides they have witnessed, referring to the disparities in access and use of digital tools by students due to economic or cultural reasons. This situation has led to a decrease in student engagement and has had a negative emotional impact on teachers (Lezama et al., 2020; Aguilar et al., 2023).

According to Alabdulaziz (2021), a crisis moment is an opportunity for all educational systems to look toward the future. In their research, they interviewed 120 mathematics teachers from different secondary schools, where 98% of participants agreed that the COVID-19 pandemic opened a door for digital learning in mathematics education. They concluded that using digital tools for learning has become an urgent and mandatory necessity in education.

Likewise, Rodríguez-Muñiz et al. (2021) considered a sample of 244 secondary mathematics teachers in Spain to analyze their perception of their preparedness for emergency remote teaching (ERT) during the COVID-19 pandemic based on their technical knowledge of pedagogical content before training in digital didactic tools, their level of digital competence for teaching mathematics, and their adaptation to ERT. Given the many resources and the high percentage of self-developed materials using educational software, mathematics teachers reflected adequate digital competence for teaching mathematics. However, the sudden transition to ERT forced teachers to slow down the pace of teaching and reduce the content taught.

On the other hand, additional studies have focused on investigating mathematics students' attitudes, perceptions, and experiences during the COVID-19 pandemic (Mukuka et al., 2021; Naidoo, 2020; Syauqi et al., 2020). These studies have explored how this experience influenced the learning and performance of mathematics students and their emotional and psychological well-being. In addition, mathematics students have faced barriers to accessing and using technology have been investigated (Chan et al., 2021).

Hodds (2021) aimed to determine if the impact of the pandemic had changed students' math ability and, if so, whether it was worse or better. The results suggest that students in 2020, despite facing pandemic-related issues, performed as well as their peers in 2018 and significantly better than their counterparts in 2019. In contrast, Schult et al. (2022) investigated fifth-grade students' reading comprehension and math competencies in Baden-Württemberg, Germany, before and after the pandemic. They used results from mandatory assessments and tests compared to the previous three years' average (2017–2019). The analysis showed that low-performing students in reading comprehension achieved pre-pandemic levels of competence. As for math competencies, students with low academic performance showed a delay in learning.

Finally, Stein et al. (2008) points out that research in mathematics education has provided evidence that learning mathematics is more effective, lasting, and deep when students engage in their learning process by participating in problem-solving activities and interacting with peers. Mathematical discussions are a crucial element in this learning process. The teacher helps to develop and construct students' personal and collective sense instead of sanctioning approaches or solving mathematical problems.

METHOD

The present research used a qualitative approach to explore and describe in-depth the perspectives and experiences of ten engineering students learning algebra and differential calculus. These subjects were selected because students from the Institute of Engineering and Technology at the Autonomous University of Ciudad Juárez had higher failure rates in algebra and calculus than other subjects in their engineering curriculum during the February–June 2022 semester.

Characteristics of the Research Participants

Ten Mexican engineering students from the Institute of Engineering and Technology at the Autonomous University of Ciudad Juárez participated in the study (see Table 14.1). To be included in the interview, it was necessary for the students to have taken an algebra or differential calculus class between August–December 2019 and August–December 2021 during the COVID-19 lockdown or to be currently taking one of these classes in February–June 2022 after the lockdown. This was done to ensure that the data obtained in the interviews were relevant to the objectives of this research.

Table 14.1

Sociodemographic Aspects of the Participant

Variable	*N* =1 0
Gender	*N* %
Male	7 (70%)
Female	3 (30%)
Age (years)	
18 to 19	3 (30%)
20 to 25	4 (40%)
27 to 30	3 (30%)
Career	
Industrial and Systems Engineering	3 (30%)
Aeronautical Engineering	2 (20%)
Manufacturing Engineering	1 (10%)
Mechatronics Engineering	1 (10%)
Biomedical Engineering	1 (10%)
Civil Engineering	1 (10%)
Computer Systems Engineering	1 (10%)

Data Collection

The data on students' perspectives and experiences were collected through semi-structured interviews. First, the students were invited to participate in an interview using the Teams platform. Once the invitation was accepted, the students were asked to sign an informed consent form authorizing the video recording of the interview for subsequent analysis. The interviews had an average duration of 26 minutes and 13 seconds.

Instrument

The instrument designed was a questionnaire with 18 questions, some of which were inspired by one used by Hyland and O'Shea (2021). The instrument that served as a guide for conducting the semi-structured interviews consisted of 5 general questions to define the sample's sociodemographic aspects and 13 questions to explore the phases of Gibbs' reflective cycle.

Questions 1 and 2 answer the description phase, while Questions 3, 4, and 5 collect information about the feelings experienced by the students during the COVID-19 lockdown. Questions 6, 7, and 8 were designed to explore the evaluation phase. For the analysis phase (positive or negative impact) on the learning of mathematics during confinement, Question 9 was used. Finally, to collect information for the conclusions phase, Question 10 was used, and Questions 11, 12, and 13 were structured for the action plan phase.[1]

Table 14.2 describes the phases and objectives of the questions designed for the instrument in this research.

Table 14.2

Phases, Questions, and Objectives of the Research Instrument Questions

Phase	Questions	Objectives
Description	1, 2	To deeply explore how algebra and differential calculus classes were conducted during the COVID-19 lockdown.
Feelings	3, 4, 5	To encourage students to reflect on their thoughts and feelings during the experience, their emotions, reactions, and overall learning experience during remote algebra and differential calculus classes.
Evaluation	6, 7, 8	To encourage students to objectively analyze what worked and did not work for learning algebra and differential calculus during this experience. To identify the positive and negative impacts of the incident, including challenging aspects of learning such as tests, class participation, interaction with classmates, and communication with the instructor.
Analysis	9	To conduct a deep examination of the benefits or damages in mathematical learning during the experience of remote classes for algebra and differential calculus, how this affected the return to in-person courses and compare personal and others' experiences.
Conclusions	10	To encourage students to reflect on the positive and negative aspects of the experience.
Action Plans	11, 12, 13	To describe possible proposals for future actions to address similar situations and to identify what students and teachers would do differently.

Data Analysis

The interviews were recorded in audio format and underwent a tape-based analysis following the approach described by Onwuegbuzie et al. (2009). Both authors actively participated in the data analysis process. Initially, we familiarized ourselves with the data by repeatedly listening to the interviews. Our goal was to identify the responses corresponding to the interview guide questions. We then transcribed only the relevant sections of the interviews that best illustrated the identified responses. Each researcher independently classified the answers for each question and grouped them accordingly. Subsequently, we compared our conclusions and held explicit discussions to address any discrepancies or uncertainties and achieve consensus on the interpretation of the answers.

Investigator triangulation (Rothbauer, 2008) was employed to ensure data reliability, where both study authors independently analyzed all data sources. Subsequently, the individual analyses conducted by each author were compared and examined for any discrepancies or differences in interpretation. This process of comparing and reconciling the analyses enhanced the overall credibility and trustworthiness of the findings.

The following section presents the results obtained from analyzing the responses to the present instrument.

RESULTS

Now we present the results obtained through the analysis of the empirical data. The presentation of results is divided into six sections: (1) Description, (2) Feelings, (3) Evaluation, (4) Analysis, (5) Conclusion, and (6) Action plan. All the interview excerpts used to illustrate the results were translated from Spanish to English.

Description

All the students had synchronous classes through a virtual platform. Microsoft Teams and the Virtual Classroom (Moodle) were the virtual platforms allowed and used by teachers and students at the Autonomous University of Ciudad Juarez (UACJ). For 90% of the interviewed students, their teachers shared their notes, PowerPoint presentations, and solved examples. 80% mentioned that the teachers also shared practice quizzes. Additionally, 70% stated that their teachers accompanied the explained topic with short videos that addressed specific questions or procedures to develop the learning of the subject.

On the other hand, 50% of the students mentioned that their teachers shared files with the solution of tasks and exams in a shared space (Microsoft Teams and Virtual Classroom). Finally, 40% of the students took some of their classes asynchronously; their classes were video recordings uploaded to a shared space through the virtual campus or Teams. All the descriptions are listed in Table 14.3.

Table 14.3

Description of mathematics classes during the COVID-19 Lockdown

Description	Yes	No
Synchronous (live) classes through a virtual platform	10 (100%)	0 (0%)
Asynchronous (recorded) lessons uploaded to a shared space	4 (40%)	6 (60%)
Written notes uploaded to a shared space	9 (90%)	1 (10%)
PowerPoint or similar presentations uploaded to a shared space	9 (90%)	1 (10%)
Solved examples uploaded to a shared space	9 (90%)	1 (10%)
Solutions to previous homework/exam questions uploaded to a shared space	5 (50%)	5 (50%)
Short videos addressing specific questions or procedures uploaded to a shared space	7 (70%)	3 (30%)
Quizzes	8 (80%)	2 (20%)

On the other hand, students expressed different opinions about using remote learning in their math classes. They mentioned that the effectiveness of this type of learning depended mainly on the preparation and support provided by the teacher. For the students, the teacher needed to address questions from the class, homework, and exams.

Student 1

> The teacher explained the subject well and prepared herself well to give us the class.

Nevertheless, students attributed their poor academic performance to the teacher's lack of skills and abilities. For example, the incompetence in handling digital technologies and the speed and pace of online classes. They also expressed their dissatisfaction with the need for more support through tutoring or academic advising.

Student 3

> The differential calculus class was challenging because there wasn't much support from the teacher, it was hard to keep up with the pace, assuming that there were things we already knew, and there was no support from the teacher regarding documents uploaded on Teams or virtual classroom.

Feelings

During the closures caused by the pandemic, the students experienced various feelings. Table 14.4 shows which feelings the students participated in.

Table 14.4

Feelings Experienced During the COVID-19 Lockdown

Sentiment	Scale				
	Nothing	Little	More or less	Quite	Too much
Anxiety	2 (20%)	3 (30%)	2 (20%)	3 (30%)	0 (0%)
Distress	1 (10%)	6 (60%)	2 (20%)	1 (10%)	0 (0%)
Depression	6 (60%)	0 (0%)	4 (40%)	0 (0%)	0 (0%)
Joy	1 (10%)	0 (0%)	3 (30%)	5 (50%)	1 (10%)
Satisfaction	0 (0%)	2 (20%)	3 (30%)	4 (40%)	1 (10%)
Hope	1 (10%)	4 (40%)	3 (30%)	1 (10%)	1 (10%)
Motivation	1 (10%)	2 (20%)	4 (40%)	3 (30%)	0 (0%)
Other Feelings	5 (50%)			4 (40%)	1(10%)
	None			Confusion, frustration, disordered eating, boredom, and sadness	Stress

Students expressed both negative and positive feelings. For instance, among the negative feelings, they indicated experiencing distress, anxiety, confusion, frustration, and depression. Several students expressed experiencing distress for various reasons. On the one hand, they indicated frequently falling asleep during class because they found it uninteresting. Likewise, they encountered difficulties in math subjects and began failing because they did not understand the topics covered in the course.

Additionally, they reported suffering from anxiety when trying to be self-taught, as the information they found on the internet sometimes did not match the teacher's explanations.

Student 10

> I felt distressed because I always got good grades and couldn't get used to the idea of failing. No matter how much I studied, I needed help understanding.

Some students expressed joy, hope, and motivation despite failing one subject, as they had received good grades in their other courses. Others felt happy and hopeful after successfully explaining a topic to a classmate, believing it would help them pass. Additionally, some students enjoyed spending more time with their families at home.

Student 5

> It caused me joy to be able to explain to my classmates the topics that they did not understand, and by presenting them, I realized that I had understood the subject and could solve the exams very quickly.

Overall, the students preferred in-person classes over online classes, as they feel more motivated, identified, and confident to ask their teachers questions. Finally, they concluded that younger teachers were the ones who adapted more quickly to technology when it came to teaching classes online.

Student 2

> It's a very different experience. Even though you have anonymity on the screen, it still limits the bond of trust with the teacher. Last semester, I failed algebra, and now I'm doing very well. Face-to-face contact generates camaraderie with classmates and a bond of trust with the teacher to express our doubts. I asked the teacher if I had any doubts at the end of class.

Regarding the challenges and difficulties of learning mathematics in-person in Algebra and Differential Calculus classes after the COVID-19 closures, the students responded that they feel more comfortable in in-person courses. The physical classroom space, and proximity to teachers and classmates, make them feel secure in asking questions, and their mathematical learning is superior to online classes.

Student 4

> In-person classes facilitate learning because being in a classroom with other people makes it easier to clarify doubts and have parts that are not understood and explained again.

Evaluation

Some of the challenging aspects mentioned by the students were the following: working in a team since, due to the pandemic, they could not meet with their classmates and found it difficult to express themselves; the multiple distractions since some students felt they were not in the right environment and did not pay attention to the classes. For others, taking notes and the way of grading the teachers was a problematic situation.

Student 8

> It was very complicated; paying attention in class was quite tricky; I sometimes took courses at work and had to solve something, or being at home, my wife wanted me to accompany her for personal things. The interaction with classmates was nonexistent; they always had their microphones turned off.

After all, the students considered that there were also several positive aspects. The main one was that they could record their classes; this allowed them to consult the recordings repeatedly to clarify their doubts or solve tasks. In addition, other students indicated that small classes forced them to be self-taught since they would not expose their suspicions to the teachers out of embarrassment. Finally, regarding the subject of exams, some pointed out that the lack of a teacher's presence allowed them to share results with their classmates.

Student 5

> The positive aspect was that I recorded the classes, and instead of asking questions, I waited until the course was over to review them. Or, if I had to do an assignment over the weekend, I would check the class to see where the topic that was causing me doubts was covered.

Finally, the students mentioned the impact of the COVID-19 lockdown on their ability to learn algebra and differential calculus. Regarding students' ability to learn mathematics, opinions were divided, with 40% considering it a somewhat negative experience and 50% considering it reasonably positive. Studying and communicating with classmates was a negative experience for 40% of the participants, as they needed help scheduling meetings and completing team activities. On the other hand, communication with teachers was more accessible, with 50% of students finding it favorable as their teachers responded to their doubts through different virtual platforms. Also, 50% stated that they could complete mathematical activities and homework as some teachers used programs in which answers could be verified, which they found fun and motivating. The majority, 70%, agreed that mathematical evaluations were positive as the teacher was more accessible given the situation being experienced.

Analysis

Some students consider that the experience during the COVID-19 lockdown has negatively affected their mathematics learning in the current in-person classes, as certain mathematical foundations acquired during that time were very deficient.

Student 6

> It affected me, for the topics I did not fully understand now hold me back.

On the other hand, the positive impacts they cited were that they learned to value the presence of the teacher and to improve their academic performance by paying more attention in class. At the same time, they felt motivated to be with their classmates doing the mathematical tasks assigned by the teacher.

Student 5

> It was very positive; I missed being in class with my teachers, talking, expressing myself, and being with someone familiar with doing the same thing: studying. I am thrilled to have returned.

Conclusion

The participants reached both positive and negative conclusions. Within the positive experiences, the students acquired or improved virtues such as responsibility, discipline, and self-teaching, and now value the presence and interaction with their teachers and classmates.

Student 7

> I had to learn independently; I taught myself probability and statistics consulting videos on the YouTube platform.

On the other hand, the negative experience was that they missed the physical relationship with their classmates and teachers.

Student 1

> Any activity is better done collectively; virtual coexistence is not the same as physical coexistence. Physical coexistence is essential for learning, as well as for any other activity.

Action Plan

In this last phase, based on their experience during the COVID-19 closures, participants proposed possible future actions better to face similar situations more effectively. Among their reflections, they mentioned the following points:

a. That the teacher has a warmer approach to students than they do in face-to-face classes.

Student 9

> I have noticed now in face-to-face classes that the teacher says, "Do you have any doubts about this problem?" because you can see the look on their face of "What are we doing?" Teachers explain better and are warmer in the classroom than in a video call.

b. Acquire better attitudes toward learning, for example: taking notes and class notes, assigning an appropriate place for study, being motivated, focusing on paying attention, avoiding distractions, and asking for tutoring when they do not understand the class.

Student 8

> In my case, I didn't take notes; I was always lying down watching the class on my phone. What I would do differently is assign a suitable place for studying, take notes, and ask my doubts.

c. Train teachers in the use and handling of technology.

Student 1

> I feel that if the pandemic were to continue, teachers should be trained to use digital tools. It's a struggle when the teacher doesn't know how to use them and tends to blame the students for their mistakes.

During the pandemic closures, students experienced various positive and negative emotions.

CONCLUSIONS

The COVID-19 pandemic continues to significantly impact the educational landscape worldwide, with teachers and students possibly being the most affected. School closures have generated challenges, particularly in teaching and learning mathematics in virtual environments. This study aims to expand our knowledge about engineering students' perspectives on the impact of COVID-19 on the learning and teaching of algebra and differential calculus, from understanding their experience in different phases to exploring potential proposals for improving such an experience in the future.

All participants in this research had synchronous classes during the COVID-19 lockdown, and their teachers shared various complementary materials to support them in their math classes. However, despite some teachers' support, others did not assist, making students believe that teachers' performance was critical in assessing the efficiency of remote learning in their math classes. During the pandemic closures, students experienced various positive and negative emotions. They reported that poor grades, failure to understand class topics, lack of interaction with teachers and peers, and not having a fixed space in their homes to take classes generated distress, anxiety, confusion, frustration, and depression. In contrast, when they understood the topics, helped their peers with the issues they did not understand, and spent more time with their families, they felt joy, hope, and motivation.

In another sense, the participants of this study evaluated their learning experience of algebra and differential calculus as both positive and negative. On the negative side, some students classified their interaction with their peers and teachers as unfavorable because communication was practically nonexistent, they felt that teachers did not dedicate enough time to resolving their doubts on the topics covered in class, and they were easily distracted while taking courses from home. On the other hand, the positive aspects were that teachers were more accessible during evaluations, there was less pressure, and they could even solve their exams with math applications, solvers they found on the internet, and collaboratively with their classmates. Another positive aspect was that they had access to video recordings of the classes and could consult them anytime, anywhere, and as many times as they deemed necessary.

The closures of educational institutions caused by the COVID-19 pandemic have led to several challenges for students, particularly in the inadequate acquisition of algebra and differential calculus knowledge during virtual classes. As a result, many students need help in their face-to-face classes due to deficiencies in these subjects. However, despite the challenges faced by students due to their insufficient knowledge of algebra and differential calculus acquired during virtual classes, one benefit they have found in returning to face-to-face courses is that they pay more attention to their math classes, as there are fewer distractions than during the COVID-19 lockdown at home. Students express happiness about being back in their face-to-face math classes and value the physical presence of both their teachers and classmates.

Finally, the participants in this study contributed possible proposals for future actions to address situations like those experienced in 2020 and identify what students and teachers would do differently. On the one hand, they suggest that teachers be trained in using digital tools, create strategies to improve student-teacher and student-student communication, and motivate students to stay active during classes. On the other hand, they consider it necessary for students to be responsible and committed to their education.

IMPLICATIONS FOR THE FUTURE

The research broadened our knowledge about the perspectives held by engineering students at the Autonomous University of Ciudad Juarez regarding the experience of learning and teaching algebra and differential calculus during the COVID-19 lockdown.

The findings of this study suggest several important implications for future educational practices. First and foremost, it is crucial to invest in teacher training and provide them with the necessary skills and knowledge to utilize digital tools in virtual learning environments effectively. This will enable teachers to deliver high-quality instruction and support to students, even in remote settings. Additionally, efforts should be made to improve communication strategies between teachers and students, as well as among students themselves, fostering a sense of connection and addressing concerns and doubts more efficiently. It is also essential to prioritize the mental health and well-being of students, and to provide the resources and support that they need to cope with the emotional challenges brought about by the pandemic.

Furthermore, flexible learning resources, such as recorded video lectures and supplementary materials, can empower students to engage in self-paced learning and to review complex topics as needed. Recognizing the potential learning deficiencies resulting from virtual classes, targeted support, and remedial measures should be implemented to address these gaps in knowledge and to ensure a solid foundation in subjects like algebra and differential calculus. Lastly, fostering student responsibility and engagement is vital, by encouraging students to take ownership of their education and to remain actively involved throughout their learning process.

SUMMARY

The research aims were: (1) to describe and analyze students' perspectives on the impact of COVID-19 on teaching and learning algebra and differential calculus and (2) to elucidate proposals that the students suggested in the case of a similar situation. From the students' perspective, knowing their teaching and understanding the learning experience during the COVID-19 lockdown is important, since issues are currently associated with high failure rates in the first semesters of engineering courses at the Autonomous University of Ciudad Juarez.

To explore the above, ten engineering students were interviewed at the Autonomous University of Ciudad Juarez, where they described their classes, expressed their feelings, and even evaluated and analyzed the experience they had in their courses during the COVID-19 lockdown. They also gave their conclusions and proposals for an action plan if a similar situation were to arise in the future. After analyzing the responses provided by the students during the interviews, it was possible to conclude that engineering students experienced various emotions, including both positive and negative emotions such as frustration, anxiety, depression, joy, and hope. In addition, it was evident that students preferred face-to-face interactions with their peers and teachers over remote instruction using digital tools. We observed a consistent pattern of behavior among the participants, who recommended that teachers improve their teaching methods and receive training on digital tools to prepare for future similar events. Additionally, the students emphasized the importance of personal responsibility and commitment to their education.

This research has allowed the perspectives of some engineering students to be heard. However, it would be important to conduct a study with a larger sample size to confirm if other engineering students share the findings reported in this research. Additionally, it would be beneficial to replicate this study in different educational levels and in different educational contexts to understand how students and parents of children studying at the basic level experienced the teaching and learning of mathematics classes during the COVID-19 lockdown and how this experience has influenced their current classroom experience.

REFERENCES

Agreement number 02/03/20 de 2020 [Secretaría de Educación Pública]. In which classes are suspended in preschool, primary, secondary, teacher training, and other schools of the National Education System, as well as those of the higher education level dependent on Secretaría de Educación Pública. 16 de marzo de 2020. Recovered: https://www.dof.gob.mx/nota_detalle.php?codigo=5589479&fecha=16/03/2020#gsc.tab=0

Aguilar, M. S., Esparza Puga, D. S., & Lezama, J. (2023). The abrupt transition to online mathematics teaching due to the COVID-19 pandemic: Listening to Latin American teachers' voices. In A. Clark-Wilson, O. Robutti, & N. Sinclair (Eds.), *The mathematics teacher in the digital era* (pp. 347–363). Springer. https://doi.org/10.1007/978-3-031-05254-5_13

Alabdulaziz, M. S. (2021). COVID-19 and the use of digital technology in mathematics education. *Education and Information Technologies*, *26*, 7609–7633. https://doi.org/10.1007/s10639-021-10602-3

Al-Mawee, W., Morgan Kwayu, K., & Gharaibeh, T. (2021). Student's perspective on distance learning during COVID-19 pandemic: A case study of Western Michigan University, United States. *International Journal of Educational Research Open*, 2. https://doi.org/10.1016/j.ijedro.2021.100080

Borba, M. C. (2021). The future of mathematics education since COVID-19: Humans-with-media or humans-with-non-living-things. *Educational Studies in Mathematics*, *108*, 385–400. https://doi.org/10.1007/s10649-021-10043-2

Bringula, R., Reguyal, J. J., Tan, D. D., & Ulfa, S. (2021). Mathematics self-concept and challenges of learners in an online learning environment during COVID-19 pandemic. *Smart Learn Environment*, *8*(22). https://doi.org/10.1186/s40561-021-00168-5

Brunetto, D., Bernardi, G., Andrà, C., & Liljedahl, P. (2022). Teaching as a system: COVID-19 as a lens into teacher change. *Educational Studies in Mathematics*, *110*(1), 65–81. https://doi.org/10.1007/s10649-021-10107-3

Chan, M., Sabena, C., & Wagner, D. (2021). Mathematics education in a time of crisis—A viral pandemic. *Educational Studies in Mathematics, 108*(1), 1–13. https://doi.org/10.1007/s10649-021-10113-5

Cusi, A., Schacht, F., Aldon, G., & Swidan, O. (2023). Assessment in mathematics: a study on teachers' practices in times of pandemic. *ZDM Mathematics Education, 55*(1), 221–233. https://doi.org/10.1007/s11858-022-01395-x

Engelbrecht, J., Borba, M. C., & Kaiser, G. (2023). Will we ever teach mathematics again in the way we used to before the pandemic? *ZDM Mathematics Education, 55*(1), 1–16. https://doi.org/10.1007/s11858-022-01460-5

Gibbs, G. (1988). *Learning by doing. A guide to teaching and learning methods*. Further Education Unit at Oxford Polytechnic.

Hill, K., & Fitzgerald, R. (2020). Student perspectives of the impact of COVID-19 on learning. *All Ireland Journal of Higher Education, 12*(2), 1–9.

Hodds, M. (2021). The early impact of the COVID-19 pandemic on mathematical competencies on entry into a UK university. *Teaching Mathematics and its Applications: An International Journal of the IMA, 40*(4), 254–262. https://doi.org/10.1093/teamat/hrab021

Hyland, D., & O'Shea, A. (2021). The student perspective on teaching and assessment during initial COVID-19 related closures at Irish universities: implications for the future. Teaching Mathematics and its Applications: *An International Journal of the IMA, 40*(4), 455–477. https://doi.org/10.1093/teamat/hrab017

Kalogeropoulos, P., Roche, A., Russo, J., Vats, S., & Russo, T. (2021). Learning mathematics from home during COVID-19: Insights from two inquiry-focused primary schools. *Eurasia Journal of Mathematics, Science and Technology Education, 17*(5), 1–16. https://doi.org/10.29333/ejmste/10830

Lezama Andalón, F. J., Flores García, R., Buendía Abalos, G., & Mariscal Vallarta, E. (2020). Docencia en matemáticas: voces latinoamericanas en la transición hacia la enseñanza a distancia por covid-19. *Investigación e Innovación en Matemática Educativa, 5*, 1–28. https://doi.org/10.46618/iime.86

Mukuka, A., Shumba, O., & Mulenga, H. M. (2021). Students' experiences with remote learning during the COVID-19 school closure: implications for mathematics education. *Heliyon*, 7(7). https://doi.org/10.1016/j.heliyon.2021.e07523

Naidoo, J. (2020). Postgraduate mathematics education students' experiences of using digital platforms for learning within the COVID-19 pandemic era. *Pythagoras, 41*(1). https://doi.org/10.4102/pythagoras.v41i1.568

Onwuegbuzie, A. J., Dickinson, W. B., Leech, N. L., & Zoran, A. G. (2009). A qualitative framework for collecting and analyzing data in focus group research. *International Journal of Qualitative Methods, 8*(3), 1–21. https://doi.org/10.1177/1609406909 00800301

Rodríguez-Muñiz, L.J., Burón, D., Aguilar-González, Á. & Muñiz-Rodríguez, L. (2021). Secondary mathematics teachers' perception of their readiness for emergency remote teaching during the COVID-19 pandemic: A case study. *Education Sciences, 11*(228), 1–18. https://doi.org/10.3390/educsci11050228

Rothbauer, P. M. (2008). Triangulation. In L. M. Given (Ed.), *The Sage encyclopedia of qualitative research methods* (Vol. 2, pp. 892–894). Sage.

Schult, J., Mahler, N., Fauth, B., & Lindner, M. A. (2022). Did students learn less during the COVID-19 pandemic? Reading and mathematics competencies before and after the first pandemic wave. *School Effectiveness and School Improvement,* 1–20. https://doi.org/10.1080/09243453.2022.2061014

Stein, M. K., Engle, R. A., Smith, M. S., & Hughes, E. K. (2008). Orchestrating productive mathematical discussions: Five practices for helping teachers move beyond show and tell. *Mathematical Thinking and Learning, 10*(4), 313–340. https://doi.org/10.1080/10986060802229675

Syauqi, K., Munadi, S., & Triyono, M. B. (2020). Students' perceptions toward vocational education on online learning during the COVID-19 Pandemic. *International Journal of Evaluation and Research in Education*, 9(4), 881–886. http://doi.org/10.11591/ijere.v9i4.20766

ENDNOTE

1. To access the complete questionnaire, you can visit: https://drive.google.com/file/d/1RNPs6FgaLR-hET_oMc57bpaYr3EcXn0T/view?usp=sharing

SECTION III

GRADUATE LEARNERS

CHAPTER 15

GRADUATE STUDENTS' MENTAL HEALTH DURING COVID-19

Parenthood and Gender

Hyeon Jean Yoo
Tennessee State University

David T. Marshall
Auburn University

ABSTRACT

Parenting in academia can be tremendously stressful. While graduate students, in general, may experience high levels of stress, time pressure, and financial difficulties, graduate students with children confront additional burdens required by the daily needs of their children. Although studies have focused on the impact of COVID-19 on higher education students, little attention has been paid to how graduate student parents were impacted by this abrupt change. Using data collected from 543 graduate students, we examined the influence of parental status and gender on graduate students' perceived helplessness, self-efficacy, and life satisfaction. In addition, we exclusively focused on the student-parent group and examined the effect of gender and minority status. We surveyed 543 graduate students and found

Examining the Cognitive and Psychological Effects of the COVID-19 Global Pandemic on High School, College, and Graduate Learners, pp. 343–366

a significant influence of parental status on graduate students. Graduate student parents reported higher levels of self-efficacy and life satisfaction while reporting lower levels of perceived helplessness than childless peers, partially supporting the role accumulation theory. We also identified a significant gender gap in each group. Specifically, female student parents reported significantly higher levels of perceived helplessness and lower levels of self-efficacy than male student parents. Similarly, female non-parents reported significantly higher levels of perceived helplessness and lower levels of self-efficacy than their counterpart. Furthermore, we found the levels of satisfaction were significantly different between the minority student parents and dominant student parents. Our findings highlight the importance of providing adequate resources and support to graduate students according to their status.

INTRODUCTION

The COVID-19 outbreak had a considerable impact on the lives of graduate students (Bal et al., 2020; Chrikov et al., 2020; Kee, 2021). Graduate students are situated in a unique position where they are challenged with financial and job insecurity while fully committing themselves to academic and professional responsibilities (Moreau & Kerner, 2015). Graduate students with dependent children may have faced additional challenges during COVID-19, as the schools and childcare facilities were no longer available (Bourne, 2021; Hicks, 2021; Spies-Upton & Hill, 2021). Children were home around the clock, forcing parents to put their additional time into childcare and homeschooling while trying to work and study full-time (Carpenter & Dunn, 2020; Marshall, 2022; Mollet & Wolf-Wendel, 2022).

While several studies have focused on the impact of COVID-19 on higher education students, little attention has been paid to how graduate student parents were impacted by this abrupt change. Studies conducted during the pandemic imply that female graduate students with children may have been impacted more significantly by the pandemic (Carli, 2020; Davis et al., 2022; Etheridge & Spantig, 2020; Gabster et al., 2020; Mollet & Wolf-Wendel, 2022; United Nations, 2020). Women reported higher mental stress (Etheridge & Spantig, 2020), increased childcare and other obligations (Carli, 2020), and decreased productivity (Ellinas et al., 2022) compared to men during the pandemic. These studies indicate that women were more vulnerable than men, juggling increased academic and caring responsibilities (Calarco et al., 2021; Ellinas et al., 2022). As little is known about how COVID-19 affected graduate student parents, it is imperative to examine their mental health and how they may differ from other graduate students who do not have children. In this study, we examined the influences of parental status and gender on graduate students' perceived helplessness, self-efficacy, and life satisfaction. In addition, we exclusively focused on the student-parent group and examined the effect of gender and minority status, as they are reported to be one of the most vulnerable populations during the pandemic (Gabster et al., 2020).

REVIEW OF LITERATURE

Parenting in Academia

Universities and colleges are often described in the literature as "greedy" institutions because academia expects exclusive and undivided loyalty and effort (Kreischer, 2017; Mollet & Wolf-Wendel, 2022; Moreau & Kerner, 2015; Wolf-Wendel & Ward, 2015; Wright et al., 2004). The institutional context operates within the ideal worker norm that expects ceaseless dedication to academic work (Mollet & Wolf-Wendel, 2022; Wright et al., 2004). The prevalence of ideal worker culture may negatively affect graduate students as they are in an "ambiguous position" where they are no longer solely students but are not yet fully professionals (Grady et al., 2014, p. 7). While they strive to fulfill their academic goals, they are constantly faced with financial challenges, time constraints, and multiple stressors. Graduate students with dependent children face additional barriers as they try to manage caregiving responsibilities while striving to be ideal workers simultaneously (Kreischer, 2017).

While the workload of graduate students is similar to that of faculty members (Chesser, 2015; Kreischer, 2017), the lack of financial resources among graduate students severely limits the options available for the parenting role (Hicks, 2021). During the COVID-19 lockdown period, faculty parents reported relying heavily on paid support, such as house-cleaning, babysitters, and tutoring for their children (Mollet & Wolf-Wendel, 2022); however, these options were not as readily available for graduate student parents due to financial constraints (Corrente, 2022; Hicks, 2021). Likewise, two graduate student parents interviewed in Spies-Upton and Hill's (2021) work shared negative and challenging experiences they faced during the pandemic as student parents, which included perceived discrimination, financial barriers, increased work, and delayed dissertation completion.

The Unequal Impact of Parenthood in Academia

Gender issues are discussed consistently in the literature on academic parents. While many studies acknowledge the challenges and struggles of parents in academia, those barriers seem much more significant for women (Coe, 2013; Davis et al., 2022; John et al., 2022; Kulp, 2020; Lisnic et al., 2019; Trussell, 2015; Wolf-Wendel & Ward, 2015). In their report, McFarland et al. (2017) note that female scholars in higher education need to catch up with their male counterparts in achieving tenure. In addition, Coe (2013) argues that marriage "accelerates a man's career" (p. 4), pointing out that married male professors tend to be promoted more quickly than their single colleagues, while it is the opposite for women.

The pandemic and the abrupt shift to online learning have had an enormous impact on women in higher education, exacerbating the existing productivity gap. Female scholars' productivity and research output were significantly affected during COVID-19 (Gabster et al., 2020; Hicks, 2021; Witteman et al., 2021). Survey data collected during COVID-19 from three countries (United States, United Kingdom, and Germany) provides evidence that women were more likely to lose their jobs than men were during the pandemic (Adams-Prassl et al., 2020). Additionally, in their quantitative research, Davis et al. (2022) suggest that female faculty experienced higher levels of stress, social isolation, and lower well-being during the pandemic, which negatively affected their research productivity.

The amount of stress and challenges experienced can be more severe for women scholars with children. Women tend to spend considerably more time on their childcare responsibilities, such as caring for and homeschooling, than men (Adams-Prassl et al., 2020). This phenomenon is explored in Mollet and Wolf-Wendel's (2022) study on academic parents during the pandemic. The authors interviewed 16 parents with young children, exploring how they navigated both professional and parenting responsibilities when childcare centers and schools were closed. While childless faculty members used the isolation period to increase productivity, this was less of an option for parents. They found that faculty experienced increased depression and anxiety, especially among single parents and those with little or no support systems around them. Similarly, Krukowski et al. (2021) conducted a study focused on faculty members and found that academic productivity differed by gender and parental status. Women scholars and faculty members with children under the age of five submitted significantly fewer articles during the pandemic than they did before the crisis.

In addition to increased gender disparities during the pandemic, studies also pointed out that COVID-19 intensified pre-existing racial/ethnic inequities in academia (Douglas et al., 2022; Doyle et al., 2021; Gabster et al., 2020). Douglas and her colleagues (2022) found that there were significant differences among academics depending on their sociodemographic identities. Women, primary caregivers, and underrepresented racial minorities reported more negative experiences, such as increased disruption due to physical health symptoms and additional caretaking, compared to their peers. In his research on historically underrepresented graduate students during COVID-19, Walsh et al. (2021) identified that these students experience a lack of support systems and difficulties in accessing adequate resources. In their longitudinal study on more than 1,000 college students between fall 2019 and spring 2020, Gopalan and his colleagues (2022) found that underrepresented racial/ethnic minority students reported a relatively lower sense of belonging compared to peers, which may lead to increased feelings of social isolation, anxiety, and depression.

Altogether, the literature suggests that academic parents often experience multiple challenges, lack of time, and financial constraints, leading to higher stress levels at home and school. Studies imply that women were more vulnerable and likely to experience poorer mental health than men due to increased workload during COVID-19. Furthermore, students of color may have been impacted more severely than others. While little is known about how the pandemic impacted graduate students, it is important to understand the extent to which their mental health was affected by their parental status, gender, and race/ethnic minority status.

THEORETICAL FOUNDATIONS

The role strain (Elliott, 2003; Goode, 1960) and the role accumulation theories (Sieber, 1974) guided the theoretical foundations of this study. While these two theories are often presented in the literature of academic parents as well as working parents, they contrast with each other. In this study, we aim to extend our understanding of graduate student parents and identify the extent to which these theories account for the experiences of graduate student parents during COVID-19.

Role Strain Theory

Role strain theory maintains that individuals have limited time and energy to perform unlimited role demands, and, therefore, role strain occurs when there is difficulty fulfilling the expectations of multiple roles (Goode, 1960). The evidence of role strain is often described in the literature on academic parents. For example, Springer et al. (2009) pointed out that student parents are confronted with "conflicting and powerful ideologies" due to social role requirements and pressure (p. 438). In other words, student parents face identity conflicts between being good parents and good students (Corrente, 2022). In their qualitative study of 20 female students, Behboodi Moghadam et al. (2017) found that a dual role of student parents as a caregiver and as a student could cause a significant dilemma for these students who wish to undertake both roles in "ideal conditions" (p. 1). Student parents who try to balance multiple roles often struggle and sometimes compromise one of the two roles. As a result, parents in graduate school often suffer from poor mental health and time pressure, trying to fulfill their academic and nonacademic duties (e.g., Dolson & Deemer, 2020).

Existing literature points out the structural barriers that women graduate students face in performing multiple roles (Lynch, 2008; Springer et al., 2009). Student parents are constantly in tension between idealized parent and idealized student. In between these roles, they often suffer from feelings of guilt when they fail to meet one of those roles (Brown, 2007). In sum, role strain theory suggests that student parents in graduate school are more likely to experience higher levels of mental stress due to multiple role demands stemming from academic and family responsibilities.

Role Accumulation Theory

Role accumulation theory suggests that people benefit by engaging in multiple roles (Barnett, 2014; Biddle, 2013; Mullen et al., 2008; Sieber, 1974). While role strain theory generally views multiple roles as a source of psychological stress, proponents of role accumulation theory argue that multiple roles may lead to positive personal well-being as people experience an increase in power, security, resources, and emotional gratification (Moen et al., 1995; Mullen et al., 2008; Sieber, 1974).

Several qualitative studies on academic parents have suggested that parents in academia partially perceive their parenting role as beneficial to their academic lives. For example, faculty parents expressed feeling decreased academic-related stress as they spent time with their children (Wolf-Wendel & Ward, 2006). A similar sentiment was noted in the literature during the pandemic that academic parents appreciated the time spent with their children despite the increased depression and anxiety stemming from their professional roles (Mollet & Wolf-Wendel, 2022). Graduate student parents and faculty parents shared developing positive self-images as they become positive role models for their children and becoming more strategic in time management and organization with dual roles (Kreischer, 2017). While acknowledging the "greedy" nature of academic life, faculty parents valued their dual role as one worked as a buffer to one another (Wolf-Wendel & Ward, 2006). Previous survey research we conducted found that graduate students with children reported higher levels of life satisfaction and lower levels of stress compared to those who do not have dependent children, highlighting the possible positive influence of parenting role (Yoo & Marshall, 2024).

Current Study

The previous literature and theoretical framework would suggest that students with dependent children may face more significant challenges during their graduate studies that may put them at risk of withdrawing from their studies. Several other studies suggest that these students may receive benefits and psychological comfort from navigating seemingly conflicting roles. Graduate student parents are often neglected in the literature on academic parents. Further, it is unclear how they are affected by their gender role, especially during the unique context of the COVID-19 pandemic. Therefore, this study aimed to examine how graduate student parents are different from their childless peers and how they are affected by their gender and race/ethnicity status. Specifically, we sought to answer the following research questions:

1. How do parental status and gender affect graduate students' perceived helplessness, self-efficacy, and life satisfaction?
2. How do minority status and gender affect graduate student parents' perceived helplessness, self-efficacy, and life satisfaction?

METHODS

Data Collection

Data were collected from March to April 2021 using an electronic survey hosted by Qualtrics. The invitation email with a link to the anonymous online questionnaire was sent to all graduate students who were enrolled and studying at a large R1 university in the Southeastern United States during the spring 2021 semester. The study was approved by the Institutional Review Board (IRB) at the university where the study was conducted. At the beginning of the data collection process, participants were informed of the purpose of the research and the expected time to take the survey. They were also informed that their participation in this survey was completely anonymous and voluntary. The sample of this study consists of 53.6% female, 64.9% Caucasian/White, and 82.1% U.S. citizens. The demographics of enrolled graduate students at the university under study in spring 2021 are presented in Table 15.1.[1]

Table 15.1

Demographic of Graduate Students in Spring 2021 at the University Under Study

	Total (N = 6,273)	
Gender	*N*	%
Female	3,361	53.6%
Male	2,912	46.4%
Ethnicity		
Asian	171	2.7%
Black or African American	499	8.0%
Caucasian or White	4,070	64.9%
Hispanic	250	4.0%
Nonresident Alien	1,123	17.9%
Others	160	2.6%

Instrumentations

The survey we administered was comprised of a demographic information section, the Perceived Stress Scale (PSS-14; Cohen et al., 1983), and one subscale of the Extended Satisfaction with Life Scale (ESWLS, Alfonso et al., 1996).

Perceived Stress Scale

The Perceived Stress Scale (PSS-14) measures the degree to which situations in one's life are perceived as stressful (Cohen, 1988; Cohen et al., 1983). It includes 14 items, with seven negative and seven positive items rated on a 5-point Likert scale. While the PSS was originally designed to test perceived stress levels, extensive research confirmed that a two-factor structure measuring perceived self-efficacy and perceived helplessness was more dominant than a one-factor structure for the PSS-14 (e.g., Safaei & Shokri, 2014). Ample research using the PSS-14 has demonstrated satisfactory internal consistency reliability (e.g., Andreou et al., 2011). Higher scores on seven negative items indicate a stronger feeling of stress, while the other seven positive items indicate higher levels of self-efficacy for higher scores.

Extended Satisfaction With Life Scale

The Extended Satisfaction with Life Scale (ESWLS) is a 50-item self-report scale that measures life satisfaction in nine domains (Alfonso et al., 1996). This study used one of its nine subscales measuring life satisfaction to measure graduate student life satisfaction. Each subscale consists of five Likert scale items, ranging from 1 (strongly disagree) to 7 (strongly agree), with higher scores indicating higher satisfaction levels. The ESWLS scale has an internal consistency that ranges from .81 to .96 and two-week test-retest reliability that ranges from .74 to .87 (Alfonso et al., 1996).

Data Analysis

IBM SPSS Statistics 28.0 was used to analyze the data. We conducted a series of factorial ANOVAs to test the main effects and interaction effects of (1) parental status and gender on graduate students and (2) minority status and gender on graduate student parents. The alpha significance level was set a priori at $p < .0167$, applying a Bonferroni correction to account for multiple tests being conducted within the same family of tests. Assumptions were tested and met for each test that was conducted.

RESULTS

A total number of 543 students participated and completed the survey. Among the participants, 133 were student parents (24.5%), and 410 were non-parents (75.5%). Regarding gender, 340 were female (62.6%), and 199 were male participants (36.7%). Four participants did not identify their gender or identified themselves as others (0.7%) and were removed from the analysis. In terms of ethnicity, 86 were Asian (15.8%), 49 were African American/Black (9.0%), 357 were Caucasian/White (65.8%), and 51 identified themselves as others (17.1%). 46.6% of student parents were between the ages of 35 and 44, while 52.7% of non-parents were between the ages of 25 and 34. Table 15.2 presents a breakdown of the characteristics of the participants divided into two categories: parents and non-parents.

Reliability

The instrument measuring perceived helplessness consists of seven items. Cronbach's alpha for perceived helplessness was .849. The instrument

Table 15.2

Demographic Information of Participants by Parental Status

Demographic	Category	Parents (n = 133)	Non-Parents (n = 410)	Total (n = 543)
Gender	Female	80 (60.2%)	260 (63.4%)	340 (62.6%)
	Male	53(39.8%)	146 (35.6%)	199 (36.7%)
	Other		4 (1.0%)	4 (0.7%)
Race/ Ethnicity	Asian	20 (15.0%)	66 (16.1%)	86 (15.8%)
	Black/African American	14 (10.5%)	35 (8.5%)	49 (9.0%)
	White/Caucasian	90 (67.7%)	267 (65.1%)	357 (65.8%)
	Other	9 (6.8%)	42 (10.3%)	51 (9.4%)
Age	18–24	1 (0.8%)	135 (32.9%)	136 (25%)
	25–34	38 (28.6%)	216 (52.7%)	254 (46.8%)
	35–44	62 (46.6%)	27 (6.6%)	89 (16.4%)
	45–54	31 (23.3%)	17 (4.1%)	48 (8.8%)
	55–64	1 (0.8%)	11 (2.7%)	12 (2.2%)
	65+		4 (1.0%)	4 (0.7%)

measuring self-efficacy comprises seven items, with Cronbach's alpha value of .854. Lastly, the instrument for measuring general life satisfaction consists of five items, with Cronbach's alpha value of .925. See Table 15.3 for reliability coefficients.

Table 15.3

Reliability of the Perceived Helplessness, Self-Efficacy, and Life Satisfaction

Variables	Number of Items	Cronbach's α
Perceived Helplessness	7	.849
Self-Efficacy	7	.854
Life Satisfaction	5	.925

Influence of Parental Status and Gender on Graduate Students' Perceived Helplessness, Self-Efficacy, and Life Satisfaction

The first research question explored the extent to which parental status and gender influenced graduate students' perceived helplessness, self-efficacy, and life satisfaction. Descriptive statistics are displayed in Table 15.4.

Table 15.4

Descriptive Statistics of Perceived Helplessness, Self-Efficacy, and Life Satisfaction by Parental Status and Gender

Variables	Parental Status	Gender	*n*	*M*	*SD*
Perceived Helplessness	Parent	Female	80	2.56	.69
		Male	53	1.86	.77
	Non-Parents	Female	260	2.63	.66
		Male	146	2.30	.70
Self-Efficacy	Parent	Female	80	2.36	.60
		Male	53	2.79	.69
	Non-Parents	Female	260	2.24	.60
		Male	146	2.38	.64
Life Satisfaction	Parent	Female	80	5.11	1.44
		Male	53	5.55	1.08
	Non-Parents	Female	260	4.79	1.32
		Male	146	4.76	1.40

According to the descriptive statistics, male student parents showed the lowest levels of perceived helplessness ($M = 1.86$, $SD = .77$), highest levels of self-efficacy ($M = 2.79$, $SD = .69$), and highest levels of life satisfaction ($M = 5.55$, $SD = 1.08$) than other groups. Female non-parents showed the highest levels of perceived helplessness ($M = 2.63$, $SD = .66$) and the lowest levels of self-efficacy ($M = 2.24$, $SD = .60$). Both female ($M = 4.79$, $SD = 1.32$) and male non-parents ($M = 4.76$, $SD = 1.40$) showed lower levels of life satisfaction than female ($M = 5.11$, $SD = 1.44$) and male parents ($M = 5.55$, $SD = 1.08$). See Figure 15.1 for a visual depiction of these findings.

Figure 15.1

The Levels of Helplessness, Self-Efficacy, and Life Satisfaction by Parental Status and Gender

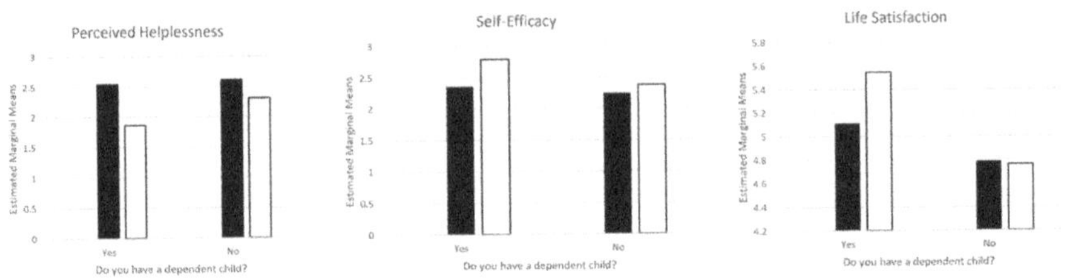

Note. Black bars = female; White bars = male.

All three dependent variables showed statistically significant correlations, as shown in Table 15.5.

Table 15.5

A Correlation Matrix of Perceived Helplessness, Self-Efficacy and Life Satisfaction

	Self-Efficacy	Life Satisfaction
Perceived Helplessness	–.655**	–.353**
Self-Efficacy		.582**

Note. **Correlation is significant at .01 level (2-tailed).

Perceived Helplessness

A factorial ANOVA was conducted to compare the main effects of parental status and gender as well as their interaction effects on perceived helplessness. The main effect of parental status and gender were statistically significant at $p < .001$. The main effect of parental status yielded a small effect size, indicating that 2.4% of the variance in perceived helplessness was accounted for by the parental status ($F(1, 535) = 13.002, p < .001, \eta^2 = .024$). The main effect of gender yielded a medium effect size, indicating that 8.9% of the variance in perceived helplessness was accounted for by gender ($F(1, 535) = 52.500, p < .001, \eta^2 = .089$). The interaction effect of parental status and gender was significant and yielded a small effect size ($F(1, 535) = 6.935, p = .009, \eta^2 = .013$). The result showed that the levels of perceived helplessness were significantly different based on students' parental status and gender. Males, in general, showed lower levels of perceived helplessness (M = 2.19, SD = .74) compared to females in graduate school (M = 2.61, SD = .67). Male and female graduate students, however, were significantly different based on their parental status. Male student parents showed significantly lower levels of perceived helplessness (M = 1.86, SD = .77) than female student parents (M = 2.56, SD = .68). Similarly, male non-parents showed significantly lower levels of perceived helplessness (M = 2.30, SD = .70) than female non-parents (M = 2.63, SD = .66).

Self-Efficacy

Main effects for parental status and gender were both found to be statistically significant. The main effect for parental status yielded a small effect size, indicating that 3.1% of the variance in self-efficacy was accounted for by parental status ($F(1, 535) = 17.254, p < .001, \eta^2 = .031$). The main effect of gender also yielded a small effect size, indicating that 3.5% of the variance in self-efficacy was explained by gender ($F(1, 535) = 19.656, p < .001, \eta^2 = .035$). The interaction effect of gender and parental status was not significant, indicating that there was no combined effect of parental status and gender on self-efficacy ($F(1, 535) = 5.498, p = .019, \eta^2 = .010$). The results indicated that the levels of self-efficacy were significantly different by students' parental status and gender. Student parents, in general, showed higher levels of self-efficacy (M = 2.53, SD = .66) than non-parents (M = 2.29, SD = .62). However, both student parents and non-parents were affected by gender, with males in each group showed significantly higher levels of self-efficacy than their female peers. Specifically, male student parents showed significantly higher levels of self-efficacy (M = 2.79, SD = .67) than female student parents (M = 2.36, SD = .60). Similarly, male non-parents (M = 2.38, SD = .64) showed significantly higher levels of self-efficacy than female non-parents (M = 2.24, SD = .60).

Life Satisfaction

The main effect of parental status yielded a small effect size, indicating that 3% of the variance in life satisfaction accounted for parental status ($F(1, 535) = 16.264, p < .001, \eta^2 = .030$). The main effect of gender was not significant ($F(1, 535) = 2.168, p = .142, \eta^2 = .004$). The interaction effect of gender and parental status was also insignificant ($F(1, 535) = 2.806, p = .094, \eta^2 = .005$). This result indicated that student parents had higher levels of life satisfaction (M = 5.29, SD = 1.32) than non-parents (M = 4.78, SD = 1.36), regardless of gender.

Influence of Minority Status and Gender on Graduate Student Parents' Perceived Helplessness, Self-Efficacy, and Life Satisfaction

The second research question looked exclusively at participants who were graduate student parents and sought to understand the extent to which perceived helplessness, self-efficacy, and life satisfaction were influenced by race/ethnicity and gender. Descriptive statistics by minority status and gender are shown in Table 15.6. Minority status was categorized by racial/ethnic background. As the study was conducted at one of the predominantly White institutions in the U.S., where the percentage of White/Caucasian students is over 60%, White/Caucasian students were categorized as dominant, and all the other students (i.e., Black/African Americans, Asians, Hispanics, and others) were categorized as racial minorities for these analyses.

Table 15.6

Descriptive Statistics of Perceived Helplessness, Self-Efficacy, and Life Satisfaction by Minority Status and Gender

Variables	Minority Status	Gender	*n*	*M*	*SD*
Perceived Helplessness	Dominant	Female	54	2.52	.68
		Male	36	1.75	.80
	Minority	Female	26	2.65	.67
		Male	17	2.11	.67
Self-Efficacy	Dominant	Female	54	2.36	.63
		Male	36	2.90	.67
	Minority	Female	26	2.36	.55
		Male	17	2.55	.62
Life Satisfaction	Dominant	Female	54	5.21	1.33
		Male	36	5.83	.99
	Minority	Female	26	4.90	1.64
		Male	17	4.95	1.05

According to the descriptive statistics, minority female student parents showed the highest levels of perceived helplessness (M = 2.65, SD = .67), lowest levels of self-efficacy (M = 2.36, SD = .55), and lowest levels of life satisfaction (M = 4.90, SD = 1.64). On the other hand, Dominant male student parents showed the lowest levels of perceived helplessness (M = 1.75, SD = .80), highest levels of self-efficacy (M = 2.90, SD = .67), and highest levels of life satisfaction (M = 5.83, SD = .99). See Figure 15.2 for a visual depiction of these findings.

Figure 15.2

The Levels of Perceived Helplessness, Self-Efficacy, and Life Satisfaction by Minority Status and Gender

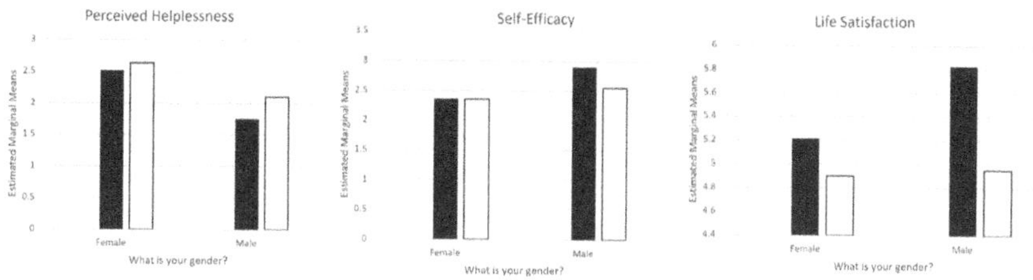

Note. Dominant shown as black, minority shown as white.

A correlation matrix of three dependent variables is shown in Table 15.7. All three dependent variables showed statistically significant correlations.

Table 15.7

Correlation Matrix of Perceived Helplessness, Self-Efficacy, and Life Satisfaction of Graduate Student Parents

	Self-Efficacy	Life Satisfaction
Perceived Helplessness	–.753**	–.502**
Self-Efficacy		.669**

Note. **Correlation is significant at .01 level (2-tailed).

Perceived Helplessness

The main effects of gender, minority status, and their interaction effect on perceived helplessness were examined by conducting a factorial ANOVA. The result of the analysis showed that the main effect of gender was significant at $p < .001$, with a large effect size ($F(1, 129) = 23.235$, $p < .001$, $\eta^2 = .153$). This indicates that 15.3% of the variance in perceived helplessness was explained by gender. The main effect of the minority status was not significant ($F(1, 129) = 3.144$, $p = .079$, $\eta^2 = .024$). The interaction effect was also not significant ($F(1, 129) = .835$, $p = .363$, $\eta^2 = .006$), indicating that there was no combined effect of gender and minority status on helplessness. The result showed that female student parents had significantly higher levels of perceived helplessness (M = 2.56, SD = .68) than male student parents (M = 1.86, SD = .77).

Self-Efficacy

The result of the analysis showed that the main effect of gender was statistically significant at p = .002, yielding a medium effect size (F(1, 129) = 9.715, p = .002, η^2 = .070), which indicates that 7.0% of the variance in self-efficacy was accounted for gender. The main effect of minority status (F(1, 129) = 2.167, p = .143, η^2 = .017) and the interaction effect of minority status and gender were not significant (F(1, 129) = 2.102, p = .150, η^2 = .016). This result indicated that the female student parents had significantly lower levels of self-efficacy (M = 2.36, SD = .60) compared to male student parents (M = 2.78, SD = .67).

Life Satisfaction

The result of the analysis showed the main effect of minority status was statistically significant, yielding a small effect size (F(1, 129) = 5.958, p = .016, η^2 = .044), which indicates that 4.4% of the variance in life satisfaction was explained by the minority status. The main effect of gender (F(1, 129) = 1.867, p = .174, η^2 = .014) and the interaction effect were not significant (F(1, 129) = 1. 320, p = .253, η^2 = .010). This result showed that dominant student parents had significantly higher levels of life satisfaction (M = 5.46, SD = 1.24) than minority student parents (M = 4.92, SD = 1.42), regardless of gender.

DISCUSSION

The findings of this study demonstrate that significant differences exist between student parents and non-parents in terms of their mental health during COVID-19. Overall, student parents showed positive mental health by reporting higher levels of self-efficacy and life satisfaction while reporting lower levels of perceived helplessness than childless peers. This result is in alignment with the role accumulation theory, suggesting that engaging in multiple roles can mutually enhance each other rather than conflict with each other (Sieber, 1984). Student parents may have developed a positive self-image of themselves by being inspiring role models for their children and effectively managing multiple roles, which may have positively influenced their mental health (Dillon, 2012; Kreischer, 2017; Moreau & Kerner, 2015; Wolf-Wendel & Ward, 2006). For example, several participants in Wolf-Wendel and Ward's (2006) study shared positive feelings about themselves as they were becoming more strategic in time management and organization (Wolf-Wendel & Ward, 2006). Consistent with Corrente's (2022) study, the graduate student parents who participated in this study demonstrated higher levels of self-efficacy than those who did not have children. Participants in this study may have developed strategies to balance multiple roles and have built confidence and belief in their abilities, which may have positively influenced their sense of well-being.

Another reason that may have contributed to the result of this study derives from the fact the majority of graduate student parents are composed of nontraditional learners who are over 25 years old and have dependent children. The literature on nontraditional learners consistently reports their unique motivation in learning, which is highly associated with mental health, that nontraditional learners may return to school with higher levels of intrinsic motivation and mastery approach to the subject matter than extrinsic motivation or grade-driven performance approach (McCollum & Kajs, 2007; Yoo & Marshall, 2022). Although the participants' motivation in academic studies was not specifically examined in this study, these nontraditional students may demonstrate a different motivation spectrum than their childless peers, which may have positively influenced their mental health during the pandemic.

The positive mental health among student parents in this study may be partially due to the psychological support that they received from their family during COVID-19. Several studies identified the positive role of psychological support on students' mental health during the pandemic (e.g., Gopalan et al., 2022). For instance, in their study of mental health during COVID-19, van den Berg et al. (2021) found that familial support was related to a decrease in stress and depressive symptoms. Similarly, Cao et al. (2020) found that students who received greater levels of psychological support during the pandemic reported lower levels of anxiety. A more focused study on underrepresented graduate students during COVID-19 found the positive role of familial support in students' persistence and motivation in pursuing their degrees (Walsh et al., 2021). These studies suggest that psychological support from family members benefits mental health, especially during stressful times. The literature prior to COVID-19 also suggests the beneficial influence of familial support (Webber & Dismore, 2020). Parenting in academia is often referred to as a "silver lining" (Mollet & Wolf-Wendel, 2022, p. 61), suggesting that academic parents experience both negatives and positives from their parenting role. During the stressful period, student parents may have been able to find positive aspects of being a parent, spend more time with their children, and appreciate the small things in life. The results of this study also imply that students without children or families near them may have felt more isolated during the pandemic compared to students with children.

We also identified a significant gender gap in each group. Female parents reported higher levels of perceived helplessness and lower levels of self-efficacy than male parents. This result is in accordance with the literature that highlighted the exacerbated challenges among mothers during COVID-19 (e.g., Gabster et al., 2020). Mothers may have experienced greater childcare responsibilities and thus were more vulnerable to unexpected situations. This gender gap was also evident in non-parent groups, as female non-parents reported significantly higher levels of perceived helplessness and lower levels of self-efficacy, suggesting a widening gender gap during COVID-19 (e.g., United Nations, 2020).

Race/ethnicity differences were identified in the levels of satisfaction. Although the effect size was small, we found evidence that student parents who were White/Caucasian showed significantly higher levels of life satisfaction than student parents of color, partially supporting the literature on racial/ethnic inequalities during the pandemic (e.g., Douglas et al., 2022). While race/ethnicity differences were not evident in the levels of perceived helplessness and self-efficacy, this result may have been derived from the number of student parents in our sample. While the overall number of participants in this study, including both parents and non-parents, was 543, the number of student parents was only 133 (24.5%). Due to the small number of participants, the analysis may not have yielded a significant result to detect the differences among the groups. As the descriptive statistics showed meaningful differences based on the minority status, a future study with a larger sample of student parents might generate a significant result.

IMPLICATIONS

Graduate student parents are often neglected as a research population, and studies exclusively focusing on this group are rare. In light of the unique struggles and challenges that they experience in pursuing their educational goals, developing a better understanding of the experiences of student parents in graduate school is important for developing policies and resources to support student parents' success. Placing an emphasis on creating a family-friendly environment throughout university campuses would help to attract competent graduate students. Therefore, universities and colleges must consider how to accommodate those who want to combine work and family throughout their study.

The findings of this study suggest important implications for institutions in higher education, professors, instructors, and policymakers to provide adequate and strategic support to assist graduate students' mental health based on their parental status and gender. Graduate students without children or family may feel more remote during the pandemic; hence it is imperative to develop a way to provide emotional and social support to those students who feel isolated and disconnected. Mental health services on campus should be available and approachable so that students make use of these resources when needed.

CONCLUSION

The purpose of this study was to examine how graduate students were impacted by COVID-19 and to investigate potential differences between parental, gender, and minority status. Based on two theoretical frameworks: (1) role strain theory and (2) role accumulation theory, we analyzed quantitative data collected from 543 graduate students in a 4-year institution in the Southeastern U.S. The findings of the current study offered support for role accumulation theory and showed results that differ from previous research in several areas. Contrary to the expectation suggested by role strain theory that student parents would demonstrate poorer mental health than their counterparts, student parents in this study, in fact, reported lower levels of perceived helplessness and higher levels of self-efficacy and life satisfaction than students without children. This result suggests that parenting may provide a beneficial influence on graduate students' mental health. During the quarantine, parents may have developed more robust relationships with their children, built increased resilience, and felt confident in multitasking. Despite the reduced productivity and anxiety from their academic roles, the stressful time may be buffered by the emotional support they gain from their parenting role.

In terms of gender disparities in academia, we found a gender gap in both student parents and non-parents. While parents may have received a positive impact from their family, this was more prominent in men than women. This result may have stemmed from the fact that women are more likely to assume more childcare responsibilities than men traditionally. In terms of the non-parent group, female graduate students also reported poorer mental health compared to their male peers. This partially supports gender inequity in higher education, which warrants gender-balanced approaches and policies.

This study was conducted in a single Southeastern research institution where the majority of students are White/Caucasian. As such, the results of this study may not be representative of all graduate students in the U.S or from other countries or cultures. Another limitation of this study is that potentially influential variables that might have affected the mental health, such as the number of children and the age of the youngest child, were not examined due to the uneven proportions of the specific groups. The department environment and the relationship graduate students had with their advisors during this time could also be influential on one's mental health. Future studies should consider including these potentially influential variables to more fully understand the experiences of graduate students.

REFERENCES

Adams-Prassl, A., Boneva, T., Golin, M., & Rauh, C. (2020). Inequality in the impact of the coronavirus shock: Evidence from real time surveys. *Journal of Public Economics, 189*, 104245.

Alfonso, V. C., Allison, D. B., Rader, D. E., & Gorman, B. S. (1996). The extended satisfaction with life scale: Development and psychometric properties. *Social Indicators Research, 38*(3), 275–301.

Andreou, E., Alexopoulos, E. C., Lionis, C., Varvogli, L., Gnardellis, C., Chrousos, G. P., & Darviri, C. (2011). Perceived stress scale: Reliability and validity study in Greece. *International Journal of Environmental Research and Public Health, 8*(8), 3287–3298.

Bal, I. A., Arslan, O., Budhrani, K., Mao, Z., Novak, K., & Muljana, P. S. (2020). The balance of roles: Graduate student perspectives during the COVID-19 pandemic. *TechTrends, 64*(6), 796–798. https://doi.org/10.1007/s11528-020-00534-z

Barnett, R. C. (2014). Role theory. In A. C. Michalos (Ed.), *Encyclopedia of quality of life and well-being research* (pp. 5591–5593). Springer. https://doi.org/10.1007/978-94-007-0753-5_2535

Behboodi Moghadam, Z., Ordibeheshti Khiaban, M., Esmaeili, M., & Salsali, M. (2017). Motherhood challenges and well-being along with the studentship role among Iranian women: A qualitative study. *International Journal of Qualitative Studies on Health and Well-Being, 12*(1), 1335168.

Biddle, B. J. (2013). *Role theory: Expectations, identities, and behaviors*. Academic press.

Bourne, R. A. (2021). *Economics in one virus: An introduction to economic reasoning through COVID-19*. Cato Institute.

Brown, R. L. (2007). College females as mothers: Balancing the roles of student and motherhood. *ABNF Journal, 18*(1), 25.

Calarco, J. M., Meanwell, E., Anderson, E. M., & Knopf, A. S. (2021). By default: How mothers in different-sex dual-earner couples account for inequalities in pandemic parenting. *Socius*, 7. https://doi.org/10.1177/23780231211038783

Cao, W., Fang, Z., Hou, G., Han, M., Xu, X., Dong, J., & Zheng, J. (2020). The psychological impact of the COVID-19 epidemic on college students in China. *Psychiatry Research, 287*, 112934. https://doi.org/10.1016/j.psychres.2020.112934

Carli, L. L. (2020). Women, Gender equality and COVID-19. *Gender in Management: An International Journal, 35*(7/8), 647–655. https://doi.org/10.1108/GM-07-2020-0236

Carpenter, D., & Dunn, J. (2020). We're all teachers now: Remote learning during COVID-19. *Journal of School Choice, 14*(4), 567–594. https://doi.org/10.1080/15582159.2020.1822727

Chesser, S. (2015). Intersection of family, work and leisure during academic training. *Annals of Leisure Research, 18*(3), 308–322.

Chrikov, I., Soria, K. M., Horgos, B., & Jones-White, D. (2020). *Undergraduate and graduate students' mental health during the COVID-19 pandemic* [Report]. SERU Consortium, University of California—Berkeley and University of Minnesota. http://conservancy.umn.edu/handle/11299/215271

Coe, A. (2013, January 17). *Being married helps professors get ahead, but only if they're male*. The Atlantic. https://www.theatlantic.com/sexes/archive/2013/01/being-married-helps-professors-get-ahead-but-only-if-theyre-male/267289/

Cohen, S. (1988). *Perceived stress in a probability sample of the United States.*

Cohen, S., Kamarck, T., & Mermelstein, R. (1983). A global measure of perceived stress. *Journal of Health and Social Behavior*, 385–396.

Corrente, M. (2022). Exploring the personal and professional realities of parenthood and graduate studies. *Alberta Journal of Educational Research, 68*(3), 340–356.

Davis, J. C., Li, E. P. H., Butterfield, M. S., DiLabio, G. A., Santhagunam, N., & Marcolin, B. (2022). Are we failing female and racialized academics? A Canadian national survey examining the impacts of the COVID-19 pandemic on tenure and tenure-track faculty. *Gender, Work, and Organization, 29*(3), 703–722. https://doi.org/10.1111/gwao.12811

Dillon, P. J. (2012). Unbalanced: An autoethnography of fatherhood in academe. *Journal of Family Communication, 12*(4), 284–299.

Dolson, J. M., & Deemer, E. D. (2020). The relationship between perceived discrimination and school/work–family conflict among graduate student-parents. *Journal of Career Development*. https://doi.org/10.1177/08948453209162

Douglas, H. M., Settles, I. H., Cech, E. A., Montgomery, G. M., Nadolsky, L. R., Hawkins, A. K., Ma, G., Davis, T. M., Elliott, K. C., & Cheruvelil, K. S. (2022). Disproportionate impacts of COVID-19 on marginalized and minoritized early-career academic scientists. *PLOS ONE, 17*(9). https://doi.org/10.1371/journal.pone.0274278

Doyle, J. M., Morone, N. E., Proulx, C. N., Althouse, A. D., Rubio, D. M., Thakar, M. S., Murrell, A. J., & White, G. E. (2021). The impact of the COVID-19 pandemic on underrepresented early-career PhD and physician scientists. *Journal of Clinical and Translational Science, 5*(1), e174. https://doi.org/10.1017/cts.2021.851

Ellinas, E. H., Ark, T. K., Kaljo, K., Quinn, K. G., Krier, C. R., & Farkas, A. H. (2022). Winners and losers in academic productivity during the COVID-19 pandemic: Is the gender gap widening for faculty? *Journal of Women's Health (2002), 31*(4), 487–494. https://doi.org/10.1089/jwh.2021.0321

Elliott, M. (2003). Work and family role strain among university employees. *Journal of Family and Economic Issues*, *24*(2), 157–181. https://doi.org/10.1023/A:1023614907886

Etheridge, B., & Spantig, L. (2020). The gender gap in mental well-being during the Covid-19 outbreak: Evidence from the UK. *ISER Working Paper Series*, Article 2020–08. https://ideas.repec.org//p/ese/iserwp/2020-08.html

Gabster, B. P., Daalen, K. van, Dhatt, R., & Barry, M. (2020). Challenges for the female academic during the COVID-19 pandemic. *The Lancet*, *395*(10242), 1968–1970. https://doi.org/10.1016/S0140-6736(20)31412-4

Goode, W. J. (1960). A theory of role strain. *American Sociological Review*, *25*(4), 483–496. https://doi.org/10.2307/2092933

Gopalan, M., Linden-Carmichael, A., & Lanza, S. (2022). College students' sense of belonging and mental health amidst the COVID-19 pandemic. *Journal of Adolescent Health*, *70*(2), 228-233. https://doi.org/10.1016/j.jadohealth.2021.10.010.

Grady, R. K., La Touche, R., Oslawski-Lopez, J., Powers, A., & Simacek, K. (2014). Betwixt and between: The social position and stress experiences of graduate students. *Teaching Sociology*, *42*(1), 5–16. https://doi.org/10.1177/0092055X13502182

Hicks, A. (2021). When the leaky pipeline erodes: Female graduate student parents and the ramifications of the pandemic. *Integrated Environmental Assessment & Management*, *17*(4), 667–668. https://doi.org/10.1002/ieam.4423

John, J. J., John, E. S., Pioppo, L., Gupta, A., Chokhavatia, S., & Tilara, A. (2022). Gender disparity in academic gastroenterology: Beginning of the end of the underrepresentation of women? *Digestive Diseases and Sciences*, *67*(2), 380–387. https://doi.org/10.1007/s10620-020-06692-7

Kee, C. E. (2021). The impact of COVID-19: Graduate students' emotional and psychological experiences. *Journal of Human Behavior in the Social Environment*, *31*(1–4), 476–488. https://doi.org/10.1080/10911359.2020.1855285

Kreischer, A. (2017). *Parents enrolled in graduate programs and their experiences with faculty* (Publication No. 10270532) [Doctoral dissertation, Iowa State University]. ProQuest. https://lib.dr.iastate.edu/etd/15341/

Krukowski, R. A., Jagsi, R., & Cardel, M. I. (2021). Academic productivity differences by gender and child age in science, technology, engineering, mathematics, and medicine faculty during the COVID-19 pandemic. *Journal of Women's Health*, *30*(3), 341–347. https://doi.org/10.1089/jwh.2020.8710

Kulp, A. M. (2020). Parenting on the path to the professoriate: A focus on graduate student mothers. *Research in Higher Education*, *61*(3), 408–429.

Lisnic, R., Zajicek, A., & Kerr, B. (2019). Work-family balance and tenure reasonableness: Gender differences in faculty assessment. *Sociological Spectrum*, *39*(5), 340–358. https://doi.org/10.1080/02732173.2019.1691097

Lynch, K. D. (2008). Gender roles and the American academe: A case study of graduate student mothers. *Gender and Education*, *20*(6), 585–605.

Marshall, D. T. (2022). *COVID-19 and the classroom: How schools navigated the great disruption*. Lexington Books.

McCollum, D. L., & Kajs, L. T. (2007). Applying goal orientation theory in an exploration of student motivations in the domain of educational leadership. *Educational Research Quarterly, 31*(1), 45–59.

McFarland, J., Hussar, B., De Brey, C., Snyder, T., Wang, X., Wilkinson-Flicker, S., Gebrekristos, S., Zhang, J., Rathbun, A., & Barmer, A. (2017). *The condition of education 2017*. NCES 2017-144. National Center for Education Statistics.

Moen, P., Robison, J., & Dempster-McClain, D. (1995). Caregiving and women's well-being: A life course approach. *Journal of Health and Social Behavior, 36*(3), 259–273.

Mollet, A. L., & Wolf-Wendel, L. E. (2022). "I don't know how they think this is possible": Work-life of academic parents during the COVID-19 pandemic. *New Directions for Higher Education, 2022*(199), 57–72. https://doi.org/10.1002/he.20455

Moreau, M.-P., & Kerner, C. (2015). Care in academia: An exploration of student parents' experiences. *British Journal of Sociology of Education, 36*(2), 215–233.

Mullen, J., Kelley, E., & Kelloway, E. K. (2008). CHAPTER 11—Health and well-being outcomes of the work-family interface. In K. Korabik, D. S. Lero, & D. L. Whitehead (Eds.), *Handbook of work-family integration* (pp. 191–214). Academic Press. https://doi.org/10.1016/B978-012372574-5.50014-4

Safaei, M., & Shokri, O. (2014). Assessing stress in cancer patients: Factorial validity of the perceived stress scale in Iran. *Psychiatric Nurs.* 2, 13–22.

Sieber, S. D. (1974). Toward a theory of role accumulation. *American Sociological Review, 39*(4), 567–578. https://doi.org/10.2307/2094422

Spies-Upton, S., & Hill, M. (2021, July 1). *Perspectives on parenting as a graduate student amid the pandemic* [The Gavel]. https://www.Apadivisions.Org. https://www.apadivisions.org/division-18/publications/newsletters/gavel/2021/07/parenting-as-grad-student

Springer, K. W., Parker, B. K., & Leviten-Reid, C. (2009). Making space for graduate student parents: Practice and politics. *Journal of Family Issues, 30*(4), 435–457.

Trussell, D. E. (2015). Pinstripes and breast pumps: Navigating the tenure-motherhood-track. *Leisure Sciences, 37*(2), 160–175.

van den Berg, Y. H., Burk, W. J., Cillessen, A. H., & Roelofs, K. (2021). Emerging adults' mental health during the COVID-19 pandemic: A prospective longitudinal study on the importance of social support. *Emerging Adulthood, 9*(5), 618–630.

Walsh, B. A., Woodliff, T. A., Lucero, J., Harvey, S., Burnham, M. M., Bowser, T. L., Aguirre, M., & Zeh, D. W. (2021). Historically underrepresented graduate students' experiences during the COVID-19 pandemic. *Family Relations, 70*(4), 955–972. https://doi.org/10.1111/fare.12574

Webber, L., & Dismore, H. (2020). Mothers and higher education: Balancing time, study and space. *Journal of Further and Higher Education, 45*(3), 1–15. https://doi.org/10.1080/0309877X.2020.1820458

Witteman, H. O., Haverfield, J., & Tannenbaum, C. (2021). COVID-19 gender policy changes support female scientists and improve research quality. *Proceedings of the National Academy of Sciences, 118*(6), e2023476118.

Wolf-Wendel, L. E., & Ward, K. (2006). Academic life and motherhood: Variations by institutional type. *Higher Education, 52*(3), 487–521.

Wolf-Wendel, L., & Ward, K. (2015). Academic mothers: Exploring disciplinary perspectives. *Innovative Higher Education, 40*(1), 19–35.

Wright, M. C., Assar, N., Kain, E. L., Kramer, L., Howery, C. B., McKinney, K., Glass, B., & Atkinson, M. (2004). Greedy institutions: The importance of institutional context for teaching in higher education. *Teaching Sociology, 32*(2), 144–159.

United Nations. (2020). *The world's women 2020: Trends and statistics.* Department of Economic and Social Affairs. https://worlds-women-2020-data-undesa.hub.arcgis.com/

Yoo, H. J., & Marshall, D. T. (2024). Understanding graduate student parents: Influence of parental status, gender, and major on graduate students' motivation, stress, and satisfaction. *Journal of College Student Retention, 26*(1), 259–282. https://doi.org/10.1177/15210251211072241

Yoo, H. J., & Marshall, D. T. (2022). Examining the relationship between motivation, stress, and satisfaction among graduate students. *Journal of Further and Higher Education, 46*(3), 409–426. https://doi.org/10.1080/0309877X.2021.1962518

ENDNOTE

1. As the demographic information of enrolled graduate students followed the U.S. Department of Education guidelines, the racial/ethnic composition of nonresident aliens is not specified. In addition, the institution under study did not provide students' parental and non-parental status.

CHAPTER 16

WALKING THE FINE LINE

First-Year Doctoral Students' Experiences During COVID-19

Deja' L. Trammell
Auburn University

Emma Quadlander-Goff
Troy University

Natalie M. Schoettler
Auburn University

Kamia F. Slaughter
Auburn University

Jessi Riel
Auburn University

Danielle L. Hudson
Auburn University

ABSTRACT

Doctoral students entering graduate programs in the midst of COVID-19 encountered several struggles with socialization, psychological well-being,

Examining the Cognitive and Psychological Effects of the COVID-19 Global Pandemic on High School, College, and Graduate Learners, pp. 367–389

and academic progress. Prior literature demonstrates the challenges that doctoral students faced prior to the pandemic; however, the nature of uncertainty during the pandemic resulted in several unforeseen circumstances. The present study utilized a collaborative autoethnography to illuminate the narratives of six doctoral students as they entered doctoral programs at the height of the COVID-19 pandemic. The researchers of the present study developed open-ended questions that reflected their lived experiences within their respective degree programs. The aim of the study was to gain insight into the psychological and emotional experiences of first-year doctoral students during the pandemic. After coding the six guided reflections, the following themes emerged: (1) Navigating Mental and Material Models of Normalcy, (2) Connecting Experiences to Emotions, (3) Developing Reactive and Reparative Self-Care Strategies. Other subthemes are discussed in the chapter. This study opens the door for dialogue among administrators, faculty, and staff to continue to create supportive environments that meet the needs of doctoral students as the socialization process continues to evolve after the pandemic.

INTRODUCTION

Since the onset of COVID-19 in the spring of 2020, a plethora of research has explored the impact of the pandemic on students and teachers alike (e.g., Marshall et al., 2022). However, little research exists on how graduate students were affected during this unprecedented time, specifically, first-year doctoral students who entered their programs during the pandemic. Doctoral students face a myriad of challenges navigating the academy, leading to more than half of them to drop out before the completion of their PhD program (Sverdlik et al., 2018). However, the challenges that doctoral students face have only been exacerbated by the pandemic and the corresponding shift to remote learning. For example, Sverdlik et al. (2022) found that doctoral students reported a variety of challenges, including the inability to visit friends and family, being stuck at home, issues with work-life balance, isolation, and decreased access to academic institutions. Bal and colleagues (2020) reflected on their experiences as doctoral students at different stages in their respective programs amid the sudden shift to remote learning and work. Their narratives highlighted the duality of each of their roles and responsibilities during this time (i.e., parent and doctoral student) and the difficulty of navigating these roles. Similarly, Colpitts et al. (2020) utilized an autoethnographic approach by soliciting the experiences of two doctoral students and their supervisors about blended learning, also known as "Hy-Flex" learning. The group's narratives revealed a lack of work-life balance that was reflected as a result of juggling professional and doctoral work, and personal responsibilities (i.e., family) in addition to touching on the importance of informal and formal support from cohort members and supervisory groups during this time (Colpitts et al., 2020). Studies such as these emphasize the different components that impact a doctoral student's experiences, along with additional challenges that could influence tenure. An examination of the literature regarding doctoral students' experiences with socialization, psychological and physical well-being, learning modalities, and academic achievement supports the present chapter's evaluation of the researchers' experiences of entering a PhD program amid COVID-19.

LITERATURE REVIEW

This study used literature surrounding doctoral student socialization to understand its impact on students' psychological well-being, academic achievement, and matriculation. The literature also illuminates the purpose of using an autoethnographic approach to guide this study.

Doctoral Student Socialization

Socialization is an important part of the doctoral journey for students. It creates a space for students to obtain the necessary knowledge, skills, and values to conduct research and to contribute to a scholarly community (Weidman et al., 2001). Khalil (2022) touched on the importance of socialization during their first year as doctoral students, in a new country with a new culture during the global pandemic. Khalil (2022) experienced a gamut of emotions, including anxiety, depression, and isolation that can be attributed to the lack of socialization. The mental and emotional stress played impacted their progress in the doctoral program in addition to adjusting to a different format of learning compared to their home country. Khalil conducted self-reflective work, comparing their journey to the country of students in Pakistan that follows the American format, coursework, and then a thesis. Since the format of the program was new, Khalil stated that they were not sure where to begin or how. This sense of confusion was experienced by the authors in this chapter as well. The researchers of this chapter did not have a clear blueprint for navigating the beginning steps of entering a doctoral program using a new modality of learning (i.e., virtual). One of the key factors that contributes to success in a doctoral program is building and establishing a relationship with a mentor or advisor to oversee the work of the graduate students (Weidman et al.,

2001). Interactions with mentors typically occur face-to-face; however, due to COVID-19, it was not safe. Mullen (2021) conducted a research study to see how the shift to online mentoring affected the progress of proposals and dissertations during the transition to online doctoral mentoring. The findings indicated that the COVID-19 pandemic had a negative effect on the progress of proposals, dissertations, and mentoring. The mentees in the study noted that the pandemic impacted their productivity due to institutional, administrative, and household changes (Mullen, 2021). Mentees also reported a disruption in the pursuit of their degree along with the daily challenges of a K–12 crisis, shifts in workplace leadership styles, and having their defenses conducted fully online with their mentor at a distance while navigating virtual communications with committee members (Mullen, 2021). Doctoral students reported that the interventive measures taken by mentors were effective and increased overall satisfaction with the online mentoring process even though there were challenges during the process (Mullen, 2021). As documented by the literature, socialization can greatly influence a doctoral student's experience in graduate programs.

Academic mentorship can impact a doctoral student's progress with regards to research, in turn, influencing a student's ability to progress in their program. Wang and DeLaquil (2020) mentioned that mentorship is a critical component of doctoral students' research opportunities, and the pandemic greatly reduced informal interactions between students and faculty. This move from on-campus to working remotely resulted in doctoral students and faculty setting formal meeting times to communicate. Although research conducted before the pandemic suggests that doctoral students reported that most of their interactions have occurred with other graduate students (Sverdlik et al., 2018), studies completed during the pandemic indicated that doctoral students have struggled with developing these social academic relationships (DeBate et al., 2021; Omar et al., 2021). Interpersonal relationships within doctoral programs are a pertinent component of success and were an additional factor that was challenging to navigate in the initial phases of the COVID-19 pandemic (Wang & DeLaquil, 2020). Moreover, a study completed by Gewalt et al. (2022) reported that "social distancing, spending most of the time at home, and e-learning via video conferences were perceived as considerable stressors for students" (p. 20). In a similar but slightly different vein, doctoral student communication via online platforms indicated a strong relationship with students' skills in academia (Omar et al., 2021). Connections and engagement between students and faculty are vital to success in graduate programs. COVID-19 impacted the availability of interactions between peers and faculty; thus, influencing the achievement and progress in graduate programs.

Impact on Psychological Well-Being

Entering a doctoral program during a pandemic can influence the mental and emotional well-being of students. Research indicates that prior to the pandemic and under normal circumstances of a doctoral program, PhD students often struggled with isolation from colleagues, friends, and family members, resulting in mental health issues (Sverdlik et al., 2018). For example, one study that assessed the mental health of doctoral students engaging in the research indicated that this population experienced increased stress and isolation from others (Hazell et al., 2020). Nevertheless, several studies have suggested that COVID-19 has impacted and or exacerbated the mental health concerns in doctoral students (Daniel et al., 2022; Kee, 2021; Wasil et al., 2021).

Research suggests that doctoral students experience heightened levels of anxiety and depression (Paucsik et al., 2022; Sideropoulos et al., 2022), as well as difficulty sleeping, increased use of alcohol and other substances, and suicidal ideations (Daniel et al., 2022). According to Wasil and colleagues (2021), graduate students in programs during COVID-19 reported major issues related to emotional health, with 55.4% being directly related to COVID-19. On the other hand, the pandemic increased rates of food insecurity in the United States to which postsecondary education students indicated issues with "psychological distress, loneliness, and suicide behavior" (DeBate et al., 2021, p. 571). The lasting effects on doctoral students' mental and emotional well-being demonstrate the need for academic institutions to integrate supportive methods into coursework to ease transitions when unprecedented events occur.

A study conducted by Hazell et al. (2020) suggested that female doctoral researchers experience higher rates of mental health issues compared to males. Moreover, women reported more disruption to their program progress, as well as higher levels of general anxiety and stress than men did (Sverdlik et al., 2022), which may be due to the multiple roles and additional responsibilities women took on in their professional and personal lives during the pandemic. Furthermore, Deryugina et al. (2021) suggests that the increased responsibilities of women could influence the time available to spend on academic endeavors in addition to fewer opportunities to practice self-care. For example, a majority of women participating in the study reported having to transition to caring for their children full-time as school systems shut down, in addition to maintaining their academic work. The psychological well-being of female doctoral students entering their first year of PhD programs during a pandemic is worth continued exploration as their roles and responsibilities were impacted by transitions from face-to-face interaction to remote learning or distance education.

A qualitative study that assessed the experiences of graduate students during COVID-19 stated that students "expressed their intentional decision to choose an academic program providing traditional face-to-face instruction" when committing to graduate programs (Kee, 2021, p. 479). Correspondingly, Sverdlik et al. (2018) noted that PhD students preferred face-to-face communication for collaboration on coursework and receiving support for the challenges of the rigorous responsibilities in a doctoral program. As a result of the pandemic, some students reported experiencing negative emotions, such as disappointment about their PhD program experiences (Kee, 2021). Furthermore, self-motivation to complete work independently is a contributing factor to success in doctoral programs (Sverdlik et al., 2018). However, likely due to the various transitions that have occurred as an outcome of the pandemic, literature documents that PhD students have been suffering from low motivation as exhibited through procrastination and avoidance of PhD responsibilities (Hazell et al., 2020). The psychological impact of the pandemic on first-year doctoral students, as documented in previous literature, demonstrates the need for understanding and insight into how academic institutions can support their students in times of uncertainty.

Academic Achievement and Program Progress

The transition from face-to-face instruction to remote learning has greatly influenced academic achievement and progress in programs for doctoral students. According to Wang and DeLaquil (2020), doctoral students often "develop aspirations and behaviors that affect their academic, career, and relationship choices in light of the opportunities, resources, and challenges that are found within and beyond our environment" (p. 1347). These aspirations align with students' academic identity, which refers to students' perceptions of themselves in academia, including self-worth and self-efficacy (Sverdlik et al., 2018). Students with low self-worth and or low self-efficacy have reported a reduction in their progress in PhD programs (Sverdlik et al., 2018). Research completed prior to the pandemic identified internal and external factors that contribute to success in PhD programs, including supervisor support, funding opportunities, motivation, and self-regulation (Sverdlik et al., 2018). Each of these factors can hinder or advance doctoral students' tenure in programs; however, COVID-19 influenced each of these factors to a varying degree. The additional responsibilities and newfound challenges that were outcomes of the pandemic caused many doctoral students to feel isolated and to struggle to stay on track with their projected program timelines. For example, Donohue et al. (2021) report that 32.3% of participants' progress as doctoral students were affected "a great deal" by the pandemic, while 29.4% reported being affected "a lot," 24.7% reported being affected "a moderate amount," and 8.9% reported being affected "a little." Only 4.7% of participants indicated that the completion of their program was unaffected by the pandemic (Donohue et al., 2021). From the literature, doctoral students' progression throughout their programs has been influenced by COVID-19.

Moreover, existing literature suggests that the pandemic affected other areas, such as food insecurity and relationships. As a result of the COVID-19 pandemic, global food production and distribution were greatly impacted (Kakaei et al., 2022) leading to 34.1% of doctoral students experiencing food insecurity (DeBate et al., 2021). Postsecondary students participating in a study assessing food insecurity reported that the pandemic led to "challenges with academics, careers, procrastination, and faculty" (DeBate et al., 2021, p. 570). Although finances are historically challenging for doctoral students (i.e., living on stipends or student loans), COVID-19 only exacerbated this aspect, resulting in increased food security.

An Autoethnographic Approach

Autoethnography is a popular approach to narrative inquiry, which focuses on a written accord drafted by the individuals of the study to which the author provides a personal story in addition to examining the cultural meaning of the story (Creswell, 2013). An autoethnographic approach allows for a multi-layered perspective that is composed of consciousness and a vulnerable and coherent self (Muncey, 2010). Colpitts et al. (2020) demonstrated that an autoethnographic approach can be useful in recording the experiences of doctoral students that have transitioned to online before and during the pandemic. This approach has proven useful in giving voice to individuals' experiences and, thus, can provide readers with insight into the narratives of doctoral students that entered their PhD programs amid a pandemic.

While being enrolled in a doctoral program during the uncertainty of a pandemic poses long-term issues on doctoral students' mental health and professional development, incoming doctoral students face additional barriers to their acclimation and socialization within their program(s), as they begin graduate programs with the intention of face-to-face interactions including coursework, mentorship, and peer engagements (Kee, 2021). There are a range of challenges that individuals face while pursuing a doctoral degree yet, the transition that occurred during COVID-19 caused additional threats to students' well-being and progress in programs. The pandemic not only influenced various areas of academic experiences for students starting and continuing their doctoral journeys but also exacerbated mental, emotional, and physical problems. An autoethnographic approach can provide further insight into the challenges of navigating academia for doctoral students during unprecedented times and provide suggestions for academic institutions to better support their doctoral students during times of hardship.

METHODS

To further explore the psychological and emotional realities of first-year incoming doctoral students during COVID-19, we utilized a collaborative autoethnographic approach (Matthews, 2021; Roy & Uekusa, 2020) to reflect on our experiences as six doctoral students who began their respective programs during the fall of 2020 at the height of COVID-19. Utilizing narrative autoethnography allows us to study ourselves in the context of the cultures we experience (Nash & Bradley, 2011) and humanizes our research instead of creating distance from our personal experiences as researchers (Bochner, 2013). Including personal narratives presents an opportunity for the researcher to be a part of the research process more iteratively and intimately, reflecting on direct experiences and emotions (Dewey, 1980). When we use narratives as a method of inquiry, we construct knowledge through the process of writing (Richardson, 1994).

To begin to reflect on our first-year experiences, we established a protocol to help guide our reflections. We held an initial meeting to discuss the experiences we recalled during our first year that held significance for us. We worked to develop and refine prompts that would speak to the mental and emotional impacts of COVID-19 and how they shaped our identity as doctoral students and researchers. Our initial reflections on the prompts included 150-word responses to develop preliminary themes surrounding our realities during COVID-19. We used monthly workshops and peer debriefing to expand upon our reflections and build a community of support that helped us work through the mental and emotional effects of COVID-19 in that first year. From our expanded 1,000-word reflections, we met for a structured peer debriefing session where we discussed our experiences during our first year as doctoral students as well as our experience engaging in this project. We recorded and transcribed our peer debriefing session creating another data point. After collecting multiple sources of data and constructing preliminary themes, four of the researchers coded three reflections each, ensuring that each expanded reflection was coded and reviewed twice. Based on our individual codebooks and peer debriefing sessions, we generated one collective codebook and further reviewed the data until we collectively agreed on and identified recurring themes and common experiences. Because of the personal experiences shared in our narratives, we decided to use pseudonyms to elaborate on the themes in our findings.

Credibility

The premise of this study seeks to understand our experiences as first-year doctoral students during COVID-19. Credibility is established through our participation in this study as experts of our own experience. The experiences accounted for in our narratives can be confirmed through our peer debriefing process and through the relationship history we bring to this study. The connection point for this research stems from the connections we made as doctoral students in our first year and have maintained over time. While our aim is to capture our unique experiences during an unprecedented time, there may be some transferability in our findings where other first-year doctoral students share similar, yet unique experiences during COVID-19.

When considering the reliability of the study and researchers' ability to replicate our findings, there are several contexts that should be accounted for (Creswell, 2013). The experiences of first-year doctoral students during COVID-19 may change depending on institution type, degree program, personal history, and background, outside responsibilities, and motivation to seek a terminal degree. Each individual brings a unique perspective and personality to their academic environment and there are many external factors that can shape how they navigate their own experience. Thus, we share our positionality and the uniqueness we bring to this study to further illuminate our findings.

Positionality

To fully understand our research and experience as incoming doctoral students during COVID-19, we must speak to the identities and experiences we bring to this study. This study involves the narratives of six women from four different disciplines: Educational Psychology, Higher Education Administration, Counselor Education, and Chemistry Education. Three of the researchers identify as Black women and three of the researchers identify as White women with ages ranging from 26 to 47. Each researcher brought their own unique experience and expertise to this research study. Two of the researchers were elementary teachers before starting their program, one researcher worked in a lab school, one researcher taught undergraduate students, one researcher transitioned into her degree right after finishing her master's, and another researcher worked as a clinical mental health counselor.

As a collective of researchers, we intentionally choose to use more personal pronouns, referring to ourselves as "we," to situate ourselves as participants and narrators of our own story while establishing collective proximity to each other through storytelling and community building. By writing our stories and sharing them, we become the narrators of the research which helps readers to interpret and understand the richness and fullness of our experience (Bochner, 1994).

FINDINGS

To better understand our own experiences as first-year doctoral students at a Southeastern R1 institution amid COVID-19, we reflected on various challenges, advantages, supports, and stressors we encountered. As a result, we organized our findings around the following themes (1) Navigating Mental and Material Models of Normalcy, (2) Connecting Experiences to Emotions, and (3) Developing Reactive and Reparative Self-Care Strategies. Each finding underscores how we were situated as students and people among our institutions and communities during the pandemic.

Navigating Mental and Material Models of Normalcy

Across the globe, COVID-19 prompted discourses around "a new normal." Public health concerns, social unrest, and the byproducts of their intersections prompted us to reconsider the standards for engaging with people, work, and everyday tasks. Broadly, the language around normalcy signified a point of departure from former ways of doing, thinking, and existing before 2020. Specifically, such conversations provided little direction for recognizing and differentiating between the old and the new. Our first finding, contextualizing normalcy, describes our experiences navigating the newness of our doctoral programs and lives as doctoral students. We had to contend with learning how to build relationships within our programs, departments, and across the institution while being confined to our respective homes for the year. The pandemic impacted the level of social support we were able to create, as some of us only interacted with faculty when we took their class. It was especially difficult to build relationships with other graduate students when the traditional programs and graduate orientation was not available.

Its core is best captured in the following sentiment that Michelle shares, "I noticed that the lack of engagement made it difficult to gauge the 'ordinary' or 'normal' experiences in coursework, professional development, research endeavors, and mentorship." Michelle spoke to the absence of in-person engagement in virtual environments, particularly it being a challenge to her doctoral student socialization. Essentially, COVID-19 impacted her and the rest of our ability to gauge the typicality of practice within our respective programs. In what follows, we discuss how we anticipated, adjusted to, and contended with normalcy amid the pandemic.

Anticipating Normalcy

For some of us, continuing our education and seeking a doctoral degree was an intentional act of resistance to change. Take Sarah, for example. She chose her institution because it functioned as a source of stability in a world that changed so effortlessly and relentlessly. She said:

> Like most of the world, I experienced lots of change during Covid. Changes with my job, living arrangement, and expectations for social gatherings greatly affected me in hindsight. I leaned on graduate school, specifically at my institution, to provide stability. It was familiar to me. I knew how the application process worked, I knew how funding and financial aid worked, I knew how to work Canvas … stuff like that. It seems basic, but I couldn't fathom learning new bureaucracies on top of new content when classes started. That would have been too much for me to handle.

For Sarah, graduate education at her institution was at home. She mentioned that she "leaned on" her graduate school, specifically positioning it as a place of comfort that supported and held her when she needed it most. Gaining two-time alumni status at her institution helped her frame the institution as familiar, ultimately impacting her choice to seek and accept admission there for a third time. In this instance, normalcy meant returning to a place of refuge and avoiding change and newness that would have been "too much … to handle." Embedded within this conversation is also the assumption that the institution would not change its core bureaucratic processes like application, financial aid, and course management (Canvas) processes, as if those were exempt from potential change. To that end, Sarah's anticipation was grounded in her institution's commitment to upholding tradition.

Adjusting to Normalcy

After being admitted to the program, we learned to adjust to our new normal. Noteworthy is that these new models of normalcy were not always explicitly or immediately evident, but we arrived at them upon reflection and after several instances of trial and error. Michelle discussed her experience re-learning how to connect with her professors. After realizing that she could no longer rely on casual, in-person office hours or pre- and post-class informal chats, she pivoted toward more formal ways of communicating with faculty through "planning and prioritization." She adapted to the virtual learning environment by scheduling, hosting, and attending meetings with faculty online.

Adjusting to normalcy also meant coming to terms with more expansive conceptions of accessibility. Ava noted, "the pandemic allowed me to attend classes that were not normally offered in a distance or virtual capacity. I was able to successfully take three courses while working my job full time because of their modality." Here, we see changes made at the institutional level to accommodate students' health and transportation needs. Doing so required institutions to reimagine what they deemed as normal course modalities. This change positively affected Ava, who is also a commuter doctoral student and a full-time employee at a different institution.

Contending With Normalcy

An institutional culture of empathy rose to normalcy during the pandemic. Faculty, staff, and students generally led with care and concern for each other's circumstances. Professors gave extensions, recorded lectures, and created flexible attendance policies. Practitioners and administrators created virtual programming for students and welcomed an influx of inquiries from institutional stakeholders. Students helped each other and extended grace to professors who needed extra time to grade and provide feedback. Though each entity sustained a culture of empathy, they realized that concessions took place. For example, Lillian said:

> While it did help me to empathize with others that nobody knew what to do, it did not always instill confidence in me that I would find my footing and understand the expectations required of me to move forward in my degree.

Here, Lillian juxtaposes collective empathy with her confidence. Though she displayed buy-in to the idea of empathy, she realized it came at a cost. She felt comfort in knowing that her general experiences navigating the pandemic mirrored others, but she understood that those experiences were not positive. Her comment broadly portrays the contention between how she reconciled with the state of the institution and her progress toward her professional development.

Further, one material effect of COVID-19 involved institutional finances. Denise recalled a few college- and department-level changes she noticed during her first year. She stated:

> One example that I have noticed, within and outside of [our institution], is high turnover in leadership and among faculty. As a result of the financial strain that COVID-19 has created, [...] several non-tenured professors have been let go, which has led to a consistent lack of course offerings due to coverage issues.

Essentially, she described a trickle-down effect of institutional decision-making. First, COVID-19 disrupted the college's finances, which led to grave budget cuts. As a result, the department was no longer able to deliver consistent course offerings. The aftermath of this spiral left students in precarious situations, forcing them to extend their timelines for matriculation, take unnecessary "filler" courses, and to search for replacement courses outside of the college. So, what initially was an example of institutions making budget cuts spiraled into an instance of students managing course cuts. The institution subconsciously modeled to students how to operate out of places of scarcity.

In sum, references to normalcy reverberated across our experiences. Whether we were anticipating, adjusting to, or contending with normalcy, we all learned to gauge our surroundings to make sense of rapid societal and institutional changes. Perhaps our current sentiments about normalcy are best captured through Ava's comments, "It still feels unsafe because COVID-19 hasn't been eradicated, but we are back to normal in our behavior." To that end, we are still grappling with the unknown, unintended consequences of the pandemic.

Connecting Experiences to Emotions

As doctoral students navigating COVID-19, we began to connect our experiences to emotions. We were not only interested in the "things" we went through; rather, we wanted to know how they affected us, socio-emotionally. Three emotions we shared were stress, anxiety, and grief. Each actualized differently for us but the essence of their manifestations resonated with all of us.

Stress

The pandemic created a lot of stress. At macro levels, the country and world failed to provide staple goods and services to consumers. At meso levels, institutions and organizations experienced turmoil and did not always communicate timely, consistent information to those who needed it most. At micro levels, we, as doctoral students, dealt with the remnants of our society, institution, and community. Often, it was difficult, burdensome, and costly. Rachel discussed the implications of the pandemic on her finances and personal well-being. She said:

> The financial strain caused by COVID-19, including supply chain issues and inflation, coupled with the financial strain of beginning a grad school program on a stipend approximately half of my income as a full-time teacher was also a source of considerable stress. I was constantly stressed about money, which made it difficult to adequately care for myself or to focus on my learning processes, especially when that learning would be above and beyond my coursework.

Rachel began by mentioning the state of the economy. COVID-19 sparked a disruption to the supply chain and inflation skyrocketed. As a citizen, Rachel had to deal with that new reality. She went on to mention her new identity as not only a doctoral student but a graduate assistant (GA). Her new professional identity from full-time teacher to part-time GA marked a change in status and pay. She was left to figure out how to make ends meet with half of her previous income. In turn, her stress affected her physical and mental health, as she mentioned the struggle of caring for herself and focusing on learning. Further, she also recounted the stress of being a doctoral student. Unlike seeking undergraduate or master's degrees, for example, pursuing doctoral degrees is accompanied by an expectation that learning extends far beyond the classroom. So, Rachel's learning stressors were expansive including coursework, research, teaching, service, and doctoral socialization skills, to name a few.

> Concerns about stress and its impact on mental health were also astounding in our journeys. Michelle spoke about her struggles with online learning by saying: Moreover, for coursework that I found more challenging such as statistics, I noticed increased stress as I struggled with application of lecture content and staying focused in Zoom lectures. The symptoms of ADHD that I experienced prior to COVID-19 were exacerbated when completing schoolwork at home. [...] This impeded my work-life balance, as I often found myself working around 12 hours a day. The lack of time management when working at home resulted in increased rates of burnout.

Though the virtual learning environment increased access to several types of students, like commuters and parents, it created stress for students like Michelle. Her ADHD collided with Zoom meetings. Additionally, her 12-hour workdays ran in addition to several faculty members' recommendations to spend approximately 3 hours per credit hour each week preparing for class. Michelle's statement reiterates the collective sentiment of feeling pressured to be available and productive that appeared in several reflections as well as the peer debriefing. Such advice does not account for students who need accommodations or additional support to maintain their course loads.

Anxiety

Being anxious was an emotion that resonated across our experiences. COVID-19 created a plethora of conditional, "what if" scenarios that rarely eased our minds. Not only were we anxious about the pandemic, itself, but we were also anxious about its effect on our families and livelihood. Denise stated:

> While I believe that transitioning into a doctoral program for the first time is challenging for anyone (especially without a previous graduate degree), the transition is even more challenging when you are living off a third of your previous wage, your partner has been laid off due to COVID-19, and you are unable to meet people and acclimate as you normally would. It is anxiety-inducing.

Denise acknowledged a general fear about beginning doctoral education but reiterated that COVID-19 complicated her experience. Seeking a PhD was concurrently her first sought graduate degree, so she had little to no prior socialization in graduate school. Like some of her peers, she began her doctoral studies after a stint in a full-time professional role, so she experienced financial distress due to a pay cut as a graduate assistant. Further, her partner had recently lost his job amid COVID-19. On top of that, she could no longer socialize with friends, family, peers, and colleagues as she normally would. The intersections of these factors made her anxious.

There were also several unknowns about doctoral student matriculation and success. Lillian posed several questions that developed as she grew anxious about the process of meeting program milestones and her professors' expectations. She said:

> Because we have never faced a pandemic like this, I had questions about how I find research opportunities and funding, what classes do I take, what is the dissertation process, and how does COVID-19 affect graduation. All these questions caused some anxiety.

Noteworthy is that Lillian mentioned the unprecedented nature of COVID-19. Though the country and world had previously encountered public health crises and the field of higher education had historically overcome plagues and ailments, COVID-19 was contemporarily unrivaled. This understanding served as the foundation for Lillian's line of questioning. First, she asked about research and funding. Several of those opportunities became contingent, as they had in-person stipulations that could not be met. Second, she asked about classes. As previously mentioned, departments experienced budget cuts, so course sequences no longer could accommodate course offerings. Then, she asked about the dissertation process. Her institution revised some of its policies for research ethics and oral exam modalities. Finally, she asked how COVID-19 would affect graduation. In 2020, several institutions altered their graduation ceremony formats and made exceptions to graduation requirements like internships, apprenticeships, co-ops, and clinical hours. All of Lillian's questions were warranted and communicated the nature of her anxiety.

Grief

Coupled with the pandemic was an immense sense of grief that manifested through death, loss, and longing. Of the hundreds of millions of people who reported contracting COVID-19, millions of them died. Some of those people were our relatives, friends, neighbors, and community members. Ava said:

> My grandmother passed away during the pandemic of natural causes, but my family couldn't participate in the ritual of gathering to grieve, sharing memories or funny stories. We couldn't allow friends to come and give us too many casseroles or tell us what she meant to them. I'm still not okay with how we had to handle her death. A lot of families had the same experience as my family, and they are not okay either.

As Ava grieved her grandmother's death, she resented the loss of the opportunity to "participate in the ritual of gathering." In this case, that likely included visitation days, a funeral, and a repast. In other contexts, rituals of gathering may include family dinners, office meetings, holidays, family reunions, vacations, weddings, birthday parties, and other events. These spaces allow us to celebrate life and love for one another. COVID-19 physically took people from us and socio-emotionally stole our rituals of gathering. Ava went on to say that she's "still not okay with how [they] had to handle her [grandmother's] death." Two points are key in that statement. First, she underscores the lingering effects of COVID-19 and the grief it ensued. One of the narratives surrounding COVID-19 and those affected was that people should deal with it and move on. Ava's comment offered an intercession and interception to such narratives and reinforced the hurt and pain she and her family still feel.

Though grief is most associated with death, we also linked it to loss and longing, more broadly. Sarah approached her doctoral education journey, in part, to compensate for experiences she grieved while obtaining her bachelor's and master's degrees.

> But I wanted to get "it" right this time … I graduated undergrad in 3 years, and I got my master's in 1 year while working full-time. Back then, I was hyper-focused on my academic well-being, which led to me not prioritizing some social activities. So, this time around, I knew I wanted to graduate, of course. But I wanted to take my time, get involved where I saw fit, meet people, and just take it slow. I wanted to see who I was as a person in school, instead of just as a student.

Sarah's grief was tied to the possibility of a different collegiate experience. Though she appreciated the fast academic track she chose, she recognized that it came at the expense of a more vibrant social life. As a result, she viewed her doctoral journey as a final attempt to make the most of her time in the academy. Sarah's approach also subconsciously represents buy-in to ideas of fatalism that were attached to the pandemic. In her case, the risk of contracting COVID-19 increased the likelihood of death. So, her desire and urgency "to get 'it' right this time," reflected a desperate—potentially final—attempt to take control of whatever life was ahead of her.

Developing Reactive and Reparative Self-Care Strategies

To cope with the plethora of new experiences and emotions we encountered, we found ourselves engaging in self-care strategies. Some of these strategies were reactive, meaning we developed them in response to various pandemic cultures. Others were reparative insofar as they helped to restore our waning physical and mental health.

Reactive Self-Care Strategies

Our reactive self-care strategies highlighted ways we intentionally formed communities of support during our first year as doctoral students. After realizing that our respective programs, departments, and institutions did not fully meet our expectations for supporting us, we made concerted efforts to find and form relationships on our own. Rachel best captured this sentiment when she said, "It has been very frustrating to feel as though my program has not worked to develop and support this community of students and faculty, and instead, my friends and I have had to put considerable effort into making it happen ourselves." She felt like there were few supports in place that were tailored specifically to students who began doctoral work during the pandemic. In turn, she and her friends performed additional labor to fill in the gaps of the institutions' shortcomings.

Community building often began organically but during formal, scheduled courses and meetings. As time passed, we transitioned to more informal means of communication. For example, Ava stated:

> I found myself messaging students in our virtual classes, introducing myself, and exchanging contact information. I created a community by reaching out to students in my classes and checking on them. In turn, I found that they would check in on me.

She created a niche community that evolved from a classroom community. By taking the initiative to message peers she did not yet know, she deliberately sought to expand her social circle. Afterward, she noted when her peers began to reciprocate energy, effort, and care by "checking in on [her]," insinuating that her community-building technique had been successful.

Like Ava, Sarah also mentioned the importance of virtual classes in sparking conversation and networking opportunities. She said:

> My program doesn't have official cohorts, but I started it with a "soft" cohort of other Black women that were coming in at the same time. It was pretty cool. We'd be in Zoom class chatting back and forth. We'd make sure we were all on our Ps and Qs when it came to keeping up with the demands of the program. That was something that I don't think any/many of us had experienced at the undergraduate level.

Though her doctoral program did not adopt the cohort model as part of its formal curriculum, Sarah still considered herself to be part of a close-knit community. She began her program with a few other Black women who held each other accountable for communicating and matriculating.

Though virtual environments sufficiently supported some of us, they did not meet all of our needs. Michelle joined campus organizations like the Graduate Student Council (GSC) and Chi Sigma Iota, a counseling honors society, where she participated in mentee-mentor programs. Similarly, Lillian joined the Black Graduate & Professional Student Association (BGPSA), connected with members of her sorority that were on campus and met with friends and peers in open, well-ventilated spaces.

Reparative Self-Care Strategies

Our reparative strategies helped us to restore, reinvigorate, and readjust our minds and bodies to support healthier lifestyles amid COVID-19. The pandemic took a toll on us all, and we are still grappling with remnants of its effects on our physical and mental health. During our first year as doctoral students, though, we developed key strategies that helped us cope. Several of us relied on exercise as an outlet. Michelle said:

> I have always used exercise as a stress reducer, so I purchased an exercise bike to work out at home. The exercise bike has the option of working out with your friends or family; thus, I also scheduled time to exercise with others. Sometimes, I even worked out with cohort members, and this helped with support.

Michelle realized that exercise was a necessity to maintain mental and physical health; thus, she prioritized a consistent routine that she could do at home. Adapting typical out-of-home activities to accommodate policy and health recommendations to stay home was an integral practice during the pandemic. She also embedded socialization into her exercises by virtually working out with her community of friends, family, and peers. Lillian and Denise also turned to exercise. In addition to walking, Denise took 15-minute mind breaks and watched movies. Beyond exercising, Denise also dedicated more time to her dogs and eating proper meals between classes and meetings.

Furthermore, the pandemic forced us to prioritize our mental health. We realized that some of our prior survival tactics were not effective enough to support them through a global public health crisis or doctoral education. Rachel stated:

> I maintained weekly virtual therapy sessions and talked frequently with my therapist about the stresses of returning to school and balancing priorities. I eventually determined with my therapist and a university-provided psychiatrist that trying an anti-anxiety medicine would be helpful to me—and it was … I do not regret that, but I do wonder if I would have needed that medical support without the stressful process of starting grad school during a pandemic.

Seeking support from medical professionals was an important support tool for Rachel. A therapist and psychiatrist were able to provide specialized support to develop coping mechanisms for her stress. That is important when considering the roles and limitations of the community. Though our loved ones are key to our success, we must realize when we need help beyond our inner circle. Rachel proceeded to contend with the relationship between her medical care, the scope of her stress, and the context of the pandemic. Like Rachel, we must be intentional in recognizing our capacity for stress and seeking expertise when needed.

DISCUSSION AND FUTURE RESEARCH

Understanding the experiences of first-year doctoral students entering their programs during COVID-19 provides insight into the actions that doctoral programs can take to support students, particularly during wide-scale events akin to a pandemic. We believe that the themes that emerged across the lived experiences listed above can serve as an important starting point in case of future unprecedented events.

From the findings explored above: (1) Navigating Mental and Material Models of Normalcy, (2) Connecting Experiences to Emotions, and (3) Developing Reactive and Reparative Self-Care Strategies, we have discussed suggestions for future departmental practice, especially during difficult global events. When matriculating new students into doctoral programs during challenging global events, institutions can learn from the insights gathered here to provide more resources to better acclimate students to graduate school during these times.

Implications

Due to the stressors and atypical situations that arise during these events, administrators should adopt policies that reflect compassion for students and instructors. This can include modifying teaching and research in ways that allow personnel to practice flexibility and self-care. For example, instructors may recognize that the physical classroom experience is not the best fit for all groups of students and decide to include virtual components or options for clinical supervision to overcome time-, transportation-, and health-related challenges. The particular challenges of COVID-19 emphasized that technological access must be prioritized so that resources can be available to all students. As seen across our reflections, technology provided pathways for not only academic learning but also cohort-building and mental health care.

Additionally, since all of our reflections addressed adjusting to the "new normal" within graduate school, part of matriculating doctoral students could include offering frequent, accessible workshops to improve advisor-advisee relationships and clarify program requirements and expectations. Recognizing the impact external challenges posed to our academic and personal experiences, institutions should also seek to point to resources for other stressors in doctoral students' lives, such as financial hardship, housing, mental health concerns, and food insecurity.

Finally, a frequent theme across our reflections was the efforts that we made to cultivate formal and informal communities in which we could find support and practice mutual care. A concurrent theme was that of frustration that the community-building process was so difficult and required so much extra effort on our part to find the support we needed. We suggest that doctoral programs proactively consider how to provide incoming students with opportunities to build relationships with colleagues, including virtually if needed. Community-building does require personal (and often meaningful) effort, but providing incoming students with a framework can ensure that they have the support that they need from the beginning.

We recognize that the novelty of COVID-19 meant that program administrators were being asked to simultaneously identify and meet students' needs while also struggling with new challenges and limited resources. We hope that the suggestions offered here provide program administrators in the future with a foundation on which to build in the event of similar crises. Additionally, by illuminating our experiences here auto-ethnographically, we hope that other doctoral students in similar circumstances will feel validated in the legitimacy of their own lived experiences.

REFERENCES

Bal, I. A., Arslan, O., Budhrani, K., Mao, Z., Novak, K., & Muljana, P. S. (2020). The balance of roles: Graduate student perspectives during the COVID-19 pandemic. *TechTrends, 64* 796–798. https://doi.org/10.1007/s11528-020-00534-z

Bochner, A. P. (1994). Perspectives on inquiry II: Theories and stories. In M. L. Knapp & G. R. Miller (Eds.), *Handbook of interpersonal communication* (2nd ed.) (pp. 21–41). Sage.

Bochner, A. P. (2013). Putting meanings into motion: Autoethnography's existential calling. In S. H. Jones, T. Adams, & C. Ellis (Eds.), *Handbook of autoethnography* (pp. 50–56). Left Coast Press.

Colpitts, B. D., Usick, B. L., & Eaton, S. E. (2020). Doctoral student reflections of blended learning before and during Covid-19. *Journal of Contemporary Education Theory & Research (JCETR), 4*(2), 3–11. https://doi.org/10.5281/zenodo.4247601

Creswell, J. W. (2013). *Qualitative inquiry and research design: Choosing among five approaches.* Sage.

Daniel, K. E., Szkody, E., Aggarwal, P., Peterman, A. H., Washburn, J. J., & Selby, E. A. (2022). Characterizing changes in mental health-related outcomes for Health Service psychology graduate students during the first year of the COVID-19 pandemic. *Journal of Clinical Psychology, 78*(11), 2281–2298. https://doi.org/10.1002/jclp.23392

DeBate, R., Himmelgreen, D., Gupton, J., & Heuer, J. N. (2021). Food insecurity, well-being and academic success among college students: Implications for post COVID-19 pandemic programming. *Ecology of Food and Nutrition, 60*(5), 564–579. https://doi.org/10.1080/03670244.2021.1954511

Deryugina, T., Shurchkov, O., & Stearns, J. E. (2021). Covid-19 disruptions disproportionately affect female academics. *AEA Papers and Proceedings, 111*, 164–168. https://doi.org/10.1257/pandp.20211017

Dewey, J. (1938). *Experience and education*. MacMillan.

Donohue, W. J., Lee, A. S. J., Simpson, S., & Vacek, K. (2021). Impacts of the COVID-19 pandemic on doctoral students' thesis/dissertation progress. *International Journal of Doctoral Studies, 16*, 533. https://doi.org/10.28945/4818

Gewalt, S. C., Berger, S., Krisam, R., & Breuer, M. (2022). Effects of the COVID-19 pandemic on university students' physical health, mental health and learning, a cross-sectional study including 917 students from eight universities in Germany. *PLoS One, 17*(8), 1–24. https://doi.org/10.1371/journal.pone.0273928

Hazell, C. M., Chapman, L., Valeix, S. F., Roberts, P., Niven, J. E., & Berry, C. (2020). Understanding the mental health of doctoral researchers: A mixed methods systematic review with meta-analysis and meta-synthesis. *Systematic Reviews, 9*(197), 1–30. https://doi.org/10.1186/s13643-020-01443-1

Kakaei, H., Nourmoradi, H., Bakhtiyari, S., Jalilian, M., & Mirzaei, A. (2022). Effect of COVID-19 on food security, hunger, and food crisis. *COVID-19 and the Sustainable Development Goals*. https://doi.org/10.1016/B978-0-323-91307-2.00005-5

Kee, C. E. (2021). The impact of Covid-19: Graduate students' emotional and psychological experiences. *Journal of Human Behavior in the Social Environment, 31*(1–4), 476–488. https://doi.org/10.1080/10911359.2020.1855285

Khalil, A. (2022). Challenges in doctoral socialisation: A researcher's reflective experience. *Waikato Journal of Education, 27*(2), 97–101. https://doi.org/10.15663/wje.v27i2.927

Marshall, D. T., Pressley, T., Neugebauer, N. M., & Shannon, D. M. (2022). Why teachers are leaving and what we can do about it. *Phi Delta Kappan, 104*(1), 6–11. https://doi.org/10.1177/00317217221123642

Matthews, A. (2021). Adapting to the transitional stage of the doctoral environment: An autoethnography of socialization. *International Journal of Doctoral Studies, 16*, 71. https://doi.org/10.28945/4685

Mullen, C. A. (2021). Online doctoral mentoring in a pandemic: Help or hindrance to academic progress on dissertations? *International Journal of Mentoring and Coaching in Education, 10*(2), 139–157. https://doi.org/10.1108/IJMCE-06-2020-0029

Muncey, T. (2010). *Creating autoethnographies*. Sage.

Nash, R., & Bradley, D. (2011). *Me-search and re-search: A guide for writing scholarly personal narrative manuscripts*. Information Age Publishing.

Omar, J. A., Ali, E. M., & Belbase, S. (2021). Graduate students' experience and academic achievements with online learning during COVID-19 pandemic. *Sustainability 13*(13055), 1–21. https://doi.org/10.3390/su132313055

Paucsik, M., Leys, C., Marais, G., Baeyens, C., & Shankland, R. (2022). Self-compassion and savouring buffer the impact of the first year of the COVID-19 on PhD students' mental health. *Stress and Health, 38*(5), 891–901. https://doi.org/10.1002/smi.3142

Richardson, L. (1994). Writing: A method of inquiry. In N. K. Denzin & Y. S. Lincoln (Eds.), *Handbook of qualitative research* (pp. 516–529). Sage.

Roy, R. & Uekusa, S. (2020). Collaborative autoethnography: "Self-reflection" as a timely alternative research approach during the global pandemic. *Qualitative Research Journal, 20*(4), 383–392. https://doi.org/10.1108/QRJ-06-2020-0054

Sideropoulos, V., Midouhas, E., Kokosi, D., Brinkert, J., Wong, K. K. Y., & Kambouri, M. A. (2022). The effects of cumulative stressful educational events on the mental health of doctoral students during the COVID-19 pandemic. *UCL Open: Environment Preprint*. https://doi.org/10.14324/111.444/000105.v1

Sverdlik, A., Hall, N. C., McAlpine, L., & Hubbard, K. (2018). The PhD experience: A review of the factors influencing doctoral students' completion, achievement, and well-being. *International Journal of Doctoral Studies, 13*, 361–388. https://doi.org/10.28945/4113

Sverdlik, A., Hall, N. C., & Vallerand, R. J. (2022). Doctoral students and COVID-19: exploring challenges, academic progress, and well-being. *Educational Psychology*, 1–16. https://doi.org/10.1080/01443410.2022.2091749

Wang, L., & DeLaquil, T. (2020). The isolation of doctoral education in the times of Covid-19: Recommendations for building relationships within person-environment theory. *Higher Education Research & Development, 39*(7), 1346–1350. https://doi.org/10.1080/07294360.2020.1823326

Wasil, A. R., Franzen, R. E., Gillespie, S., Steinberg, J. S., Malhotra, T., & DeRubeis, R. J. (2021). Commonly reported problems and coping strategies during the COVID-19 crisis: A survey of graduate and professional students. *Frontiers in Psychology, 12*, 1–14. https://doi.org/10.3389/fpsyg.2021.598557

Weidman, J. C., Twale, D. J., & Stein, E. L. (2001) *Socialization of graduate and professional students in higher education: A perilous passage?* Jossey-Bass.

CHAPTER 17

STRESSES OF COVID-19 FOR DOCTORAL STUDENTS IN ENGINEERING

Jennifer G. Cromley
University of Illinois at Urbana-Champaign

Karin J. Jensen
University of Michigan

Joseph F. Mirabelli
University of Michigan

ABSTRACT

Building on a small body of mostly questionnaire research collected in 2020 about stresses of COVID-19 on doctoral students, in 2021–2022 we interviewed 55 PhD engineering students four times each. Coding for various COVID-19 related stressors suggested a similar set of stressors as found across the whole set of previous papers reporting on early-COVID-19 stresses, but with more prominent worry for self, family, and friends, perhaps due to the Omicron surge in January 2022. A nexus of visa/travel/family/quarantine stressors was found in our more highly-international sample, who had been separated from family for longer. Concerns about getting research done waned and waxed as conditions on campus changed. Similar to undergraduates, these students missed social interactions and relied greatly on family for coping.

Examining the Cognitive and Psychological Effects of the COVID-19 Global Pandemic on High School, College, and Graduate Learners, pp. 391–410

Keywords: doctoral advising, research progress, international students, social relations

INTRODUCTION

A number of American education researchers rapidly shifted to researching COVID-19 impacts in 2020–2021. This shift has led to quite a few studies on stresses of COVID-19 on students in K–16 education, but little research has considered stresses for doctoral students (Börgeson et al., 2021; Cornell University, 2021; Covington & Jordan, 2022; Melnyk et al., 2021; Ogilvie et al., 2020; Rutledge-Prior & Casey, 2023; Scorsolini-Comin et al., 2021; Sverdlik et al., 2022; Walsh et al., 2021; Wasil, et al., 2021; Zhao et al., 2022). COVID-19 added additional insecurity to the already-stressful undertaking of PhD studies, in which students must learn to conduct and publish research that creates new knowledge, to teach undergraduates, to work in a large bureaucracy, and to balance these with taking courses and exams, home life, household responsibilities, recreation, and social engagement.

GOALS OF THE RESEARCH

In fall 2021, our team began an interview study of stressors affecting PhD students in engineering, and because of the ongoing pandemic, COVID-19 was frequently named as a stressor. This chapter therefore represents a small part of the data collected on that larger project. Within the few published studies of COVID-19 stressors for doctoral students, most administered researcher-developed surveys in March–December, 2020 and none were longitudinal. Thus, our research contributes a longitudinal October, 2021–December, 2021–February, 2022–April, 2022 interview-based lived experience perspective which includes the large Omicron variant peak of disease and death in the United States.

LITERATURE REVIEW

The small 2020–2023 literature on COVID-19 stressors for doctoral students suggests that this more-mature working group was affected in some ways, similar to other adults in the United States. The majority of these studies on stressors used questionnaires, where the researchers wrote items based on what they thought COVID-19 stressors might be. Those researchers stated that they based the questions on stressors from the general doctoral student stressors literature and from media reports of how people generally were affected by the COVID-19 pandemic. In the present research, we wanted to build on researcher perspectives and hear from students themselves what they perceived the biggest COVID-19 stressors to be, and how these stressors played out in their personal (e.g., friends, family, and lab), organizational (e.g., university policies), and larger sociopolitical (e.g., rules about masking, travel, visas) contexts.

Eight themes emerge from the small, published literature on early COVID-19 effects. *First,* doctoral students highly endorsed items about worrying about family or friends who were infected with COVID-19 (Walsh et al., 2021). Like the public at large, many doctoral students had family or friends who were infected or at risk of infection, and especially in the early days of the pandemic (when data from most published studies was collected) rates of severe illness and hospitalization were high, even among younger people, presumably inducing higher levels of worry. *Second,* doctoral students highly endorsed items about worrying about themselves getting infected with COVID-19 (Wasil et al., 2021). Again, similar to the public at large, doctoral students were unsure about how to protect themselves and were worried about what might happen to them if they were infected. Similarly, the early-stage studies collected data before methods of transmission were understood and before treatments and vaccines were identified or developed, so high levels of worry about infection would be expected.

Third and fourth, doctoral students doing empirical research were affected in contradictory ways. On the one hand, their responses conveyed some urgency about returning to research and delays in their research (Börgeson et al., 2021; Rutledge-Prior & Casey, 2023; Scorsolinin-Comin et al., 2021; Sverdlik et al., 2022; Wasil et al., 2021). On the other hand, many, especially those who worked in labs, highly endorsed items about worrying about whether others around them would follow recommended precautions (Börgeson et al., 2021). Early in the pandemic there was concern among many members of the public about whether people would or could follow changing public health recommendations, such as early advice to make a cloth mask, followed by recommendations to wear N95 type masks, which were not always affordable or available. These general societal concerns were reflected in doctoral students' responses but were perhaps framed within university policies that could be both more universal across a campus setting, as well as more stringent than county/city-level or business-specific policies.

Fifth, in some contexts, but not all, students lost jobs or salary (Covington & Jordan, 2021; Ogilvie et al., 2020; Scorsolini-Comin et al., 2021). Some U.S. universities obtained and used COVID-19 relief funds to pay students who could not work due to campus or lab closures, but not all universities were eligible and not all chose to pay doctoral students specifically. These institution-specific conditions frame the present work, but also speak to greater difficulty generalizing top stressors found at one institution to top stressors at other institutions. *Sixth,* in part due to lost income, some doctoral students rated severe levels of strain on availability of appropriate food and suitable housing (Ogilvie et al., 2020). As with the general public, universities in areas with high COVID-19-related unemployment (e.g., cities highly dependent on tourism and entertainment such as New York City or Los Angeles) and areas with the highest housing costs (e.g., large cities, California) had doctoral students who experienced higher levels of stress around getting affordable food and housing.

Seventh, as they did in the general public, female students reported increased family responsibilities that made work-life balance more difficult (Borgeson et al., 2021; Scorsolini-Comin et al., 2021; Walsh et al., 2021) and students of color reported more economic impacts and more depression (Cornell University, 2021; Melnyk et al., 2021). This was not just due to loss of the students' own income and the students' own expenses, but also due to effects on extended family and in some cases the need to replace income lost by parents, siblings, or other family members.

Eighth, later-stage surveys identified concerns about future job prospects and finishing the degree as disruptions wore on (Covington & Jordan, 2021; Ogilvie et al., 2020; Rutledge-Prior & Casey, 2023).

These findings in many ways mirror impacts on working Americans, and at the same time highlight four differences between COVID-19 stressors for doctoral students and working Americans more broadly. First, doctoral student employment and finances are more precarious than for similarly educated working adults. Second, COVID-19 more strongly affected research, particularly in laboratory settings, than it did class-taking or teaching.. Third, students had to rely on their own campus—rather than their own family, employer, county, and so forth, separately—to make COVID-19 safety decisions that students felt comfortable regarding work, recreation, classrooms, housing, and health care. Fourth, there were unique aspects of doctoral programs (e.g., need for ongoing data collection) and employment for PhD graduates (e.g., increased biomedical jobs, stalled hiring for faculty jobs) that caused stress for doctoral students in this small literature to date.

Beyond COVID-19 stressors, doctoral students face many stressors that can vary by their stage in the program. Towards the beginning of a PhD program, students are more likely to be taking classes, getting to know their advisor, learning a variety of research techniques, and preparing for departmental exams (called variously qualifying exams or comprehensive exams or preliminary exams at different institutions). In the middle of their program, they are likely to be designing their own research, thinking about their research trajectory, and thinking about dissertation/thesis design. They may begin presenting at conferences and/or writing for publication in this middle stage. In the late stage, they are focused on their dissertation and career with very intense research activity and writing. Students might serve as teaching assistants at any stage and might also engage in grant proposal writing at any stage, depending on their academic discipline. International students face additional stresses due to culture shock and visa policies, and those who are not native English speakers also face stresses from speaking and writing challenges (Le & Gardner, 2010). Engineering students specifically are likely to seek out corporate summer internships, to work in laboratories where most experiments fail and great perseverance is required, and to work in large teams where they do a presentation to the lab on a weekly or bi-weekly basis (though this can vary for very small labs; Burt, 2019; Osbeck et al., 2010). These characteristics of doctoral programs and of engineering doctoral education also framed how we recruited participants for the study.

The 2021–2022 COVID-19 Context

Our study is also contextualized within the specific COVID-19 responses in the 2021–2022 academic year at the large, Midwestern U.S. research-intensive university where we collected our data. The first evidence of an effective treatment for COVID-19 (with dexamethasone) was published in July 2020 (RECOVERY Collaborative Group, 2020). Travel bans had lifted, and many universities had re-opened at least partially by Fall 2020, albeit with varied requirements to mask and show a negative COVID-19 test from a physician. The Pfizer vaccine received emergency use approval in December 2020, and health care workers and high-risk populations began receiving vaccines in spring 2021. Fall 2021 represented something of a return to normal on many campuses, following 1.5 years of very disrupted research and teaching at universities. In fall 2021, some courses at the research site were still being taught online. Although the fall 2021 return to campus did not bring a large wave of disease, as had been feared, the Omicron variant wave began in December 2021 and crested in January 2022. Throughout the 2021–2022 year, the university where we conducted the research required masking in classrooms, dormitories, recreation, and health care settings, but not in laboratories. All unvaccinated students, faculty, and staff on campus were required to take a COVID-19 test at a university facility at least twice per week.

In the present study, we provide updated doctoral student perspectives, using interviews that enable us to contextualize comments in personal and larger organizational contexts, tracing the entire 2021–2022 school year, and drawing on a more international and gender-balanced sample than previous research.

METHOD

Participants were 55 PhD students in a range of engineering programs at a large Research I university in the Midwestern region of the United States. They were recruited using general email announcements to a variety of doctoral Teaching Assistant training workshops and courses, to student engineering interest groups (e.g., Society for Women in Engineering, National Society of Black Engineers), and to offices serving specific populations (e.g., International Student Services). They were sampled to represent the population of PhD students at the university, and students who expressed interest but whom we could not accommodate in the interview study were offered the chance to participate in a questionnaire study on doctoral student stress. No potential participant contacted us and then stated they did not wish to participate.

Participants identified as 56% male, 42% female and 2% nonbinary. They were 53% domestic and 47% international students; 38% were in the early stage (before qualifying/comprehensive exam[s]) of their doctoral program, 42% were in the middle stage (before preliminary/dissertation proposal exam), and 20% were late stage (see Table 17.1 for more details about the sample). For the purpose of anonymity, pseudonyms are reported for participants and specific departmental or demographic data are not simultaneously tied to participants. Participants chose to either specify a pseudonym or allow our team to generate one.

Procedure. After obtaining online consent per an approved IRB protocol, we conducted individual online Zoom interviews, video recorded but without the interviewer's or participant's face. Initial October 2021 interviews lasted about 40 minutes, and participants were compensated $40 each. Follow-up December 2021, February 2022 (including one COVID-19 question), and April 2022 interviews with the same participants each lasted about 10 minutes, and participants were compensated $10 for each completed interview.

Measures. Measures comprised a semi-structured individual interview protocol and a demographics form. The demographic form was completed after Interview 1, and participants also completed monthly questionnaires on level of stress, level of anxiety, and intention to remain in an Engineering PhD program, whose results are not reported here.

Table 17.1

Participant Demographics

	Longitudinal study sample ($N = 55$)	Population at the institution
Department size		
Small	20 (36%)	36%
Medium	18 (33%)	31%
Large	17 (31%)	33%
Race		
White, Caucasian	26 (47%)	74%
Asian or Pacific Islander	20 (36%)	
Black/African American	2 (4%)	
Hispanic	7 (13%)	
Indian subcontinental	5 (9%)	
Arab/Middle Eastern	2 (4%)	
American Indian	1 (2%	

Notes: All demographic questions were made optional for participants; however, information was complete from these longitudinal participants. Options from the demographic questionnaire with no responses have been omitted from this table. *Cutoff values for department size were determined by the team before recruiting participants. The site institution's large departments (400+ graduate students) were considered to be Mechanical Engineering, Electrical and Computer Engineering, and Computer Science; the medium departments (150–400 students) were considered to be Civil and Environmental Engineering, Materials Science and Engineering, and Physics; all other departments were considered to be small size (< 150 students). ** For Race and for Gender, multiple options could be selected.

Interview protocol. The open-ended interview protocol about PhD student stressors (available at https://hdl.handle.net/2142/117275) began with general questions about housing and life in town; we then asked about stresses related to advisor, research, taking classes, and teaching; the third part of the interview focused on how the participant perceived these stresses to affect them, what they did to cope with the stresses, and any changes they proposed to lessen such stresses for PhD students in engineering. In the February 2022 interview just past the Omicron peak we added a question about any specific COVID-related stresses or impacts of the Omicron wave on working conditions.

Data analysis. The research team began coding the entire corpus—not just these COVID-19 statements—with codes from previous research on general doctoral stressors. One member of the team wrote an expanded COVID-19 code list with definitions after thoroughly reading all transcribed interviews; the entire team then provided modifications to that code list. The COVID-19 coding scheme was developed from the data, though codes did overlap with questionnaire items in the literature published after we conducted our emergent coding. It included 31 codes (full coding scheme with examples at https://hdl.handle.net/2142/117275). All coding was reviewed by the interviewer who had conducted all 212 interviews, and who had formerly been an engineering doctoral student who left their program due to stressful advisor, lab, and course-taking experiences. We took a qualitative negotiated agreement approach to inter-rater reliability (Garrison et al., 2021).

Codes were applied using Atlas.ti software and raw counts are reported here. Analyses using the Atlas.ti "normalized counts" (to account for the brevity of the last three interviews compared to the first lengthy interview) showed almost identical patterns.

After presenting results at the level of the most frequent single codes (mentioned eight or more times), we present larger themes we found across sets of codes.

RESULTS

COVID-19 was reported by these PhD students to affect all aspects of their work, student, and personal lives. The most prominent stressors were related to travel, family, and fear of oneself/others getting sick. Next most prominent were stresses of family and friends actually getting COVID-19; general effects of COVID-19; slowing of research activity; and decreased exercise. Next most prominent were decreased social interactions, stresses of online classes, financial strain, effects on life plans, getting sick oneself, effects on advising, and getting to know the community (see Table 17.2 for counts). Other COVID-19 stressors represented 1% or less each of coded statements. We close our Results section with three meta-themes that pull together specific micro-level themes below.

Travel. Doctoral students spoke of simultaneously wanting to travel (coded 46 times) but being hindered by many different issues related to COVID-19, to travel restrictions, to U.S. visa rules, and even to advisor flexibility with regard to being away from the lab. As Sue, a middle-stage student in a small department noted:

> I cannot renew my visa in this country while staying here, even though I'm legally okay to stay here. And as I said, embassies outside the country, because of COVID reasons, they're not efficient. So, I cannot go home, and I've been trying to like schedule an appointment since the past six months. (Sue)

Table 17.2

Counts of Stressor Codes by Interview Wave, From Most to Least Total Prevalence

Code (and Meta-Theme, if applicable)	Hour-long Interviews	Follow-Up 1	Follow-Up 2	Follow-Up 3	Total
Fear of getting sick (self and others) or long-term effects of COVID illness	6	3	19	2	30
Inability to see family (1)	5	7	9	4	25
Slowing progress of research (2)	12	1	11	1	25
General added stress	13	3	4	2	22
Death or illness of family member or friend	2	5	11	1	19
Lack of informal or social interactions at work (3)	14	0	4	1	19
Online classes not effective	16	0	0	1	17
Decreased physical activity or exercise	5	3	4	2	14
Inability to go out or socialize (non-work; 3)	5	1	5	2	13
Inability to get to know community	10	0	1	0	11
Financial stress	6	1	2	1	10
Sick with COVID	0	0	8	1	9
Decreased interaction or feedback from advisor	4	0	3	1	8
Decreased formal research group meetings	7	0	1	0	8
Adding uncertainty to life planning	3	3	2	0	8
Online classes/meetings save time	3	0	4	0	7
Blurred lines between work and home	6	0	1	0	7
Advisor is flexible/understanding of COVID challenges	5	1	0	0	6
Instructors not adjusting well to online	5	1	0	0	6
Need to find coping activities	6	0	0	0	6
Challenges of working at home	4	0	2	0	6
Decreased Motivation	4	0	0	0	4

(Table continued on next page)

Table 17.2 (Continued)

Counts of Stressor Codes by Interview Wave, From Most to Least Total Prevalence

Code (and Meta-Theme, if applicable)	Hour-long Interviews	Follow-Up 1	Follow-Up 2	Follow-Up 3	Total
Decreased stress presenting online	3	0	1	0	4
Starting new hobbies or exercise	3	0	0	0	3
Stress symptoms due to COVID	3	0	0	0	3
COVID - Side effects of vaccine/ booster shots	0	3	0	0	3
Increased uncertainty about work hours/expectations (1)	1	0	1	0	2
Drinking alcohol because of COVID	1	0	0	0	1
Inability to participate in previous hobbies other than exercise	1	0	0	0	1
TAing more challenging	1	0	0	0	1
TAing online as a positive	1	0	0	0	1
Total	166	42	114	23	345

The prospect of travel was stressful not only because of visa rules, but also because of the length of travel (e.g., 18 hours flying each way), the in-country quarantine rules, and advisor demands regarding the duration of vacations/breaks. Kimmi, a student in a medium-sized department who was nearing her thesis defense, described her travel concerns:

> I will admit that I cannot go back … [it's a] very long process if you want to go home, especially to my country to [pay] to quarantine this kind of thing. And because of this, I haven't been home for more than two years. It makes me feel really bad about this. Because I know my advisor will not allow me a very long time on my vacation. They usually only [give] three weeks on … vacations, like the usual case. And if I choose to go home, like during this pandemic, I probably need more than one month. (Kimmi)

Re-entry to the U.S. was also a concern. For example, Melinda described not knowing if she would be able to return from her break until the last possible moment, saying: "It was a, yeah, a huge source of stress because you have to get, you have to have a negative test right before you board internationally."

Decreased Social Interactions. Because many classes, labs, meetings, and other activities were canceled or moved online, many participants spoke of decreased social interactions (coded 19 times for work social interactions and 13 times for personal social interactions). One participant, a domestic student in a small department who preferred to only be referenced by his participant number, described waiting for his wife to be able to arrive in the United States.

> [Having] little to no, like interaction with people in the real world, was difficult. Like I—I live—I lived alone, because, I was just—I was living in the apartment that we were going to live in together ... [and] there would be days where I would go, without really talking to someone. Like I would—I would end up going out and picking up food from like [name of restaurant]. And realize, when I went to talk to the teller, that that was the first conversation I had had, like all day. And that was a big stressor for me. (Participant 107)

In some cases, students yearned for a more normal social life including going out in the evenings. Naomi, a domestic middle-stage student in a small department, described:

> I'm a part of our graduate student [redacted] committee. And so, the, what we are in charge of our recruitment. And so, one of the things that, we would do in a non-COVID world is, take all of the recruits out to the bars in downtown.... I was like, no, no, we're not, we're not doing that, absolutely not. Like we're not going bar hopping with a bunch of kids we don't know when there's COVID running rampant like that's just asking to get sick. (Naomi)

Inability to see family. Inability to see family in person was a stressor coded 25 times; some students reported being separated from family for two or more years, including being separated from their own children. Vijay, an international student, reflected "being away from family and wife was a bit tricky. So like coping and talking to your family each day and feeling alone at some point, like, will of course affect your productivity." Even domestic students like Naomi were affected, "We were going to go up to [state] and visit [my partner's] family, but unfortunately his brother got COVID. And then, we were going to be seeing like on the order of 30 people, and this was right when Omicron was hitting.... So, we ended up staying here."

Fear of oneself/others getting sick. Doctoral students were concerned about getting sick themselves, and also afraid that they might make others sick (coded 30 times). Gabriella explained, "I have been vaccinated fully but I still don't really go out just because I'm scared of the virus still. I heard that even if you're vaccinated, you should still wear a mask and everything, because you could still like give it ... to someone else." Kenji described, "because my parents are older, I think every time they come to visit ... it makes me want to be more careful. And so then, sometimes I'll opt to go to class online instead of like in person." Students described concern for their spouse/partner, for parents, grandparents, siblings, aunts and uncles; for roommates, classmates, fellow residents, and co-workers in the lab—faculty, staff, graduate, and undergraduate students.

Family and Friends get COVID. Nineteen students (35% of participants) described family members, friends, roommates, or labmates/friends from the lab getting COVID-19. In two cases, family members died from COVID-19; more often, participants described their worry about family and friends potentially having long-term health or financial effects. Louise, a domestic early-stage student, depicted this tense family situation:

> My parents ended up catching COVID and there was like a big like family fight about it, because like my aunt hosted people for Christmas dinner and didn't tell anyone that her son had COVID. So yeah, my parents got COVID and my mom was very upset about it. (Louise)

Gabriella experienced the stress more around family finances, "I'm also trying to help my family through financial hardships due to COVID because their jobs were impacted by COVID."

In some cases, labmates were infected with COVID-19 and then passed along the illness in the workplace, such as in Priya's wet lab in a small department:

> Basically, once with the new variant kind of came along about a fourth of my lab ended up getting COVID so there was one case right before I left for break and then that was kind of worrisome, because that was someone I was like in close contact with. And then luckily, they were the only case like within our group, but then unfortunately their COVID got like, kind of passed on to some other people in my friend group. (Priya)

Research Activity Affected. Progress of experiments or presentations were affected in a multitude of ways (coded 25 times)—by labmates getting sick, supply chain issues with lab supplies, university rules reducing the number of people in the lab and/or participants coming in person, or not being able to travel to present at conferences (sometimes because of visa rules). As Priya noted, "I'm an experimentalist. So, it was kind of hard once I joined a lab last October, we were kind of limited in the amount of time we could interface with the rest of the group. So, starting research was a little rocky, but once ... everyone started getting more vaccinated and stuff, we were able to come in more, and then that's definitely helped out a lot."

General Effects of COVID-19. Twenty-two statements described general added stress from COVID-19 such as having "cabin fever," conferences being poorly attended, interference with plans (e.g., planning a wedding), masking concerns interfering with a course, and not being able to work immediately after receiving a booster vaccine dose.

Decreased Exercise. Participants spoke of decreased exercise (coded 14 times), due to both not feeling motivated to exercise, and worries about being infected by other students at the university gymnasium. Helen said, "Weightlifting, ... that was something I really liked, but well once we got back to campus, I stopped doing that ... because COVID cases were so high and I didn't feel like going to the weight room and getting COVID from the dudes there." On the other hand, some students spoke of purchasing at-home exercise equipment (e.g., a yoga mat, a pull-up bar) and substituting exercise alone and at home.

Stresses Of Online Classes. Though some doctoral engineering students liked the switch to online classes, more (coded 17 times) had difficulty with online learning. In some cases, participants like Naomi attributed this to poor use of technology, "So this particular professor would show up late to class, would come unprepared, would have—had no grasp on technology whatsoever." In other cases, students like Mohammed attributed the difficulties more to their own time management. "All the lectures are recorded. And sometimes you procrastinate watching one lecture. And then before you know it, like two or three weeks later, you're behind like four or five lectures and you need to catch up."

Financial Strain. Despite a university-wide 100% salary protection program, participants experienced financial strain (coded 10 times) either from family losing income and the student needing to contribute, or from not being able to get a summer internship. Gabriella, an early-stage domestic student noted, "It's not that the stipend isn't enough for like my personal living, because honestly, if I was only caring about myself, like the stipend is more than enough, but I'm also trying to help my family through financial hardships due to COVID because their jobs were impacted by COVID." Sayeed noted more generally, "I have like a [redacted fellowship] appointment, like if I have an internship or something except last summer during the pandemic, I had a little bit shortage of funding."

Effects On Life Plans. Participants found it harder to move ahead with plans for the future (coded 8 times) due to a number of causes, including obstacles to partners traveling/moving, job openings reduced, and supply chain issues, all of which made the future seem much less sure. Planning a wedding or a partner move could be much more stressful due to visa, travel (e.g., testing requirements), and unavailability of services and goods. Matthew, for example, had to re-design his dissertation research:

> I had a couple of experimental phases of my later portion of the PhD, pretty much planned out that I was, that I was already in the middle starting. And as soon as [COVID] hit, you know access to labs and kind of the confusion of like, who gets access, who's supposed to be on campus.... So, I was kind of pushed out and so we had to do a lot of re-planning and a lot of the confusion of how long is this going to be, how long, like, is kind of going to be done and over. Is this going to keep going? (Matthew)

Getting COVID-19. This stressor was coded nine times and was overall reported as a mild stressor. Participants spoke of missing in-person meetings of classes because of being sick, but online options were available. They spoke of not being able to go into the lab to work, but perhaps even more so of not knowing when they should go back in order to protect others. Sue said, "I'm sitting at home. And then when can I start my work? I have no idea. So yeah, those two things happened. I got infected. And then one of—like a week after that, my undergrad got infected. So, I was just thinking about this, 'Ooh, what is the right thing to do?'"

Effects on Advising. Eight participants mentioned a decrease in quantity or quality of advisor interaction because of the pandemic. Jan, who had previously worked in industry, said, "My style is to kind of show up at your office and talk to you. It's kind of how I learned to operate before the pandemic. And there's really not a good equivalent with Zoom." Karina noted stress from "dealing with my advisor. He's also been busier with like COVID [...] Yeah, he wanted to shorten meetings to like 15 minutes." Natasha noted "The situations have changed largely because COVID.... So, he hasn't been very available partially because it has impacted [redacted]. But it's kind of impacted the way he runs the lab. In the sense of, we used to have meetings available for 30 minutes if we'd like them. We could schedule them anytime. Last semester, most of those got canceled kind of with little notification and/or were cut short drastically."

Getting to Know the Community. This was coded 11 times, mostly for first-year students who had only recently moved to the community. This included both exploring around town (e.g., seeking a grocery store that carries favored ingredients) and connecting with others living in the same town. As Grace, an early-stage student noted, "COVID kind of just makes everything online. So, with people not being able to go into a lab ... the generic interactions that kind of like happen when you're coworking in [the same space], just like got minimized ... the feeling of community really comes from being in the same place or going out for dinner after a whole day in the lab."

Summary of Findings

Here we elaborate on three meta-themes that crossed multiple code categories.

(1) The family/visa/lab workload/quarantine/air travel nexus. Five themes from our interviews coalesced into an especially stressful situation for international students—family pressures, visa rules, heavy workload in the lab, quarantine rules, and air travel rules. In some cases, the combination of not being able to get a visa appointment, having an inflexible advisor, facing quarantine rules in the home country, and concern about needing a negative COVID-19 test to fly led to participants being separated from family in person for more than two years.

(2) Unclear COVID-19 Guidelines, Precautions. Another overarching theme regarding worry about getting COVID-19 was a set of changing federal, county public health, and university policies. By the time we conducted our last interview, masking was not required at the university in labs or athletic facilities, but was required in all classrooms; likewise, testing requirements had dropped to once per week but rapid tests were still expensive. This changing landscape led students to worry more about getting COVID-19. Leo, a middle-stage student in a large department, said:

> It directly affects my research because I've been trying to avoid to be in the lab whenever there's a lot of people there, for safety, right. [...] We need a lot of people [coming into the lab] and sometimes that means that it's not safe for me to be in the lab, lots of undergrads too, especially undergrads. And since there's no like testing requirements now, we're just relying on people's self-judgment. (Leo)

Changing travel policies, such as being required to quarantine on arrival or not, requiring a negative COVID-19 test to board of a flight or to enter the U.S., masks being required or not required on transportation, visas being issued or not also caused stress. Cyrus, an early-stage domestic student, described the impact of COVID-19 on his vacation plans:

> I was like, considering trying to get a visa to go to [country]. And then, because they opened up, like, if you have like relatives who are willing to like, say, oh, yeah, we want them to come from there, you can go. And then they just said, oh, there's a new COVID variant, no. (Cyrus)

These policies were based on sound science, but the constant changes were experienced as stressors by these PhD students.

(3) Social Interactions Affected. Another overarching theme is that students frequently commented on how stay-at-home orders and university policies made it difficult to meet new people, or to interact socially with friends or

labmates, many of whom were the friendship pool for doctoral students. This was found across five themes: fear of oneself/others getting sick, research activity, general social interactions, advising, and getting to know the community. Overall, doctoral students were more affected socially than they were in their work or classroom lives.

CONCLUSIONS

Our main themes are all present in one or more prior doctoral student COVID studies, but show different prevalence across a number of codes; we found more travel stress (Walsh et al., 2021) and less financial (Covington & Jordan, 2021; Ogilvie et al., 2020; Rutledge-Prior & Casey, 2023), family responsibilities (Borgeson et al., 2021; Scorsolini-Comin et al., 2021; Walsh et al., 2021), course grades (Cornell, 2020), housing/groceries (Walsh et al., 2021), dislike of precautions (Zhao et al., 2022), qualifying exam (Sorsolini-Comin et al., 2021), and microaggressions stress (Zhao et al., 2022) than other studies. We believe this is because COVID-19 prevalence, precautions, and policies were different by 2021–2022 than in the studies that had been done one to one-and-a-half years earlier, and perhaps due to conditions at our specific institution.

Stress from limited social contact (Cornell University, 2021; Covington & Jordan, 2021; Melnyk et al., 2021; Scorsolini-Comin et al., 2021; Wasil et al., 2021;) and counting on family for support (Cornell University, 2021; Melnyk et al., 2021; Walsh et al., 2021; Wasil et al., 2021) were found in our study and were also strongly supported in research on doctoral students earlier in the pandemic. Concern about research progress (e.g., participant cannot access the lab or it is not safe to go into lab) was found in our study and in the prior doctoral student stress literature (Borgson et al., 2021 Ogilvie et al., 2020; Rutledge-Prior & Casey, 2023; Scorsolini-Comin et al., 2021; Sverdlik et al., 2022; Wasil et al., 2021). Fear for one's own health/health of others was also prominent concern in our study as well as in the prior literature (Cornell University, 2021; Melnyk et al., 2021; Walsh et al., 2021; Wasil et al., 2021).

Other trends in our study may be more due to the population, context, and timing of our study. We had a large international student sample who had been separated from family for a long time, hence the prevalence of travel/visa stresses. The geographic area where the study was conducted has a relatively reasonable cost of living, so loss of housing or sudden unaffordability was never shared by our participants but was found in the literature in high-cost regions. Our doctoral sample never lost income, because federal funds were used for income protection before any research groups/labs re-opened and student research assistant salaries resumed. The peak of disease concerns in February interviews coincides with the Omicron disease peak in the U.S. in January, making concerns for self and others larger than found in some other studies.

Our results contribute to the stress and coping literature, in that they show that doctoral students are simultaneously living in more adult settings, with concerns revolving around their jobs as researchers, and family and work friends with whom they live and work and care about. At the same time, like undergraduates, they may feel the lack of in-person social contact as a more severe stressor than do faculty or staff.

Other researchers studying doctoral students during COVID-19 should consider how results are situated in time, city/state, and specific university and even national (i.e., CDC) policies which change over time. Our interview protocol and coding scheme are linked here and could be used by other researchers.

IMPLICATIONS FOR THE FUTURE

Advisors, staff, and counselors should all be aware of these stressors and how they change with the prevalence of disease, government and university policies, student identities, and the local context. Unlike some education research topics—for example, the effects of socio-economic status on academic achievement—an identical COVID-19 stressor seems to have somewhat different effects in different contexts. For example, finances were present in our sample as a stressor, but it was not so much a student's difficulty making ends meet—as had been found in other studies done at other times in other contexts—but having to make up for lost family income.

What would we recommend that universities and advisors do if there were a new pandemic (respiratory or enteric)? Clearly, every policy and action has benefits and costs—some of which are emotional. For example, the decision to shut down labs protects everyone in the lab from infection; on the other hand, it interferes with progress towards the PhD and also interferes with social supports that can help people cope during an emergency. With 20/20 hindsight, it might have been better to severely limit the number of people in a lab (perhaps with rotating shifts), increase ventilation, and strictly enforce masking and vaccination when those became available, rather than any shutdown (Morris, 2023). Our study informs these decisions by showing that doctoral engineering students are trying to balance social needs—to see family, be with friends, and get support—with the need to progress in their research.

The payment policies of the university where we gathered data were probably successful in keeping the financial stresses of doctoral students to a minimum; policies like these should be continued, especially to support students who cannot work—or need to reduce their work hours—due to getting ill or suffering long-term effects from getting sick.

In a future pandemic, advisors could intentionally foster social connections, particularly for newly recruited students; this could be done with outdoor activities or dining, by hosting backyard events, and with precautions such as masking, hand-washing, testing, using disposable plates, and/or asking for proof of vaccination. Individual departments or colleges at a university could do this as well, but are not as close to students which seemed to matter to our participants.

Advisors could also be more flexible with international students, who likely would face a similar travel/visa/transport/quarantine nexus in another pandemic. Creative solutions might include "banking" lab hours in advance to allow for longer holiday breaks or determining whether any aspects of remote work (e.g., writing up results while quarantined abroad) would be permissible and feasible. Advisors can also be more empathetic, reflecting back the student's specific experiences in difficult times that cause stress for everyone; that it is understandable to be stressed during a pandemic. This might be especially needed around social stresses, which might not be at the forefront for faculty, but are more salient for doctoral students who are mostly close in age to undergraduates.

Universities should consider how their policies might affect doctoral students differently from undergraduates. Doctoral students are simultaneously affected by employment policies and by student policies, and this created a complex patchwork of rules and enforcement which were different in class vs. at the gym vs. in the lab vs. in university housing. A more consistent set of policies and more consistent enforcement might be better received by doctoral students, even if some of those policies—such as masking in the lab—might have a weaker rationale from a public health standpoint.

If these lessons learned from the 2020–2023 COVID-19 pandemic can be implemented by advisors, departments, colleges, and universities, doctoral students should be able to weather subsequent pandemics with fewer effects on well-being.

SUMMARY

In sum, most of the stressors that were themes in the doctoral student COVID-19 questionnaire literature using data collected before the end of 2021 were also present in our large U.S. longitudinal interview study that included more international students. Doctoral students who are focused on learning how to do empirical research experienced stress from delays in the research process. These students in emerging adulthood both counted greatly on family for supports, and felt stress around not being able to travel, and this was especially true for international students. These stressors were exaggerated for international students because of the intersection of COVID-19 rules, research demands, and advisor decisions. Doctoral students also wanted more social interaction, but in safe ways, and they found it difficult to navigate the constantly changing landscape of late-pandemic information and guidelines about how to interact safely.

ACKNOWLEDGMENT

The research reported here was supported by the U.S. National Science Foundation, through Grant #2034800 to University of Illinois, Urbana-Champaign. The opinions expressed are those of the authors and do not represent views of the National Science Foundation.

REFERENCES

Börgeson, E., Sotak, M., Kraft, J., Bagunu, G., Biörserud, C., & Lange, S. (2021). Challenges in PhD education due to COVID-19-disrupted supervision or business as usual: a cross-sectional survey of Swedish biomedical sciences graduate students. *BMC Medical Education, 21*(1), 294.

Burt, B. A. (2019). Toward a theory of engineering professorial intentions: The role of research group experiences. *American Educational Research Journal, 56*(2), 289–332.

Cornell University. (2021). Fall 2020 mental health and well-being survey. https://health.cornell.edu/sites/health/files/docs/QuantitativeReport_MentalHealthWell-BeingSurvey_Fall2020.pdf

Covington, N. V., & Jordan, L. M. (2022). Impact of the COVID-19 pandemic on PhD students in communication sciences and disorders. *Perspectives of the ASHA Special Interest Groups*, 7(2), 512–522.

Garrison, D. R., Cleveland-Innes, M., Koole, M., & Kappelman, J. (2006). Revisiting methodological issues in transcript analysis: Negotiated coding and reliability. *The Internet and Higher Education*, 9(1), 1–8.

Le, T., & Gardner, S. K. (2010). Understanding the doctoral experience of Asian international students in the Science, Technology, Engineering, and Mathematics (STEM) fields: An exploration of one institutional context. *Journal of College Student Development, 51*(3), 252–264.

Melnyk, B. M., Tan, A., Hsieh, A. P., Amaya, M., Regan, E. P., & Stanley, L. (2021). Beliefs, mental health, healthy lifestyle behaviors and coping strategies of college faculty and staff during the COVID-19 pandemic. *Journal of American College Health*, 1–11.

Morris, B. (2023, March 11). If we knew then what we know now about COVID, what would we have done differently? *Wall Street Journal*.

Ogilvie, C., Brooks, T. R., Ellis, C., Gowen, G., Knight, K., Perez, R. J., Rodriguez, L. S., Schweppe, N., Smith, L. L., & Smith, R. A. (2020). NSF RAPID: Graduate student experiences of support and stress during the COVID-19 pandemic. *Montana State University, Bozeman, MT, USA, White Paper*. https://www.montana.edu/covid19_rapid/updated%20NSF_RAPID_GraduateStudentExperiences_Covid19_White_Paper.pdf

Rutledge-Prior, S., & Casey, D. (2023). "An isolating experience aggravated by COVID": Exploring disconnections between political science PhD candidates and supervisors. *PS: Political Science & Politics*. https://doi.org/10.1017/S1049096523000161

Osbeck, L. M., Nersessian, N. J., Malone, K. R., & Newstetter, W. C. (2010). *Science as psychology: Sense-making and identity in science practice*. Cambridge University Press.

Scorsolini-Comin, F., Patias, N. D., Cozzer, A. J., Flores, P. A. W., & Von Hohendorff, J. (2021). Mental health and coping strategies in graduate students in the COVID-19 pandemic. *Revista Latino-Americana de Enfermagem, 29*, e3491.

Sverdlik, A., Hall, N. C., & Vallerand, R. J. (2022). Doctoral students and COVID-19: exploring challenges, academic progress, and well-being. *Educational Psychology, 43*(5), 545–560.

RECOVERY Collaborative Group. (2021). Dexamethasone in hospitalized patients with Covid-19. *New England Journal of Medicine, 384*(8), 693–704.

Walsh, B. A., Woodliff, T. A., Lucero, J., Harvey, S., Burnham, M. M., Bowser, T. L., Aquirre, M., & Zeh, D. W. (2021). Historically underrepresented graduate students' experien□es during the COVID 19 Pandemi□ *Family Relations, 70*(4), 955–972.

Wasil, A. R., Franzen, R. E., Gillespie, S., Steinberg, J. S., Malhotra, T., & DeRubeis, R. J. (2021). Commonly reported problems and coping strategies during the COVID-19 crisis: A survey of graduate and professional students. *Frontiers in Psychology, 12*. https://doi.org/10.3389/fpsyg.2021.598557

Zhao, Y., Ding, Y., Shen, Y., Failing, S., & Hwang, J. (2022). Different coping patterns among us graduate and undergraduate students during COVID-19 pandemic: A machine learning approach. *International Journal of Environmental Research and Public Health, 19*(4), 2430.

CHAPTER 18

GENDER DIFFERENCES IN GRADUATE STUDENTS' ADJUSTMENT, MENTAL HEALTH, MOTIVATION AND LEARNING STRATEGIES DURING THE COVID-19 GLOBAL PANDEMIC

Jianwei Dong, Kailea Q. Manning, Yan Dai, Chih-hsuan Wang, Jill D. Salisbury-Glennon, David T. Marshall, and Deja' Trammell
Auburn University

ABSTRACT

Graduate students face adjustment, motivation, and mental health issues just like undergraduate students, yet there are fewer studies that explore their experience. Their adjustment has been exacerbated by the COVID-19 global pandemic, which has resulted in increased reports of stress, anxiety, and depression, leading to the use of different self-regulated learning strategies to cope. What is even less understood is whether the impact of the COVID-19

Examining the Cognitive and Psychological Effects of the COVID-19 Global Pandemic on High School, College, and Graduate Learners, pp. 411–434 pandemic produced any gender-related differences. Thus, the present study sought to examine whether female students differ in their levels of adjustment, mental health, motivation, and self-regulated learning as compared to male students. To examine these differences, an anonymous survey was administered through Qualtrics to graduate students at a large Southeastern university. The survey included a demographic questionnaire, College Adjustment Test (CAT), Depression, Anxiety, and Stress Scale (DASS21), and selected subscales from the Motivated Strategies for Learning Questionnaire (MSLQ). A total of 301 graduate students completed the survey. Results indicated that female graduate students suffered higher levels of Negative Affect, Homesickness and Stress, whereas the motivation and cognitive strategy use levels did not differ significantly from those of male graduate students during the COVID-19 global pandemic. The present study corroborated the results of prior research that demonstrated no gender differences in motivation and self-regulated learning strategies and further demonstrated that female graduate students experienced more mental health issues during the COVID-19 global pandemic.

Keywords: COVID-19 global pandemic, adjustment, stress, depression,

anxiety, motivation, self-regulated strategy.

INTRODUCTION

The COVID-19 pandemic caused upheaval on college and university campuses across the United States during the spring semester of 2020, and instruction rapidly shifted online as a result (Chirikov et al., 2020; Okado et al., 2023). While higher education institutions quickly adapted their courses from face-to-face to online instructional modalities, students reported adjustment issues, higher levels of stress, anxiety, and depression, and subsequently needed to use different self-regulated learning strategies (Daniel, 2020; Halliburton et al., 2021; Huckins et al., 2020; Liu, Frazier, et al., 2022b; Okado et al., 2023; Son et al., 2020; Wang et al., 2020). Chirikov et al. (2020) surveyed 15,346 graduate and professional students at research universities and reported that 32% of graduate students had depression during the pandemic, a significant increase from 15% before the pandemic. Similarly, anxiety showed a 13% increase among graduate and professional students.

The graduate student community faces unique challenges that can include financial burdens and family responsibilities. While graduate students are often seen as more mature and capable of being self-managed, the COVID-19 pandemic compounded the difficulties that graduate students face, which can be overwhelming (Jabbari et al., 2022; Pyne & Grodsky, 2020; Walsh et al., 2021). Frequently responding to adjustment could cause mental health issues and decrease motivation for academic performance during the campus closure. Walsh et al. (2021) conducted focus groups via Zoom with historically underrepresented graduate students and their families from April to May 2020 and found that students' motivation and academic effort were impeded by the increased workload and technological requirements due to the abrupt transition. Because of the intermittent reopening and teaching modality changes, students' coping with the continuous demand of varying accommodations (Liu, Pinder-Amaker, et al., 2022a) had to employ higher levels of self-regulated strategies. While adjustment, mental health, motivation, and self-regulated strategies are associated with each other and impact the academic outcome, few studies explore them systematically.

What is even less understood is whether the impact of the COVID-19 pandemic produced any gender-related disparities in adjustment, mental health, motivation, and self-regulated learning. Numerous studies suggest females' mental health was more susceptible to being affected by COVID-19 pandemic compared to males (Deryugina et al., 2021; Sharma & Vaish, 2020; Vloo et al., 2021; Xue & McMunn, 2020). These studies provide a consensus view that the COVID-19 pandemic has led to a disproportionate burden on women in terms of their roles as primary caregivers for their families across nations. With the closure of schools and childcare facilities, women have had to take on a greater share of household and caregiving responsibilities, which led to increased stress, anxiety, and burnout. Chirikov et al. (2020) similarly found that female graduate and professional students reported had nine percent greater levels of anxiety than their male peers. Prowse et al. (2021) studied undergraduate students and found that the COVID-19 pandemic caused more stress, greater isolation, and a greater negative impact on females' academic performance than males.

Pre-pandemic studies on gender differences in self-regulated learning in motivation, self-regulated learning strategies, and self-efficacy beliefs have shown inconsistent results. For instance, Balam (2015) studied 139 graduate students at a Southeastern university and found no gender differences in motivation and learning strategies. By contrast, Virtanen and Nevgi (2010) found that female students who majored in the sciences reported higher levels of self-regulated skills. However, the significant difference may be due to an imbalanced number of participants in each discipline. Moreover, few studies have investigated the gender differences in motivation and learning strategies during the COVID-19 pandemic. Hussein et al. (2020) conducted a case study to explore students' difficulties during online learning at a university in the United Arab Emirates. While students frequently mentioned assignment overloads and a lack of online support, one female student specified that family duties often distracted her from working on courses. Although the case study did not delve into academic engagement difficulties caused by women's family roles, the experiences that female students encountered offered a glimpse into the specific disadvantages that they experienced as compared to male students.

OBJECTIVES AND RESEARCH QUESTIONS

Graduate education is a critical pathway for individuals to advance their careers and to achieve professional success (Balam, 2015; Pyne & Grodsky, 2020; Wade et al., 2021; Walsh et al., 2021; Wang et al., 2020). However, completing a graduate program requires significant intellectual, academic, and financial resources. Female graduate students may face increased challenges in achieving academic success when the unexpected challenge imposed by the COVID-19 pandemic intersects with existing gender disparities (Deryugina et al., 2021; Jabbari et al., 2022; Wade et al., 2021). The current study aimed to examine whether female graduate students differ in their levels of adjustment, mental health, motivation, and self-regulated learning as compared to male students during the COVID-19 pandemic period. Specifically, this study was guided by the following research questions:

RQ1: Are there gender differences in adjustment issues among graduate students during the COVID-19 pandemic?

RQ2: Are there gender differences in mental health issues among graduate students during the COVID-19 pandemic?

RQ3: Are there gender differences in motivation among graduate students during the COVID-19 pandemic?

RQ4: Are there gender differences in self-regulated learning strategies among graduate students during the COVID-19 pandemic?

LITERATURE REVIEW

This study was guided by the existing literature on college adjustment, mental health, and motivation and learning strategies.

College Adjustment

College adjustment refers to how well students are able to adapt to college life, including their thoughts and feelings about the transition process (Anderson et al., 2016; Baker & Siryk, 1984; Pennebaker et al.,

2013). Research has shown that students who leave their hometowns to pursue higher education face a range of challenges, including intellectual, psychological, social, and financial issues (Credé & Niehorster, 2012; van der Zanden et al., 2018). Successful adjustment to college requires positive affection, a sense of belonging, and psychological well-being, which can ultimately lead to academic success. Conversely, negative emotions and homesickness can have a detrimental impact on coping strategies and adjustment (Garr et al., 2021; Terry et al., 2013; van der Zanden et al., 2018). The COVID-19 pandemic caused disruption in the lives of college students. Those who were in the U.S. were required to quickly adapt to online learning and widely reported a sense of uncertainty for undergraduate students due to frequent transitions to different learning and living conditions (Liu, Frazier, et al., 2022b; Okado et al., 2023; Prowse et al., 2021; Usher et al., 2021). While there have been several studies conducted into undergraduate students' experiences, there has been considerably less discussion of graduate students' possible adjustment challenges.

Several studies have reported the concerns of graduate students during the pandemic, such as accessing academic and financial support, losing control of graduation plans, and struggling to access laboratory and hands-on activities (Ebell et al., 2020; Kee, 2021; Walsh et al., 2021). For example, students enrolled in graduate-level teacher preparation programs engaged in virtual experiences, since in-person student teaching was not an option (Love & Yesbeck, 2022; Marshall et al., 2022; McKnight et al., 2022; VanLone et al., 2022). Walsh et al. (2021) found that historically underrepresented graduate students reported insecurity about their academic and personal lives, expressing concerns about accessing academic and financial support during the COVID-19 pandemic. Graduate students also worried about being unable to fulfill academic activities and lost control of graduation plans due to limited access to labs and hands-on activities (Kee, 2021).

While there is limited research on gender differences in adjustment during the COVID-19 pandemic among graduate students, previous studies investigating gender differences among undergraduate students have shown mixed results. van der Zanden et al.'s (2018) systematic review of literature on college student adjustment found that female students had more difficulties adapting to the university environment, particularly in their first year, than their male counterparts. By contrast, other research has suggested that female students had higher psychological and emotional well-being than males (Bowman, 2010; Strayhorn, 2012). It is important to note that these findings from studies on undergraduate students may not necessarily apply to graduate students since they are at different stages of their academic and professional development. Nonetheless, these prior studies serve as a foundation for investigating gender differences in adjustment among graduate students during the COVID-19 pandemic. Therefore, the first research question aimed to examine whether female graduate students experience more challenges in adjusting than male graduates.

Mental Health

The onset of the COVID-19 pandemic has brought numerous changes for college students. Amid the personal, social, and academic challenges that college students face, their mental health has been significantly impacted due to the closure of campuses (Chirikov et al., 2020; Gruber et al., 2021; Halliburton et al., 2021; Zhai & Du, 2020). For instance, students who relied on on-campus counseling services may have lost access to them, which could exacerbate their psychological symptoms. Additionally, campus closures may have created a financial strain for some students who lost their on-campus jobs. Leaving campus can lead to some students feeling a sense of loss, as they may have lost connections with friends as well as a safe space. Furthermore, when students were forced to move out of their dorms or even back home, they were often isolated and may have lost the peer socialization and support they had on campus (Liu, Pinder-Amaker, et al., 2022a; Zhai & Du, 2020).

Previous studies have focused more on undergraduate students and showed a decline in mental health, including increased levels of stress, anxiety, and depression during the pandemic. Limited attention has been given to graduate students' mental health (Jabbari et al., 2022; Kee, 2021; Walsh et al., 2021). The rate of increased mental problems was notably higher among graduate students than undergraduates during this time. According to Chirikov et al.'s (2020) longitudinal survey of students' experiences, both undergraduate and graduate students experienced a significant increase in mental health problems in 2020. The prevalence of major depressive disorder among graduate and professional students was found to be twice as high as in 2019, and the prevalence of anxiety was 1.5 times higher than 2019.

Students who previously reported low risk of mental health suffered more psychological problems due to the unprecedented situation (Borelli et al., 2021; Hamza et al., 2021). Hamza and colleagues (2021) conducted a quantitative study comparing college students with and without pre-existing mental health issues. The results showed that students without pre-existing mental health challenges reported an increase in depression, anxiety, loneliness, isolation, and disorientation after the onset of the

COVID-19 pandemic (Walsh et al., 2021). This finding is consistent with a case study conducted by Gruber et al. (2021), which also found evidence of increased depression, anxiety, and loneliness among participants who initially reported no clinical depression and mild stress. These students reported a significant increase in depression scores, ranging from mild to moderate.

Although the COVID-19 pandemic has been acknowledged as a stressor for students in general, it is still unknown whether female graduate students in the U.S. have experienced gender-related disparities. The previous literature has reviewed that female students may be more vulnerable to emotional fluctuation and struggle to adjust during times of transition (van der Zanden et al., 2018). Kilius et al. (2021) assessed the dreams of 71 female students in a Canadian university during the lockdown period. The results showed that these female participants frequently reported nightmares. These dreams reflected heightened negative emotions, such as anxiety, academic worry, and a sense of threat. Gewalt et al. (2022) conducted a survey in German universities to investigate gender differences in college students' physical and mental health. The results indicated that female students experienced a significantly greater decline in mental health compared to their male counterparts. In particular, 58.7% of female students reported a deterioration in mental health, whereas the corresponding figure for male students was 46.8%. Although the study did not specify the exact percentage of graduate students within the female sample, there was a noticeable trend of higher stress levels among female students.

Research on gender differences in mental health issues during the COVID-19 pandemic among graduate students is limited. However, previous research has shown that females and males respond differently to stressful events (Mallinckrodt & Leong 1992; McLean et al., 2011). In a study on the social support needed by graduate students to cope with stress, Mallinckrodt and Leong (1992) found that female graduate students were more affected by recent stressful life events than their male counterparts were. As a result, they reported experiencing more perceived stress and diagnosed stress symptoms. The study also revealed that depression and anxiety were severe psychological symptoms exacerbated by heightened stress levels in female graduate students. Therefore, female graduate students required more support from both their academic departments and family environments to cope with stress effectively. The COVID-19 pandemic has triggered a series of life stressors, and it is crucial to provide meaningful and appropriate support to graduate students experiencing heightened stress levels and mental health issues. The second research question aimed to examine whether female graduate students experience more stress, anxiety, and depression than male graduates as the result of the COVID-19 global pandemic.

Motivation and Learning Strategy

The academic routine in higher education has been disrupted due to changes in course modality in response to the outbreak of the COVID-19 pandemic (Kilius et al., 2021; Liu, Pinder-Amaker, et al., 2022a; Okado et al., 2023; Usher et al., 2021). Students are required to be highly motivated to engage in academic activities and to practice self-regulated strategies to adapt to new academic management. Zimmerman (1986) defined the self-regulated learner as being a metacognitively, motivationally, and behaviorally active participant in his or her learning. Additionally, Pintrich and colleagues (1991, 1993, 1999) integrated the role of motivation and proposed the self-regulated learning model that assumed two important categories of strategies: (1) cognitive and metacognitive learning strategies (rehearsal, elaboration, organization, critical thinking, and metacognitive self-regulation), and (2) resource management strategies (time and study environment, effort regulation, peer learning, and help-seeking). Motivation plays a critical role in promoting and sustaining self-regulated learning, as previous studies have shown a positive association between self-regulated learning, motivation, and academic achievement (Kryshko et al., 2022; Waldeyer et al., 2022). Schunk and Dibenedetto (2020) explored the concept of motivation from the perspective of Bandura's social cognitive theory, highlighting self-efficacy as the personal dimension of motivation that drives individuals to focus on achieving their goals. Students with higher self-efficacy are more likely to engage in effective learning strategies, manage their time and environmental resources, and seek support when needed.

There is a paucity of research that systematically explores the self-regulated learning and motivational components of graduate students and graduate gender differences (Balam, 2015; Virtanen & Nevgi, 2010). During the COVID-19 pandemic, numerous research has shown that college students encountered difficulties in being motivated and practicing self-regulation to engage in learning activities (Chirikov et al., 2020; Daniel, 2020; Walsh et al., 2021). Usher et al. (2021) conducted a survey study involving 358 undergraduate college students during the 2020 spring semester in the U.S. and found increases in sleep, social media use, online gaming, and procrastination, as well as decreases in academic motivation and self-regulation. The students attributed their decreased learning to internal factors, such as self-regulatory and motivational difficulties, as well as external factors, including a decline in instructional quality and communication following the shift to online instruction. Like undergraduate students, graduate students also faced changes in course modality. However, graduate students pursuing advanced degrees may experience different difficulties. Studies emphasizing graduate students have often focused on domain-specific academic topics to catch up with the nuance of their fields and delve deeper into the challenges and opportunities in their disciplines (Muñoz, 2021; Sifri et al., 2022). In a systematic literature review of 23 studies, Muñoz (2021) explored the role of self-efficacy in graduate nursing students' enrollment, retention, and graduation. The analysis identified that self-efficacy is sourced in perceived positive experiences, and it leads to productive thoughts, feelings, and actions, resulting in successful degree completion. Moreover, the shift to online classes disproportionately affected graduate and doctoral students in scientific fields requiring access to laboratory environments. These students have expressed concerns about disruptions to their academic routines and difficulties in continuing their research (Sifri et al., 2022). According to Sifri et al. (2022), graduate students reported a decreased amount of time and effort spent on class work and research, resulting in a significant lack of research progress.

In the current research, the third and fourth research questions aimed to examine whether gender as a factor differs in the impact of the COVID-19 pandemic on the motivational and self-regulated learning strategy components among graduate students. Specifically, the study explored critical thinking, metacognitive self-regulation, and resource management strategies using the Motivated Strategies for Learning Questionnaire (MSLQ; Pintrich, 1991). Additionally, the study investigated intrinsic and extrinsic motivation, as well as self-efficacy as key motivational components.

METHODS

In this study, we used a quantitative approach to investigate the gender differences that distinguish graduate students' adjustment, mental health, motivation, and self-regulated strategies during the COVID-19 pandemic in the U.S. This study received Institutional Review Board (IRB) approval.

Procedure and Participants

An anonymous online survey hosted by the Qualtrics platform collected data that measured variables and participants' demographic information from November to December 2021. The online survey invitation link was distributed through the Graduate Office mail list at a large university in the Southeast. We also relied on snowball sampling, encouraging participants to forward the survey link to other graduate students they knew. The survey was completed by 301 graduate students, with a high completion rate of 97.7%. The majority of participants (52%, n = 156) reported being currently enrolled in a master's degree program. Among the participants,

66% were female (n = 199), 33% were male (n = 98), and 1% (n = 4) self-identified as "other." The participants ranged in age from 18 years to 77 years, with a mean of 28.5 years (SD = 7.5). The most ethnic group was White (63%, n = 188). Demographic information is detailed in Table 18.1.

Table 18.1

Participant Demographic Information

Demographic	*n* (%)	Mean (*SD*)	Min	Max
Age		28.44 (7.49)	19	77
Sex				
Female	199 (66%)			
Male	98 (33%)			
Other	4 (1%)			
Degree				
Master	156 (52%)			
Doctorate	136 (45%)			
Specialist	9 (3%)			
Ethnicity				
White	188 (63%)			
Asian or Pacific Islander	57 (19%)			
Hispanic or Latinx	20 (7%)			
African American	17 (6%)			
Other	19 (6%)			

Measurements

The survey included a demographic questionnaire, the College Adjustment Test (CAT, Pennebaker, 2013), the Depression, Anxiety, and Stress Scale, (DASS21, Lovibond & Loibond, 1995), and selected subscales from the Motivated Strategies for Learning Questionnaire (MSLQ, Pintrich, 1991).

College Adjustment Test (CAT). The College Adjustment Test (CAT) was developed by Pennebaker (2013) and consists of three subscales. Participants use a Likert scale ranging from 1 (*Not at all*) to 5 (*A great deal*) to indicate the extent to which they experienced positive affect (6 items), negative affect (9 items), and homesickness (6 items) in the past week. Higher scores on the scale indicate stronger feelings towards the items.

Depression, Anxiety, and Stress Scale (DASS21). The Depression, Anxiety, and Stress Scale (DASS21) was developed by Lovibond and Lovibond (1995) and has been widely used in both clinical and research settings to assess psychological distress in various populations. The DASS21 consists of 21 items, with seven items each for depression, anxiety, and stress. Participants rate the frequency and severity of symptoms experienced in the past week on a Likert scale ranging from 1 (Did not apply to me at all) to 4 (Applied to me very much or most of the time). Higher scores indicate greater levels of depression, anxiety, and stress.

Motivated Strategies for Learning Questionnaire (MSLQ). The Motivated Strategies for Learning Questionnaire (MSLQ, Pintrich, 1991) is a self-report instrument designed to measure students' motivation and self-regulated learning strategies. The MSLQ originally included 81 items includes range of scales that measure different aspects of motivational and self-regulation components. The present study selected intrinsic (4 items) and extrinsic (4 items) motivation, and self-efficacy beliefs (8 items) to measure motivation. Moreover, critical thinking (5 items), metacognition and self-regulation (12 items), and resource management strategies (i.e., time and study management (8 items), peer learning (3 items), and effort regulation (4 items)) were included to measure the utility of self-regulated strategies. Participants rated their level of agreement with each item on a Likert scale ranging from 1 (not at all true of me) to 7 (very true of me), with higher scores indicating higher levels of motivation or self-regulated learning.

Data Analysis

Data were analyzed using SPSS 28 to provide descriptive statistics and correlations. First, the mean scores and bivariate correlation of the following scales were calculated: College Adjustment (Positive Affect, Negative Affect, and Homesickness), Mental Health (Stress, Anxiety, and Depression), Motivation (Intrinsic Goals, Extrinsic Goals, and Self-efficacy), and the cognitive Strategy used for learning (critical thinking, metacognition and self-regulation, time and study environment management, effort regulation, and peer learning). Next, multivariate analyses of variance (MANOVA) were conducted to compare if female graduate students differ on levels of the following subscales with male graduate students.

RESULTS

The reported values for Cronbach's Alpha ranged from .66 to .94 (see Table 18.2), indicating acceptable to excellent internal consistency reliability (Hair et al., 2006). Table 18.3 summarizes the mean, standard deviation (SD), and bivariate correlation coefficients of the 14 subscales.

The negative affect in college adjustment was found to have a significant and moderate correlation with homesickness, stress, anxiety, and depression (r = .60 ~.67, p < .01), and a negative correlation with self-efficacy, time and environment, and effort regulation (r = –.20 ~ –.24, p < .01). The three mental health scales had positive and moderate correlations with each other (r = .43 ~ .67, p < .01). The correlation showed that depression was significantly and negatively correlated with self-efficacy (r = –.23, p < .01), time and environment regulation (r = –.33, p < .01), and effort regulation (r = –.22, p < .01). Of the three motivation subscales, only self-efficacy had a significant and moderate correlation with the five self-regulated strategies examined (r = .16 ~.46, p < .01). Four out of five self-regulated strategy subscales were positively and moderately correlated, except for the peer learning strategy, which showed low correlation with the other four strategies. Table 18.2 presents the internal consistency reliability Cronbach's Alpha and the number of items for each of the 14 subscales.

Table 18.2

Reliability Result for Each Measure (Internal Consistency Cronbach's Alpha)

Measure	Num. of Items	Cronbach's Alpha
College Adjustment		
Positive Affect	6	.70
Negative Affect	9	.83
Home Sickness	6	.72
Mental Health		
Stress	7	.84
Anxiety	7	.81
Depression	7	.88
Motivation		
Intrinsic Goals	4	.82
Extrinsic Goals	4	.74
Self-Efficacy	8	.94
Self-regulated Learning Strategy		
Critical Thinking	5	.88
Self-Regulated	12	.80
Time & Environment	8	.75
Effort-Regulated	4	.66
Peer Learning	3	.79

Table 18.3

Means, SD, and Correlation Variables (N = 301)

	DV	*M*	*SD*	1	2	3	4	5	6	7	8	9	10	11	12	13
1	Positive Affect	3.45	0.69	–												
2	Negative Affect	3.09	0.86	–.28**	--											
3	Homesickness	3.06	0.77	–.11	.67**	–										
4	Stress	2.31	0.73	–.35**	.67**	.43**	–									
5	Anxiety	1.81	0.67	–.24**	.60**	.48**	.66**	–								
6	Depression	1.93	0.74	–.40**	.66**	.48**	.66**	.64**	–							
7	Intrinsic	4.98	1.33	.32**	–.06	–.09	–.04	–.03	–.05	–						
8	Extrinsic	4.87	1.47	.14*	.16**	.14*	.18**	.18**	.07	.28**	–					
9	Efficacy	4.23	1.34	.35**	–.24**	–.18**	–.21**	–.18**	–.23**	.52**	.20**	–				
10	Critical	4.45	1.40	.17**	.05	–.03	.09	.07	.04	.43**	.13*	.46**	–			
11	Self_reg	4.47	0.97	.28**	–.09	–.02	.01	.06	–.09	.51**	.24**	.46**	.52**	–		
12	Time	4.91	1.06	.26**	–.21**	–.15**	–.11	–.19**	–.33**	.32**	.27**	.34**	.19**	.45**	–	
13	Effort	5.27	1.11	.20**	–.20**	–.13**	–.09	–.12*	–.22**	.35**	.20**	.41**	.21**	.43**	.58**	–
14	Peer	3.85	1.75	.18**	.04	.16**	.04	.11	–.03	.18**	.20**	.16**	.18**	.27**	.15**	.08

Note. Critical: Critical Thinking, Self_reg: Metacognitive Self_regulation, Time: Time_Environment Management, Effort: Effort Regulation, Peer: Peer Learning

** $p < .01$, * $p < .05$.

Four MANOVA tests were conducted to investigate whether female graduate students differed from male graduate students in scores on adjustment factors, mental health factors, motivational factors, and self-regulated strategy factors. Box's M test of equality of covariance indicated heterogeneity of the four MANOVA procedures. Wilks' Lambda was used to evaluate the multivariate significance (Hair et al., 2006). The results showed that female and male graduate students had different levels of adjustment (Box's $M = 10.72, p = .10, F(3,293) = 4.14, p = .01, \eta^2 = .04$) and mental health (Box's $M = 13.53$ $p = .04, F(3,293) = 6.43, p < .001, \eta^2 = .06$), with small to moderate effect sizes, respectively. Follow up analyses indicated that female graduate students had higher levels of homesickness ($F(1,295) = 11.14, p < .001, \eta^2 = .04$), negative affect ($F(1,295) = 6.68, p = .01, \eta^2 = .02$), and stress ($F(1,295) = 7.30, p = .01, \eta^2 = .02$) with small effect sizes. However, there were no significant differences between female and male graduate students in positive affect, anxiety, depression, and all subscales in motivation and the use of self-regulated learning strategies. Table 18.4 summarizes the four hypotheses testing results.

CONCLUSIONS

In the current study, MANOVA results indicated that the first and second hypotheses tested partially held. Female graduate students showed statistically higher negative affect, homesickness, and stress levels than their male peers. The negative affect and homesickness are two subscales that are designed to evaluate a student's level of negative emotional experiences related to adjusting to college life, particularly those who are living away from home (Pennebaker, 2013). The negative affect scale measures a student's level of worry that may be impacted by external factors such as academics and intimate relationships or a negative sense of self internally (Credé & Niehorster, 2012; van der Zanden et al., 2018). Besides, homesickness characterizes the distress that students missing their home and familiar surroundings when moving away to attend college. Homesickness can pose a significant challenge to students' adjustment to attachment and overall well-being during the transition period (Terry et al., 2013).

The gender differences in adjustment observed in the present study were consistent with previous research on first-year college adjustment. van der Zanden et al. (2018) found that female undergraduate students had more difficulties adapting to the university environment, especially in their first year, than male students. Given that many graduate students have likely experienced disruptions in their routines and have been separated from their familiar surroundings (Halliburton et al., 2021; Liu, Frazier, et al., 2022b; Okado et al., 2023), the higher homesickness showed

Table 18.4

MANOVA Results

Scale	Female	Male n = 98 M (SD)	Box's M (p)	MANOVA				ANOVA			
				F	df	p	η^2	F	df	p	η^2
College Adjustment			10.72 (.102)	4.14	3,293	.007**	.04				
Positive Affect	3.42 (0.67)	3.54 (0.73)						2.19	1,295	.140	.07
Negative Affect	3.18 (0.80)	2.90 (0.96)						6.68	1,295	.01**	.02
Home Sickness	3.16 (0.69)	2.85 (0.88)						11.14	1,295	<.001***	.04
DASS			13.53 (.038)	6.43	3,293	<.001***	.06				
Stress	2.38 (0.71)	2.14 (0.73)						7.30	1,295	.007**	.02
Depression	1.91 (0.70)	1.97 (0.83)						0.44	1,295	.15	.01
Anxiety	1.85 (0.69)	1.73 (0.62)						2.09	1,295	.51	.00
Motivation			0.85 (.991)	2.47	3,291	.062	.03				
Intrinsic Goal	4.88 (1.32)	5.18 (1.32)									
Extrinsic Goal	4.91 (1.48)	4.80 (1.46)									
Self-Efficacy	5.25 (1.35)	5.18 (1.34)									
Learning Strategies			18.77 (.244)	1.33	5,289	.25	.02				
Critical Thinking	4.39 (1.46)	4.54 (1.30)									

(Table continued on next page)

Table 18.4 (Continued)

MANOVA Results

Scale	Female	Male n = 98 M (SD)	Box's M (p)	MANOVA				ANOVA			
				F	df	p	η^2	F	df	p	η^2
Self-Regulation	4.52 (1.00)	4.37 (0.91)									
Time Environment	4.97 (1.05)	4.79 (1.09)									
Effort Regulation	5.34 (1.11)	5.10 (1.11)									
Peer Learning	3.84 (1.77)	3.87 (1.72)									

Note. * $p < .05$; ** $p < .01$; *** $p < .001$

that female graduate students might be more susceptible to feelings of isolation and uncertainty due to frequent transitions to different learning and living conditions. Moreover, the gender difference in stress among graduate students in the context of the COVID-19 pandemic is consistent with previous research in academic settings (Prowse et al., 2021; Wade et al., 2021). The current study also revealed that while there were no gender differences in anxiety and depression, there was a moderate correlation between adjustment and mental health problems (see Table 18.3), indicating that negative adjustment and increased stress may have contributed to the worsening of anxiety and depression issues.

The third and fourth hypotheses were not supported, as no significant gender differences were found in motivation and cognitive strategy levels between female and male graduate students during the COVID-19 pandemic. These findings are consistent with prior research that also showed no gender differences in motivation and self-regulated learning strategies (Balam, 2015; Virtanen & Nevgi, 2010). However, the present study has uncovered potential issues that could undermine motivation and self-regulated learning. One notable factor in mental health, namely depression, showed a significant and moderate negative correlation with self-efficacy, time and environment management, and effort regulation ($r = -.23, -.33, -.22, p < .001$). Given the reported increase in depression among graduate students, the adverse impact on learning warrants attention. On the other hand, it has been widely reported that professional women bear more household and caregiving responsibilities across nations (Sharma & Vaish, 2020; Xue & McMunn, 2020; Wade et al., 2021). According to Deryugina et al. (2021), who conducted a global survey of academics, COVID-19 pandemic disruptions disproportionately affect the productivity of female academics.

IMPLICATIONS FOR THE FUTURE

In response to the pandemic, scholars have recommended that administrators collaborate with students to create interventions, proactive programs, and enhanced services to support the mental health and well-being of graduate students (Chirikov et al., 2020; Gruber et al., 2021; Huckins et al., 2020; Liu, Pinder-Amaker et al., 2022a). The COVID-19 pandemic has been a stressful time for everyone, but research indicates that female students at all levels reported greater levels of stress than their male peers (Centers for Disease Control and Prevention, 2023; Lee et al., 2021; Marshall, 2023). Graduate students may be experiencing additional stress due to increased caregiving responsibilities and financial instability. Providing mental health support tailored to the needs of women and experiences can help address gender inequalities in graduate education issues and promote positive adjustment. We share some initial gender-informed ideas as a basis for further refinement and development. One way to support female graduate students is by offering flexible work arrangements (Jabbari et al., 2022). Many women are juggling multiple responsibilities, such as caregiving, work, and school. Having the opportunity to work part-time or remotely can help them manage these responsibilities while still pursuing their academic and professional goals. Another way to support female graduate students is by promoting mentorship and networking opportunities. Female graduate students may face additional barriers to networking and mentorship due to gender-based biases and stereotypes biases (Mallinckrodt & Leong, 1992; Sifri et al., 2022). By providing opportunities for female graduate students to connect with mentors and peers who can offer guidance and support, these barriers can be addressed, and academic success can be promoted.

The present study provides a basis for future researchers to gather more comprehensive data and to delve deeper into graduate students' academic experiences. It is recommended that future studies consider the impact of the post-pandemic landscape on their academic journey. One potential area of investigation could focus on its impacts on female graduate students' academic productivity and graduation processes. To capture a more nuanced understanding of their experiences, a combination of survey and follow-up interviews, for instance, could be employed to analyze significant changes and sustained effects. However, it remains unclear whether differences found among female graduate students are due solely to gender or if they navigate gender-biased relationships and societal perceptions. Therefore, in addition to the gender factor, it is also essential to explore the intersectionality of other factors, such as race and socioeconomic status, to understand how these factors affect graduate students. Furthermore, demographic questionnaires should be supplemented with personal information such as marital status, number of children, or financial support sources to fully understand graduate students' experiences.

SUMMARY

Graduate students, like their undergraduate counterparts, face challenges related to adjustment, motivation, mental health, and self-regulated learning strategies engagement, yet they are understudied (Jabbari et al., 2022; Walsh et al., 2021). These issues have been compounded by the COVID-19 pandemic, leading to a widely reported increase in negative adjustment, stress, anxiety, and depression among students. Prompting the use of various self-regulated learning strategies can help students overcome these challenges.

The pandemic has brought to light the disproportionate disadvantages that women face. Disrupted routines and instability can be particularly challenging for female students who place a higher value on emotional connections and support systems. As a result, they were more vulnerable to emotional fluctuations and experienced greater levels of homesickness and stress during the COVID-19 pandemic. Despite the absence of significant gender differences in motivation and self-regulated learning strategies in the current study, attention should be given to the possibility that the COVID-19 pandemic could exacerbate the existing gender gap in academia.

In addition to the emotional difficulties faced by female graduate students, female graduate students may also be disproportionately affected by their caregiver identity (Prowse et al., 2021; Deryugina et al., 2021). The instability caused by the pandemic has widened the gap of gender inequality (Jabbari et al., 2022; Sharma & Vaish, 2020; Walsh et al., 2021; Xue & McMunn, 2020). During the COVID-19 pandemic, the closure of schools and childcare facilities has led to women, in general, taking on a greater share of household and caregiving responsibilities across cultures. Sharma and Vaish's (2020) studied India female professionals aged 22 and older through online survey. Results revealing that women working from home while also managing household chores experienced an increase in both physical and mental load. As a result, women have experienced an increased workload that has been associated with higher levels of stress, anxiety, and burnout. This may have worsened existing gender disparities and added to the challenges faced by female graduate students in achieving academic success. Xue and McMunn (2020) examined a household longitudinal dataset with a gender perspective in the U.K. Among 6,166 participants who were parents and caregivers, women reported spending on average five more hours per day on housework and 10 more hours per week on childcare compared to men during the lockdown. Results from the present study indicated that female graduate students suffered higher negative affect, homesickness, and stress levels.

It is uncertain whether the high levels of negative adjustment and mental health issues experienced by graduate students during the COVID-19 pandemic will immediately decrease in the aftermath of the pandemic. While the pandemic has been a major stressor for many graduate students, other factors such as financial difficulties, academic pressure, and personal circumstances may continue to affect mental health and well-being even after the pandemic subsides. Recognizing that recovery is a complex and ongoing process, and the effects of the pandemic on maladjustment may be long-lasting, universities administrators and psychological professionals may need to provide targeted support and resources to graduate students. This support should be provided in the aftermath of the pandemic to address graduate student mental health, academic engagement, and well-being.

REFERENCES

Anderson, J. R., Guan, Y., & Koc, Y. (2016). The academic adjustment scale: Measuring the adjustment of permanent resident or sojourner students. *International Journal of Intercultural Relations, 54*, 68–76. https://doi.org/10.1016/j.ijintrel.2016.07.006

Baker, R. W., & Siryk, B. (1984). Measuring adjustment to college. *Journal of Counseling Psychology, 31*,179–189.

Balam, E. M. (2015). Learning strategies and motivation of graduate students: is gender a factor?. *Institute for Learning Styles Journal, 1*, 1–9.

Borelli, J., Lai, J., Yunusova, A., Rivera, A. P., Labbaf, S., Hu, S., Jain, R. C., & Rahmani, A. (2020). *Nine months in the life of a college student during 2020: A case study using multi-modal assessments to capture personalized contexts of well-being*. https://doi.org/10.31234/osf.io/wb4ds

Bowman, N. A. (2010). The development of psychological well-being among first-year college students. *Journal of College Student Development, 51*, 180–200. http://dx.doi.org/10.1353/csd.0.0118

Centers for Disease Control and Prevention [CDC]. (2023). *Youth risk behavior survey: Data summary & trends report 2011–2021*. https://cdc.gov/healthyyouth/data/yrbs/pdf/YRBS_Data-Summary-Trends-Report2023_508.pdf

Chirikov, I., Soria, K. M., Horgos, B., & Jones-White, D. (2020). *Undergraduate and graduate students' mental health during the COVID-19 pandemic*. SERU Consortium, University of California—Berkeley and University of Minnesota. https://cshe.berkeley.edu/seru-covid-survey-reports

Credé, M., & Niehorster, S. (2012). Adjustment to college as measured by the student adaptation to college questionnaire: A quantitative review of its structure and relationships with correlates and consequences. *Educational Psychology Review, 24*(1), 133–165.https://doi.org.10.1007/s10648-011-9184-5

Daniel, S. J. (2020). Education and the COVID-19 pandemic. *Prospects, 49*, 91–96. https://doi.org/10.1007/s11125-020-09464-3

Deryugina, T., Shurchkov, O., & Stearns, J. (2021, May). COVID-19 disruptions disproportionately affect female academics. In *AEA Papers and Proceedings* (Vol. 111, pp. 164–168). 2014 Broadway, Suite 305, Nashville, TN 37203: American Economic Association. https://doi.org/10.1257/pandp.20211017

Ebell, M. H., Bierema, L., & Haines, L. (2020). Graduate students significantly more concerned than undergraduates about returning to campus in the era of COVID-19. *medRxiv*, 2020-07. https://doi.org/10.1101/2020.07.15.20154682

Garr, K., Odar Stough, C., Godfrey, L. M., & Ley, S. L. (2021). Weight change predicts college adjustment and depressive symptoms among first-year college students. *Journal of American College Health*, 1–7. https://doi.org/10.1080/07448481.2021.1950729

Gewalt, S. C., Berger, S., Krisam, R., & Breuer, M. (2022). Effects of the COVID-19 pandemic on university students' physical health, mental health and learning, a cross-sectional study including 917 students from eight universities in Germany. *Plos One, 17*(8). https://doi.org/10.1371/journal.pone.0273928

Gruber, J., Prinstein, M. J., Clark, L. A., Rottenberg, J., Abramowitz, J. S., Albano, A. M., Aldao, A., Borelli, J. L., Chung, T., Davila, J., Forbes, E. E., Gee, D. G., Hall, G. C. N., Hallion, L. S., Hinshaw, S. P., Hofmann, S. G., Hollon, S. D., Joormann, J., Kazdin, A. E., ... Weinstock, L. M. (2021). Mental health and clinical psychological science in the time of COVID-19: Challenges, opportunities, and a call to action. *American Psychologist, 76*(3), 409–426. https://doi.org/10.1037/amp0000707

Hair, J. F., Black, W. C., Babin, B. J., Anderson, R. E., & Tatham, R. L. (2006). *Multivariate data analysis* (6th ed.). Pearson.

Halliburton, A. E., Hill, M. B., Dawson, B. L., Hightower, J. M., & Rueden, H. (2021). Increased stress, declining mental health: Emerging adults' experiences in college during COVID-19. *Emerging Adulthood, 9*(5), 433–448. https://doi.org/10.1177/21676968211025348

Hamza, C. A., Ewing, L., Heath, N. L., & Goldstein, A. L. (2021). When social isolation is nothing new: A longitudinal study on psychological distress during COVID-19 among university students with and without preexisting mental health concerns. *Canadian Psychology, 62*(1), 20–30. https://doi.org/10.1037/cap0000255

Huckins, J. F., DaSilva, A. W., Wang, W., Hedlund, E., Rogers, C., Nepal, S. K., Wu, J.-L., Obuchi, M., Murphy, E. I., Meyer, M. L., Wagner, D. D., Holtzheimer, P. E., & Campbell, A. T. (2020). Mental health and behavior of college students during the early phases of the COVID-19 pandemic: Longitudinal smartphone and ecological momentary assessment study. *Journal of Medical Internet Research, 22*(6). https://doi.org/10.2196/20185

Hussein, E., Daoud, S., Alrabaiah, H., & Badawi, R. (2020). Exploring undergraduate students' attitudes towards emergency online learning during COVID-19: A case from the UAE. *Children and Youth Services Review, 119*. https://doi.org/10.1016/j.childyouth.2020.105699

Jabbari, J., Ferris, D., Frank, T., Malik, S., & Bessaha, M. (2022). Intersecting race and gender across hardships and mental health during COVID-19: a moderated-mediation model of graduate students at two universities. *Race and Social Problems*, 1–19. https://doi.org/10.1007/s12552-022-09379-y

Kee, C. E. (2021) The impact of COVID-19: Graduate students' emotional and psychological experiences. *Journal of Human Behavior in the Social Environment, 31*(1–4), 476–488, https://doi.org/10.1080/10911359.2020.1855285

Kilius, E., Abbas, N. H., McKinnon, L., & Samson, D. R. (2021). Pandemic nightmares: COVID-19 lockdown associated with increased aggression in female university students' dreams. *Frontiers in Psychology, 12*, 644636. https://doi.org/10.3389/fpsyg.2021.644636

Kryshko, O., Fleischer, J., Grunschel, C., & Leutner, D. (2022). Self-efficacy for motivational regulation and satisfaction with academic studies in STEM undergraduates: The mediating role of study motivation. *Learning & Individual Differences*, 93. https://doi.org/10.1016/j.lindif.2021.102096

Lee, J., Jeong, H. J., & Kim, S. (2021). Stress, anxiety, and depression among undergraduate students during the COVID-19 pandemic and their use of mental health services. *Innovative Higher Education, 46*, 519–538. https://doi.org/10.1007/s10755-021-09552-y

Liu, C. H., Pinder-Amaker, S., Hahm, H. C., & Chen, J. A. (2022a). Priorities for addressing the impact of the COVID-19 pandemic on college student mental health. *Journal of American College Health, 70*(5), 1356–1358. https://doi.org/10.1080/07448481.2020.1803882

Liu, Y., Frazier, P. A., Porta, C. M., & Lust, K. (2022a). Mental health of US undergraduate and graduate students before and during the COVID-19 pandemic: Differences across sociodemographic groups. *Psychiatry Research, 309*. https://doi.org/10.1016/j.psychres.2022.114428

Love, S. M., & Yesbeck, D. (2022). Lessons learned from a liberal arts teacher preparation program. In D. T. Marshall (Ed.), *COVID-19 and the classroom: How schools navigated the great disruption* (pp. 213–230). Lexington Books.

Lovibond, S. H., & Lovibond, P. F. (1995). *Manual for the depression, anxiety, & stress scales* (2nd ed.). Psychology Foundation.

Mallinckrodt, B., & Leong, F. T. (1992). Social support in academic programs and family environments: Sex differences and role conflicts for graduate students. *Journal of Counseling & Development, 70*(6), 716–723. https://doi-org.spot.lib.auburn.edu/10.1002/j.1556-6676.1992.tb02154.x

Marshall, D. T., Trammell, D. Shetty, P., & Woods, S. (2022). How an alternative licensure program pivoted during the pandemic. In D. T. Marshall (Ed.), *COVID-19 and the classroom: How schools navigated the great disruption* (pp. 231–246). Lexington Books.

Marshall, D. T. (2023) COVID-19 and school closures: A narrative review of pediatric mental health impacts. *Journal of School Choice,* 1–10. https://doi.org/10.1080/15582159.2023.2201734

McKnight, K., Hope, S., Marrs, S., & Pitre-Martin, M. (2022). Lessons learned from an urban teacher residency. In D. T. Marshall (Ed.), *COVID-19 and the classroom: How schools navigated the great disruption* (pp. 247–262). Lexington Books.

McLean, C. P., Asnaani, A., Litz, B. T., & Hofmann, S. G. (2011). Gender differences in anxiety disorders: prevalence, course of illness, comorbidity and burden of illness. *Journal of Psychiatric Research, 45*(8), 1027–1035. https://doi.org/10.1016/j.jpsychires.2011.03.006

Muñoz, L. R. (2021). Graduate student self-efficacy: Implications of a concept analysis. *Journal of Professional Nursing, 37*(1), 112-121.https://doi.org/10.1016/j.profnurs.2020.07.001

Okado, Y., Scaramella, C., Nguyen, H. M., Mendoza, B., & Watarastaporn, T. (2023). Psychosocial adjustment of U.S. college students in the early months of the COVID-19 pandemic. *Journal of American College Health, 71*(4), 1281–1292. https://doi.org/10.1080/07448481.2021.1926268

Pennebaker, J. W., (2013). The college adjustment test (CAT). *Measurement Instrument Database for the Social Science.* http://www. midss.ie

Pintrich, P. R. (1991). A manual for the use of the Motivated Strategies for Learning Questionnaire (MSLQ). https://doi.org/10.1037/t09161-000

Pintrich, P. R. (1999). The role of motivation in promoting and sustaining self-regulated learning. *International Journal of Educational Research, 31*(6), 459–470. https://doi.org/10.1016/s0883-0355(99)00015-4

Pintrich, P. R., Smith, D., Garcia, T., & Mc Keachie, W. (1993). Predictive validity and reliability of the Motivated Strategies for Learning Questionnaire (MSLQ). *Educational and Psychological Measurement, 53*(3), 801–813. https://doi.org/10.1177/0013164493053003024

Prowse, R., Sherratt, F., Abizaid, A., Gabrys, R. L., Hellemans, K. G., Patterson, Z. R., & McQuaid, R. J. (2021). Coping with the COVID-19 pandemic: examining gender differences in stress and mental health among university students. *Frontiers in Psychiatry, 12.* https://doi-org.spot.lib.auburn.edu/10.3389/fpsyt.2021.650759

Pyne, J., & Grodsky, E. (2020). Inequality and opportunity in a perfect storm of graduate student debt. *Sociology of Education, 93*(1), 20–39. https://doi.org/10.1177/0038040719876245

Schunk, D. H., & DiBenedetto, M. K. (2020). Motivation and social cognitive theory. *Contemporary Educational Psychology, 60.* https://doi.org/10.1016/j.cedpsych.2019.101832

Sharma, N., & Vaish, H. (2020). Impact of COVID–19 on mental health and physical load on women professionals: an online cross-sectional survey. *Health Care for Women International, 41*(11–12), 1255–1272. https://doi.org/10.1080/07399332.2020.1825441

Sifri, R. J., McLoughlin, E. A., Fors, B. P., & Salehi, S. (2022). Differential impact of the COVID-19 pandemic on female graduate students and postdocs in the chemical sciences. *Journal of Chemical Education, 99*(10), 3461–3470. https://doi.org/10.1021/acs.jchemed.2c00412

Son, C., Hegde, S., Smith, A., Wang, X., & Sasangohar, F. (2020). Effects of COVID-19 on college students' mental health in the United States: Interview survey study. *Journal of Medical Internet Research, 22*(9). https://doi.org/10.2196/21279

Strayhorn, T. L. (2012). Exploring the impact of Facebook and Myspace use on first-year students' sense of belonging and persistence decisions. *Journal of College Student Development, 53*(6), 783–796. http://dx.doi.org/10.1353/csd.2012.0078.

Terry, M. L., Leary, M. R., & Mehta, S. (2013). Self-compassion as a buffer against homesickness, depression, and dissatisfaction in the transition to college. *Self and Identity, 12*(3), 278–290. http://dx.doi.org/10.1080/15298868.2012.667913

Usher, E. L., Golding, J. M., Han, J., Griffiths, C. S., McGavran, M. B., Brown, C. S., & Sheehan, E. A. (2021). Psychology students' motivation and learning in response to the shift to remote instruction during COVID-19. *Scholarship of Teaching and Learning in Psychology.* https://doi.org/10.1037/stl0000256

van der Zanden, P. J., Denessen, E., Cillessen, A. H., & Meijer, P. C. (2018). Domains and predictors of first-year student success: A systematic review. *Educational Research Review*, *23*, 57–77. https://doi.org/10.1016/j.edurev.2018.01.001

VanLone, J., Panse-Barone, C., & Long, K. (2022). Teacher preparation and the COVID-19 disruption: Understanding the impact and implications for novice teachers. *International Journal of Educational Research Open, 3*. https://doi.org/10.1016/j.ijedro.2021.100120

Virtanen, P., & Nevgi, A. (2010). Disciplinary and gender differences among higher education students in self-regulated learning strategies. *Educational psychology, 30*(3), 323–347. https://doi.org/10.1080/01443411003606391

Vloo, A., Alessie, R. J. M., Mierau, J. O., Boezen, M. H., Mierau, J. O., Franke, L., ... & Jankipersadsing, S. A. (2021). Gender differences in the mental health impact of the COVID-19 lockdown: Longitudinal evidence from the Netherlands. *SSM-population Health, 15*, 100878. https://doi.org/10.1016/j.ssmph.2021.100878

Wade, M., Prime, H., Johnson, D., May, S. S., Jenkins, J. M., & Browne, D. T. (2021). The disparate impact of COVID-19 on the mental health of female and male caregivers. *Social Science & Medicine*, *275*. https://doi.org/10.1016/j.socscimed.2021.113801

Waldeyer, J., Dicke, T., Fleischer, J., Guo, J., Trentepohl, S., Wirth, J., & Leutner, D. (2022). A moderated mediation analysis of conscientiousness, time management strategies, effort regulation strategies, and university students' performance. *Learning and Individual Differences*, 100. https://doi.org/10.1016/j.lindif.2022.102228

Walsh, B. A., Woodliff, T. A., Lucero, J., Harvey, S., Burnham, M. M., Bowser, T. L., Aguirre, M., & Zeh, D. W. (2021). Historically underrepresented graduate students' experiences during the COVID-19 pandemic. *Family Relations*, *70*(4), 955–972.

Wang, X., Hegde, S., Son, C., Keller, B., Smith, A., & Sasangohar, F. (2020). Investigating mental health of US college students during the COVID-19 pandemic: Cross-sectional survey study. *Journal of Medical Internet Research*, *22*(9). https://10.2196/22817

Xue, B., & McMunn, A. (2021). Gender differences in unpaid care work and psychological distress in the UK Covid-19 lockdown. *PloS One, 16*(3), e0247959. https://doi.org/10.1371/journal.pone.0247959

Zhai, Y., & Du, X. (2020). Addressing collegiate mental health amid COVID-19 pandemic. *Psychiatry Research*, *288*. https://doi.org/10.1016/j.psychres.2020.113003

CHAPTER 19

A SELF-STUDY ON PROMOTING SELF-REGULATED LEARNING USING TECHNOLOGY DURING REMOTE INSTRUCTION

Héfer Bembenutty
Queens College of the City University of New York

Charles Raffaele
NYU Steinhardt School of Culture, Education, and Human Development

Daniel R. Pisari
The Graduate Center, City University of New York

ABSTRACT

In response to the COVID-19 pandemic, teacher candidates were challenged to adopt new technologies and to adjust to the unique demands of online learning as well as to the social and emotional difficulties of navigating a dangerous pandemic. For teacher educators, this also necessitated a redesign of instruction, curriculum, and assessment to best suit the new needs of their

Examining the Cognitive and Psychological Effects of the COVID-19 Global Pandemic on High School, College, and Graduate Learners, pp. 435–465

learners. In this chapter, three teacher educators shared the findings of self-study research when they taught undergraduate educational psychology courses in a teacher preparation program at a college in the United States. Changes to the courses described in this chapter include adjustments to self-regulatory processes, such as social and emotional learning, self-efficacy, and academic delay of gratification. It also describes pedagogical approaches, including technology implementation, lesson implementations, validity and reliability of assessment, and feedback. These adjustments enhanced the three teacher educators' successful development of self-regulated learning skills and supported teacher candidates' academic success in the transition to learning during a pandemic. Three themes derived from their self-study: (a) the importance of teacher educators in promoting social and emotional learning, delay of gratification, and self-regulated learning, (b) the importance of utilizing established pedagogical approaches, particularly during crises, and (c) the importance of being reflective and overcoming challenges as teacher educators during difficult situations in teacher education programs.

Keywords: self-study, COVID-19, self-regulated learning, teacher education, emergency remote teaching, self-efficacy, classroom management, online learning

The COVID-19 pandemic transformed how instruction was conducted with learners, which resulted in an education challenging in which teaching and learning shifted to online distance learning (Calamlam et al., 2022; Dai et al., 2022). To slow the spread of the COVID-19 pandemic, in March–April 2020, schools around the world were switched abruptly to remote, online formats, which affected a billion learners worldwide (UNESCO, 2020a). Learners' disruptions included school closures, societal safety measures, social distancing, stress, and anxiety (UNESCO, 2020b). Nevertheless, educators promoted self-regulated learning with technology to help students cope with the pandemic (Dai et al., 2022). *Self-regulated learning* involves activating and sustaining motivation, actions, behaviors, and affect to pursue worthwhile goals (Zimmerman, 2013).

This chapter presents self-study research conducted by three teacher educators. We describe, analyze, and reflect on our use of various educational psychology and pedagogical approaches to support teacher candidates' self-regulated learning during the COVID-19 pandemic. Such approaches included technology implementations and social and emotional support. Teacher educators also have ways to maximize the fidelity of lesson conductance, assessment validity, feedback relevance, and self-efficacy. A critical internal motivational process is self-efficacy beliefs. In academic settings, self-regulated learning is associated with students' *self-efficacy*—learners' beliefs about their competence to perform designated tasks (Bandura, 1997). We reflected on how the COVID-19 pandemic impacted our instruction, and how our pedagogical adaptations promoted the self-regulated learning of our teacher candidates.

In the following sections, we first provide an overview of the impact of the COVID-19 pandemic on our educational system worldwide. We then describe various self-regulatory processes and highlight the vital role self-regulated learning played during the transition from in-person instruction to distance learning. We review the literature on self-study research to provide a comprehensive understanding of our self-study and how it is contextually situated within a trustworthy, valid, and reliable qualitative methodology. After this, we describe the methodology guiding our study and the significant research findings. In the discussion, we describe three noteworthy themes derived from our experience during this transitional experience, reflect on the educational outcomes, and offer practical educational implications.

LITERATURE REVIEW

The COVID-19 Pandemic and Teacher Preparation

In the summer of 2020, teachers reported having anxiety and depressive symptoms (Hirshberg et al., 2023). Boyer-Davis (2020) showed that college educators reported increased technostress from their inability to adapt to new technologies healthily (Brod, 1984). Other difficulties adjusting to online learning included a lack of experience and training regarding teaching online, adjusting existing assignments to work online, and designing accessible online learning environments (Guilbaud et al., 2021). At the college level, many challenges faculty faced in dealing with the pandemic may be generalized as concerns regarding new technology implementations, lesson implementation, students' social and emotional well-being, the validity of assessments, and providing effective feedback (Mandouit & Hattie, 2023). Some teacher educators have attempted to address these challenges in teacher education programs by promoting students' self-regulated learning in online classes (Choate et al., 2021; Dai et al., 2022).

Teacher preparation courses required specific changes in the transition to emergency remote teaching. Student teaching requirements were often waived or vastly reduced for teacher candidates, with possible long-term effects on candidates' career trajectories (Choate et al., 2021). Other field observation requirements for teacher candidates faced similar difficulties, and teacher educators made great efforts to adapt using technological innovations (Hartshorne et al., 2020). More generally, teacher educators have focused on applying learning technologies to accommodate the difficulties of the pandemic—facilitating communication with students, synchronous and asynchronous instruction, and new approaches to assessment (Quezada et al., 2020).

Following the onset of the pandemic, promoting teacher candidates' self-regulated learning became particularly challenging due to concerns with health issues, income instability, and caring for family members. Regular access to technology was difficult for some students. Maintaining attention during online classes became complicated, too. In general, teacher educators struggled to secure teacher candidates' opportunities to gain experience and to apply new knowledge and skills during instruction and school settings (Rosenberg et al., 2021). Students may need to improve self-regulated learning skills to succeed in environments with many disruptions.

Self-Regulated Learning Processes

Recent research into COVID-19 has focused on the crucial role that self-regulated learning plays in helping learners to cope with the pandemic's adverse effects (Dai et al., 2022; Hensley et al., 2022). Recently, Xu and her associates synthesized research and confirmed self-regulated learning as effective for promoting academic achievement in online or blended learning (Xu et al., 2023). Self-regulated learners purposefully use cognitive, metacognitive, and affective regulation strategies (Schunk & Greene, 2018; Zimmerman, 2013) and focus on development through a feedback loop (Zimmerman, 2008).

Self-regulated learning involves multidimensional processes. Theorists from diverse perspectives have developed valuable models to explain its various processes (Bembenutty, 2011; Bembenutty et al., 2013; Panadero, 2017; Schunk & Greene, 2018; Vohs & Baumeister, 2016; Zimmerman & Schunk, 2011). The theories share common perspectives about how learning, teaching, and performance happen (Schunk & Greene, 2018). One of the common features is that learners can be behaviorally, cognitively, and motivationally active in their pursuit of goals. They also can set goals and have at their disposal a myriad of strategies helpful to reach learning and successful performance.

The literature on self-regulated learning reveals that students can learn how to become self-regulated and proactive learners (Zimmerman, 2013). They set goals and select learning strategies. At the same time, teachers and college educators and faculty can promote self-regulated learning in their classrooms (Pintrich, 1995, 2004). According to Pintrich (1995), there are three major characteristics of self-regulated learners. He proposed that self-regulated learners can control, monitor, regulate, and adjust their behavior, motivation, affect, and cognition. He emphasized that self-regulated learners are working to achieve a desirable goal. He further posited that self-regulated learners control their own actions and behavior rather than their parents or teachers. Pintrich concluded that (a) students can learn to be self-regulated, (b) self-regulated learning is controllable, (c) self-regulated learning is appropriate to the college context, and (d) self-regulated learning is teachable.

Pintrich (1995) conceptualized academic delay of gratification as part of the self-regulated learning processes. *Academic delay of gratification* refers to learners' postponing receiving immediately available rewards to achieve valuable academic goals later on (Bembenutty & Karabenick, 1998). Successful teacher candidates are willing to delay gratification to pursue goals or rewards for which they need to wait (Bembenutty, 2016). Academic delay of gratification is correlated to self-regulatory behaviors such as selecting specific goals, use of learning strategies, and resulting academic performance among regular college students (Bembenutty, 2022) and teacher candidates enrolled in educational psychology classes (Bembenutty, 2016). Remaining task-focused required high task value placed on the rewards for successfully staying goal-committed. Human agency is a function of self-efficacy beliefs and self-regulatory competencies.

Bembenutty (2016) examined teacher candidates' motivation and self-regulated learning during their teaching training. The results revealed that delay of gratification was associated with academic performance. Further, Bembenutty (2016) found that preservice teachers who used self-regulatory strategies reported high self-efficacy beliefs and high intrinsic motivation. Preservice teachers with a positive attitude toward help seeking preferred to delay gratification and had a low tendency to engage in self-handicapping behavior. Furthermore, White and Bembenutty (2013) examined the use of help-seeking strategies and beliefs for preparing to pass a state certification examination. They found that help seeking varies according to learners' self-efficacy beliefs and use of self-regulatory strategies, such as their willingness to delay gratification.

Pintrich also proposed that faculty can be models of self-regulated learning. This view is consistent with the culturally self-regulated pedagogical model (Bembenutty, 2022; White & Bembenutty, 2014, 2016), which proposes that both teachers and students are proactive self-regulated learners and model each other. Students also need to practice using self-regulatory learning strategies. Self-regulated learning involves a developmental process that grows across time, effort, self-discipline, and delayed gratification. The selection and use of strategies could help learners over time. Students' proactive and self-initiated tasks during instruction should promote self-regulated learning. Self-regulation is also construed as cyclical in that learners can start by identifying goals and strategies, monitoring progress, assessing performance outcomes, and then adapting to start the process again (Zimmerman, 2013) based on received feedback (Hattie & Timperley, 2007; Mandouit & Hattie, 2023).

Self-Regulated Learning and College Teaching During the Pandemic

Research has been conducted on the utility and characteristics of college students' self-regulated learning during the COVID-19 pandemic. Dai et al. (2022) conducted a cross-cultural study comparing self-efficacy, self-regulation, and resilience between college students in the United States and China. Multivariate analyses of variance (MANOVA) revealed that self-efficacy, self-regulation, and resilience differed between U.S. and Chinese college students. U.S. students' self-efficacy was reported as being higher than that of Chinese students. U.S. college students' self-regulation was slightly lower than their Chinese counterparts'. However, the researchers concluded that effective teaching and learning strategies could be used to establish supportive learning environments for both student groups from diverse cultural backgrounds. These findings suggest that learners can use self-regulation to sustain effort and goals even during challenges such as the pandemic. A significant contribution of this study to the literature is that it highlights the essential association between self-efficacy and self-regulation as a buffer to challenges during the COVID-19 pandemic—also crucial for teacher candidates.

Hilpert et al. (2021) assessed college students' coping self-regulated skills during the transition to remote instruction, during the first week of the semester, immediately after the disruption, and through the end of the semester. The researchers found significant decreases in student motivation, increases in students' perceived costs, and changes in coping strategies and mental depletion during disrupted learning. Students' self-efficacy, perceptions of cost, and feelings of anger and personal responsibility for family explained significant variance in course performance. Again, Hilpert et al.'s findings revealed that self-efficacy is an agentic solid belief vital for college students' coping challenges during the COVID-19 pandemic.

Hensley et al. (2022) investigated the effects of switching from in-person to online classes on undergraduates' engagement in self-regulated learning. They had two research questions: (a) How does a sudden change of context to online instruction impact students' engagement in self-regulated learning? and (b) What elements of instructors' responses to emergency remote education do college students perceive as supporting or hindering their engagement in self-regulated learning? Students responded to six open-ended questions about the COVID-19 pandemic and changing the instructional format. Students' responses revealed four themes related to their remote learning: (a) feeling disconnected, discordant, and distracted; (b) struggling to engage amid lost autonomy and personal stressors; (c) experiencing academic burden and burnout; and (d) meeting both caring and disregard from instructors. These findings highlight that self-regulated learning, and particularly emotional regulation, is a critical aspect of students significantly affected by the transition to distance instruction.

Emotional regulation and coping strategies during the pandemic has challenged learners and educators. Gaeta and her associates (Gaeta et al., 2021) examined the relationships between students' emotions, coping strategies, and self-regulated learning in online learning during COVID-19. They were interested in finding whether college students could manage their emotions and take greater responsibility for their learning during the health crisis. They found that students' self-regulated learning was positively related to gratitude, joy, and hope, and negatively related to loneliness and disinterest. Students' primary coping strategy was focused on facing and reassessing the situation. Tranquility, hope, gratitude, and joy were positively related to self-regulated learning. Coping strategies mediated the relationship between emotions and self-regulated learning. The researcher concluded that promoting self-regulated learning during online learning is essential when students are bound at home.

Shidler (2023) examined the perceptions of teacher candidates' assessments of self-efficacy beliefs during the preparation and changes that have taken place in schools since 2020. Shidler found that teacher candidates expressed a lower level of self-efficacy in working with children with special needs and in working and communicating with parents. Taken together, the studies of Hensley et al. (2022), Gaeta et al. (2021), and Shidler (2023) reveal that self-regulated learning involves a positive and crucial process that helps students in general, and teacher candidates specifically, to deal effectively with obstacles that transform our daily routines and educational system.

Türkan et al. (2020) report that candidates' concerns about assessment and evaluation involved uncertainty, infrastructure, fair examination, and assessment methods (e.g., online exams), while teacher educators were concerned about candidates' social and emotional uneasiness in their personal lives and family relationships. *Social and emotional learning* (SEL) involves the management of emotions, building and maintaining relationships, prosocial skills, and effectively handling intrapersonal and interpersonal situations (Jones & Bouffard, 2012). Despite methodological challenges in SEL research, there is widespread acceptance of the benefits of promoting it for learners (Frydenberg et al., 2017).

An influential SEL model, consistent with self-regulated learning models (Alexander & Vermette, 2019), is that of the Collaborative for Academic, Social, and Emotional Learning (CASEL, 2012). CASEL's model includes five SEL core competencies: self-awareness, self-management, social awareness, relationship skills, and responsible decision-making. *Self-awareness* and *self-management* refer to recognizing and regulating one's emotions and thoughts, including as to how they influence behavior. *Social awareness* and *relationship skills* refer to the understanding of others' viewpoints and the ability to maintain healthy relationships with others. *Responsible decision-making* is making constructive and respectful choices about personal behavior and social interactions. Our self-study will explore how SEL impacted our teaching experience during the pandemic. Türkan et al.'s (2020) work and CASEL's social and emotional learning spotlight that self-regulation is more than learning skills but that it also involves assessment and evaluation of learning and affect, which were vital in helping to cope with social and emotional stressors during the COVID-19 pandemic for teacher candidates and teacher educators.

SELF-STUDY RESEARCH ON SELF-REGULATED LEARNING DURING THE COVID-19 PANDEMIC

During the onset of the COVID-19 pandemic, Berry and Kitchen (2020) stated that self-study "has important contributions to make in these times for documenting the experiences and insights that come from radical educational change" (p. 124). *Self-study* is defined as "a research approach in the domain of teacher education which can be typified as follows: self-study focuses on one's own practice as a teacher educator; for this reason, it privileges the use of qualitative research methods; collaborative interactions are constitutive for the research process; and its validation is based on trustworthiness" (Vanassche & Kelchtermans, 2015, p. 522). Our utilization of self-study would thus inform a rich knowledge of how our instructional adaptations to the unexpected COVID-19 circumstances operated. This would be particularly true for the collaborative environment, where the three instructors developed vital aspects of our adaptations. Such a research method would also fit well with studying such an unexpected situation since it does not require developing in advance a study design with randomization to different conditions or with only descriptive quantitative data available.

Vanassche and Kelchtermans (2015) conducted a systematic review of self-study of teacher education practices research literature published between 1990 and 2012. They indicated that teacher educators design self-study research to assess and improve their practice and to validate their professional expertise. They also identified challenges in self-study work, the tension between relevance and rigor on the one hand, and effectiveness and understanding on the other. They identified four themes related to self-study research. The first theme concerned the impact of particular pedagogical interventions on student teachers' learning and development to promote the ongoing improvement of practice with student teachers and their self-oriented nature. The second theme involves the contradictions between teacher educators' knowledge, beliefs, and practices. The third theme indicates that teacher educators are trying to make their practice a more socially just learning environment. The fourth theme reflects that teacher educators seek and explore diverse theoretical–pedagogical approaches.

Kwon and Yeo (2022) conducted a collaborative self-study during the COVID-19 pandemic's transition to the new online environment and redesigned their courses. They reflected on their experiences in appropriating, transforming, reconstructing, and changing their teacher education pedagogies. Their self-study revealed three themes: (a) using virtual manipulatives; (b) creating collaborative, interactive, and shared learning experiences for preservice teachers; and (c) making preservice teachers engaged in student thinking. In their shared collaborative learning spaces, they used Google Slides, Web Whiteboard, Zoom Whiteboard, Jamboard, Padlet, Poll Everywhere, and Canvas Discussion to enhance online communication to share their strategies. They experienced transformative knowledge as teacher educators focusing more on pedagogical improvement in teaching mathematics.

Self-study research aims to understand teaching and learning better and "become better informed, gain expanded understanding, and make an effort to improve oneself as a professional educator and one's own practice" (Hauge, 2021, p. 2). Self-study helps search for the gap and contradictions between personal theory, beliefs, thoughts, ideas, and how one teaches and is initiated and carried out by practitioners (Hauge, 2021). It also aligns practices with intended goals and teaching methods.

Pithouse-Morgan (2022) analyzed ten self-study research articles to examine professional practice as a scholarship and method. She identified 10 self-study characteristics in the articles (e.g., self-study research begins with a sense of curiosity rooted in practice, entails making a positive commitment to change, and requires bravery and resilience). She uncovered three broad self-study research contributions: (a) teachers and teacher educators advance practice and knowledge by becoming accomplished researchers of their work, (b) a self-directed professional learning paradigm benefits teachers' and teacher educators' professional development initiatives, and (c) teachers and teacher educators help themselves and others when they commit to their professional growth in supportive communities. The present self-study aims to make these three contributions to benefit teacher candidates, our communities, and our professional growth.

Bullough and Pinnegar (2001) proposed that self-study emerged from converging at least four developments within educational research in their guidelines for quality in autobiographical forms of self-study research. One is "the remarkable transformation that followed the introduction of naturalistic and qualitative research methods into education, and the redefinition of validity as trustworthiness or accuracy" (p. 13). They also addressed the importance of standards for self-study research, stating that the "self-study researcher has to edit the text and yet not present an interpretation that contradicts or would be contradicted and repudiated by a complete reading of the data. This is an issue of conscience as well as of reliability and honesty" (p. 19). In the present study, following this guidance and that of Moorhouse and Tiet (2021) and Feldman (2003), we will examine validity, trustworthiness, accuracy, and reliability, giving honest reports and interpretations of at-times contradictory experiences.

Self-study is thus key to understanding learning and teaching during the COVID-19 pandemic. Self-study research was crucial because it gave us, in a timely fashion, low-cost, valid, and reliable data, which were easily accessible. Self-study gave us immediate helpful feedback to adapt our instruction without waiting years for results from a longitudinal study or experimental results with control and randomized participants. A self-study methodological approach was prime for understanding a health, educational, and social phenomenon without precedent in our current society. Our self-study involved creating changes and improvements for teacher candidates and ourselves (Hauge, 2021). The value of this approach rests in its innovative experimentations using primarily qualitative methods that afford self-reflection, self-evaluation, and self-adaptation in a feedback loop while being available to the professional community. The value of our self-study rests in that it allowed us to practice building the plane as we fly. Our study met all the necessary conditions to conduct self-study research based on our teaching experiences.

METHOD

Participants

Three educational psychology educators of secondary education (Grades 7–12) teacher candidates reflect on their teaching experiences during the pandemic transition to online instruction. In the early semesters of the pandemic, we corresponded via email and Zoom sessions regarding how to teach best in emergency remote conditions. This included preparing and implementing a video-watching replacement for Grades 7–12 school observations by teacher candidates. Then, we decided to perform the present study by reflecting on our experiences by collaborating via email, Zoom, and Google Docs to describe our shared and different experiences and to analyze those data.

Instructor 1 is an Associate Professor of Educational Psychology at a college in the northeast of the United States. He received his PhD in educational psychology from The City University of New York. He has taught undergraduate and graduate courses in educational psychology, cognition, instruction and technology, human development and learning, classroom management, and multicultural education in-person for over 20 years and online for 2 years. Instructor 2 has a PhD in educational psychology and is an adjunct assistant professor at a college in the northeast of the United States. He has taught undergraduate educational psychology courses online for two years and in person for five years. The instructor's teaching philosophy emphasizes skill-building through writing and group discussion. Instructor 3 is a doctoral student and graduate teaching fellow at a college in the northeastern United States and has been teaching undergraduate educational psychology courses online for three years and in person for one year. His teaching philosophy centers on collaborative production and developing student autonomy.

Although we are the primary focus of our self-study, it is vital to observe that we taught around 25 teacher candidates during the pandemic in every class, between one to three sections per semester. Candidates aspired to teach science, English, world languages, mathematics, art, physical education, music, English as a second language, social studies, or nutrition. Our focus was on secondary education, Grades 7–12. Candidates were in similar numbers of males and females, and they were all from diverse backgrounds consistent with the city's population in which we teach. We also followed a consistent curriculum, including similar readings and common assessments (see Table 19.1).

Data Sources

We found it helpful to organize the myriad data of our teaching efforts and students' reactions to them into categories of self-regulatory processes (focusing on students' experiences) and pedagogical approaches (focusing on techniques we used to promote self-regulated learning).

Table 19.1

Teacher Educators' Pedagogical Approaches and Corresponding Self-Regulated Learning (SRL) Processes

Instructor's Description and Rationale	Candidate's SRL Processes and Examples
Social and Emotional Support	
• Instructors include whole-class discussion and small-group activities using Zoom's breakout rooms function. • Instructors promote collaborative activities alleviating candidates' dearth of human connection in a time period of isolation. • Instructors focus on situating self-regulation within multiple social and emotional contexts of teachers, learners, and the social context in which learning is happening. • Instructors serve as models and co-regulators of candidates' emotions and social and emotional behavior.	• Candidates' social and emotional skills of relating and connecting with other people were a central focus on the classroom objectives. • Candidates' social interaction with others more successfully increases their ability to perform functions such as self-regulated learning. • Candidates' willingness to delay gratification to engage in social and emotional regulation enhances collaborative activities throughout the classes, engendering a camaraderie among all participating. Candidates show social and emotional adaptation to the new normal. • Candidates engage in emotion regulatory behavior when experiencing technological challenges.
Self-Efficacy	
• Instructors communicate the beliefs that they can learn and acquire content knowledge, and skills. • Instructors model the behavior for students to emulate while providing scaffolding for them. • Instructors use verbal persuasion to instill in students a belief that they can put in effort and persist through challenges. • Instructors use teaching methods connecting candidates' interests, including appealing and informative audio and visuals, and eliciting candidates' active participation with low-stakes grading. • Instructors to increase engagement, adapt to candidates' keeping their webcams off and having strong temptations to do activities unrelated to the class.	• Candidates engage in observational learning and emulation of behavior displayed by the instructors and peers. • Candidates read articles describing the behavior and actions of self-efficacious learners. • Candidates experience intrinsically and extrinsically motivating course instruction that may lead them to attend to class instruction even when the temptation to disengage is high. • Candidates generally engage with the class, as shown by consistent rates of participation when called upon. • Candidates' positive relationships with the instructor's classroom climate on numerous outcomes are observed, including student social and emotional behavior and development. • Candidates reinforce their belief system with statements such as "I can do it."

(Table continued on next page)

Table 19.1 (Continued)

Teacher Educators' Pedagogical Approaches and Corresponding Self-Regulated Learning (SRL) Processes

Instructor's Description and Rationale	Candidate's SRL Processes and Examples
Academic Delay of Gratification	
• Instructors promote sustaining goal-directed learning under pressure and challenges over time, requiring practice of strategic planning. • Instructors encourage the use of self-monitoring forms and homework logs. • Instructors describe the psychological value of remaining task-focused and avoiding instances of task distractions. • Instructors recommend making an honest effort to avoid getting distracted by cell phones, searching the internet, and distractions in home environments. • Instructors impart the value of persistence in spite of the challenges presented by the pandemic.	• Candidates try to remain task focused and judge the value of immediately available rewards and temporally distant rewards after the pandemic is over. • Candidates find interest in academic tasks reflecting on how the challenges of their current circumstances will not last forever. • Candidates put in effort to engage in class activities even when there are distractions in the environment. • Candidates utilize learning tools (e.g., homework logs, self-monitoring forms) to monitor their academic progress and manage their time and effort.
Technology Implementations	
• Instructors change to require candidates to choose a technology to use during presentation assignments. • Instructors institute this requirement for candidates to increase proficiency in modes of communicating information that are increasingly crucial.	• Candidates experience online environments conducive to enhance self-efficacy beliefs about their ability to perform designated online tasks. • Candidates display higher self-efficacy for techniques of practical value, helping them be capable of success. • Candidates utilize technologies such as Kahoot, Google Jamboard, YouTube videos, and Mentimeter in their presentations, improving their abilities to use these technologies when they teach.

(Table continued on next page)

Table 19.1 (Continued)

Teacher Educators' Pedagogical Approaches and Corresponding Self-Regulated Learning (SRL) Processes

Instructor's Description and Rationale	Candidate's SRL Processes and Examples
Lesson Implementation	
• Instructors adapt to technical issues in the technology of remote learning in various ways (e.g., by describing what was in a video that could not be shown to candidates, letting candidates with microphone malfunctions participate by writing in the chatbox). • Instructors use diverse technologies to support the intended instruction. • Instructors look to make sure candidates still have the necessary materials and practice for successful learning. • Instructors endorse a culturally self-regulated pedagogy, ingraining the values, traditions, and beliefs of both candidates and teachers within the learning environment since self-regulated learning is a culturally bounded process.	• Candidates learn about the benefits of cyclical self-regulated learning, including forethought, performance, and self-reflection phases. • Candidates' access to necessary materials and practice opportunities informs their setting of realistic and adequate goals, self-monitoring accurately during performance, and having self-reflection that is accurate and self-efficacy-building. • Candidates follow along with spontaneous changes to instruction; some changes require further accommodation (e.g., delay of viewing chatbox-writers' responses until they finish, and press send). • Candidates adopt a proactive and agentic approach to develop, adapt, change, and control the situations and environmental conditions while engaging in forethought, performance, and self-reflection processes during learning.
Validity and Reliability of Assessment	
• Instructors replace required references in candidates' written assignments from in-person observations at schools to video observations of recorded content relevant to educational psychology. • Instructors use video observations as the best available replacement for enriching content for candidates to reference in their written assignments.	• Candidates experience instruction and assessment with high validity evidence that taps skills and knowledge. • Candidates receive writing assignments that maintain a high level of validity and reliability drawing from videos as from in-person observations regarding authentic educational happenings and enriching pedagogical information. • Candidates successfully complete fieldwork-referencing parts of written assignments.

(Table continued on next page)

Table 19.1 (Continued)

Teacher Educators' Pedagogical Approaches and Corresponding Self-Regulated Learning (SRL) Processes

Instructor's Description and Rationale	Candidate's SRL Processes and Examples
Feedback	
• Instructors provide feedback, which includes praise for student efforts while also noting areas needing improvement. • Instructors offer encouragement alongside critique that may promote candidates' continuing efforts and bolster their value and interest in making progress. • Instructors promote self-efficacy concomitantly with self-regulatory skills that assist in pursuing goals.	• Candidates sustain self-efficacy beliefs in their ability to perform class tasks and online activities. • Candidates receiving feedback with positive comments, while noting areas needing improvement, may experience support for their self-efficacy in performing assigned tasks. • Candidates gain or maintain interest and utility values in their coursework and persevere despite generational challenges of COVID-19.

Self-Regulatory Processes

Social and Emotional Support

We utilized collaborative activities, including whole-class discussions and small-group work. Candidates were given time to prepare answers (either through low-stakes writing or in their groups) and then called on to share their answers with the class. Candidates faced the risk of isolation (Fruehwirth et al., 2021). The collaborative activities we employed were meant to help candidates engage in otherwise potentially unavailable SEL and model how candidates could promote SEL for their future students. We targeted all of CASEL's (2012) competencies by promoting emotional reflection and planning on educational experiences, synchronous discussion with other teacher candidates, and professional choices for their future careers as educators.

Self-Efficacy

Self-efficacy influences learners' effort, self-discipline, time spent on tasks, persistence, and ability to delay gratification to pursue valuable rewards. Among teacher candidates, self-regulated learning is a significant predictor of academic performance (Bembenutty et al., 2015). During the COVID-19 pandemic, U.S. college students reported high self-efficacy (Dai et al., 2022). Learners with high self-efficacy tend to persist in challenging tasks and situations because they believe they can do it and have the necessary skills and knowledge. In contrast, students with low self-efficacy beliefs would tend to give up during challenging tasks, such as those presented by the COVID-19 pandemic. When an attractive alternative to self-identified goals arises, learners will have a high sense of efficacy and remain-tasks focused, while those with a low sense of beliefs could succumb to temptations, resulting in low academic performance on tasks. In our self-study, we communicated the beliefs that they could learn and acquire content knowledge and skills. We modeled the behavior for students to emulate while providing scaffolding for them. We used teaching methods connecting candidates' interests, including appealing and informative audio and visuals, and eliciting candidates' low-stakes graded active participation. Candidates engaged in observational learning and emulation of behavior displayed by the instructors and peers and their positive relationships with the instructor's classroom climate on numerous outcomes were observed, including their social and emotional behavior and development. Candidates reinforced their belief system with statements such as "I can do it."

Academic Delay of Gratification

During the pandemic, students have many tasks besides our classes. Some lost their jobs, some families were sick, and some were sick with COVID-19. They lost many social interactions with the required social isolation or the need to care for sick children or sick parents. That is why we provide concrete datelines for completing tasks while offering extra time opportunities when appropriate. We encouraged them to delay gratification by remaining task-focused during class or turning the camera on during instruction. We also assigned some tasks to be completed during class time. We invited them to self-monitor their tasks, keep weekly planners or use homework logs. We also encouraged them to attend office hours to discuss their concerns.

Pedagogical Approaches

Technology Implementations

We required candidates to choose a technology to incorporate into their presentation assignments (e.g., Google Jamboard, Kahoot, YouTube, Mentimeter). The technology requirement was meant to expand the options available to them as future teachers, as their self-efficacy increased to implement various levels and types of technology that are increasingly available in the classroom. Practice with technology may increase a teacher's mastery of using the technology in the future, mainly when situated within authentic and situated pedagogical tasks (Hughes, 2005). Thus, we sought to increase candidates' future teaching implementations of technology by giving them as-similar-as-possible practice by presenting it to their classmates.

Lesson Implementation

When technology malfunctioned, we adapted instructions to accommodate our new limitations. Some adaptations included describing the content of a video that could not be shown or letting candidates type responses in the chat when microphones stopped working. It could be more challenging to gauge class comprehension and to adjust pacing during video lectures due to students' lack of visual feedback, particularly those who did not use their cameras. Instead, we relied more on monitoring comprehension by having students respond to quick knowledge checks and self-efficacy reflections using polling and chat features.

Validity and Reliability of Assessment

Our assessments required candidates to reference the fieldwork of relevant videos watched. These videos were meant to fill the gap to the extent possible of candidates witnessing authentic educational occurrences as they would experience in-person fieldwork. This substitute would maintain the validity of the candidates' analyses of fieldwork in the written assignments. Implementing multiple-choice tests online remains challenging using current best practices (e.g., Şenel & Şenel, 2021), let alone those hastily developed during emergency remote teaching during the pandemic. Nevertheless, we used methods to increase the validity and reliability of their administration. We had students perform a mock mini-test during class before the first test to familiarize them with the remote administration interface. We also randomized question-and-answer choice orders to reduce the impact of students' conferencing with each other mid-test (e.g., Arnold, 2016; Şenel & Şenel, 2021).

Feedback

When reviewing candidate work, we followed Hattie and his associates' (Hattie & Timperley, 2007; Mandouit & Hattie, 2023) feedback guidelines, which they classify as reducing the discrepancies between current understanding or performance and a desired goal. They also make clear that the quality of feedback can make the difference between learners' increasing effort and improving strategies or abandoning, blurring, or lowering their goals. We sought to affirm learners' efforts while noting areas for improvement—coaching rather than judging approach to feedback (Bean, 2011). This targeted, accurate, and supportive feedback was intended to counterbalance candidates' often fraught life experiences during the COVID-19 pandemic. A recent meta-analysis has shown that effective feedback enhances academic achievement in technology-rich environments (Cai et al., 2023).

Procedures

After working with teacher candidates throughout the transitional period of moving instruction to online environments, the three authors reflected on experiences and notes from each of our courses relevant to self-regulatory processes and pedagogical approaches, including social and emotional support, self-efficacy, delay of gratification, technology implementations, lesson implementation, validity and reliability of assessment, and feedback. We then synthesized our notes and collaboratively analyzed our reflections for the emergence of latent themes.

RESULTS

Our self-study revealed two primary categories of findings. The first category was *self-regulatory processes* focused on psychoeducational factors important for proactive and self-directed learning. Our first category stemmed from research on self-regulated learning, which we found helpful for students in various ways. Pandemic-related circumstances and students' limitations in adapting quickly were sometimes present. However, the efforts we managed to make, and students' efforts to self-regulate, were largely successful. Our second category was *pedagogical approaches* focused on teaching methods and assessments helpful to facilitate instruction and learning. Our second category emerged from the success of using established pedagogical approaches (e.g., unique capabilities of technology taken advantage of, maximizing validity and reliability), often developed collaboratively between instructors, in promoting self-regulated learning. We discussed these categories next.

Self-Regulatory Processes

Our inclusion of collaborative teaching (e.g., whole-class discussion, small-group discussion) successfully built camaraderie in the classes, facilitating positive emotions and relationships. Particularly at the end of the spring 2020 semester, candidates involved in the classes generally reported and showed strong interpersonal attachments with each other as they departed from the last class session. Thus, we successfully fostered positive relationships among teacher candidates. Candidates cold-called after time to prepare answers generally responded, despite many having their screens black. Though this was partly incentivized through participation grades, the chance of a student in a class of 20 to 30 getting called on was low, suggesting high participation rates were also a function of engagement with the lessons.

In their participation, candidates shared evocative reflections on their own past educational experiences (self-awareness competency). They planned to maintain composure even when their teaching of Grade 7–12 students would become trying (self-management competency). Synchronous discussions showed candidates taking stock of others' statements as they built off each other and contributed to a positive class climate (social awareness and relationship skills competencies). Candidates in both in-class comments and their portfolio writings related to professionalism demonstrated commitment to developing consistent and competent conduct when they would become teachers (responsible decision-making competency).

We aimed to help candidates sustain their self-efficacy beliefs during the pandemic transition. We know self-efficacy is sensitive to the situation and context (Bandura, 1997). We understood that self-efficacious candidates in an in-person class might not be during an online class. COVID-19 brought significant challenges for us as instructors and our students. That is why we provide opportunities for candidates to master the tasks of the classes by providing frequent feedback about their performance on class presentations, written assignments and during office hours. We also orally expressed our beliefs that they were reaching their goals and performing at satisfactory levels. When anxious, nervous, uncertain, or unconfident, we assured them with words such as, "You can do it" and "We believe you can do it." When candidates appeared distracted and concerned about the class tasks or their circumstances associated with the pandemic, we assured them that they would be fine, could relax, and that a low level of anxiety was acceptable. We also paired them for group projects and presentations with peers so they could learn vicariously from each other. We also showed videos and assigned them to watch videos of successful teachers to learn vicariously from experienced teachers.

Our effort to promote self-regulated learning helped teacher candidates to remain focused on their goals. We reminded them of tasks due and encouraged them to use self-monitoring forms and homework logs. When they construed their goals as having value, they would not give up at the first instance of task distractions. We understood that to sustain goal-directed learning under pressure and challenges over time, our students needed to be willing to engage in academic delay of gratification to secure the successful completion of tasks and reach goals and rewards. We observed their effort to avoid getting distracted by cell phones, searching the internet, and distracting home environments. For some students, the comfortable home environment, with other exciting things to do, represented significant distractions. Our success during the pandemic was partly a function of our effort to convey to candidates the importance of academic delay of gratification and assure them that their effort and commitment will pay off well later.

Another self-regulated learning approach vital for us as teacher educators is our ability to promote willingness to delay gratification among teacher candidates. We promoted sustaining goal-directed learning under pressure and challenges over time. We practiced strategic planning while candidates tried to remain task focused and judge the value of immediately available rewards and temporally distant rewards after the pandemic. We encouraged using self-monitoring forms and homework logs while describing the psychological value of remaining task-focused and avoiding instances of task distractions. Consequently, candidates found interest in academic tasks by reflecting that the challenges of the current circumstances will not last long and engaging in class activities, even when there are distractions.

Pedagogical Approaches

Following Zimmerman's (2013) model, we emphasized self-reflection and self-assessment as pedagogical approaches. Having writing assignments require references to video fieldwork instead of in-person fieldwork was an adequate replacement. To promote self-regulated learning, candidates self-reflected on their experiences that, though lacking affordances of in-school observations, had other more impactful affordances (e.g., viewing students' home environments). As such, the validity of the writing assignments was maintained for candidates' reflections on authentic and enriching educational observations. Our increasing adaptations for online multiple-choice exam implementations improved their validity and reliability. Our mock mini-tests clarified the format, so students rarely had to send format-related questions during exams. When we started randomizing question-and-answer orders, the effects of between-students conferencing mid-test were reduced, as shown by results having more normal curves rather than near-ceiling effects. Questioning—another of Zimmerman's (2013) self-regulatory approaches requiring content application—demonstrated its appropriateness for the open book exam contexts, also shown by a lack of ceiling effects given the availability of all the course materials at the test-takers' fingertips.

Conducting assessments online offered benefits. For instance, we saved class time by using the flexibility in scheduling formative assessments asynchronously, preparing feedback to be displayed dynamically to teacher candidates immediately following an online quiz. However, digital assessment is not without challenges. Amongst other issues, we struggled with consistently being unable to monitor students who do not use their cameras during online classes (Al-Maqbali & Raja Hussain, 2022). In particular, the asynchronous assessment was challenging to monitor. Assessment can create opportunities for students to discuss an assessment that should be completed alone or to consult notes and online resources during an assessment. Digital assessment tools required class time to train students to set up accounts or use the platforms and introduced extraneous reliance on digital devices that some students may find difficult to access or navigate. These difficulties threaten the authenticity of the evidence of learning in digital classrooms, requiring many assessments designed for in-person classes to be adjusted for online environments to protect validity and reliability.

Our requirements for candidates to choose a technology to implement in their presentations resulted in candidates' self-regulation by implementing technologies such as Kahoot, Google Jamboard, and Mentimeter. The candidates generally demonstrated success in their implementations. These performances occurring in a presentation assignment increased their alignment with the context we sought for teacher candidates to develop self-efficacy in their future teaching. Such contextual alignment increases the chance of teachers learning the technology (Hughes, 2005). Many students elected to implement their chosen technology in the demo lesson portion of their presentation assignment, further enhancing it being contextually situated in school-based learning.

We generally adapted successfully to the technological issues that arose. This success was aided by candidates' sympathy for such problems (particularly early in the pandemic). Additional accommodation was necessary, such as filling time while a candidate with microphone problems was typing their responses. Self-efficacy and comprehension checks through polling and chat invited candidates to exercise self-reflection and provided instructors' feedback. Success in communicating information to candidates and ensuring their ability to participate promoted candidates' proactive and agentic approaches to develop, adapt to, change, and control the situations and environmental conditions while engaging in forethought, performance, and self-reflection processes during learning. Utilizing "coaching" style feedback in responding to candidates' work gave candidates a strong base of confidence. They learned from their errors and took pride in their successes, understanding that their achievements demonstrated perseverance through generational challenges. Our approach to feedback supported their goals of becoming teachers and encouraged them not to lower or compromise those goals.

DISCUSSION

In this chapter, we presented a variety of alterations, guided by self-regulated learning principles, to our instruction and curriculum. These changes are documented and categorized in terms of social and emotional support, self-efficacy, academic delay of gratification, technology implementations, lesson implementation, validity and reliability of assessment, and feedback. These self-regulatory processes and pedagogical approaches have helped promote success for undergraduate teacher candidates and increased our awareness of caring for our students during unexpected transitions and crises. They also enhanced our beliefs that to be effective teacher educators we need to be self-regulated learners. Consistent with Dembo (2001), we embraced the notion that learning to teach was not enough—our teacher candidates and we also needed to learn how to learn, and self-regulation helped us to reach that goal during the pandemic. For us, the cornerstone of successfully helping candidates requires understanding their goals and revising or identifying new strategies. We refocused our assessment and measurement to ensure that they reflect sustained validity and reliability. Adopting a renewed form of social and emotional learning tendencies within a self-regulated learning framework, renewed self-efficacy beliefs and willingness to delay gratification were imperative while embracing a culturally self-regulated pedagogy (Bembenutty, 2022; White & Bembenutty, 2014, 2016). These approaches lead us to reflect on the success and effectiveness of our teaching.

Themes of Our Self-Study

From our self-study research, three themes emerged reflecting major takeaways we extrapolated from our experience. The first theme is *embracing self-regulated learning for successfully coping with challenging circumstances matters*. As our self-study reveals, self-regulated learning is crucial first for us as teacher educators. Teaching educational psychology theories, such as Piaget's theory of cognitive development or Vygotsky's sociocultural theory of human learning, was not enough. We needed to be self-regulated learners, too. We must set goals, select strategies, be self-efficacious, monitor our tasks, and reflect on outcomes. We must design, impart, and assess instruction as self-regulated teacher educators. Through this self-study, we discovered that during crises like the pandemic, we needed to be compassionate with candidates' social and emotional situations that affected their learning and academic performance. We also experienced self-efficacy's influence on us educators and teacher candidates. As Bandura (1997) observed, self-efficacy has a causal effect on effort and persistence. During the pandemic, that was obvious when we experienced that it assured the students to keep trying and believing in their capabilities. We encouraged our teacher candidates to remain task-focused, and it helped them to defer immediately available distractions or put their eyes on the future.

The second theme is *collaboratively implementing established pedagogical approaches, particularly during crises, matters*. What started as experimenting with short-term emergency accommodations quickly evolved into collaborative development between faculty members to ensure proper and productive learning opportunities for teacher candidates. For example, recordings of classroom practices contribute to teacher candidates' self-efficacy (Karsenti & Collin, 2011), so we worked together to curate lists of videos to serve as fieldwork observation material, which provided authentic observation experiences and valid sources to reference on assessments. Not only did we teacher educators need to adjust, but candidates also gained valuable experience in being flexible with their adaptations to learning processes (Brinia & Psoni, 2022). Candidates planned and reflected on online teaching processes by including technology implementation criteria in the rubric for presentations and classroom activities demonstrations.

The third theme is *teacher educators' practice of reflective teaching matters*. Iterative refinement of teaching methods, useful in typical times, becomes crucial when an emergency requires sudden accommodations and ongoing updates. Reflective teaching was indispensable to our accommodative processes as the pandemic required the sudden shift to, and semesters of development of, emergency remote teaching. Increasing abilities of technological implementation in lessons by ourselves and our teacher candidates, heightening sensitivity to candidates' social and emotional learning needs, and other adaptations led to candidates receiving instruction close to regular standards despite the strained conditions. If teachers practice reflection on their pedagogical approaches regularly, they will be more ready to practice it on a grander scale during trying times.

Practical Implications

Our self-study led to three important principles that have crucial implications for teacher education programs. These principles guided us during our transition to remote instruction and will continue directing us to make decisions based on what is practical and can benefit our future teacher candidates. Our teaching will be conducted in manners consistent with these principles, carrying on through new experiences and providing a sense of direction and purpose.

First Principle: *Affordances and constraints of online teaching environments can be improved by ingraining self-regulated learning in all aspects of teacher education programs.* We recommend assessing the affordances and constraints of online teaching environments for opportunities to promote self-regulated learning skills. Our experience serves as a guide to reflect on instructional practices and how teacher educators may introduce self-regulated learning principles to best serve students in new learning environments during significant challenges. In educating teacher candidates, it is vital to take a comprehensive approach of caring, flexibility, and adaptivity to the new circumstances we encounter, and the challenges experienced by teacher candidates. This process is facilitated by emphasizing the importance of establishing goals, strategic planning, self-monitoring, and promoting self-efficacy beliefs and self-reflection.

Second Principle: *New technological approaches can be embraced to enhance instruction, learning, and performance.* Computer programs, social software, and various computer-based learning environments can support students' self-regulated learning. The instructors can integrate artificial intelligence (e.g., ChatGPT), social networking tools (e.g., Facebook), communication tools (e.g., Zoom, Skype), and resource-sharing tools (e.g., YouTube) to design instruction and assessments and facilitate instructor-student and student-student interaction and self-regulated learning—particularly when students are socially isolated as was the case during the pandemic transition (Kitsantas & Dabbagh, 2011).

Third Principle: *Social and emotional learning can be embedded as a self-regulated learning process.* The promotion of social and emotional learning has widely been accepted for its educational benefits, despite methodological issues in research of it (e.g., its assessment—Frydenberg et al., 2017). Social and emotional learning thus can be recognized for its role in self-regulated learning. Managing emotions, building, and maintaining relationships, developing prosocial skills, and effectively handling intrapersonal and interpersonal situations (Jones & Bouffard, 2012) help the learner deal with challenges and crises as they attempt to self-regulate their learning. An integrated approach to self-regulated learning can include social and emotional learning within a culturally self-regulated pedagogy (White & Bembenutty, 2014, 2016). In this approach, teachers and students embrace goal setting, strategic planning, help-seeking skills, willingness to delay gratification and engagement in self-reflection. These practices of teachers and students within classroom environments can contribute to and be predicated on successful affective and interpersonal adjustments, facilitating learners' expressing values and beliefs that reflect their cultures, identities, and traditions.

Limitations and Future Directions

Our self-study had some limitations. We had no direct assessments of students' perceptions of our efforts. Also, since the study emerged spontaneously during the pandemic (out of our interactions as instructors), it was not pre-planned. We also did not keep journals of our experiences, so we relied on our memories and existing records. We did not incorporate such supported anti-invigilation tools as randomized question pools (Baron & Crooks, 2005) or during-test video conferencing (e.g., CCTV on a mobile phone set to the side for viewing candidate and the computer screen they are taking the test on—Tuah & Naing, 2021). Our methods, though largely effective, were not always successful. Though the sudden situation of the pandemic explains the imperfection of our adaptations, we must develop safeguards for predictable crises that may impact teacher education in the future. Improvements to synchronous online teaching systems in the future could ease any necessary transitions back to emergency online education. For instance, better ways to shield candidates from distractions in their remote settings (both in their physical environment and on the computer) and improved remote invigilation approaches would reduce currently existing endemic challenges.

Derived from our self-study are expected challenges and opportunities based on our findings:

1. These findings have opened opportunities for other teacher educators to conduct self-study to find solutions to their challenges. That solution, we expect, should make self-regulated learning an essential element in their research.
2. Future studies should explore the theoretical and empirical grounds between self-regulated learning and social and emotional learning. These two crucial psychological domains have produced benefits for educators and learners, but they remain substantially as two parallel lines.
3. More studies are needed to explore the principles of academic delay of gratification in academic settings. Since academic delay of gratification is not conceptualized as a trait but rather a competence, how it can develop, and its benefits need further exploration.

4. Clarifying the self-regulatory structures and processes and refining its measurement instruments is vital.
5. It is crucial to conduct longitudinal studies to explore whether the self-regulatory approaches implemented by teacher educators and adopted by teacher candidates produce a lasting effect that transfers to different conditions, courses, and health and social events.

Conclusion

Transitioning from traditional in-person classrooms to online instructional environments has been challenging for faculty and teacher candidates alike. Embracing the adaptations outlined in this chapter affords opportunities to benefit teacher educators, teacher candidates, and other faculty and learners in similar situations. The evidence provided here is limited to our experiences, and continued investigation of the unique benefits of self-regulated learning during the COVID-19 pandemic is necessary. It is imperative to share these reports of our ongoing experiences as teacher educators during an unprecedented shift in instructional needs. Still, an upcoming challenge will be that the next global crisis will have similarities and differences to the COVID-19 pandemic, such that our current implications must be adapted to fit the situation's particulars.

Our experiences show the opportunities for using a self-regulatory pedagogical approach to sustain effective instruction at a time of abrupt technological transition. Although our self-study focused on us as teacher educators in teacher education programs, our experiences can contribute to the ongoing challenges all educators and students experience during and after the pandemic. Future research should investigate the effectiveness of COVID-19 pandemic-era self-regulation promotion by teacher educators on the successes of teacher candidates in their future teaching careers and how well they transfer the skills they learned from teacher education to their teaching practices, as well as how they inspire their prospective students to adopt self-regulated learning as a process that guides lifelong learning.

Teacher educators should continue embracing and researching self-regulated learning, integrated with technology, to become better educators and instill in our future students the importance of remaining task-focused during crises and challenges. There are great possibilities for further improvement of digital teaching methods in fostering self-regulated learning, increasingly valuable for the more digital and remote world that remains as the pandemic has receded.

REFERENCES

Alexander, K., & Vermette, P. (2019). Implementing social and emotional learning standards by intertwining the habits of mind with the CASEL competencies. *Excelsior: Leadership in Teaching and Learning, 12*(1), 3–16. https://doi.org/10.14305/jn.19440413.2019.12.1.03

Al-Maqbali, A. H., & Raja Hussain, R. (2022). The impact of online assessment challenges on assessment principles during COVID-19 in Oman. *Journal of University Teaching & Learning Practice, 19*(2), 73–92. https://doi.org/10.53761/1.19.2.6

Arnold, I. J. (2016). Cheating at online formative tests: Does it pay off? *The Internet and Higher Education, 29*, 98–106. https://doi.org/10.1016/j.iheduc.2016.02.001

Bandura, A. (1997). *Self-efficacy: The exercise of control*. Macmillan.

Baron, J., & Crooks, S. M. (2005). Academic integrity in web based distance education. *TechTrends, 49*, 40–45. https://doi.org/10.1007/BF02773970

Bean, J. C. (2011). *Engaging ideas: The professor's guide to integrating writing, critical thinking, and active learning in the classroom* (2nd ed.). Jossey-Bass.

Bembenutty, H. (2011). Self-regulated learning. *New directions for teaching and learning, 2011*(126). Jossey-Bass.

Bembenutty, H. (2016). Motivation and self-regulated learning among preservice and in-service teachers enrolled in educational psychology courses. *Scholarship of Teaching and Learning in Psychology, 2*(4), 231–244. http://dx.doi.org/10.1037/stl0000068

Bembenutty, H. (2022). Sustaining motivation and academic delay of gratification: Analysis and applications. *Theory Into Practice, 61*(1), 75–88. https://doi.org/10.1080/00405841.2021.1955555

Bembenutty, H., Cleary, T. J., & Kitsantas, A. (Eds.). (2013). *Applications of self-regulated learning across diverse disciplines: A tribute to Barry J. Zimmerman*. Information Age Publishing.

Bembenutty, H., & Karabenick, S. A. (1998). Academic delay of gratification. *Learning and Individual Differences, 10*(4), 329–346. https://doi.org/10.1016/S1041-6080(99)80126-5

Bembenutty, H., White, M. C., & Vélez, M. R. (2015). *Developing self-regulation of learning and teaching skills among teacher candidates*. Springer. https://doi.org/10.1007/978-94-017-9950-8

Berry, A., & Kitchen, J. (2020). The role of self-study in times of radical change. *Studying Teacher Education, 16*(2), 123–126. https://doi.org/10.1080/17425964.2020.1777763

Boyer-Davis, S. (2020). Technostress in higher education: An examination of faculty perceptions before and during the COVID-19 pandemic. *Journal of Business and Accounting, 13*(1), 42–58.

Brinia, V., & Psoni, P. (2022). Online teaching practicum during COVID-19: The case of a teacher education program in Greece. *Journal of Applied Research in Higher Education, 14*(2), 610–624. https://doi.org/10.1108/JARHE-07-2020-0223

Brod, C. (1984). *Technostress: The human cost of the computer revolution*. Addison-Wesley. https://doi.org/10.1177/089443938600400428

Bullough, R. V., Jr., & Pinnegar, S. (2001). Guidelines for quality in autobiographical forms of self-study research. *Educational Researcher, 30*(3), 13–21. https://doi.org/10.3102/0013189X030003013

Cai, Z., Gui, Y., Mao, P., Wang, Z., Hao, X., Fan, X., & Tai, R. H. (2023). The effect of feedback on academic achievement in technology-rich learning environments (TREs): A meta-analytic review. *Educational Research Review*. https://doi.org/10.1016/j.edurev.2023.100521

Calamlam, J. M., Ferran, F., & Macabali, L. G. (2022). Perception on research methods course's online environment and self-regulated learning during the COVID-19 pandemic. *E-Learning and Digital Media, 19*(1), 93–119. https://doi.org/10.1177/20427530211027722

Choate, K., Goldhaber, D., & Theobald, R. (2021). The effects of COVID-19 on teacher preparation. *Phi Delta Kappan, 102*(7), 52–57. https://doi.org/10.1177/00317217211007340

Collaborative for Academic, Social, and Emotional Learning (CASEL). (2012). *2013 CASEL guide: Effective social and emotional learning programs—Preschool and elementary school edition.*

Dai, Y., Jang, H. S., Salisbury-Glennon, J. D., Wang, C. H., & Strunk, K. K. (2022). A cross-cultural comparison of college student self-efficacy, self-regulation, and resilience between the US and China during the COVID-19 pandemic. In M. M. Merviö (Ed.), *Handbook of research on interdisciplinary studies on healthcare, culture, and the environment* (pp. 21–40). IGI Global. https://doi.org/10.4018/978-1-7998-8996-0.ch002

Dembo, M. H. (2001). Learning to teach is not enough—Future teachers also need to learn how to learn. *Teacher Education Quarterly, 28*(4), 23–35.

Feldman, A. (2003). Validity and quality in self-study. *Educational Researcher, 32*(3), 26–28. https://doi.org/10.3102/0013189X032003026

Fruehwirth, J. C., Biswas, S., & Perreira, K. M. (2021). The Covid-19 pandemic and mental health of first-year college students: Examining the effect of Covid-19 stressors using longitudinal data. *PloS One, 16*(3). https://doi.org/10.1371/journal.pone.0247999

Frydenberg, E., Liang, R., & Muller, D. (2017). Assessing students' social and emotional learning: A review of the literature on assessment tools and related issues. In E. Frydenberg, A. J. Martin, & R. J. Collie (Eds.), *Social and emotional learning in Australia and the Asia-Pacific: Perspectives, programs and approaches* (pp. 55–82). Springer. https://doi.org/10.1007/978-981-10-3394-0_4

Gaeta, M. L., Gaeta, L., & Rodriguez, M. D. S. (2021). The impact of COVID-19 home confinement on Mexican university students: Emotions, coping strategies, and self-regulated learning. *Frontiers in Psychology, 12*, 1323. https://doi.org/10.3389/fpsyg.2021.642823

Guilbaud, T.C., Martin, F., & Newton, X. (2021). Faculty perception on accessibility in online learning: Knowledge, practice and professional development. *Online Learning, 25*(2), 6–35. https://doi.org/10.24059/olj.v25i2.2233

Hartshorne, R., Baumgartner, E., Kaplan-Rakowski, R., Mouza, C., & Ferdig, R. E. (2020). Special issue editorial: Preservice and inservice professional development during the COVID-19 pandemic. *Journal of Technology and Teacher Education, 28*(2), 137–147. https://www.learntechlib.org/primary/p/216910/

Hattie, J., & Timperley, H. (2007). The power of feedback. *Review of Educational Research, 77*(1), 81–112. https://doi.org/10.3102/003465430298487

Hirshberg, M. J., Davidson, R. J., & Goldberg, S. B. (2023). Educators are not alright: Mental health during COVID-19. *Educational Researcher, 52*(1), 48–52. https://doi.org/10.3102/0013189X221142595

Hauge, K. (2021). Self-study research: Challenges and opportunities in teacher education. *Teacher Education in the 21st Century-Emerging Skills for a Changing World.* https://doi.org/10.5772/intechopen.96252

Hughes, J. (2005). The role of teacher knowledge and learning experiences in forming technology-integrated pedagogy. *Journal of Technology and Teacher Education, 13*(2), 277–302. https://www.learntechlib.org/primary/p/26105/

Hensley, L. C., Iaconelli, R., & Wolters, C. A. (2022). "This weird time we're in": How a sudden change to remote education impacted college students' self-regulated learning, *Journal of Research on Technology in Education, 54*, S203–S218. https://doi.org/10.1080/15391523.2021.1916414

Hilpert, J. C., Bernacki, M. L., & Cogliano, M. (2022). Coping with the transition to remote instruction: Patterns of self-regulated engagement in a large post-secondary biology course. *Journal of Research on Technology in Education, 54*(sup1), S219–S235. https://doi.org/10.1080/15391523.2021.1936702

Jones, S. M., & Bouffard, S. M. (2012). Social and emotional learning in schools: From programs to strategies. *Social Policy Report, 26*(4), 1–33. https://doi.org/10.1002/j.2379-3988.2012.tb00073.x

Karsenti, T., & Collin, S. (2011). The impact of online teaching videos on Canadian pre-service teachers, *Campus-Wide Information Systems, 28*(3), 195–204. https://doi.org/10.1108/10650741111145724

Kitsantas, A., & Dabbagh, N. (2011). The role of Web 2.0 technologies in self-regulated learning. *New Directions for Teaching and Learning, 126*, 99–106. http://dx.doi.org/10.1002/tl.448

Kwon, M., & Yeo, S. (2022). Beyond adaptation: Transforming pedagogies of teaching elementary mathematics methods course in the online environment. *Mathematical Education, 61*(4), 521–537. http://doi.org/10.7468/mathedu.2022.61.4.521

Mandouit, L., & Hattie, J. (2023). Revisiting "The Power of Feedback" from the perspective of the learner. *Learning and Instruction, 84*. https://doi.org/10.1016/j.learninstruc.2022.101718

Moorhouse, B. L., & Tiet, M. C. (2021). Attempting to implement a pedagogy of care during the disruptions to teacher education caused by COVID-19: A collaborative self-study. *Studying Teacher Education, 17*(2), 208–227. https://doi.org/10.1080/17425964.2021.1925644

Panadero, E. (2017). A review of self-regulated learning: Six models and four directions for research. *Frontiers in Psychology*, 8. https://doi.org/10.3389/fpsyg.2017.00422

Pintrich, P. R. (1995). Understanding self-regulated learning. *New Directions for Teaching and Learning, 63*, 3–12. https://doi.org/10.1002/tl.37219956304

Pintrich, P. R. (2004). A conceptual framework for assessing motivation and self-regulated learning in college students. *Educational Psychology Review, 16*, 385–407. https://doi.org/10.1007/s10648-004-0006-x

Pithouse-Morgan, K. (2022). Self-study in teaching and teacher education: Characteristics and contributions. *Teaching and Teacher Education, 119*. https://doi.org/10.1016/j.tate.2022.103880

Quezada, R. L., Talbot, C., & Quezada-Parker, K. B. (2020). From bricks and mortar to remote teaching: A teacher education Program's response to COVID-19. *Journal of Education for Teaching, 46*(4), 472–483. https://doi.org/10.1080/02607476.2020.1801330

Rosenberg, M. S., Mason-Williams, L., Kimmel, L., & Sindelar, P. T. (2021). Addressing teacher shortages in the COVID-19 landscape: Viewing teacher candidates as assets. *Excelsior: Leadership in Teaching and Learning, 13*(2), 86–95. https://doi.org/10.14305/jn.19440413.2021.13.2.01

Schunk, D. H., & Greene, J. A. (2018). Historical, contemporary, and future perspectives on self-regulated learning and performance. In D. H. Schunk & J. A. Greene (Eds.), *Handbook of self-regulation of learning and performance* (2nd ed., pp. 1–15). Routledge.

Şenel, S., & Şenel, H. C. (2021). Remote assessment in higher edu□ation during COVID-19 pandemic. *International Journal of Assessment Tools in Education, 8*(2), 181–199. https://doi.org/10.21449/ijate.820140

Shidler, L. (2023). Teacher education in 2022: Teacher candidates' echos of the past with a pathway for future preparation. *Social Sciences & Humanities Open*, 7(1). https://doi.org/10.1016/j.ssaho.2023.100427

Tuah, N. A. A., & Naing, L. (2021). Is online assessment in higher education institutions during COVID-19 pandemic reliable? *Siriraj Medical Journal, 73*(1), 61–68. https://doi.org/10.33192/Smj.2021.09

Türkan, A., Leblebi□i, H., & Önal, I. (2020). Opinions of tea□her □andidates on distance education implemented during the COVID-19 pandemic period. *European Journal of Education Studies*, 7(11), 328–353. https://doi.org/10.46827/ejes.v7i11.3355

UNESCO. (2020a). *COVID-19 impact on education*. https://en.unesco.org/COVID19/educationresponse

UNESCO. (2020b). *Nurturing the social and emotional wellbeing of children and young people during crises*. https://unesdoc.unesco.org/ark:/48223/pf0000373271

Vanassche, E., & Kelchtermans, G. (2015). The state of the art in self-study of teacher education practices: A systematic literature review. *Journal of Curriculum Studies, 47*(4), 508–528. https://doi.org/10.1080/00220272.2014.995712

Vohs, K. D., & Baumeister, R. F. (Eds.). (2016). *Handbook of self-regulation: Research, theory, and applications*. Guilford.

White, M. C., & Bembenutty, H. (2013). Not all avoidance help seekers are created equal: Individual differences in adaptive and executive help seeking. *Sage Open, 3*(2), 1–14. https://doi.org/10.1177/2158244013484916

White, M. C., & Bembenutty, H. (2014, October). *Teachers as culturally proactive agents through cycles of self-regulation* [Paper presentation]. The Department of Secondary education and Youth Services' Research Symposium, Queens College. New York, NY.

White, M. C., & Bembenutty, H. (2016, April). *Transforming classroom practices of teachers and students through training in self-regulation* [Paper presentation]. The American Educational Research Association, Washington, DC, United States.

Xu, Z., Zhao, Y., Liew, J., Zhou, X., & Kogut, A. (2023). Synthesizing research evidence on self-regulated learning and academic achievement in online and blended learning environments: A scoping review. *Educational Research Review*. https://doi.org/10.1016/j.edurev.2023.100510

Zimmerman, B. J. (2008). Investigating self-regulation and motivation: Historical background, methodological developments, and future prospects. *American Educational Research Journal, 45*(1), 166–183. https://doi.org/10.3102/0002831207312909

Zimmerman, B. J. (2013). From cognitive modeling to self-regulation: A social cognitive career path. *Educational Psychologist, 48*(3), 135–147. https://doi.org/10.1080/00461520.2013.794676

Zimmerman, B. J., & Schunk, D. H. (2011). *Handbook of self-regulation of learning and performance*. Routledge. https://doi.org/10.4324/9780203839010

CHAPTER 20

COGNITIVE AND PSYCHOLOGICAL EFFECTS OF COVID-19

Insights From a Systematic Meta-Review of Systematic Reviews and Meta-Analyses

Martin Daumiller
Ludwig Maximilian University of Munich

Raven Rinas
University of Augsburg, Germany

Ingrid Schoon
University College London

Marko Lüftenegger
University of Vienna, Austria

ABSTRACT

The COVID-19 pandemic had a profound impact on education globally, from primary to tertiary levels. Many studies have been conducted to better understand the cognitive and psychological effects of this pandemic, including

Examining the Cognitive and Psychological Effects of the COVID-19 Global Pandemic on High School, College, and Graduate Learners, pp. 467–506

research on a variety of topics (e.g., school closures, online teaching and learning, mental and physical health), populations (e.g., students and instructors), and educational levels (e.g., school, higher education). Numerous systematic reviews and meta-analyses provide both qualitative and quantitative summaries of the literature on specific effects of the pandemic on education. In this chapter, we present a systematic meta-review of these reports to synthesize and combine this existing database and derive broader and more comprehensive insights that can aid educational stakeholders moving forward. We identified 5806 records, and after screening abstracts and full-texts, a total of 55 reports were included in our review: 43 systematic reviews, 4 meta-analyses, and 8 combined systematic reviews and meta-analyses published until November 2022. Through thematic synthesis, we identified six groups of psychological and cognitive variables: mental health, emotional experiences, attitudes and worries, social relationships, achievement-related variables, and meaning. For each of these groups, we discuss key findings to provide a detailed narrative of psychological and cognitive implications of COVID-19 that can inform future educational practices and policies.

INTRODUCTION

The COVID-19 pandemic disrupted the socioeconomic order of the world and posed unprecedented challenges for education on a global front. At its peak, this crisis affected 63 million teachers and around 1.6 billion students across all educational levels in more than 190 countries on all continents (United Nations, 2020). Students missed an estimated 2 trillion hours of in-person instruction (United Nations Children's Fund et al., 2022), which is expected to have far-reaching consequences for the global economy in the years to come (Psacharopoulos et al., 2021).

The COVID-19 pandemic led to a global lockdown consisting of extended closures of educational institutions from pre-primary to higher education. As a consequence, exams were canceled, admission processes were delayed, and international student enrollment declined, strongly impacting intellectual, emotional, and multicultural aspects of education (Tilak & Kumar, 2022). Following this, the subsequent response phase involved emergency remote teaching and learning, which required significant adjustments for teachers and students alike (Daumiller et al., 2021; Pelikan et al., 2021; Turnbull et al., 2021). With the distribution of vaccines, educational institutions gradually resumed in-person operations by the end of 2022. However, the pandemic exposed inadequacies of established practices, highlighted areas for growth, and necessitated new educational requirements. Moreover, vast differences were exposed in how students, teachers, and parents were affected in terms of their psychological and cognitive functioning during this unprecedented crisis. By analyzing these differences, we can develop educational policies to better manage and mitigate future crises.

Throughout all stages of the pandemic, researchers made significant efforts to better understand the impact of the COVID-19 pandemic on education through primary research studies. Since the beginning of 2020, the quantity of COVID-19-related research articles has soared, with pandemic-related works accounting for a considerable amount of all published articles (Brainard, 2022). According to the Web of Science database, between 2020 and 2022, almost 8,000 articles were published with the terms COVID and school, university, or education in their title alone. Many journals welcomed this surge of research by waiving publishing costs and expediting publication processes for COVID-19-related topics (Palayew et al., 2020). While quick delivery of research output was crucial for sharing new findings, it may have come at a cost in terms of quality due to reduced objectivity and less rigorous peer review processes in order to support speed of knowledge dissemination. Moreover, the sheer volume of papers makes keeping up with research on this topic difficult (Brainard, 2022). As a result, meta-analyses and systematic literature reviews have been conducted to draw conclusions about the vast amount of unique research works that have analyzed COVID-19-related educational experiences and subject them to quality control. These reviews were undertaken at various points throughout the pandemic, and given the wealth of research on COVID-19 and education, they often addressed rather specific and overlapping topics, necessitating a comprehensive overview.

We address this with the present chapter by drawing on a systematic review that combines the information from existing meta-analyses and systematic reviews. As such, this review brings together diverse and abundant findings in one place to be compared, allowing for thorough conclusions about the current research state regarding how COVID-19 affected education, as well as prospective directions moving forward. The overarching aim of this meta study was thereby to provide a comprehensive overview to better understand the psychological and cognitive effects of COVID-19 on education, expose gaps in current research and its quality, and ultimately to provide researchers, practitioners, and policymakers with a synopsis of key outcomes and future directions. Following this book's focus, we specifically examined the role of cognitive and psychological variables. Besides other, such as economic and technological, consequences of the pandemic, this focus on cognitive and psychological effects of COVID-19 is particularly important to address the widespread mental health concerns, support vulnerable populations, and devise effective strategies to promote overall well-being and resilience in individuals and communities.

METHODS

We conducted a systematic meta-review of systematic reviews and meta-analyses that investigated the impact of COVID-19 on education (for details, see Daumiller et al., 2023). Specifically, two of the authors independently conducted a search of systematic reviews and meta-analyses between January 2020 and November 2022 using SCOPUS as well as the first 250 results from Google Scholar. We specifically selected these databases in order to cover a wide range of disciplines and academic fields. The reference lists of the collected reviews were also scanned. We searched for systematic reviews and meta-analyses of COVID-19-related educational experiences among students and educators at elementary, secondary, and postsecondary levels. Our search keywords were as follows: "TITLE-ABS-KEY((corona OR covid OR "cov-19" OR pandemic) AND (school* OR university OR college OR instructor OR pupils OR teacher OR teaching OR learner OR learning OR educat* OR undergraduate OR faculty) AND (meta-analysis OR review)) AND PUBYEAR AFT 2019." We included peer-reviewed articles, book chapters, conference proceedings, and preprints published in English. We excluded works that were retracted or only review protocols, as well as works that focused on a highly specific sample (e.g., dentistry students in Austria) or a general sample (i.e., the general population and not students, teachers, or parents specifically), as their generalizability to education was unclear.

To support the literature screening, we used ASReview (van de Schoot et al., 2021), a machine-learning application that aids the selection process by grouping the records based on their relevance, thus facilitating a more effective and error-free screening process (van de Schoot et al., 2021). Against the background of the accelerated publication processes during the pandemic, we explicitly also considered the quality of the respective reports. To this end, two trained raters coded each of the reports with regard to the quality criteria specified in AMSTAR 2, a widely used and confirmed instrument for both systematic reviews and meta-analyses (Shea et al., 2017). We modified this instrument slightly in order to align with the scope of included reports (yielding good inter-rater reliability: $\kappa = .84$). Discrepancies were consensually resolved through discussion between the coders as well as a third researcher. To provide a full overview of the covered research, we considered all works, irrespective of their quality, but used the ratings to assess overall confidence in the results of the review when interpreting their findings.

We originally conducted this systematic review to identify overarching themes that these research works addressed (well-being of students, well-being of educators, school closures and other school measures, e-teaching and learning, interventions, individual factors, as well as at-risk groups; see Daumiller et al., 2023. With the present secondary analysis, we focused on the relevant psychological and cognitive variables that have been addressed and synthesize how they have been impacted. To this end, we used thematic synthesis (Thomas & Harden, 2008), a systematic and transparent method to move from the findings of multiple individual reports to synthesis. We used the key findings noted in the included reports as primary codes to inductively create descriptive themes, which were in turn used to identify analytical themes through an inductive and deductive process in which we also considered existing classifications of cognitive and psychological variables and resolved unclear classifications through discussion within the author group (including PERMA, Seligman, 2018; and BESSI, Soto et al., 2022).

We present a PRISMA flow diagram detailing the reports identified and included in our review in Figure 20.1. The covered literature database is provided in an open repository at https://osf.io/9gudy/

RESULTS

Our literature search identified 5,806 records. After we removed duplicates and retractions, we examined the abstracts of the remaining 5,589 entries, and subsequently gathered the full texts of 174 records (two of which we were unable to retrieve). After reading the full texts, we excluded 118 reports: 65 were not systematic reviews or meta-analyses, 9 were not about COVID-19 and education, 2 were not in English, 38 were about a specific population, and 3 were about a general sample rather than students or educators. The systematic review therefore comprised 55 studies in total. The majority of them (n = 43) were systematic literature reviews, followed by meta-analyses (n = 4) or combined systematic reviews and meta-analyses (n = 8). They primarily focused on secondary (n = 29) and tertiary education (n = 26). Only a few considered primary education (n = 8). In terms of investigated populations, the reports included students (n = 37), teachers (n = 18), other school personnel (n = 2), and parents (n = 3) (see Table 20.1).

All individual reports and their findings are summarized in Table 20.1. Table 20.2 summarizes the quality criteria for these reports. We found that a substantial number of reviews addressed the same topic and were even published within the same year and journal, with some having subpar quality. More than two-thirds of the reviews failed to meet basic criteria such as the provision of review questions, a search strategy, inclusion/exclusion criteria, or did not ensure reliability in terms of study inclusion and data extraction. Despite this, we included all reviews to provide a comprehensive overview of the covered research, and used quality ratings to determine overall confidence in the review results when interpreting their conclusions (see Table 20.2).

Figure 20.1

PRISMA Flow Diagram Illustrating the Reports Identified and Included in the Systematic Review

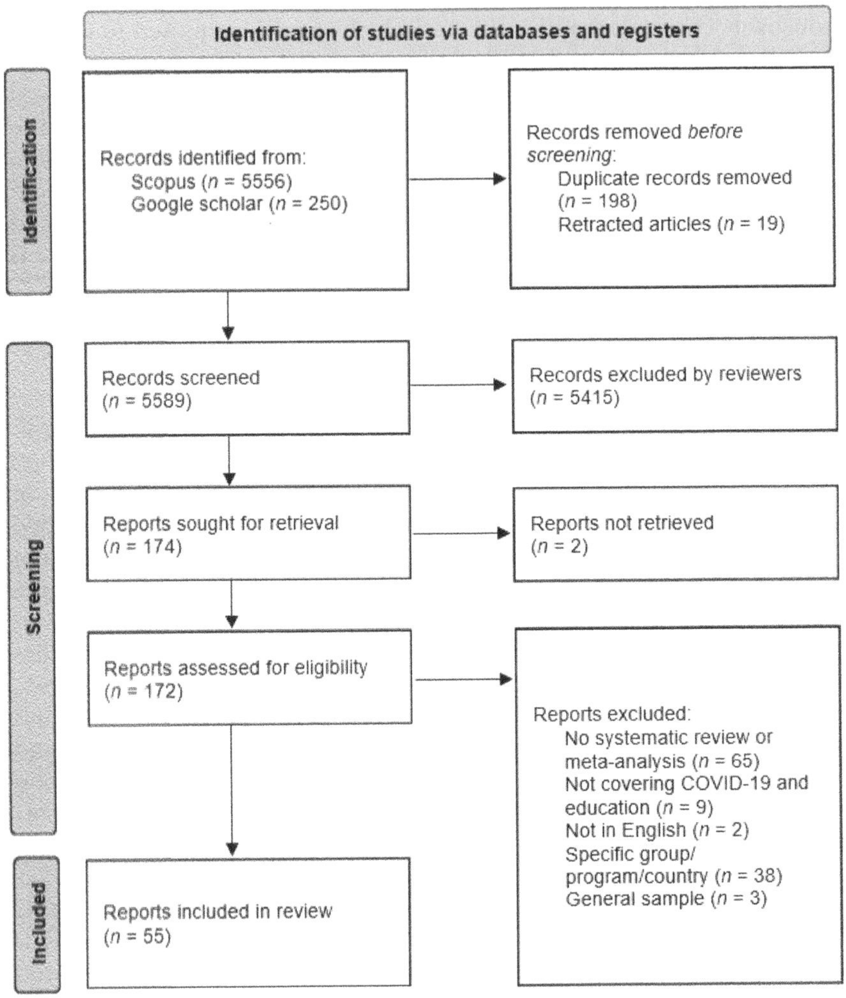

Table 20.1

Overview of the Reviewed Studies

	Study	Type	*k*	Focus	Sample	Period	Key findings
A	Aisha and Ratra (2022)	SLR	19	Opportunities, challenges and psychological impacts of sudden shift to e-teaching	Primary, secondary, and tertiary education students + teachers	Jul '20 to May '21	- Online education influenced interests and experiences of students and teachers with an immense impact on their overall psychology - For effective implementation of online and blended education, psychological well-being of students and teachers should be taken care of with properly designed instructions, adequate infrastructure or resources and satisfactory technological skills
A	da Silva et al. (2022)	SLR	13	Online group interventions for mental health promotion	College students	Dec '19 to Jan '22	- Online interventions were effective in helping the mental health of college students during social isolation and in reducing symptoms of anxiety, depression, and stress - All identified group intervention methods showed satisfactory and promising results
A	Fekih-Romdhane et al. (2022)	SLR + MA	59	Prevalence and risk factors of psychotic experiences	High school and college students	Until Jan '22	- Lower self-reported psychotic episode rates (12.50%, 95%CI: 7.06%–21.19%) for high school and college students during COVID-19 than before
A	Haddad et al. (2021)	SLR	6	Impact of social media on mental health	College students	Jan '20 to Jan '21	- Excessive or problematic social media use during the COVID-19 pandemic was correlated with worse mental health outcomes that could be mitigated by dialectical thinking, optimism, mindfulness, and cognitive reappraisal
A	Ma et al. (2022)	SLR + MA	54	COVID-19 pandemic-related anxiety, stress, and depression	School teachers	Dec '19 to Jul '21	- Prevalence of stress: 62.6%, 95%CI: 46.1–76.6%; anxiety: 36.3%, 95%CI: 28.5–44.9%; depression: 59.9%, 95%CI: 43.4–74.4% - Experiences of psychological issues associated with gender, online teaching, job satisfaction, teaching experience, and workload - Protective factors included regular exercise and provision of technical support for online teaching

(Table continued on next page)

Table 20.1 (Continued)

Overview of the Reviewed Studies

	Study	Type	*k*	Focus	Sample	Period	Key findings
A	Nang et al. (2022)	SLR	52	Teacher technostress and coping mechanisms	School and higher ed teachers	Dec '19 to Aug '21	- Teachers used coping strategies to deal with the ramifications of the pandemic - The most frequently used coping strategies entailed reaching out for social support, physical exercise, taking part in leisure and spiritual activities, reading, and listening to music - Seeking social support was marked as the most popular strategy.
A	Valenzuela et al. (2022)	SLR	72	Sleep	Undergrads	Jan '20 to Dec '21	- Undergraduates experienced increased sleep duration, as well as sleep pattern disruption during lockdowns - Several psychological, behavioral, environmental, demographic, and socioeconomic factors were associated with sleep changes
A	Westphal et al. (2022)	SLR	17	Stress and burnout	K−12 teachers	Jan '20 to Aug '22	- Some indication that burnout increased during the COVID-19 pandemic - Little differen□es in stress and burnout experien□ed by K−12 tea□hers compared to other occupational fields - Individual factors associated with burnout: personality, self-efficacy in online teaching, and perceived vulnerability to COVID-19
A	Zheng et al. (2022)	SLR	52	Techno stress for online activities	University teachers	Dec '19 to May '21	- Teachers experienced techno stress during the COVID-19 pandemic - Absence of infrastructure, lack of guidance and assistance for non-expert online teachers increased techno stress
A B	Buizza et al. (2022)	SLR	17	Changes in mental health and lifestyle	College students	Jan '20 to May '21	- College students experienced more anxiety, mood disorders, alcohol use, sedentary behavior, and internet use, as well as decreased physical activity when comparing their pre- and post-COVID-19 data - Female students, as well as sexual and gender minority youth reported poorer mental health conditions

(Table continued on next page)

Table 20.1 (Continued)

Overview of the Reviewed Studies

	Study	Type	*k*	Focus	Sample	Period	Key findings
A B	Chaabane et al. (2021)	SLR	10	Impact of school closure on child and adolescent health	-	Jan '20 to Sep '20	- Critical school-based services inaccessible (e.g., healthcare, programs for children with disabilities, nutrition programs) - Significant decline in hospital admissions and pediatric emergency department visits - Impacts on child and adolescent mental (e.g., anxiety, loneliness, sadness, frustration) and physical (e.g., increased BMI) health - Increase in child stress, sadness, frustration, indiscipline, and hyperactivity; alteration or breakdown in daily routines - Widening educational disparities due to the lack of support (parents, remote learning)
A B	Chang et al. (2021)	MA	16	Prevalence of anxiety and depressive symptoms	College students	Jan '20 to Nov '20	- Prevalence of anxiety symptoms during COVID-19 was 31% (95%CI: 23–39%) across the studies sampled - Prevalence of depressive symptoms was 34% (95%CI: 27–41%) - Prevalence of anxiety and depressive symptoms differed across students from different countries - Prevalence of depressive symptoms was higher in females compared to males
A B	Deng et al. (2021)	SLR + MA	89	Depressive symptoms, anxiety symptoms, and sleep disturbance	Higher ed students	Jan '20 to Jan '21	- Prevalence of depressive symptoms, anxiety symptoms, and sleep disturbances was 34%, 32% and 33%, respectively - Differences based on location, diagnostic criteria, education, study year, financial situation, living arrangements and gender - Prevalence of depressive and anxiety symptoms higher compared to pre-pandemic prevalence in similar populations
A B	Ebrahim et al. (2022)	SLR + MA	90	Psychological well-being	University students	Jan '20 to Sep '20	- Prevalence of anxiety symptoms was 29.1% (95%CI: 20.9–39.0%) - Prevalence of depression symptoms was 23.2% (95%CI: 15.7–32.9%)

(Table continued on next page)

Table 20.1 (Continued)

Overview of the Reviewed Studies

	Study	Type	*k*	Focus	Sample	Period	Key findings
A B	Elharake et al. (2022)	SLR	16	Mental health	School and college students	Jan '20 to Jul '21	- Students reported feeling more anxious, depressed, fatigued, and distressed compared to pre-pandemic times - Risk factors such as living in rural areas, low family socioeconomic status, and being a family member or friend of a healthcare worker were associated with worse mental health
A B	Fang et al. (2022)	SLR + MA	104	Prevalence of psychological stress	School and higher ed students	Jan '20 to Mar '22	- Prevalence of depressive symptoms: 32.0% (95%CI: 28.0–37.0%), anxiety symptoms: 28.0% (95%CI: 24.0–32.0%) - Prevalence of stress symptoms was 31.0% (95%CI: 23.0–39.0%), fear symptoms: 33.0% (95%CI: 20.0–49.0%) - Prevalence differed by gender, epidemic stage, region, education stage, student major and assessment tool
A B	Li et al. (2021)	SLR + MA	27	Mental health	College students	Dec '19 to Oct '20	- Prevalence of depression was 39% (95%CI: 27–51%), prevalence of anxiety was 36% (95%CI: 26–46%) - Prevalence of depression (60%, 95%CI: 46–74%) and anxiety (60%, 95%CI: 46–74%) in non-Chinese students higher than Chinese students (26%, 95%CI: 21–30% and 20%, 95%CI: 14–26%) - Prevalence of depression (54%, 95%CI: 40–67%) and anxiety (37%, 95%CI: 26–48%) higher after March 1 than before (21%, 95%CI: 16–25% and 19%, 95%CI: 13–25%)

(Table continued on next page)

Table 20.1 (Continued)

Overview of the Reviewed Studies

	Study	Type	*k*	Focus	Sample	Period	Key findings
A B	Malinauskas and Malinauskiene (2022)	MA	10	Psychological interventions for reducing stress, anxiety, and depression	University students	Jan '20 to July '22	- The random control trials (RCTs) of interventions reviewed indicated a trend in effectiveness of internet-based interventions for reducing stress, anxiety, and depression in university students during COVID-19 - Significant effects from the included RCTs with interventions for reducing stress and depression were established - Psychological internet-based interventions may reduce depression and stress among university students; more research is needed to determine their effectiveness in reducing anxiety
A B	Ozamiz-Etxebarria et al. (2021)	SLR + MA	8	Prevalence of anxiety, depression, and stress	School and higher ed teachers	Dec '19 to Jun '21	- Prevalence of anxiety, depression, and stress: 17% (95%CI: 9–28%), 19% (95%CI: 15–24%, and 30% (95%CI: 17–46%) - Higher anxiety in Asia compared to other continents and in school teachers compared to university teachers - Higher stress levels in university teachers compared to school teachers
A B	Riboldi et al. (2022)	SLR	8	Digital mental health interventions for anxiety and depressive symptoms	University students	Jan '20 to Jan '22	- Regarding anxiety symptoms, digitally delivered cognitive behavioral therapy, dialectical behavior therapy, and mind-body practice techniques emerged as valid strategies, while digital positive psychology and mindfulness-based interventions showed mixed results - For depressive symptoms, digitally delivered dialectical behavior therapy and positive psychology interventions have some efficacy
A B	Silva et al. (2021)	SLR	6	Prevalence of anxiety, depression, and stress	School and higher ed teachers	Jan '20 to Aug '21	- Prevalence of anxiety in school and higher ed teachers from 10% to 49.4%, considerably higher in a study conducted in Europe - Prevalence of depression ranged from 15.9% to 28.9%, being considerably higher in a study with teachers who worked in schools - For stress, a considerably higher prevalence was found in Europe (50.6%) compared to studies conducted in the Americas (12.7%)

(Table continued on next page)

Table 20.1 (Continued)

Overview of the Reviewed Studies

	Study	Type	*k*	Focus	Sample	Period	Key findings
A B	Viner et al. (2022)	SLR	36	Health and well-being outcomes associated with school closures during first wave	Students, teachers, and parents	Jan '20 to Sep '20	- High psychological distress (18% to 60% of children and adolescents above thresholds for risk of psychological difficulties) - No significant increases in suicides; increased anxiety and trauma, increased sense of connection with school (but not peers and family), worsening student behavior, inattention and hyperactivity, increased sleep problems, lower life satisfaction and well-being - Associations between school closure and health outcomes could not be separated from broader lockdown measures
A B	Zhu et al. (2021)	MA	176	Mental health	Post-secondary students	Until May '21	- Prevalence estimates of clinically elevated depressive and anxiety symptoms were 30.6% (95%CI: 27.4–34.0%) and 28.2% (95%CI: 24.6–32.1%), respectively - Month of data collection and geographical region were significant moderators
A	Jehi et al. (2022)	SLR	37	Anxiety	Higher ed students	Mar '20 to Jun '21	- More than one-third of higher ed students suffered from anxiety during the early stages of the pandemic - Being a female, living in rural areas, facing financial hardship, working full-time, spending the quarantine in isolation, worrying about infection, uncertainty of future, reduced sleep quality, and transitioning to online learning associated with increased anxiety
A	Liyanage et al. (2022)	SLR	36	Prevalence of anxiety	University students	Sep '20 to Feb '21	- Prevalence of anxiety in university students was 41% (95%CI: 0.34–0.49%) - Prevalence lowest in Asia: 33% (95%CI: 0.25–0.43%), Europe: 51% (95%CI: 0.44–0.59%), USA: 56% (95%CI: 0.44–0.67%) - Prevalence of anxiety in females: 43% (95%CI: 0.29–0.58%), males: 39% (95%CI: 0.29–0.50%)

(Table continued on next page)

Table 20.1 (Continued)

Overview of the Reviewed Studies

	Study	Type	*k*	Focus	Sample	Period	Key findings
B	Wang et al. (2022)	SLR + MA	16	Prevalence of fear	College students	Dec '19 to Nov '21	- Moderate amount of fear, according to average score across studies being 17.60 (95%CI: 16.4–18.8) on the Fear of COVID-19 Scale (interpretation: mild fear ≤ 17, moderate fear 18–23, severe fear ≥ 24) - The mean of COVID-19 fear in women (17.1, 95%CI: 16.6–17.6) higher than in men (15.2, 95%CI: 14.3–16.1) - Highest fear in Israel, Russia, and Belarus (21.6, 95%CI: 20.8–22.3), lowest in Europe (16.5, 95%CI: 15.3–17.8)
C E	Masalimova et al. (2022)	SLR	27	Students' attitudes about e-learning	University students	N/S [Jan '20] to N/S [Nov '21]	- Mixed findings on students' attitudes (some positive, some negative) - Mostly moderate to high levels of satisfaction - Students articulate preferences for face-to-face learning
CD	Amate et al. (2021)	SLR	13	Repercussions of COVID-19 measures on primary education	Primary school students + teachers	Jan '20 to N/S [Jul '21]	- Problems identified: right to education, repercussions for teachers, students, and family spheres, emergence of social inequalities that were less noticed before - Challenges for teachers: transition from face-to-face to e-teaching, remote work - Role of family enhanced for teaching-learning processes
D	Bakaniene et al. (2022)	SLR	17	Challenges of online learning for children with special educational needs	School-age children, their caregivers and school staff	Jan '20 to May '21	- Main challenges: inequities of resources and access to technology, lack of accommodations, routine change, and social isolation - Faced by families and school professionals were the same in all countries regardless of differences between the educational systems and living conditions - Main strategy implemented to address barriers and/or challenges: communication and collaboration between teachers and parents

(Table continued on next page)

Table 20.1 (Continued)

Overview of the Reviewed Studies

	Study	Type	*k*	Focus	Sample	Period	Key findings
D	Dobosz et al. (2022)	SLR	11	Home-schooling of children with special educational needs and disabilities	Parents of students with special needs	Jan '20 to Sep '21	- Children with special needs faced additional challenges - Substantial minority found that pandemic yielded positive effects (time spent together), whereas most parents with children with special needs reported being negatively impacted by the pandemic - increase in difficulties due to COVID-19 may have hindered parents' ability to cope with stress of parenting special needs children
D E	Ibna Seraj et al. (2022)	SLR	45	Pedagogical trends and assessment practices in emergency e-teaching	Students and teachers	Mar '20 to Apr '21	- Advantages: teachers'-students' positive experience, cost-saving, flexible learning, time-saving, collaborative learning, conductive learning, effectiveness, good medium, synchronous teaching methods - Challenges: course integration with technology, internet issues, lack of interaction, technical infrastructure, devices, training, motivation, distraction, time management, lack of technological literacy, increased workload, organizational preparedness, limited communication, unequal learning changes
E	Aljedaani et al. (2022)	SLR	34	Barriers of deaf and hard-of-hearing students	Students	Jan '20 to N/S [Jun '22]	- Technology-related challenges: unavailability of hearing devices, disruptions during online lessons, lack of familiarity with online devices - Education system-related challenges: e-learning as a significant barrier for deaf students, lipreading restricted due to masks - Physical accessibility challenges: especially in underdeveloped countries, remote learning as significant struggle for students with auditory access needs - Health-related challenges: mental health as most critical challenge, students with hearing disabilities showed four times more symptoms of anxiety, depression, and emotional challenges than other students

(Table continued on next page)

Table 20.1 (Continued)

Overview of the Reviewed Studies

	Study	Type	*k*	Focus	Sample	Period	Key findings
E	Aznam et al. (2022)	SLR	50	Motivation and satisfaction in online learning	School and higher ed students + teachers	Dec '19 to Dec '20	- Significant change in motivation and satisfaction with online learning during pandemic in which students struggled with limited learning - Special efforts should made by policy makers in addressing and meeting the needs of student learning activities, especially increasing their motivation and level of satisfaction
E	Boström et al. (2021)	SLR	46	Effects of pandemic on students' study strategies	Higher ed students	Jan '20 to Jan '21	- Students' study strategies changed to some extent during pandemic, with more emphasis on own responsibility and need for a developed teaching strategy to align with the changing framework related to the emergency provision of distance education - Students should develop metacognitive strategies
E	Camilleri and Camilleri (2022)	SLR	31	Costs and benefits of e-learning technologies	-	Jan '20 to Mar '22	- Costs: mixed satisfaction with quality of online learning, lacking preparedness/training of instructors, vast differences in quality of e-teaching formats, worries about academic progress, increasing divide due to lacking internet access, physical problems due to increased time in front of screen - Benefits: potential to foster learning and retention, provision of support, more convenient access
E	Fernández-Batanero et al. (2022)	SLR	29	Impact of shift to e-teaching	Students and teachers in higher ed	Jan '20 to Apr '22	- Benefits: flexibility, self-efficacy, remote learning, social distance, ease of use - Limitations: lack of resources, mental health, digital literacy of teachers, student assessments, workload, communication quality, student engagement and motivation, technical aspects, financial aspects, lack of experience
E	Hammerstein et al. (2021)	SLR	11	General and differential effects of school closures in spring 2020 on achievement	Primary + secondary school students	Mar '20 to Apr '21	- Negative effect of COVID-19-related school closures on student achievement, comparable in size to findings of research on summer losses ($d = -0.005$ SD to -0.05 SD per week; see Kuhfield & Tarasawa, 2020) - Positive effects on achievement primarily observed for students who already worked with online learning software before and increased its use during school closures

(Table continued on next page)

Table 20.1 (Continued)

Overview of the Reviewed Studies

	Study	Type	*k*	Focus	Sample	Period	Key findings
E	Morfaki and Skotis (2022)	SLR	9	Online learning experiences under the lens of broad personality	Higher ed students	Sep '21 to Feb '22	- Students' personality traits impacted their learning experiences and well-being throughout the pandemic - Agreeableness was linked to learning and perceived anxiety - Openness was associated with learning, self-efficacy, and satisfaction, yet also anxiety - Extraverted students reported lower course achievement and intrinsic motivational regulation as well as increased anxiety - Conscientiousness was associated with academic achievement, self-efficacy beliefs, and effective learning styles
E	Na and Jung (2021)	SLR	8	Challenges in online teaching and design opportunities	University instructors	Jan '20 to May '21	- Challenges: managing/conducting online classes, using online learning platforms/software, teaching class effectively, interacting with students, making students participate and learn, course preparation, solving technical issues - Causes: lack of skills, infrastructure issues, need for adjustment, external distractions, facility issues, not being in the same place, lack of support/direction, rapid transition, software issues
E	Nakhoda et al. (2021)	MA	24	E-Learning satisfaction	University students	N/S [Jan '20] to N/S [Mar '21]	- Overall moderate levels of satisfaction - Medical students less satisfied than others, possibly due to more practical courses
E	Nasution et al. (2022)	SLR	53	Effectiveness, outcomes, challenges of emergency online learning	-	Jan '20 to Aug '20	- Effectiveness: largely noted as high - Learning outcomes: mixed results on students' achievement - Learning challenges: lack of internet access, teachers' incapacity to use technology, nervousness when using technology, teacher interaction, students restricted learning facilities, pressure and disturbances

(Table continued on next page)

Table 20.1 (Continued)

Overview of the Reviewed Studies

	Study	Type	*k*	Focus	Sample	Period	Key findings
E	Ndibalema (2022)	SLR	11	Constraints of transition to online distance learning in in developing countries	Higher ed students in developing countries	Jan '20 to N/S [Dec '21]	- Major issues in developing countries: blind turning to online distance learning solutions, lacking personal and institutional readiness to e-learning, little consideration of social-emotional challenges - Individual teacher factors: technological literacy, lack of technical support, lack of pedagogical ICT knowledge, reluctance to adopt new technological solutions, lack of readiness - Individual student factors: digital divide due to economic disparities, lack of digital culture, lack of readiness, anxiety, fear and stress due to sudden change, lack of devices due to economic disparities, poor home learning environment - Individual institutional factors: inadequate equipment, poor and unreliable internet access, missing standards, policies, and guidelines for e-teaching, administrative hindrances, lack of digital culture
E	Panagouli et al. (2021)	SLR	42	Academic performance during online learning and modified educational methods	Students, aged 8-22	N/S [Jan '20] to N/S [Nov '21]	- Mixed findings regarding effectiveness: some reporting learning losses, few reporting benefits - Good communication between teachers and parents, and interactive and interesting learning material, supportive for learning gains - High-achieving and older students profited more than disadvantaged and younger students - Students from non-privileged areas less likely to participate at all in online lessons - Parents report difficulties of their students regarding discipline and self-regulation despite parental support - Students with neurodevelopmental disorders or special education needs struggled the most (e.g., ADHD, dyslexia)

(Table continued on next page)

Table 20.1 (Continued)

Overview of the Reviewed Studies

	Study	Type	*k*	Focus	Sample	Period	Key findings
E	Turnbull et al. (2021)	SLR	26	Role of educational technologies in the transition from face-to-face to online teaching and learning activities	-	Feb '20 to Oct '20	- Technologies used: role of Zoom to replicate face-to-face instruction online, adapting learning management systems as "first points of access", use of social media in online delivery - Challenges regarding transition: reconciling synchronous/asynchronous delivery, technology access, online competence, academic dishonesty, privacy and confidentiality - Lessons learned: institutional support, training, blended learning, learning communities
E	Xue and Crompton (2022)	SLR	50	How the pandemic influenced educational technology research	Mostly undergrads	Dec '19 to Jan '22	- Influencing factors: online teaching self-efficacy and multimodality of materials as central factors triggering student participation and success - Effectiveness: multiple aspects of success (experience, adaptation, more positive attitudes towards live chat as help-seeking tool) - Challenges: social isolation, lack of interactivity, self-regulated learning, technical problems, methodological aspects - Role of teachers: professional development required, teachers' proficiency, confidence, and motivation in using digital technology improved
F	Abu Talib et al. (2021)	SLR	47	Impact of shift to e-learning in early 2020 on education	-	Jan '19 to N/S [Oct '20]	- Mixed recommendations regarding merits of e-teaching - Key disadvantages: inequality of access, inadequacy of online teaching, poor communication quality, technical difficulties, increased workload and stress, low technological literacy, difficulty in assessment of student engagement and performance, poor work-life balance, and some privacy concerns - Key advantages: flexibility and convenience, discussion and communication, effectiveness as a didactic tool, efficiency, decreased costs, increased exposure to technology, impetus for change

(Table continued on next page)

Table 20.1 (Continued)

Overview of the Reviewed Studies

	Study	Type	*k*	Focus	Sample	Period	Key findings
F	Susilaningsih et al. (2021)	SLR	5	Quality of work-life	Lecturers	Jan '20 to June '21	- Online learning during COVID-19 reduced the quality of work-life of lecturers - Causative factors include poor psychological well-being, frustration regarding IT use, and reduced work-life balance
X	Amelia et al. (2021)	SLR	21	Digital transformation and impact of e-learning on pedagogy in primary schools	-	Jan '20 to N/S [Sep '21]	None articulated
X	Coles et al. (2022)	SLR	69	Factors for poorer educational outcomes exacerbated by COVID- 19	Disadvantaged school students in Australia	Jan '20 to Jul '20	- Key disadvantaged groups: young children who started school behind, older students already at risk of disengagement from school, children and young people who have had contact with the child protection system - Individual factors: health (early health problems, early developmental delay, poorer home learning environments, poor parenting practices, neglect, abuse, and maltreatment), social (lack of peer connectedness, acceptance, and social exclusion), economic (increased family stress, poor family relationships, less access to high quality care and support programs), educational (academic, behavior, mental health difficulties and truancy, lack of teacher support, poor peer, school, teacher connection)
X	Cortés-Albornoz et al. (2022)	SLR	21	Effects of remote learning on visual health	School students	Jan '20 to Jan '22	- Children had more rapid myopia progression, increased frequency of dry eye and visual fatigue symptoms, and signs of vergence and accommodation disturbances such as acute acquired concomitant esotropia and convergence insufficiency during the pandemic

(Table continued on next page)

Table 20.1 (Continued)

Overview of the Reviewed Studies

	Study	Type	*k*	Focus	Sample	Period	Key findings
X	Deepika et al. (2021)	SLR	45	E-learning modalities used during onset of COVID-19	-	Jan '20 to Mar '20	- E-learning as convenient way to continue teaching and learning during the pandemic and beyond - Learning management systems can integrate content delivery, record maintenance, assessment and feedback processes - Though many barriers and challenges are in the way of successful implementation of e-learning, necessary to step forward with e-learning technology
X	Khan (2021)	SLR	39	Evaluation of school measures following the lockdown	-	Mar '20 Jul '20	- Increased levels of disruption in teaching, especially in the migration from face-to-face teaching to online learning - Importance of the social contact between educational institutions, the communities in which they operate, and the stakeholders that they serve
X	Kratzer et al. (2022)	SLR	18	Unintended consequences of measures implemented in the school setting	Primary and secondary school students and staff	Jan '20 to Mar '21	- Broad range of unintended consequences, including educational (e.g., hearing difficulties due to masks, disruptive behaviors of students), physical, physiological, environmental, and socioeconomic outcomes - However, unintended consequences only sparsely researched and no evidence of a comprehensive or coherent body of research on these outcomes
X	Krishnaratne et al. (2020)	SLR	42	Measures implemented in the school setting	Primary and secondary school students and staff	Jan '20 to Oct '20	- Structural and environmental measures include physical distancing, ventilation, removal of furniture, cleaning schemes - Surveillance and response measures included testing, tracing, and symptom screening as well as isolation, quarantine, and reactive school closures - Most of the studies were mathematical modelling studies with varying quality - Relatively few studies focused on structural/ environmental measures and surveillance and response measures - Most studies considered the presence (and sometimes varying intensity) of other non-school-related co-interventions

(Table continued on next page)

Table 20.1 (Continued)

Overview of the Reviewed Studies

	Study	Type	*k*	Focus	Sample	Period	Key findings
X	Saikat et al. (2021)	SLR	22	Benefits and challenges of mobile learning	Learners and educators	Jan '20 to N/S [Jun '21]	- Benefits: adaptability, saving time, flexibility at own time, more participants in given course possible - Challenges: content issues, lack of technological literacy, lack of resources, preparing materials time-consuming and complicated (especially for older instructors), lack of communication, evaluation, connectivity, data protection and privacy, as well as increased motivational, problem-solving, psychological, and economical issues

Note. Unless otherwise specified, all findings are directly related to the COVID-19 pandemic. The first column indicates which of the six identified groups of psychological and cognitive variables were primarily addressed, with "A" referring to mental health, "B" emotional experiences, "C" attitudes and worries, "D" social relationships, "E" achievement-related variables", "F" meaning, and "X" no clear emphasis on any of these aspects. Regarding the characteristics of the reports themselves, "SLR" denotes systematic literature review, "MA" meta-analysis, and "*k*" refers to the number of included primary studies. The "sample" column specifies if the authors restricted their report to a specific sample, if this was not the case, this is denoted with "-". Some studies did not mention their search period. We specify this with the acronym N/S, followed with a maximum estimate in square brackets that is based on the publication dates of the included articles as well as the submission date of the review itself.

Table 20.2

Quality Assessment of the Reviewed Studies

Study	1.1	1.2	1.3	1.4	2.1	2.2	2.3	2.3	2.4	2.5	2.6	3	4.1	4.2	4.3	4.4	5.1	5.2	6.1	6.2	7.1	7.2	8.1	8.2	8.3	8.4	8.5	9.1	9.2	10	11	12
Abu Talib et al. (2021)	0	NA	NA	1	1	0	0	0	0	0	0	1	1	0	0	0	0	0	0	0	0	0	NA	NA	1	0	NA	NA	0	0	0	0
Aisha and Ratra (2022)	1	NA	NA	1	0	0	0	0	0	0	0	1	1	0	1	0	0	0	0	0	0	1	NA	NA	2	2	NA	NA	0	0	0	1
Aljedaani et al. (2022)	1	NA	NA	1	1	1	1	0	1	0	0	1	1	1	0	0	0	1	0	0	0	2	NA	NA	2	1	NA	NA	1	0	0	1
Amate et al. (2021)	1	NA	NA	1	0	0	0	0	0	0	0	1	1	0	0	1	1	1	1	0	1	2	NA	NA	2	0	NA	NA	0	0	0	1
Amelia et al. (2021)	0	NA	NA	1	0	0	0	0	0	0	0	1	0	0	0	0	0	0	0	0	0	1	NA	NA	0	0	NA	NA	0	0	0	0
Aznam et al. (2022)	1	NA	NA	1	0	0	0	0	1	0	1	1	1	1	0	0	0	0	0	0	0	2	NA	NA	1	1	NA	NA	0	0	0	1
Bakaniene et al. (2022)	1	NA	NA	1	1	0	0	0	1	0	0	1	1	1	0	1	0	0	0	0	0	2	NA	NA	2	2	NA	NA	0	1	0	1
Boström et al. (2021)	1	1	1	1	0	0	0	0	0	0	0	1	1	0	0	0	0	0	0	0	0	1	1	1	1	1	NA	NA	0	1	0	1
Buizza et al. (2022)	1	NA	NA	1	1	1	1	0	0	0	1	1	1	0	0	1	0	1	0	0	0	2	NA	NA	2	1	NA	NA	1	1	0	1

(Table continued on next page)

Table 20.2 (Continued)

Quality Assessment of the Reviewed Studies

Study	1.1	1.2	1.3	1.4	2.1	2.2	2.3	2.3	2.4	2.5	2.6	3	4.1	4.2	4.3	4.4	5.1	5.2	6.1	6.2	7.1	7.2	8.1	8.2	8.3	8.4	8.5	9.1	9.2	10	11	12
Camilleri and Camilleri (2022)	0	NA	NA	1	0	0	0	0	0	0	0	0	1	0	0	0	0	0	0	0	0	1	NA	NA	0	1	NA	NA	0	0	0	0
Chaabane et al. (2021)	1	1	NA	1	1	1	1	0	1	0	0	1	1	1	1	0	0	0	0	0	0	2	2	1	2	2	0	0	0	0	0	1
Chang et al. (2021)	1	NA	NA	1	0	0	0	0	0	0	0	1	1	0	0	1	0	1	0	0	0	2	NA	NA	2	1	0	1	0	1	1	1
Coles et al. (2022)	1	NA	NA	1	0	0	0	0	0	0	0	1	1	0	0	0	0	0	0	0	0	1	NA	NA	1	0	NA	NA	0	0	0	1
Cortés-Albornoz et al. (2022)	1	NA	NA	1	0	0	0	0	0	0	0	1	1	0	0	0	0	0	0	0	0	1	NA	NA	1	1	NA	NA	1	0	0	1
da Silva et al. (2022)	1	1	NA	1	1	0	1	0	0	0	0	1	1	0	0	1	0	0	0	0	0	2	2	1	1	1	NA	NA	0	0	0	1
Deepika et al. (2021)	0	NA	NA	1	0	0	0	0	0	0	0	1	1	0	0	1	0	1	0	0	0	0	NA	NA	0	0	NA	NA	0	0	0	0
Deng et al. (2021)	1	NA	NA	1	1	1	1	1	1	0	0	1	1	1	0	0	0	0	0	0	0	2	NA	NA	2	1	0	1	0	1	1	1
Dobosz et al. (2022)	1	NA	NA	1	0	0	0	0	0	0	0	1	1	0	0	0	0	0	0	0	0	2	NA	NA	0	1	NA	NA	0	0	0	1
Ebrahim et al. (2022)	1	NA	NA	1	0	0	0	0	0	0	0	1	1	0	0	0	0	1	0	0	0	2	NA	NA	2	1	0	1	1	1	1	1

(Table continued on next page)

Table 20.2 (Continued)

Quality Assessment of the Reviewed Studies

Study	1.1	1.2	1.3	1.4	2.1	2.2	2.3	2.3	2.4	2.5	2.6	3	4.1	4.2	4.3	4.4	5.1	5.2	6.1	6.2	7.1	7.2	8.1	8.2	8.3	8.4	8.5	9.1	9.2	10	11	12
Elharake et al. (2022)	1	NA	NA	1	0	0	0	0	0	0	0	1	1	0	0	0	0	0	0	0	0	2	NA	NA	2	1	NA	NA	0	0	0	1
Fang et al. (2022)	1	NA	NA	1	0	0	0	0	0	0	0	1	1	0	0	0	0	0	0	0	0	2	NA	NA	2	1	0	1	1	0	0	1
Fekih-Romdhane et al. (2022)	1	NA	NA	1	1	1	1	1	1	1	0	1	1	1	0	1	0	1	0	0	0	2	NA	NA	2	1	1	1	1	1	0	1
Fernández-Batanero et al. (2022)	1	NA	NA	1	0	0	0	0	0	0	0	1	1	1	0	0	0	0	0	0	0	1	NA	NA	1	0	NA	NA	0	0	0	1
Haddad et al. (2021)	1	NA	NA	1	0	0	0	0	0	0	0	1	1	0	0	0	0	0	0	0	0	2	NA	NA	2	2	NA	NA	0	0	0	1
Hammerstein et al. (2021)	1	NA	NA	1	0	0	0	0	0	0	0	1	1	1	0	1	0	1	0	0	0	1	NA	NA	1	1	0	0	1	1	1	1
Ibna Seraj et al. (2022)	1	NA	NA	1	0	0	0	0	0	0	0	1	1	0	0	0	0	0	0	0	0	1	NA	NA	1	1	NA	NA	0	0	0	1
Jehi et al. (2022)	1	NA	NA	1	0	0	0	0	0	0	0	1	1	1	0	0	0	0	0	0	0	1	NA	NA	2	1	0	0	1	0	0	1
Khan (2021)	1	NA	NA	1	0	0	0	0	0	0	0	1	1	0	0	0	0	0	0	0	0	1	NA	NA	1	0	NA	NA	0	0	0	1
Kratzer et al. (2022)	1	1	NA	1	1	1	1	0	1	0	1	1	1	1	1	0	0	0	0	1	1	2	2	NA	2	2	NA	NA	0	0	0	1

(Table continued on next page)

Table 20.2 (Continued)

Quality Assessment of the Reviewed Studies

Study	1.1	1.2	1.3	1.4	2.1	2.2	2.3	2.3	2.4	2.5	2.6	3	4.1	4.2	4.3	4.4	5.1	5.2	6.1	6.2	7.1	7.2	8.1	8.2	8.3	8.4	8.5	9.1	9.2	10	11	12
Krishnaratne et al. (2020)	1	1	NA	1	1	1	1	0	1	0	0	1	1	1	1	0	0	0	0	1	1	2	2	NA	2	2	NA	NA	0	0	0	1
Li et al. (2021)	1	NA	NA	1	1	1	1	1	1	1	0	1	1	1	0	1	0	1	0	0	0	2	NA	NA	2	1	1	0	0	0	0	1
Liyanage et al. (2022)	1	NA	NA	1	0	0	0	0	0	0	0	1	1	1	0	0	0	1	0	0	0	1	NA	NA	1	1	1	1	0	1	0	1
Ma et al. (2022)	1	NA	NA	1	0	0	0	0	0	0	0	1	1	1	0	1	0	1	0	0	0	2	NA	NA	2	1	0	1	1	1	1	1
Malinauskas and Malinauskiene (2022)	1	1	1	1	0	0	0	0	0	0	0	1	1	1	1	1	0	1	1	0	0	2	2	2	2	2	0	1	0	1	1	1
Masalimova et al. (2022)	1	NA	NA	1	0	0	0	0	0	0	0	0	1	0	0	0	0	1	0	0	0	1	NA	NA	0	1	NA	NA	0	0	0	1
Morfaki and Skotis (2022)	1	NA	NA	1	1	1	1	0	0	0	0	1	1	0	0	0	0	0	0	0	0	2	NA	NA	2	2	NA	NA	0	1	0	1
Na and Jung (2021)	1	NA	NA	1	0	0	0	0	0	0	0	1	1	0	0	0	0	0	0	0	0	2	NA	NA	1	1	NA	NA	0	0	0	1
Nakhoda et al. (2021)	1	NA	NA	1	0	0	0	0	0	0	0	1	1	0	0	0	0	0	0	0	0	2	NA	NA	0	0	0	1	0	1	0	1

(Table continued on next page)

Table 20.2 (Continued)

Quality Assessment of the Reviewed Studies

Study	1.1	1.2	1.3	1.4	2.1	2.2	2.3	2.3	2.4	2.5	2.6	3	4.1	4.2	4.3	4.4	5.1	5.2	6.1	6.2	7.1	7.2	8.1	8.2	8.3	8.4	8.5	9.1	9.2	10	11	12
Nang et al. (2022)	1	NA	NA	1	0	1	0	0	0	0	0	1	1	0	0	0	0	0	0	0	0	1	NA	NA	0	0	NA	NA	1	NA	NA	0
Nasution et al. (2022)	1	NA	NA	1	1	0	0	0	0	0	0	1	1	0	0	0	0	0	0	0	0	1	NA	NA	0	0	NA	NA	0	1	0	1
Ndibalema (2022)	1	NA	NA	1	0	0	1	0	0	0	0	1	1	0	0	0	0	0	0	0	0	0	NA	NA	0	0	NA	NA	0	0	0	1
Ozamiz-Etxebarria et al. (2021)	1	NA	NA	1	0	0	0	0	0	0	0	1	1	1	1	0	0	0	0	0	0	2	NA	NA	2	1	0	1	1	1	1	1
Pana-gouli et al. (2021)	1	NA	NA	1	0	0	0	0	0	0	0	1	1	1	0	0	0	1	0	0	0	1	NA	NA	0	1	NA	NA	0	1	0	1
Riboldi et al. (2022)	1	1	1	1	0	1	1	0	0	0	0	1	1	0	0	1	0	1	0	0	0	2	2	2	2	2	0	0	0	0	0	1
Saikat et al. (2021)	0	NA	NA	1	0	0	0	0	0	0	0	1	1	0	0	0	0	0	0	0	0	1	NA	NA	0	1	NA	NA	0	0	0	0
Silva et al. (2021)	1	NA	NA	1	1	1	1	0	1	1	0	1	1	1	0	1	0	1	0	0	0	2	NA	NA	2	1	1	1	0	1	0	1
Susilaning-sih et al. (2021)	1	NA	NA	1	0	0	0	0	0	0	0	1	1	0	0	0	0	0	0	0	0	1	NA	NA	0	1	NA	NA	0	0	0	1
Turnbull et al. (2021)	1	NA	NA	1	0	0	0	0	0	0	0	1	1	0	0	0	0	0	0	0	0	1	NA	NA	0	0	NA	NA	0	0	0	1

(Table continued on next page)

Table 20.2 (Continued)

Quality Assessment of the Reviewed Studies

Study	1.1	1.2	1.3	1.4	2.1	2.2	2.3	2.3	2.4	2.5	2.6	3	4.1	4.2	4.3	4.4	5.1	5.2	6.1	6.2	7.1	7.2	8.1	8.2	8.3	8.4	8.5	9.1	9.2	10	11	12
Valenzuela et al. (2022)	1	NA	NA	1	0	0	0	0	0	0	0	1	1	0	0	1	0	1	0	0	0	2	NA	NA	2	2	1	0	1	1	0	1
Viner et al. (2022)	1	1	0	1	1	1	1	1	1	0	0	1	1	1	0	1	0	1	0	0	0	2	1	0	1	2	NA	NA	1	0	0	1
Wang et al. (2022)	1	NA	NA	1	0	0	0	1	1	1	0	1	1	1	0	1	1	0	0	0	0	2	NA	NA	2	2	1	1	1	1	1	1
Westphal et al. (2022)	1	NA	NA	1	0	1	0	0	0	0	0	1	1	1	1	1	1	1	0	0	0	2	NA	NA	2	1	NA	NA	0	1	0	1
Xue and Crompton (2022)	0	0	0	0	0	0	0	0	0	0	0	0	1	0	0	1	1	0	0	0	0	1	1	1	1	1	NA	NA	0	0	0	0
Zheng et al. (2022)	1	NA	NA	1	0	0	0	0	0	0	0	1	1	0	0	0	0	0	0	0	0	1	NA	NA	0	0	NA	NA	0	0	0	1
Zhu et al. (2021)	1	NA	NA	1	0	1	1	1	1	1	0	1	1	1	0	1	0	1	1	0	0	2	NA	NA	2	2	1	1	1	1	1	1

(Table continued on next page)

Note. For better interpretability, the cells are colored reflecting whether the respective criterium was fully (dark gray), partially (medium gray), or not (light gray) satisfied. The criteria are:

Q1: The research questions and inclusion criteria for the review mentioned (Yes = 1 OR No = 0 OR NA): Q1.1: Population, Q1.2: Intervention, Q1.3: Comparison group, Q1.4: Outcome (variables of interest)

Q2: The authors state that they had a written protocol or guide established prior to conducting the review that included (Yes = 1 OR No = 0): Q2.1: Review question(s), Q2.2: Search strategy, Q2.3: Inclusion/exclusion criteria, Q2.4: A risk of bias assessment, Q2.5: A meta-analysis/synthesis plan, if appropriate, Q2.6: A plan for investigating causes of heterogeneity

Q3: Did the authors explain their selection of the study designs for inclusion in the review? (Yes = 1 OR No = 0)

Q4: Did the review authors use a comprehensive literature search strategy? (Yes = 1 OR No = 0): Q4.1: Searched at least 2 databases, Q4.2: Provided key words and/or search strategy, Q4.3: Searched the reference lists / bibliographies of included studies, Q4.4: Searched for grey literature

Q5: Did the review authors state that they performed study selection in duplicate? (Yes = 1 OR No = 0): Q5.1: At least two reviewers independently agreed on selection of eligible studies and achieved consensus on which studies to include, Q5.2: Two reviewers selected a sample of eligible studies and achieved good agreement (at least 80 percent), with the remainder selected by one reviewer

Q6: Did the review authors perform data extraction in duplicate? (Yes = 1 OR No = 0): Q6.1: At least two reviewers achieved consensus on which data to extract from included studies, Q6.2: Two reviewers extracted data from a sample of eligible studies and achieved good agreement (at least 80 percent), with the remainder extracted by one reviewer

Q7: Did the review authors provide a list of excluded studies and justify the exclusions? (Yes = 1 OR No = 0): Q7.1: Provided a list of all potentially relevant studies that were read in full-text form but excluded from the review, Q7.2: Justified the exclusion from the review of each potentially relevant study

Q8. Did the review authors describe the included studies in adequate detail? (Yes in detail = 2, Yes somewhat = 1, OR No = 0 OR NA): Q8.1: Populations, Q8.2: Interventions, Q8.3: Comparators, Q8.4: Outcomes, Q8.5: Research designs

Q9: If meta-analysis was performed did the review authors use appropriate methods for statistical combination of results? (Yes = 1 OR No = 0 OR NA): Q9.1: The authors justified combining the data in a meta-analysis, Q9.2: They used an appropriate weighted technique to combine study results, adjusting for heterogeneity if present (Yes = 1 OR No = 0 OR NA)

Q10: Did the review authors account for risk of bias in individual studies when interpreting/ discussing the results of the review? (Yes = 1 OR No = 0)

Q11: Did the review authors provide a satisfactory explanation for, and discussion of, any heterogeneity observed in the results of the review? (Yes = 1 OR No = 0)

Q12: Did the review authors carry out an adequate investigation of publication bias and discuss its likely impact on the results of the review? (Yes = 1 OR No = 0)

Through the thematic synthesis, we identified the following six categories regarding psychological and cognitive variables that were addressed in these reports: (A) mental health, (B) emotional experiences, (C) attitudes and worries, (D) social relationships, (E) achievement-related variables, (F) meaning. Most reports primarily focused on one of these aspects, while 17 focused on two aspects. Only eight reports did not assess any of these aspects, which we interpret as evidence of the relevance of psychological and cognitive variables in general, and the identified categories in particular, for characterizing the relevant effects of the COVID-19 pandemic on education. In the following sections, we describe the six aspects and summarize the main findings as well as immediate implications provided in these reports. In the final discussion section, we then elaborate on overarching implications and recommendations.

Mental Health

Most of the reports ($n = 25$) focused on the mental health of students and teachers. These reviews identified significant impacts of the pandemic on aspects such as burnout, depressive symptoms, anxiety (as a diagnosable psychiatric disorder), psychotic episodes, hyperactivity, trauma, mood disorders, as well as overall well-being and more specific aspects such as techno-stress and sleep disturbances. Female students, sexual and gender minority youth, and students who lived in rural areas or who faced financial hardships reported poorer mental health conditions during the pandemic. Furthermore, the lack of access to critical school-based services, such as healthcare and programs for children with disabilities exacerbated the mental health issues faced by students.

The pooled prevalence estimates of depression ranged from 23%–39% in students and from 16%–59.9% in educators. Moreover, the pooled estimates of anxiety ranged from 28%–41% in students and 10%–49.4% in educators. For stress, similar levels were observed. Notably, studies identified lower prevalence rates of mental health issues in pre-pandemic times. For example, a large-scale survey of 13,984 college students across eight nations before the pandemic reported 12-month prevalence rates of anxiety and depression as 16.7% and 18.5%, respectively (Auerbach et al., 2018). This is consistent with longitudinal evidence from Buizza et al. (2022), who found that most studies (12 out of 17) in their review reported an increase in depression, mood disorders, or personality disorders in students before and during the pandemic. Furthermore, Westphal et al. (2022) reported that teachers experienced a decrease in feelings of accomplishment and an increase in depersonalization and emotional exhaustion (see Weißenfels et al., 2022; Zadok-Gurman et al., 2021). Positive psychological effects, such as resilience-building factors during the pandemic, were not frequently addressed.

Emotional Experiences

The second most prevalent category was emotional experiences (n = 15), which encompassed more immediate emotional reactions such as fear, frustration, and sadness. Similar to anxiety and depression, rates of fear were documented as being high, with pooled estimates of 33% in students (Fang et al., 2022). Furthermore, with critical school-based services having become inaccessible, studies reported that educational disparities widened, exacerbating differences in students' emotional reactions during the pandemic.

To assist students in dealing with these emotional burdens, support measures and programs were developed to aid in effective emotion regulation and the fostering of mental health. Specifically, three reviews identified with our search summarized the effectiveness of various forms of online interventions used to address emotional experiences and mental health in students. It is worth noting that the interventions described in these reviews were primarily aimed at supporting students in higher education. However, we did not come across any reviews that focused on interventions tailored to the specific needs of school students or teachers.

Attitudes and Worries

Few reviews (n = 2) addressed attitudes and worries in relation to education during the COVID-19 pandemic. One review focused on students' attitudes towards e-learning, revealing both positive as well as negative appraisals (Masalimova et al., 2022). Meanwhile, faculty members also reported the transition to e-teaching to be challenging. While many research syntheses identified in our review compiled challenges and opportunities associated with the transition from face-to-face to e-learning during the pandemic, they generally considered the effects of digital learning and not students' and teachers' attitudes and worries specifically. However, such personal experiences hold a key position for the implementation and use of digital teaching/learning and should therefore not be neglected in endeavours focused on supporting digital teaching and learning processes (Sailer et al., 2021). Moreover, the included works reflected very little on how attitudes might have changed over the course of the pandemic, from the forced transition to remote learning and students' lack of online learning readiness to increased familiarity with such learning environments.

Social Relationships

Only four studies investigated the effects of the pandemic on social relationships. The respective studies included effects on relationships and collaboration between students, parents, and teachers. Challenges such as inequities in resources and access to technology, lack of accommodations, routine change, and social isolation were faced by families and school professionals in all countries, regardless of differences in the educational systems and living conditions. In the educational context, communication and collaboration between students, teachers, and parents were considered a key solution to effectively handle these problems. Especially for younger students as well as for students with special educational needs, the family and how well they collaborated with teachers emerged as a decisive factor for successful teaching-learning processes.

Achievement-Related Variables

Many of the included reviews focused on achievement-related variables ($n = 16$). These include self-efficacy beliefs, technological literacy, workload, actual achievement, learning experiences, strategies, study satisfaction and challenges, as well as academic dishonesty. To this end, the respective studies were concerned with the effects of school closures as well as e-teaching specifically. Although a few studies attempted to evaluate the effectiveness of digital teaching and learning in general, such as the research by Camilleri and Camilleri (2022), most researchers have been cautious about comparing the digital education brought about by COVID-19 with regular digital education (Hodges et al., 2020). The ad hoc emergency remote teaching was characterized by a rapid transition that often lacked adequate preparation for curricula, timetables, guidelines, and technology infrastructure, but also by professional development for teachers and students to ensure successful teaching and learning (Bergdahl & Nouri, 2021). These lessons learned from emergency remote teaching should be used to guide future preparedness strategies, enabling faster transitions and more effective remote education delivery if similar circumstances arise again.

Despite implementing remote learning, the results suggest that students experienced a decline in learning similar to what is typically observed during the summer break for students who receive no instruction ($d = -0.005$ *SD* to -0.05 *SD* per week; see Kuhfield & Tarasawa, 2020). A recent meta-analysis also confirmed this trend, reporting a pooled effect size of $d = -0.14$ (Betthäuser et al., 2023). This means that students lost approximately 35% of a regular school year's learning, indicating that most remote learning efforts during the initial school closures in the spring of 2020 were ineffective for student learning. Specifically, during the early stages of the pandemic, learning deficits appeared which have not significantly accumulated or decreased since then (Betthäuser et al., 2023). Although some studies found that online learning tools can improve student achievement, the positive effects are usually limited to students who are already experienced with such tools and do not have to adapt to a new learning environment. This finding is consistent with the reported satisfaction and challenges that both students and educators have experienced while using digital technology for teaching and learning.

Meaning

While the pandemic had an existential impact on many individuals, only a small number of reviews ($n = 2$) examined the effects of the pandemic on meaning, including factors such as individuals' sense of purpose, sense of belonging, sense of self, and their perceived work-life balance. However, even in these reviews, these variables were often discussed as secondary concerns, with a greater emphasis placed on the challenges of achieving a satisfactory work-life balance during the pandemic. By overlooking individuals' sense of meaning, we miss out on a deeper understanding of how the pandemic affected students, educators, and educational systems as a whole. Addressing such existential concerns, in turn, is crucial for promoting resilience in times of uncertainty.

DISCUSSION

The COVID-19 pandemic had a profound impact on education worldwide, and the research conducted in the first three years of the pandemic shed light on its effects. While the pandemic showcased the ability of science to adapt in times of crisis, there remains a deficiency in efficient methods to select, organize, and present new discoveries in a manner that optimizes comprehension and practical application. Consequently, even experts find it challenging to keep abreast of the multitude of COVID-19 papers published, hindering the acquisition of crucial information. This predicament is particularly problematic during crises where urgent overviews are required for policy and practice, and existing research syntheses may not be adequate for policy transfer (van de Schoot et al., 2021).

Based on this, the present chapter aimed to provide an overview of systematic reviews and meta-analyses that examined education during COVID-19 with a focus on psychological and cognitive variables.

Specifically, our analysis identified six distinct and partially overlapping categories, including mental health, emotional experiences, attitudes, social relationships, achievement, and meaning. Within this, the respective studies primarily focused on the perspectives of higher education students, and to a lesser extent, also those of school students and teachers. While many works assessed variables pertaining to mental health, emotional experiences, and achievement, considerably fewer examined attitudes and meaning, highlighting the need for further research in these areas. It is worth noting that our meta-review only covers categories that other researchers have deemed relevant to include in existing reviews. Thus, although the abundance of systematic reviews and meta-analyses focused on these topics highlight their importance, it is crucial to acknowledge that gaps still exist in our understanding of psychological and cognitive impacts of the pandemic.

Related to this, it is worth noting that our meta-review was based on reviews assessing research available at the time of our literature search, however, new studies are continuously being generated that have not yet been published or included in systematic research syntheses. The scarcity of studies on attitudes and meaning might be a function of the need to address tangible and measurable outcomes, limited resources, expertise, and the long-term nature of these aspects, which may take time to fully emerge. However, it is critical to recognize the importance of studying all aspects of human experiences to gain a complete understanding of the effects of the pandemic. Furthermore, our review identified that the quality of existing syntheses varied significantly, which is a concerning limitation. Despite the necessity of rapid research syntheses regarding the pandemic, the increased pace of publications and the urgency for reliable results may decrease their usefulness and limit the conclusions that can be drawn. In some reviews, studies were falsely included that equated expected projections to actual losses and conclusions were primarily based on this information (Zierer, 2021). Such practices are highly misleading and can negatively impact public discourse and trust in science. Lastly, the long-term impact of the pandemic on education is still uncertain, and thus, caution must be exercised when making predictions based on the currently available evidence.

Taken together, our meta-review suggests that the COVID-19 pandemic was a challenging time for many students and teachers. Factors such as lockdowns, closures, worries about education, and poor job prospects all contributed to mental health issues and emotional distress. The challenges associated with distance learning, technology issues, and lack of social interaction further strained their psychological well-being and increased risk of dropout and attrition. The economic background of institutions and students significantly determined the quality of online learning and teaching, widening educational inequalities worldwide and highlighting another aspect of educational disparity revealed by the pandemic that transcends geographic and economic disparities (Tilak & Kumar, 2022). Despite these challenges, the pandemic also spurred advancements in educational technology and online learning that will likely have long-lasting effects on the future of education. Notably, the accessibility and spread of remote learning, along with the increased integration of technology in education, are paving avenues for flexible, personalized, and adaptive learning. To prepare for future crises, the science community should prioritize reliable research practices and findings, which may necessitate a trade-off between speed and rigor in conducting research. While many researchers already worked in a highly collaborative manner regarding research during the pandemic, further collaboration between researchers and disciplines is needed, along with increased open science and a focus on higher quality outputs. This will help inform policymakers and the public, who have shown a willingness to listen to researchers throughout the pandemic. Researchers pooling their efforts will be an important asset in steering future crises. Looking ahead, it is imperative for national educational policymakers to prioritize their collaboration with education and psychology experts. Together, they must develop robust policies aimed at reversing the profound negative effects of the pandemic. This unequivocally stands as our most significant responsibility in the post-COVID era.

REFERENCES

(The references of all studies identified in the review are provided in the OSF repository)

Abu Talib, M., Bettayeb, A. M., & Omer, R. I. (2021). Analytical study on the impact of technology in higher education during the age of COVID-19. *Education and Information Technologies, 26*(6), 6719–6746. https://doi.org/10.1007/s10639-021-10507-1

Aisha, N., & Ratra, A. (2022). Online education amid COVID-19 pandemic and its opportunities, challenges and psychological impacts among students and teachers. *Asian Association of Open Universities Journal, 17*(3), 242–260. https://doi.org/10.1108/AAOUJ-03-2022-0028

Aljedaani, W., Krasniqi, R., Aljedaani, S., Mkaouer, M. W., Ludi, S., & Al-Raddah, K. (2022). If online learning works for you, what about deaf students. *Universal Access in the Information Society*. https://doi.org/10.1007/s10209-022-00897-5

Amate, J. J. S., de la Rosa, A. L., Cáceres, R. G., & Serrano, A. V. (2021). The effects of COVID-19 in the learning process of primary school students. *Education Sciences, 11*(10), Article 654. https://doi.org/10.3390/educsci11100654

Amelia, R., Dwiningrum, S. I. A., Haryanto, Zamzani, & Mustadi, A. (2021). *Pandemic pedagogy in the era of digital transformation*. 5th International Conference on Learning Innovation and Quality Education: ICLIQE 2021.

Auerbach, R. P., Mortier, P., Bruffaerts, R., Alonso, J., Benjet, C., Cuijpers, P., Demyttenaere, K., Ebert, D. D., Green, J. G., & Hasking, P. (2018). WHO world mental health surveys international college student project. *Journal of Abnormal Psychology, 127*(7), 623–638. https://doi.org/10.1037/abn0000362

Aznam, N., Perdana, R., Jumadi, J., Nurcahyo, H., & Wiyatmo, Y. (2022). Motivation and satisfaction in online learning during COVID-19 pandemic. *International Journal of Evaluation and Research in Education, 11*(2), 753–762. https://doi.org/10.11591/ijere.v11i2.21961

Bakaniene, I., Dominiak- wigo , M., Meneses da Silva Santos, M. A., Pantazatos, D., Grammatikou, M., Montanari, M., Virgili, I., Galeoto, G., Flocco, P., Bernabei, L., & Prasauskiene, A. (2022). Challenges of online learning for children with special educational needs and disabilities during the COVID-19 pandemic. *Journal of Intellectual and Developmental Disability*. https://doi.org/10.3109/13668250.2022.2096956

Bergdahl, N., & Nouri, J. (2021). COVID-19 and crisis-prompted distance education in Sweden. *Technology, Knowledge and Learning, 26*(3), 443–459.

Betthäuser, B. A., Bach-Mortensen, A. M., & Engzell, P. (2023). A systematic review and meta-analysis of the evidence on learning during the COVID-19 pandemic. *Nature Human Behaviour*, 1–11.

Boström, L., Collén, C., Damber, U., & Gidlund, U. (2021). A rapid transition from campus to emergent distant education: Effects on students' study strategies in higher education. *Education Sciences, 11*(11), Article 721. https://doi.org/10.3390/educsci11110721

Brainard, J. (2022). Pivot into COVID-19 research eases as publishing surge starts to level off. *Science, 376*(6595), 782–783.

Buizza, C., Bazzoli, L., & Ghilardi, A. (2022). Changes in college students mental health and lifestyle during the COVID-19 pandemic. *Adolescent Research Review*, 7(4), 537–550. https://doi.org/10.1007/s40894-022-00192-7

Camilleri, M. A., & Camilleri, A. C. (2022). *A cost-benefit analysis on the use of remote learning technologies*. 6th International Conference on E-Education, E-Business and E-Technology, ICEBT 2022.

Chaabane, S., Doraiswamy, S., Chaabna, K., Mamtani, R., & Cheema, S. (2021). The impact of COVID-19 school closure on child and adolescent health. *Children, 8*(5), Article 415. https://doi.org/10.3390/children8050415

Chang, J. J., Ji, Y., Li, Y. H., Pan, H. F., & Su, P. Y. (2021). Prevalence of anxiety symptoms and depressive symptoms among college students during COVID-19 pandemic. *Journal of Affective Disorders, 292*, 242–254. https://doi.org/10.1016/j.jad.2021.05.109

Coles, L., Johnstone, M., Pattinson, C., Thorpe, K., Van Halen, O., Zheng, Z., Bayliss, O., Lakeman, N., Western, M., Povey, J., & Staton, S. (2022). Identifying factors for poorer educational outcomes that may be exacerbated by COVID-19. *Australian Journal of Social Issues, 58*(1), 13–40. https://doi.org/10.1002/ajs4.236

Cortés-Albornoz, M. C., Ramírez-Guerrero, S., Rojas-Carabali, W., De-La-Torre, A., & Talero-Gutiérrez, C. (2022). Effects of remote learning during the COVID-19 lockdown on children's visual health: a systematic review. *BMJ Open*, *12*(8), Article e062388. https://doi.org/10.1136/bmjopen-2022-062388

da Silva, G. C. L., Rossato, L., Correia-Zanini, M., & Scorsolini-Comin, F. (2022). Online group interventions for mental health promotion of college students. *Counselling and Psychotherapy Research*, *22*(4), 844–852. https://doi.org/10.1002/capr.12561

Daumiller, M., Rinas, R., Hein, J., Janke, S., Dickhäuser, O., & Dresel, M. (2021). Shifting from face-to-face to online teaching during COVID-19. *Computers in Human Behavior*, *118*. https://doi.org/10.1016/j.chb.2020.106677

Daumiller, M., Rinas, R., S□hoon, I., & Lüftenegger, M. (2023). How did COVID-19 affect education and what can be learned moving forward? *Zeitschrift für Psychologie*, *231*(3), 192–204. https://doi.org/10.1027/21512604/a000527

Deepika, V., Soundariya, K., Karthikeyan, K., & Kalaiselvan, G. (2021). Learning from home. *Postgraduate Medical Journal*, *97*(1151), 590–597. https://doi.org/10.1136/postgradmedj-2020-137989

Deng, J., Zhou, F., Hou, W., Silver, Z., Wong, C. Y., Chang, O., Drakos, A., Zuo, Q. K., & Huang, E. (2021). The prevalence of depressive symptoms, anxiety symptoms and sleep disturbance in higher education students during the COVID-19 pandemic. *Psychiatry Research*, *301*, Article 113863. https://doi.org/10.1016/j.psychres.2021.113863

Dobosz, D., Gierczyk, M., & Hornby, G. (2022). Parental perspectives of home-schooling of children with special educational needs and disabilities during the COVID-19 pandemic. *Journal of Research in Special Educational Needs*, *23*(1), 3–11. https://doi.org/10.1111/1471-3802.12575

Ebrahim, A. H., Dhahi, A., Husain, M. A., & Jahrami, H. (2022). The psychological well-being of university students amidst COVID-19 pandemic. *Sultan Qaboos University Medical Journal*, *22*(2), 179–197. https://doi.org/10.18295/squmj.6.2021.081

Elharake, J. A., Akbar, F., Malik, A. A., Gilliam, W., & Omer, S. B. (2022). Mental health impact of COVID-19 among children and college students. *Child Psychiatry and Human Development*, *54*, 913–925. https://doi.org/10.1007/s10578-021-01297-1

Fang, Y., Ji, B., Liu, Y., Zhang, J., Liu, Q., Ge, Y., Xie, Y., & Liu, C. (2022). The prevalence of psychological stress in student populations during the COVID-19 epidemic. *Scientific Reports*, *12*(1), Article 12118. https://doi.org/10.1038/s41598-022-16328-7

Fekih-Romdhane, F., Pandi-Perumal, S. R., Conus, P., Krebs, M. O., Cheour, M., Seeman, M. V., & Jahrami, H. A. (2022). Prevalence and risk factors of self-reported psychotic experiences among high school and college students. *Acta Psychiatrica Scandinavica*. https://doi.org/10.1111/acps.13494

Fernández-Batanero, J. M., Montenegro-Rueda, M., Fernández-Cerero, J., & Tadeu, P. (2022). Online education in higher education. *Heliyon*, *8*(8), Article e10139. https://doi.org/10.1016/j.heliyon.2022.e10139

Haddad, J. M., Macenski, C., Mosier-Mills, A., Hibara, A., Kester, K., Schneider, M., Conrad, R. C., & Liu, C. H. (2021). The impact of social media on college mental health during the COVID-19 pandemic. *Current Psychiatry Reports, 23*(11), Article 70. https://doi.org/10.1007/s11920-021-01288-y

Hammerstein, S., König, C., Dreisörner, T., & Frey, A. (2021). Effects of COVID-19-related school closures on student achievement. *Frontiers in Psychology, 12*, Article 746289. https://doi.org/10.3389/fpsyg.2021.746289

Hodges, C. B., Moore, S., Lockee, B. B., Trust, T., & Bond, M. A. (2020). *The difference between emergency remote teaching and online learning*. http://hdl.handle.net/10919/104648

Ibna Seraj, P. M., Chakraborty, R., Mehdi, T., & Roshid, M. M. (2022). A systematic review on pedagogical trends and assessment practices during the COVID-19 pandemic. *Education Research International, 2022*, Article 1534018. https://doi.org/10.1155/2022/1534018

Jehi, T., Khan, R., Dos Santos, H., & Majzoub, N. (2022). Effect of COVID-19 outbreak on anxiety among students of higher education. *Current Psychology, 42*, 17475–17489. https://doi.org/10.1007/s12144-021-02587-6

Khan, M. A. (2021). COVID-19's impact on higher education. *Education Sciences, 11*(8), Article 421. https://doi.org/10.3390/educsci11080421

Kratzer, S., Pfadenhauer, L. M., Biallas, R. L., Featherstone, R., Klinger, C., Movsisyan, A., Rabe, J. E., Stadelmaier, J., Rehfuess, E., Wabnitz, K., & Verboom, B. (2022). Unintended consequences of measures implemented in the school setting to contain the COVID-19 pandemic. *Cochrane Database of Systematic Reviews, 2022*(6), Article Cd015397. https://doi.org/10.1002/14651858.CD015397

Krishnaratne, S., Pfadenhauer, L. M., Coenen, M., Geffert, K., Jung-Sievers, C., Klinger, C., Kratzer, S., Littlecott, H., Movsisyan, A., Rabe, J. E., Rehfuess, E., Sell, K., Strahwald, B., Stratil, J. M., Voss, S., Wabnitz, K., & Burns, J. (2020). Measures implemented in the school setting to contain the COVID-19 pandemic. *Cochrane Database of Systematic Reviews, 2020*(12), Article Cd013812. https://doi.org/10.1002/14651858.CD013812

Kuhfield, M., & Tarasawa, B. (2020). The COVID-19 slide. Brief. *NWEA*. https://doi.org/10.3102/0013189X20965918

Li, Y., Wang, A., Wu, Y., Han, N., & Huang, H. (2021). Impact of the COVID-19 pandemic on the mental health of college students. *Frontiers in Psychology, 12*, Article 669119. https://doi.org/10.3389/fpsyg.2021.669119

Liyanage, S., Saqib, K., Khan, A. F., Thobani, T. R., Tang, W. C., Chiarot, C. B., Alshurman, B. A., & Butt, Z. A. (2022). Prevalence of anxiety in university students during the COVID-19 pandemic. *International Journal of Environmental Research and Public Health, 19*(1), Article 62. https://doi.org/10.3390/ijerph19010062

Ma, K., Liang, L., Chutiyami, M., Nicoll, S., Khaerudin, T., & Ha, X. V. (2022). COVID-19 pandemic-related anxiety, stress, and depression among teachers. *Work (Reading, Mass.), 73*(1), 3–27. https://doi.org/10.3233/WOR-220062

Malinauskas, R., & Malinauskiene, V. (2022). Meta-analysis of psychological interventions for reducing stress, anxiety, and depression among university students during the COVID-19 pandemic. *International Journal of Environmental Research and Public Health, 19*(15), Article 9199. https://doi.org/10.3390/ijerph19159199

Masalimova, A. R., Khvatova, M. A., Chikileva, L. S., Zvyagintseva, E. P., Stepanova, V. V., & Melnik, M. V. (2022). Distance learning in higher education during COVID-19. *Frontiers in Education, 7*, Article 822958. https://doi.org/10.3389/feduc.2022.822958

Morfaki, C., & Skotis, A. (2022). Academic online learning experience during COVID-19 - a systematic literature review based on personality traits. *Higher Education, Skills and Work-based Learning, 13*(4). https://doi.org/10.1108/HESWBL-03-2022-0062

Na, S., & Jung, H. (2021). Exploring university instructors' challenges in online teaching and design opportunities during the covid-19 pandemic. *International Journal of Learning, Teaching and Educational Research, 20*(9), 308–327. https://doi.org/10.26803/ijlter.20.9.18

Nakhoda, K., Ahmady, S., Fesharaki, M. G., & Azar, N. G. (2021). Covid-19 pandemic and e-learning satisfaction in medical and non-medical student. *Iranian Journal of Public Health, 50*(12), 2509–2516.

Nang, A. F. M., Maat, S. M., & Mahmud, M. S. (2022). Teacher technostress and coping mechanisms during COVID-19 pandemic. *Pegem Egitim ve Ogretim Dergisi, 12*(2), 200–212. https://doi.org/10.47750/pegegog.12.02.20

Nasution, A. K. P., Nasution, M. K., Batubara, M. H., & Munandar, I. (2022). Learning during COVID-19 pandemic. *International Journal of Evaluation and Research in Education, 11*(2), 639–648. https://doi.org/10.11591/ijere.v11i2.21917

Ndibalema, P. (2022). Constraints of transition to online distance learning in higher education institutions during COVID-19 in developing countries. *E-Learning and Digital Media, 19*(6), 595–618. https://doi.org/10.1177/20427530221107510

Ozamiz-Etxebarria, N., Mondragon, N. I., Bueno-Notivol, J., Pérez-Moreno, M., & Santabárbara, J. (2021). Prevalence of anxiety, depression, and stress among teachers during the COVID-19 pandemic. *Brain Sciences, 11*(9), Article 1172. https://doi.org/10.3390/brainsci11091172

Palayew, A., Norgaard, O., Safreed-Harmon, K., Andersen, T. H., Rasmussen, L. N., & Lazarus, J. V. (2020). Pandemic publishing poses a new COVID-19 challenge. *Nature Human Behaviour, 4*(7), 666–669.

Panagouli, E., Stavridou, A., Savvidi, C., Kourti, A., Psaltopoulou, T., Sergentanis, T. N., & Tsitsika, A. (2021). School performance among children and adolescents during COVID-19 pandemic. *Children, 8*(12), Article 1134. https://doi.org/10.3390/children8121134

Pelikan, E. R., Lüftenegger, M., Holzer, J., Korlat, S., Spiel, C., & S□hober, B. (2021). Learning during COVID-19: The role of self-regulated learning, motivation, and procrastination for perceived competence. *Zeitschrift für Erziehungswissenschaft, 24*(2), 393–418. https://doi.org/10.1007/s11618-021-01002-x

Psacharopoulos, G., Collis, V., Patrinos, H. A., & Vegas, E. (2021). The COVID-19 cost of school closures in earnings and income across the world. *Comparative Education Review, 65*(2), 271–287.

Riboldi, I., Cavaleri, D., Calabrese, A., Capogrosso, C. A., Piacenti, S., Bartoli, F., Crocamo, C., & Carrà, G. (2022). Digital mental health interventions for anxiety and depressive symptoms in university students during the COVID-19 pandemic. *Revista de Psiquiatria y Salud Mental*. https://doi.org/10.1016/j.rpsm.2022.04.005

Saikat, S., Dhillon, J. S., Ahmad, W. F. W., & Jamaluddin, R. A. (2021). A systematic review of the benefits and challenges of mobile learning during the COVID-19 pandemic. *Education Sciences, 11*(9), Article 459. https://doi.org/10.3390/educsci11090459

Sailer, M., Schultz-Pernice, F., & Fischer, F. (2021). Contextual facilitators for learning activities involving technology in higher education. *Computers in Human Behavior, 121*. https://doi.org/10.1016/j.chb.2021.106794

Seligman, M. (2018). PERMA and the building blocks of well-being. *The Journal of Positive Psychology, 13*(4), 333–335. https://doi.org/10.1080/17439760.2018.1437466

Shea, B. J., Reeves, B. C., Wells, G., Thuku, M., Hamel, C., Moran, J., Moher, D., Tugwell, P., Welch, V., & Kristjansson, E. (2017). AMSTAR 2. *BMJ, 358*. https://doi.org/10.1136/bmj.j4008

Silva, D. F. O., Cobucci, R. N., Lima, S. C. V. C., & de Andrade, F. B. (2021). Prevalence of anxiety, depression, and stress among teachers during the COVID-19 pandemic a PRISMA-compliant systematic review. *Medicine, 100*(44), Article e27684. https://doi.org/10.1097/MD.0000000000027684

Soto, C. J., Napolitano, C. M., Sewell, M. N., Yoon, H. J., & Roberts, B. W. (2022). An integrative framework for conceptualizing and assessing social, emotional, and behavioral skills. *Journal of Personality and Social Psychology, 123*(1), 192. https://doi.org/10.1037/pspp0000401

Susilaningsih, F. S., Komariah, M., Mediawati, A. S., & Lumbantobing, V. B. M. (2021). Quality of work-life among lecturers during online learning in COVID-19 pandemic period. *Malaysian Journal of Medicine and Health Sciences, 17*, 163–166.

Thomas, J., & Harden, A. (2008). Methods for the thematic synthesis of qualitative research in systematic reviews. *BMC medical research methodology, 8*(1), 1–10.

Tilak, J. B. G., & Kumar, A. G. (2022). Policy changes in global higher education. *Higher Education Policy, 35*(3), 610-628. https://doi.org/10.1057/s41307-022-00266-0

Turnbull, D., Chugh, R., & Luck, J. (2021). Transitioning to e-learning during the COVID-19 pandemic. *Education and Information Technologies, 26*(5), 6401–6419. https://doi.org/10.1007/s10639-021-10633-w

United Nations. (2020). *Policy brief: Education during COVID-19 and beyond*. https://unsdg.un.org/resources/policy-brief-impact-covid-19-children

United Nations Children's Fund, UNESCO, & World Bank. (2022). *Where are we on education recovery?* UNICEF.

Valenzuela, R. L. G., Velasco, R. I. B., & Jorge, M. P. P. C., II. (2022). Impact of COVID-19 pandemic on sleep of undergraduate students. *Stress and Health, 39*(1), 4–34. https://doi.org/10.1002/smi.3171

van de Schoot, R., de Bruin, J., Schram, R., Zahedi, P., de Boer, J., Weijdema, F., Kramer, B., Huijts, M., Hoogerwerf, M., & Ferdinands, G. (2021). An open source machine learning framework for efficient and transparent systematic reviews. *Nature Machine Intelligence, 3*(2), 125–133.

Viner, R., Russell, S., Saulle, R., Croker, H., Stansfield, C., Packer, J., Nicholls, D., Goddings, A. L., Bonell, C., … & Minozzi, S. (2022). School closures during social lockdown and mental health, health behaviors, and well-being among children and adolescents during the first COVID-19 wave: A systematic review. *JAMA Pediatrics, 176*(4), 400–409. https://doi.org/10.1001/jamapediatrics.2021.5840

Wang, F., Zhang, L., Ding, L., Wang, L., & Deng, Y. (2022). Fear of COVID-19 among college students. *Frontiers in Public Health, 10,* Article 846894. https://doi.org/10.3389/fpubh.2022.846894

Weißenfels, M., Klopp, E., & Perels, F. (2022). Changes in teacher burnout and self-efficacy during the COVID-19 pandemic. *Frontiers in Education, 6*. https://doi.org/10.3389/feduc.2021.736992

Westphal, A., Kalinowski, E., Hoferi□hter, C. J., & Vo□k, M. (2022). K−12 tea□hers' stress and burnout during the COVID-19 pandemic. *Frontiers in Psychology, 13*, Article 920326. https://doi.org/10.3389/fpsyg.2022.920326

Xue, S., & Crompton, H. (2022). Educational technology research during the COVID-19 pandemic. *Interactive Technology and Smart Education*. https://doi.org/10.1108/ITSE-05-2022-0067

Zadok-Gurman, T., Jakobovich, R., Dvash, E., Zafrani, K., Rolnik, B., Ganz, A. B., & Lev-Ari, S. (2021). Effect of inquiry-based stress reduction (IBSR) intervention on well-being, resilience and burnout of teachers during the COVID-19 pandemic. *International Journal of Environmental Research and Public Health, 18*(7). https://doi.org/10.3390/ijerph18073689

Zheng, M., Asif, M., Tufail, M. S., Naseer, S., Khokhar, S. G., Chen, X., & Naveed, R. T. (2022). COVID academic pandemic. *Frontiers in Psychology, 13*, Article 895371. https://doi.org/10.3389/fpsyg.2022.895371

Zhu, J., Racine, N., Xie, E. B., Park, J., Watt, J., Eirich, R., Dobson, K., & Madigan, S. (2021). Post-secondary student mental health during COVID-19. *Frontiers in Psychiatry, 12*, Article 777251. https://doi.org/10.3389/fpsyt.2021.777251

Zierer, K. (2021). Effects of pandemic-related school closures on pupils' performance and learning in selected countries. *Education Sciences, 11*(6), 252. https://doi.org/10.3390/educsci11060252

CHAPTER 21

EXAMINING THE COGNITIVE AND PSYCHOLOGICAL EFFECTS OF THE COVID-19 GLOBAL PANDEMIC ON HIGH SCHOOL, COLLEGE AND GRADUATE LEARNERS

What Have We Learned and How Can We Be Better Prepared for the Future?

Jill D. Salisbury-Glennon, Chih-hsuan Wang, David M. Shannon, and Yan Dai
Auburn University

As we stated at the very beginning of this co-edited book, in Chapter 1, the effects of the COVID-19 global pandemic on colleges and universities around the world have been greater than any event in recent history (Alexander et al., 2020; Rashid & Yadav, 2020). At the peak of the pandemic, 63 million teachers and around 1.6 billion students at all educational levels from more than 190 countries on all continents were affected (United Nations, 2020, as cited in Daumiller et al. (Chapter 20). Further, students missed an estimated

Examining the Cognitive and Psychological Effects of the COVID-19 Global Pandemic on High School, College, and Graduate Learners, pp. 507–528

2 trillion hours of in-person instruction (United Nations Children's Fund et al., 2022, as cited in Daumiller et al. (Chapter 20). During 2019–2020 alone, approximately 12 million full-time college students were impacted by the COVID-19 global pandemic (IPEDS, 2020, as cited in Sherif et al., Chapter 7). At the time of this writing, we remain in the midst of this global pandemic and thus, we can barely even begin to comprehend the far-reaching effects that this pandemic will have on education. This co-edited book represents one of the initial efforts to synthesize the research into the cognitive and psychological effects of the COVID-19 global pandemic on high school, college and graduate-level learners.

The present co-edited book serves to synthesize the diverse research conducted by the authors included in this edited book with a focus on the cognitive and psychological effects of the COVID-19 global pandemic on high school, college, and graduate learners. This research has been conducted in multiple countries across multiple continents, using multiple diverse populations, using several different research methodologies, along with an emphasis on both the challenges as well as the positive outcomes that have resulted from this unprecedented event. Specifically, the present volume includes research that was conducted across four continents from the following countries: The United States of America, Taiwan, Mexico, Germany, The United Kingdom and Australia. In addition, the present volume includes research with students enrolled in a variety of majors, including nursing, a STEM academy, engineering, and education. Further, in addition to a focus on more typical learners, this volume includes a focus on more underrepresented and marginalized participant populations such as first-generation college students, learners with ADHD, multilingual learners, underserved and underrepresented college student populations, graduate-student parents, first-year doctoral students, and teacher educators. Finally, the research presented in this co-edited volume synthesizes studies that have been conducted using quantitative research approaches such as survey methodologies, qualitative research methodologies including semi-structured interviews, case-study designs, and a qualitative collaborative ethnography, mixed methodological approaches such as an explanatory sequential design as well as a systematic meta-review of systematic reviews and meta-analyses. The following section will summarize the theoretical frameworks, research methodologies, participant populations, research findings, and challenges as well as the positive outcomes of each research study conducted in the midst of the COVID-19 global pandemic. The section will conclude with a more general thematic summary as well as implications for future inevitable world crises, lockdowns, and other unprecedented events.

SUMMARY

High School Learners

One common practice that has existed for many years as we bridge the transition from high school to higher education learning environments is that of standardized assessment. Standardized assessment is one area that remains in an altered state as the result of the COVID-19 global pandemic at the time of this writing. First, since the onset of the COVID-19 pandemic, many colleges and universities have become test-optional. Second, we are really just beginning to understand the full magnitude of the COVID-19 pandemic on standardized test scores. For example, preliminary research has shown that since the onset of the pandemic, standardized test scores such as the ACT and SAT have dropped significantly. It is not uncommon to read a quote in the media such as:

> The graduating class of 2023 was in their first year of high school when the COVID-19 global pandemic forced classrooms to shut down and forced students to learn at home through emergency remote instruction. The data show that the percentage of these 2023 seniors meeting none of the college-readiness benchmarks- goals for English, math, reading and science reached historic highs with 43% failing to achieve any of these goals. (Gore, 2023, para. 5)

Thus, in Chapter 2, "Effects of the COVID-19 Pandemic on College and Career Planning, Social and Emotional Skills and College and Career Readiness: Evidence From the ACT, Inc.," Allen et al. (Chapter 2) sought to investigate the effects of the pandemic on: (a) college and career readiness, (b) student achievement, (c) social and emotional skills, (d) college preparation during the COVID-19 global pandemic and e) student reflections regarding the effects of the COVID-19 global pandemic across student groups and especially amongst underrepresented learners. During the time-span of 2019–2022, from pre-pandemic to post-pandemic, using surveys and quantitative data analyses, Allen et al., (Chapter 2) found that ACT scores declined significantly for all learners in all grade levels. Further, these researchers found that with regards to instructional modality, these scores declined most severely for the virtual group, followed by the hybrid group, and then followed by the onsite group (Allen et al., Chapter 2). Further, with regards to their specific learning aptitude, these students reported that the pandemic had a negative impact on their self-management, socializing, college and career readiness, motivation and learning, focus and discipline, relationships with friends, involvement in extracurricular activities, time management and organizational skills.

While students' reports of the impacts of the global pandemic on their academic learning, motivation, mental health and socialization were overwhelmingly negative, it is important to note that students also stated that they had made gains in their use of: digital tools and technology, personal self-reliance, and their appreciation for education and for their teachers Allen et al. (Chapter 2). The authors concluded that these high school students demonstrated some evidence of positive social and emotional skill development as a function of the pandemic.

In Chapter 3, "Examining the Academic and Psychological Experiences of Students and Educational Stakeholders in a High School STEM Academy during the COVID-19 Pandemic," Fletcher et al. (Chapter 3) implemented a qualitative case-study design using 25 interviews from stakeholders and 23 from high school students enrolled in an engineering academy in an effort to investigate the effects of the COVID-19 global pandemic on black male high school students, many of whom came from disadvantaged circumstances. The results of these interviews were classified into four themes: (a) a lack of student engagement and social interaction, (b) growing pains: school stakeholders and students as adaptive learners, c) work-based learning implementation challenges, and (d) the NAF Lab as an intervention. While both stakeholders and students reported challenges due to the lack of student engagement during the pandemic, the researchers also concluded that the pandemic caused both scholars and practitioners to create new ways to increase their students' engagement and work-based learning opportunities through the use of emerging technologies. The researchers further concluded that The NAF Future Ready Lab provided an example of an effective approach that was instrumental in providing a work-based learning simulated environment for disadvantaged learners during these unprecedented times (Fletcher et al., Chapter 3).

In Chapter 4, "The Effects of Mental Health, Motivation, and Learning Strategies on High School Students' Grades During COVID-19" (Wang et al., Chapter 4), sought to investigate the effects of the COVID-19 global pandemic on high school students' motivation and learning. They asserted that while adolescent populations are a population known to have adjustment and mental health issues (Wang et al., Chapter 4), relatively little is known regarding the effects of the pandemic on high school learners' motivation and learning strategies. Further, this study was conducted using Taiwanese high school students enrolled in distance learning courses. In this quantitative study, the participants completed a demographic survey, the DASS21 (Lovibond & Lovibond, 1995), The MSLQ (Pintrich et al., 1991) and indicated their expected final grade. Results of structural equation modeling (SEM) indicated that high school students' mental health directly impacted their motivation, which then impacted their levels of learning strategies, which ultimately affected their final grades.

Undergraduate Learners

In Chapter 5 "Instructional Support and the Student-Teacher Relationship in Higher Education: Lessons Learned From Students' Perceptions of Instruction During Emergency Remote Learning," Miller et al. (Chapter 5) sought to examine the factors that contributed to the satisfaction and frustration of college students' psychological needs during this transition to emergency remote instruction in an effort to better understand the role of the student-teacher relationships and instructional support during learning. Grounded in self-determination theory (SDT; Deci & Ryan, 1991), the researchers hypothesized that perceived instructor competence during an emergency remote instructional setting will relate positively to students' needs satisfaction and negatively to the frustration of their basic needs. Results of both qualitative and quantitative analyses suggested that as the result of this transition to emergency remote learning, student perceptions of the learning environment were directly related to their basic psychological need satisfaction and thus, lent support for self-determination theory (SDT; Deci & Ryan, 1991). Finally, the results of this study suggested that as the result of the COVID-19 global pandemic, more students and instructors are choosing and using on-line instruction since their initial introduction during emergency remote learning (Miller et al., Chapter 5).

In Chapter 6, "College During COVID: A Mixed Methods Study Examining Undergraduate Students' Academic Experiences and Responses" (Sewell et al., Chapter 6) sought to investigate the effects of the COVID-19 global pandemic on the academic experiences of first-generation college students. Overall, the research conducted thus far has suggested that while navigating the pandemic was challenging for most learners, it was especially challenging for underserved, marginalized and underrepresented populations, as the pandemic seemed to exacerbate existing inequalities. First-generation college students have been demonstrated to experience such challenges as: greater financial hardships, increased living and technology expenses, more difficulty with on-line learning, an increased incidence of mental health issues, and an insecurity regarding their ability to continue enrollment (Sewell et al., Chapter 6). Grounded in a transactional model of stress and coping and self-determination theory, Sewell et al. (Chapter 6) conducted an explanatory sequential mixed-methods design. Results of quantitative analyses followed by qualitative analyses indicated that the largest areas of impact of the COVID-19 global pandemic noted by first-generation college students were stress, interactions with family members and friends, daily routines, and academics. Interestingly, first-generation college students actually experienced a significantly lower negative impact of the COVID-19 global pandemic on daily routines, stress and interaction with family and friends.

It was believed that it may be possible that first-generation college students may have been more resilient during the COVID-19 global pandemic. Despite the overwhelmingly negative impact of the pandemic that was reported, some participants noted positive impacts and even employed adaptive coping responses. For example, these participants noted that the pandemic afforded them more study time, that professors checked on them more and/or were more empathic with deadlines, and so forth, due to the pandemic. Further, some participants indicated that they enjoyed more time at home with their family, and the extra support from the relationships that they did have access to, which resulted in a sense of community for some.

In Chapter 7, "The Impact of the COVID-19 Pandemic on First-Generation Undergraduate Students' Participation in Campus Activities," Sherif et al. (Chapter 7), sought to examine fist-generation college students' involvement and participation in campus activities during the pandemic. While research to date has elucidated the effects of the COVID-19 global pandemic on such factors as student mental health, socialization, academic achievement and engagement in learning (e.g., Lee et al., 2021; Mucci-Ferris et al., 2021; Potts, 2021; Salta et al., 2021; Vaterlaus et al., 2021; Wester et al., 2021; Wu & Teets, 2021, as cited in Sherif et al., Chapter 7), there remains a paucity of research into the effects of the pandemic on student on-campus engagement. While the importance of student involvement has been very well-established, Sherif et al. (Chapter 7) suggest that first-generation college students often face unique challenges in college such as having less financial resources, a lower graduation rate, and less extracurricular engagement. One reason for this may be that many first-generation college students may be living at home and not on campus, thus making campus involvement more challenging. The results of this quantitative study suggested that campus involvement was important for first-generation college students and that it would be helpful for university administrators to encourage more involvement among first-generation college students as we move into the post-pandemic phase.

In Chapter 8, "The Impact of the COVID-19 Pandemic on College Students with ADHD: Implications and Interventions," Quadlander-Goff et al. (Chapter 8), sought to investigate the impact of the COVID-19 global pandemic on college students diagnosed as having attention-deficit hyperactivity disorder (ADHD). College students diagnosed with ADHD tend to demonstrate higher incidences of learning challenges such as not submitting assignments on time, a lack of organizational skills, having a hard time paying attention in class and/or focusing during studying and/or exams, and a lack of time management. During the COVID-19 global pandemic, on many campuses, many undergraduate students were forced to learn almost exclusively online for almost an entire academic year

(Birmingham, 2023). While the transition to emergency remote instruction was difficult for many college students to cope with, this instructional format created an especially challenging situation for many college students with ADHD as the result of common challenges such as their executive functioning challenges, procrastination, avoidance and emotional dysregulation (Bodalski et al., 2022, as cited in Quadlander-Goff et al., Chapter 8). Further, due to the pandemic campus shut-downs, many of the campus resources that were normally available to college students, such as tutoring, accommodations during testing, quiet library study rooms, and so forth, were no longer available. Many precautions were put into place to mitigate the spread of the COVID-19 virus. However, it is important to note that while these precautions were developed to promote better physical health, these precautions often inadvertently resulted in decreased psychological health for many college students as indicated by increases in depression, stress and anxiety for many college students (Jorales et al., 2020, as cited in Quadlander-Goff et al., Chapter 8). Thus, college students with ADHD were found to experience even greater difficulties due to the sudden shift to on-line learning. It was suggested that cognitive behavioral therapy may serve as one means to assisting college students with ADHD to cope with the learning challenges created by the COVID-19 global pandemic.

In Chapter 9 "Trade-Offs of Seeking Support for University Students During the Pandemic," Rosen et al. (Chapter 9) sought to investigate both the adaptive and maladaptive outcomes of support seeking during the pandemic. In this quantitative study, the following surveys were administered: (a) Co-Rumination Questionnaire (CRQ, Davidson et al., 2014; Rose, 2002), (b) Network of Relationships Inventory (NRI; Buhrmester & Furman, 2008), (c) Perceived Coronavirus Threat Questionnaire (Conway et al., 2020), (d) The Center for Epidemiological Studies Depression Scale (CESD; Radloff, 1977), and (e) The Coronavirus Health and Impact Survey (CRISIS; Nikoladis et al., 2020). The results of Structural Equation Modeling (SEM) demonstrated that co-rumination had a significantly positive relationship with the mediators of perceived COVID threat and friendship closeness. Perceived COVID threat was also significantly positively related to both depression and psychological distress. The researchers concluded that co-rumination appeared to make a positive contribution to friendship closeness. However, it also increased anxiety and psychological distress, and thus, had both positive and negative effects.

In Chapter 10 "Balancing Work and School During the Time of COVID-19: Lessons Learned from Online Pre- and In-Service Teacher Training," Tackett et al. (Chapter 10), discussed the use of Bronfenbrenner's ecological systems theory (1979) to interpret the experiences of preservice and in-service teachers engaged in teacher-education courses during the COVID-19 global pandemic. The shift to on-line instruction was a contributor to the widening of the achievement gap due to race/ethnicity and school poverty status. For example, higher poverty schools experienced 50% more achievement loss than low-poverty schools (Goldhaber et al., 2022, p. 2). In the present study, written responses from 211 pre and post in-service teachers were analyzed and coded using themes from Bronfenbrenner's theory. Results indicated that in-service teachers were more likely to report negative experiences due to increased or constantly changing family roles. On the other hand, preservice teachers were more likely to report missing the peer interaction from their classes.

In Chapter 11, "Underserved and Underrepresented College Students' Resilience During COVID-19," Tyler et al. (Chapter 11) sought to investigate the resilience of undergraduate STEM students from disadvantaged backgrounds in the Alabama Black Belt Region. While the transition to on-line learning impacted instructional quality, which often created academic challenges for many college students, these challenges were especially significant for disadvantaged students. Further, disadvantaged students enrolled in science classes with required labs faced even more significant challenges due to the lack of lab access during the pandemic (Beck et al., 2021; Parker et al., 2021; Wang et al., 2021b, as cited in Tyler et al., Chapter 11). Thus, a Mentoring Bridge Model was developed in an effort to provide additional academic and social support through peer mentoring to underrepresented, minority and/or lower-income college students enrolled in STEM courses with their classwork during this challenging time (Dunn et al., 2021; Qazi et al., 2016). This Mentoring Bridge Model was developed to help further develop students' resilience, time management, and persistence skills, enabling them to navigate the academic and social challenges posed by the pandemic. Results of this study demonstrated that the COVID-19 global pandemic presented many challenges to college students, especially underrepresented college students. However, many of the underrepresented college students began to adapt to overcome these challenges as the result of their participation in The Bridge Model due to its emphasis on resilience, academic and social support.

In Chapter 12, "Perceptions and Attitudes of Nursing Students' Transition to Remote Instruction During COVID-19," Manning et al. (Chapter 12) sought to investigate the shift to on-line learning for nursing students in the midst of the COVID-19 global pandemic. While nursing is generally a field that emphasizes social skills and direct personal contact and communication, the shift to emergency remote learning resulted in a loss of face-to-face clinical opportunities and the ability to practice these skills in a hands-on environment. In the summer and fall of 2020, nursing students enrolled in a Nursing Skills Bootcamp. In this Bootcamp, students participated in small group labs, and practiced basic skills on manikins. Results of a related-samples Friedman's analysis of variance indicated that students' overall perceptions of readiness in performing the skills required for their clinical service were significantly higher after completing the skills Bootcamp.

In Chapter 13 "Exploring the Online Academic Acculturation of Multilingual Learners During COVID-19," Williams and Diamond (Chapter 13) sought to investigate how multilingual students demonstrated the various stages of acculturation as they transitioned to online instruction. These researchers used thematic analyses of international students' written assignments in an effort to study student perceptions as they made the unexpected transition to distance education. International students already face a vast array of challenges as they learn in a foreign country, often in a new language. Learning online can further exacerbate these challenges faced by international students. As the result of the COVID-19 global pandemic, these international students often arrived at their university expecting to engage in in-person classes and social interactions, but instead, were forced to learn through emergency remote instruction using online platforms such as Zoom, and so on. The results of thematic analyses revealed that multilingual learners experienced linguistic and autonomous learning challenges. Specifically, some multilingual learners expressed difficulty communicating with their peers and instructors due to their language barriers. Further, many multilingual learners found that the online learning environment slowed their language growth. With regards to positive outcomes, most of the multilingual learners studied were able to develop their own personal strategies to become autonomous learners.

In Chapter 14 "Perspectives of Engineering Students on the Impact of COVID-19 on the Learning and Teaching of Algebra and Differential Calculus," Gutierrez and Puga (Chapter 14) sought to investigate engineering students' perspectives on the impact of COVID-19 on the teaching and learning of algebra and differential equations. The results of a qualitative approach using the triangulation of semi-structured interviews revealed that these engineering students experienced a wide range of emotions, from frustration, anxiety and despair to joy and hope. Overall, the engineering majors preferred face-to-face interactions with their peers and teachers as opposed to remote digital instruction. Engineering students enrolled in algebra and differential calculus also mentioned that there were some positive outcomes as the result of the change to emergency remote instruction. Specifically, the lack of teacher presence seemed to encourage more peer interactions in an effort to understand the concepts. Participants also mentioned that they were forced to develop more responsibility, discipline and self-teaching as the result of the pandemic. Finally, participants mentioned that this experience enabled them to develop a greater appreciation of their teachers and the peer interactions that occur in face-to-face classrooms.

Graduate Learners

In Chapter 15, "Graduate Students' Mental Health During COVID-19: Parenthood and Gender," Yoo and Marshall (Chapter 15) sought to investigate the effects of parental status and gender on graduate students' perceived helplessness, self-efficacy and life satisfaction as a function of the COVID-19 global pandemic. While the nature of graduate school in general can create a high degree of stress for graduate students, this stress may be exacerbated for graduate students who are also parents. In general, graduate students may experience many stressors, such as finances, time constraints and the need to juggle the demands of a job, such as a GTA, along with the demands required of being a student. These stressors were even more challenging to manage for those graduate students during the pandemic who were also parents, as children were home 24/7 when the world shut down in 2020. Yoo and Marshall (Chapter 15) asserted that in addition to increased gender disparities as a function of the abrupt shift to online learning, the COVID-19 pandemic also exacerbated existing racial and ethnic inequalities in academia (Douglas et al., 2022; Doyle et al., 2021; Gabster et al., 2020; as cited in Yoo and Marshall, Chapter 15). Yoo and Marshall theoretically grounded their research in the tension between role strain theory (Elliot, 2003; Goode, 1960, as cited in Yoo & Marshall, Chapter 15), and the role accumulation theories (Sieber, 1974) which do technically offer opposing perspectives regarding roles. According to role strain theory, individuals have limited time and energy, which makes it difficult to fill multiple roles (Goode, 1960). Student parents often face the conflict between being a good parent, and being a good student, which can result in poor mental health (e.g., Dolson & Deemer, as cited in Yoo and Marshall, Chapter 15). Thus, from the perspective of role strain theory, graduate student parents are more likely to face stress due to the conflict of their multiple roles. In contrast, role accumulation theory suggests that people can benefit from juggling multiple roles (Bennett, 2024). Thus, the present study sought to examine how graduate student parents differ from graduate student non-parents, as well as whether this tension is different as a function of gender and ethnicity. In this quantitative study of 543 graduate students, Yoo and Marshall (Chapter 15) found that female non-parent graduate students demonstrated the highest level of perceived helplessness and the lowest levels of self-efficacy. Overall, results indicated that graduate student parents showed positive mental health as demonstrated by higher levels of life satisfaction and self-efficacy than their graduate peers without children. These results supported the role accumulation theory which suggests that engaging in multiple roles can actually enhance mental health (e.g., Sieber, 1974).

In Chapter 16, "Walking the Fine Line: First-Year Doctoral Students' Experiences During COVID-19," Trammell et al. (Chapter 16) sought to investigate the lived experiences of six female doctoral students as they transitioned to graduate school during the COVID-19 global pandemic using a qualitative collaborative autoethnography. While graduate students entering a doctoral program pre-pandemic have been shown to demonstrate a variety of mental health issues (e.g., Daniel et al., 2022; Koci, 2021, Wasil et al., 2021) as well as an increased level of anxiety or depression (Pacsik et al., 2022, as cited in Trammell et al., Chapter 16), graduate students who entered their doctoral studies during the pandemic appeared to demonstrate even more severe mental health issues (e.g., Donohue et al., 2021). Findings indicated that during the pandemic entering doctoral students during the pandemic had to navigate building relationships with peers and faculty while being confined to their homes during their first year of their doctoral studies. Thus, the pandemic affected the level of social support that these doctoral students received. A second theme centered around the decreased resources as the result of the pandemic. Specifically, graduate students indicated increased financial stress due to increased inflation, yet limited graduate funding through assistantships, along with limited course offerings. A third theme centered around grief, anxiety and stress. One participant mentioned that the learning conditions of the pandemic, in particular emergency remote learning, was especially challenging due to her ADHD. In addition, while students were anxious about the pandemic itself, they were also anxious about the effects of the pandemic on their family members. With regards to positive outcomes as the result of the COVID-19 global pandemic, several doctoral students mentioned that due to the conditions of the pandemic, faculty, staff and students generally developed a deep sense of care and concern to help each other to navigate these challenging circumstances. For example, faculty were more likely to give grace on an assignment date, while students were more likely to give grace to faculty who may have needed more time for grading, and so forth. Further, doctoral students were able to develop informal communities, to use exercise and self-care strategies to decrease their stress and anxiety, and to attend therapy sessions to help them to decrease their stress levels during this challenging time.

In Chapter 17 "Stresses of COVID-19 for Doctoral Students in Engineering," Cromley, Jensen, and Mirabelli (Chapter 17) interviewed 55 engineering doctoral students, four times each in an effort to better understand their direct lived experiences regarding the stressors that they experienced during the COVID-19 global pandemic. The data which was derived from semi-structured interviews and monthly questionnaires throughout the study revealed the following stressors experienced by engineering doctoral students. Doctoral students mentioned that the COVID-19 pandemic affected all aspects of their work, student and personal lives. The data was analyzed using Atlas ti and revealed three major themes. First, many doctoral students found issues related to travel to be very stressful. In many instances, international doctoral students wanted to go visit their families in other countries, or their family wanted to come visit them, but that was not possible in the peak of the pandemic. This resulted in some doctoral students being away from their own children and families for up to two years. There was also a fear of being able to travel, but not being able to reenter the country, which was also a cause for stress and concern. Second, the lack of social interaction due to the pandemic was a significant stressor for most doctoral students. Some students mentioned that they could go for days without talking to anyone else. Third, the pandemic resulted in significant and prevailing health concerns. Specifically, many doctoral students worried about family members, friends or themselves contracting COVID-19, which at the start of the pandemic, could have devastating health consequences, especially before the availability of vaccines. Fourth, there was a general concern about their research, in particular, about getting into research labs, and about the safety of research labs if one could enter. Relatedly, several doctoral students worried about getting their research done and staying on track in their doctoral studies.

In Chapter 18, "Gender Differences in Graduate Students' Adjustment, Mental Health, Motivation and Learning Strategies During the COVID-19 Global Pandemic," Dong et al. (Chapter 18) examined whether female students differ in their levels of adjustment, mental health, motivation and self-regulated learning as compared to male graduate students. In this quantitative study, 301 graduate students completed the College Adjustment Test (CAT; Pennebaker, 2013), the Depression, Anxiety, and Stress Scale (DASS-21; Lovibond & Lovibond, 1995), and selected subscales of the Motivated Strategies for Learning Questionnaire (MSLQ; Pintrich et al., 1991). Results indicated that female graduate students suffered higher levels of negative affect, such as homesickness and stress. Further, results indicated that there was not a significant difference in motivation and self-regulated learning between male and female graduate students.

In Chapter 19, "A Self-Study on Promoting Self-Regulated Learning Using Technology During Remote Instruction," Bembenutty et al. (Chapter 19) examined the effects of the COVID-19 global pandemic, in particular the effects of the curriculum redesign as a function of the pandemic on teacher candidates' self-regulated learning. Thus, in the present study, 3 educational psychology educators of secondary education teacher candidates (Grades 7–12) reflected on their teaching experiences during the pandemic, with emphasis on their transition to online instruction. During the pandemic, these three educators provided social emotional support in their classroom through collaborative activities, whole-class discussions, small group work and attempted to model self-efficacy when possible. Further, they encouraged the delay of gratification, provided scaffolding, and invited teacher candidates to self-monitor their progress by keeping planners and logs. Their self-study revealed the following two primary categories of findings. First, students' efforts to self-regulate were largely successful. Second, pedagogical approaches focused on teaching methods and assessments were helpful to facilitate instruction and learning. Bembenutty et al., (Chapter 19) concluded that implementing self-regulated learning strategies helped the instructors to teach learning to learn rather than merely learning to teach during the COVID-19 global pandemic. In conclusion, the researchers posited that self-regulated learning strategies were instrumental in helping learners to cope with challenging circumstances.

In Chapter 20, "Cognitive and Psychological Effects of COVID-19: Insights from a Systematic Meta-Review of Systematic Reviews and Meta-Analyses," Daumiller et al. (Chapter 20) presented a systematic meta-review in an effort to synthesize and combine 55 reports highlighting the educational effects of the COVID-19 global pandemic. Specifically, this study sought to better understand the psychological and cognitive effects of the COVID-19 global pandemic on education. Through thematic analysis, the researchers identified the following six groups of psychological and cognitive variables: mental health, emotional experiences, attitudes and worries, social relationships, achievement related variables and meaning. With regards to mental health, the COVID-19 pandemic significantly impacted learners, as they had indicated significant increases in burn-out, depression, anxiety, technostress, and sleep disturbances. With regards to the emotional experiences as the result of the pandemic, participants indicated significant increases in sadness, frustration, and fear. With regards to attitudes and worries, participants indicated significant increases in both positive and negative views towards e-learning. With regards to social relationships, overall results indicated a lack of communication. The authors concluded that the challenges associated with the emergency remote instruction as the result of the COVID-19 global pandemic resulted in an overall decrease in psychological well-being along with an increased risk of dropout and attrition. The authors further noted that despite these challenges, the pandemic also fostered significant advances in educational technology and on-line learning that will likely have long-lasting effects on the future of education (Daumiller et al., Chapter 20).

THEMATIC CONCLUSION

While we are in the midst of this global pandemic, we can barely even begin to comprehend the far-reaching effects that this pandemic will have on education. This co-edited book represents one of the initial efforts to synthesize the research into the cognitive and psychological effects of the COVID-19 global pandemic on high school, college and graduate-level learners. The results of each of the aforementioned chapters presented in this co-edited volume will be elucidated below. As the result of a thematic analysis, the findings of these chapters have been organized into the following seven themes which elucidate the extensive effects of the COVID-19 global pandemic on: (a) socialization, (b) mental health and well-being, (c) self-regulated learning, self-directed learning, autonomy and responsibility, (d) the experiences of underrepresented and underserved learners, (e) technology, (f) familial effects, (g) and academic achievement, academic progress and research. For each theme, both the challenges and the positive outcomes of each of these themes will be discussed. Finally, this section will conclude with implications for the future.

Theme 1—Socialization

With regards to challenges associated with socialization, Fletcher et al. (Chapter 3) found that both stakeholders and high school students from disadvantaged circumstances enrolled in a STEM academy reported challenges due to a lack of engagement as the result of the pandemic. Further, Cromley et al. (Chapter 17) found that a lack of social interaction due to the pandemic was a significant stressor for most engineering doctoral students. Some mentioned that they could go for days without talking to anyone in the peak of the pandemic, for example.

With regards to positive outcomes associated with socialization, Allen et al. (Chapter 2) asserted that the high school students demonstrated learned positive social and emotional skill development as the result of the pandemic, as indicated by a greater appreciation for their teachers and in-person instruction. Sewell (Chapter 6) found that some first-generation students enjoyed more time with their family and that the extra support from the relationships that they did have access to helped them to form a sense of community. Similarly, to help them through the pandemic, a group of entering doctoral students actually developed an informal community to help decrease their stress during their transition to graduate school in the midst of the pandemic (Trammell et al., Chapter 16).

Theme 2—Mental Health and Well-Being

With regards to the challenges associated with mental health during the peak of the pandemic, while many precautions were put into place in an effort to promote better physical health, and to mitigate the spread of the COVID-19 virus, these very precautions often inadvertently resulted in decreased psychological health for many college students as they indicated increases in depression, stress and anxiety (Jorales et al., 2020, as cited in Quadlander-Goff et al., Chapter 8). As a means of coping, while co-rumination appeared to foster better and closer relationships with friends, it also actually increased anxiety and psychological distress (Rosen et al., Chapter 9). Daumiller et al. (Chapter 20) found that with regards to mental health, the COVID-19 pandemic significantly negatively impacted learners as they had increases in burn-out, depression, anxiety, technostress, and sleep disturbances. These authors concluded that the COVID-19 global pandemic resulted in an overall decrease in psychological well-being.

With regards to positive outcomes associated with the pandemic, the results of Structural Equation Modeling (SEM) indicated that high school students' mental health directly impacted their motivation which then impacted their levels of learning strategies, which ultimately affected their final grades (Wang et al., Chapter 4). Sewell et al., (Chapter 6) asserted that the participants in her study noted that the pandemic afforded them more study time, and that professors were more empathic. Finally, Yoo and Marshall (Chapter 15) found that graduate student parents actually demonstrated higher levels of life satisfaction and self-efficacy than their graduate peers without children. This finding provided support for the role accumulation theory (e.g., Sieber, 1974).

Theme 3—Self-Regulated Learning, Self-Directed Learning, Autonomy, and Responsibility

With regards to challenges associated with self-regulated learning, self-directed learning, autonomy and responsibility, many college students struggled to learn in distance learning settings as the result of emergency remote instruction since they did not have the self-regulation and discipline to learn the material without having the direct guidance of an instructor in a face-to-face classroom.

With regards to the positive outcomes associated with self-regulated learning, self-directed learning, autonomy and responsibility, Williams et al. (Chapter 13), found that many multilingual learners were able to develop their own personal strategies to become autonomous learners. Gutierrez et al. (Chapter 14) found that engineering majors enrolled in Algebra and

Differential equations taught through emergency remote instruction were forced to develop more responsibility, discipline and self-teaching as the result of the pandemic. Bembenutty et al. (Chapter 19) concluded that implementing self-regulated learning strategies in secondary education courses for teacher candidates was instrumental in helping these learners to cope with the challenging circumstances inherent in the pandemic.

Theme 4—The Experiences of Underrepresented and Underserved Learners

With regards to the challenges associated with the experiences of underrepresented and underserved learners; due to the campus shut-downs, many of the needed campus resources that were normally available to college students such as tutoring, accommodations, quiet library study areas, access to advanced technological resources and extracurricular activities were not available during the peak of the pandemic (Quadlander-Goff et al., Chapter 8). With regards to the positive outcomes associated with the pandemic, The Naf Lab intervention provided one example of an effective approach that was instrumental in providing a work-based simulated environment for disadvantaged learners during these unprecedented times (Fletcher et al., Chapter 3). Similarly, a study by Tyler et al. (Chapter 11) sought to investigate the resilience of undergraduate STEM students from disadvantaged backgrounds. They implemented a Mentoring Bridge Model in an effort to further develop college students' resilience, time management, and so on, enabling them to adapt to the academic and social challenges presented by the pandemic. Many of the underrepresented college students began to adapt to overcome these challenges as the result of their participation in the Bridge Model (Tyler et al., this volume).

Theme 5—Technology

With regards to the challenges experienced as the result of the transition to emergency remote instruction during the pandemic, many learners around the world found the immediate reliance on technology to be challenging. Allen et al. (Chapter 2) found that from 2019 to 2022, from pre-pandemic to post-pandemic, ACT scores declined significantly for all learners at all grade levels. Further, with regards to instructional modality, these scores declined most for the virtual group, followed by the hybrid group, and then followed by the onsite group (Allen et al., Chapter 2). While this rapid shift to on-line learning was challenging for many learners around the world, college students with ADHD were found to experience even greater difficulties (Quadlander-Goff et al., Chapter 8). Further, this shift to online instruction created a widening of the achievement gap. For example, some students did not have adequate computers, laptops, Wi-Fi or other technological resources in their homes to adequately complete their assignments during the shut-down (Quadlander-Goff et al., Chapter 8). Tyler et al., (Chapter 11) also suggested that while the transition to online learning was challenging for so many learners, it was especially difficult for already disadvantaged learners (e.g., Williams et al., Chapter 13).

With regards to positive outcomes related to the abrupt switch to emergency remote instruction during the pandemic, Miller et al. (Chapter 5) have asserted that as the result of the COVID-19 global pandemic, more students and instructors are choosing and using on-line instruction since their forced introduction to emergency remote instruction. Finally, Daumiller et al. (Chapter 20) concluded that the pandemic has fostered significant increases in educational technology, and on-line learning that will have long-lasting effects on the future of education (Daumiller et al., Chapter 20).

Theme 6—Familial Effects

With regards to the challenges associated with familial factors as a function of the COVID-19 global pandemic, in-service teachers reported that they were more likely to have negative experiences due to the constantly changing or even increasing family roles as the result of the pandemic. Cromley et al. (Chapter 17) asserted that several graduate students mentioned that they hadn't seen close family members in over two years due to COVID-19 global travel restrictions.

With regards to the positive outcomes related to familial effects due to the COVID-19 global pandemic, Sewell et al. (Chapter 6) found that some participants indicated that they enjoyed more time at home with their families, and the extra support from the fewer relationships that they still did have access to. The results of Yoo and Marshall's research (Chapter 15) supported role accumulation theory as graduate student parents showed positive mental health, as demonstrated by higher levels of life satisfaction and self-efficacy than graduate students without children.

FUTURE IMPLICATIONS

A thematic analysis based on the results and conclusions of each of the research studies included in this co-edited book revealed the following six themes or areas that were most significantly affected by the COVID-19 global pandemic: (a) socialization, (b) mental health and well-being,

(c) self-regulated learning, self-directed learning, autonomy and responsibility, (d) experiences of underrepresented and underserved learners, (e) technology, and (f) familial effects. Based on these six themes, the following implications are suggested for college and university faculty, staff, and administrators should we ever find ourselves in a similar unprecedented situation.

With regards to socialization, several learners in the present study mentioned that they experienced significant isolation and loneliness as the result of the pandemic, especially during the mandated government shut-downs. It is suggested here that faculty not only use emergency remote devices for learning and instruction but also that they use these to check in with their students in an effort to foster not only learning but also the socialization necessary to facilitate learning. For example, in this type of emergency pandemic situation, faculty could schedule either virtual office hours with mandatory attendance, or individual Zoom sessions with each learner if feasible.

With regards to mental health and well-being, as the result of the pandemic, there was a significant increase in depression, anxiety and other mental health issues, yet also a shortage of mental health resources. Even if a mental health professional him/herself was available to students during the pandemic, these offices were often mandated to be closed. It is suggested here that mental health professionals be available via Zoom or other related accessible resources such as Telehealth.

With regards to self-regulated learning, self-directed learning, autonomy and responsibility, it is recommended that faculty put more responsibility on their learners while providing effective scaffolding for using emergency remote forms of instruction regularly in case this unexpectedly needs to become the norm. Relatedly, with regards to technology, various forms of technology should be used regularly as teaching tools even in face-to-face classrooms, so that faculty and students are both skilled in using these tools, so there isn't an emergency switch with little to no training for faculty or students. Finally, additional efforts should be made to find innovative and creative means for providing the necessary resources to underserved and underrepresented learners during times of crisis, as these were frequently the students who suffered the greatest learning losses. For example, accommodations such as tutoring, study groups, and extra resources and support could all be provided virtually if needed. While it is not ideal, extracurricular clubs and organizations could also still hold meetings on Zoom and other platforms, as the research suggested that this may be especially important for underrepresented college student populations such as first-generation college students who can be somewhat reluctant to get involved, especially in the midst of a crisis.

REFERENCES

Alexander, B., Darby, F., Fischer, K., Jack, A. A., Le Sane, C. B., Staisloff, R., & Stout, K. A. (2020). *The post pandemic college and the future of: The academic enterprise, teaching and learning, the student experience, enrollment, business models and community colleges.* The Chronicle of Higher Education. Washington, DC.

Allen, J., Schnieders, J. Z-Y., Murano, D., Walton, K., Casillas, A., & Burrus, J. (2025). Effects of the COVID-19 Pandemic on college and career planning, social and emotional skills, and college and career readiness: Evidence from ACT, Inc. In J. D. Salisbury-Glennon, C.-H. Wang, & D. M. Shannon (Eds.), *Examining the cognitive and psychological effects of the COVID-19 global pandemic on high school, undergraduate and graduate learners.* Information Age Publishing.

Bembenutty, H., Raffaele, C. & Pisari, D. R. (2025). A self-study on promoting self-regulated learning using technology during remote instruction. In J. D. Salisbury-Glennon, C.-H. Wang, & D. M. Shannon (Eds.), *Examining the cognitive and psychological effects of the COVID-19 global pandemic on high school, undergraduate and graduate learners.* Information Age Publishing.

Birmingham, W. C., Wadsworth, L. L., Lassetter, J. H., Graff, T. C., Lauren, E., & Hung, M. (2023). COVID-19 lockdown: Impact on college students' lives. *Journal of American College Health, 71*(3), 879–893. https://doi.org/10.1080/07448481.2021.1909041

Bridges, M. E. S., & Duffy, M. C. (2025). College during COVID-19: A mixed methods study examining undergraduate students' academic experiences and responses. In J. D. Salisbury-Glennon, C.-H. Wang, & D. M. Shannon (Eds.), *Examining the cognitive and psychological effects of the COVID-19 global pandemic on high school, undergraduate and graduate learners.* Information Age Publishing.

Buhrmestr, D., & Furman, W. (2008). *The Network of Relationships Inventory: Relationships Qualities Version* [Unpublished measure. University of Texas at Dallas].

Conway, L. G., Woodward, S. R., & Zubrod, A. (2020, April 7). *Social psychological measurements of COVID-19: Coronavirus perceived threat, government response, impacts, and experiences questionnaires.* https://doi.org/10.31234/osf.io.z2x9a

Cromley, J. G., Jensen, K. J., & Mirabelli, J. F. (2025). Stresses of COVID-19 for doctoral students in engineering. In J. D. Salisbury-Glennon, C.-H. Wang, & D. M. Shannon (Eds.), *Examining the cognitive and psychological effects of the COVID-19 global pandemic on high school, undergraduate and graduate learners.* Information Age Publishing.

Daniel, K. E., Szkody, E., Aggarwal, P., Peterman, A. H., Washburn, J. J., & Selby, E. A. (2022). Characterizing changes in mental health-related outcomes for Health Service psychology graduate students during the first year of the COVID-19 pandemic. *Journal of Clinical Psychology, 78*(11), 2281–2298. https://doi.org/10.1002/jclp.23392

Daumiller, M., Rinas, R., Schoon, I., & Luftenegger, M. (2025). Cognitive and psychological effects of COVID-19: Insights from a systematic meta-review of systematic reviews and meta-analyses. In J. D. Salisbury-Glennon, C.-H. Wang, & D. M. Shannon (Eds.), *Examining the cognitive and psychological effects of the COVID-19 global pandemic on high school, undergraduate and graduate learners*. Information Age Publishing.

Davidson, C. L., Grant, D. M., Byrd-Craven, J. Mills. A. C., Judah, M. R., & Lechner, W. V. (2014). Psychometric properties of the Co-Rumination Questionnaire. *Personality and Individual Differences, 70*, 171–175. https://doi.org/10.1016/j.paid.2014.07.002

Deci, E. L., & Ryan, R. M. (1991). A motivational approach to self: Integration in personality. In R. A. Dienstbier (Ed.), *Current theory and research in motivation* (pp. 237–288). University of Nebraska Press.

Donohue, W. J., Lee, A. S. J., Simpson, S. & Vacek, K. (2021). Impacts of the COVID-19 pandemic on doctoral students' thesis/dissertation progress. *International Journal of Doctoral Studies, 16*, 533, https://doi.org/10.28945/4818

Dong, J., Manning, K. Q., Dai, Y., Wang, C. -H., Salisbury-Glennon, J. D., Marshall, D. T., & Trammell, D. (2025). Gender differences in graduate students' adjustment, mental health, motivation and learning strategies during the COVID-19 global pandemic. In J. D. Salisbury-Glennon, C.-H. Wang, & D. M. Shannon (Eds.), *Examining the cognitive and psychological effects of the COVID-19 global pandemic on high school, undergraduate and graduate learners*. Information Age Publishing.

Dunn, C. Shannon, D., McCullough, B., Jenda, O., Qazi, M., & Pettis, C. (2021). A mentoring bridge model for students with disabilities in science, technology, engineering and mathematics. *Journal of Postsecondary Education and Disability, 34*(2), 163–177.

Fletcher E. C., & Ford, D. Y. (2025). Examining the academic and psychological experiences of students and educational stakeholders in a high school STEM academy during the COVID-19 Pandemic. In J. D. Salisbury-Glennon, C.-H. Wang, & D. M. Shannon (Eds.), *Examining the cognitive and psychological effects of the COVID-19 global pandemic on high school, undergraduate and graduate learners*. Information Age Publishing.

Goode, W. J. (1960). A theory of of role strain. *American Psychological Review, 25*(4), 483–496. https://doi.org/10.2307/2092933

Goldhaber, D. , Kane, T. J., McEachin, A., Morton, E., Patterson, T., & Staiger, D. O. (2022). *The consequences of remote and hybrid instruction during the pandemic*. National Bureau of Economic Research. https://doi.org/10.3386/w30010

Gore, L. (2023, November 16). Here's the average ACT score in Alabama and the U.S. *AL.com*. http://tinyurl.com/28useeb3

Gutiérrez, V. C., & Puga D. S. E. (2025). Perspectives of engineering students on the impact of COVID-19 on the learning and teaching algebra and differential calculus. In J. D. Salisbury-Glennon, C.-H. Wang, & D. M. Shannon (Eds.), *Examining the cognitive and psychological effects of the COVID-19 global pandemic on high school, undergraduate and graduate learners*. Information Age Publishing.

Lovibond, S. H., & Lovibond, P. F. (1995). Manual for the Depression Anxiety & Stress Scales (2nd ed.). Psychology Foundation.

Manning, K. Q., Wang, C. -H., Lambert, A., Jones, M. C., Chidume, T., Dong, J., Curtis, A., & Brown. L. G. (2025). Perceptions and attitudes of nursing students' transition to remote instruction during COVID-19. In J. D.

Salisbury-Glennon, C.-H. Wang, & D. M. Shannon (Eds.), *Examining the cognitive and psychological effects of the COVID-19 global pandemic on high school, undergraduate and graduate learners*. Information Age Publishing.

Miller, A. D., Vomund, J., Buehl, M. M., Brophy, N. S., & Broeckelman-Post. M. (2025). Instructional support and the student-teacher relationship in higher education: Lessons learned from students' perceptions of instruction during emergency remote learning. In J. D. Salisbury-Glennon, C.-H. Wang, & D. M. Shannon (Eds.), *Examining the cognitive and psychological effects of the COVID-19 global pandemic on high school, undergraduate and graduate learners*. Information Age Publishing.

Nikolaidis, A., Paksarian, D., Alexander, L., De Rosa, J., Dunn, J., Nielson, D. M., Droney, I., Kang, M., Douka, I., Bromet, E., Milham, M. P., Stringaris, A., & Merikangas, K. R. (2020). The Coronavirus Health and Impact Survey (CRISIS) reveals reproducible correleates of pandemic-related mood states across the Atlantic. *medRxiv: The Preprint Server for Health Sciences*. https://doi.org/10.1101/2020.08.24.20181123

Pintrich, P. R. (1991). A manual for the use of the Motivated Strategies for Learning Questionnaire (MSLQ). *International Journal of Educational Research, 31*(6), 459–470. https://doi.org/10.1037/t09161-000

Qazi, M., Shannon, D., Jenda, O., McCullough, B., Griffin, G., Lunn, A. (2016). A mentoring bridge model to prepare students with disabilities in the STEM fields at Tuskegee University. *Journal of Women and Minorities in Science and Engineering, 22*(3), 183–197. https://doi.org/10.1615/jwomenminorscieneng.2016015452

Quadlander-Goff, E., LaPolla, M., & Marshall, D. T. (2025). The impact of the COVID-19 pandemic on college students with ADHD: Implications and interventions. In J. D. Salisbury-Glennon, C.-H. Wang, & D. M. Shannon (Eds.), *Examining the cognitive and psychological effects of the COVID-19 global pandemic on high school, undergraduate and graduate learners*. Information Age Publishing.

Radloff, L. S. (1977). The CES-D scale: A self-report depression scale for research in the general population. *Applied Psychological Measurement, 13*, 385–401. https://doi.org/10/1177%2F014662167700100306

Rashid, S., & Yadav, S. S. (2020). Impact of the COVID-19 pandemic on higher education and research. *Indian Journal of Human Development, 14*(2), 34043. https://doi.org/10.1177/0973703020946700

Rosen, L. H., Rubin, L. J., Higgins, M., & Yeatts, P. (2025). Trade-offs of seeking support for university students during the pandemic. In J. D. Salisbury-Glennon, C.-H. Wang, & D. M. Shannon (Eds.), *Examining the cognitive and psychological effects of the COVID-19 global pandemic on high school, undergraduate and graduate learners*. Information Age Publishing.

Sherif, V., Patterson, J. A., & Redger-Marquardt, C. (2025). The impact of the COVID-19 pandemic on first-generation undergraduate students' participation in campus activities. In J. D. Salisbury-Glennon, C.-H. Wang, & D. M. Shannon (Eds.), *Examining the cognitive and psychological effects of the COVID-19 global pandemic on high school, undergraduate and graduate learners*. Information Age Publishing.

Sieber, S. D. (1974). Toward a theory of role accumulation. *American Sociological Review, 39*(4), 567–578. https://doi.org/10.2307/2094422

Tackett, S., Arrastía-Chisholm, M., & Torres, K. M. (2025). Balancing work and school during the time of COVID-19: Lessons learned from online pre- and in-service teacher training. In J. D. Salisbury-Glennon, C.-H. Wang, & D. M Shannon (Eds.), *Examining the cognitive and psychological effects of the COVID-19 global pandemic on high school, undergraduate and graduate learners.* Information Age Publishing.

Trammell, D. L., Quadlander-Goff, E., Schoettler, N. M., Slaughter, K. F., Riel, J. & Hudson. D. L. (2025). Walking the fine line: First-year doctoral students' experiences during COVID-19. In J. D. Salisbury-Glennon, C.-H. Wang, & D. M. Shannon (Eds.), *Examining the cognitive and psychological effects of the COVID-19 global pandemic on high school, undergraduate and graduate learners.* Information Age Publishing.

Tyler, J. M., Collins, J., Shannon, D. M., Carney, J., LaPolla, M. (2025). Underserved and underrepresented college students' resilience during COVID-19. In J. D. Salisbury-Glennon, C.-H. Wang, & D. M. Shannon (Eds.), *Examining the cognitive and psychological effects of the COVID-19 global pandemic on high school, undergraduate and graduate learners.* Information Age Publishing.

Wang, C, -H., Dai, Y., Dong, J., Manning, K. Q., Salisbury-Glennon, J. D., Tseng, C.-M., & Marshall, D. T. (2025). The effects of mental health, motivation, and learning strategies on high school students' grades during COVID-19. In J. D. Salisbury-Glennon, C.-H. Wang, & D. M. Shannon (Eds.), *Examining the cognitive and psychological effects of the COVID-19 global pandemic on high school, undergraduate and graduate learners.* Information Age Publishing.

Wasil, A. R., Franzen, R. E., Gillespie, S., Steinberg, J. S., Malhotra, T., & De Rubeis, R. J. (2021). Commonly reported problems and coping strategies during the COVID-19 crisis: A survey of graduate and professional students. *Frontiers in Psychology, 12*(598557), 1–14. https://doi.org/10.3389/fpsyg.2021.598447

Williams, G. M., & Diamond, M. S. (2025). Exploring the online academic acculturation of multilingual learners during COVID. In J. D. Salisbury-Glennon, C.-H. Wang, & D. M. Shannon (Eds.), *Examining the cognitive and psychological effects of the COVID-19 global pandemic on high school, undergraduate and graduate learners.* Information Age Publishing.

Yoo, H. J., & Marshall, D. T. (2025). Graduate students' mental health during COVID-19: Parenthood and gender. In J. D. Salisbury-Glennon, C.-H. Wang, & D. M. Shannon (Eds.), *Examining the cognitive and psychological effects of the COVID-19 global pandemic on high school, undergraduate and graduate learners.* Information Age Publishing.

ABOUT THE CONTRIBUTORS

Jeff Allen is a statistician in ACT's Applied Research Department.

Meagan Arrastia-Chisholm is an associate professor of educational psychology and an associate licensed counselor at Valdosta State University. Her research and counseling interests include diverse and neurodivergent learners, first-generation college students, and parental separation.

Héfer Bembenutty is an associate professor in educational psychology at Queens College of City University of New York in the Department of Secondary and Youth Services, where he is the department coordinator of the Educational Psychology courses and Educational Psychology Lecture Series. Dr. Bembenutty obtained his doctorate from The City University of New York Graduate Center in educational psychology. His research focuses on academic delay of gratification and the cyclical and self-regulated culturally proactive pedagogy model. He has also published studies on teachers' self-efficacy beliefs and self-regulation and has served as an editor for many special issues of various journals. He has authored and co-edited seven books.

Melissa Broeckelman-Post is the Basic Course Director and Professor in the Department of Communication and a Senior Scholar in the Center for the Advancement of Well-Being at George Mason University. She is responsible for planning, supervising, assessing, and improving the communication courses that meet the general education requirement at GMU. Broeckelman-Post is the co-author of two national communication textbooks, The Speaker's Primer and Communication Pathways. She is also a quantitative methods and mixed-methods research specialist who conducts research in communication assessment, communication pedagogy, and instructional communication.

Mary Elizabeth Sewell Bridges is a Teaching Assistant Professor of Psychology at East Carolina University. She earned her PhD in Educational Psychology and Research from the University of South Carolina, where she examined students' academic emotions, resilience, and experiences during the COVID-19 pandemic. Dr. Bridges focuses on enhancing academic performance and student well-being, with particular interests in researching resilience, coping styles, and positive psychological resources—such as hope, optimism and self-efficacy—that significantly impact student success. With over 20 years of experience in higher education, Dr. Bridges has dedicated her career to supporting students and promoting their academic persistence.

Nate S. Brophy is a doctoral candidate in Communication at George Mason University. His research focuses on basic psychological needs and fulfilment in higher education.

Lynn Greenleaf Brown is an associate clinical professor at Auburn University. Her research interests include women's health, older adults, and student success.

Michelle M. Buehl is a Professor of Educational Psychology at George Mason University. Her research focuses on the role of student and teacher beliefs in relation to learning, motivation, and academic development. She teaches courses to undergraduate, masters, and doctoral students related to learning and cognition, motivation, and research methods with a focus on helping students make connections between research, theory, and practice.

Jeremy Burrus is a social psychologist on the SEAL team in ACT's Research Department.

Jamie Carney is a retired Humana Germany Sherman Distinguished Professor at Auburn University. Dr. Carney is a retired Professor in the Counselor Education program. She has extensive experience in counselor training and supervision. This work includes curriculum development and assessment focused on program and learning factors in counselor education. Dr. Carney's research has included the examination of variables corresponding to attitudes and beliefs related to working with individuals from underrepresented and diverse backgrounds.

Alex Casillas is a Principal Research Psychologist on the SEAL team in ACT's Research Department.

Tiffani Chidume is an associate clinical professor and simulation center coordinator at Auburn University College of Nursing. As the simulation center coordinator, she engages students as active learners who reflect critically on what they have learned to apply it to the ongoing development of their critical-thinking skills. She also works to demonstrate innovation and excellence within simulation-based education. She received Best Research Award in Nursing and Health Professions (2021) as well as the Alabama Nurses Foundation Scholarship for Academic Excellence and Leadership (2020). She is a reviewer for multiple nursing and simulation journals.

Joanna Collins is a Doctoral Candidate in the Counselor Education Doctoral Program at Auburn University. She has several years of teaching experience, including teaching master's level counselors. Her work has also involved development of training and preparing graduate students to work with students from diverse backgrounds. She is a licensed practicing counselor with extensive experience in counseling practice and supervision.

Jennifer G. Cromley is a Professor of Educational Psychology in the College of Education at the University of Illinois Urbana-Champaign (UIUC). She holds a 2005 PhD in Human Development and a Certificate in Educational Measurement and Statistics from the University of Maryland College Park. Cromley's research focuses on cognitive and motivational predictors of STEM grades and retention, including research in biology, chemistry, and calculus, as well as research on learning from biology text and diagrams. She has conducted basic processes research, longitudinal, and multi-method studies including interview, think-aloud, and eye tracking research with students in middle school through postsecondary education.

Amy Curtis is an assistant clinical professor in the Auburn University College of Nursing, where she coordinates the Fundamentals of Nursing and Health Assessment courses for junior nursing students. She also teaches in both the MSN and RN to BSN Graduate Programs. She is a Certified Healthcare Simulation Educator (CHSE) with over 11 years of simulation experience. Her research interests include best practice in simulation-based education, best practice in nursing education, holistic admission practices, and breast cancer education.

Yan Dai is a doctoral student in the Educational Psychology program in the Department of Educational Foundations, Leadership & Technology

(EFLT), Auburn University. Her research interests focus on motivation (particularly on self-efficacy and self-regulation), resilience, online learning, and cross-cultural compassion research. She also works under a critical theoretical frame using ethnographic and auto-ethnographic methods.

Martin Daumiller is a professor of Educational Psychology at the Ludwig Maximilian University of Munich (LMU). His research interests include motivation and the fostering of motivation in educational settings, academic dishonesty, learning with digital media, and experiences, as well as the behaviors and performances of teachers and researchers. He has successfully obtained grant funding as PI and Co-PI in competitive calls (including two DFG grants) and has published the outcomes of his research in more than 70 empirical journal articles, books, and book chapters. He has pursued multiple research stays abroad, including the University of Rochester (USA) and the University of Korea (South Korea). He has received multiple prizes for his research, such as the Robert J. Menges New Research Award 2020 granted by the AERA FTED SIG.

Mary S. Diamond is an instructor at Auburn Global, an English language program for international students who wish to learn English.

Jianwei Dong is a doctoral student in Educational Psychology at Auburn University. Her research interests focus on college students' motivation and self-regulated learning in technology-related or online learning contexts.

Melissa C. Duffy is an assistant professor in Educational Psychology and Research at the University of South Carolina. Her program of research focuses on the intersection between motivation, emotion, and learning across higher education and professional training settings. Her research has examined how learners' emotional states relate to cognitive processes and performance; the impact of students' achievement motivation and engagement within online and computer-based environments; and relations between teacher beliefs, instructional practices, and student beliefs. More recently, her work has focused on academic resilience and how college students navigate academic setbacks, including challenges during COVID-19.

Edward C. Fletcher Jr., is an Education and Human Ecology Distinguished Professor of Workforce Development and Education in the College of Education and Human Ecology at The Ohio State University. He serves as Editor for the Career and Technical Education Research journal. Dr. Fletcher has received over $5 million in funding from the National Science Foundation. His research focuses on the role of high school career academies in promoting students' engagement and school experiences as well as postsecondary and labor market transitions, particularly for ethnically and racially diverse learners and those who come from economically disadvantaged backgrounds.

Donna Y. Ford is a Distinguished Professor of Education and Human Ecology and Kirwan Institute Faculty Affiliate at The Ohio State University. She is in the Department of Educational Studies, Special Education Program. She has earned all degrees from Cleveland State University. Ford focuses primarily on the underrepresentation of Black and Hispanic students in gifted education and advanced classes. She is a leader in urban education. Dr. Ford has authored more than 400 publications and 14 books. She presents in school districts and organizations on opportunity gaps, equity, multicultural curriculum, antiracism, and cultural competence.

Valeria Cornejo Gutiérrez obtained a degree in Accounting from the Ciudad Juárez Technological Institute in 1997. Later, in 2012, she obtained a master's degree in Administration from the Autonomous University of Ciudad Juarez (UACJ). Currently, she is a candidate for a doctorate in Administrative Sciences and a master's degree in Mathematics Education at the Autonomous University of Ciudad Juárez. Her research focuses on decision-making and intellectual capital.

Meredith Higgins is a doctoral student in the Counseling Psychology program at Texas Woman's University. Her research has focused on how the pandemic has affected students and families.

Danielle L. Hudson is a doctoral student in the Curriculum and Instruction department at Auburn University. Her research interest is equity in STEM education, particularly as it relates to girls and women in STEM fields. Danielle has 15 years of experience in higher education teaching non-traditional and traditional learners in a variety of settings.

Karin J. Jensen is an Assistant Professor of Biomedical Engineering and a member of the Engineering Education Research Program in the College of Engineering at the University of Michigan Ann Arbor. Her research interests include mental health and wellness, engineering student career pathways, and engagement of engineering faculty in engineering education research. Jensen is also a member of the ASEE Commission on Diversity, Equity, and Inclusion. She is currently an associate editor for the Journal of Women and Minorities in Science and Engineering. She earned a bachelor's degree in Biological Engineering from Cornell University and a PhD in Biomedical Engineering from the University of Virginia.

Meghan C. Jones is an associate clinical professor at Auburn University College of Nursing and the director of clinical simulation and skills labs. Her work focuses on simulation excellence and best practice and creating environments that foster the growth of both simulation educators and learners. Her research interests include pre-briefing, psychological safety, and anxiety among reproductive-age women.

Ann Lambert is an associate clinical professor at Auburn University College of Nursing. She teaches primarily in the junior level Maternity Course and Pediatric nursing content within the integrated curriculum. Her research focuses on nursing education, sudden infant death syndrome (SIDS) prevention, pediatric oncology and shaken baby syndrome (SBS), community support for breastfeeding, play therapy, and alternative therapies.

Madeline LaPolla is a doctoral candidate in the Counselor Education program at Auburn University. She works as a clinical mental health counselor at a community mental health organization, providing therapy to adults with serious mental illness. Madeline's research interests include exploring the impact of intolerance of uncertainty (IU) on mental health within undergraduate college students, an interest that predominantly arose from the COVID-19 pandemic.

Marko Lüftenegger is an associate professor for developmental and educational psychology of school age at the University of Vienna, Austria. His research interests include the identification of malleable characteristics in educational settings and how they contribute to beneficial development of motivational, cognitive, and socio-emotional student outcomes. Additionally, he focuses on the development and evaluation of intervention programs in different educational contexts. He published the outcomes of his research in more than 80 empirical journal articles, books and book chapters, and successfully obtained grant funding as PI and Co-Pl in competitive calls (Total: > 2.100.000 €).

Kailea Q. Manning, is a doctoral student at Auburn University in the Educational Psychology PhD program within the Educational Foundations, Leadership, and Technology department. She received her master's degree in Experimental Psychology from Augusta University, where she gained experience with program evaluation and educational research. Her research interests include motivational theories in graduate student success and in faculty job satisfaction. Currently, she is assisting in projects examining undergraduate and graduate student's academic and psychological adjustment during COVID-19.

David T. Marshall is an associate professor of educational research in the College of Education at Auburn University. His research has focused on the impact that the COVID-19 pandemic has had on K–12 education and charter schools. His first book, *COVID-19 and the Classroom: How Schools Navigated the Great Disruption*, focused on the impact that the pandemic had on K–12 stakeholders, education policy, and teacher preparation from March 2020 through June 2021. Previously, Dr. Marshall worked with teacher residency programs in Virginia for seven years, serving in several capacities. He began his career in education as a middle and high school social studies teacher in Philadelphia, Pennsylvania. He recently served two terms as the chair of the Alabama Public Charter School Commission.

Angela D. Miller is an Associate Professor in Research Methods and Educational Psychology at George Mason University. Her research encompasses both teacher and student aspects of the classroom context and has two overlapping lines of inquiry: the influence of classroom context on student motivation and using student perceptions to better understand classroom dynamics. She examines student motivation and behavior in a classroom as a function of student beliefs and goals about learning, prior experiences in classrooms and the meaning they make out of teacher messages and behaviors.

Joseph F. Mirabelli is a doctoral student in the Department of Educational Psychology at the University of Illinois Urbana-Champaign (UIUC). Mirabelli's research interests include retention, culture, and mental health and well-being for engineering students at undergraduate and graduate levels, and additionally mentorship and professional development for graduate students and faculty. He conducts mixed methods research with a focus on measurement development using interview data. He holds an MS in Physics from the University of Indiana at Bloomington and a BS in Engineering Physics from the University of Illinois Urbana Champaign.

Dana Murano is an educational psychologist on the Social, Emotional, and Academic Learning (SEAL) team in ACT's Research Department.

Natalie M. Schoettler received her doctorate in Educational Psychology at Auburn University. Natalie received her Master of Science in Educational Research, Measurement, and Evaluation, as well as a Graduate Certificate in Program Evaluation from Auburn University. Before coming to Auburn, Natalie worked as a research assistant for Emory University in an inclusive preschool lab school at the Marcus Autism Center, where children with and without autism learn together and from each other. Currently, Natalie serves as a graduate assistant in Research and Instruction Services at Auburn's Ralph Brown Draughon Library. Her research interests encompass school choice for parents of children with special needs, including charter schools, and the academic and social inclusion of children on the spectrum.

Jean A Patterson is a Professor of Educational Leadership at Wichita State University. Her areas of expertise are qualitative inquiry, K–12 and higher education organizations and policy, and educational equity. She is co-editor of the forthcoming book *Differentiated Academic Advising Strategies for Students Beyond the Margins*, under contract with Rowman-Littlefield. Recent publications include A distributed leadership perspective on implementing instructional reform: A case study of an urban middle school published in the *Journal of School Leadership* and the book chapter "It CAN Happen Here:" Addressing school safety and security after a mass shooting in a small Kansas town.

Danny Pisari is a doctoral student in Educational Psychology at the City University of New York Graduate Center. He is currently a Graduate Teaching Fellow in the department of Secondary Education and Youth Services at Queens College, City University of New York, where he teaches educational psychology to preservice teacher candidates online and in person. His research interests include multimedia design practices and digital learning through social and interactive media.

Danelly Susana Esparza Puga, obtained a bachelor's degree in mathematics at the Autonomous University of Ciudad Juárez (UACJ) in the year 2011. Later in 2014, she earned a master's degree in mathematics education from the UACJ and obtained her PhD in mathematics education at the National Polytechnic Institute of Mexico in 2018. She is a member of the National System of Researchers of Mexico, and her research interests develop around the use of digital tools in teaching and learning mathematics.

Emma Quadlander-Goff is a doctoral candidate in the Counselor Education and Supervision program at Auburn University. She obtained her Master of Science in Counseling and Psychology with an emphasis on Clinical Mental Health Counseling in 2019 from Troy University. She works as a clinical mental health counselor in private practice, providing treatment to college students with ADHD and those who are bereaved. Emma is currently a clinical researcher for Harmonex Neuroscience Research and her interests include grief, unexpected loss, trauma, and ADHD. Emma also works as an adjunct faculty member at Troy University in the Counseling, Rehabilitation, and Interpreter Training Division.

Charles Raffaele obtained a PhD in educational psychology from the Graduate Center, City University of New York. He is an adjunct assistant professor in the Secondary Education and Youth Services department at Queens College, City University of New York. His research is focused on second language learning with digital games and multimedia. He has presented at the American Educational Research Association on an app for promoting college enrollment. He has served as a reviewer for *Journal of Interactive Technology and Pedagogy*. He has published chapters on games-based learning and writing implementation in psychology instruction.

Chelsea Redger-Marquardt is an Assistant Professor of Organizational Leadership & Learning at Wichita State University. Dr. Redger-Marquardt also holds a joint faculty appointment and serves as the Assistant Dean in the Dorothy and Bill Cohen Honors College. Her research interests include experiential leadership education, immersive service-learning, leadership identity construction, and the scholarship of teaching and learning. She is the Director of the Lead for Tomorrow Cohen Honors Leadership academy and collaboratively instructs the connected courses with an interdisciplinary team of colleagues. She leads several immersive service-learning travel seminars and co-coordinates the university service-learning efforts as a Service-Learning Faculty Fellow.

Jessi Riel is a doctoral student in the Educational Psychology program at Auburn University and formerly a public school teacher in the Arkansas Delta, where she focused on community development through education and youth sports. Now living in Auburn, Alabama, Riel continues to work in community engagement and education as Program Director at O Grows, a community-university outreach committed to increasing local students' access to experiential learning and community knowledge-sharing pathways while also working for food justice through cultivating students' food literacy and providing affordable produce for local residents. Her research interests center on communal pedagogy and how community-driven educational programs can foster student and community thriving, particularly in rural and/or marginalized settings.

Raven Rinas is a research and teaching associate in the Department of Psychology at the University of Augsburg, Germany. Her research interests include fostering motivation and well-being in students and teachers, with a focus on the higher education context.

Lisa H. Rosen is an Associate Professor and Director of the Undergraduate Psychology Program at Texas Woman's University. Her research focuses on parent-child communication and exploring ways that parents can best support victimized youth. Her more recent work has focused on how the effects of the COVID-19 pandemic.

Linda J. Rubin is a Professor of Psychology and Licensed Psychologist at Texas Woman's University. Her research, clinical, and teaching interests target traumatic stress and violence against women. She has offered empirically-based intervention to college students who experience domestic/dating violence, sexual assault/rape, and stalking.

Jill D. Salisbury-Glennon, is a Professor of Educational Psychology at Auburn University. Her research focuses on student motivation and achievement. Her specific research interests include: college students' learning and study strategies, self-regulated learning, metacognition, motivation, attachment, and academic achievement; as well as creating learner-centered contexts at the university level. More recently, she has been involved in a fairly large-scale research project that investigates the effects of the COVID-19 global pandemic on college students' parental and peer relationships and how these impact college students' learning, motivation, resilience and academic performance. She is currently co-editing two books on the COVID-19 global pandemic entitled: *Examining the Cognitive and Psychological Effects of the COVID-19 Global Pandemic on High School, Undergraduate and Graduate Learners*; and *Instructional Survival in the Midst of the Perfect Storm: The Experiences of K–12 Teachers During the COVID-19 Global Pandemic.*

Joyce Schnieders is an educational psychologist in ACT's Applied Research Department.

Ingrid Schoon is a Professor of Human Development and Social Policy at the Institute of Education, University College London, a Fellow of the UK Academy of Social Science (FAcSS) and since June 2014 Research Fellow at the Wissenschaftszentrum Berlin. She has lead a number of large scale research projects and has served as an expert advisor on government policies and a range of national and international panels, including the OECE 2030 Competencies Framework Working Group. Her research focuses on the study of risk and resilience in the transition to adulthood, social inequalities in skill development, attainment and wellbeing, asking (1) to what extent and how do social conditions, in particular socioeconomic adversity, affect individual thinking, feeling and behavior; (2) to what extent and in what circumstances can individuals succeed against the odds and steer their own life? She has published widely, including a monograph on "Risk and Resilience" (2006) and co-edited books on *Transitions from School to Work* (with Rainer K. Silbereisen, 2009), *Gender Differences in Aspirations* *and Attainment* (with Jacquelynne S. Eccles, 2014), and with John Bynner on *Young People's Development and the Great Recession: Uncertain Transitions and Precarious Futures*—all published by Cambridge University Press.

David M. Shannon is a retired Humana-Germany-Sherman Distinguished Professor in Educational Research. His research interests are focused on issues related to quantitative research methods, program evaluation, and broadening participation in the STEM disciplines. He has research publications in top educational research and evaluation professional journals and he has served as the lead researcher or evaluator, or investigator for over 30 funded projects while at Auburn. Current funded projects are focused specifically on low-income students, students with disabilities, and other underrepresented populations in STEM.

Victoria Sherif is an Assistant Professor of Educational Leadership in Intervention Services and Leadership in Education at Wichita State University. Her research interests center around the issues of leadership of youth, early childhood administrators, and superintendents, as well as qualitative secondary analysis as a research methodology. She teaches research foundations and methods, leadership theories, and educational policy courses. Dr. Sherif has served as a dissertation research chair and consultant on program-based projects related to student and youth leadership, student voice, early childhood, and workforce development.

Kamia F. Slaughter is a doctoral student in the Administration of Higher Education program at Auburn University and serves as a Graduate Research Assistant in the Department of Educational Foundations, Leadership, and Technology. Her research centers around sociopolitical landscapes in Black, rural communities and the work that institutional, organizational, and community practitioners engage in to support Black students. She also gleans from former professional experiences as an elementary teacher, and federal program analyst intern, and outreach practitioner to engage in work.

Samantha Tackett is the Proactive Referral and Engagement Program Director at Florida State University. Her professional and research interests include academic motivation, engagement, persistence, and retention of students and the academic experiences of first-generation and other underrepresented student populations within the U.S. educational systems.

Kelly M. Torres is the Department Chair of the Educational Psychology and Technology program at TCSPP. Her research interests are focused on international education, graduate student retention, innovative technologies, and online learning.

Deja' L. Trammell is a native of Montgomery, Alabama who has dedicated her career to the advancement of students of color in higher education through academic and professional supportive services. She received her Bachelor of Science in Psychology from Alabama State University, her Master of Social Work from Clark Atlanta University, and her Master of Science in Education Research, Measurement, and Evaluation from Auburn University. She is a third-year doctoral student at Auburn University pursuing her degree in Educational Psychology with a focus in Higher Education Administration. Her research focuses on the identities and experiences of Black students throughout academia and how culturally responsive practices in education can foster student agency and success. She is committed to enhancing the growth and development of students of color in education by providing diverse, equitable access to institutional resources and programming.

Chin-Meng Tseng is an Associate Professor in the Department of International and Comparative Education at National ChiNan University in Taiwan. Her research focuses on educational media and technology, and student mental health, motivation, and learning.

Jessica Melendez Tyler is an Associate Professor of Practice in the Department of Human and Organizational Development at Vanderbilt. Dr. Tyler is a Counselor Educator with extensive supervision and clinical experience. She is a Licensed Counseling Supervisor, Licensed Professional Counselor and EMDR Trained with a background in training, research and teaching related to trauma and trauma-informed care.

Jeffrey Vomund is a doctoral candidate in Educational Psychology at George Mason University. His research investigates the impact of student perceptions on their motivation, achievement, and well-being. Specifically, he focuses on the impact of student perceptions of empathy within a classroom setting.

Kate E. Walton is a Principal Research Scientist on the SEAL team in ACT's Research Department.

Chih-hsuan Wang is a Professor in Educational Psychology at Auburn University. She teaches research methods and data analysis courses. Dr. Wang's research focuses on enhancing learning using technology as well as motivation assessment and learning outcomes within an online learning environment and its impacts on the teaching and learning process. Her other research interests include K–12 STEM education and evaluation, factors that influence international students' motivation and learning, and topics related to health psychology and nursing education.

Gwendolyn M. Williams is an associate professor of ESOL Education at Auburn University. Her research interests include issues related to multilingual learner access to instruction, and teacher preparation for educating multilingual learners. She teaches courses in methods of educating multilingual learners in reading and writing, cultural issues of multilingual learners, and assessment of multilingual learners.

Paul Yeatts serves as the Director of the Center for Research Design and Analysis (CRDA) at Texas Women's University. His research efforts have been focused in the area of exercise psychology and statistical analysis.

Hyeon Jean Yoo is an Assistant Professor in the Department of Teaching and Learning at Tennessee State University, Nashville, TN, United States. She received her PhD in Adult Education and an MS in Educational Research, Measurement, and Evaluation from Auburn University, Auburn, AL, United States. Her research interests include nontraditional learners, minority populations, and parenthood and gender inequality in higher education.

Printed and bound by CPI Group (UK) Ltd, Croydon, CR0 4YY

16/09/2026

14963374-0003